American Government and the Economy

EMMETTE S. REDFORD
Ashbel Smith Professor of Government
The University of Texas

Chapters 9, 20, and 22 by

CHARLES B. HAGAN
Professor of Political Science
University of Illinois

The Macmillan Company, New York
Collier–Macmillan Limited, London

© Copyright, THE MACMILLAN COMPANY, 1965

All rights reserved. No part of this book
may be reproduced or utilized in any form
or by any means, electronic or mechanical,
including photocopying, recording
or by any information storage
and retrieval system, without permission
in writing from the Publisher.

First Printing

Library of Congress catalog card number: 65–10959

THE MACMILLAN COMPANY, NEW YORK

COLLIER-MACMILLAN CANADA, LTD., TORONTO, ONTARIO

Printed in the United States of America

DESIGNED BY ANDREW P. ZUTIS

Preface

GOVERNMENT'S ROLE in the economy of the United States has been, is now, and will continue to be extensive and significant. It is the purpose of the authors to provide a comprehensive view of this role, with greatest emphasis on what is now done, but with attention also to why and how we got where we are and where we may be going.

It is not easy to acquire a comprehensive view of the relationships between government and the economy. Past experience, present conditions, pressures of groups, concepts of thought, administrative mechanisms, and constitutional framework must all be blended into one's vision, or the picture will be incomplete and unbalanced. All of these are considered, separately and compositely, in the chapters of this book.

A book that is to be used as a text for students must contain reasonably thorough factual summaries. The authors provide such summaries, but their objective is to offer more than that. From the first to the last page, their aim is to interpret events and encourage thought about them. It is hoped that the student will be led to think about what will be and what may be (or what need not be), about means that men have at hand to meet problems which press upon them, even about the way they should view the whole course of events in their time. A book written with such purposes differs from most books that survey public policy on economic matters, but its justification must be that:

> He who teaches facts and facts alone
> Lives only for today and dies when
>   facts have changed,
> But he who teaches men to think
> Lives for the future and survives as
>   long as thought doth reign.

Nearly all the major fields of government legislation are covered in this book. Not included are regulation and promotion of foreign trade, and maintenance of standards on food and drugs. The need to restrict the size of the book, and the belief that enough areas of legislation were included to reveal virtually all the types of problems, led to the omission of these two fields of government activity.

The completion of the task has been made possible by the participation of Charles Hagan. He has written Chapters 9, 20, and 22, on Monetary and Fiscal Policy, Communications, and Agriculture, respectively. I am deeply indebted to him for these chapters.

I am grateful for the assistance given me by colleagues and other friends. A number of chapters have been read by my colleagues in the Department of Government and the School of Law at the University of Texas: Chapters 4 and 5 by Professor Malcolm Macdonald; Chapters 6, 7, and 8 by Professor Wallace Mendelson; Chapters 10, 11, and 12 by Professor Ernest Goldstein; Chapters 13 and 14 by Professor Jerre S. Williams; and Chapter 21 by Professor William Huie. Professor Charles Hagan read all of my chapters. My own chapters were also read by my former student and research assistant, Mr. Orion White. Professor Michael D. Reagan read the manuscript for the publisher. All of these readers have helped to prevent errors and have made suggestions for revision.

I must add some other expressions of appreciation. The University of Texas generously granted me freedom from teaching duties for a semester. My colleague in the next office, Professor Howard A. Calkins, has advised me on innumerable occasions. My wife has graciously tolerated my absorption in the enterprise and assisted with many details.

I can only hope that the book will be useful enough to justify all of these many courtesies extended to me.

EMMETTE S. REDFORD

The University of Texas

Contents

Part I. The Role and Process of Government (policies + programs)

Chapter 1. The Early Period: 1776 to the Civil War   3

Early American Conditions 3 · The Place of Government 6 · The Attitudes of Men 12

Chapter 2. The Conditions of Our Time   17

The Disappearance of Unoccupied Resources 17 · Technological Dynamics 19 · Nationalization of the Economy 21 · The Industrial Structure 23 · The New Power of Labor 26 · Organizational Functions and Market Rigidities 28 · The Security Motive 34 · Defense, Foreign Relations, and Space 35 · Broadening Social Objectives 37 · Development of the Public Sector 37

Chapter 3. Economic Interests and the Governmental Process   40

The Economic Basis of Politics 40 · Analysis of the Interest Basis 42 · Governmental Structure 53 · Some Conclusions on the Political Process 60

Chapter 4. The Role of Government: Patterns of Thought   63

The Old Individualism 63 · *Laissez Faire* with Exceptions: The Rationalistic Approach 71 · The Modern Idealists 74 ·

CHAPTER 4. THE ROLE OF GOVERNMENT:
PATTERNS OF THOUGHT—Continued

Laissez Faire with Exceptions: The Empirical Approach 76 · Elements of Skepticism 80 · Modern Revolutionary Philosophies: Communism and Fascism 81

CHAPTER 5. SEARCH FOR A TWENTIETH-CENTURY SYSTEM OF THOUGHT   85

Liberalism, Socialism, Conservatism, and Neoliberalism 85 · The Indigenous American Approach 90 · The Synthesis of Individual Right and Public Interest 91 · Approaches in Policy in a Mixed Economy 92 · The Ultimate Beneficence of a Mixed Economy 98 · Summary 100

Part II. The Constitution and the Economy

CHAPTER 6. THE CONSTITUTION AND THE NATIONAL ECONOMY   105

Interstate Citizenship 106 · Full Faith and Credit 108 · Money 109 · Contracts 110 · Commerce 111 · Miscellaneous Aids to Economic Enterprise 115 · Foreign Affairs 115 · Supreme Law and Supreme Judiciary 116 · A National Government with Strength 117 · Conclusion 117

CHAPTER 7. THE CONSTITUTION, SOCIAL INTERESTS, AND ECONOMIC RIGHTS   119

The Constitution 119 · From the Constitution to the Civil War 121 · After the Civil War: Crystallization of Constitutional Doctrine 126 · The Economic Significance of Due Process: From the 1880's to the 1930's 129 · From the Thirties to the Present: Revision of the Court's Position 132 · Conclusion 134

CHAPTER 8. POWERS OF THE NATIONAL AND STATE GOVERNMENTS   136

National Powers 137 · State Powers 151

Part III. Policies Affecting the Economy Generally

CHAPTER 9. MONETARY AND FISCAL POLICY 157
Policies Before the Great Depression 157 · Fiscal Policy During the Depression 164 · Post-Depression Developments 174

CHAPTER 10. THE SHERMAN ACT AND
  ITS INTERPRETATION 184
The Meaning of Words 184 · The Rule of Reason 187 · Close Combinations and Single-Firm Power 188 · Loose-Knit Combinations 195 · Patents and the Antitrust Act 202 · Conclusion 206

CHAPTER 11. ADDITIONAL LEGISLATION ON
  COMBINATIONS AND BUSINESS PRACTICES 208
The Federal Trade Commission Act, As Amended 209 · Unfair Methods of Competition and Deceptive Acts 215 · The Clayton Act, As Amended 216 · A Special Problem: Basing-Point Pricing 232 · Exemptions from Antitrust 236 · Summary and Conclusions 242

CHAPTER 12. PROBLEMS OF INDUSTRIAL
  POLICY AND ENFORCEMENT 244
Competition as the Regulator 244 · Policy Answers Which Minimize the Role of Antitrust 247 · Effectiveness in Antitrust 253 · The Issues Broadened and Sharpened: Government and Steel in 1962 265

CHAPTER 13. GOVERNMENT PRESCRIPTION OF
  CONDITIONS, RIGHTS, AND BENEFITS
  OF EMPLOYMENT 269
Prevention of Fraud 269 · Safety, Health, and Rehabilitation 270 · Freedom of Labor 271 · Insurance for Workers 275 · Child Labor, Maximum Hours, and Minimum Wages 283 · Conclusions 290

CHAPTER 14. GOVERNMENT POLICY ON EMPLOYER-
EMPLOYEE RELATIONS   295

Government Action Prior to 1926 296 · Legislation on Railway Labor 300 · The Labor Injunction: The Norris-LaGuardia Act, 1932 305 · The Antitrust Act in a New Period 308 · National Legislation on Industrial Labor: Labor's Rights 309 · National Legislation on Industrial Labor: Comprehensive Policy 312 · Problems for the Future 323

CHAPTER 15. ECONOMIC CONTROLS IN WARTIME   329

The Change to a Wartime Economy 330 · Production Programming 332 · Allocation 336 · Stabilization 342 · Problems of Organization and Coordination 353 · Planning for Future Emergencies 355

Part IV. Regulation and Promotion of Industries

CHAPTER 16. INDUSTRY REGULATION AND
PROMOTION: A PREVIEW   359

Panorama of Industry Regulation and Promotion 359 · Substantive Types of Regulatory Action 361 · Substantive Types of Promotion 367 · General Qualities of Government Action 368

CHAPTER 17. RAILROAD REGULATION   371

Background of Interstate Commerce Act 371 · The Interstate Commerce Act of 1887 373 · The Strengthening of Rate Regulation 375 · Comprehensive Regulation: The Transportation Act of 1920 378 · Regulatory Legislation Since 1920 382 · Comments on Railroad Regulation 389

CHAPTER 18. GOVERNMENT AND THE
TRANSPORTATION NETWORK   395

Elements in the Transportation Network 395 · Motor Carriers 398 · Air Carriers 404 · Water Carriers 414 · Pipelines 415 · Problems in Transportation Policy 416

American
Government
and the
Economy

CHAPTER 19. PUBLIC UTILITY REGULATION   425

Municipal Control 428 · State Regulation 428 · National Regulation: Electric and Gas Utilities 430 · Regulation of Rates 438 · Concluding Comments 449

CHAPTER 20. THE REGULATION OF
      COMMUNICATIONS   451

The Telegraph 451 · The Telephone 453 · International Cables 458 · Broadcasting 459 · Conclusion 473

CHAPTER 21. OIL AND GAS: PRODUCTION,
      PRODUCERS' PRICES, AND NATIONAL POLICY   474

Petroleum Production and Its Regulation 475 · Producers' Prices 486 · National Policy 492

CHAPTER 22. AGRICULTURE   499

Nineteenth-Century Policies 499 · The Twentieth-Century Surplus 500 · Regulation of Middlemen 503 · Cooperatives for Farmers 509 · Equality for Agriculture 510 · Commentary 522

CHAPTER 23. FINANCIAL INSTITUTIONS
      AND MARKETS   527

Commercial Banking 527 · Regulation of Insurance 533 · The Securities Markets 537

Part V. The Regulatory System

CHAPTER 24. THE SYSTEM OF ADMINISTRATIVE
      REGULATION   547

Administrative Agencies 548 · Administrative Development of Regulatory Programs 552 · Administrative Procedure 556 · Elements of Administrative Strength 561 · Responsibility 565

CHAPTER 25. PROBLEMS IN REGULATORY
      ADMINISTRATION   568

Internal Process 569 · Organization and Responsibility 575 · Interest Associations 582 · Public-Private Balances 588

Part VI. Public Enterprise

Chapter 26. The Scope of Public Enterprise 593

Arguments and Motivations 594 · Areas of Public Enterprise 599 · Miscellaneous Enterprises 607 · Mixed Enterprise 608 · Conclusion 612

Chapter 27. Policies and Methods in Business-Type Enterprises 614

Finance 614 · Organization 619 · Miscellaneous Aspects 627

Part VII. Summary and Conclusions

Chapter 28. Final Observations 631

Realities of Our Time 631 · Public Policy in the Mixed Economy 633 · The Processes of Government 636

Selected References 640

Table of Cases 657

Index 665

American
Government
and the
Economy

Part I. The Role and Process of Government

Chapter 1. The Early Period: 1776 to the Civil War

THE ROLE OF GOVERNMENT at any given time results from the interaction of three factors. First, it will depend mainly on the existing or previous social and economic conditions that have left their imprint on current behavior. Second, it will be influenced by the effectiveness of group demands in the political sphere. Third, it will depend also upon the ideas of people as to what is proper, necessary, or expedient. These three factors—ecological, political, and ideological—are intertwined so tightly that the precise effect of each, and the extent to which each is cause rather than effect, cannot be determined. (The three as factors in our day are discussed separately in chapters immediately following this one.) Preliminarily, this chapter examines these several factors in the early part of our history. "The past is prelude to the present": what exists now is affected profoundly by the conditions, successful group demands, and ideas of the antecedent period.

EARLY AMERICAN CONDITIONS

Foremost among the circumstances which determined thought and the course of events in nineteenth-century America was the abundance of undeveloped and unoccupied resources. Lands, forests, and minerals of immeasurable richness lay westward and beckoned capital, labor, and organizing genius. The vast, untouched American resource domain made this the incomparable land of opportunity for individuals and also the setting for unprecedented expansion in the production of goods.

Many of the other factors in the development of this nation's economy in the first hundred years of independence either derive from or are closely associated with this prime factor. Likewise, the attitudes of Americans toward the role of government in the economy, though affected by other factors, were in considerable measure the result of this first one.

A second and complementary factor was the freedom the individual had, under the American institutional system, to acquire and develop these resources. The western resources were national domain to which citizens of every state and immigrants from abroad could move freely. The lands became available first at low cost and later without cost to homesteaders,

3

4   The Role and Process of Government

and hence passed to millions of individual proprietors. These proprietors were largely unhampered by legal inhibitions; restrictive covenants in titles to property were almost nonexistent, as were regulations affecting production or commerce.[1] Similarly, forests, minerals, and waterfalls awaited the hand of the business enterpriser, and the legal and social system gave him freedom, prestige, and access to favorable political action. The lack of restraint was, of course, a response to frontier conditions, but at the same time the freedom allowed under the inherited governmental and legal systems facilitated the rapid development of the nation's resources. (In other words, from the beginning there was a political base for economics; law and public policy fostered individual enterprise.)

Third, the use of resources was affected tremendously by the technological developments which marked the beginnings in this country of the industrial revolution. In agriculture the cotton gin and the reaper are well-known spectacular introductions, but there were also the increasing substitution of the plow for the hoe, the introduction of the cast-iron and later the steel-alloy plow, and the development of harrows, cultivators, mowers, sowers, and other implements. In ranching there were the windmill and the barbed-wire fence. These many improvements facilitated the cultivation of large areas (for example, wheat and cotton production increased a thousandfold from 1790 to 1860), reduced man-hour requirements in production, and made possible the development of a large export trade in agricultural products. Similar technological developments were occurring in industry. Thus, the substitution of coal for charcoal, for example, worked a revolution in the iron industry, bringing a tenfold increase in productive capacity in many cases by 1860 and allowing concentration of the industry in locations close to coal. Similar developments in technique occurred in other industries, such as textile and arms manufacture.[2]

Fourth, the period was one of tremendous expansion in multiple directions. Between 1790 and 1860 the population increased from about 4 million to about 31½ million (approximately a 35-per-cent average increase each decade); millions of immigrants arrived from Germany, Ireland, and other places; the line of settlement moved from the Alleghenies to the Pacific; foreign markets absorbed greater quantities of American agricultural produce; internal improvements—canals and roads, then railroads—were made on a scale hitherto undreamed of; and manufacturing expanded. Parallel to the development of the West was the growth of cities as centers of industry, finance, and merchandising. In 1790 no city had over 50,000 population, but by 1860, 9.8 per cent of the people lived in thirty-five cities of this size

---

[1] For an account of the political effects of the lack of feudal institutions in this country, see Louis Hartz, *The Liberal Tradition in America: An Interpretation of American Thought since the Revolution* (New York: Harcourt, Brace & World, Inc., 1955).

[2] A good account of technological developments in this period can be found in Chapters 6 to 12 of Harold F. Williamson (ed.), *The Growth of the American Economy: An Introduction to the Economic History of the United States*, 2nd ed. (Englewood Cliffs, N.J.: Prentice-Hall, Inc., 1951).

and 4.4 per cent in two cities of over 500,000.³ The economy developed, however, at an uneven pace, with tremendous spurts of activity being interrupted by periods of depression, such as after the War of 1812 and again in 1837 and 1857.

Fifth, the economy was atomistic. Except for the Southern plantation system, it was built, in the main, of small individual enterprises or partnerships. "Even by 1860 only 6 industries averaged more than 100 employees per plant, and of these only cotton textiles (with an average of about 120) consisted of many establishments." ⁴ The corporate system had begun to develop, particularly in finance, transportation, and manufacturing, and large undertakings were increasing. Nevertheless, individual rather than corporate, small rather than large, enterprises predominated. The kind of society assumed in eighteenth- and nineteenth-century philosophy, of which the units of social organization were the individual man (in politics) and the small individual concern (in economics), really existed in the formative period of this country. Where law ran counter to the system—as in the rule of primogeniture or in provisions for sale of western land in large, high-priced portions—it was changed to conform to the spirit of equality; and when trends toward large, controlling economic power seemed evident— as in the Second United States Bank—the spirit of antagonism was strong.

Sixth, the social characteristics of the period varied considerably from section to section. On the agrarian frontier, individual, family, and community self-sufficiency was predominant, and hence there was a lack of dependence on central political or social organization, or even substantial dependence on formal local organization. Frequently a man dug his own well, cut his own fuel from the forest, made his own whiskey, had his own gun handy for defense, and built his home and cut his path through the forest alone or with the cooperation of his neighbors. In the cities in the older sections of the country, big fortunes were being made in finance, industry, and trade, and at the same time there were poverty, the beginnings of slum areas, and twelve- to fourteen-hour workdays. In the South the plantation was the dominant social institution, but beside it stood the small holdings of the poorer whites, a considerable number of whom constantly sought opportunity farther west. In many local communities there was little competition in merchandising and service trades (a single village general store, a blacksmith, and a few other establishments were the business world), but as time passed, improved transportation facilities and continuing settlement increased the number of merchandising outlets and thus the amount of competition. Surveys indicated that life expectancy increased from twenty-five years in 1790 to about forty years just prior to the Civil War. A relatively large measure of equality—in economic opportunity, suffrage, social

---

³ *Statistical Abstract of the United States, 1958* (Washington, D.C.: 1958), pp. 20 and 21.
⁴ Harold F. Williamson (ed.), *The Growth of the American Economy: An Introduction to the Economic History of the United States*, 2nd ed. (Englewood Cliffs, N.J.: Prentice-Hall, Inc., 1951), p. 291.

life, and the attention and regard of one's fellows—existed on the frontier, and democratic philosophy spread through all parts of the nation, reflected, for example, in the changing requirements for voting and holding office in the seaboard states.

Finally, the conditions of the time made for fluidity in the economic and social system. All was in flux, rapid flux: the frontier moved ever westward, technology brought steamboats, reapers, and other implements, the public school developed, new religious movements started—unitarianism and deism being followed by a spate of new denominations, political parties died and new ones were born, the democrats took political control from the aristocrats, the immigrant flow increased, the Orient was opened, the slave economy of the South was destroyed. The most distinctive aspect, however, of the fluidity was the opportunity of the enterprising man to do new things, to establish his own enterprise (farm, mill, store), to use the capital and the labor of others in manufacturing, transportation, and commerce, to rise from humble to high station. Movement, change, opportunity—here was the converse of the Old World systems built on caste, custom, and legal restraint.

THE PLACE OF GOVERNMENT

THREE GREAT POLITICAL EVENTS. Independence, the Constitution, and the Civil War were three political events which affected the development of the economy.

The Economic Importance of Independence. The first great contribution of political action to the economy of this country was the winning of independence. The effect was to free the people from the shackles of the mercantilist system and the dependence of a colonial status. The American Revolution won more than political independence; it won the economic independence of a people and cut loose a vast and rich economic domain for development without Old World restrictions.

The Economic Importance of the Constitution. Chapter 6 summarizes the notable contributions made to the development of the American economy by the framers of the Constitution. It will suffice here to note a few of their greatest contributions.

1. They laid the foundation for a strong national government that could preserve tranquillity, protect commerce, and aid in the development of the western territory.

2. They made certain decisions which were necessary to allow the free flow of persons, investment money, and commerce over the nation as a whole, thus opening a vast area and a vast market to the entrepreneurial genius of Americans, wherever located. This they did through a multitude of related provisions, including retention of the interstate citizenship pro-

vision of the Articles of Confederation (see pages 106–108), prohibitions on the states, and grants of power to the national government.

3. Building upon and adding to the Articles of Confederation, they made possible national uniformity in certain facilities for commerce, such as coinage, patents and copyrights, uniform weights and measures, and a postal system.

4. They established a framework for government under which—save only for the events leading to the Civil War—the conflicting demands of the various sections of a growing country could be accommodated and compromised. The resulting tranquillity provided security and continuing opportunity for the entrepreneur.

The effect of these changes was to create one large economic area for development—the United States as an economic as well as politically unified reality. It is evident that the most important contribution of government to the development of the economy was the Constitution. It may not be too much to say that the Constitution of the United States was the greatest single political contribution to economic development in history. Never, perhaps, has positive, forward-looking political decision meant so much to the development of an economy.

The Economic Importance of the Civil War. The great schism in the nation was not political only; it was basically economic. The nation started with two economic systems, one based on slave labor, the other on free labor. The conflict between the two divided the nation politically, but beneath it was the economic division. The Southern economy was distinct from, and out of accord with, the dominant trend in the nation.

The Civil War left this nation with one economy, based everywhere on free and mobile labor, paid with cash. The South could now participate in the development of the diversified, capitalistic American economy. Unfortunately, the full transition of the South into the ebullient overflow of economic energy which characterized the nation was difficult and delayed by many factors. But ultimately the South would benefit from industrialization and diversification of its economy, and would become indistinguishable from the rest of the country in its economic characteristics.

THE CORE OF GOVERNMENT FUNCTIONS. Certain government functions have been continuously performed in this country from the beginning. They could be referred to as traditional functions, continuous functions, or as the core of government functions having a close relation to the economy. The first two of these are the maintenance of order and the administration of justice. Included in the latter is the protection given to property and the sanction given to contracts. Some regulation is involved in protection of property, because property rights must be defined and choices made from among alternative rights of ownership and transmission; some regulation is also necessary in safeguarding contracts, because government does not enforce all contracts (for example, contracts for slavery, child marriage, or in restraint of trade).⁵ Third is the provision of a money system, to serve as a medium of exchange and a standard for deferred payments. This has long been accepted by most persons as a proper government function. In England, for example, the efforts to provide a dependable coinage reach back to Anglo-Saxon days; penalties, such as cutting off a man's hand, were imposed for debasing the coinage. Americans readily accepted this age-old function of government, and today have expanded it into a complex currency and credit system. Fourth is government provision of a postal system, an enterprise which, in the days of its origin, seemed to meet Adam Smith's test of a type of service which could not be provided successfully by private enterprise.⁶ Fifth are certain facilities of commerce, such as patents and copyrights and uniform weights and measures, authorized as functions of Congress in our Constitution. Sixth is the protection of the home market and the promotion of foreign trade. The former, by the device of a protective tariff, ran counter to the ideas of theoretical free traders and many citizens' views on public policy, but it has now existed for so long and is so widely accepted that it can be thought of as a traditional function of government in this country. Seventh is the provision of internal aids to commerce through internal improvements, such as canals and roads. This too conforms with Adam Smith's test, and was early accepted in this country as a proper function of state and national governments.

STATE ECONOMIC POLICIES. The preceding summary of the generally accepted core of government functions should not obscure the fact that governments have always engaged in many other types of activity. In the period we are surveying, the additional scope of government functions can best be indicated by reference to the states, which were then the chief centers of legislative action. Recognizing this fact, Louis Hartz, in his *Economic Policy and Democratic Thought: Pennsylvania, 1776–1860*,⁷ has analyzed one state's legislation relating to economic matters. From his discussion we can summarize the chief types of economic legislation in a major American state.

The chief aim of state policy in Pennsylvania was to aid and promote the development of resources and the expansion of trade. This promotional aim was reflected in three types of activity. First, private corporations were granted charters for such enterprises as mining, manufacturing, banking, and transportation. At a time when charters were granted by special act of the legislature, the various sections of the state contested for charter grants to corporations which would be active in their respective areas. Second, state enterprises were established for the construction of internal improve-

---

⁵ "While the theorists were talking about laissez faire, men were buying and selling legal titles to property, were chartering corporations, were making and enforcing contracts, were suing for damages. In these transactions, by means of which the work of society was carried on, the state was implicated at every vital point." Walter Lippmann, *The Good Society* (London: Little, Brown & Co., Inc., 1937), p. 187.

⁶ See pages 595–596.

⁷ Cambridge, Mass.: Harvard University Press, 1948.

ments, including canals, roads, and railroads. Third, the state invested money in mixed companies—that is, companies in which some of the stock was owned by private investors and some by the state. Mixed companies were established for such purposes as banking and bridge or road construction. Hartz says the state participated in these companies for three reasons: to make a profit, to promote economic development, and for "partial guidance of corporate policy." Hartz has summarized the trends in state promotional activity in the state of Pennsylvania as follows:

(1) The period immediately after the Revolution in which the state assumed complete responsibility for the construction and operation of turnpikes. (2) The period from 1791 to 1825 when the state began to rely increasingly upon private and mixed corporations and when complete public ownership was challenged on practical grounds. During this period public ownership was universally acknowledged, as before, as being within the legitimate sphere of state action. (3) The period of the initiation of the public-works system when public ownership was not only accepted as legitimate but was believed by the overwhelming mass of Pennsylvanians to be practical and desirable as well. (4) The period after 1830 when, in controversies over the use of the public railways, the legitimacy of ownership as a governmental function began to be challenged for the first time and in a vague way.[8]

Ultimately, the failure of state enterprise and the drive of "the emergent railroad capitalists" led to the liquidation of state enterprise and the turn toward development by private corporations.

In addition to promotional activity, the state government in Pennsylvania, like other state governments of the time, engaged in a considerable amount of regulatory activity. Particularly noteworthy was the extent of inspection and licensing. "The inspection program," says Hartz, "included such articles as flour, fish, beef, pork, hogslard, flaxseed, butter, biscuits, harness and leather, tobacco, shingles, potash and pearlash, staves, heading and lumber, ground black-oak bark, pickled fish, spirituous liquors, and gunpowder."[9] "Licensing governed a variety of businessmen, e. g., inn-keepers, peddlers, retailers of foreign goods, liquor merchants, brokers of various kinds, wharfage pilots, and auctioneers."[10] Debtor-creditor relations were regulated by such measures as the abolition of imprisonment for debt, "stay laws" (allowing delay of payment), and bankruptcy. Labor regulations were passed—for example, prohibitions on child labor and on labor beyond ten hours a day, and mechanics' lien laws (giving the laborer-contractor a lien on buildings for labor and materials used in their construction). Corporate charters contained regulatory conditions of various kinds, the most notable being price-fixing clauses, such as those concerning rates of charge in railroad corporation charters.

[8] *Ibid.*, pp. 165–166.
[9] *Ibid.*, p. 205.
[10] *Ibid.*, pp. 206–207.

10   *The Role and Process of Government*

All in all, the period surveyed by Hartz was one in which state governments, and local governments as well, were extremely active in the promotion and regulation of economic activity.[11]

ISSUES OF NATIONAL POLICY. Great issues of national politics arose out of the conflicting economic interests of sections and groups. During the revolutionary period there was a kind of populist social revolt which resulted in the enactment of state laws favorable to debtor and small-farmer groups. The interests of other groups were adversely affected, and led to a conservative reaction against the unlimited powers of state legislatures. The commercial and financial interests desired a stronger national government for protection and advancement of their economic interests. "In fact, most of our political evils may be traced to our commercial ones . . . ," wrote Madison prior to the meeting of the Philadelphia convention.[12] One need not agree with all the arguments of Charles A. Beard in his *An Economic Interpretation of the Constitution* (particularly his imputations of direct personal interest to the members of the Convention [13]) to accept the essential accuracy of Beveridge's statement that "Finance, commerce, and business assembled the historic Philadelphia convention. . . ."[14] Within the Convention many compromises had to be made among the conflicting economic interests of the different sections of the country. In the struggle for ratification, there was conflict between those interests which had suffered most and those which had gained or suffered little under the pre-Convention system.

[11] Books on state policy in three other states tell a similar story. Oscar and Mary Flug Handlin, *Commonwealth: A Study of the Role of Government in the American Economy: Massachusetts, 1774–1861* (New York: New York University Press, 1947), shows how in the beginning "all looked to the Commonwealth, the guardian of the common interest, to breathe new life into the productive system" (p. 53); and how, with the passage of time, "regulatory, police" action expanded and a reform spirit arose and dominated the state after 1850 (p. 217), but how the diffusion of opportunities to obtain charters had weakened their use as instruments of state policy, and had given them a private character. Thus, the stage was set for new developments and new notions. James Neal Primm, *Economic Policy in the Development of a Western State: Missouri, 1820–1860* (Cambridge, Mass.: Harvard University Press, 1954), concludes that in Missouri "the state took an active, positive role in the economic affairs during the period before the Civil War" (p. 125), with promotional and regulatory activities both being important. The state was "not hampered appreciably" by *laissez faire* notions (p. 125), nor motivated "by a theory of state action," for "Missourians . . . were essentially pragmatic" (p. 127). Milton Sydney Heath, *Constructive Liberalism: The Role of the State in Economic Development in Georgia to 1860* (Cambridge, Mass.: Harvard University Press, 1954), concludes that "although the spirit of *laissez faire* was ever pervasively present and its influence reflected repeatedly, it enjoyed no extended period of ascendancy" (p. 389). ". . . it was accepted that individual development was a social process, the product of many sorts of group action as well as individual initiative. The state was only one among the former . . ." (p. 390).

[12] Letter to Jefferson, March 18, 1786, in Gaillard Hunt (ed.), *Writings of James Madison* (New York and London: G. P. Putnam's Sons, 1900–1910), Vol. 2, p. 228.

[13] *An Economic Interpretation of the Constitution of the United States* (New York: The Macmillan Company, 1913); on personal interests of members, see Edward S. Corwin's review of Beard's volume in *History Teachers Magazine,* **V** (February 1914), pp. 65–66.

[14] A. J. Beveridge, *The Life of John Marshall,* 4 vols. (Boston: Houghton Mifflin Company, 1916–19), Vol. I, p. 310.

Following the Convention, differences on economic policy separated the Hamiltonians and the Jeffersonians. And down through the succeeding years, most of the political issues arose from the conflicting interests of men in government's economic policy. The major issues deserve brief reference in this discussion.

Tariffs for Protection. Even before the Convention there was agitation for government protection of home industry from foreign competition. The first Congress adopted a tariff measure which was protectionist in purpose and moderately protectionist in fact. After the War of 1812 the demand for protection increased, and the struggles over the question cut deep rifts among the sections and even led to the threat of nullification by South Carolina. Tariff laws were passed in 1816, 1824, 1828, 1832, 1833, 1842, 1846, and 1857, and bills were introduced in other years. From 1816 to 1832 the protectionists carried the day, though with much quarreling on particulars among the sections favorable to protection. Following the Compromise Tariff Act of 1833 there was a period of decline in rates, interrupted briefly from 1842 to 1846, and the bitterness that had characterized the struggles from 1819 to 1833 subsided.[15]

Development of the West. The conquerors of the West wanted government aid for their enterprise. The majority wanted western lands to be made accessible to them. They demanded, first, the sale of land in small portions at low prices, and they achieved it. Later, the Free Soil party advanced the idea of "free soil and free labor," which was taken over by the new Republican Party in 1856; and the Homestead Act, under which men could acquire title by residence, was passed in 1862. A parallel demand from the West was for easy credit, which was reflected in the liberal policy of governments in regard to the establishment of banks and their operation. The demand for internal improvements arose with and accompanied the expansion westward. The development of foreign markets, the protection of home markets, and the further expansion of the western area were also included in the demands of western settlers.

Money. Easy money versus hard money and debtor versus creditor have been constant or ever-recurring polarities in American politics from Revolutionary days to the present. In early politics it was reflected in the struggles over the two national banks and in the evolution of state banking policies. The adoption of the Constitution, with its prohibitions of state coinage, or state bills of credit, and of state impairment of contracts, seemed to be a victory for the creditor interests; but the trends in policy in the ensuing years demonstrated the superior political power of those who needed easy money. The dominant trend was to meet the needs in the developing economy for credit and easy access to banking facilities.

SLAVE VERSUS FREE LABOR. The issue of slave versus free labor was the dominant issue in politics during much of this period. From the

---

[15] See F. W. Taussig, *The Tariff History of the United States* (New York: G. P. Putnam's Sons, 1923).

beginning, in the Constitution itself, compromises had to be made between the slave- and free-labor areas (an example is the provision in the Constitution that the importation of slaves could not be prohibited before 1808). Before long, the conflict centered on the issue of slavery in the territories —on the expansion or nonexpansion of slavery. Statesmen struck compromises between the sections in 1820 and 1850, but the intensification of the conflict continued, and the issue was resolved by blood rather than by ballot and compromise. In the course of this struggle, governments regulated the labor supply of the nation: first, by protecting and enforcing property rights; second, by compromises on the extension of slavery to the territories; and third, by abolishing slave labor.

THE ATTITUDES OF MEN

The spirit of the developing nation was inevitably one of optimism. The doleful views of Malthus and all other Old World pessimists were alien to the spirit of the New World. Here men could retain the eighteenth-century belief in progress and burgeon forth an ebullient faith in the power of the individual and the destiny of the nation.

The center of the picture was the individual. Individualism as we have known it in America never had a chance in the Old World, where prescriptive rights to resources were already established and where social organization had fixed distinctions among men. But in this country the opportunity of the individual with initiative and diligence to make his own place in the world was for many a *fact*, and inevitably, therefore, it became a *creed*. The fact was boldly illustrated, not alone in such epic illustrations as the rise of Lincoln from log cabin to presidency and of the immigrant boy to a position of economic power, but also in the life stories of innumerable men witnessed daily in the communities of the nation. The creed was therefore simple and unequivocal: an industrious man could get ahead in America, and if he were thrifty, he could make provision for his material needs. Industry and thrift were therefore the chief virtues. They had the sanction of religion and sound lay thought: they were emphasized in Calvinistic theology (Puritan in this country) and in Franklin's *Poor Richard's Almanac;* they stood the test of experience in the lives of many in this country; they became, therefore, the core of American ethics.

Though New World conditions set the stage for individualism, Old World theory provided the basic *ideas*. Transferred from Europe to America, Calvinistic theology could join plain common sense in support of the ideas of industry and thrift. Beyond this was the secular-religious idea of a higher moral law which was the test of the justice or goodness of the worldly acts of men. The idea was old. The Greeks and the Romans developed the idea of natural law, which was a universal law of reason; the medieval theologians emphasized the existence of divine or natural law;

and early English judges looked not alone to custom, but also to reason and natural equity for their decisions. The modern Western Europeans transmitted a secular notion of natural law to America, where it was buttressed by the Christian doctrine that God had created a moral law to bind the actions of men. In America, however, the idea of a higher, fundamental law, more basic than the civil law of time and place, took a distinctive turn, for written documents came to be regarded as the fundamental law—first the colonial charters, and then the written constitutions of states and nation. Nevertheless, there still remained the idea that there was a moral law, derived from God or inherent in nature and discoverable by reason. This moral law was higher than man-made law, even if the latter was in constitutions or statutes. In its discovery one would find the test of the legitimacy of human action.

Already by the seventeenth century the idea of natural law was in large measure being transmuted into an idea of natural rights. The law of nature conferred rights on men. This idea, which had served the cause of religious, economic, and political dissent in Europe, was well known in this country through the writings of Locke and other political philosophers. It was popularized in the Revolution, notably in the Declaration of Independence and other state papers.

The doctrines of industry, thrift, and natural right, and the opportunity (or vision thereof) created by American conditions, all tended to support the vibrant individualism of the nineteenth century. It is significant, nevertheless, that the creed and sentiment of individualism can lead in divergent directions where state policy is concerned. The initial trend of individualism in this country was *not* toward *laissez faire,* in theory or in practice. Government was regarded as a support for the individual. It should provide *aid* in the development of the nation's resources: "To aid, encourage, and stimulate commerce, domestic and foreign, is a duty of the sovereign, as plain and as universally recognized as any other." [16] Moreover, *regulation* was not regarded as contrary to natural right if its direction and effect in a particular instance was to foster opportunity for men.

Hartz' useful book has not only shown the practice of the early period, but provided much insight into the attitudes of men. In the first half of the nineteenth century there was a strong fear of the private corporation and a belief that state-granted corporate rights ran counter to the natural rights of men. Accompanying this was the belief that the social contract (that is, the existence of civil society) strengthened the power of the individual and provided him with an opportunity to use the state for promotion of enterprise, for prevention of excess private power, and even as an alternative to corporate enterprise in such areas as banking and transportation. A House committee report in Pennsylvania in 1830 could even state

---

[16] Quoted by Louis Hartz, *Economic Policy and Democratic Thought: Pennsylvania, 1776–1860* (Cambridge, Mass.: Harvard University Press, 1948), p. 122, from the majority opinion in *Sharpless et al. vs. Mayor of Philadelphia,* 21 Pa. St. Rep. 147, 182 (1853).

that private charters should be granted only if it was shown "that it is inexpedient for the state to proceed in the undertaking as a public measure." [17]

The fact that government action in the economy was accepted is revealed in the politics of the period. The discussion above shows that men did not hesitate to press for state or national action which would be helpful to their section or to the economic group to which they belonged. Moreover, the leading statesmen believed that government had an important role to play in the economy of the nation.

To Madison, often called the father of the Constitution, this role was one of holding a balance among the interests. He accepted the fact that there would be division and conflict—"faction," he called it—in society. Also he, unlike Marxists, saw that there could be many causes for faction, such as "A zeal for different opinions concerning religion, concerning government, and many other points, as well of speculation as of practice; an attachment to different leaders. . . ." But in one of the most perceptive statements in the literature of political science, he recognized both the reality of the economic basis of politics and of the regulatory function of government:

But the most common and the most durable source of faction has been the various and unequal distribution of property. Those who hold and those who are without property have ever formed distinct interests in society. Those who are creditors, and those who are debtors, fall under a like discrimination. A landed interest, a manufacturing interest, a mercantile interest, a moneyed interest, with many lesser interests, grow up of necessity in civilized nations, and divide them into different classes, actuated by different sentiments and views. *The regulation of these various and interfering interests forms the principal task of modern legislation,* and involves the spirit of party and faction in the necessary and ordinary operations of government.

The danger, he thought at the time those words were written, was that a majority would form a faction and carry its interests into legislation, and he sought to find means in the structure of government to prevent this.[18]

Other statesmen favored the tilting of the scales in support of certain forms of enterprise. Hamilton and Jefferson alike recognized the importance of the role of government in determining the course of the economy. Hamilton definitely favored a policy of intervention that would strengthen the financial and manufacturing interests. In presenting his plans for funding of the public debt at par and for creating a national bank, he argued both the fiscal advantages for government and the benefits to the economy,[19] and he contemplated the mutual strengthening of government and private finance through the interrelation of the two. In his "Report on Manufactures" in 1791 he argued for a government policy to foster manufacturing

---

[17] *Ibid.,* p. 72.
[18] The summary of Madison's views is from *The Federalist,* No. 10. Italics supplied. Madison's recommendations for containing a majority faction are given in No. 10.
[19] *American State Papers* (Chicago: Encyclopaedia Britannica), Vol. VII, pp. 15–25, 67–76.

by a protective tariff and bounties, and for aid to industry by such means as payments to induce discoveries of new methods and the migration of artisans.[20] Jefferson, on the other hand, believed that agriculture should form the economic basis of the good society. This involved less government intervention in his day than did the fostering of manufacturing. The purchase of Louisiana, of course, was government action which strengthened the influence of agriculture. Moreover, the abolition of primogeniture, the spreading of educational opportunity, a limited and inexpensive government, and other Jeffersonian ideals would have the effect of fostering that individualistic type of society which Jefferson desired. John Adams and Webster believed that government should give special representation to the holders of property; and Webster, in the Hamiltonian tradition, said, "I am looking . . . for a law that shall induce capitalists to invest their capital in such a manner as to occupy and employ American labor."[21] Henry Clay wanted an "American System" of protective tariffs which would protect manufacturing and certain types of agriculture, and build a home market for the latter. It is clear, indeed, that the men of the first half of the century saw no inconsistency between individualism and the use of government to advance the economy (their cause).

Nevertheless, near the end of the period, developments were occurring which presaged the spread of *laissez faire* notions. Two of them were in the area of large-scale enterprise. First, state investment in railroads and other projects began to be looked upon with disfavor. This was due in part to imprudent, even reckless and extravagant, state investments in public projects and in the stock of private ones, and in part to amateur administration in state projects. Some states incurred obligations beyond their ability to pay, and the panics of 1837 and 1857 pointed up the excessive debt structure; hence, in many state constitutions provisions were added or old provisions strengthened to limit the power of legislatures to incur debts or invest in private enterprise. Second, the capacity of private enterprise to handle large undertakings, such as the construction of railroads, was beginning to be demonstrated. The day for the lapse of public enterprise and the extension of private enterprise was at hand.

Paralleling these developments was the imposition of new limitations on legislatures in the direction of *laissez faire.* The idea that acquired or vested property rights were protected by a higher moral law, even though not embodied in constitutional prohibitions, had been stated near the beginning of the period here considered by Justice Chase (in *Calder v. Bull,* 1798) and was repeated later by Justices Marshall, Johnson, and Story (all on the Supreme Court of the United States), Justice Kent of the New York courts, and others. The idea was that there were implied limitations on legislatures which grew out of natural law or natural rights, or, as

---

[20] *Ibid.*, pp. 123–144.
[21] Quoted in Charles A. and Mary R. Beard, *The Rise of American Civilization* (New York: The Macmillan Company, 1927), Vol. I, p. 673.

Justice Chase argued, out of the nature of the social compact and of free republican government.²² Such ideas had faded into the background with the rise of the Jeffersonian and Jacksonian democracies. But in the decades preceding the Civil War, the ideas of higher law were being revived and given concrete meaning in state courts.²³ And already some judges were seeing in the words "due process of law" a constitutional basis for restricting the role of government.²⁴

Thus, at the end of this period there was (1) disillusionment about government economic activity resulting from the failures of state enterprise and state investment in private undertakings, (2) the beginning of the great demonstration of the capacity of corporate enterprise, and (3) the development of legal doctrines into which could be poured the *laissez faire* ideas of the late nineteenth and early twentieth centuries.

²² *Calder v. Bull*, 3 Dallas 386, 388 (1798).
²³ For the story of higher-law limits in American courts, see Charles Grove Haines, *The Revival of Natural Law Concepts* (Cambridge, Mass.: Harvard University Press, 1930).
²⁴ For a detailed discussion of the developments in law, see Chapter 7 of this book.

Chapter 2. The Conditions of Our Time

WRITING IN 1911, Frederick J. Turner declared, "it is with a shock that the people of the United States are coming to realize that the fundamental forces which have shaped their society up to the present are disappearing." [1] He was speaking of one change in our society, but fifty years later we can note many changes. And we may see also how these changes "coerce us," as John M. Gaus has put it, "into the use of government." [2]

THE DISAPPEARANCE OF UNOCCUPIED RESOURCES

Turner was referring to the end of the American frontier of unoccupied land, which is generally said to have occurred about 1890. He had placed great emphasis on the change in his influential lecture in 1893: "The existence of an area of free land, its continuous recession, and the advance of American settlement westward, explain American development." [3] A school of historians accepted this thesis, arguing that the frontier accounted for the increase in goods, opportunity for the individual, and the growth of democracy and individualism.

More recently, Walter P. Webb has written *The Great Frontier*.[4] This title refers to the area, with all its wealth, which was opened to Europe (the "Metropolis") by geographical discovery beginning in the fifteenth century. Regarding the frontier, Webb stated this hypothesis: "This sudden, continuing, and ever-increasing flood of wealth precipitated on the Metropolis a business boom such as the world has never known before and probably never can know again." [5] The boom lasted from about 1500 to about 1900. Webb found in "the great frontier" the dynamism for the Western world, through four centuries, which Turner and his disciples found for the United States in its own frontier.

---

[1] "Social Forces in American History," *The American Historical Review* (January 1911), XVI, p. 217.
[2] *Reflections on Public Administration* (University, Ala.: University of Alabama Press, 1947), p. 5.
[3] "The Significance of the Frontier in American History," *Annual Report of the American Historical Association for the Year 1893* (Washington, D.C.: 1894), pp. 197–227, at p. 199.
[4] Walter P. Webb, *The Great Frontier* (Boston: Houghton Mifflin Company, 1952).
[5] *Ibid.*, p. 13.

To many scholars the explanation of the frontier historians has seemed grossly partial. Some have found in the frontier thesis, as developed by the Turner school of historians, an overemphasis on land and insufficient attention to other unoccupied and undeveloped resources, such as minerals, forests, and water. Others have criticized the apparent denial of the influence of the Old World heritage of ideas on the development of American individualism and democracy. Still others have argued the importance of technological advances. Many have thought that the thesis was too simple, and that the full explanation of American development would be found in a complex set of physical and cultural factors.[6]

Finding the explanation for past growth in a factor which no longer existed, the frontier historians looked to the future with a new Malthusian pessimism. The basis for progress having disappeared, the continuance of individual freedom and democracy was regarded as uncertain. Although many have not shared this pessimism, all recognize that the passing of the frontier has had momentous consequences.

The disappearance of the frontier has accentuated the shift to urban living and the congestion of men in cities. The trend is registered in language: first, men talked of urbanism, then of metropolitanism, now of megalopolis —a term used to describe, for example, that whole area of congestion from north of Boston to south of Washington. The trend is registered also in the expansion of municipal functions and the complexity of municipal problems: transportation, supply of utility service, slum clearance, police effectiveness, health protection, recreation, and many others. The growth of municipal functions is even greater perhaps than that of national functions![7]

The passing of the frontier has contributed, along with industrialization and urbanization, to man's dependence on social organization. While once he battled against nature's ill fortune and sought its gratuities, now he struggles within an intricate social structure and harbors the hope that its effects will be beneficial. For he is dependent upon economic development in a social order for his job, the level of his sales, or the solvency of his investments. In adversity he is dependent upon private insurance, public insurance or assistance, or other social mechanisms.

The disappearance of the frontier has also been a major factor in the development of a self-conscious labor movement. It is not accidental that the American labor organizations began to develop strength at about the same time the frontier began to disappear.

Also, President Theodore Roosevelt and others recognized our momentous

---

[6] For a summary of criticisms, see David M. Potter, *People of Plenty: Economic Abundance and the American Character* (Chicago: University of Chicago Press, 1954), Chapter VII.

[7] See the table of expansion of functions of the City of Detroit in William Anderson and Edward W. Weidner, *American City Government*, rev. ed. (New York: Holt, Rinehart & Winston, Inc., 1950), pp. 73–84.

conservation problem just as the great reservoir of unoccupied resources was finally disappearing. Nature's bounty being less, man's care increased. Today dozens of government agencies, at national and state levels, work to conserve soil, forests, minerals, water. Elimination of waste is one objective. Another is to obtain fuller and more effective use of resources in order to meet new industrial and population needs. To accomplish these ends, governments and private institutions plan for the future on the assumption that resources may be short.

With the passing of the frontier, the wellhead of government's benevolence changed. Webb has graphically demonstrated the vertical flow of wealth from sovereign to people between 1607 and 1900.[8] He thus pictures the give-away age, the period when sovereigns could give much more than they took. The resources of the West were a huge gift barrel, from which payments to settlers and development companies could be made. It was a means of stimulating new enterprise and bringing new wealth into the economy. Also, the free resources were used for the support of government functions. Texas gave 3,025,000 acres, about one-fiftieth of its huge area, for the construction of its capitol building! Education and railroads got vast support out of the public lands. Today the gift barrel as the free source of support for government functions is gone. What government bestows or what services it renders now must be produced from existing resources. Additional governmental undertakings use resources of labor and capital that must be drawn from the economy. This the sovereign may do by taxes, by allowing a measure of inflation to reduce the burden of debt, or by acting as the entrepreneur through ownership, and each of these creates new problems for government and society. Government is not now the giver of nature's bounty, but the distributor of social income drawn from the economy.

TECHNOLOGICAL DYNAMICS

Since the Civil War, the pace of technological change has quickened at a continuously—lately an enormously—accelerated rate. Technological advance, important from the eighteenth century onward, has become by now unquestionably the new dynamism for the economy. It has also brought an outpouring of goods such as was never before contemplated, even in Utopian visions.

Early inventions and their utilization occurred in small shops, were exceptional events, were marked with the names of individual geniuses such as Fulton, Whitney, Howe, McCormick, and Bell, and were achieved by private persons. Today the systematic methods and trained skill of specialized scientists are employed in laboratories of business, government, univer-

---

[8] *The Great Frontier* (Boston: Houghton Mifflin Company, 1952), p. 151.

sities, and foundations. Now the discovery of new processes and new products is a normal occurrence and vital to growth of the economy. Now research is institutional: business firms may spend as much as 15 to 30 per cent of their gross income for research; the United States government in 1963 spent over $12 billion on research and development—about one-third more than its annual peacetime budget prior to World War II. Now, indeed, government is the dominant factor, the national government paying about two-thirds of the cost of all research and development in the country. Now, also, by the government's practice of contracting out research, government and business jointly contribute to technological advance and become mutually dependent.

In the thirties, as men raised their heads above the tragedy of depression, they caught a new vision. They began to talk of new technological frontiers which might sustain the dynamic quality of the economy. Technological advances might keep alive the change, expansion, and opportunity which had existed in the frontier era. Then World War II initiated a new explosion in science, technology, and management. Today's realities have run beyond man's visions of yesterday. A historian writes of America as a "land of plenty," [9] and an economist asserts that economic problems now arise from abundance rather than scarcity.[10]

Competition takes a new form, unanticipated by Adam Smith—namely, the search for new products and new methods of lowering cost and improving quality, and the effort to make these new advances profitable by mass advertising. And government stands at the center of the picture, sponsoring new developments such as communication satellites and atomic energy which will create new challenges for entrepreneurs who can think largely and plan boldly.

Yet the visions of a scientific world are not entirely comforting. It is not merely that Malthusian pessimism remains because of the population explosion, and that fear of annihilation through the new weapons of war clouds all golden visions. Beyond these fearful contingencies many questions remain unanswered. First, will men's capacity to consume the output of the technological revolution continue to be sufficient to maintain an expanding economy? Will a faltering of consumption and the accompanying investment lead to depression and unemployment? Would a failure to maintain employment lead to vast government efforts to compensate for the lack of internal dynamics in the economy? Would such efforts be successful? Could the required adjustments be made without fundamental revision of the present legal and political institutions? Second, even if the pace of the technological revolution continues, can the institutional features of individualism and democracy be maintained? Will a new aristocracy of science and

---

[9] David M. Potter, *People of Plenty: Economic Abundance and the American Character* (Chicago: University of Chicago Press, 1954).

[10] John Kenneth Galbraith, *The Affluent Society* (Boston: Houghton Mifflin Company, 1958).

management arise? Will the technological skill of society fall into the control of small groups of managers, as James Burnham predicted?[11] Or is the power of society passing from politicians and managers to the technical specialists, as Victor Thompson has recently argued?[12] Can instruments of democracy be maintained or new ones devised through which new bureaucracies of managers and specialists can be made to serve the public interest? Can the frontiers of management and science be kept open to men of talent, as the western frontier was to men of strength, courage, and vision? Third, what problems of social policy must be faced by the governors of society? How drastic will be the changes, as old industries die and new ones are born, and as computers and other technologies reduce the need for manpower? Can the gains from technological advances be widely distributed so as to sustain the expansion of enterprise? Will wise and farsighted social policies be needed to buttress the inherited system of individual opportunity and social democracy which were natural phenomena in the frontier era?

These questions need not lead to despair, but rather to at least a feeble grasp of the challenges to be faced by men who have responsibility for making public policy.

NATIONALIZATION OF THE ECONOMY

In 1869, Union Pacific and Central Pacific locomotives "touched noses," marking the completion of the first transcontinental railway. This, as much as Appomattox four years earlier, symbolized the unification of the nation. A few decades later the great railway network was practically completed, and the products of the nation could move with new speed to distant markets. This gave impetus to the industrial revolution by broadening markets, opening the inland areas not reached by waterways, and allowing for expansion of industry at locations which were favorable in terms of raw products, labor availability, and other factors.

Later the development of railway express and the establishment of parcel post by the Post Office Department in 1913 facilitated the reach of merchandisers to wider markets. Great mail-order houses became new American institutions, and their catalogues a common rural possession. National merchandising brought new choices to consumers and new competition in the distribution of goods.

Then came the building of highways, facilitated, as had been the spread of railroads, by the national government. In 1916 the national government began its system of grants-in-aid for highway construction. The building of roads and the extensive sale of automobiles enabled the consumer to buy

---

[11] James Burnham, *The Managerial Revolution: What Is Happening in the World?* (New York: John Day Company, Inc., 1941).
[12] Victor A. Thompson, *Modern Organization* (New York: Alfred A. Knopf, Inc., 1961).

merchandise in a broader market and made the American market still more competitive. The development of highway transportation over the nation brought commercial trucking on a vast scale. Thus, new means of distributing products filled gaps in railroad service and brought lowered transportation costs for many products and areas.

Recently there has been a third wave of transportation development—air transport. Also, the oil and gas pipeline and shipping on the rivers and along the coastline provide still other means of transportation.

In addition to the movement of goods, new modes of transportation have led to more rapid communication of information and orders for merchandise. These developments and the use of the telephone and telegraph have facilitated the sale of merchandise, quickened the tempo of economic enterprise, and contributed to effective managerial control of dispersed industries.

The developments in transportation made possible the location of factories at great distances from markets and encouraged the development of large-scale enterprise. Combined with radio and television, they made possible mass advertising of standardized, trademarked products. This advertising is done increasingly on a national scale, and encourages the further development of national markets for consumer goods.

One effect of these changes has been to make for greater interdependence between the sections of the nation and the parts of the economy. Another effect has been to shift the center of promotion and regulation of economic interests to the national capital. The dramatic juncture of Union and Central Pacific in 1869 was evidence of a new day not only of giant private enterprise, but also of national action, for these railroads had had their large subsidies from Washington instead of state capitols; and the Wabash decision of the Supreme Court in 1886,[13] holding that the states could not regulate interstate railroad rates, followed by the act for national regulation in 1887, symbolized the fact that a nationalized economy brings a shift of political power from state to nation. As the further nationalization of the economy proceeded, the growth of national regulation followed in its wake. Today each of the means of transportation and communication is regulated (or managed—for example, the post offices) from Washington, and the productive and distributive industries are subject to national regulation of various sorts. Although interest groups have not overlooked the continued importance of the states (for example, as taxing jurisdictions, or in regulation of such diverse matters as banks, motor carriers, and labor), they now center their attention on Washington as the major source of policy affecting the economy. This is because it has been generally recognized that effective promotion or regulation is possible only from a jurisdiction as wide as the existing economic market.

[13] *Wabash, St. Louis, & Pacific Railway Co. v. Illinois,* 118 U.S. 557.

THE INDUSTRIAL STRUCTURE

The American economy is predominantly a *wage-basis, business, corporate* economy. In 1960, compensation of employees constituted over 83 per cent of all disposable personal income.[14] Agricultural employees totaled only about 8.6 per cent of all employed civilians, a decline from approximately 20 per cent in 1940, and from about 12.6 per cent as late as 1950.[15] Other sectors of the economy, private and public, have been absorbing both new workers and former agricultural workers. Of the nonagricultural civilian employees, about five-sixths were in private employment and about one-sixth in government employment.[16] As for corporate development, it was estimated that by 1929, corporations contributed 57 per cent of the income produced by private enterprise, a rise from approximately 21 per cent in 1870.[17]

In the corporate sector of the economy, perhaps the most impressive features are the size and significance of a small percentage of the corporations. Both of these features are, of course, difficult to measure; nevertheless, something may be revealed by some selected figures. In 1938, Dr. Willard Thorp described a large corporation as one with assets of $5 million or more,[18] and Berle and Means, in their exhaustive analysis in 1932, thought that the two hundred corporations each with $90 million or more assets had achieved a dominating position in the American economy.[19] In 1954 A. D. H. Kaplan considered "the big business sector" to include about eleven hundred industrial firms, each with assets in excess of $50 million or net income in excess of $5 million.[20] However, this big-business sector of eleven hundred firms did not include finance and insurance companies, which, according to Kaplan, accounted in 1948 for nearly half of the total assets of corporate enterprise.

Truly, this is a day of large corporations, and expansion of their businesses and inflation of prices have increased their dollar assets. What

[14] Computed from figures in U.S. Department of Commerce, *Survey of Current Business,* Annual Review Number (February 1961), Table 1, p. 4.

[15] Computed from figures in U.S. Department of Commerce, *Business Statistics,* 1961 Edition, p. 61.

[16] *Ibid.,* pp. 62–63.

[17] See A. D. H. Kaplan, *Big Enterprise in a Competitive System* (Washington, D.C.: Brookings Institution, 1954), p. 113. Kaplan draws his figures from Alfred L. Bernheim (ed.), *Big Business: Its Growth and Its Place* (New York: Twentieth Century Fund, 1937), p. 17, and Robert R. Doane, *The Measurement of American Wealth* (New York: Harper and Row, Publishers, Inc., 1933), Table 18, p. 53.

[18] *Hearings before the Temporary National Economic Committee* (Washington, D.C.: 1941), Part I (Dec. 2, 1938), p. 106.

[19] Adolf A. Berle, Jr., and Gardiner C. Means, *The Modern Corporation and Private Property* (New York: The Macmillan Company, 1932), Chapter III.

[20] *Big Enterprise in a Competitive System* (Washington, D.C.: Brookings Institution, 1954), p. 115.

position do they occupy in the total economy? Is their importance increasing as the years pass?

On the latter question, Berle and Means stated in 1932 that from 1909 to 1928 the largest two hundred corporations had had an annual rate of growth of 5.4 per cent, while other corporations had grown at a rate of only 2.0 per cent.[21] The period of World War II, in which the bulk of government contracts went to about seventy-five large concerns,[22] might have been expected to accentuate this stated trend that large corporations were growing more rapidly than small ones. Yet authorities were unable to agree that such a trend had continued. More recently, figures on manufacturing industries indicate the continuation of the trend noted by Berle and Means. The two hundred largest manufacturing companies increased their percentage of the value added to products by manufacturing from 30 per cent in 1947 to 38 per cent in 1958.[23]

Undoubtedly, the significance of the large corporation is tremendous. In banking, insurance, mining, transportation, and utilities the giants are dominant. For manufacturing, the Federal Trade Commission reported the percentages of total value of shipments of products accounted for by the largest companies in 1950. For the five largest companies the percentage was 11.4, for the fifty largest it was 26.6 per cent, and for the two hundred largest it was 40.5 per cent. The comparable figures for 1935 were 10.6, 26.2, and 37.7.[24] Kaplan found that the percentage of total corporate assets of industrial corporations held by the one hundred largest firms was 26.7 per cent in 1948, in comparison with 24.6 per cent in 1909 and 25.5 per cent in 1929.[25]

A different measure of concentration in American industry is the extent to which oligopoly has developed. Kaysen and Turner analyzed 1954 census data for manufacturing against two measures of oligopoly.[26] Type I oligopoly was defined as existing when eight or fewer firms made 50 per cent or more of shipments of products and the first twenty made 75 per cent or more of the shipments. Type II oligopoly existed when eight firms made 33 per cent of shipments and the first twenty made less than 75 per cent. Their figures show for national markets (in contrast to local or regional ones, or markets in which some products of the industry were sold on

[21] Adolf A. Berle, Jr., and Gardiner C. Means, *The Modern Corporation and Private Property* (New York: The Macmillan Company, 1932), p. 35.

[22] See *Economic Concentration in World War II: Report of the Smaller War Plants Corporation to Study Problems of American Small Business.* Sen. Doc. 206, 79th Cong., 2nd Sess. (1946).

[23] *Concentration Ratios in Manufacturing Industries, 1958,* Report Prepared by the Bureau of the Census for the Subcommittee on Antitrust and Monopoly of the Committee on Judiciary. U.S. Senate, 87th Cong., 2nd Sess., Part I (1962), p. 8.

[24] *Report of the Federal Trade Commission on Changes in Concentration in Manufacturing, 1935 to 1947 and 1950* (Washington, D.C.: 1954), pp. 16–17.

[25] A. D. H. Kaplan, *Big Enterprise in a Competitive System* (Washington, D.C.: Brookings Institution, 1954), p. 126.

[26] Karl Kaysen and Donald F. Turner, *Antitrust Policy: An Economic and Legal Analysis* (Cambridge, Mass.: Harvard University Press, 1959), pp. 29–32.

regional and some on national markets) that approximately 25 per cent of the shipments were made by companies in Type I oligopoly and approximately 40 per cent were made by those in Type II. In addition, twelve companies with shipments of more than one billion dollars in Type I oligopoly made nearly one-sixth of the shipments, and twenty-nine in Type I and Type II with shipments of over one billion accounted for about 47 per cent of the total shipments. In other words, nearly half the manufacturing shipments were made in concentrated markets by billion-dollar companies. A Federal Trade Commission report in 1949 showed that four companies had over 50 per cent of the net capital assets in nineteen of twenty-six fields of production analyzed.[27] A study for 1958 showed percentages of dollar volume of shipments by the largest four manufacturing companies. It was 77 for motor vehicles and parts, 32 for petroleum refining, 53 for steel works and rolling mills, 34 for meat packing, 56 for aircraft engines, 55 for organic chemicals, 79 for cigarettes, 46 for pulp mills, 80 for tin cans and other tinware, 76 for synthetic fibers, 79 for tractors.[28] Clearly, in many segments of American industry, production and commerce are highly concentrated in a small number of firms.

Figures on percentage of assets, shipments, etc., still do not give a full picture of the significance of the large corporation. First, they do not show the power of the large corporations in dealing with smaller concerns, either as buyer, seller, borrower, or lender. Second, the figures given on shipments do not show the extent of influence that can be brought to bear in multiple markets by the conglomerate enterprise—that is, the enterprise which operates in several industries. Third, power is concentrated through interlocking relationships among corporations—that is, through corporations owning stock in other corporations and through interlocking of directors and officers. These interlockings create close interrelationships between corporations and reduce the total number of persons in whom control over large enterprise is vested. And finally, the figures do not reveal the leadership of the officers and large stockholders of the giant corporations in the corporate community and in the larger society of which it is a part. The corporate community is organized in national associations, such as the U. S. Chamber of Commerce, the National Association of Manufacturers, and the many trade associations. There is a sharing of sentiment and opinion within the corporate community and much influence from within this community on the organs of opinion and on government; in the fostering of this opinion, the leadership of the big and powerful among corporate leaders is undoubtedly of great significance.

These corporate developments have created new social relationships of great significance. Law has always been the moderator and regulator when social relationships created new claims of right and new elements of conflict.

[27] *Report of the Federal Trade Commission on the Concentration of Productive Facilities* (Washington, D.C.: 1949), p. 21.
[28] *Concentration Ratios in Manufacturing Industries, 1958*, pp. 43–47.

And new law has had to be forged for the relationships arising from corporate growth. First, there are the claims of right and the conflicts of interest within the structure of corporate finance. There are relations between investors and managers; among types of investors (holders of common stock, preferred stock, bonds, debentures, etc.); between sellers and buyers of securities; between holding company and operating company; and so on. As in the feudal period, when a hierarchy of persons held rights in the same land, so here many groups hold rights or claims of interest in the same, or related, corporate entities. A vast network of corporate law has evolved to embody the policy of the state in protecting these various interests. To a large extent, this evolution has occurred within the courts, but through such legislation as the Securities Act of 1933 and the Securities Exchange Act of 1934, legislative and administrative regulation have been superimposed on the judically created network of rules. Second, new relationships between employers and employees were created. In their early period, corporations dealt harshly and on an impersonal basis with labor. Labor, facing the new power, lacked rights. This did not continue. The idea that law should aid the weaker party gained currency in legislatures, and to some extent in courts. This was reflected in waves of labor legislation of two types: one to protect labor by legislation on such matters as safety, hours, and even wages; the other to protect labor in its effort to establish in labor organization a countervailing power. Still later, the power of labor was checked by additional legislation. The results are another new network of law and administration and another set of issues of public policy. Third, corporate development has brought new relationships between industrial giants and those who would compete with them or deal with them as seller or buyer. To meet these new situations, legislatures have enacted antitrust laws and a variety of other measures to protect the public from concentrated power.

All in all, corporate growth has been perhaps the most fertile source of new relationships and of new claims and conflicts of interest, and hence of law and issues of public policy, in the last three generations.

THE NEW POWER OF LABOR

Developments similar to those in industry have occurred in labor. Here they came later, but more rapidly. There were less than four million members of labor unions when the National Labor Relations Act (1935) was passed, but afterwards the number was approximately quadrupled rather quickly. Today there are approximately 17 million union members. In recent years the number has been relatively unchanged, although as a proportion of the total labor force it has declined.

Union membership includes only about one-third of nonagricultural employees, but the power of organized labor is greater than the figures on proportion of membership indicate. Its power is apparent, first, in the tremendous size of some unions. In 1960 three unions had more than 1,000,000 members, four had 500,000 to 1,000,000, and fourteen had 200,000 to 500,000.[29] Unions of this size, with large accumulations of funds to aid members during strikes and with strong, centralized leadership, are great centers of private power. Second, in a large part of the economy, concentration in labor organization has gone far beyond that in industry. Thus, one union faces four major automobile manufacturers; a single miners' union, teamsters' union, and musicians' union faces in each case thousands of employer units. Third, union membership in many fields of labor is often virtually compulsory. This may result either from the existence of union membership contracts with employers or from the mere gain of control of the field of employment by unions. Fourth, unions may possess great strategic advantages. They may be able to use a monopoly position to tie up a whole industry, or choose a particular employer or segment of the industry on whom demands can be made which can be later extended to the whole industry. Fifth, labor's community of interest is represented by a giant federation (namely, the AFL-CIO) and affiliated political-action organizations, in the same way that capital's community of interest is represented through Chambers of Commerce and trade associations. Finally, the power of labor organization is revealed in the extent to which the pattern for new advances in labor benefits is set in union demands and negotiations in key situations. A rise in wages in the steel industry or others as a result of the concentration of labor pressure at one point brings a new round of wage and (ultimately) also salary increases throughout the whole economy; the establishment of welfare funds in a key industry strengthens the movement for employee retirement plans and other welfare measures in all industries. Thus, the policy-making function of the nation centers, at particular moments, around a negotiating table where a few representatives of labor and industry sit. Neither the market nor the sovereignty—though each may exert an influence—determines the next step in policy; it is, by the course of events and not by delegation, in commission to strategic positions of private power.

The new relationships resulting from union development are similar in kind to those arising from corporate development. Here, too, there are relationships within the newly developed structure. These are not as complex as the rights within corporate organization which are governed by corporation law; but law has already had to give attention to intralabor relationships. Thus, the National Labor Relations Act provided for elections to determine which union the employees desired as their representative; the Taft-Hartley Act added other provisions for vote of union membership; and the Labor Management and Disclosure Act extensively

---

[29] U.S. Department of Commerce, *Statistical Abstract of the United States, 1962*, Table 321, p. 242.

regulated the rights of members of labor organizations.[30] Here, too, new social relationships are created vis-a-vis the other party in the bargaining struggle. As big management has come to be faced by big labor, the law of industrial relations—evolved legislatively, administratively, and judicially—has become complex and the problems of public policy difficult and sometimes exasperating. And here, too, new aspects of public interest are created. There is a strong public interest if production and commerce are interrupted by stalemate in industry-labor bargaining; and there is a strong public interest in the types of decisions made to settle the disputes. For out of these decisions may come inflation or, oppositely, lag in purchasing power, or disproportionate benefits for some in relation to others, or other effects of general community concern. As the contract of men has taken the place of the arbitrament of the market, the question has arisen: Where and how does the public interest find representation in policy-making?

ORGANIZATIONAL FUNCTIONS AND MARKET RIGIDITIES

The consequences of the growth of corporations and unions have been stated above in the simplest and most familiar terms: they create new relationships which generate public controls. Yet this familiar way of stating consequences, though enlightening, does not by itself portray the full and unique significance of corporate and union growth.

These two developments exemplify—indeed, largely constitute—a great change in the nature of society, to which government responds. Modern economic and political theory have alike centered on man (the microcosmic unit) and the community at large (the macrocosmic unity of the state and the public interest). Rousseau and Locke in their seminal notions about government, and Adam Smith in his notions about the economy, share these foci of interest and either ignore or abhor the existence of intermediary associations between man and the state. Yet these are now with us, and the effects upon the functions of government, and on the economy with which it deals, are tremendous. It is primarily the latter which is of interest at this point.

The heart of the matter is that corporations and unions are organizations and that the economy must now be interpreted in terms of organizational behavior. The *structural* changes exhibited in big corporations and big unions, and in federations and liaisons within the corporate and the labor communities, give rise to an economy in which organization *behavior* is the central feature.[31]

---

[30] See Chapter 14.
[31] For fuller discussion, the student is referred to Kenneth E. Boulding, *The Organizational Revolution* (New York: Harper and Row, Publishers, Inc., 1953), and Wilbert E. Moore, *The Conduct of the Corporation* (New York: Random House, Inc., 1962).

The organizations are large and complex structures, and a variety of interests exists within them. Within the labor union there may be conflicts of interest between executives and workers, or, depending upon the union's composition, among other constituent elements. The business firm is an operating coalition of groups of people with objectives which are not entirely concordant—stockholders, bondholders, managers, laborers.[32] Moreover, these complex organizations operate within a matrix of associated and conflicting organizations to which they must adjust or from which they will demand adjustment.

In traditional organization theory the corporate executive is in a command position, and in traditional economic theory, he is in a position to make decisions toward the single objective of maximizing profits. Actually, as an administrator he is a broker compromising with, and hence yielding to, groups within the firm, and as an entrepreneur he is reconciling the goal of profit maximization with the other objectives of groups within the organization. He is more broker than commander or economist. Moreover, as presumed head of the enterprise, he must bargain with a conflicting labor power which is in one way within the firm and in another way outside of it. Even stockholders often appear to be an outside group to the executive, who is concentrating attention on management of an enterprise and who is bestowing large rewards on the managers. Finally, irrespective of where the bounds of the enterprise are, the corporate executive must represent this entity in a multitude of bargaining relationships with independent or semi-independent bankers, suppliers, affiliates, even with governments which award contracts, regulate prices, or move in other ways, and he must sometimes trim his sails to that outer force called public opinion.

The position of organization executive, either the corporate or the union, is a double one of agent for groups and broker among groups. His conduct is determined by an environment of men and institutions, perhaps much more than that of a market. The role is best described in words drawn from the realm of politics: representation, bargaining, compromise, and command.[33] It is this change from entrepreneur to organization man that Boulding had in mind when he wrote:

> One can almost describe the history of the present era as a continuous encroachment of politics on economics. We mean here by "politics" the conscious organization and planning through the instruments of authority and subordination, *private and public;* by "economics" the conscious and automatic coordination of human activity through the market and the price-profit mechanism.[34]

Although Boulding here overstates the role of "authority and subordination" (in contrast to representation and bargaining, which he emphasizes

---

[32] See James G. March, "The Business Firm as a Political Coalition," *The Journal of Politics* (November 1962), **XXIV**, pp. 662–678.
[33] James G. March, *ibid*.
[34] Kenneth E. Boulding, *The Organizational Revolution* (New York: Harper and Row, Publishers, Inc., 1953), p. 49. Italics supplied.

elsewhere), his statement significantly summarizes the shift from market to organization controls over the economy. He might have added that these organization controls are highly centralized in what another author has called "concentrates" of power and influence.[35]

Boulding himself has stated one of the effects of organization behavior: "In regard to economic life, the main impact of the development of large economic organizations has been to make prices and money wages more 'sticky' and less flexible than they would otherwise have been." [36] This effect first became the subject of wide discussion with the distribution in 1935 of a brochure on price inflexibility prepared by Gardiner C. Means.[37] It contained a table showing the *variations* in percentages of decline of prices and of production during the depression. The table showed, for example, that agricultural production had declined 6 per cent and agricultural prices 63 per cent, while for iron and steel the figures were 83 per cent for production and 20 per cent for prices, and for agricultural implements 80 per cent for production and 6 per cent for prices. The brochure explained that men in industry were able to limit production and maintain prices, while this could not be done in agriculture. In other words, prices of many industrial products were, in Means' words, "administered prices" (that is, determined by men), while other prices (for example, of farm products) were fixed in the market. Part of the economy was governed by men in organizations, while other parts were market-controlled.

Meeting a decline in demand by reducing output increases unemployment. Moreover, unions resist the downward adjustment of wages, thereby keeping costs high and thus contributing to price inflexibility and to the resulting unemployment in a period of declining demand. Since avoidance of an increase in unemployment must be an objective of government, the relatively high rigidity of wages and prices is one of the factors which forces government to adopt such policies as may avert recession. Moreover, wage and price rigidity pushes government toward demand-increasing, rather than cost-decreasing, policies. There is, in other words, a built-in tendency toward wage and price maintenance and increased government expenditures.

The impact of organizational decisions may be seen in another way: namely, in the transmittal and pattern effects of organization decisions. A negotiated wage increase, at least if it is greater than increases in productivity in the industry, will normally lead to price increases. Moreover, a wage settlement in one collective-bargaining contract may set a pattern for a round of wage increases throughout the economy. Similarly, a company

---

[35] Adolf A. Berle, Jr., *The 20th Century Capitalist Revolution* (New York: Harcourt, Brace & World, Inc., 1954), p. 26.

[36] Kenneth E. Boulding, *The Organizational Revolution* (New York: Harper and Row, Publishers, Inc., 1953), p. 208.

[37] *Industrial Prices and Their Relative Inflexibility.* Sen. Doc. 13, 74th Cong., 1st Sess. (January 1935).

with a strong position of price leadership may initiate changes in prices which will spread throughout the industry and effect prices in other industries which buy its products. Since persons acting in a representative capacity, such as corporate executives or union leaders, are under constraint to get additional benefits for those they represent, there is in these transmittal and pattern effects a built-in inflationary tendency. Also, since these decisions may take place first, or more rapidly, or to the greatest extent, in highly organized sectors of the economy, the organization decisions may result in imbalances in the economy and may limit the operation of market forces in the distribution of income and allocation of resources.

The substantial substitution of organizational controls for market controls has given rise to issues of responsibility. It is now widely recognized that private organizations are private governments whose decisions have large effects on the interests of diverse groups of men. It is also recognized that power is centered in corporate managers and labor leaders, rather than in the owners of corporate property. Adolf Berle has discussed this development regarding the corporation in a book appropriately entitled *Power without Property,* and Father Harbrecht calls our society a "paraproprietal society"—that is, one which "has passed from a property system to a power system." [38] A financial commentator has discussed an "erosion in stockholder status" and an overprivileged executive class with "power to overpay themselves." [39] Some authors have proposed stockholder democracy as the answer, which implies that the purpose of the corporation is the pursuit of profit for its owners.[40] Others have accepted the fact of the brokerage function of corporate management—the power to allocate benefits among groups; they have accepted the fact of multiple responsibilities—to workers, managers, investors, and the community. As a result, the corporate manager is regarded as the trustee of the interests of the various groups affected by his function. But how impress upon the trustee the obligations implicit in his position? The restraint of conscience has been suggested.[41] Also, the possibilities of corporate constitutionalism have been discussed.[42] A corporate constitution would restrain corporate management as public constitutions restrain public managerial power. It is recognized that such a constitution would emanate in part from the law of the state, but the hope is expressed that there will be "active efforts within the leading business corporations

---

[38] Adolf A. Berle, *Power without Property: A New Development in American Political Economy* (New York: Harcourt, Brace & World, Inc., 1959); Paul P. Harbrecht, *Pension Funds and Economic Power* (New York: Twentieth Century Fund, 1959). And see the Berle-Harbrecht pamphlet, *The Paraproprietal Society* (New York: Twentieth Century Fund, 1959).

[39] J. A. Livingston, *The American Stockholder* (New York: J. P. Lippincott Co., 1958), pp. 218 and 222.

[40] See Louis D. Kelso and Mortimer J. Adler, *The Capitalist Manifesto* (New York: Random House, Inc., 1958).

[41] See pages 248–249.

[42] See particularly Richard Eells, *The Government of Corporations* (New York: Free Press of Glencoe, Inc., 1962) and his discussion of the views of others at pages 39–52.

to bring their internal governmental systems into line with prevailing norms of equitable procedure." [43] The design for a corporate constitution has not been developed, though some elements in such a constitution may be apparent: the check of labor power upon corporate power, and the definition of legal rights and limitations in the law of the state are two. The main problem in developing a constitution for the corporation is the same one that is central to republican government—that of representation. Since corporate managers and union leaders do not represent all the constituencies affected by their acts, and since they over-represent particular interests, means other than their own action would be necessary to insure representation of all interests.[44]

In the absence of a modern, constitutionalized system of representative government in economic organizations, through which all interests can be given representation, government remains the channel through which the varied and conflicting interests will seek representation. As indicated in the two preceding sections, the inevitable effect of the rise of industrial and labor power is to create new problem areas within which government must serve as broker among interests. The result is that there is already considerable public law circumscribing the discretion of organization executives, which some may regard as elements in a public constitutional system for the economy.

The most important issue of the future is not whether government will surround the exercise of private power with restrictions and regulations, but whether the decision-making function will be properly allocated between the privately organized and the publicly organized sectors of the political economy. Collective bargaining allocates labor policy to private organizations, but along with it go both procedural and substantive limitations in law; government also has set minimum labor standards. Present policy allows price decisions to be made by corporate managers, but within a framework of antitrust; government also regulates some prices. Welfare policy is divided between the private and public sectors, provisions for labor welfare being included both in labor contracts and in legislation. Subsequent chapters will show the policies that government has followed—collective bargaining, antitrust, minimum welfare standards (only)—in order to preserve the right of private decision. Nevertheless, there remains a question as to whether the brokerage function of private organizations will be held in check sufficiently by competition, countervailing powers between organizations, and business and labor conscience (see the discussion at pages

---

[43] *Ibid.*, pp. 278–279.

[44] Generally on the function and position of the corporation, see Richard Eells, *The Meaning of Modern Business: An Introduction to the Philosophy of Large Corporate Enterprise* (New York: Columbia University Press, 1960); and on the relation of private and public power, Michael D. Reagan, *The Managed Economy* (New York: Oxford University Press, 1963). Reagan's discussion includes reference to the extensive literature on the subject.

244–252) to prevent further substitution of public organizational for private organizational decisions on such key matters as wages and prices.

The other aspect of organizational influence mentioned above has a significant effect upon public economic policy. The economy is a medley of flexible and inflexible, stabilized and unstabilized, human-managed and market-influenced factors. The degrees of inflexibility vary in different parts of the economy. The existence of corporate and union organization is not the only factor making for inflexibility. Debt charges, fixed tax charges, investments in assets which are nontransferable, government-regulated utility rates and government-supported agricultural prices, mortgaged incomes through installment buying, established salary scales, custom pricing (merchants often regard traditional margins of mark-up as sacrosanct), and the habit of cost-plus pricing are some of the additional factors which have created elements of rigidity in the economy. Nevertheless, organizational behavior which creates the labor contract and resists unstabilizing effects on prices is the prime factor in producing rigidities. At the same time, however, market factors operate with little impediment in other parts of the economy.

These facts are now widely understood. Every intelligent farmer knew in the Great Depression that his difficulties arose not alone from the decline in his prices, but also from the fixed level of his debt charges, taxes, and many of the things he bought. And every intelligent salary earner and bond clipper knew that his declining standard of living in the inflation of the forties was the result of the different impact of market changes on his income and on his costs.

The concurrent existence of flexible and inflexible elements, and the intermingled impact of human management and market influence on the economy, create new pressures on government. How will it react to factors which limit the automaticity of market controls? Will it try to pulverize the economy so that it will function as classical economists assumed it would? Will it break up big business and big labor unions to prevent price and wage rigidities and price and wage leadership? Will it abolish regulation of utility rates? Will it make all taxes—local, state, and national—flexible? What about cost accounting and debt charges? Or will it, as an alternate policy, seek to put stability in unstabilized areas, as it has done for agriculture and oil since the thirties? Policies in either direction on a scale large enough to be fully effective would involve government in more activity than men would accept, and policies of the first type would even involve control of so forceful a nature as to appear tyrannical. Or will government try to exercise some influence in both directions, making the market a more effective governor in some areas and at the same time seeking to protect other areas from the full impact of market changes?

The question may be stated in another way: What will men demand of government in an economy which is a medley of conflicting features? Will some demand that government seek to strengthen market controls by antitrust and other policies? Will some, on the other hand, demand that government support a measure of stabilization in some areas, as it has in farm prices, oil production, and utility rates? Will government policies be responses to conditions and pressures in particular situations? And, shifting the question from what appears to be inevitable to what may be good, is it possible that such varied responses are more reasonable and will be more beneficial to man than consistent support of market control or, oppositely, of a totally managed economy?

THE SECURITY MOTIVE

Men must always have been interested in security. Yet they have become more conscious of the word, more conscious (under recent democratic and humanitarian impulses) of all men's desire for it, and more conscious of new ways to achieve it.

The security motive stands behind many public policies. Security is provided to the property holder and his heirs. Security for the nation and the way of life to which men have become accustomed are dominating considerations in national policy. Security against violent upheavals in the economy is an ever-present objective in domestic affairs. Security for industries, and for investments therein, is a motive in regulation of industry.

The security motive is strongly revealed in the socialization of entrepreneurial and investment risks through government action. Here are some outstanding instances:

1. The means provided in the Federal Reserve Act of 1913 for individual banks to find security in the banking system as a whole, through central reserves and discounted paper.
2. The insurance of bank deposits.
3. The insurance of savings up to $10,000 for each depositor in thrift and home-financing institutions.
4. The insurance of housing loans made by private lending institutions (through the Federal Housing Administration).
5. Crop insurance under the Federal Crop Insurance Act.
6. Loans by the Commodity Credit Corporation to finance withholding of farm commodities from the market.

It appears that in such fields as banking, housing, and agriculture the risks of enterprise have been to a considerable extent lifted from the investor's or entrepreneur's shoulders under programs set up by government.

The search for security is even more strongly revealed in legislation aimed at providing safeguards to individuals for two types of situations: first, normal expectancies, such as old age; second, hazards of life, such as injury and unemployment. Government has provided in this country for insurance of individual risks in the following programs: [45]

Workmen's compensation—that is, compensation for injuries occurring in the course of employment.
Retirement, survivors, and disability insurance.   OASDHI
Unemployment insurance.

In these and the programs of public assistance (for example, aid to needy aged), men generally find a measure of the security always found by some in private property. The costs are spread by government to the economy as a whole, and the burden is distributed by government through its tax and insurance policies.

DEFENSE, FOREIGN RELATIONS, AND SPACE

World War II was a breaking point in American history. Among the many changes it brought was the greater impact of public affairs upon the economy.

The biggest factor has been the tremendous increase in the defense budget. The budget for defense has been the main cause of the national budget's rising to a $100 billion level. National-defense expenditures have in recent years run around 9 per cent of total expenditures in the nation for goods and services. They are the biggest item in allocation of resources by public decision.

The effects are many. The postwar economy has been stimulated by the sheer quantity of government expenditure. Resources that might be used for domestic welfare are channeled into weapons systems. And a nation which negotiates on disarmament is at the same time fearful of the potential effects of disarmament on employment and economic growth. Some would be fearful that government would not (others that it would) expand its social expenditures to close the gap in production that would thereby be created. In simple terms, the economy has become dependent upon a high level of government spending, and it might be difficult or impossible to sustain it without these high levels.

The relationships of much of industry to government have been changed by the huge expenditures initiated at the beginning of the war. A large part of American industry is dependent upon government contracts, and the government is dependent upon these contractors for the performance of its functions. The contracts are made by bargaining between organizations—between a monopolistic buyer and oligopolistic sellers. The contract is an instrument that defines the relationships between government and business. It is a means by which the buyer can regulate sellers, for it deter-

[45] See Chapter 13.

mines the product, the terms of settlement, and the means of supervision. Not only is there a new relationship, but the line between public and private is indistinct. The contracting firm shares in a public purpose, though it has also a private aim. It may take on some of the conditions of public organizations, such as security clearances, tight accounting of funds, and rules concerning conflicts of interests. Although the attributes of the new relationship have not been the subject of depth study by scholars, it appears that there is in this development a substantial modification of the usual industry-government relationships.

One product of the new defense age is the tremendous impetus toward greater technological development. It began with nuclear fission, which, too, meant large government expenditures and close public-private relationships by contract, but which also would ultimately mean new product and process developments within the private economy. And so also with missiles and other technological developments: research and development would bring about mutual dependence of government and industry and also overflow effects on the private economy.

Defense appropriations and contracting constitute only one aspect of the impact that foreign relationships have upon the American economy. A first development was the allocation of some American resources for foreign aid, both military and economic. Recently, there have been three other significant developments. First, the economies of Western Europe and Japan have now been restored to vitality, and their products now compete successfully, not only in world markets, but also in the American market, with American-made products. Second, the economic union of six Western European countries in the Common Market will further strengthen the competitive power of Western Europe, and will raise questions as to the extent to which the European market will be open to American trade. Third, by 1960 the American deficit on the balance-of-payments ledger was leading to a withdrawal of gold from this country in alarming proportions. All of these changes marked the extent to which the welfare of the American economy had become linked to world developments.

Yet now it is linked also to developments reaching beyond this globe. The advent of the space age is registered in the rapid increase in public expenditures for space exploration. No one can now foretell what the scale of expenditures for space development will be in the future, nor what effects space exploration and technology will have on the economy. Already one large example of change is before us: a new communications revolution is ahead, and a new administrative arrangement for public and private co-investment and collaboration on Telstar has been authorized by Congress.[46]

The relationship of government to the economy is as inexorably influenced by developments in defense, atomic energy, foreign competition, and space as it once was by the frontier. The difference is that with the frontier

[46] See page 612.

reduced, these changes increase the dependence of the economy upon government. The balance of payments and the Common Market accentuate the age-old problems of government with respect to foreign trade and investment; defense, nuclear fission, and space exploration are more revolutionary, for whatever may be the role of private industry in these projects, they bring public expenditure, public planning and initiative, and public control.

BROADENING SOCIAL OBJECTIVES

Whether as the result of the changes in economic and social conditions or the result of movements in ideas, the objectives men seek to obtain through government have been enlarging. This development need only be illustrated with a few examples. Education is perhaps the outstanding one. It is sought for all, even the mentally retarded; it is given to increasing numbers at higher levels; its curriculums are constantly being expanded. It has been the most distinctive American enlargement of the function of government. Elimination of child labor is another example; except for agriculture, newspaper delivery, confectionery employment, and a few other areas, it has now been practically eliminated. A third example is protection against the sale of injurious foods and drugs; this is one example of how prevention of fraud and protection of health underlie much modern legislation. One need only recall the earlier references to conservation, the security objective, and space exploration, or mention such things as minimum wages, public hospitals, housing, and public parks and playgrounds, to convey some consciousness of the enormous broadening of objectives sought to be attained through public action.

The largest leap, however, in public objectives is the one represented by the Employment Act of 1946. Although this act was carefully framed to recognize the joint responsibilities of private enterprise and government for the condition of the economy, it did assert the responsibility of government to coordinate its own efforts toward "maximum employment, production and purchasing power." The Employment Act came about as the result of three things: the fight against depression in the thirties, the one against inflation in the forties, and the fear of postwar unemployment. Henceforth, men would expect government to use its resources to maintain the well-being of the economy.

DEVELOPMENT OF THE PUBLIC SECTOR

As a result of the changes highlighted in the preceding sections, the nature and impact of the public sector of the economy has changed radically. Today the public sector consists first of public expenditures, and second of a battery of regulatory and promotional tools.

The increased significance of public expenditures is revealed in their sheer magnitude. Total government purchases of goods and services rose from 8.5 per cent of the gross national product in 1929 to 20.4 per cent in 1963.

The effect of government expenditures on the economy has been summarized as follows:

Public expenditures for defense, social welfare, public works, and foreign rehabilitation and relief have become so large a part of the total income of society that they may at times be the largest single influence on economic operations. Their rate, timing, and direction, and their effect on government's fiscal operations are significant. Their rate and timing may coincide with other forces in a business cycle and thus accentuate inflationary or deflationary trends; or their rate and timing may have a compensatory effect, raising the level of economic activity in depressed periods. Their direction may have a selective influence on industries, as when purchases for foreign aid create domestic shortages and inflation of prices in particular industries, or when public works expenditures stimulate the building trades and their supply sources.[47]

Normally, the costs of government are paid out of revenues from taxes. Taxes have now reached such a level that they are one of the largest elements of cost in the private sector of the economy. Moreover, the effects of taxes are among the major considerations in the determination of business policy. The entrepreneur may find that his choice between alternative courses of action is materially affected, or even determined, by comparison of tax liabilities. On government's side, the practical and ethical considerations in choice of taxes to be levied, and in determining their levels and the apportionment among groups in the population, have become exceedingly complex and laden with political consequences.

The battery of regulatory and promotional tools has also become more significant. These provide many ways in which government may affect trends and benefits in the economy. The federal budget itself is perhaps the chief of these tools. Tax policy is another. The monetary controls exercised by the Federal Reserve Board influence interest rates, the volume of loans, the amount of speculative risk, and the tempo of business activity. The guides for wage increases set forth by the Kennedy administration in 1961 added another tool to the battery of political weapons. Even in 1945 Harold D. Smith, then director of the Bureau of the Budget, was able to present a long list of things in a " 'Tool Chest' of Government Activities" to assure full employment.[48]

Not only does government have a considerable kit of tools with which to influence the economy as a whole; legislation has now set forth a large variety of tools for regulation and promotion of particular industries.

[47] Emmette S. Redford, *Administration of National Economic Control* (New York: The Macmillan Company, 1952), p. 131.
[48] *Hearings before a Subcommittee of the Committee on Banking and Currency*. U. S. Senate, 79th Cong., 1st Sess., "Full Employment Act of 1945," pp. 681, 691–696.

Among these are various forms of licensing, production control and price fixing, as well as a considerable number of ways to give assistance to industries. Although such tools were used in the early part of our history, particularly by local and state governments, they have now been incorporated into comprehensive national systems of industry promotion and regulation.

The result of these developments in the public sector, growing out of the many changes sketched earlier in this chapter, is to create a *mixed economy*—that is, one in which there is both private enterprise and public action. In this *mixed system* the health of industries and of the economy as a whole will be dependent not merely upon the self-generative and self-corrective operations of a market economy, but also upon the wisdom of the decisions made both by men in organizational positions in the private sector and by other men in the organizational centers of government.

Chapter 3. Economic Interests and the Governmental Process

WE HAVE SEEN that even in the simple conditions of our early national history, different economic groups made demands on government, and tariffs, money, land, and other economic subjects were the main stuff of politics. Later chapters of this book will show in detail how the more complex conditions sketched in the last chapter have created new demands and how governments have responded to them. At this point it is desirable to show how economic groups press their demands upon government and how the governmental process is organized for response. Such a discussion will unveil some of the attributes of governmental decision for a politicized economy, and will also raise a question of deep concern to all which recurs throughout this volume—the extent to which an American may reasonably expect governmental intervention in the economy to be beneficial.

THE ECONOMIC BASIS OF POLITICS

The basic reason why politics exists is that some people are dissatisfied with the operation of things as they are, or have aspirations beyond what they can achieve by other means, and other people are satisfied and wish to preserve their positions and prerogatives. It is just as simple and natural as that. Just as a man decides that a saw works better than an ax and drops the latter to pick up the former, so an entrepreneur sees that competition gives him trouble and cannot be avoided by joint action with his fellows, and hence appeals to government. A farmer wants good prices, and if he cannot get them either by acting alone or by cooperative action, he may follow the lead of those who tell him that he can get them through government action. This is aggressive politics, and it is paralleled by the defensive politics of those who are seeking to preserve their advantages. Politics is just a tool, and man may use it as readily as he would use a saw. He may be deterred to some extent by theoretical arguments that it is better to suffer without politics than to enjoy life with it, or that politics is a deceitful weapon from which ultimately more woe than joy will emerge. But when politics has become a customary and accepted pursuit of men generally, man, suffering an immediate malady or entertaining aspirations for something better, is unlikely to be deterred by arguments, even though buttressed with reference (relevant or irrelevant) to historical experience. There is much truth in Walter Lippmann's comment that "The controlling principle of our time is that the peoples of the world will not let nature take its course." [1]

Another factor contributing to politics is the existence of leadership groups and organizations which try to represent economic groups or solve their problems. In a democracy there are groups, such as association executives, political parties, legislators, and government executives, which seek to retain or obtain support from other groups of people. These either serve, or aspire to serve, in a representative capacity. In reaching for support, they may activate group demands which were dormant or semi-dormant, and may generate expectancies of political solutions for problems. This is only possible, however, where the primary substance of politics—dissatisfactions or unrealized aspirations—exists, for political leaders must, to be successful, be conscious of real and potential sources of concern among the people. In addition to leadership groups, there are also governmental administrative instrumentalities (for example, regulatory commissions) which have been created for, or have emerged into, a position in which they work on economic problems. The very existence of these instrumentalities creates expectancies that they will do something about economic affairs within their respective jurisdictions, and their activities generate dissatisfactions or raise new expectancies. Hence, these administrative instrumentalities, like the leadership groups, activate and expand demands on government. Since these demands threaten other groups with restrictions and/or costs, the opposition of these groups is generated and political conflict ensues.

Recognition of the fact that men will use government to achieve their economic objectives need bring no sense of reproach to man as to either his own nature or the nature of government. For in the first place, this fact can be recognized without acceptance of a completely materialistic interpretation of human events. Karl Marx based his analysis on a completely materialistic interpretation. But Madison, in what most men will regard as deeper insight, argued that men may be motivated by factors other than material ones. While he did say that "the most common and durable source of factions [divisions in politics] has been the various and unequal distribution of property," he also noted that

A zeal for different opinions concerning religion, concerning government, and many other points, as well of speculation as of practice; an attachment to different leaders ambitiously contending for pre-eminence and power; or to persons of other

---

[1] Quoted by Clyde Kluckhohn, *Mirror for Man: The Relation of Anthropology to Modern Life* (New York and Toronto: Fawcett Publications, Inc., 1949), p. 263.

descriptions whose fortunes have been interesting to the human passions, have, in turn, divided mankind into parties. . . .²

Second, man's material existence is unquestionably an important part of his life, and therefore his desire to use all appropriate means to satisfy his material wants is not only natural but intelligent. Finally, citizens of this country can be grateful that the nation has been spared deep political controversy over such fundamental questions as the relationship of government to religion, the republican form of government, and the existence of private economic enterprise, and hence grateful that politics has dealt with economic issues, measures which—except for the slavery conflict—did not create divisions among the people that could not be reconciled within the political process.

ANALYSIS OF THE INTEREST BASIS

SECTIONALISM, CLASSISM, AND FUNCTIONALISM. Already in the society of the eighteenth century, conflict of economic interests along three lines was recognized. The framers of the Constitution spent much of their time at the Convention of 1787 in reconciling *sectional* interests—North versus South, East versus West. Madison, in Federalist Paper No. 10, took note of *class* interests—referring to the conflict between rich and poor. He also referred to *functional*, or *group*, interests—"a landed interest, a manufacturing interest, a mercantalist interest, a moneyed interest." ³

Today the structure of economic interests is much more complex than in the eighteenth century, along all three lines—sectional, class, and functional. Madison, for example, took no notice of a middle class. And he could not foresee the extent to which manufacturing, merchandising, labor, and agriculture would be broken into a multitude of interests. Within the functional group of cotton producers today, for example, the deep cleavages of interest between the old producing sections of the South and the new producing areas of the West have been reflected in Senatorial debates over production allotments. Beyond this are the differences of interest between large and small planters; among owners, sharecroppers, and wage earners; between efficient and inefficient operators.

The complexity of interest divisions is revealed in the many-sided nature of American politics. "National politics is inseparable from sectional politics," wrote Holcombe in 1924.⁴ He found that the great unities of interest

---

² Benjamin Fletcher Wright (ed.), *The Federalist* (Cambridge, Mass.: Harvard University Press, 1961), No. 10.

³ *The Federalist*, No. 10. See also Madison's speech on the Senate in the Convention on June 26, as reported in Madison's notes and Yates' notes, *Documents Illustrative of the Formation of the Union of the American States* (Washington, D.C.: 1927), pp. 279–281, 810–811, respectively.

⁴ Arthur N. Holcombe, *The Political Parties of To-day* (New York: Harper and Row, Publishers, Inc., 1924), p. 40.

were geographical and grew out of the economic specializations in the several sections. "In general, those industries which are the most evenly distributed throughout the country must have the least proportionate influence in national politics." [5] The "primary producers, especially the agricultural interests, the manufacturing interests, and the mining interests," would have the most influence, because other interests would be dependent upon them.[6] Of these, the agricultural interests had been the most significant because of the large numbers engaged in agriculture and the greater representation accorded to agriculture in our constitutional system, particularly in the Senate. Hence, the study of politics must center around such sectional unities as the cotton area, the corn belt, the hay and pasture region, etc. After a thorough analysis of the history of American politics, he concluded that "National parties . . . can be formed only on the basis of durable combinations of sectional interests." [7]

The historians of the frontier also were expounding a sectional view of politics and, indeed, of American development. Their leader, Frederick J. Turner, said that the task of statesmanship in this country "consists not only in representing the special interests of the leader's own section, but in finding a formula that will bring the different regions together in a common policy." [8]

Writing again in 1933, Holcombe expounded a second basis for economic-interest groupings—class interest. "The old sectional interests are changing and the old sectional alliances are breaking down. The old party politics is visibly passing away. The character of the new party politics will be determined chiefly by the interests and attitudes of the urban population. It will be less rustic than the old and more urbane. There will be less sectional politics and more class politics." [9] He analyzed the composition of American classes, and found this to be much more complex than Marxian bipolar analysis. He found a strong middle class, and concluded, "If the leading American politicians continue to manifest middle-class habits of thought, the middle class should continue to hold a commanding position in urban as well as in rural areas." [10]

Twenty years after Holcombe's second book we can see that politics is much more complex than either of his books revealed. The catering of parties to lower, middle, and upper classes is itself complex, with attempts being made to appeal to those in all three groups. Beyond this, modern industrialization has brought diverse specializations within sections, so that the unities of interest which seemed to prevail within these are now less existent. This specialization has done more than divide men into lower,

[5] Holcombe, *ibid.*, p. 56.
[6] Holcombe, *ibid.*, p. 53.
[7] Arthur N. Holcombe, *ibid.*, p. 355.
[8] Quoted by Arthur N. Holcombe, *The New Party Politics* (New York: W. W. Norton & Company, Inc., 1933), p. 15.
[9] Holcombe, *ibid.*, p. 11.
[10] Holcombe, *ibid.*, p. 110.

middle, and upper classes. It has created within the sections many functional or group interests. As one rides, for example, through the South, he will see that the cotton belt has been changed by oil, manufacturing, dairying, army camps, and other influences. Moreover, modern communication has made it possible to link functional interests by organizations extending across sections. Thus, farmers in cotton and corn belts are brought together in the American Farm Bureau, manufacturers across the nation in the National Association of Manufacturers, and musicians in every city in the National Musicians Union.

There is, then, an overlaying of functional interest on sectional interest, and of class interest on both. All three are significant. Sectionalism is revealed as South opposes North on minimum wages; classism, as dividend receivers oppose wage earners on tax reductions; groupism, as powerful sections of the petroleum industry contend with others over reduction in oil imports. The demands of people on government are made by section, by class, and by functional grouping. The national parties must seek durable combinations of *sectional, class,* and *functional* interests.

Each of the major political parties is a coalition of interest groupings that are not completely consistent one with the other, and internal friction is the usual result. There have been times when the sectional and functional groupings largely coincided; and when the coalition held, stable programs emerged—for example, in the Jackson period or again in 1860. Internal frictions continued within the parties, but a dominant grouping of interests maintained control of the party machinery. At present, both major parties have serious internal bickerings, and often public policy at Washington results from coalitions across party lines. The outstanding example at present is the Southern Democratic–Republican coalition on some issues. Some issues of public policy are decided mainly along party lines, but on many issues there is no clearly defined party cleavage, functional groupings gaining their support and opposition in both parties. In these instances informal coalitions provide the leadership and support, within Congress, the executive, and the country.

THE REPRESENTATION OF INTERESTS. In what ways do the interests have access to government? How are they represented in the political process?

In the early development of modern European states emphasis was placed on class representation. The aristocracy and the common people were represented in separate legislative chambers. This was in accord with the social structure of society and with ideas of mixed government—that is, that government should be organized so as to balance the interests of the rich and the poor. The ideas of mixed government were strong in this country in the eighteenth century, and hence there were built-in protections for the well-to-do in our first state and national governments. Suffrage was limited. In the national government the only direct representation the enfranchised population had was the House of Representatives. The Senate was regarded as a bulwark for the propertied classes. The President and the judiciary were selected by special processes which removed them from direct control by the electorate. In the states many similar arrangements existed to protect the propertied against the nonpropertied classes.

The protections for wealth in the formal structure of government have now disappeared. Rich and poor alike may vote, although poll taxes or the color bar in some areas present obstacles. The presidency has been popularized, the Senate is directly elected, parties have been partially democratized through conventions and primaries, even judges are popularly elected in most states, and the national judiciary has become responsive to the needs of the underprivileged. Through the ballot and direct representation both the poor and the well-to-do, those with hopes for the future as well as those with an established stake in society, may make demands to which government will respond. Free public education and mass-communication media have made the public more literate, and this has undoubtedly made government still more responsive to the wider public.

What wealth has lost in the formal structure of government, it now seeks in the informal political process. Money still has ways of gaining influence in politics. Campaign contributions is one way. A political candidate may find that he is responsive both to the ballot box and the dollar box. Money speaks also through the influence of the corporate community. The lobby, the cultivation of public opinion through friendly news channels, and maintenance of social contacts with politicians are some of the other ways by which those with money can exert influence. If the same means are also employed by associations of people with little wealth, it is yet true that wealth provides means of influence that can offset to some degree the political influence based on number of voters.

Representation based on districts and states has provided representation for sectional interests. Sectional interests are directly represented in the formal structure of government. Particular interests that are concentrated in a section have direct representation in Congress and state legislatures. The agricultural interests, in particular, are safeguarded through geographical representation, first because of their concentration, and second because of the over-representation of rural areas. Other interests, such as the silver interests, which have been concentrated in states with small population, have found that equal representation of states in the United States Senate gave them strong representation in the formal structure of government.

Functional interests, like upper-class interests, are not represented formally in legislative bodies, but, like the monied class, they find other means of representation. Indeed, the development of their access to government is a striking phenomenon in twentieth-century politics, comparable to the substitution of democratic for class representation in the nineteenth century. In the first description of this development, it was concluded "that the system of geographic representation as outlined in the fundamental law of the land has been supplemented by a new and spontaneous and at the same time systematic form of representation based upon various interests of various groups of like-minded people." [11]

Functional interests are represented indirectly in government through the activities of associations. Trade associations, professional associations, unions and their affiliated organizations, farmers' organizations, and other similar groupings are the usual channels for representation of interests. The extent of this development is most clearly revealed in the location of association offices in the national capitol. Herring reported in 1929 that over five hundred organizations had offices in Washington,[12] and by 1961 the number had grown to over a thousand. Often the home office of an association is located in Washington, convenient to those upon whom influence is sought. In the states also one will usually find a concentration of associational offices in capital cities.

These associations are units in the "lobby." This formerly was called the "Third House" of the legislative branch, but the lobby now works also with the bureaus and departments of the executive branch of the government. As governmental power has been delegated to the bureaucracy and the overhead policy-making officials of the executive branch, these too have become objects of attention from the lobby. The components of the lobby are sometimes referred to as "pressure groups," because of the relentless pressure they exert, and those they represent are referred to as "interest groups"—though not all interest groups are fortunate enough to be represented by special organizations and lobbies.

The lobby provides a channel of representation *before* government. This does not mean that the interests forego efforts to obtain representation *within* government. On the contrary, they seek representation on advisory boards and the appointment of favorable persons to administrative positions. Also they try to insure that favorable persons are nominated for and elected to public office. By campaign contributions to, and close associations with, legislators and executives they may hope to put in government persons who will at least listen attentively, and at most serve as their advocates. Moreover, in a multitude of ways they carry their views of public policy to the people in the hope that public opinion will serve as an additional means of support. Thus, indirect as well as direct approaches to government are employed.

These modern means of seeking representation in government are, of course, not used only by functional interest groups. As we have noted, class groups use the same means. Sectional interests also use these approaches to supplement their access to government through geographical representation. The result is that the system of representation has become very complex. Groups of all kinds have found ways to make their interests known and get them considered.

---

[11] E. Pendleton Herring, *Group Representation Before Congress* (New York: McGraw-Hill Company, Inc., 1929), pp. 17–18.

[12] Herring, *ibid.*, p. 19.

LIMITATIONS ON ORGANIZED GROUPS. The rise of organizations with large memberships, with huge funds at their disposal, or with strategic position which are bent upon using the political process for their own ends, has led to fears or misgivings concerning the political process. Some fear that organization will create an imbalance of political power among groups or even a dominance over government by special groups. It has been noted, in addition, that there is a class bias in organization, since persons in the upper economic and social levels tend, more than those in the lower levels, to join and support organizations.[13] It is also known that leaders of organizations often have to adopt strong and highly biased positions in order to maintain their leadership positions. It may, finally, be thought that governmental policy is likely to be merely a composite of the demands of strong groups.

There are, however, certain safeguards in American society and its political processes which limit these undesired effects of group action. These safeguards moderate and limit the influence of particular special-interest organizations. They create greater flexibility than will be found in the demands of the interest organizations. They broaden the conflict of interests beyond the interest groups to the community at large and its representatives. They infiltrate new considerations of policy into the matrix of policy deliberation.

What are these safeguards? The first is the very multiplicity of groupings, already noted. This multiplicity creates a kind of check-and-balance system within society. The desirability of this feature has been emphasized by some noted political scientists. Rousseau, though arguing "that there should be no partial society within the state," had another thought: "If there are partial societies, it is best to have as many as possible and to prevent them from being unequal." [14] John Stuart Mill said that the "desirable object" was "that no class, and no combination of classes likely to combine, should be able to exercise a preponderant influence in the government." [15] And James Madison thought that republican government could operate successfully if there was diversity of interests sufficient to prevent the dominance of any one interest.[16] In American industrialized and pluralistic society this safeguard does exist.

The second safeguard is what Professor David Truman calls "overlapping memberships." He notes that "No tolerably normal person is totally

---

[13] See Paul Felix Lazarsfeld, Bernard Berelson, and Hazel Gaudet, *The People's Choice* (New York: Columbia University Press, 1924), p. 145; and E. E. Schattschneider, *The Semisovereign People: A Realist's View of Democracy in America* (New York: Holt, Rinehart & Winston, Inc., 1960), Chapter 2.

[14] Jean Jacques Rousseau, *The Social Contract*, Everyman's ed. (New York: E. P. Dutton & Co., Inc., 1913), Chapter III.

[15] *Representative Government,* Everyman's ed. of *Utilitarianism, Liberty, and Representative Government* (New York: E. P. Dutton & Co., Inc., 1910), p. 255.

[16] B. F. Wright (ed.), *The Federalist* (Cambridge, Mass.: Harvard University Press, 1961), Number 10.

absorbed in any group in which he participates." [17] He has multiple memberships and hence multiple loyalties. This creates lack of unity within organizations. The leader of an organization will find that he must exercise the role of political broker among internal groups. He will find that he is limited in the positions he can take because of the lack of internal unity. And the representatives of the people in legislative and executive positions will know that claims by organization leaders that their members are united behind a particular position must be discounted.

Yet Truman recognizes that this safeguard will not be dependable in the case of organizations with cohesive memberships, as "of the National Association of Manufacturers and the United Steelworkers of America, or of the American Farm Bureau Federation and the United Automobile Workers." He sees, however, another safeguard in the unorganized interests.[18] By this he means the shared attitudes of people, what he prefers to call the "rules of the game," or what he says others have called "systems of belief," "general ideological concensus," or "a broad body of attitudes and understandings regarding the nature and limits of authority." [19] Some of these "systems of belief" are represented and preserved in institutions such as courts or regulatory commissions. The additional significance of these shared beliefs is that the political leader can appeal to these in his search for support. When, for example, organized industry or organized labor pushes its hand too far, the political leader may find in such concepts as fair play or the public interest a rallying point for support of a policy opposed by either or both. In effect, the shared beliefs in the public provide an opportunity to extend the forum of discussion beyond the organized to the unorganized interests in society.

A further safeguard is that the political system places some men in a position in which they find it advantageous to make a cross-sectional, cross-class, and cross-group appeal. There are two devices of our electoral system that are so important in this respect as to make them key elements in the political system itself. The first is the requirement of a majority electoral vote for election of the President. This means that no man can be President without appealing to many groups and to the shared beliefs of the society; thus he must find positions on current issues which, though they might not satisfy any of the highly organized special groups fully, will satisfy each sufficiently to make the search for solutions possible. The high position of the office of President further strengthens this tendency of the holder of the position to look for solutions which accord with the shared interests of

[17] David B. Truman, *The Governmental Process: Political Interests and Public Opinion* (New York: Alfred A. Knopf, Inc., 1951), pp. 508–510.

[18] Truman, *ibid.*, pp. 510ff.

[19] He refers to the following: Clyde Kluckhohn, *Mirror for Man: The Relation of Anthropology to Modern Life* (New York: Fawcett Publications, Inc., 1949), p. 248 and *passim;* Sebastian de Grazia, *The Political Community: A Study of Anomie* (Chicago: University of Chicago Press, 1949), pp. ix, 80, and *passim;* Gabriel A. Almond, *The American People and Foreign Policy* (New York: Frederick A. Praeger, Inc., 1950), p. 158; and Charles E. Merriam, *Systematic Politics* (Chicago: University of Chicago Press, 1945), p. 213.

the nation. The other electoral device is the single-member congressional constituency. Although some representatives and senators are, in effect, agents of special viewpoints, and although probably all are captives of these on some issues, many who go to Congress represent districts so diverse in their composition that they are constrained, like the President, to find policy positions that build majorities out of diversity.

A final safeguard in the political system is that expert and creative intelligence sets boundaries on group demands. The interests may make demands, but the experts must discover what is feasible. The experts may differ, but their knowledge may nevertheless have narrowed the scope of conflict. Their discovery of what is possible may infiltrate new elements into policy deliberation, alter the positions of contending groups, and raise new standards that will appeal to the unorganized and, perhaps, also the organized. It seems probable that the more complex problems become, the more impact the discoveries and judgments of the experts will have on the policies adopted.

These several safeguards may possibly be blended together in one politician whose actions merits the accolade, "statesmanship." When a political leader can look, on the one hand, at what the experts say is feasible and, on the other, at the group demands and the shared attitudes and expectancies in the community at large, and can compound these two into a politically and administratively feasible solution, then he may merit the title of "statesman."

THE PUBLIC INTEREST. Through the political process policy choices will be made. Toward what end? Is there a public interest? Is there any basis, after all, for being concerned whether a single organized interest prevails in the political process? Is the idea of the common good merely a myth?

Although the concept of the public interest has been accepted and, indeed, been regarded as vital by politicians, publicists, political scientists, and men in general, it has recently been attacked by "realist" political scientists.[20] One argument is that because there is no commonly accepted definition of the public interest, the social scientist will find the concept to be of no value. One author notes that it has been defined variously as "Commonly-Held Value," as the "Wise or Superior Interest," as "Moral Imperative," as a "Balance of Interests," as the public interest "undefined," and adds another of his own which he calls "Compromise as Method," meaning the settlement of conflicts by democratic and orderly rules and procedures.[21] The reply is that although variety of definition does undoubtedly make it difficult or impossible to determine with scientific accuracy what the public interest is in any given situation, such variety does not by itself prove that

---

[20] See especially Glendon Schubert, *The Public Interest: A Critique of the Theory of a Political Concept* (New York: Free Press of Glencoe, Inc., 1960).

[21] Frank J. Sorauf, "The Public Interest Reconsidered," *The Journal of Politics*, XIX (November 1957), pp. 616–639.

the concept has no value as a goal of human effort. "Justice," too, is a concept that has been defined variously. Thus it has been argued that it is the right of the stronger, the protection of the weak against the strong, or the maintenance of the balances which exist in society. But the will to search for justice has been a compass for the judiciary. A single definition of the public interest may indeed be impossible, both because of the philosophical implications and because it is, as Justice Frankfurter has said, "A texture of multiple strands." [22] Another argument is that the accepted standards of the public interest are so general that they offer no operational standard for determining a particular conflict. Thus, though good education is a commonly accepted standard of public welfare, this general goal does not resolve the issue as to whether public aid should be given to parochial schools. The reply may be made that the search for the common good may narrow the limits of many controversies or may supply guides for action. Thus, there may be a point in a strike at which the stoppage of essential production or transportation is recognized to be of general interest; whatever the disagreement as to the desirable terms of settlement, the recognition of the social interest creates a new framework of issues and leads to actions for the protection of general interests. Finally, it is said that the term "public interest" is merely a term used by the special interests to sanctify their own goals. There is indeed an effort of each special interest to identify its goals with the public interest, but this does not necessarily mean that there is no validity in the concept itself.

While these attacks on the concept of public interest warn of the need for caution in its use, it is inevitable that men will seek some standard for determination of the general good. It is suggested that men do search for the public interest and that this fact alone indicates that the concept has real value. It is suggested further that this search is conducted on three levels.

The first is the reconciliation of group interests. Pendleton Herring has said that "the purpose of the democratic state is the free reconciliation of group interests." [23] Some scholars conceive of this reconciliation as a compromise process. Sorauf, arguing for the "modest conception of the public interest" as "compromise as method," says, "We are bound together, therefore, in accepting the process of democracy and the method of compromise, *regardless of the policies it may produce*." [24] Some use the term "balancing process" to imply that the purpose of the state is to balance the interests, and some describe the function of politics as brokerage—that is, the middleman function of resolving conflicts between groups. Others, however, see it as more than a mere balancing process. "But usually," writes Paul Appleby, "the interests are so numerous and unlike that the process is not umpiring

---

[22] *Federal Power Commission v. Hope Natural Gas Co.*, 320 U.S. 591, 627 (1944).

[23] E. Pendleton Herring, *Public Administration and the Public Interest* (New York: McGraw-Hill Company, Inc., 1936), p. 9.

[24] Frank J. Sorauf, "The Public Interest Reconsidered," *The Journal of Politics*, **XIX** (November 1957), p. 22. Italics supplied.

at all. Rather it is a process of distilling out of those private interests something approximating the general interest." [25] Herring, without arguing (as Sorauf does) that consequences are to be dismissed, asserts the compromise thesis: "Hence the public interest cannot be given concrete expression except through the compromise of special claims and demands finally effected." [26] He believes, however, that government may find some standard of public interest which gives it some independent weight among contenders for power. Merle Fainsod presses the point on independent weight when he says that government may be able to "tilt the scale" among contenders.[27] At the same time, Herring does more than argue for compromise among groups; he advances the idea that a compromise must be effected between the state and the special interests: "The solution of the democratic state must lie in establishing a working relationship between the bureaucrats and the special interests—a relationship that will enable the former to carry out the purpose of the state and the latter to realize its ends." [28] Avery Leiserson has expressed a similar view. Speaking only of administration of public programs, he suggests "that a satisfactory criterion of the public interest is the preponderant acceptance of administrative action by politically influential groups." [29]

In summary, the argument is that government umpires the conflicts among interests, is broker among the groups, and must find acceptance for its policies among the groups that have political influence. This umpire-broker-acceptance theory of the nature of politics is accepted generally by political scientists and recognized as one element, at least, in the search for the public interest. They will differ, however, in their views as to how far government may be more than broker, for there may be a wide difference between a conservative view of the brokerage function, as reflected by Sorauf and some of Herring's statements, and a more positive view of the function of the state, as reflected in Appleby's comment that the state does more than umpire, or Fainsod's that it may "tilt the scale," or in Herring's suggestion that government may find a standard which gives it some independent weight.

Yet men do search for the public interest on another plane also. Though they may be, as Sorauf avers, devoted to the rules of the game in American democracy, they will also be concerned with the policies produced. They will seek for the public interest by looking for policies that are for the

[25] Paul H. Appleby, *Morality and Administration in Democratic Government* (Baton Rouge, La.: Louisiana State University, 1952), p. 95.
[26] E. Pendleton Herring, *Public Administration and the Public Interest* (New York: McGraw-Hill Company, Inc., 1936), p. 209.
[27] "Some Reflections on the Nature of the Regulatory Process," in C. J. Friedrich and Edward S. Mason, *Public Policy, 1940* (Cambridge, Mass.: Harvard University Press, 1940), p. 320.
[28] E. Pendleton Herring, *Public Administration and The Public Interest* (New York: McGraw-Hill Company, Inc., 1936), pp. 24–25.
[29] Avery Leiserson, *Administration Regulation: A Study in Representation of Interests* (Chicago: University of Chicago Press, 1942), p. 16.

common good. They will not be deterred by the fact that it may be only 95 or 85 or some other percentage of the public that actually benefits, nor by the fact that there is some tilting of the scales in favor of some groups against others, nor by the fact that there will be no scientific way of determining whether their search was successful.

This search will be for the ways in which the expectancies of the community may be realized. There will be widely-shared objectives for the economy, such as maintenance of employment, economic growth, and the prevention of boom-and-bust cycles. These are generally shared objectives of people in the community, even though it may be true that a few would profit by failure to attain the objectives. There will also be widely shared attitudes (or values [30]), such as belief in the dignity of man, opportunity for all, good living standards, fair play among competitors, and security against the hazards of life. Some may see moral imperative in these ends, while others will see them as expectancies arising out of the conditions of plenty and the social and cultural history of the nation. In the present discussion this issue is immaterial; the point is that whatever their origin and basis, they are indeed interests of the public at large, and the search for means to implement them is part of man's search for the public interest.

It can be argued that this search is only part of the process of brokerage of interests. Common interests are but another set of interests that will be compromised in the political process with the special interests. This, of course, is true. It may be true also that the conscience of man will regard as ethical some compromise of the general interests with specially affected interests. On the other hand, most persons will believe that, in certain exigencies at least, there should be certain priority given to community-shared interests over those more narrowly shared. Hence, men do seek ways of achieving public interests in this sense of widely-shared substantive interests.

These questions directly lead to the third level of search for the public interest. It is a level on which the process goal of successful brokerage of interests and the substantive goal of attainment of community objectives are blended. It is the search for organization and process through which these two may be attained continuously and peacefully in the society. It is the search for effective political institutions (that is, organizations and processes)—in essence, a search for a desirable constitution for the polity.

This search is sought in this country within a framework of moderated democracy. In such a framework one may discern three primary elements of a political constitution. The first is political due process for the groups in society. This has been well expressed in Ordway Tead's *"principle of the representation of interests,* which says that every group which has a clearly identifiable set of interests is safeguarded in its dealings with other groups only as it has the opportunity for an explicit voicing of its interests

---

[30] Various words may be used interchangeably: "objectives," "attitudes," "values," "needs," "expectancies."

in councils where the common problems of the several groups are under consideration." [31] This principle asserts the right of access, the right to be heard. The second element is the principle of comprehensive consideration, which says that all claims of interest must be considered in a forum or set of forums that alone or together will provide attention to the diverse group and common interests of men. This principle asserts the need of a general, community, or public orientation of political instrumentalities. The third element is the principle of intelligence, which says that provision should be made for the study of problems and for injection of the expert knowledge so gained into the decisional process. This principle merely asserts that decision shall not be made until the effects of action are traced as far as possible.[32]

It is now possible to state two broad tests of the public interest with respect to government action affecting the economy. The first two principles above may be combined into a standard of responsiveness. The second is a standard of rationality. A system of political intervention in the economy can be beneficial to man only if it is responsive to his needs, and only if it is rational in the sense that it is based on correct analysis of the consequences of decisions. These two standards may not always lead in the same direction—the society may make demands that are not rational. Community responsiveness is the ultimate goal in a political system, but the beneficence of its operations will be dependent also upon the willingness of the community and its agents to be rational.

GOVERNMENTAL STRUCTURE

What is the structure of government in which decisions on the interests of men are made? Where are the powers of decision located? How, in other words, is government organized for responsiveness and rationality? Although later sections of this book will contain details related to these questions, it will be useful to answer them in a general way at this point. Since the most vital decisions affecting the economy are now generally made at the national level, the discussion will be limited largely to the structure at that level.

THE JUDICIARY. The judiciary has had a large role in the making of economic policy in this country. First, it has developed and applied much of the law relating to such matters as property ownership, contracts, liability to suit, corporations, and employer-employee relations. It has done this through the development of the common law and equity, which are

---

[31] His *New Adventures in Democracy: Practical Applications of the Democratic Idea* (New York: McGraw-Hill Book Co., Inc., 1939), p. 5.

[32] "But the essence of public interest is awareness of that web ['society's seamless'] and the constant impulse to trace things as far as possible before acting and as a guide to action where choices otherwise unguided must be made." Arthur W. Macmahon, "Specialization and the Public Interest," in O. B. Conaway, Jr. (ed.), *Democracy in Federal Administration* (Graduate School, U. S. Department of Agriculture, 1956), p. 49.

systems of judge-made law developed on a case-to-case basis over a period of centuries. While the common law and the supplementary system of jurisprudence called equity originated in England, American judges have, through their decisions, adapted it to the conditions and ideals of their country. Much of this law has developed in the state courts, and much of it is still applied there. Second, the judges, in applying statutes to particular cases, often find them ambiguous and must fill in the meaning of the statutes by interpretation of the meaning of the words or the intent of the legislative organs which used them. Third, in this country the judges have had the function of interpreting and declaring the meaning of constitutional provisions as these affected the decision of particular cases. Through the process of interpreting the national Constitution, the national courts have had an unusually large role in determining basic economic policies of the nation.

One view of the function of the judiciary places emphasis on the judge as an impartial, objective decision maker. Undoubtedly, the conditions under which he operates do contribute to this kind of an attitude in judicial decision making. On the other hand, judges have to make new policy decisions to deal with new situations, and their own values will unavoidably affect their decisions. In the long run, it is probably true that the judges respond to the prevailing ideals of the community at large. Yet they can tilt the scales toward groups struggling to make their ideas prevail in law.

The opportunities of the judges to determine economic policy have been greatly narrowed by a series of recent developments. First, the Supreme Court's interpretations of the Constitution, largely since 1937, have substantially transferred from the Court to Congress the responsibilities it once held of determining the role of government, specifically the role of the national government, in the economy. Second, legislatures have been more active in the making of policy. Whereas much of the new law of society was once made by the slow, precedent-to-precedent procedure of the courts, the center of lawmaking in a rapidly changing society is now in the legislatures. These erect entirely new edifices of law in statutes. Third, when legislatures have found it difficult to fix the details of policy, they have vested in administrative agencies the discretion for these details. This is, in a sense, a search for rationality, for it is believed that specialized agencies can give more expert attention to economic matters. The courts have supported this practice by upholding the rules and orders of the agencies, unless they violate certain minimum standards.

The result of these trends, which are described in detail in later chapters (particularly Chapters 24 and 25), has been to increase the importance of the executive and legislative departments in the determination of economic policy.

THE EXECUTIVE AND THE LEGISLATURE: THE POLITICS OF FUNCTION. Most descriptions of the executive and legislative branches of the government start with the President and the Congress and proceed with a top-to-bottom analysis. The assumption is that what is, or should be, characteristic of these branches is unity, and that the elements of disunity should be considered only as a part of the description of the branch as a whole. This kind of discussion fits well into a discussion of separation of powers (among legislative, executive, and judicial branches) and checks and balances among the three branches. An alternative is to begin with the units of organization within the executive and legislative branches established for each area of government activity.

Within the executive department, separate units of organization are set up for each major area of government activity. First, there are departments with bureaus. In some cases the departments have a considerable amount of unity in their functions. In others they are federations of bureaus which have distinct functions. For example, the Comptroller of the Currency in the Treasury, the Antitrust Division of the Department of Justice, and the Food and Drug Administration of the Department of Health, Education and Welfare each have functions separable from the other functions of the departments within which they are included. Each of these can be included under the general term "bureau" (that is, subdivision within a department). Second, there are so-called independent regulatory commissions, which generally are outside departments and are less subject legally to presidential direction than the departments and bureaus. Third, there are government corporations for the operation of some of the business (loan and sale) operations of the government. Fourth, there are presidential agencies—that is, agencies outside the cabinet departments but unquestionably subject to the President's control.

A similar organization of subunits exists in the Congress. The main subunits are the standing committees and their subcommittees. The Legislative Reorganization Act of 1946 reduced the number of standing committees in the House and Senate. Today there are twenty such committees in the House, sixteen in the Senate, and eleven joint committees of the two houses. But in 1961 there were 131 subcommittees in the House, 109 in the Senate, and 13 subcommittees of joint committees.[33] There are also special committees in each house. Most of the committees are legislative—that is, they exist for the consideration of bills introduced in the houses. Somewhat different is the committee in each house, with its many subcommittees, which considers appropriations. There are also committees of investigation and others, such as the powerful Rules Committee in the House, for administration of the business of each of the houses.

The subunits of the executive and congressional systems now have specialized expert assistance. The merit system for the executive branch has brought into that branch experts in every field of activity of the government. Also, the bureau chiefs are usually experts in their respective fields,

---

[33] George Goodwin, Jr., "Subcommittees: The Miniature Legislatures of Congress," *American Political Science Review*, **LVI** (September 1962), pp. 596–604, at p. 596.

and some expertness may be expected from the heads of other types of executive agencies. The Legislative Reorganization Act provided for staff aid for the committees, and they can obtain additional help from the Legislative Reference Service (now staffed with considerably more than a hundred staff specialists) and from the bureaus or other executive agencies. Finally, some of the committee and subcommitte chairmen have held their positions for a sufficient length of time that they have become, with bureau chiefs, the "cream of the career crop in the federal government," as V. O. Key has said.[34] Thus the subunits are equipped to examine practicalities and hence, formally at least, to achieve rationality in their decisions.

When the government takes on a function, the function is usually assigned for administration to a subunit in the executive branch. This subunit will then be brought into continuous relationships with the subunits in the congressional system that are concerned with the function. This liaison results from the fact that the committees and subcommittees will exhibit a continuing interest in the activity assigned to the agency. They will be considering new legislation or appropriations, or will be trying to see how the administrative unit is conducting its affairs. The liaison results also from the fact that the agencies must play defensive and offensive politics. They will try to build a relationship with the committee members which will result in favorable appropriations, or favorable consideration of the new legislation they desire, or which will avoid hostile intrusions into the work of the agency.

Each administrative unit will be in continuous relationship with four working centers in the Congress. The first is composed of the two legislative committees having jurisdiction over matters related to the agency. Thus, the Department of Agriculture will be in constant contact with the Committee on Agriculture in each House and with its subcommittees; the Civil Aeronautics Board with the Committee on Commerce in each House and with the Subcommittee on Aviation in the Senate and the Subcommittee on Transportation and Communications in the House; the Antitrust Division of the Department of Justice with the Judiciary Committee and subcommittees thereof in each House; and the Treasury Department with the Finance Committee of the Senate and the Ways and Means Committee of the House and their subcommittees. Similarly, the agencies will be in constant contact with the subcommittees of the two appropriation committees. These agency-committee contacts may be made at the staff level, or they may be made between principals. Particularly important are the chairmen of the committees and subcommittees, for they occupy strategic positions through which they can exert power and influence.

Outside of the government are groups which have a continuing interest

---

[34] In Fritz Morstein Marx, *Elements of Public Administration,* 2nd ed. (New York: Prentice-Hall, Inc., 1959), p. 319.

in each of the fields of government activity. They are the clienteles of the agencies. Businessmen are interested in the Department of Commerce; labor-union leaders in the Department of Labor; farm groups in the Department of Agriculture; airlines and pilots in the Civil Aeronautics Board; railroads, truckers, and coastal shippers in the Interstate Commerce Commission. An agency may have a single strong clientele, but it is likely to face either a number of clienteles or a lack of cohesion in a dominant one. These outside groups maintain more or less continuing contacts with the subunits in the executive and congressional systems. This is, for them, defensive and aggressive politics.

It is possible to summarize the results of the development of subordinate governmental structure in certain descriptive terms. When government embarks on a function, it creates a new "universe of activity." [35] The regular continuing business of government, with respect to each universe, is conducted through specialized subdivisions in the executive and congressional systems. The relations among the subunits in the executive and congressional systems create what one author has called "subsystems of the larger political system." [36] But this bilateral relationship of administration and committees is converted into a triangular one by the contacts that outside groups have with the executive agencies and the committees. The result is to create what Ernest Griffith has called "whirlpools or centers of activity focusing on particular problems." Griffith believes "that ordinarily the relationship among these men—legislators, administrators, lobbyists, scholars—who are interested in a common problem is a much more real relationship than the relationship between congressmen generally or between administrators generally." [37] It can be added that in addition to other arenas of politics, we have a *politics of function,* the politics which swirls around each universe of activity in the government.

It can be said also that there is created a continuing mechanism of decision for each function. This mechanism allows for some rationality through the participation of the expert and provides for a large measure of responsiveness to interested groups. It also provides in several ways for some responsiveness to the community at large. This larger responsiveness comes, first, from the position and attitudes of congressional participants who represent constituencies with multi-interest memberships and who must seek answers that can be identified with the general good; also, the agency will

---

[35] The phrase is basic in the author's "A Case Analysis of Congressional Activity: Civil Aviation, 1957–58," *The Journal of Politics,* **XXII** (May 1960), pp. 228–258.

[36] J. Leiper Freeman, *The Political Process: Executive Bureau-Legislative Committee Relations* (Garden City, N.Y.: Doubleday & Company, Inc., 1955), p. 1. See also, with respect to the type of relationships here discussed, Arthur Maass, *Muddy Waters* (Cambridge, Mass.: Harvard University Press, 1951).

[37] Ernest S. Griffith, *The Impasse of Democracy* (New York: Harrison-Hilton Books, 1939), p. 182, and *The American System of Government* (London: Frederick A. Praeger, Inc., 1954), p. 127.

represent some conception of the public interest embodied in its enabling legislation and its own line of development; and finally, the experts may infuse a broadened perspective into the deliberations on policy.

THE EXECUTIVE AND THE LEGISLATURE: MACROPOLITICS. The subsystem based on function merges into and is part of a larger arena of politics. It is possible to distinguish, on the basis of scope of participation or involvement, three levels of open politics: (1) micropolitics, in which individuals, firms, or communities make efforts to obtain benefits, such as a job, license, or airport, for themselves only; (2) an intermediate level of politics—that is, the politics of function, involving the interrelationships of bureaus and other administrative operating agencies, the parallel congressional committee structure, and the interest organizations, trade press, and lobbyists concerned with a particular area of activity; and (3) the top level, *macropolitics,* which arises when the leaders of the government as a whole or the community at large are brought into the discussion and determination of issues. An issue affecting persons or groups may be considered at any of the three levels or may move from one to another. For example, a person's effort to obtain the aid of his congressman in getting a license, which is micropolitics at this stage, may draw the attention of the congressional committees, the administrative agency, and interest organizations, thus becoming part of the politics of a subsystem, and may ultimately force upward questions for consideration by the party leaders in Congress, the President, the press, and the public, thus becoming macropolitics.

The intermediate level merges into the top level in a number of ways. First, the participants in the more specialized spheres are themselves connected in many ways to macropolitics, the highest level of policy making. Members of the committees are forced by the single-member district system to think of the varied interests of their respective constituencies and, by their party memberships, to give some attention to the party leadership. Even though they work on a specialized function, they are shareholders in the larger arena of macropolitics. As for the administrative participants, the law under which they operate has set objectives for them. These objectives, defined in the arena of macropolitics, will have become part of their own thinking, and will limit the adaptations they can make under the compulsions of the influences in the triangular system. Second, the leaders in the subsystems must obtain consent of and approval by (or avoid veto or disapproval by) the superstructure—the Congress, department heads, the President, above them. Third, there is the conflict between subsystems, or merely the need to correlate two or more of such systems. In the executive branch there is the need to correlate such systems as defense and international relations, or health and welfare, or defense and economic policy. Moreover, the frequent splintering of the organization of closely related activities, such as the division of monetary controls and fiscal policy between the Federal Reserve Board and the Treasury Department, itself creates need for coordination. Within the Congress the separate subsystems may come into conflict. For example, over a period of years the interest of the military in retaining a large Military Air Transport (MATS) as a reserve defense force, and the conflicting interest of the commercial airlines in taking over some of this transport, led to conflict within Congress between the committees responsible for the defense function and those responsible for civil airline policy. Fourth, issues are constantly being pushed out of the arena of intermediate politics into that of macropolitics by the actions of officials in the systems. Bureau chiefs seek help from department heads and the President, they and committee chairmen seek new legislation from Congress, dissentient members of the committee structure stir up controversies, and special investigating committees air issues before the public at large. Finally, there are interventions in the subsystems from the political overhead—that is, from congressional leaders and the higher levels of the executive branch.

Who are the chief participants in this larger arena of politics, referred to here as macropolitics? On the congressional front the first are the party leaders and their associated aides in the Congress. This leadership is centered for the majority party in the speaker of the House and the majority floor leader of the Senate, and for the minority party in the minority floor leader in each house. But it is also distributed among the party leaders who form the party policy or steering committees, the committee chairmen, the Rules Committee of the House, and other persons who have acquired influence. It is exercised both within parties and across party lines, for within the Congress many issues are not decided by strict party divisions. The party leaders will have small corps of aides who analyze problems and assist in liaison with the working units of the Congress.

The mainspring in the system of macropolitics is the President. The President is the chief formulator of public policy. He prepares the program of legislation for Congress and sends bills to Congress embodying his proposals. He sets lines of policy for the departments within the executive branch and has ways of influencing even the independent regulatory commissions. He may even determine, on his own initiative, policies which influence or bind the organization leaders in the private economy, as he did in 1961 when he set guidelines on wage increases; or as he has done at times in orders—applicable to those holding government contracts—relating to security, discrimination in employment, or other matters; or as he did in his order in 1962 against discrimination in housing financed through funds of the federal government. He is the policy leader of the nation—on defense and international affairs, on social welfare, and on economic problems.

Because of the central position of the President, the hopes of the nation for responsiveness of government and for rationality in policy rest heavily on him personally and on the operation of the presidency as an institution. As for responsiveness, it can be said on the one hand that the presidency tends to complement the system of group representation in Congress. The President today must be responsive to urban populations and minority

60 *The Role and Process of Government*

races because of the importance of these in determining election results in the large states; the Congress perhaps gives greater representation to rural viewpoints and, because of the existence of a Southern bloc and of its strong representation in positions of leadership (as a result of the seniority system for selecting committee chairmen), reflects a somewhat different viewpoint on race problems. On the other hand, it can be said that the presidency is the chief organ for responsiveness to the unorganized interests—that is, to the shared attitudes and demands of the community at large. This, as we noted earlier, is the result primarily of our electoral system and of the great burden of responsibility placed on the President. As for rationality, the President is today able to draw on many sources of expert information. He can appoint *ad hoc* committees or task forces. He can call on the departments of the government for studies and reports. He has at hand an institutional aggregation of staff aides to anticipate problems, make studies, define issues, and aid in deliberations on policy. Many of these men will be among the top experts in the nation on policy problems. Others will be expert advisers on political feasibilities. The policy positions that result stem from these diverse sources of information on policy alternatives, on the political feasibilities, and on the President's capacity to synthesize these into viable programs.

To some extent the political leaders and the President are merely dealing with the management of the political subsystems. The political leaders in Congress arrange the business of Congress so that the decisions made in the substructures have an opportunity to be approved by the Congress, and the presidency encompasses arrangements for legislative clearance, through which the proposals of any bureau are considered, in order to determine their relationship to other activities of the government. Yet the top political figures are engulfed primarily in macropolitics. This game is played before the whole public. Macropolitics deals with issues that have become of general public concern or that someone is trying to make a matter of such concern. It therefore encompasses from outside the government political platforms and campaigns, the press and other forums of general public discussion, and the ballot of the people. Macropolitics is the politics which delivers the discussion of public issues into the broader forums of public consideration and thus forces some measure of responsiveness of government to the larger unities of interest in the nation.

SOME CONCLUSIONS ON THE POLITICAL PROCESS

Complexity is the basic characteristic of political decision making for the economy. The substructures of interests, the means of their access to government, the organization of government, and the interrelationships of all of these in the political system are exceedingly complex.

Within this complexity there are many variations. One is the extent to which the community at large becomes involved in a matter. Politics itself relegates certain functions to private action.[38] The organized groups will expend considerable effort toward keeping government out of certain functions, and they will be supported by much unorganized opinion favorable to this end. An example is the antagonism within industry and labor to any system by which government itself determines the wage settlement, combined with the considerable public support for this position. When government does embark on a function, it creates arrangements for specialization. One or more administrative agencies will administer the function, and certain congressional committees will give it their more or less continuous attention. Because of the diversity of the tasks of government, much minor policy is virtually determined within the areas of functional specialization. To illustrate, the decision in 1955 to substitute permanent for temporary certificates (authorizations to serve communities) to local service airlines was to all intents finalized in the deliberations of the congressional committees on the basis of information gained from the Civil Aeronautics Board and the industry; there was little interest in the matter at the presidential level and little discussion of it on the floors of the houses. Sometimes there is considerable cohesion among the administrative agencies, the congressional committees, and the organized interest groups. Thus, there is much cohesion of interest among the Department of Agriculture, the Committees on Agriculture, and certain farm organizations. Yet even in this case there must be compromises among different farm interests and with other interests. In other cases, there may be much less cohesion of interest, and hence conflict and more necessity for mediation among groups. Nevertheless, specialization, like privatization, reduces the number of matters which will attract the interest of the political overhead and the community at large. Yet any matter can erupt into this larger arena. It does so when it becomes one of general interest. The political system allows for any issue to come full force into the arena of macropolitics at any time.

The system of political decision making for the economy is often criticized. To some extent this comes from those who distrust the whole process in which economic decisions are made in a political system. Many people have greater confidence in the arbitrament of the market than they do in the compromises of politics, even perhaps when the economy itself has been politicized by organization. To some extent the criticism comes from those who accept the utility of the system of political decision making but recognize, nevertheless, its distinctive features. Some think the process is too "political"—that is, that it responds too much to group or uninformed mass opinion and allows insufficient opportunity for rationality to prevail. Some think the range of interests given consideration in the subsystems is

---

[38] See E. E. Schattschneider, *The Semisovereign People: A Realist's View of Democracy in America* (New York: Holt, Rinehart & Winston, Inc., 1960), Chapter 1.

often too narrow. Some think the dispersal of power in the system makes it too difficult to obtain leadership and prompt action. Some think that the system has a class bias because of the power of organizations and the failure of nearly half the people to vote, while others think political decision gives too much opportunity for the "have nots" to take from the "haves."

The system works differently at different times and on different issues. Sometimes it produces benefits for labor, at other times for industry; sometimes for the well-to-do, at other times for the poor; sometimes under the spur of leadership, sometimes with resistance to it; sometimes perhaps with more rationality than at others. It should be judged in the entirety of its effects. Judged this way, it can be said that the American system does provide much responsiveness on many fronts, and that it does provide many opportunities for the infusion of rationality into the process.

One thing, however, is certainly clear. Complete consistency among economic decisions cannot be expected. The American political system operates in a pluralistic society and through pluralistic political institutions. Power is shared among many centers, public and private, and the balances of power among the centers shift constantly. "Within government, moves made contemporaneously at different points may not be synchronized—may even have conflicting effects—and moves made over a period of time may reflect great changes in purposes and effects. The processes of administrative and political decision are sensitive in too many directions for men to hope or to fear for the congruency of policies anticipated in a planned society. The realized public interest in a free society is no neat package of consistent elements." [39]

On the other hand, large trends in economic decision may be established, as will be shown in Chapter 5.[40] Goals may guide action to a substantial extent. Techniques may be evolved for handling problems. Conflicts may be settled. Problems may be solved with reasonable satisfaction to society. Some matters will be reduced to routine or simple management. For other problems, patterns of solution will be evolved and new problems handled by the processes of incremental decision. On some other matters man will move on to new plateaus of confusion and problem.

Whether the political process or the market process is the more beneficial is probably undeterminable. Stated this broadly, the question is also probably irrelevant. For in a mixed economy, men use both the political process and market controls. Their unavoidable task is to decide through political decision what shall be private and what public, and what kinds of decisions shall be made for the areas that are public.

---

[39] Emmette S. Redford, *Ideal and Practice in Public Administration* (University, Ala.: University of Alabama Press, 1958), p. 136.
[40] Pages 94–98.

Chapter 4. The Role of Government: Patterns of Thought

THIS CHAPTER PRESENTS an analysis of six large patterns of thought about government's role in the economy which have emerged in the Western world in the past two centuries. We begin with the *old individualism,* which in its politico-economic aspects emphasized the doctrine of *laissez faire.* There follows a discussion of a representative pattern of thought in a transition period (that of John Stuart Mill) which was a closely reasoned statement of *laissez faire with exceptions.* Next come two reflections of the modern or new individualism, or new liberalism: one the *idealist attitude,* the other the *empirical approach.* Then, following a summary of the elements of skepticism surrounding the promise of a better life through state control (as presented or assumed by idealists or empiricists), there is a sketch of radical attacks contained in *communism* and *fascism.*

All of these patterns of thought reflect ideas that groups of men have held about the relationship of government to the economy, and they are referred to so often in the literature of political science and economics, and in the everyday language of journalism and politics, that they should be familiar to the student of political economy. Some comments about their utility as frameworks of thought on government's role in the economy are made throughout this chapter, and additional comments on the relevance of these large patterns of thought and of certain other ideas to American experience are made in the following chapter.

THE OLD INDIVIDUALISM

The old individualism is like a central image seen from the three faces of a prism. The three faces are natural rights, utilitarianism, and *laissez faire* economics. The central image is a negative and restricted role for government.

NATURAL RIGHTS. The Declaration of Independence states that it is self-evident that "all men are endowed by their Creator with certain inalienable rights, among which are life, liberty, and the pursuit of happiness."

This is a restatement of the view (which, though expressed earlier, had flowered in the seventeenth and eighteenth centuries) that man's rights have a more permanent basis than civil grant. They come to him by virtue of his existence—because of his nature as a man. They are the result of a higher morality, which binds governments as well as men. They derive from nature, or from its Creator, and have been commonly referred to as "natural rights."

The Declaration of Independence put no specific economic content in "inalienable rights." The question was whether they included rights of property. Many argued in the eighteenth century that property ownership was not a natural right, but only a civil one. Blackstone considered property in its fundamental character to be a natural right, but stated that the modifications of it in existence, the modes of acquiring and transmitting it, were derived from society.[1] Many Americans went further: Marshall argued, in 1796, "Property is a creature of civil society, and in all respects subject to the disposition and control of civil institutions."[2] Justice Chase, for the Supreme Court, said, "I think it is the better opinion that the right, as well as the mode . . . of acquiring property, and of alienating or transferring, inheriting, or transmitting it, is conferred by society, is regulated by civil institution, and is always subject to the rules prescribed by positive law."[3]

But the opposite view was also stated. Thus, the Massachusetts Constitution of 1780 included "acquiring, possessing, and protecting property" in the list of inalienable rights. The conditions of the eighteenth century being what they were, it must have seemed clear to men that the possession of property was essential for "the pursuit of happiness." As a result, they could easily concur with Samuel Adams that "The security of right and property is the great end of government." Madison, however, with deeper understanding and with unconscious prediction of the coming American emphasis on opportunity, put it differently: "The first object of government is the protection of the diversity in the faculties of men, from which the rights of property originate."[4]

It was not until the last half of the nineteenth century that this doctrine of natural rights became a significant means of limiting the economic functions of government. In the post–Civil War period, lawyers and judges asserted that the rights to acquire property, to use it without unreasonable restrictions, and to make contracts concerning it were natural rights. Natural rights became, then, in this country, one of the buttresses of *laissez faire*.[5]

---

[1] See, on his views, Guido de Ruggiero, *History of European Liberalism*, translated by R. G. Collingwood (New York: Oxford University Press, 1927), pp. 28–29.

[2] Before the Supreme Court in *Ware v. Hylton*, 3 Dall. 199, 211.

[3] *Calder v. Bull*, 3 Dall. 386, 394 (1798).

[4] B. F. Wright (ed.), *The Federalist* (Cambridge, Mass.: Harvard University Press, 1961), No. 10.

[5] For the story of this development, see Chapter 7. On the lack of influence of *laissez faire* notions in the first half of the century, see Chapter 1.

The practical strength and weaknesses of the idea of natural rights are rather obvious. The strength of the claim of natural right rests in this country's traditional belief in a higher law. Natural right is merely a way of stating a belief in a higher law that should control government in favor of the rights of men. Men, therefore, fall back on a claim of natural right when government goes beyond what they think is "reasonable." The Declaration of Independence used natural right as a justification for revolution; Americans since have often referred to it as a test of government acts. Two big weaknesses in application are apparent. The first is that counterclaims of right can be made. If one man can assert that government should not in wartime regulate his rents because his use of his property is a natural right, another can assert that a right to have living quarters at a reasonable rate is an even more basic right; if one man can assert that he has a natural right to employ whomever he will in his own business, another can assert that he has a natural right to be considered for employment without discrimination because of color, religion, or politics. The second weakness is that the contributions of a man, whether through capital, management, or labor, cannot be accurately measured. Society has contributed protection, education, and other benefits which are significant in the process of production and distribution. Moreover, wealth is cooperatively produced.

In view of these weaknesses, a referee is needed to pass upon rival claims of moral right. Acceptance of the function by society is inevitable. Some may argue that society has only a right to take an equivalent of its contribution (as in the benefit theory of taxation); others may say that society has contributed so much that it has unlimited rights of regulation and of allocation of benefits. Most would probably take the middle view that the complexities of the economic structure and the rival claims of moral right that men may make within it justify regulation, but within the limits set by the conscience of the men who compose the society. If so, then natural right as a justification for *laissez faire* has lost its force; it remains only as an idea that whatever is done or not done should be fair, just, and reasonable.

UTILITARIANISM. What American antagonists of government control found in natural rights English antagonists found in utilitarianism. Though the two sets of ideas led in the same direction, they arose from opposite conceptions. To test the legitimacy of governmental action, the natural-rights philosophy looks backward to a system of natural equity—or upward, as Justice Holmes said, to "a brooding omnipresence in the sky"— to the laws of the Creator of nature. To test legitimacy, the utilitarian looks forward to the consequences of acts. He determines the validity of government acts by trying to measure the probable results.

It was a unique brand of this philosophy which had its influence in England—Benthamite utilitarianism. Jeremy Bentham, father of utilitarianism, stated its fundamental premises in his *Principles of Morals and Legislation* (1789) and other writings. There were three basic assumptions in his philosophy—and assumptions they were.⁶ First, the aim of legislation is to produce "the greatest happiness of the greatest number." Bentham did not create this apt phraseology, but his greatest long-run ideological contribution was its popularization. Second, legislation is a science. This science is the anticipation and measurement of the results of legislation in terms of its effects on happiness. Third, Bentham believed that "the greatest happiness of the greatest number" could be best attained if each individual, who would be the best judge of his own happiness, were allowed to pursue his own self-interest.

These doctrines became the dominant opinions influencing the law of England for nearly half a century after the 1820's. Bentham himself was one of the greatest legal reformers of all history; he sought and attained the removal of aristocratic privileges and inhuman elements from the criminal law of his country. Others, such as his friend James Mill, worked on the doctrines' implications for self-government. If each man is the best judge of his own happiness, how can restricting the suffrage to a few be justified? The Bentham creed supported the Reform Act of 1832, under which suffrage rights were expanded. Most Benthamites, however, were not willing to follow the doctrines to their logical conclusion in this regard. They trusted only a middle class with voting rights and left to others, the Chartists, the task of beginning the movement for worker suffrage. In the economic area, the Benthamite doctrines were on the side of liberty. The utilitarians favored the repeal of the corn laws, and many of them also opposed the beginnings of factory legislation on the ground that it was contrary to the self-interest principle. Thus, they stood on the side of the short period of reform which tore away the old restrictions, and their doctrines made them wary of the new collectivism, which was to bring new restrictions —public-spirited leaders such as John Bright and Richard Cobden defending the labor of children and other factory conditions against regulation by government.

Though utilitarianism in its inception was a doctrine of individualism and *laissez faire,* the long-run effect of the first two of its theses could run toward collectivism.⁷ The principle of "the greatest happiness of the greatest number" is egalitarian and has often been used as a justification for social legislation. The "science" of legislation can be used for positive social aims as well as for removal of restraints. These two parts of utilitarianism could stand alone if men ceased to believe in the third principle—that the pursuit of self-interest by each would produce the greatest happiness of the greatest number. In the absence of belief in the last principle, utilitarianism can, like natural rights, be a means of justifying state intervention.

⁶ See A. V. Dicey, *Lectures on the Relation between Law and Opinion in England* (New York: The Macmillan Company, 1905), pp. 125–209.

⁷ Dicey says that utilitarianism gave English collectivism of the late nineteenth century three things: a creed (the greatest happiness of the greatest number); an instrument (parliamentary sovereignty); and a tendency (the reform of government). *Ibid.,* pp. 302–309.

LAISSEZ FAIRE ECONOMICS. What utilitarianism assumed, and what many believers in natural rights thought was self-evident, Adam Smith's *Wealth of Nations* (1776) sought to prove by reason and reference to historical experience.

There are two basic and complementary ideas in the *Wealth of Nations*. The first is that there is a "natural order of things" which derives its energy from the "natural liberty" of man to pursue his own self-interest. The second is that the natural order operates for the general good. It has been observed that one could accept the idea of a natural order without believing in its beneficence, but that Adam Smith argued for both.[8]

Smith started with the argument that the division of labor was the great cause of the increase in production. But this division was the result of the tendency to barter, which arose out of man's effort to better himself. Hence, the true cause of the increase in opulence was this regard of every man for his own interest.[9]

The principle of self-interest was asserted repeatedly and forcefully. As to the tailor, the shoemaker, and the farmer, "All of them find it for their interest to employ their whole industry in a way in which they have some advantage over their neighbors," purchasing with the gains of their industry from the production of others.[10] Society's "capital has been silently and gradually accumulated by the private frugality and good conduct of individuals, by their universal, continual, and uninterrupted effort to better their own condition." [11] "It is not from the benevolence of the butcher, the brewer, or the baker, that we expect our dinner, but from their regard to their own interest. We address ourselves, not to their humanity but to their self-love, and never talk to them of our own necessities but of their advantage." [12]

Equally forcefully, the beneficent results are stated. "The natural effort of every man to better his own condition, when suffered to exert itself with freedom and security, is so powerful a principle, that it is alone, and without any assistance, not only capable of carrying on the society to wealth and prosperity, but of surmounting a hundred impertinent obstructions with which the folly of human laws too often incumbers its operations." [13] Society need not be concerned about capital. If some individuals will be prodigal, their tendency will be more than compensated by the frugality of others.[14] As to the use of capital: "Every individual is continually exerting himself to find out the most advantageous employment for whatever capital he can command. It is his own advantage, indeed, and not that of society,

---

[8] Man does not always accept natural law as beneficent—for example, someone has noted that man is willing to use a parachute or wear a pair of suspenders.

[9] Adam Smith, *An Inquiry into the Nature and Causes of the Wealth of Nations*, Edwin Cannan (ed.), 6th ed. (London: Methuen & Co., Ltd., 1950), Vol. **I**, Chapters 1, 2.

[10] Smith, *ibid.*, **I**, p. 422.

[11] Smith, *ibid.*, **I**, pp. 327–328.

[12] Smith, *ibid.*, **I**, p. 16.

[13] Smith, *ibid.*, **II**, p. 43. Compare **I**, p. 325, and the preceding pages.

[14] Smith, *ibid.*, **I**, p. 323.

which he has in view. But the study of his own advantage naturally, or rather necessarily leads him to prefer that employment which is most advantageous to the society." [15] Though he does not intend "to promote the public interest," "he is in this, as in many other cases, led by an invisible hand to promote an end which was not part of his intention." [16] Nor need society be concerned about supply and demand, for these will be adjusted to each other. When supply exceeds demand, market price falls below natural price; and when supply is below demand, market price rises above natural price. Hence, "The quantity of every commodity brought to market naturally suits itself to the effectual demand." [17] As for foreign trade, the same considerations which lead an individual to concentrate his industry on what he can do best should lead a nation to prefer free trade, buying from abroad what can be purchased more cheaply than it can be produced at home.[18]

If the natural order operates so beneficially, then it follows that the state should free the system from restraint. "All systems either of preference or of restraint, therefore, being thus completely taken away, the obvious and simple system of natural liberty establishes itself of its own accord. Every man, as long as he does not violate the laws of justice, is left perfectly free to pursue his own interest his own way, and to bring both his industry and capital into competition with those of any other man, or order of men." [19] To this, which is implicit in the whole argument, other arguments against state interference are added. There is, first, the argument of private right. To restrict the use of a poor man's labor "in what manner he thinks proper without injury to his neighbor," is a "manifest encroachment upon the just liberty" of the workman and the employer.[20] There is, in addition, the argument of utility. As to employment of capital, Smith said that "every individual . . . can, in his local situation, judge much better than any statesman or lawgiver can do for him." [21] And whereas right and utility argued for individual freedom, the state itself was incompetent: ". . . no human wisdom or knowledge could ever be sufficient" for "superintending the industry of private people, and of directing it towards the employments most suitable to the interests of society." [22] Governments are "always, and without any exception, the greatest spendthrifts in society." As for government engaging in business operations, Smith declared, "No two characters seem more inconsistent than those of trader and sovereign." [23] When government regulates foreign trade, it is not the science of a legislator that prevails, but "the skill of that insidious and crafty animal, vulgarly called

---

[15] Smith, *ibid.*, **I**, p. 419.
[16] Smith, *ibid.*, **I**, p. 421.
[17] Smith, *ibid.*, **I**, p. 59.
[18] Smith, *ibid.*, **I**, p. 422.
[19] Smith, *ibid.*, **II**, p. 184.
[20] Smith, *ibid.*, **I**, p. 123.
[21] Smith, *ibid.*, **I**, p. 421.
[22] Smith, *ibid*, **II**, p. 184.
[23] Smith, *ibid.*, **II**, p. 304.

a statesman or politician, whose councils are directed by the momentary fluctuations of affairs." [24]

Smith offered a statement of the duties of the sovereign: [25]

... first, the duty of protecting the society from the violence and invasion of other independent societies; secondly, the duty of protecting, as far as possible, every member of the society from the injustice or oppression of every other member of it, or the duty of establishing an exact administration of justice; and, thirdly, the duty of erecting and maintaining certain public works and certain public institutions which it can never be for the interest of any individual, or small number of individuals, to erect and maintain; because the profit could never repay the expense to any individual or small number of individuals, though it may frequently do much more than repay it to a great society.

Smith preferred, however, as much use of the self-interest stimulus as possible. He thought the diligence of judges should be encouraged by paying them by fee, that the state need not have to supply all education, and that some public works might be maintained better by private persons.

On the other hand, Smith was realistic enough to accept various other types of state action. Thus, he justified certain regulations of banking, an act of Parliament preventing paper money from being legal tender in the colonies, regulation of the interest rate, tariffs on foreign commerce to protect an industry which was essential for defense, supporting the faith of contracts and enforcing the payment of debts, requiring knowledge of science and philosophy of those who exercised any liberal profession or held any honorable office of trust or profit.[26]

There is also a considerable admission in the following statement: "Such regulations [against small notes of bankers] may, no doubt, be considered as in some respect a violation of natural liberty. But those exertions of the natural liberty of a few individuals, which might endanger the security of the whole society, are, and ought to be, restrained by the laws of all governments; of the most free, as well as of the most despotical." [27]

Smith had, nevertheless, created a system of thought which was to be the main ideological basis for *laissez faire.* The system fitted the patterns of thought of the eighteenth century, for it assumed a natural order and dealt with the natural relationships among things.[28] It also fitted certain requirements of thought in the late nineteenth century, for it was the basis for a new science, the principles of which could be studied, expanded, and restated. It conformed with the interests of business, for it, like utilitarianism, combined egoism and altruism. Man could do what seemed best for himself

---

[24] Smith, *ibid.*, **I**, pp. 432–433.
[25] Smith, *ibid.*, **II**, p. 185.
[26] Smith, *ibid.*, **I**, pp. 307–312, 310, 338, 427; **II**, pp. 395–396, 281. The list is not intended to be complete.
[27] Smith, *ibid.*, **I**, p. 307.
[28] Thorstein Veblen called it a "taxonomic science." "Why Is Economics not an Evolutionary Science," and "The Preconceptions of Economic Science," *Quarterly Journal of Economics*, **XII** (July 1898), pp. 372–397, and **XIII** (January 1899), pp. 121–150.

and yet realize that he was working for the common good. It would be hard to visualize a more comforting doctrine for a man of conscience or a more convenient escape from conscience for a buccaneer. And it provided, in reason as well as in apparent foundation in experience, a basis for opposition to governmental regulation.

Though the system of thought has validity, within limits, as an explanation of portions of the economy of our day, and some validity as a tool of analysis for the economy as a whole, it is by itself inadequate as an explanation of the *operation* of the economy and hence inadequate also as a basis for determining the proper scope of government action. First, man does not always know his self-interest or, knowing it, find it possible to promote it by his own efforts. Even in the employment of capital, about which Adam Smith said so much, the consequences of the acts of men may be catastrophic for society because they may have moved with a tide of enthusiasm without any knowledge of future markets and economic trends. The inability of men acting alone to promote their own interest is reflected in the many forms of joint effort and in many appeals to government.[29] Second, the ultra-materialistic psychology of the *Wealth of Nations* is too simple. Men may be motivated by the desire for service, or the desire to do a good job ("instinct of workmanship," as Thorstein Veblen called it), or the desire to excel, as well as (or in some cases even more than) by self-interest. If so, they may work effectively in a variety of institutional arrangements. Smith's assumption that a man would not work well in a corporation or in a government because he would not be motivated sufficiently by self-interest does not take account of the opportunities of organizations to take advantage of the many types of impulses to work and to work effectively. Third, Smith argues for a kind of economic society which does not and cannot exist in our day. He assumes a society in which the constituent units are individual men. He grudgingly accepted joint-stock companies (corporations) for a few types of industry, just as he grudgingly accepted some government. He said, "The directors of such companies, however, being the managers rather of other people's money than of their own, it cannot be well expected, that they should watch over it with the same anxious vigilance with which the partners in a private copartnery frequently watch over their own." He concluded that joint-stock companies had "seldom succeeded" when not granted monopolies, and "frequently" had not succeeded when they had monopolies.[30]

Smith could not see the need for, nor the great potentialities for benefit from, large-scale organizations. He offers little understanding about them, such as would now be available from experts in industrial and public management, and from economists who have learned about the politicizing of

---

[29] See the discussion of Mill's ideas at p. 73. The student may think of such things as unions, open-competition plans, and efforts of farmers to deal with the problem of excess production.

[30] Adam Smith, *The Wealth of Nations*, Cannan, Edwin (ed.), 6th ed. (London: Methuen & Co., Ltd.), **II**, p. 233. See also **II**, pp. 246–248.

private organizations and "imperfect competition." [31] Nor does he provide understanding of the diversity in economic life processes in the twentieth century. To attain such understanding, one has to accept the fact of the great changes outlined in Chapter 2 and to study the ways in which different industries are organized, the diversity of interrelationships among organizations, groups, and individuals, and the extent and limitations on adjustability of parts of the economy. Smith's grand pattern of thought is, like Rousseau's, that of the eighteenth century: it assumes men and the state. The twentieth-century realist has a more difficult task: he must recognize organization, group relations, built-in resistances to change. Recognition of these facts makes the task of building a theory about government's relation to the economy more difficult. *Laissez faire* becomes only one tool of thought, to be balanced with other notions.

LAISSEZ FAIRE WITH EXCEPTIONS: THE RATIONALISTIC APPROACH

It is apparent that complete *laissez faire* is a Utopian dream. Any attempt to explain the proper role of government on the basis of *laissez faire* philosophy alone would be exceedingly unrealistic. Even its most ardent historical advocates, including Adam Smith, have admitted exceptions to the doctrine.

"*Laissez faire* with exceptions" may be a more tenable doctrine. A second-generation utilitarian, John Stuart Mill (son of James Mill, a disciple of Bentham) developed, more than a century ago, this doctrine as an explanation of the proper role of government. This he did in Chapters 1 and 11 of Book VI of his *Principles of Political Economy*.[32]

Mill, under the influence of utilitarianism, considered that consequences of acts, rather than assumed natural rights, should be the test of the appropriateness of government action. At the same time, he proceeded on the assumption that by reason one could lay down general principles or guides by which he could determine the appropriateness of governmental intervention in particular instances. He was, therefore, in dealing with the relationship of government to the economy, more rationalist than empiricist, and undoubtedly had an influence on judges and others in the United States who sought to determine particular issues by reasoning from general assumptions.

Mill begins (Chapter 1) by distinguishing between the "necessary" and the "optional" functions of government, and shows that the former are "considerably more multifarious than most people are at first aware of." But his logic breaks down, for he is soon discussing "admitted" rather than "neces-

---

[31] See pages 29ff. and 245–246.
[32] First published in 1848. Quotations which follow are all from Chapters 1 and 11 of Mill's seventh and last edition, that of 1871, W. J. Ashley, ed. (New York: Longmans, Green and Co., Inc., 1909).

sary" functions and concludes that "it is hardly possible to find any ground of justification common to them all, except the comprehensive one of general expediency. . . ." This might reasonably have deterred him from advancing further; but, believing that the rules of expediency are discoverable, he proceeded to search for them.

In a new chapter (Chapter 11) Mill states a pair of conclusions:

Laissez faire, in short, should be the general practice: every departure from it, unless required by some great good, is a certain evil.

We have observed that, as a general rule, the business of life is better performed when those who have an immediate interest in it are left to take their own course, uncontrolled either by the mandate of the law or by the meddling of any public functionary.

These statements carry realistic qualifications: "the general practice," "as a general rule." Each is a form of statement of the conclusion, *"laissez faire* with exceptions."

The pages preceding these conclusions contain a famous summary of the reasons for limiting the functions of government:

1. ". . . there is a part of the life of every person who has come to years of discretion, within which the individuality of that person ought to reign uncontrolled either by any other individual or by the public collectively." This is the part which concerns the inward life of the individual and "does not affect the interests of others," except perhaps by example. But in his essay *On Liberty* (Chapter 5) Mill said, "trade is a social act"—that is, economic relations affect the interests of others. Hence Mill adds that even in the case of actions affecting others, "the onus of making out a case always lies on the defenders of legal prohibitions." Why? Because coercion cramps the soul of man, and legal restraints upon the conscience of the individual "partake . . . of the degradation of slavery."

2. ". . . every increase of the functions devolving on the government is an increase of power, both in the form of authority, and still more, in the indirect form of influence."

3. It is desirable to maintain a division of labor. The government may be "overcharged with duties," with the consequence "that most things are ill done."

4. Even if the force of the foregoing objection were diminished by "better organization of government," it would still be true that individuals would do things better than government because of their greater interest in the result.

5. ". . . one of the strongest" reasons is that the "business of life is an essential part of the practical education of the people," that their faculties will be "only half developed" if they "look habitually to their government to command or prompt them in all matters of joint concern," that it is desirable to encourage management of "joint concerns by voluntary co-operation."

The Role of Government: Patterns of Thought

In these arguments—liberty, fear of government power, inefficiency of government, superior motivation of self-interest, the advantages of a pluralistic society—Mill has stated arguments which many will believe are persuasive reasons for limiting government functions. He is much less successful, however, when he tries, in his subsequent discussion, to state the kinds of exceptions to *laissez faire* that are justified. We summarize below his principles of exception, his examples of government action which are justified by his exceptions, and some examples from recent legislation which could be justified by his exceptions.

Mill's Principles of Exception	Mill's Examples	Our Examples
1. Where the buyer is not qualified to judge the commodity	Education of children	Food and Drug Act Prevention of misbranding and false advertising Wool Labelling Act Prescription of standards of quality Regulation of professions and trades Securities Act
2. Where the interest and judgment of the agent cannot be relied on		
(a) Where he is incapable	Idiots, lunatics, children	Child Labor Laws
(b) Where he makes irrevocable decisions for distant time	Contracts in perpetuity	
(c) Where he acts through delegated agency, as in joint stock companies	Regulation or ownership of monopolies, preferably the former	Regulations over all large-scale corporate enterprise
(d) Where law is required so that individuals can give effect to their interests	Labor laws Wakefield system of colonization	Price supports for agriculture Laws to give large number of people with common interests "what they want"—for example, parks, playgrounds, and highways
(e) Where the person acts for the benefit of others	Poor relief: "The claim to help, therefore, created by destitution is one of the strongest which can exist; and there is *prima facie* the amplest reason for making the relief of so extreme an	Welfare legislation, including social security laws

Mill's Principles of Exception	Mill's Examples	Our Examples
	exigency as certain to those who require it as by any arrangements of society it can be made"	
(f) Where the consequences of individual acts extend "indefinitely beyond them, to interests of the nation or of posterity"	Colonization	Conservation, physical and human Control of discharge of wastes in streams or exhausts in the air (smog)
(g) Where no individual could or would be interested in performing an important public service	Voyage of geographical or scientific exploration Endowment of a learned class	Public works Loans to business and agriculture Defense production
(h) Where actions are clearly injurious to others	Prohibiting force, fraud, and negligence	Various uses of property

Mill concluded:

The intervention of government cannot always practically stop short at the limit which defines the cases intrinsically suited to it. In the particular circumstances of a given age or nation, there is scarcely anything really important to the public interest, which it may not be desirable, or even necessary, that the government should take upon itself, not because private individuals cannot effectually perform it, but because they will not.

Others may draw additional conclusions from Mill's discussion. Some may think that his basic premise of *laissez faire* as the general rule is vitiated by the scope of his exceptions and that a different approach to the problem of the role of government is required. Others may still believe that a preference for *laissez faire* should exist, and that whether or not it can be the general rule, it should at least be retained where good reasons for departures from it are not advanced. All will recognize that Mill's discussion shows that one who undertakes to rationalize the legitimate functions of government may find that their scope is exceedingly extensive.

THE MODERN IDEALISTS

The modern idealists have offered a new approach. The term is used not merely to refer to the English school of idealists, but to a pattern of thought shared by many. In general, it may be said that idealists begin with the assumptions that there need be no conflict between state authority and liberty, and that the practical objections to state interference advanced by Mill and others can be met by the establishment of efficient, democratic, and responsible political institutions.

A good brief exposition of the idealist viewpoint is given in Leonard T. Hobhouse's *Liberalism*.[33] We use his exposition here because of the clarity, simplicity, and comprehensiveness of his statement of idealist faith.

Hobhouse based his argument on the "organic, or, . . . harmonic conception" of society. The ideal is liberty. "The foundation of liberty is the idea of growth." On the one hand, society depends upon the growth of the individual: "The self-directing power of personality" becomes "a necessity of society." On the other hand, the "life of the individual . . . would be something utterly different if he could be separated from society"; "he finds his own good in the common good."

Hobhouse said that he was not assuming, as did the older economists, that there was an "actually existing harmony"; "this assumption was too optimistic." He was stating an ethical ideal for man: "only that there is a *possible ethical harmony,* to which, partly by *discipline,* partly by the *improvement of the conditions of life,* men might attain, and that in such attainment lies the social ideal" (italics supplied). This seems to mean, simply put, that one's opportunity for growth in harmony with society depends first upon his disciplining himself to life with others, and second upon the existence of favorable conditions.

What, then, is the place of the state? The state is "one among many forms of human association for the maintenance and improvement of life." This statement keeps Hobhouse on the side of a pluralistic society and draws a line between him and totalitarians, who would have the state assume the full responsibility for favorable conditions. But it did lead him to what he calls "the 'positive' conception of the State." What is the peculiar role of the state? "The object is to secure certain conditions which it believes necessary for the welfare of its members, and which can only be secured by an enforced uniformity." "Enforced uniformity" involves compulsion. What should be the "sphere of compulsion"? The answer is in strictly functional terms: "The reply is that compulsion is of value where outward conformity is of value, and this may be in any case where the non-conformity of one wrecks the purpose of others." What is the proper limit of compulsion? The answer is: ". . . its own incapacity to achieve its ends." The area where force cannot be effective is in matters of the spirit. Hence, "The object of compulsion is to secure the most favourable *external* conditions of inward growth and happiness *so far as* these conditions depend on combined action and uniform observance" (italics supplied). "The true opposition is between the control that cramps the personal life and the spiritual order, and the control that is aimed at securing the external and material conditions of their free and unimpeded development." And hence further, nothing in the doctrine of liberty prevents state action "in the sphere in which it is really efficient."

---

[33] L. T. Hobhouse, *Liberalism* (New York: Holt, Rinehart & Winston, Inc., 1911), particularly at pp. 116–213.

Hobhouse did not believe that the ethical ideal could be approached in practice except in a democratic society. Self-government is both essential to and results from freedom: "Liberty and compulsion have complementary functions, and the self-governing state is at once the product and the condition of the self-governing individual." And the freedom must be that in which all men share: ". . . the old idea of equality has its place. For the common good includes every individual. It is founded on personality, and postulates free scope for the development of personality in each member of the community. This is the foundation not only of equal rights before the law, but also of what is called equality of opportunity."

We need not sketch the details of Hobhouse's application of his assumptions to economic legislation, for we offer his analysis only as an example of a type of approach, and those who advocate the approach may differ on details of application. The general lines of application should, however, be indicated. He said that there were two lines for state action: "One would consist in providing access to the means of production, the other in guaranteeing to the individual a certain share in the common stock [that is, of social income]." He put great emphasis on the first of these, but he had also a place for public assistance or social insurance, because wages would not be likely to cover all the misfortunes of life.

It can be seen that Mill and Hobhouse both believed in liberty and self-development. But where Mill built from fear of the state, Hobhouse set out the ideal of a state which works for the common good. Both leave us in the same position: the state is there, and a large area of authoritative state control is justified. Both, therefore, leave us with the same question: Will the state in its economic legislation really act in a beneficial way? Hobhouse says that the economists gave us too optimistic a view. But is the modern idealist's view too far from the realities of politics to be acceptable?

Every student should have some kind of answer to this question. More will be written about it on succeeding pages.

LAISSEZ FAIRE WITH EXCEPTIONS: THE EMPIRICAL APPROACH

It can be said that all of the foregoing approaches are rationalistic. This does not mean that the men who explained the approaches did not take note of experience and current needs of men. But each was rationalistic in the sense that he sought to develop by reason a comprehensive framework on the basis of which men might find answers to particular issues or problems.

There is another approach which is distinctly different. This is the empirical approach. In this approach the wisdom of governmental action is to be determined *separately in each particular case from the circumstances*. That government action is appropriate which is a reasonable response to a situation. Such action may have to be adjusted from time to time because of changes in circumstances. Thus public policy is made because of felt needs, and it is made experimentally. The ultimate test of the legitimacy of the policy will be found, borrowing Justice Holmes' words, in "experience rather than logic."

The approach can be illustrated best by reference to the use of a so-called sociological method by American courts in determining the reasonableness of what other men have done—that is, in determining the constitutionality of the acts of legislatures alleged to be in violation of general constitutional provisions such as the due process clauses. The Fourteenth Amendment, for example, says that no state shall "deprive any person of life, liberty, or property without due process of law." If an act of a legislature seems to be a deprivation of someone's liberty, how can a court determine whether it is "without due process of law"? By the end of the nineteenth century, the Supreme Court had interpreted this to mean that the act must be reasonable both as to its purpose and as to the means used to attain that purpose. Now how can a court determine whether the legislature acted reasonably? The empirical approach, referred to in jurisprudence and particularly in constitutional law as the sociological approach, is to see if there was an evil, a set of conditions, or a problem which concerned the public, and whether the legislature adopted reasonable means to meet the evil, the conditions, or the problem. This means in essence that the decision is to be determined by the facts in the particular instance.

The sociological approach has always been used to an extent by judges in passing upon issues before them. It is not surprising, therefore, that its use is apparent in some of the earliest due process cases. Thus, in *Munn v. Illinois* in 1876 the Supreme Court was asked to pass upon the constitutionality of a state statute that fixed the rates of charge for grain-elevator services supplied in Chicago. The Court upheld the legislation. And though it reasoned in part from history and a bit of dogma in an old and forgotten treatise, it took note of conditions of monopoly within the industry and said: "This indicates very clearly that during the twenty years in which this particular business had been assuming its present 'immense proportion', something had occurred which led the whole body of the people to suppose the remedies such as are usually employed to prevent abuses by virtual monopolies might not be inappropriate here." [34] But it took Attorney Louis Brandeis' brief, in *Muller v. Oregon* (1908—involving the constitutionality of a state statute limiting the hours that women could work), to make men familiar with the sociological approach in constitutional law. His brief concentrated on facts about the effect of long hours on women's health rather than on legal doctrine.

A good example of the method will be found in Justice Stone's dissents in *Tyson v. Banton* (1927) and *Ribnik v. McBride* (1928).[35] The Supreme

---

[34] 94 U.S. 113, 132.
[35] *Tyson v. Banton,* 273 U.S. 418; *Ribnik v. McBride,* 277 U.S. 350.

Court had held invalid a New York statute limiting resale mark-up by theater-ticket brokers and a New Jersey statute providing for regulation of employment agencies' fees. By reference to history and doctrine, the Court majority reasoned that these industries were not "affected with a public interest." Stone thought that in using this phrase, the Court "was begging the question to be decided." He thought the Court should use the sole test of the reasonableness of the means of price fixing to meet the kind of situation which the legislature found to exist. In *Ribnik v. McBride* he took note of the economic data on employment agency charges and said that the legislation of many states "may not be disregarded in determining, first, whether the conditions peculiar to the business under consideration makes it one in which . . . there is a paramount public concern; and second, whether the regulation adopted is reasonably calculated to safeguard that interest." [36]

Stone went further, however. He placed this methodology in a context which again can be called "*laissez faire* with exceptions." He thought that competition should be accepted when it was working beneficially, but that the state should be allowed to regulate it whenever it was not. In *Ribnik v. McBride,* referring to previous decisions on price fixing, he said: "As I read those decisions, such regulation is within the state's power whenever any combination of circumstances seriously curtails the regulative force of competition, so the buyers and sellers are placed at such a disadvantage in the bargaining struggle that a legislature might reasonably anticipate serious consequences to the community as a whole." [37] And why should this be the test? In *Tyson v. Banton* he said: "The constitutional theory that prices normally may not be regulated rests upon the assumption that the public interest and private right are both adequately protected when there is 'free' competition among buyers and sellers, and that in such a state of economic society, the interference with so important an incident of the ownership of private property as price fixing is not justified and hence is a taking of property without due process of law." [38]

On price fixing, Stone's logic *as a test for the judiciary to use* was not accepted, for in 1934, Holmes' doctrine (stated in a dissent by him in *Tyson v. Banton*) that the legislature should be allowed to regulate the price in *any* industry finally came to prevail. But we have used Stone's logic only as an example of an approach which is used in a wider area. It is an approach used constantly *in legislatures to determine* what they should do. Facts are gathered on a situation, and an attempt is made to find a solution which is appropriate for the situation and which meets the requirements of group demands. It is problem solving. It is the method inherent in every attempt to base legislation on economic and social facts.

Some guide in purpose is, however, needed in determining what action should be taken on facts. This has been found in the United States in the

---

[36] 277 U.S. 350, 372.
[37] 277 U.S. 350, 360.
[38] 273, U.S. 418, 451.

concept of the public interest. This concept has rarely been defined. Some would define it as the best attainable compromise among the conflicting interests; others would say that it is the shared interests of the people; and perhaps most would recognize that it included some element of both.[39] But however defined, or whether defined, the idea that the public interest should prevail, with proper concessions to private right, has supplied the moral test for the American legal or political empiricist. He has believed that the analysis of economic and social data in the particular context of a problem by those who believed in the common weal provided the only satisfactory method of determining whether government should act and, if so, in what manner.

This type of approach may lead men far away from *laissez faire*. If private concentrations of power, misuses of economic position, economic depression, and the uncertainties of life create evils with which people are concerned, the legislator may be influenced to seek appropriate ways of meeting the observed evils. Hence, empiricism has in our day become collectivist.

But not entirely so. Legislatures have tended to accept the *status quo* and act only where evils were revealed or problems presented. In practice, industries are left alone unless there is a belief that government action is necessary to meet some paramount need. The breach in *laissez faire* may be very wide indeed; *laissez faire* may even cease to be the general rule; nevertheless, *laissez faire* is the basic condition from which departures are made, and the burden of making a case rests upon those who favor some new government intervention.

This practical, problem approach is more understandable to Americans than the more abstract approach of the idealists. Yet some will wonder whether the philosophy is fully satisfactory. One group may believe that it does not provide a sufficient basis for faith in results unless it is supplemented by idealist assumptions. They may accept empiricism on the level of method —that is, that action should be taken in response to conditions and for the correction of these—and still believe that it offers promise only if conducted under conditions under which it can be assumed that there is a high degree of consonance between the welfare of each and the welfare of all. Empiricism will appear to many to be a barren philosophy if not supplemented by some philosophy of goals. In this country men have seldom sought to combine their ideas in a coordinated system of beliefs. If those who have faith in public action did so, their acceptance of empiricism in public policy would probably be accompanied not merely by an assumption of the goal of the public interest, but also by an assertion of faith in democratic collectivism— that is, faith that in a democratic nation such as the United States, social action will contribute to individual growth. On the other hand, there are some who lack this faith, and they too may raise questions about the empirical approach. If they accept it, they will do so with reservations. They, like a

---

[39] For fuller discussion, see pages 49–53.

justice once on the Supreme Court, would have us "beware beginnings"; they would fear that we could not retreat from errors; and they would be concerned over whether the cumulative and total effect of interventions to correct evils would be good or bad for the economy and man.

Some, then, will return to the questions of the idealists. Under what conditions may it be hoped that government action will create opportunities for human development? Others will return to the questions of Mill. Skeptically they will ask: Does state intervention in particulars cumulatively bring unavoidable evils?

ELEMENTS OF SKEPTICISM

The questions of the skeptics may be given immediate attention. What are the elements of this skepticism? Four possible ones deserve attention.

Two elements of skepticism from Old World thought have not bothered Americans much. One is the doctrine of the iron law of oligarchy. It is the doctrine that society will always be ruled by an oligarchy, that no oligarchy can avoid interpreting its own interests as those of society, and that any social change which destroys one oligarchy will produce another. This doctrine is an answer of European skeptics to the promise of a new life in such sweeping reform movements as socialism and communism. To the American who has never lived under the iron rule of oligarchy and who has contemplated no revolutionary changes in his society, this fear of oligarchy has not seemed particularly relevant. He is likely to believe still that any threat of a managerial or scientist oligarchy will not be serious in this society of pluralism, flexibility, and individual opportunity.[40]

The second element of skepticism arises from the fear of statism—that is, that the economy will be controlled for state purposes. This is a normal European fear, and it has been voiced also by American critics of government intervention in the economy. These, however, have had to draw their examples from Old World experience, and hence the danger they have cited has seemed remote. Recently, there has developed some cause for skepticism, not among critics of government intervention, but among those who have hoped that government action would result in social gains. The basis for this is the possibility that the social income of society, which might have been available for social betterment, will continue to be needed for military pur-

---

[40] Burnham's argument that power is passing to a managerial group is met by Thompson's argument that power is passing to the specialists because of managers' lack of ability to direct and supervise them. When two interpreters differ so completely, and both overlook the checks in society on the tendencies argued, some will believe that neither is fully correct and that there is still a healthy check and balance among trends in the society. See James Burnham, *The Managerial Revolution: What is Happening in the World* (New York: John Day Company, Inc., 1941), particularly Chapters 4 and 16, and Victor A. Thompson, *Modern Organization: A General Theory* (New York: Alfred A. Knopf, Inc., 1961).

poses, and that promotional and regulatory measures of government would likewise have as their primary aim the strengthening of our national unity and military strength. This, of course, would not be a matter of choice, but one of necessity growing out of foreign danger.

Two other elements of skepticism have deep roots in American soil. One is the belief that a government bureaucracy will be inefficient and bungling. The American frontier notions on bureaucracy corresponded with those stated by Smith and Mill, and the recent overcoming of the spoilsmen and the contemporary development of effective personnel administration have not overcome the frontier notions. Today, however, this old set of notions seems outmoded. A more modern aspect of this element of skepticism arises from the fear that government will lack the ability successfully to cope with the tremendously complex and changing economic forces, that it will not be able to foresee the future, to foretell the effects of its actions, to handle the problems of coordination and leadership of its own agencies, to keep initiative and vision in its personnel, and to act for the larger public interests.

This last set of fears about bureaucracy is part of an element of skepticism about government as a whole. It is the fear that governmental policy will only be a series of things done for the strong special interests, and that the total result for the economy will be unpredictable and probably the sacrifice of the general good.

Those who answer the skeptics are forced to reason as follows. We cannot escape the problems of our day, whatever the uncertainties as to our capacity for self-government. As for the latter, the skeptics overlook the merits of the American system of government, with its multiple responsiveness to the varieties of interest in the society and its capacity to bring intelligence into the solution of problems.

MODERN REVOLUTIONARY PHILOSOPHIES: COMMUNISM AND FASCISM

The communist and the fascist go beyond the skeptics. Most of the latter accept the traditional Western ideal of the state as the servant of man, and only raise questions as to the degree to which it should intervene in the economy. The communist and fascist deny completely the old ideal views of the state and government.

The ideal view of the state has taken many forms of expression. The basic ideal, central in Greek, Roman, medieval, and modern Western thought, is that the state may be an instrument of justice among men. A further idea is that the state may be a means of promoting the common weal or public interest. To these ideals, which have their roots in antiquity, has been added another—that the state may work for the amelioration of economic and social ills, for improvement of the conditions of life. This has been paralleled by another idea—that the state can best achieve its ideal aims if it is democratic in structure and operation.

The communist says that this is all nonsense. He interprets the history of man and his institutions in strictly materialistic terms. More particularly, he accepts the conclusion of the *Communist Manifesto* (1848): "the history of all hitherto existing society is the history of class struggles." In his view, the state is neither an instrument of justice nor a promoter of common interests or social betterment; democracy itself cannot make it such in a class society. The state is only the means by which the ruling *class* in society dominates other classes. In modern society, where, according to Marx, the class struggle is simplified, the bourgeoisie (owning and managing class) exploit the proletariat (working class). The police, the army, and the bureaucracy are to the communist the characteristic instruments of the state, and these are all used by the state to preserve the subjection of the worker.

To this unhappy view of the state the communist adds a doleful interpretation of the economy. Marx and Engels argued that competition among laborers would keep wages at a subsistence level, and that the surplus value produced by labor would be appropriated by the bourgeoisie. Moreover, the "lower strata of the middle class"—shopkeepers, handicraftsmen, and peasants—would "sink gradually into the proletariat, partly because their diminutive capital does not suffice for the scale on which modern industry is carried on, and is swamped in the competition with the large capitalists, partly because their specialized skill is rendered worthless by new methods of production" (*Communist Manifesto*). Also, capitalism would be repeatedly convulsed because its gigantic production could not be absorbed: "The conditions of bourgeois society are too narrow to comprise the wealth created by them" (*Communist Manifesto*).

But to this gloomy picture the communist adds a promise of the future for the dispossessed of society. At times his gods, Marx and Engels, prophesy that a revolt of the masses is inevitable, but in doing so, they do not discount the necessity for initiative on the part of the masses: "Workmen of the world, unite!" was the closing call of *The Communist Manifesto*. The proletarian revolution which follows does not immediately change the nature of the state. It brings the dictatorship of the proletariat, and this new dominant class uses the state and its weapons of power to eliminate the bourgeoisie. Only when this is accomplished can the state serve the interests of all. When classes have disappeared, the weapons of coercion will cease to exist; the state will "wither away." The political utopia is thus one of freedom from state compulsion, one in which the affairs of men are managed by cooperation without compulsion. The economic utopia is one in which each supplies work according to his ability, and obtains benefits according to his needs.

Three comments may be made about this view of the relationship of the state to the economy. First, though Marx has been called the father of "scientific socialism" (in contrast with the utopian models of socialistic society that preceded him), this set of dogmas falls short of the standards of scientific analysis and prediction. The materialistic interpretation, in Marx as in Smith, assumes too simple a view of human motivation and human institutions. The criticisms of existing society are grossly overstated, whether of capitalism or of the nature of political authority. Predictions are made without substantiating evidence. The hope of the future is stated dogmatically, without question as to whether a new autocracy might emerge from a dictatorship of the proletariat, or whether the goal of "from each according to his ability, to each according to his needs" was not beyond the nature of man. Communism as a doctrine is propaganda, not science.

Second, it gives no hope without a terrible social convulsion, and thus overlooks the possibilities for internal change in capitalism and in social policies by governments. It is here that the unscientific nature of the predictions is most clearly revealed. Capitalism has changed. Marx was correct in seeing the decline of certain elements of an old middle class. But he overlooked the continuance in the interstices of society of remnants of these classes. More significant, he did not foresee the development of new elements in the middle class. These are the salaried and fee-taking professional and semiprofessional workers—accountants, clericals, lawyers, engineers, doctors, nurses, teachers, entertainers, and others. These thrive in ever-increasing numbers in American capitalism. Also, Marx denied that the wages of workers and the standards of life of people generally could be raised under capitalism, and hence did not see that the ownership of homes and other goods—even of stocks and bonds—might be widely distributed. Nor could he foresee welfare programs in industry, with security plans for those injured, reaching retirement age, and so on. Not only capitalism, but also government has changed. Legal recognition and protection are given to trade unions, social security legislation has been passed, the state seeks to avoid the horrors of depression. There are, therefore, other hopes—much better hopes—for the worker than communism.

All of this means that the proletariat in the United States need not conduct a revolution in order to achieve its goals. The worker has received many benefits under capitalism and government policy, including the opportunity for his children to take new positions in the social structure.

Third, this does not mean that communism is not a threat to our country. It does mean that the threat takes different forms from that predicted by Marx. It is a threat of encirclement from the outside and of subversion from within, not of internal collapse of capitalism from within.

Fascism makes a different kind of attack on traditional ideal views of the state. It is more movement than philosophy, and its specific manifestations have varied in different fascist countries. But elements of a common manner of thinking are evident, nevertheless. The tendency of such movements has been to reverse the means-ends relation between the state and the individual. Fascism is statism and anti-individualism. It places emphasis on state aims, state honor, state unity, usually also on state expansion. It is often presented with a biological emphasis, as in Hitler's racism or in an Italian Fascist's definition of the Italian state as "the recapitulating unity of successive generations." Against such a macrocosmic unity as this, a fascist will think, what independent value can a single microcosmic unity such as the individual have? Fascism, therefore, attacks the Western notion of freedom against the state. It has also been authoritarian in flavor, dictatorial in technique, and antidemocratic in attitude. And by appealing to the emotional drives in men, it has sometimes, as in Germany, let loose the most bestial passions in man.

On its economic side fascism has been an antiliberal movement. It has been supported by those who were opposed to unionism and to liberal or socialist reform movements. Repression of organized labor and a reactionary attitude to social reform have characterized fascist movements. Ultimately, however, fascism creates state control and authoritarianism in more and more areas, with the result that freedom for the business entrepreneur and the farmer, as well as the laborer, is lost.

Is a fascist movement a possibility in our country? Its distinct manifestations, if on the way to development in this country, would probably be these: a movement for a distinctly nationalist foreign policy (perhaps combining isolationism and the brandishing of the big stick), an attack upon labor unions and the welfare state, a disregard of traditional American liberties, and effort to create suspicion of the operation of democratic institutions, and appeal to emotions—arousing the hates and fears of the people.[41] Of course, it is clear that no one of these, or even several in combination, would constitute a fascist movement; but the combination of all of these would produce an indigenous American fascist movement whose opportunities for success might be enhanced by hard times and a leader capable of stirring large masses of people and obtaining funds from friendly sources.

Fascism, of course, arises when there is a decline in patience and hope for the solution of problems by democratic methods. It will not appeal to men until this condition exists. Fascism, therefore, like communism, is a challenge to freedom and democracy—a challenge to us to find solutions for social-economic problems in the basic framework of freedom and democracy, and to retain the traditional American faith in the values of freedom and democracy against the day when patience, reason, understanding, and good will may be sorely pressed.

[41] For an analysis of the possible characteristics of an indigenous American fascism, see H. Arthur Steiner, "Fascism in America?" *American Political Science Review*, **XXIX** (October 1935), pp. 821–830.

Chapter 5. Search for a Twentieth-Century System of Thought

IT IS POSSIBLE that some students will accept one of the patterns of thought outlined in the preceding chapter as a reasonably satisfactory answer concerning the role of government in the economy. Most persons, however, draw their philosophy from many sources. For these, it is hoped that the suggestions in this chapter will aid in the development of individual syntheses of ideas.

LIBERALISM, SOCIALISM, CONSERVATISM, AND NEOLIBERALISM

Communism and fascism would be radical breaks with the American tradition and would bring violent convulsions within society. The American student will recognize these as movements or systems of ideas to be avoided. He will search for the answer to the problem of the role of government in ideas that are closer to the trends of the past. For his basic attitudes he may find help in the traditional trends of liberal and conservative thought. Some students will lean strongly toward one or the other of these; others will find that they are liberal conservatives or conservative liberals.

Liberalism has been a historical movement, or series of movements, and has constituted a leaven of change in Western society. In general, liberalism has been optimistic in attitude. It has been a doctrine of progress which encompassed a belief that the conditions of existence for men generally could be improved, that man's nature was inherently good and could be perfected under conditions of freedom and material well-being, and that government's role was necessarily related to these aims.

For a long time the liberal idea was reflected in the movement to liberate the mind and physical existence of man from governmental restraints. In its economic aspects it was initially a movement toward freeing the economic initiative of man from outmoded systems of state restraint. Through the ideas of natural right, utilitarianism, and *laissez faire* economics, it was an attack upon state preservation of feudal privileges, of mercantilist restraints (which had arisen in the era of modern state building), and newer forms of control which hampered initiative and private gain. The leaven of liberal ideas fitted the needs and spirit of the time, for the great frontier described by Webb, the technological revolution, the spirit of entrepreneurs (what Veblen called the "masterless men"), and the idea of the freedom of man all called for release of human energy from the tutelage or restriction of government.

This type of idea is still called "economic liberalism," "economic individualism," or "traditional liberalism." Long ago, however, it was accepted by conservatives and may today satisfy many who are called reactionaries. A new phase developed in so-called liberal thought which has been referred to as the "new liberalism," the "new individualism," or "reform liberalism." It is reflected in two patterns of thought discussed in the preceding chapter—that of the idealist, and that of the empiricist. Both reflect concern with the ills of mankind, and both reflect the idea that government may be a useful instrument with which to attack these ills. Both reflect new notions about liberty: that it is more than absence from restraint by government; that it may be hampered by private economic acts or institutions, or by unfavorable conditions, as well as by government; and that government action may be needed to counteract private encroachments upon freedom or to create a favorable basis for human initiative. Both reflect the idea of equality—that is, that all men have a valid claim on government. The idealist states it; as for the empiricist, it is implicit in his doctrine of the public interest, which assumes that the welfare of all is the object of government. Behind the new liberalism in a broad way are the modern trends toward humanitarianism, equality, and the effort to use government to promote human well-being.

The trend of this movement in ideas has been toward the regulatory and welfare state. In this country the new liberalism, which seeks freedom and welfare through state action, though presaged in government control in the Granger period, has been reflected mainly in the Progressive movement, the New and Fair deals, and the New Frontier.

Modern democratic socialism is in considerable measure a product of the same trend. It has, however, also drawn ideas and inspiration from the Marxist creed. This has been more true of some countries than of others; for example, in Germany the democratic socialist movement (Social Democratic Party) broke away from revolutionary Marxism, while in England Fabian socialism rose substantially from the roots of liberalism. Socialist thought has differed from liberal thought in one other respect. It has placed great emphasis on state ownership as the means of correcting the evils of capitalism. Socialism, it would appear, has suffered from a dogmatism of thought—partly the dogmatism of Marxism, and partly the dogmatism of belief in state ownership as a cure-all. On the other hand, Western socialists have been liberal in that they have accepted gradualism in reform, have been ardent supporters of democratic government, and have treasured the ideal of freedom, albeit with a different concept of economic liberty than that of the business entrepreneur.

Conservatism, like liberalism, changes its colors with the passage of time and reflects different shades at any one moment in time. But, again like liberalism, it also has a central core of attitude. If one accepts change readily, the other places emphasis on order and stability, continuity, caution, and prudence. Conservatives have less faith than liberals in a happy lot for all or in the perfectibility of the nature of man. Conservatism has often reflected the attitude that the masses of men must find their salvation in obedience to a higher law of morality rather than in the perfection of social conditions. It has consistently placed emphasis on the values of property ownership, on protection of acquired property rights, and on government by people with a stake in things.

In this country the conservative attitude was reflected, in the Constitution-framing period, in the struggle for a balanced government in which the rights of property would receive protection; in the pre-Civil War period, in the struggle to preserve the position of property (through constitutions, courts, appeals to higher law) against the advancing democracy; in the post-Civil War period, in antagonism to regulatory measures, to Populism, and to the Progressive movement; and lately, in opposition to the New and the Fair deals, to the growth of labor power, to the extension of the welfare state, to the centralization of power in Washington, and in ideological support for the "free enterprise" system.

It should, of course, be recognized that the lines between liberal and conservative positions have not always been as clear-cut as they are in a statement of their basic attitudes. Each position has accepted much from the other over the course of time. And today each is challenged at a new stage in human affairs to reconsider its policy objectives. Those who have thought of themselves as liberals can see that antitrust has not been fully successful, that regulation has not achieved as much as many had hoped for, that social security and public works cannot be substitutes for initiative in the private sector of the economy, that giantism in government and labor raise as many problems as giantism in industry. Those who have thought of themselves as conservatives can recognize that "free enterprise" must not be a slogan that denies the need to enforce antitrust laws or the need for appropriate regulation, that social security provides a security that not everyone can find in property ownership, that public works are an essential supplement to private initiative, and that concentration of power in government is essential.

There will be many issues which create conflict between those with liberal and those with conservative points of view. Among these, for example, will probably be the division of taxes among classes of the population, the role of the state in housing and power development, the breadth and depth of regulation, the degree of state support for minimum living standards, and the extent of deficit financing by government. But American politics has been characterized by general acceptance, after a time, of the basic steps in policy. Thereafter controversy and struggle have centered on smaller issues of application of policy, or of its elaboration or contraction.

In recent years another form of liberal thought, called "neoliberalism," has been expressed. Neoliberalism is an intellectual movement associated with such names as Henry C. Simons, Friedrich A. Hayek, Frank Knight, Wilhelm Röpke, and Alexander Rüstow.[1] Although each author may not have stated them all, the general themes of neoliberal thought can easily be delineated. Neoliberals attack collectivism, authoritarianism, socialism, government coercion, and arbitrary decision. Their central theme is that all efforts should be directed toward a market economy, in contrast to a directed or planned economy. Competition and the price system should be the mechanisms of social control. They regard "competition as superior not only because it is in most circumstances the most efficient method known but even more because it is the only method by which our activities can be adjusted to each other without coercive or arbitrary intervention of authority."[2] But the neoliberal accepts a considerable sphere of government activity and distinguishes himself from the doctrinaire advocate of *laissez faire*. He may advocate a "positive program for *laissez faire*"—that is, a "program of economic reconstruction" involving a radical attack by government on monopoly and the other means by which private persons prevent the operation of a free market.[3] He distinguishes between " 'compatible' and 'incompatible' interventions—that is, those that are in harmony with an economic structure based on the market and those which are not."[4] He accepts government action to maintain the framework of the economy, such as rules on contracts and property. A particularly strong point of emphasis is on the need for government to act through general rules to which the economy can make its adjustment, rather than through changing bureaucratic, detailed, "arbitrary" actions.[5] Thus, he will accept a tariff more willingly than quota controls, for the former may be less detailed and may allow opportunity for adjustment to the fact of its existence.[6] The neoliberal may

---

[1] For typical works, see Henry C. Simons, *A Positive Program for Laissez Faire* (Chicago: University of Chicago Press, 1934), and *Economic Policy for a Free Society* (Chicago: University of Chicago Press, 1948); Friedrich A. Hayek, *The Road to Serfdom* (Chicago: University of Chicago Press, 1944), *The Constitution of Liberty* (London: William Hodge & Co., 1960); Wilhelm Röpke, *Civitas Humana (A Humane Order for Society)*, translated from the German by Cyril Spencer Fox (London: William Hodge & Co., 1948), *The Social Crisis of Our Time*, translated from the German by Annette and Peter Schiffer Jacobsohn (Chicago: University of Chicago Press, 1948), and *A Humane Economy: The Social Framework of the Free Market*, translated from the German by Elizabeth Henderson (Chicago: Henry Regnery Co., 1960); and Carl J. Friedrich's essay on the first two volumes of Alexander Rüstow's major work, *Ortsbestimmung der Gegenwart* (Erlenbach-Zürich: E. Rentsch, 1952), in *American Political Science Review*, XLIX (June 1955), pp. 509–525.

[2] Friedrich A. Hayek, *The Road to Serfdom* (Chicago: University of Chicago Press, 1944), p. 36.

[3] The first quotation is from the title of Henry C. Simons' publication in 1934, and the second is from the opening sentence of that publication.

[4] Friedrich A. Hayek, *The Social Crisis of Our Time*, op. cit., p. 160.

[5] See particularly Friedrich A. Hayek, *The Constitution of Liberty*, op. cit., pp. 224ff.

[6] Friedrich A. Hayek, *The Social Crisis of Our Time*, op. cit., p. 160.

even accept social legislation of the type advocated by the reform liberal, such as social security, but he will want the system hedged to keep it as compatible as possible with the conditions of a market economy.[7] He may even urge that "There should be a strong state, aloof from the hungry hordes of vested interests . . . ," which can exert the force necessary to maintain the basic element (in his opinion) of freedom—namely, the free competitive market.[8] Hayek even accepts as "in accordance with the market economy" such things as "readjustment of income levels in order to effect a more equitable distribution," subsidies out of tax revenues for workmen's housing, and state management of enterprises or "whole branches of production." [9]

There is in this new intellectual movement (stemming largely from German scholars) two broad aims which may appeal to both reform liberals and conservatives. The first is the ideal of limiting the role of government by making the market economy operable. Liberals may say, "We do not argue for complete economic planning; we favor minimizing the load on government by making antitrust more effective; we are for the market where it really operates and without social injury." Conservatives may say, "This is, indeed, the goal for which we have argued." The second is the ideal that government should function through known, general rules to which the economy may make its adjustments. All Americans can say, "We have always had a predisposition toward avoidance of detailed, variable decisions made by bureaucrats."

Yet there is a certain tone of unreality and impracticality in much that the neoliberals write. They have aimed their guns at "socialism," "economic planning," and "arbitrary" intervention rather than at the kinds of restrained interventions that have characterized American government. Even then, like Adam Smith and John Stuart Mill before them, they have riddled their theory with exceptions when they have come to the level of consideration of specific policies. They have failed to recognize the inexorable pressures toward, and frequent necessity of, discretion in the administration of law (which the student will be able to observe as the separate programs are discussed in succeeding chapters). Beyond all this, the neoliberal assumes the adaptability of eighteenth-century remedies to twentieth-century conditions. He fails to recognize the durability of the organizational revolution. The "positive program for *laissez faire*" would probably involve so drastic a breakup of organization power as to constitute a political revolution against the economic and social revolution that has already occurred, and if so, would involve political power not available in pluralistic democracy. The neoliberals desire a strong state which stands above interest groups, recognizing, apparently, that only such a state could put into effect the

[7] Friedrich A. Hayek, *The Constitution of Liberty*, op. cit., Chapter 19.
[8] Friedrich A. Hayek, *The Social Crisis of Our Time*, op. cit., p. 181.
[9] Hayek, *ibid.*, pp. 189–190.

"positive program for *laissez faire*." What they seem not to realize is that American pluralistic democracy, in which groups exercise political influence, really makes impossible a pattern of complete economic planning (which they attack) and also prevents the establishment of a full pattern of market control (which they favor). The organizational revolution and other great changes (discussed in Chapter 2) and American pluralistic democracy (discussed in Chapter 3) make inevitable a mixed-economy system. Consequently, it may be said that the neoliberals re-emphasize goals which liberals and conservatives alike will treasure, but which both, when brought face to face with problems, will find are only partially achievable.

THE INDIGENOUS AMERICAN APPROACH

If we look beneath the conflict between ideological systems to the trends in accepted ideal and method in this country, we can see six elements in thought which have been significant and which may still form a core of realistic approach for a citizen of the United States.

1. The first is the *opportunity ideal*. The American ideal has been that every boy and girl should have a good opportunity to develop and use his talents. Americans have not been much concerned whether each person had an *equal* opportunity, but they have believed that each should have a *good* opportunity.

This is only another mode of expressing individualistic thought. Adam Smith and others of the eighteenth century could talk in terms of natural right, Mill in terms of liberty, Hobhouse in terms of growth. Each of these expressions has meaning for an American. But in the climate in which he has lived these have not appeared to be distant visions, for all appeared to be realities in the "land of opportunity." The measure and dispersion of opportunity has given him an optimistic belief that opportunity does and can continue to exist. For him, as David Potter has said, liberty means "freedom to grasp opportunity."

2. The second is the ideal of *material well-being*. In different language, it is the ideal of high consumption, mass buying power, or wide distribution of goods. This is an ideal in the stage of high production in this country. Life on the frontier and for the laborer in the early days was hard. Money was scarce, and conveniences and comforts were few. But the twentieth century has produced the vision of material well-being for all. It is the goal of mass retailers, advertisers, and producers as well as of the humanitarian, liberal philosopher, and politician.[10] Its general acceptance, and the similarly general acceptance of the opportunity ideal, mark the

---

[10] David M. Potter has sought the secret of American character in "the abundance of usable goods" produced from our resources. *People of Plenty: Economic Abundance and the American Character* (Chicago: University of Chicago Press, 1954). See particularly page 67. John Kenneth Galbraith has called for contemporary Americans to accommodate their

extension of hopes for material welfare beyond any dreams that would have been possible for the liberal optimists of the eighteenth century.

3. The third element is the *empirical approach.* Most Americans have believed that individual opportunity can exist without radical transformation of the existing order. Hence, the empirical approach has been more acceptable to the American than general, sweeping doctrines such as socialism and complete economic planning. He will take things as they are until problems are presented or evils revealed, and will limit his solutions to these problems or evils. But he will reject *laissez faire* also in cases where he experiences evils which he believes government can alleviate or remove. The empirical approach, like the opportunity ideal, has been a natural response to favorable American conditions.

4. A fourth element in American thought is the *public interest* concept. This is the concept which gives moral significance to the empirical approach. The legislator, administrator, or judge believes that the motive in problem solving is the public interest. Whether the public interest is definable or whether it is myth or reality,[11] it is the object of search. The term is a way of expressing another ideal of higher morality: *salus populi suprema lex esto* (the welfare of the people is the highest law).

5. The idea of the public interest has been balanced by the concept of *minority rights*. The American has never been a 100-percenter for any single ideal. While accepting the ideal of the public interest, he has also recognized that minority interests should be considered. The effort to reconcile these two ideals is one of the largest chapters in American judicial history, and is told in Chapter 7; the reconciliation is now achieved through the operation of pluralistic democracy, described in Chapter 3.

6. Americans have sought the attainment of the public interest ideal through democratic institutions, but they have embraced *moderated democracy* rather than simple majority rule. Moderated democracy in the beginning was a system of internal checks and balances within government; more recently it is pluralistic government resting on a pluralistic society and working in complex ways toward the satisfaction of demands and the solution of problems.

THE SYNTHESIS OF INDIVIDUAL RIGHT AND PUBLIC INTEREST

Two of the nonrevolutionary systems of thought discussed in the preceding chapter assume a harmonic society in which the interest of each is the interest of all. The old economics assumed that the harmony between

---

thinking to the fact recorded in his title *The Affluent Society* (Boston: Houghton Mifflin Company, 1958).

[11] See pages 49–53.

individual interest and general good could be achieved without the action of public authority. This assumption, though comforting, is far "too optimistic" (as Hobhouse said) for the economy as a whole, though it may be acceptable—at least as the best attainable—for parts of the economy. The idealist tells us that *our ideal,* which we may in part attain, must be to legislate in such a way as to avoid disharmony between the individual and society. Can one realistically place his hopes so high?

Mill saw clearly the possibilities of conflict between social control and individual interest and liberty. The assumption that such a conflict could exist has been the basis of much American thought. This is revealed in the story told in Chapter 7 on "The Constitution, Social Interests, and Economic Rights." Judicial decisions have often been made upon the assumption of conflict, but quite rarely from the positive conception that regulation was the basis of liberty.

It appears that there is a basis for both idealistic and realistic thinking on this problem of social control and liberty. Thus, idealist assumptions of the harmony of interests appear valid regarding the Employment Act of 1946. Legislation that helps maintain high employment, production, and purchasing power works for the opportunity of each. The general goal may be acceptable to all, even though some may argue that the general good will not be fostered if "high" employment means no unemployment. On the other hand, realistic thinking will show conflict of interest on certain labor proposals. A rise in minimum wages may well cause loss of income to some. Decision on an increase in minimum wages may, therefore, call for *measuring the losses of some against the gains of others.* In legislation on labor relations, management and labor are not likely to agree on such things as the closed shop, the secondary boycott, and unionization of supervisory personnel. Legislators may not succeed in finding solutions which will make both labor and management happy. In such cases, the unhappy losers may either continue to press for amendments or will need to discipline themselves to life under an arrangement which seems unsatisfactory.

On the whole, the legislator may hope that his work helps produce social arrangements that aid the freedom, growth, and well-being of all. At the same time, he may recognize that his help to Peter may restrain Paul, perhaps to his disadvantage. However, he may also hope that the adjustments called for will not be so great as to prevent each party from disciplining himself with good grace to accept the imposed conditions.

APPROACHES IN POLICY IN A MIXED ECONOMY

In the mixed economy of our day, in a nation in which people are accustomed to both freedom and responsiveness of government to the people's needs, four factors of circumstance and idea may be significant as basic considerations concerning policy approaches.

First, the people depend basically for opportunity and material well-being upon the successful operation of the private sector of the economy. Not only does the private sector supply the preponderant portion of goods and services, but it must also supply the surplus revenue from which the major part of the cost of the public sector is paid.

Second, the state must respond positively to the great demands for service and control. On the service side, the great needs for defense, highways, education, maintenance of law and order, development of resources, and other benefits have outmoded any negative view of grudging acceptance of a role for government. On the control side, the interdependence of the parts of the economy, the concentration of economic power, the recurrence of elements of imbalance, the need of production for defense objectives, and other factors also demand a positive view of the function of government.

Third, to maintain the pluralistic nature of the mixed economy and the mainsprings of private initiative, and also to avoid overburdening the government, some of Mill's arguments may be of real significance today. He argued, it will be recalled, the dangers of overloading government. We have, through progress in managerial science and art and through experience in World War II, become better equipped as a nation for the problems of big government. We also have at hand many devices for distributing the load of government, such as the federal system, the area authority (for example, T.V.A.), and the government corporation. Nevertheless, suggestions in recent years for complete and detailed economic planning involving the setting of production schedules and the control of price and wage throughout industry, such as exist in some foreign nations and was necessary in this country during World War II, have not appealed to American thinkers. They have thought in terms of a system in which positive government effort and independent private initiative would each make a significant contribution.

Mill also noted what we could call the psychological element in freedom —the fact that men do not like to feel restrained. There is in our society a need for men to recognize that they must discipline themselves to accept restraint. If men are to be happy in society, they must learn how to accept the red traffic light without anger, and to accept the idea that most regulations are probably indeed for the general welfare. On the other hand, the multiplication of detailed restrictions that seem to interfere with day-to-day decisions may be exasperating and may inculcate a feeling of frustration. These feelings may, in turn, dampen initiative. It would appear, therefore, that for a mixed economy there is an advantage in government policies that center at the bridgeheads—which determine general lines of policy to which business must make its adjustment, but which try to avoid the necessity of continuing, detailed prescription.

Fourth, the choices available in a mixed economy are not simply those of state control or the absence of such control; they include, on the contrary, a considerable range of possibilities. Robert Dahl and Charles Lindblom, political scientist and economist, have show that there are four central sociopolitical processes involved in the relationship of the state to the economy.[12] One is the price system—what we have referred to frequently as market controls. A second is hierarchy, which means "a very high degree of unilateral control" by leaders over nonleaders.[13] The third is polyarchy, which is the "untidy" system in which "nonleaders exercise a relatively high degree of control over leaders" and which provides a rough and crude approximation of democracy in some societies.[14] The fourth is bargaining, which is "a form of reciprocal control among leaders" and is generally "inversely related to the amount of hierarchy and the extent of initial agreement."[15] This form of control may exist among economic leaders, political leaders, or both. "All modern industrialized economies combine, though in different ways, the four central sociopolitical processes. . . ."[16] Also, to the extent that man has alternatives, he may seek suitable choices of combinations of these processes.

In addition to this scheme of basic processes, Dahl and Lindblom advance the idea of "continuums." In a number of charts they illustrate the continuum (or range) of choices between such things as government and private action, voluntary and compulsory action, direct and indirect controls. These charts show multiple choices between polar extremes. For example, on the continuum between public and private there are, among other things, the government lease and contract with private persons, government ownership, regulated private utilities, joint government-private firms, subsidized private corporations, corporations subject to miscellaneous regulations (for example, of labor and securities), corporations only subject to corporate regulations, small proprietors subject only to the common law.[17] All of these, it may be added, exist in the United States. Obviously, in a mixed economy there are many alternatives from which political choices may be made.

Against this background of considerations, it is appropriate to note the outstanding directions that government policy has taken or is taking in the mixed economy of this country.

ANTITRUST POLICY. Antitrust has been the basic American policy regarding business enterprise. It has as its chief objective the maintenance of free and fair competition in the market. Woodrow Wilson argued that the purpose of antitrust was to preserve the freedom of men—their freedom

---

[12] Robert A. Dahl and Charles E. Lindblom, *Politics, Economics and Welfare* (New York: Harper and Row, Publishers, Inc., 1953), Part IV.
[13] Dahl and Lindblom, *ibid.*, p. 227.
[14] Dahl and Lindblom, *ibid.*, p. 275.
[15] Dahl and Lindblom, *ibid.*, p. 324.
[16] Dahl and Lindblom, *ibid.*, p. 369.
[17] Dahl and Lindblom, *ibid.*, p. 10.

to engage in enterprise.[18] Chief Justice Hughes called it "a charter of freedom." [19] Another argument has been that the enforcement of antitrust laws was the only way to prevent such concentration of controls in industry as would lead to popular pressure for government control. The policy thus has been interpreted as one designed to maximize the self-regulatory features of the economy. Both to the person who believes in the maximum retention of the system of "natural" freedom and to the one who is fearful that the load on government may be increased too rapidly, antitrust will appear to be a form of government control which conserves the use and the force of government and maintains initiative and self-regulatory forces in the private sector of the economy. The objections to the argument, particularly in terms of the historical ineffectiveness of enforcement and the amount of power that would now be needed to implement antitrust fully, are not without force; but it is nevertheless true that, to the extent that antitrust prevents market control by private power, it is working toward the preservation of a market-controlled economy.

REGULATION. Regulation has been the typical approach in this country when there was dissatisfaction with the operation of industries. In many areas this was not the only approach possible; a much greater use of government production and sale through government-owned enterprise would have been feasible. The English, whether ruled by Conservatives or Laborites, have leaned, in those cases in which the market did not operate successfully, toward government management rather than government regulation. But in this country the initial experimentation with ownership and management of railroads by the states was followed by a trend toward regulation instead of ownership by government. Regulation became the typical, though by no means the exclusive, American approach in handling the problems created in particular industries.

Three different types of motivation in the growth of regulation have been significant. An early one was the moral motivation. Liquor, gambling, prostitution, and fraud in sale of commodities were combatted by regulation in its extreme form—prohibition. This nation was too strongly Puritan for "natural liberty" to survive against claims of the community in the so-called "unlawful industries" or where fraud was practiced. Second, regulation has arisen as a means of protecting the community against abuses in industries. It was to protect the community, or segments thereof, that regulation of railroads, utilities, banking, and insurance was instituted. Third, regulation has sometimes been set up to protect industries or persons therein. This is the motivation for regulation of oil and agriculture, and to a large extent for licensing requirements to engage in learned professions and service trades.

---

[18] Woodrow Wilson, *The New Freedom* (Garden City, N.Y.: Doubleday & Company, Inc., 1913).
[19] *Appalachian Coals, Inc. v. U.S.*, 288 U.S. 344, 360 (1933).

Regulation has been accepted not because it was regarded as something to be desired in an economy, but, like other steps in a nation following an empirical approach, because of revealed need (unsatisfied interests), frequently after a strong struggle to achieve it, and often also with less use of power by government initially than proved to be essential for the long pull.

SERVICE AND PROMOTION. Defense, administration of justice, education, and public works were forms of service which Adam Smith accepted for the state. All of these have been rendered in this country. The public works have taken many forms, such as constructing canals, improving harbors and river navigation, and building railways, roads, irrigation projects, and power-generating facilities. These and many other services have been rendered to the economy as a whole. Also, many methods of promoting, protecting, or insuring particular industries have been adopted.

Service and promotion involve either no coercion or only incidental forms of coercion, except insofar as taxes may be collected to meet the expenses. Except for the latter, they bring ordinarily no sense of restraint to the individual. They conserve the power of government and extend its service. They involve use of government, but in ways which ordinarily raise less objection than regulation. Moreover, in these areas there are opportunities for government to perform great service to the people when private industry could not or would not without subsidy, or when the cost through private enterprise might be higher, or when the government unit concerned has seen other advantages in government management.

MAINTAINING MINIMUM STANDARDS OF WELL-BEING. In this country we have (though much later than some countries that were industrialized earlier) moved rapidly in recent years toward making the relief from extreme exigencies "as certain to those who require it as by any arrangements of society it can be made." [20] This we have done through workmen's compensation, old-age and survivors' insurance, unemployment insurance, crop insurance, through provision of methods of extending help to dependent children, aged and blind, through charity hospitals, veterans' medical care, public housing, and by other means. We have also set minimum wages and maximum hours and outlawed child labor.

Except for those mentioned in the last sentence, most of these have been forms of service. They have involved some competition in instances with private enterprise and some coercion through the taxing power. In the main, however, they have been service rather than control. They have been exceptions to the rule that individuals should take care of all their own needs by their own efforts, and are charges on the income of the total economy to meet strongly felt human needs. The ability of the economy

---

[20] John Stuart Mill, *Principles of Political Economy*, 7th ed. (1871), W. J. Ashley (ed.) (New York: Longmans, Green and Co., Inc., 1909), Chapter 11. See above, pages 73–74.

to provide them is part of the measure of its ability to meet the American demand for a high standard of material well-being for all.

COMPENSATORY ACTION. In recent years the most significant tendency in thought about government policy in a mixed economy is toward the acceptance of the idea of compensatory policy. By compensatory policy is meant "the control of expenditures, taxes, and borrowing so as to promote *stability*" [21]—that is, to prevent depression or inflation.

Initially this idea was explained in the writings of John Maynard Keynes. Keynes was an English economist whose writings spanned the second, third, and fourth decades of this century.[22] His writings had great practical significance for this country in the thirties in that they gave a theoretical underpinning to the pump-priming efforts of the government. Keynes lifted economic thought from the microeconomic approach, which concentrated attention on equilibriums between economic units, to the macroeconomic approach, which centers attention on the aggregate flow of national income. Depression and unemployment resulted from an inadequate total demand, and depression could be combatted by increasing the total national income that became available for expenditure. An increase in total national income could be brought about by an increase in government expenditures. These would, in fact, have a much larger effect than the number of dollars expended, for, as explained in the concept of the multiplier, a dollar spent by government would be in part respent several times, thus multiplying the effect of the initial expenditure.

In this country, economists such as Alvin Hansen and organizations such as the Committee for Economic Development [23] have outlined an extensive battery of antidepression weapons that are compensatory in nature. Most of these could be referred to as part of fiscal and monetary policy, for they assume that government fiscal policy (taxes, expenditures, and interest rate on government securities) and monetary policy (rediscount rates and other policies of the Federal Reserve system) should, in the case of a threat of depression, be adjusted so as to maintain a high level of national income. Taxes that limited purchasing power would be reduced, government expenditures increased, interest rates depressed, and so on, to increase total national expenditure.

The idea of compensatory policy now extends also to anti-inflation efforts.[24] Policies converse to those followed in a depression are recommended to prevent inflation. When inflation threatens, taxes are to be

---

[21] Alvin H. Hansen, *Economic Policy and Full Employment* (New York: McGraw-Hill Company, Inc., 1947), p. 11. Hansen's italics.

[22] For an analysis see Seymour E. Harris (ed.), *The New Economics: Keynes' Influence on Theory and Public Policy* (New York: Alfred A. Knopf, Inc., 1947).

[23] See the report by its Research and Policy Committee, *Defense Against Recession: Policy for Greater Economic Stability* (New York: Committee for Economic Development, 1954).

[24] See Alvin H. Hansen, *Economic Policy and Full Employment* (New York: McGraw-Hill Company, Inc., 1947), Chapter 1.

raised, government expenditures reduced, interest rates raised, and so forth.

Further discussion of antidepression and anti-inflation policies is included in succeeding chapters. It is sufficient now to make two points. The first is that action of a compensatory type has become a notable—perhaps the most significant—part of government economic policy in our mixed economy. Anyone who studies Federal Reserve Board policy, reports of the Council of Economic Advisers, or statements of our political leaders will see that the idea is widely accepted that government policy in fiscal and monetary matters should be *adjusted* to the ebb and flow of the economic tide. Second, compensatory action accords with the objectives in policy stated at the beginning of this section. True, it assumes that there shall be some economic planning by government—that is, that the government will look at the trends in the economy as a whole and plan its own action to meet foreseen dangers. Nevertheless, it is a concept of conservation of government, for it seeks to avoid detailed government intervention on matters of production and price, and reserves the intervention of government to the bridgeheads of finance and money in order to keep the economy on an even keel.

THE ULTIMATE BENEFICENCE OF A MIXED ECONOMY

Both the old and the new individualism provided man with grand visions of a good society. The first placed hope in the initiative of man applied independently at many points. The second placed hope in public action taken by a democratically constituted government. Both visions have been stated in forms which drew the criticism of realists—one on the ground that it did not picture the economic system as it is, the other on the basis that it did not show the political process as it operates, and both on the ground that the visions assumed too complete a harmony between individual and general good. Yet both contain elements of hope for our day. To locate the elements of hope, one must move to new planes of discussion, coming closer to the realities of the day.

On the side of public action, one must hope that the decision-making process will be an efficient one. This process in government is so complex that its efficiency cannot be judged by any single criterion. In general, it must meet the two tests of responsiveness and rationality. Economic policies must satisfy reasonably well group demands on government; if policies fail to meet this end, they will be reversed or applied without vigor. Economic policies must also meet the broad demands of the general public that the economy be kept functioning so as to provide opportunity and a high standard of material well-being. These are the standards for the policy maker. To meet these tests, there must be expert analyses of facts, of prospective trends, and of mechanisms of control, and these analyses must be brought to the attention of the policy maker. The political problem of our day is to make the process of decision as effective, in terms of economic effect and human response, as possible. The factors that lead to economic control by government challenge us to improve continuously the governmental process.

The objectives in public decision making may be illustrated from a few areas of public policy. One, not peculiarly economic, is traffic regulation. The experts have learned how, with stop signs, red and green lights, one-way streets, and other devices, to expedite the travel of city dwellers toward various destinations. They have learned how, through a combination of high-speed, controlled-access freeways and parallel low-speed, outside lanes, to expedite both through and local traffic. They have met the objectives of the idealist: the individual has opportunity to attain his objectives in a social order. It is achieved by the two methods suggested by the idealist: by the discipline of each person to accept the restrictions for the common good without feeling frustrated, and by the establishment of conditions (a framework of regulations) under which each is able to reach his goal with reasonable safety and speed. These conditions have been developed under democratic assumptions of equality—that is, that there should be no effort to gear the system toward favoritism for rich or poor, north or south travelers, or any other group. Yet it is achieved by something the idealists did not stress—effort of the experts. The system works well when it shows responsiveness to the needs of all and when it is expertly designed. The other example is labor-management relations. Here, realists can see that the difficulties of establishing a regulatory system are much greater. Nevertheless, the means to solution are similar. If any system is to be successful, there must be self-discipline. It will not work if it calls for collective bargaining and then labor leaders refuse to bargain, or if industrial leaders carry the sentiment of one who said, "All hell will freeze over before I go to the bargaining table." Also, the system will be successful only if workable means are found for protecting and balancing the various interests involved—management, labor, public. The expert's job is tougher, and the decision maker finds that the welfare of each is not identifiable with the welfare of all. Yet the tests of the efficiency of the process are the same as in traffic regulation: it must be responsive to the interests, must also be workable, and therefore expertly designed.

On the side of private action, one must hope that initiative and creativeness may be preserved in the actions of men. This side of the picture is complex too—much more complex than Adam Smith assumed. The test of efficiency in the economy must be made by more diverse measuring rods than he anticipated. There is still need for the initiative of the individual entrepreneur (operating under the corporate form or otherwise) to open new lines of enterprise and to expand or improve service in many old lines. There is need also for the initiative of the large corporation in research on new techniques and products, in improvement of management, in expansion of production, and in search for new markets. There is need for keeping alive all the motivations that move men to useful effort—not just the drive of self-interest, but the urge to expand (is this a characteristic of Americans?), to discover, to excel, to do something constructive. It would seem that the real significance of the term "free enterprise" lies in the maintenance of an economy in which opportunities for new developments and the multiple stimuli for human effort are fostered.

This quality of initiative is needed, also, on the public side. There are opportunities for public enterprises (public works, education, etc.), public-welfare activity, and discovery of techniques of regulation that can be met, or met most effectively, only by public effort. Historically, in spite of the negative emphasis on the function of government in economic theory, politics has been what politics may be expected to be: an effort to make a positive response to felt human needs that can be satisfied by government service and control. In this case, what may be expected appears also desirable. Initiative, vision of opportunities, positive action in both the private and public sectors of the economy may be essential for satisfaction of the wants of the people, which is the objective of an economic system.

The ultimate beneficence of the economy of the future is thus dependent upon the successful operation of the mixed system of public and private enterprise. It may be hoped that the relative weight and methods of each form of enterprise will not be determined entirely by what is inevitable under the new conditions, but in part by sound judgment of men on the utility of feasible approaches to satisfying human wants. It will necessarily be man's hope that the empirical approach in methodology, the democratic methods of establishing responsiveness and combining this with expertness, and the notion that government action must meet a higher-law standard of fairness and reasonableness will lead to generally satisfactory results in the public sector, and that the freedom to exercise initiative—freedom from restraints both within and from without the private sector—will be large enough to insure a vigorous private sector in the economy.

The mixed economy is the only alternative today to a totalitarian economy. Whether the one or the other creates more difficult problems may be a question difficult or impossible to answer. But for the American the preference, on the basis both of value judgments and of past performance in terms of the opportunity and high-consumption ideals, will be in favor of the mixed economy, and he will therefore accept the challenge to prove its workability.

SUMMARY

The preceding chapter analyzed some of the main theoretical frameworks of thought about the relationship of government to the economy. This chapter has sought to draw from ideas and trends in this country additional elements of thought which might help the student acquire a theoretical preview of government's position before moving into the analyses of control and service in the succeeding chapters.

American policy has been motivated by a combination of liberal and conservative ideas. The basic liberal ideas, accumulated from many historical sources, have, in concert with current dissatisfactions, moved Americans toward many steps in public policy designed to improve the conditions of their material existence. There have, indeed, been powerful liberal thrusts toward new developments in policy. But these changes have not been made without regard for the values which conservatives have emphasized. The most clearly observable trends in indigenous development of ideas have been the ideals of opportunity and material well-being, and the empirical approach toward the public interest without overlooking the rights of minorities. The society has not been thoroughly organic, with complete reconciliation of public and private interests, either as assumed by Smith or set up as ideal by men such as Hobhouse; but the adjustments in society have been made in such a way as to lead to a general acceptance of main trends in policy after a time. The hope for a beneficent economy is not sought either in complete *laissez faire,* which was the eighteenth-century ideal, or in complete economic planning, which has been offered as a twentieth-century solution, but in a mixed economy. In the mixed economy, approaches in policy will be varied, but will reveal a combination of public endeavor and private enterprise, of social control and self-operative forces, of freedom and regulation. The ultimate beneficence of such an economy will depend, in the main and over the long pull, both upon the maintenance of initiative in individuals, corporations, and government in an expanding economy and upon the quality of the decision-making process in government.

Part II. The Constitution and the Economy

Chapter 6. The Constitution and the National Economy

THERE HAS BEEN a sharp contrast between Western Europe and the United States in the political conditions affecting economic development. In the former, the beneficial use of resources and the expansion of markets have been severely limited by the European state system. As late as the eighteenth century, a multitude of sovereignties or quasi-sovereignties chopped Western Europe in little pieces; and even today, after the consolidations of the nineteenth and late eighteenth centuries, the largest states of Western Europe are smaller than some of the constituent states of the U.S. The separate states have restricted commerce in favor of their own citizens, and wars and threats of war have interrupted the development of commerce and industry for peaceful ends and imposed heavy burdens upon the economies. Leaders of successive generations have taken steps to diminish the deleterious effects of the organization of states upon the economies. The French Revolutionists, in a cry for unity, broke the restrictions of provincial governments on trade. The Germans formed the *Zollverein* (Customs Union), which set up a larger area of free trade, and Bismarck consolidated the system (without Austria) through political unity. Italy was united politically and therefore commercially. In 1952 the European Coal and Steel Community created a single market for the coal and steel production of Belgium, France, West Germany, Italy, Luxembourg, and the Netherlands; and the subsequent establishment of a common market for these countries reflects the conviction that the old state system is obsolete.

In this country it has been different. The vast resources of a tremendous area have been open to citizens of all our states, and trade has moved freely across state lines. Coal moves across state lines to iron ore, steel across state lines to manufacturers of finished products, and finished products across state lines to consumers in every state. In this country Detroit could be the hub of the nation for automobiles, mail-order houses could distribute goods across the nation, specialization could develop in agriculture—and all of this without significant interference by local sovereignties. Ours is a national economy in spite of the size of the nation and the federal system of government. The development of this large-scale national economy has created large opportunities for producers and distributors and great benefits for consumers.

These facts are matters of common knowledge. It is not generally recognized, however, that the national economy could not have developed without a foundation in political organization. The framers of the Constitution, accepting certain arrangements in the Articles of Confederation and adding others, laid the basis for the development of a national economy. From their deliberations and the subsequent course of history there emerged a "grand pattern." The grand pattern is largely the creation of the Constitution and subsequent court decisions. The pattern constitutes the highest contribution of politics to economics in the history of this nation.

What are the elements in the grand pattern? What are the separate contributions of political deliberation and action which fit so neatly into a larger design? What, in contrast also, are the factors allowing the exercise of local sovereignty?

INTERSTATE CITIZENSHIP

"The citizens of each state shall be entitled to all privileges and immunities of citizens in the several states" (Article IV, Section 2). This provision, a contraction of longer wording with similar import in the Articles of Confederation (Article IV), means in its economic implications that John Jones can live in State X and can acquire property and do business in State Y *on the same conditions as citizens of that state.* In *Corfield v. Coryell* it was said that the privileges and immunities included, among others:

the right to acquire and possess property of every kind. . . . The right of a citizen of one State to pass through, or to reside in any other State, for purposes of trade, agriculture, professional pursuits, or otherwise . . . ; to institute and maintain actions of any kind in the courts of the State; to take, hold and dispose of property, either real or personal; and an exemption from higher taxes or impositions than are paid by the other citizens of the State. . . .[1]

The guarantee against discrimination, according to Justice Miller in the Slaughterhouse Cases, is a declaration "to the several States, that whatever these rights, as you grant or establish them to your own citizens, or as you limit or qualify, or impose restrictions on their exercise, the same, neither more nor less, shall be the measure of the rights of citizens of other States within your jurisdiction."[2] Thus the clause gives individuals *a right of access to resources* and *a right of trade* without limitation of state boundaries.

There are some significant limits on the scope of this so-called comity clause. First, it does not limit the taxing and regulatory powers of the state when these are applied without discrimination between its citizens and those of other states. It does not, therefore, protect persons from having to

---

[1] 6 Fed. Cas. No. 3,230, 546, 552 (1823).
[2] 16 Wall. 36, 77 (1873).

do business under different laws in different states. Second, it does not prevent the states from passing regulations applying particularly to citizens of other states, provided these are reasonably related to public needs. Thus, for example, the state can require an outside person doing business in the state or travelling on its highways to consent to service of legal process on an agent,[3] or a period of residence before one can sell insurance,[4] or subjection to reasonable quarantine regulations at the state border. Third, it does not prohibit the states from imposing residence requirements for political rights, including the suffrage and the right to hold office within the state. Fourth, it does not give rights of access to resources in which the state holds a kind of proprietary interest for its citizens, such as fish,[5] wild game, and running water. Fifth, the comity clause does not apply to corporations, since it is a guarantee to "citizens."

The rule that a corporation was not a citizen within the meaning of the "privileges and immunities" clause evolved early in the nineteenth century.[6] As a result, a state could prevent a corporation chartered in another state (called a "foreign corporation") from doing business within the state. This was restated in oft-quoted language in *Paul v. Virginia* in 1869: [7]

> The corporation being the mere creation of local law, can have no legal existence beyond the limits of the sovereignty where created. . . . They [the states] may exclude the foreign corporation entirely; they may restrict its business to particular localities, or they may exact such security for the performance of its contracts with their citizens as in their judgment will best promote the public interest. The whole matter rests in their jurisdiction.

States, therefore, could require that foreign corporations obtain a license and meet special conditions. Or they could expel a foreign corporation for violation of state laws, as was done, for example, in *Waters-Pierce Oil Corporation v. Texas* for violation of the state's antitrust laws.[8]

There are, however, many constitutional restrictions on state power over foreign corporations. First, a foreign corporation cannot be denied the right to sue in federal courts.[9] Second, the Fourteenth Amendment limits the state's taxing and regulatory powers over foreign corporations admitted to the state. Thus, for example, a state cannot, under the guise of taxing the privilege of engaging in business within the state, levy a tax on property outside the state. Nor can it arbitrarily throw a corporation out of the state after it has acquired a position within the state. Third, the doctrines

---

[3] *Doherty and Co. v. Goodman,* 294 U.S. 623 (1935); *Hess v. Pawloski,* 274 U.S. 352 (1927).
[4] *La Tourette v. McMaster,* 248 U.S. 465 (1919).
[5] Except, says the Supreme Court, free-swimming fish in the marginal seas. *Toomer v. Witsell,* 334 U.S. 385 (1948).
[6] See Marshall's opinion in *Bank of U.S. v. Deveaux,* 5 Cr. 61 (1809) and Taney's in *Bank of Augusta v. Earle,* 13 Pet. 519 (1939).
[7] 8 Wall. 168, 181.
[8] 177 U.S. 28 (1900).
[9] After vacillation, the Supreme Court made the point clear in *Terral v. Burke Construction Co.,* 257 U.S. 529 (1922).

of *Paul v. Virginia,* and other cases following a similar line, do not apply to that portion of a foreign corporation's business which is interstate commerce. A state cannot require a license for conducting interstate business, or levy a privilege tax thereon. Concerning a foreign corporation engaged in both intrastate and interstate commerce, it is difficult to state precisely the position of the Supreme Court. Thus, in one case involving a license on an interstate bus line, the Court said: "In order that the fee or tax shall be valid, it must appear that it is imposed solely on account of the intrastate business done, that the amount exacted is not increased because of the interstate business done; that one engaged exclusively in interstate commerce would not be subject to the imposition; and that the person taxed could discontinue the intrastate business without withdrawing also from the interstate business." [10] On the other hand, in a telephone case the Court said: "No decision of this Court lends support to the proposition that an occupation tax upon local business, otherwise valid, must be held void merely because the local and interstate branches are for some reason inseparable." [11]

The Supreme Court, by protecting interstate commerce, and corporations under the Fourteenth Amendment, has to a considerable extent removed the disabilities of corporations under the doctrine of *Paul v. Virginia* and earlier cases. Moreover, states have created corporations in great number, and other states have generally admitted these corporations without significant encumbrance. An easy admission policy for foreign corporations has paralleled an easy incorporation policy for domestic corporations. Thus, the practice of the states has had the effect of extending the rights of access to resources and trade to foreign corporations; further encouragement is thereby given to the development of a national economy.[12]

FULL FAITH AND CREDIT

"Full faith and credit shall be given in each State to the public acts, records, and judicial proceedings of every other State" (Article IV, Section 1). This provision also was substantially copied from the Articles of Confederation (Article IV). It states, moreover, a principle of comity among states embodied in private international law, which would therefore, in the

---

[10] *Sprout v. South Bend,* 277 U.S. 163, 171 (1928).

[11] *Pacific Telephone and Telegraph Co. v. Tax Commission,* 297 U.S. 403, 415 (1936). For further discussion see *The Constitution of the United States: Analysis and Interpretation,* Edward S. Corwin (ed.). Sen. Doc. No. 170, 82nd Cong., 2nd Sess. (Washington, D.C: Government Printing Office, 1953), pp. 196–198.

[12] For an able summary, somewhat dated, see Gerald Carl Henderson, *The Position of Foreign Corporations in American Constitutional Law: A Contribution to the History and Theory of Juristic Persons in Anglo-American Law* (Cambridge, Mass.: Harvard University Press, and New York: Oxford University Press, 1918).

absence of constitutional statement, have had such effect among the American states as international practice required.

The Constitution added to the provision in the Articles of Confederation the following: "And the Congress may by general laws prescribe the manner in which such acts, records and proceedings shall be proved, and the effect thereof." Congress has, beginning in 1790, enacted legislation to implement the principle of full faith and credit.

The principle has considerable significance for business enterprise. For example, when a person obtains a judgment on a debt in State X, he can secure execution in any state in which the defendant has property. The records of contracts, mortgages, deeds, charters, and other legal instruments must, when properly authenticated, be given the same force and effect as in the state where these originated. Congress has, moreover, established rules concerning the authentication of documents.

There are, nevertheless, technical limitations on the applicability of full faith and credit. In order to carry out in one state the judgment of another state, it is necessary to institute a new suit in the former. In such a suit the jurisdiction of the court awarding the judgment may be questioned. Also, congressional legislation has not determined the effect to be given to constitutions and statutes of other states; and where conflict in statutory policy exists among the states, the courts may be called upon to measure the interests of each jurisdiction before deciding on the scope of the "full faith and credit" provision. These limitations on the application of the clause could presumably be removed by congressional legislation, and it has even been suggested that Congress could, by legislation concerning the effect to be given to acts, records, and proceedings of states, "enact standards whereby uniformity of state legislation may be secured." [13]

MONEY

A uniform medium of exchange and standard for settlement of accounts is a first essential of commerce. The grand pattern of the Constitution, supplemented by judicial decision and congressional enactments, has provided a uniform currency system for the nation as a whole.

The Constitution contains positive and negative provisions related to this end. On the one hand, it vested in Congress the power "to coin money, regulate the value thereof"; and on the other hand, it said, "No state shall . . . coin money, emit bills of credit, make anything but gold and silver coin a tender in payment of debts. . . ." [14] As used in this provision, the

---

[13] *The Constitution of the United States of America: Analysis and Interpretation*, Edward S. Corwin (ed.). Sen. Doc. No. 170, 82nd Cong., 2nd Sess., 1953, p. 684.

[14] Article 1, Sections 8 and 10. The Articles of Confederation had provided that the Congress should "have the sole and exclusive right and power of regulating the alloy and value of coin struck by their own authority, or by that of the respective states."

term "bills of credit" means a paper medium of exchange to be used in transactions between individuals, or between individuals and the government.

A breach a yard wide and more was rent in the pattern of the framers by the decision of the Supreme Court in *Briscoe v. Bank of Kentucky* in 1837.[15] In this case it was held that the prohibition against bills of credit (paper money) did not extend to state banks, even though a state was the sole owner of the bank's stock and though it appointed the bank's officers. This decision, allowing a state to create an agent to do what it could not do itself, encouraged the issuance of state bank notes. In the absence of a national banking system or national currency in the pre–Civil War period, state banks issued most of the currency needed for trade.

The evils resulting from state bank issuances were overcome by a law of Congress, enacted in 1866, which levied a 10 per cent tax on circulating notes issued by state banks. This statute drove state bank notes out of existence. It was upheld by the Supreme Court in *Veazie Bank v. Fenno* in 1869.[16]

While the states are excluded from the creation and regulation of currency, the grants to Congress have been sufficient (with liberal judicial construction) to enable it to develop a currency system which would meet the needs of an expanding economy. The coinage provision and the fiscal powers (to tax, to borrow money) of Congress have been expansively interpreted through the use of the "necessary and proper" clause.[17] *McCulloch v. Maryland* provided a constitutional foundation for a national banking system,[18] as did the Legal Tender Cases for paper notes that could be made legal tender.[19] Thus, this nation not only was provided with a uniform standard of value, but also had a firm constitutional base for a flexible and adequate currency.

CONTRACTS

"No state shall . . . pass any . . . law impairing the obligation of contracts" (Article 1, Section 10). The right of access to resources and the right of trade would have had little meaning if buyer and seller, borrower and lender, could not assume the validity of contracts. The states had passed debtor relief laws in the Revolutionary period—laws which provided for the issuance of paper money and for making this paper legal tender in payment of debts, which postponed date of payment of obligations, or which

---

[15] 11 Peters 257.
[16] 8 Wall. 533.
[17] And even of a doctrine of inherent powers in The Legal Tender Cases, 12 Wall. 457 (1871).
[18] 4 Wheaton 316 (1819).
[19] The Legal Tender Cases, 12 Wall. 457 (1871); *Juilliard v. Greenman*, 110 U.S. 421 (1884).

allowed payment in commodities. To meet this situation, the Framers included the provisions prohibiting the states from coining money, issuing bills of credit, or making anything but gold or silver legal tender in payment of debts. The specific effect intended by the Framers for the clause on impairment of contracts is obscure,[20] but Gerry said (in the Convention) that it would emphasize "the importance of public faith," and Madison declared (in Federalist Paper No. 44) that it would "inspire a general prudence and industry, and give a regular course to the business of society."

The clause was early interpreted to apply to public as well as private contracts, and to prevent impairment of public grants to individuals or to corporations in their charters or otherwise.[21] Its significance as a limitation on the states has been qualified by judicial decisions and other developments, which can be discussed best in another chapter.[22] It can be said here, however, that although the clause does not operate as a complete prohibition against legislation affecting contracts retroactively, it does inhibit some legislation of this type. Thus, although laws passed during the last depression staying the date of foreclosure were upheld,[23] other such laws which did not preserve the essential rights of creditors were held invalid.[24] The restrictions of the clause have been held applicable also to the national government as a part of the limitation of the due process clause of the Fifth Amendment.[25] As a restriction on the states, it has tended to merge with the due process clause to prevent unreasonable legislation affecting vested rights. A disposition against legislation having an unreasonable effect on such rights is deeply ingrained in the thinking of the people, and this disposition is probably more important today than the constitutional provisions in maintaining confidence in contracts. On the other hand, wars, their aftermath, and the threat of war have made inflation and the danger of further inflation more significant as threats to creditors' rights than the kind of laws enacted during the Revolutionary period.

COMMERCE

As in the case of money, so in commerce the constitutional pattern is constructed from grant to the national government and restrictions on the

---

[20] For an analysis of the little available information, see Benjamin Fletcher Wright, *The Contract Clause of the Constitution* (Cambridge, Mass.: Harvard University Press, 1938), Chapter I.

[21] *Fletcher v. Peck,* 6 Cranch 87 (1810); *Dartmouth College v. Woodward,* 4 Wheaton 518 (1819).

[22] In the next chapter at pages 123–124.

[23] *Home Building & Loan Association v Blaisdell,* 290 U.S. 398 (1934), and the recent case of *East New York Savings Bank v. Hahn,* 326 U.S. 230 (1945).

[24] *Worthen Co. v. Thomas,* 292 U.S. 426 (1934); *Worthen Co. v. Kavanaugh,* 295 U.S. 56 (1935).

[25] *Perry v. U.S.,* 294 U.S. 330 (1935); *Louisville Joint Stock Bank v. Radford,* 295 U.S. 555 (1935).

states, express or implied. The primary grant to Congress is broad: "to regulate commerce with foreign nations, among the several states, and with the Indian tribes." The restrictions on the states include prohibition of tonnage duties or of "imposts or duties on imports or exports." An exception was made in the latter case for duties "absolutely necessary" for executing inspection laws, but the net produce of such duties would go to the Treasury of the United States, and Congress has a reserved right of revision and control.

It is obvious, however, that the express restrictions on the states did not, as in the case of money, extend as far as the grant to the national government. There is no express prohibition against state duties on interstate commerce,[26] or against state regulatory legislation affecting foreign or interstate commerce, or even prohibiting or restricting such commerce. A question was therefore inevitable: Did the grant to Congress "to regulate" imply that states could not regulate? Put differently, was the power to regulate foreign and interstate commerce an exclusive power of Congress, or a concurrent power of Congress and the states?

By the supremacy clause (Article VI), which made "laws of the United States which shall be made in pursuance" of the Constitution supreme over state laws and constitutions, congressional legislation on foreign and interstate commerce would supersede conflicting state legislation. Chief Justice Marshall, in *Gibbons v. Ogden* in 1824 (9 Wheaton 1), asserted, in a resounding precedent for future decisions, the overriding supremacy of a congressional enactment over a state law which affected foreign or interstate commerce—and this whether the state law was passed as a concurrent regulation of foreign or domestic commerce, or as a domestic regulation of trade and other matters. This early case illustrated the benefits of a central power of regulation over commerce, for New York State had granted a monopoly over steam navigation in its waters, and neighboring states were passing retaliatory measures. By upholding the force of a coasting license granted to a rival of the monopolists by the national government, Marshall, for the Supreme Court, gave notice that state-granted monopolies and other state measures could not interfere with foreign and interstate commerce *when Congress had exercised its jurisdiction as to the specific situation.*

But commerce is so extensive and varied that congressional acts cannot reach all its aspects. Where Congress had not acted, could the states regulate? In the areas of congressional "silence" could states legislate, even to the extent of trying to favor their own citizens?

Undoubtedly, the Framers intended that interstate and foreign commerce should not be burdened by state restrictions. Indeed, it was said by Madison

---

[26] It has recently been argued that the imports-and-exports provision was intended to protect interstate as well as foreign commerce. William W. Crosskey, *Politics and the Constitution in the History of the United States* (Chicago: University of Chicago Press, 1953), 2 vols. But this is not the generally accepted view concerning the purpose of the provision.

The Constitution and the National Economy 113

that the purpose of the grant to Congress was mainly "a negative and preventive provision against injustice among the States." [27] But what about state legislation primarily aimed to meet a real local need (such as protection of local safety or health) but having an incidental effect on commerce? The Supreme Court, in 1851, tried to balance the obvious objective of the Framers for freedom of trade against the apparent need for local legislation. Involved in the case before it (*Cooley v. Board of Wardens of the Port of Philadelphia* [28]) was the issue of constitutionality of a Pennsylvania statute of 1803 that regulated pilots in the port of Philadelphia. The Court held the statute valid on the grounds that the matter was local in its nature and did not require uniform national legislation, and that Congress had not acted. In line with this leading case, the Court has decided subsequent issues of constitutionality of state regulatory legislation in the light of these questions: (1) Is the legislation designed to meet a local need? (2) Does it impede, obstruct, interfere with, or burden interstate or foreign commerce? (3) Has Congress legislated on the subject in such a way as to cover the thing on which the state was legislating? If the answer to the first question is "yes" and to the second and third "no," then the state legislation is upheld.

Did this decision create dangers similar to those arising from the Briscoe case on state banks? Would state legislation burden the flow of commerce, and would Congress be forced to pass acts to nullify the state acts, as in the case of state banks? If so, could Congress meet all the situations created by state legislation?

The answer is that the Supreme Court still sits. It is the perpetual arbiter between the legitimate claims of the states and the freedom of commerce from state interference. Thus, for example, it has, in the absence of congressional requirements, upheld state laws or orders requiring interstate railroads to use electric headlights of stated minimum strength, to eliminate grade crossings, or to use state-licensed engineers.[29] On the other hand, it has held invalid an Arizona Train Limit Law which limited trains to fourteen passenger cars or seventy freight cars.[30] It has recognized the right of states to limit the load of trucks moving in interstate commerce,[31] but has denied the right of a state to require a certificate of public convenience from a concern operating solely in interstate commerce, as a condition of using the highways for regular routes or between fixed termini.[32] Some think that some of the Court's decisions, such as those upholding quarantine and inspection laws of the states, have provided the states with opportunities

---

[27] James Madison, *Letters and Other Writings,* **IV**, pp. 14–15 (Philadelphia: J. B. Lippincott Co., 1865).
[28] 12 Howard 299.
[29] *Atchison, T. & S. F. R. Co. v. Rr. Comm.,* 283 U.S. 380 (1931); *Erie Rr. Co. v. Public Utility Commrs.,* 254 U.S. 394 (1921); *Smith v. Alabama,* 124 U.S. 465 (1888).
[30] *Southern Pacific Co. v. Arizona,* 325 U.S. 761 (1945).
[31] *Sproles v. Binford,* 286 U.S. 374 (1932).
[32] *Buck v. Kuykendall,* 267 U.S. 307 (1925).

to favor their local industries under the guise of avoiding diseased plants or animals from entering the state. But the Court still has power to say when a state goes too far, and Congress also has overriding power of legislation, for congressional statutes on interstate commerce override state laws on the subjects covered.

More difficult, perhaps, has been the problem of state taxation. A leading source says that the Court's judgments on this have "often been fluctuating and tentative, even contradictory," and follows with this summary:

> States, therefore, may not tax property in transit in interstate commerce. A nondiscriminatory tax, however, is permitted if the goods have not yet started in interstate commerce, or have completed the interstate transit even though still in the original package, unless they are foreign imports in the original package; and States may also impose a nondiscriminatory tax where there is a break in an interstate transit, and the goods have not been restored to the current of interstate commerce.[33]

This does not answer the question as to when goods are really at rest and out of current of commerce, nor does it answer many other questions with respect to varied forms of taxation—use, property, income, and others. This whole area is so complicated that it is possible to say here only that the Court recognizes that the states must have revenue, and that it would be unfair for purely intrastate business to carry all the burden of state and local government; but on the other hand, the decisions avoid any tax which would make engaging in interstate commerce a privilege or license of the state, or which would impose a burden on interstate or foreign commerce deemed unjustified by the Court.

In spite of the allowance by court decisions of state regulation incidentally affecting interstate and foreign commerce, and of powers of state taxation as well, the significant conclusion can be reached that this has not impeded the development of interstate and foreign commerce. This nation has benefited from a system under which interstate and foreign commerce was either completely free, or was subjected only to a single uniform regulation by Congress, or was subjected only to such state regulations or taxes as did not impair its essential freedom. "The power over commerce," said Marshall in *Gibbons v. Ogden,* "was one of the primary objects for which the people of America adopted their government." It may be added that the power, with its negative as well as its positive effects, was an important contribution of the Framers to domestic tranquillity and national prosperity.

It should be noted, nevertheless, that the states have the power to regulate production and intrastate commerce insofar as its regulations do not come into conflict with constitutional prohibitions or with regulations constitutionally imposed by the national government. The state's powers extend also to the regulation of the rights of property ownership and to the main body of our commercial law. These several types of regulation differ ma-

---

[33] *The Constitution of the United States of America: Analysis and Interpretation,* Edward S. Corwin (ed.). Senate Document 170, 82nd Cong., 2nd Sess., pp. 179, 180.

terially among the states. Much has been done through the National Conference of Commissioners of Uniform State Laws and actions of the states individually to bring uniformity in many aspects of commercial law and other aspects of state law. Nevertheless, American business must operate under separate and diverse state regulations and tax laws. Some entrepreneurs will prefer to avoid these multiple systems of law by restricting their operations to one or a few states. Those who operate in intrastate as well as interstate business in a number of states will find that there is considerable expense and inconvenience in keeping informed about the diversity of laws applicable to their businesses and in adapting their operations to the requirements of the several states.

MISCELLANEOUS AIDS TO ECONOMIC ENTERPRISE

By virtue of certain grants to the Congress, the nation has had the benefit of complete or substantial uniformity on a number of matters besides money and commercial regulation. Congress was given power to "fix the standard of weights and measures," "to establish post offices and post roads," to pass "uniform laws on the subject of bankruptcies throughout the United States," [34] and "to promote the progress of science and useful arts" by grants of exclusive rights for limited periods (patents and copyrights). Uniformity on these matters is of considerable significance for the economy of the nation.

FOREIGN AFFAIRS

Special note should be made of the fact that the Constitution, in a large number of provisions, united this nation with respect to matters of foreign relations. Not only the power to regulate foreign commerce, but the treaty-making power and the power to establish a force sufficient to protect American foreign trade and entrepreneurial enterprise abroad were granted to the national government. Moreover, the states were prohibited from making treaties, granting letters of marque and reprisal, laying imposts and duties on imports or exports to enhance their revenue or protect local business, and laying tonnage duties without the consent of Congress. There have been some cases in which the domestic regulations of the states, such as those preventing alien ownership of land, have created difficulties in international

---

[34] It was held, however, judicially that the states could pass insolvency measures which would have effect until Congress passed bankruptcy legislation, but the significance of these holdings has been destroyed by congressional bankruptcy legislation, which provides uniform requirements for the nation. There are, however, many state laws which affect the rights of insolvent persons.

relations; but the power of the national government to protect, encourage, and regulate foreign trade and investment has not been materially impaired by local sovereignties.

SUPREME LAW AND SUPREME JUDICIARY

To safeguard the pattern of the Constitution, certain arrangements for the conclusive establishment of uniform law for the nation were necessary. Significant in this regard are the following:

1. The Constitution defined the supreme law: "This Constitution, the laws of the United States which shall be made in pursuance thereof, and all treaties made, or which shall be made, under the authority of the United States, shall be the supreme law of the land."

2. The Constitution defined the judicial power of the United States broadly to include two classes of cases: (1) on the basis of subject matter, "all cases, in law or equity, arising under" the Constitution, laws and treaties of the United States, and all cases of admiralty and maritime jurisdiction; (2) on the basis of parties involved, "all cases affecting ambassadors, other public ministers and consuls"; "controversies to which the United States shall be a party"; "controversies between two or more states; between a state and citizens of another state; between citizens of different states; between citizens of the same state claiming lands under grants of different states, and between a state, or the citizens thereof, and foreign states, citizens or subjects."

3. The Constitution provided for one supreme court and such inferior courts as Congress would establish.

4. Congress set up levels of inferior courts to handle in original jurisdiction the bulk of the cases arising under the grant of judicial power, though it has also provided for the handling of some types of federal cases in state courts.

5. The Constitution made it the duty of all state judges to uphold the three categories defined as supreme law, "any thing in the Constitution or laws of any state to the contrary notwithstanding" (Article VI).

6. But state judges might fail to do this, or might differ among themselves on the interpretation of the national constitution, laws, or treaties. To meet this possibility, statutes provide, in appropriate cases, for removal of cases to federal courts or appeal to the United States Supreme Court from the highest state court.

7. By three methods, therefore, cases might move from other courts to the Supreme Court: (1) by trial initially in federal courts and appeal to the Supreme Court; (2) by removal from a state court to a federal court and appeal to the Supreme Court; (3) or by appeal from the highest court of

the state to the Supreme Court of the United States, as provided in the Judiciary Act of 1789.

By these means, then, it is assured that a Supreme Court can define and apply national law for the nation as a whole, and thus provide a national jurisprudence for the conduct of interstate business.

State law is maintained in those matters to which it is applicable, even when cases are tried in the federal courts. When cases are tried in the federal courts because of the diverse citizenship (different states) of the parties, rather than because there is federal law involved, then the federal courts follow the rules of law applied in the courts of the state.[35] Once again the right of the states to maintain their separate systems of law with respect to matters within their jurisdiction is maintained.

A NATIONAL GOVERNMENT WITH STRENGTH

All of the separate and particular provisions of the Constitution that have effect on the economy would have been meaningless except for the larger aim and total effect of the Constitution. The Framers intended, and the Constitution provided, elements of strength for the government of the nation. Here was a government which could almost immediately insure protection against pirates on the seas and against Indians, French, and Spanish on the western frontier. Here was a government which could, through a bold Supreme Court in its early years, strike down state laws impairing the obligation of contract and creating local monopolies. Here was a government which could, through the ensuing years, obtain respect abroad, establish unity at home, and maintain domestic tranquillity—all of which were essential for the economic advance of the nation.

CONCLUSION

The constitutional system of the United States, by and large, has protected interstate and foreign commerce from interference by local sovereignties; prevented state exclusion of citizens of the several states from resources and trade within the states; protected contracts from impairment by the states; allowed development of uniform facilities for commerce, such as money, standards of weights and measures, patents and copyrights, a postal system, and rules of bankruptcy; provided for maintenance of a supreme law by a supreme judiciary; and set the stage for a government

---

[35] *Erie Railroad v. Tompkins,* 304 U.S. 64 (1938), overruling the long-standing case of *Swift v. Tyson,* 16 Pet. 1 (1842).

of sufficient strength to preserve (except for the Civil War period) domestic tranquillity and freedom from foreign aggression. In doing these things, the Framers and the interpreters of the Constitution have contributed greatly to the American opportunity system. At the same time, the constitutional system has left to the states certain powers over foreign corporations engaged in intrastate business within their borders and powers of local legislation and taxation, even though there may be some effect on interstate and foreign commerce. These powers of local legislation lead to much diversity in state law, which may cause inconvenience and expense to business concerns operating nationally. On the other hand, these local powers have not been sufficient, as restrained by the Supreme Court and overriding laws of Congress, to impede the development of industry and commerce for a national market.

Chapter 7. The Constitution, Social Interests, and Economic Rights

WE HAVE NOTED that the egoistic philosophy of the eighteenth century, which assumed a natural harmony between individual self-interest and social welfare, and the idealist philosophy of the twentieth century, which assumed the possibility that a harmony could be achieved by social legislation, were both too optimistic. Social theory must take account of the reality of conflicts of interests. These conflicts may be presented as section against section, group against group, or as individual against society. This chapter deals with this last type of conflict, as unfolded in our constitutional history and related to the function of government in the economy. It discusses the effort to reconcile in a superior constitutional law the claims of private economic right and those of public interest. The discussion is broad in order to show the philosophical bases, but it is focused on the great issues of power over things economic in nature. It is a historical story and deals in part with some trends that have now been reversed, but it contains much of the history of the relationship of government to industry in this country.

THE CONSTITUTION

The Convention of 1787 was assembled for the purpose of creating governmental power, not of limiting it. The task of the Framers was to establish a government through which the great social interests of the nation could be promoted. But the very protection of these social interests involved the placing of limitations on government. In the limitations imposed, we can see three types of purpose.

First, some limitations were imposed for the purpose of reconciling sectional economic interests or of insuring that the new government would not favor one section against another. In some cases, the limitations were the result of compromise. To protect the interests of sections, there were prohibitions against taxing exports, stopping the importation of slaves before 1808, levying direct taxes without apportionment. To insure equal treatment, there were provisions that "all duties, imposts and excises shall be uniform throughout the United States," and that "no preference shall be given by any regulation of commerce or revenue to the ports of one state over those of another."

Second, some limitations were imposed solely or in part to protect the national government's sphere of power over state action. Thus, states were prohibited from entering any treaty, alliance, or confederation; granting letters of marque and reprisal; coining money, emitting bills of credit, or making anything but gold or silver legal tender in payment of debts; laying imposts or duties, except for executing their inspection laws (and this subject to restrictions); laying tonnage duties; engaging in war; and taking other actions.

Third, limitations were imposed to protect individual rights. Thus, both Congress and the states were prohibited from passing bills of attainder and ex post facto laws; the states were prohibited from impairing the obligation of contracts; the national government was required to try crimes by jury and in the state in which they were committed; and restrictions were placed on definition of, procedure in, and punishment for treason.

It is apparent that some of the limitations in the first two groups have the effect of protecting individual rights. For example, prohibitions on the states regarding money undoubtedly had as part of their purpose the protection of creditor rights. But it is interesting to observe how far the Framers stuck with their business of doing what was necessary to establish a government, and how little attention they gave to limitations in favor of private right. Those favoring the Constitution promised addition of a bill of rights in order to obtain ratification. But what is significant in regard to *economic rights* is how little was added in the first eight amendments. The rights guaranteed in these amendments are chiefly those of person. Only two or three have particular significance as far as economic rights are concerned. The Fifth says: "nor shall private property be taken for public use without just compensation." The Fifth also says that no person shall "be deprived of life, liberty, or property, without due process of law," but at that time this undoubtedly referred only to rights of procedure. The Fourth prohibited unreasonable searches and seizures.

It would seem, then, that the oft-made arguments that the Framers were economic individualists cannot be substantiated from the Constitution. Take, for example, the great power to regulate commerce. Where are the significant limitations to protect individuals from the exercise of the power? Or of the great powers over money, including that to "regulate the value thereof"? The prohibitions in this case are on the states.

On the other hand, it need not be concluded that the Framers were economic paternalists. Rather, the Constitution indicates that they saw many facets to this problem of the relationship of government to individual rights. First, they used prohibitions on government to preserve many rights which English, colonial, and state experience had taught them to value. To a large extent, though not exclusively, these were rights of person. Second, they sought to balance the economic interests of the nation in the compromises concerning power. Third, they framed a Constitution—containing grants of power, not a code of detailed provisions—and left to the future the problems of extent and direction of use of power. Finally, they thought that protections for different interests could be provided in the structure of government. This is clear, for example, in the thought of Madison. He thought that minority interests would be protected by the inability of one interest to dominate in a large nation and by the device of representation.[1] In the Convention also he showed his concern for the protection of minority interests. He predicted that the power under the laws of suffrage would slide into the hands of those who sighed for a more equal distribution of life's blessings, and argued for a Senate whose members would have age and long tenure. A Senate with "permanence and stability" could "secure the permanent interests of the country against innovation."[2] Others in that day besides Madison, notably John Adams, saw in the whole system of separation of powers and checks and balances, and in the arrangement for balancing the power of the people of wealth with that of the people generally, a protection for the rights of minorities against majorities. Less evident to them was the converse problem of protecting majorities from minorities. And less evident to them also was the future course of the development of power in the courts.

FROM THE CONSTITUTION TO THE CIVIL WAR

GENERAL DEVELOPMENTS. In the main, the battle between assertions of private right and claims of social interest was fought in this period over state legislation, for it was in the states primarily that regulatory and other powers were being exercised.[3] Also, the battle was fought, by and large, over the issue of the vested rights of property.[4]

In this period the protections given to property in the structure of the state governments disappeared. Property qualifications for voting and holding office were abolished everywhere. The national government, too, was being democratized. Manhood suffrage for the House of Representatives, popular election of presidential electors, and the convention system for making nominations brought the government closer to the common man; only the Senate remained (until 1913) a bulwark for property.

---

[1] Benjamin Fletcher Wright (ed.), *The Federalist* (Cambridge, Mass.: Harvard University Press, 1961), No. 10.
[2] *Documents Illustrative of the Formation of the Union of the American States* (Washington, D.C.: Superintendent of Documents, 1927), pp. 279–281, 810–811.
[3] See pages 8–10.
[4] See, in regard to the general developments, Edward S. Corwin (ed.), *The Constitution of the United States of America: Analysis and Interpretation* (Sen. Doc. No. 170, 82nd Cong., 2nd Sess., 1953), Ch. III; Corwin, *The Twilight of the Supreme Court: A History of Our Constitutional Theory* (New Haven, Conn.: Yale University Press, 1934), Ch. II; and Charles Grove Haines, *The Revival of Natural Law Concepts* (Cambridge, Mass.: Harvard University Press, 1930), Part II.

In the states, conservatives looked with horror on the new developments. Typifying their attitude was a speech of Chancellor Kent in the New York constitutional convention in 1821, in which he appealed for the retention of property qualifications for voting for the state Senate. He condemned "our apparent disposition to vibrate from a well-balanced government to the extremes of democratic doctrines." He foresaw the day when men of no property might dominate the assembly and was worried over the possible loss of the Senate. "The apprehended danger from the experiment of universal suffrage, applied to the whole legislative department, is no dream of the imagination. It is too mighty an excitement for the moral condition of men to endure." He added: "We stand, therefore, on the brink of fate, on the very edge of a precipice. If we let go our present hold on the Senate, we commit our proudest hopes and our most precious interests to the waves." [5]

But this speech, like Madison's in the Philadelphia convention, overemphasized the importance of a senate and overlooked the potentialities of protection from the judiciary. The "precious interests" of which Kent spoke were to be the special concern of the judiciary.

The power of judicial review had been well established by the time Kent spoke. Benjamin Wright found seven cases in which the power was exercised in state courts before the Convention of 1787.[6] But the bold stroke that established the power was taken by the U.S. Supreme Court in *Marbury v. Madison* in 1803.[7]

In that case and other opinions, Marshall stated what has been the conventional justification of judicial review. In essence, the justification is this: the Constitution emanates from the people; it is the paramount law and places limits on legislatures; it is the function of the judiciary, in cases of conflict between the paramount law and the ordinary law, to give effect to the former. This justification makes popular sovereignty the supreme principle and judicial review an instrument for protecting it.

But the "people's" law in national and state constitutions did not contain as much limitation on state legislatures as the friends of vested property rights desired. Hence, the idea was expressed that there were other limits on state legislatures. Daniel Webster argued: "If at this period, there is not a general restraint on legislatures, in favor of private rights, there is an end to private property. *Though there may be no prohibition in the Constitution, the legislature is restrained* from committing flagrant acts, from acts subverting the great principles of republican liberty, and of the social compact. . . ." [8] Justice Story said, "The fundamental maxims of a free govern-

---

[5] D. R. Fox, *The Decline of Aristocracy in the State of New York* (1919), p. 251, quoted by Edward M. Sait, *American Parties and Elections* (New York: Appleton-Century-Crofts, Inc., 1927), pp. 13–14.

[6] Benjamin Fletcher Wright, *The Growth of American Constitutional Law* (New York: Holt, Rinehart & Winston, Inc., 1942), p. 14.

[7] 1 Cr. 137 (1803).

[8] As attorney in *Wilkinson v. Leland*, 2 Pet. 627, 645 (1829). Italics supplied.

ment seem to require that the rights of personal liberty and private property should be held sacred." [9] And Chief Justice Marshall, holding an act of a state legislature void in *Fletcher v. Peck*, was not sure of the ground for the decision, for he said it was the unanimous decision of the Court that the state "was restrained, *either by general principles,* which are common to our free institutions, or by the particular provisions of the Constitution of the United States. . . ." [10]

It appears, then, that many thought that there were two kinds of higher law which courts could enforce over legislatures—the higher law of the people, and the higher law of nature and reason—and that judicial review had two justifications, one given by Marshall in 1803, the other deriving from the philosophy of natural law. Justice Iredell protested against the latter in 1798 on the ground that "ideas of natural justice are regulated by no fixed standards; . . . and all that the court could properly say, in such an event, would be, that the legislature (possessed of an equal right of opinion) had passed an act which, in the opinion of the judges, was inconsistent with the abstract principles of justice." [11] The doctrine protested by Justice Iredell was described later by Justice Holmes as decision based on "some brooding omnipresence in the sky."

It appears, therefore, that in the pre–Civil War period, judges found it necessary to give specific meaning to general phrases of constitutions, and at the same time groped for the content of a higher moral law which they thought limited government. In both cases, the opportunity for judicial creativeness was exceedingly great.

JUDICIAL CREATIVENESS AND THE IMPAIRMENT OF CONTRACT. One of the opportunities for creativeness was in the interpretation of the clause which prohibited the states from impairing the obligation of contracts. The Marshall Court (1801–1835) gave the clause an expansive interpretation. First, it held in *Fletcher v. Peck* in 1810 that public as well as private contracts were safeguarded by the clause, and that a grant by a state (in this case of land) was a contract within the meaning of the clause.[12] Second, it held in *Dartmouth College v. Woodward* in 1819 that a charter granted by a state was a contract protected by the clause.[13] Though in this case it was a nonbusiness corporation, the decision was applicable also to business corporations. Third, the Court held that the taxing power of the state was alienable; that is, a contract in which the state agreed not to tax was protected by the contract clause.[14]

The Court in which Taney sat as Chief Justice (1836–1864) was also creative. It should be noted first that the Taney Court held a considerable

---

[9] *Ibid.,* 2 Pet. 627, 657 (1829).
[10] 6 Cr. 87, 139 (1810). Italics supplied.
[11] 3 Dall. 386, 399 (1798).
[12] 6 Cr. 87.
[13] 4 Wheat. 518.
[14] *New Jersey v. Wilson,* 7 Cr. 164 (1812).

number of state laws invalid under the contract clause, usually because they adversely affected creditor rights (debtors' relief legislation) or because they violated contractual exemptions from taxation.[15] The creativeness of the Taney Court, however, was shown in limitations on the protection given by the clause. The first limitation was in the doctrine that all grants by the state, in cases of doubt as to meaning and effect, were to be strictly construed in favor of the public—that is, that nothing could be construed to have been given away by implication, but only by express provision. This was in 1837 in the leading and highly significant case of *Charles River Bridge v. Warren Bridge Co.*[16] The Massachusetts legislature had granted to the Charles River Bridge Company the right to operate a toll bridge on the Charles River for a stated number of years, and subsequently (and prior to the expiration period) had provided for construction of a free bridge only a few rods away. This, of course, reduced the commercial value of the right to maintain a toll bridge. But the Supreme Court denied the contention of the Charles River Bridge Company that the obligation of contract had been impaired, since there was no express provision in the contract that the company's grant to maintain a bridge was exclusive. The Court, quoting an English case, said "that any ambiguity in the terms of the contract must operate against the adventurers and in favor of the public," and thus arrived at its rule of strict construction of contractual provisions granting rights or privileges.

A second limitation on the scope of the contract clause came from the decision in *West River Bridge v. Dix* in 1848.[17] The Court held that the power of eminent domain was an inalienable power: no contract could give this power away. It was always, therefore, one held in reserve by government. Thus, for example, whatever rights a state may give to private utility corporations, it can never give away its right to purchase their property through eminent domain proceedings.

In sum, the Taney Court, though applying the contract clause according to its previously established meaning, placed two significant limits on it in favor of the public interest. It also defined the public interest in broad terms, stating that "the object and end of all government is to promote the happiness and prosperity of the community by which it is established."[18]

In addition to these judicial developments, state constitutions very early began to place limits on legislative power to make grants in perpetuity or in ways that would be detrimental to public interests, and the legislatures—whether limited by constitutions or not—developed the practice of inserting in corporate charters a reservation of legislative power to amend or cancel these.

---

[15] See Benjamin Fletcher Wright, *The Contract Clause of the Constitution* (Cambridge, Mass.: Harvard University Press, 1938), Ch. III, for an analysis of the cases.
[16] 11 Pet. 420, 547.
[17] 6 How. 507.
[18] *Charles River Bridge v. Warren Bridge Co.*, 11 Pet. 546.

JUDICIAL CREATIVENESS ON OTHER ISSUES. In the absence of contracts, what limitations existed on state legislatures other than those on money?

In the early case of *Calder v. Bull* (1798) [19] an attempt was made to get the the Supreme Court to interpret the ex post facto clauses [20] as forbidding legislation with retroactive effects on vested rights. Such an interpretation would have given great protection to acquired property rights. The Supreme Court held, however, that the clauses were applicable only to criminal penalties.

It was nevertheless in this decision that Justice Chase stated that legislatures were limited by "the general principles of law and reason." The search for such principles continued—chiefly among the state judges, who enunciated their views of concepts of justice which limited legislatures. Chief among these was Chancellor Kent, who, as a judge in New York State and as author of his *Commentaries,* had a great influence on the law. In 1811 Kent used against a state statute an old maxim that "a new law should apply to future matters and not to things past"; he gave birth to the idea that eminent domain and taxing powers should be used only for public purposes; and he and Justice Shaw of Massachusetts both used the term, "so use your own as not to injure another," as though it were a test of the scope of government power.[21]

This search for "general principles of law and reason," which, after *Calder v. Bull,* departed from the provisions of constitutions, was to be brought back to the language of these documents before the Civil War. New content was to be found in the clauses "law of the land" or "due process of law," which appeared in the state constitutions and in the Fifth Amendment as a limitation on the national government. These clauses, in their dictionary and historical meanings, would seem to refer only to procedure; they would seem to mean that a legislature could not deprive people of rights except by fair procedure, usually at least in the courts. But prior to the 1850's some judges began to impute to the clauses a broader meaning. Then, just before the Civil War, it was given a substantive meaning in two important cases. In the first, *Wynehamer v. State of New York* in 1856, the highest New York court held invalid a state prohibition statute on the basis that it violated due process in its effects relative to liquor already in existence.[22] In the second, the Dred Scott case, Chief Justice Taney made the due process

---

[19] 3 Dall. 386.

[20] Article 1, Section 9, prohibited ex post facto laws by Congress; Article 1, Section 10, by states.

[21] For illuminating summaries of these developments and the larger struggle between vested-right doctrine and public-interest doctrines, see Edward S. Corwin, *The Twilight of the Supreme Court* (New Haven, Conn.: Yale University Press, 1934), Chapter II, and *Liberty Against Government* (Baton Rouge, La.: Louisiana State University Press, 1948), Chapter III.

[22] 13 N.Y. 378 (1856).

126   *The Constitution and the Economy*

clause of the Fifth Amendment one of the bases for holding invalid the Missouri Compromise.²³

Concurrent with the search for constitutional limitations were continued statements of the sovereignty of legislatures. Judicial creativeness was chiefly revealed in the origin of the term "police power." First used by Marshall in *Brown v. Maryland* to refer to the internal regulatory power of the state, as contrasted with power it did not possess over interstate or foreign commerce, it came to be an American phrase to define the power of state legislatures to protect the public interest. Just as Romans could say, *"Salus populi supreme lex esto"* ("the welfare of the people is the highest law"), Americans could have their own term to refer to the power of legislatures to promote the public health, morals, safety, and welfare.

Both trends—the search for constitutional limitations, and the statement of legislative power (either in cases affecting contracts or otherwise)—probably fitted the general trend of ideas in the nation. As Professor Wright has said, the nineteenth century was one in which the average American expected to become a man of property, and hence he could believe in protection for vested property rights; ²⁴ on the other hand, he did not yet believe in *laissez faire,* he had antagonisms toward any special monopolistic rights which might develop, and he therefore looked to his legislature for promotion of the general interest.

AFTER THE CIVIL WAR: CRYSTALLIZATION OF CONSTITUTIONAL DOCTRINE

An eminent constitutional historian has noted the concurrence of two events in 1868.²⁵ The first was the publication of Justice Cooley's *Constitutional Limitations,*²⁶ which summarized the trends in constitutional doctrine to that time. Cooley set forth the rights of the legislatures in a chapter on "The Police Power of the States." He argued also that courts could not hold legislation invalid merely because it violated "fundamental principles of republican government"; legislation was void only when there was violation of the words of constitutions.²⁷ On the other hand, he argued that "The maxims of Magna Charta and the common law are the interpreters of constitutional grants of powers." ²⁸ His chapter on protection of property

---

²³ *Scott v. Sandford,* 19 How. 393 (1857).
²⁴ Benjamin F. Wright, *The Contract Clause of the Constitution* (Cambridge, Mass.: Harvard University Press, 1938), pp. 354–355.
²⁵ Edward S. Corwin, *The Twilight of the Supreme Court* (New Haven, Conn.: Yale University Press, 1934), p. 71.
²⁶ Thomas M. Cooley, *A Treatise on the Constitutional Limitations Which Rest Upon the Legislative Power of the States of the Union,* 6th ed. (Boston: Little, Brown & Company, 1890).
²⁷ Cooley, *ibid.,* Chapter VII.
²⁸ Cooley, *ibid.,* p. 208.

asserted that the phrase "the Law of the Land" and the due process clauses were intended to protect against arbitrary exercises of power and particularly to protect "vested rights." [29] As Professor Corwin has shown, Cooley's summary gave judges a set of doctrines under which they could rule either way as to the constitutionality of legislation.

Cooley's *Treatise* shows that constitutional doctrine had developed to the point where state judges could undertake the role of balancing the rival claims of private and social interests. But how did this function accrue also to the *federal* judiciary? This was the aftermath of the second event of 1868, the adoption of the Fourteenth Amendment. By judicial interpretation of this amendment, the Supreme Court of the United States assumed the role of superior balancer.

The Amendment said that no state shall: (1) "make or enforce any law which shall abridge the privileges or immunities of citizens of the United States"; (2) "deprive any persons of life, liberty, or property, without due process of law"; (3) "deny to any person within its jurisdiction the equal protection of the law."

The first issue arose over the privileges-and-immunities prohibition. Louisiana had granted a monopoly of the slaughtering of animals in and around New Orleans to a corporation, and other butchers alleged that this deprived them of the privileges and immunities of United States citizenship. By 5 to 4 the Supreme Court overruled this contention.[30] The majority saw that a decision against the state grant would work a substantial alteration in the American federal system. Previously the protection of civil rights had rested with the states. If now the civil rights of men were to be called privileges and immunities of U.S. citizenship, then those who disliked state legislation could carry their cases to the U.S. Supreme Court. This, said Justice Miller for the majority, would make the Court "the perpetual censor upon all legislation of the states." This would indeed diminish the sovereignty of the states and broaden the scope of federal judicial review. The majority shrank from the result, and decided that privileges and immunities of U.S. citizenship were limited to those activities related to national functions, such as travel to the seat of government, access to its functions, use of the navigable waters of the United States, or related to a limited number of specific rights guaranteed by the national Constitution.

In this case the majority gave little attention to due process and equal protection clauses. The Court was soon pressed, however, to give a broader meaning to the due process clause, to enable it to pass on the substance of state legislation. It refused at first to do so, in one case giving a kind of lecture to lawyers to quit bringing such claims to the Court. After pointing out that while few cases had been brought to the Supreme Court under the due process clause of the Fifth Amendment, many had been brought under

---

[29] Cooley, *ibid.*, Chapter XI.
[30] Slaughterhouse Cases, 16 Wall. 36.

this clause of the Fourteenth within a few years. The Court said, "There is here abundant evidence that there exists some strange misconception of the scope of this provision as found in the Fourteenth Amendment." [31] Apparently the Court majority wanted acceptance for the doctrine stated in 1876 in *Munn v. Illinois,* when it upheld the right of a legislature to set grain elevator rates without judicial review of their reasonableness: "We know that this is a power which may be abused; but that is no argument against its existence. For protection against abuses by legislatures the people must resort to the polls, not to the courts." [32]

These affirmations of state sovereignty and legislative power were not acceptable to a minority of the Court in *Munn v. Illinois* and in the first and second Slaughterhouse Cases (1873 and 1883). In dissenting opinions in the first Slaughterhouse case, and in concurring opinions in the second, the justices cited all three guarantees in the Fourteenth Amendment as basis for unconstitutionality, but said also that the statute was "against all public law" and that the right to engage in a common calling was an inalienable right included in "the pursuit of happiness" of the Declaration of Independence and was an implied limitation on all free governments.

These statements show the continued groping for doctrines under which legislatures could be limited, and also the confusion of constitutional provisions with extraconstitutional sources. That the majority itself was not entirely free of this confusion was shown in 1875 in *Loan Association v. Topeka.*[33] Here the Court held invalid a state statute authorizing the City of Topeka to grant money to a bridge-manufacturing concern (to induce it to locate there) on the ground that "There are limitations on such [state] power which grow out of the essential nature of all free governments. Implied reservations of individual rights. . . ." This was a strange foundation for judicial review in a nation which had regarded constitutions rather than natural law as the supreme law of the land.

In the period from the middle seventies to the nineties, two things are evident in the positions of the Court. First, it established the supremacy of certain elements of the public interest—namely, public health and morals, to which safety was added with the passage of time. It did this first and most clearly with respect to the contract clause. In *Stone v. Mississippi* the Court unanimously upheld state revocation of previously granted rights to operate lotteries, declaring that neither the legislature nor the people could bargain away the power to protect the public health and morals.[34] And the Court was to find neither in the contract clause nor in the due process clause significant limitation on the prohibition against sale of liquor, even though property values were destroyed. Perhaps Puritanism is a stronger American motivation than the protection of private rights.

[31] *Davidson v. New Orleans,* 96 U.S. 97, 104 (1878).
[32] 94 U.S. 113, 134.
[33] 20 Wallace 655.
[34] 101 U.S. 814 (1880).

The second development was the reversal of the position of the Court in the Slaughterhouse Cases and *Munn v. Illinois*. The change is evident in *Mugler v. Kansas* in 1887, in which the Court, though upholding a state liquor prohibition act, nevertheless limited the paramount police power to health, safety, and morals, and revealed its intention to examine the circumstances to determine whether state legislation has "real or substantial relation to these objects, or is a palpable invasion of rights secured by the fundamental law."[35] The due process clause was the provision of the Constitution which permitted this extension of judicial authority, and was shortly to be used by the Supreme Court in holding invalid state regulation of railroad rates deemed unreasonable.[36]

Constitutional law had now advanced (or regressed) to a point where judges, using the due process clause of the Fourteenth Amendment, could pass upon the reasonableness of legislation. Each case involved the determination of whether legislation was for a proper purpose, and if so, whether the methods used to attain the purpose were reasonable. The judges could thus determine whether legislation was against "common right and reason,"[37] but in doing so were only applying the words of the Constitution— the ambivalent due process of law. To state it differently, just as the common law and "common right and reason" were identified by some early English judges, so natural law and the popular-sovereignty–judicial-instrumentality concept announced by Marshall were made identical by the Supreme Court through the alchemy of due process. Two kinds of higher law—that of the people and that of natural right—were existent and identified. And more than this, one Supreme Court made itself the supreme "censor," and thus prevented the states from circumventing, even by amendment of their constitutions, the higher law of reason as determined by a central judiciary.

THE ECONOMIC SIGNIFICANCE OF DUE PROCESS: FROM THE 1880's TO THE 1930's

All the words of the due process clause were given an expansive interpretation in this fifty-year period. Due process itself referred to substance, content, purpose, as well as to procedure. "Person" was interpreted to include corporation,[38] so that the guarantees of the clause for individuals were in general extended to corporations. Liberty came to include the rights implicit in the economics of Adam Smith[39]: the right to engage in common

---

[35] 123 U.S. 623, 661.

[36] *Chicago, M. & St. P. R. Co. v. Minnesota*, 134 U.S. 418 (1890).

[37] Words used in Bonham's Case in 1616 by an English justice—Sir Edward Coke—who had great influence on American thought.

[38] First decided by the Supreme Court, with respect to the words of the equal protection clause, in *Santa Clara Co. v. S.P.R. Co.*, 118 U.S. 394, 396 (1886).

[39] For a summary of the growth of the definition "liberty," see Charles Warren, "The 'New Liberty' under the Fourteenth Amendment," *Harvard Law Review*, **XXXVIII** (February 1926), pp. 439–465.

callings, liberty of contract between buyer and seller, liberty of contract in labor relations, and the "right to work." Property came to include not only physical possession of physical assets, but incorporeal assets, rights of use of property, and rights of fair return.

None of these rights were absolute; all were qualified by the right to protect the public interest by reasonable means. Thus, the right to engage in common callings was paralleled by the right of society to regulate or prohibit entry into the businesses which the state could make unlawful—for example, liquor, pool halls, prostitution, lotteries, and others; by the right of society to establish qualifications for professions or even for service trades; by the right of society to require certificates for entry into the public-service industries. But the right to run private employment exchanges, though subject to regulation, could not be prohibited,[40] nor could the right to sell ice be limited to those holding a license.[41] Or again, liberty of contract between buyer and seller could be limited by price regulation for grain elevators, railroads, utility companies, insurance companies, stockyards, tobacco warehouses, the interest rate, and for housing in emergencies. But it could not be so limited in the case of the resale prices of theater-ticket brokers,[42] or the charges of employment agencies [43] or gasoline retailers.[44] And liberty of contract in labor relations did not prohibit regulations deemed reasonable by the Court to prevent fraud in payment of wages, to limit hours of labor, or to protect the safety of the worker. On the other hand, it did prevent, in 1905, limitation of the hours of bakery and confectionery workers to ten per day or sixty per week; [45] in 1923, the setting of minimum wages for women; [46] in 1908 and in 1915, protection for the laborer in joining a union; [47] in 1923, a system of compulsory arbitration of labor disputes for the industries of a state.[48]

What the court did in the fifty years between 1887 and 1937 was to enforce a doctrine of *laissez faire* with exceptions. It had written the rule of reason into the Constitution by way of the due process clause of the Fifth and Fourteenth Amendments. This meant that legislatures could do nothing that was unreasonable, and that judges—nay, five judges or a lesser number forming a majority—could determine what was reasonable. This in itself was the greatest curtailment of the sovereignty of the states, which were then the chief repositories of regulatory power, in the history of the country—for the Supreme Court was the censor of state legislatures

---

[40] *Adams v. Tanner*, 244 U.S. 590 (1917).
[41] *New State Ice Co. v. Liebmann*, 285 U.S. 262 (1932).
[42] *Tyson and Brothers v. Banton*, 273 U.S. 418 (1927).
[43] *Ribnik v. McBride*, 277 U.S. 350 (1928).
[44] *Williams v. Standard Oil Co.*, 278 U.S. 235 (1929).
[45] *Lochner v. New York*, 198 U.S. 45.
[46] *Adkins v. Children's Hospital*, 261 U.S. 525.
[47] *Adair v. U.S.*, 208 U.S. 161 (1908); *Coppage v. Kansas*, 236 U.S. 1 (1915).
[48] *Wolff Packing Co. v. Industrial Court*, 262 U.S. 522 (1923), 267 U.S. 552 (1925); *Dorchy v. Kansas*, 264 U.S. 286 (1924).

on economic legislation. The content of the limitations was to be determined by a judicial assumption that the rights implicit in an individualistic economic order, such as liberty of contract and right to use one's property, were those to be protected against unreasonable legislation. The Court did not enforce these rights without limitation, for it lived in a Puritan society and in one where change led to new types of legislation. It took the double answers of Cooley—there were police powers and there were vested rights —and evolved a middle ground (or so it must have seemed to the judges) of *laissez faire* with exceptions. The strands of judicial history running through Kent and other creators of constitutional limitations were united with the economics of John Stuart Mill. And the result was that for fifty years, government through the judiciary "tilted the scale" in favor of the entrepreneur who sought freedom to build without social interference.

Many of the decisions of the Supreme Court holding state regulatory legislation invalid were made in a closely divided court, and many were widely criticized. There were, in addition, many lines of general criticism, either of the role assumed by the Court or of the way it acted in that role. First, though the Court often restated its official doctrine that it passed only upon the existence or nonexistence of power, it was obvious that issues of reasonableness really involved questions of wisdom. To many, such questions seemed to belong to the legislatures rather than to the courts. Second, an even broader attack on the Court's role was made by Justice Holmes in *Lochner v. New York* in 1905. He argued that "a constitution is not intended to embody a particular economic theory, whether of paternalism and the organic relation of the citizen to the state, or of *laissez faire*." [49] To him, a Constitution was a frame of government under which men of different opinions could live and battle for the supremacy of their notions concerning proper public policy.

Other criticisms were less basic. A third related to the restriction of the scope of the police power in decisions of the Court. Although some legislation was upheld which related to economic well-being or to other elements of the general welfare besides health, morals, and safety, there was a strong tendency on the Court both to disregard the relation of legislation to these latter purposes and to deny validity to legislation which apparently served other purposes. Thus, in *Lochner v. New York*, in holding invalid a state statute limiting the hours of bakery and confectionery workers, the majority of the Court thought it sufficient to point out that the statute was not a health law but purely a regulation of labor; [50] and in holding minimum-wage legislation invalid in 1923, the majority again thought it was enough to point out that the law was not related to health and morals. [51] The Court majority regarded labor legislation not related to health, morals, and safety as "arbitrary interference with the liberty

[49] *Lochner v. New York*, 198 U.S. 45, 75 (1905).
[50] 198 U.S. 45.
[51] *Adkins v. Children's Hospital*, 261 U.S. 525.

of contract which no government can legally justify in a free land." [52] Though Justice Holmes, in 1910, said that "the police power extends to all the great public needs," [53] the Court had not arrived at the position where economic well-being was accepted as equivalent to public health, morals, and safety as a justification for legislation; and Justice Brandeis thought it desirable, in dissenting in a case in 1932, to re-emphasize the inclusion of "the general welfare" in the definition of the police power.[54] Fourth, many thought that the discretion of the Court in its new role was too broad. As Justice Iredell had said in 1798, "ideas of natural justice are regulated by no fixed standard." Justice Holmes thought a decision in a particular case depended "on a judgment or intuition more subtle than any articulate major premise." [55] And in 1934 Professor Corwin pointed out that the Court had a double set of answers—that is, could go either way on issues under the Fourteenth Amendment and "cite an ample array of precedents in justification of either approach." [56] Fifth, critics found the Court in a strained position on many matters. Thus, it had never placed any restrictions on the power of the state to enter businesses. It could apparently enter businesses in which price regulation was illegal, either assuming a monopoly or a competitive position. Many thought the Court's doctrines on valuation prevented effective regulation in the areas in which it allowed regulation. Or, for another example, some thought the Court was oversolicitous about some, and overlooked other, liberties. Thus, in 1915, the majority thought that state legislation outlawing the yellow-dog contract deprived employers of liberty, but some would have agreed with the minority position of Justices Day and Hughes that such legislation was designed to protect the worker's right to join associations.[57]

FROM THE THIRTIES TO THE PRESENT: REVISION OF THE COURT'S POSITION

Whatever the merits of the Supreme Court's restraining role vis-a-vis economic regulation in the half-century before the late thirties, it has now substantially withdrawn from its role of restricting the regulatory power of government. Judgment on the wisdom of legislation is again the function of representative assemblies, with only occasional restraints from the judiciary. The power to regulate has now been established.

In the main, this result was attained by a line of decisions reversing

---

[52] *Adair v. U.S.,* 208 U.S. 161, 175 (1908).
[53] *Noble State Bank v. Haskell,* 219 U.S. 104, 111 (1911).
[54] *New State Ice Co. v. Liebmann,* 285 U.S. 262, 304 (1932).
[55] *Lochner v. New York,* 198 U.S. 45, 76 (1905).
[56] Edward S. Corwin, *The Twilight of the Supreme Court* (New Haven, Conn.: Yale University Press, 1934), p. 86.
[57] *Coppage v. Kansas,* 236 U.S. 1 (1915).

the positions of the past. The new decisions came in response to national and state legislation, whereas most of the earlier decisions were rendered on state legislation. In 1930 the Court reflected a changed view on legislation to protect laborers in choice of their representatives for collective bargaining. In upholding the Railway Labor Act, the minority view of Day and Hughes in 1915 (that such legislation was designed to protect a right of labor) was written by Chief Justice Hughes into the opinion of the Court.[58] The acceptance by the Court in 1937 of the National Labor Relations Act completed this reversal of position.[59] In 1934 the Court did away with the doctrine that prices could be regulated only in industries "affected with a public interest." [60] In 1937 it reversed the decision of 1923, in which it had held minimum-wage legislation invalid.[61] In 1944 it declared that "fair return upon fair value," which had been the Court's criterion in utility rate cases since 1898,[62] was no longer the test of the reasonableness of rates.[63]

These reversals were accompanied by new positions on new types of legislation. Thus, in 1937 the Court upheld social-security legislation, saying in one case, "It is too late today for the argument to be heard with tolerance that in a crisis so extreme the use of the moneys of the nation to relieve the unemployed and their dependents is a use for any purpose narrower than the promotion of the general welfare." [64] It also upheld the depression moratorium laws—that is, laws that allowed postponement of payment of debts (though with preservation of the rights of creditors to interest and to final payment of principal);[65] and similarly it upheld the national prohibition against payment of debts in gold, even for contracts providing for such payments.[66]

The Court has now yielded to the legislative branch of government the choice of economic interests to be protected. This is pointedly revealed in certain labor cases. In upholding the power of the state to prohibit the closed shop, the Court said, "Just as we have held that the due process clause erects no obstacle to block legislative protection of union members, we now hold that legislative protection can be afforded non-union members." [67] In regard to picketing of employers by laborers or labor organizations, the Court began in 1940 by holding that prohibition of all peaceful

---

[58] *Texas & N.O.R. Co. v. Brotherhood of Railway & S.S. Clerks,* 281 U.S. 548.
[59] *National Labor Relations Board v. Jones & Laughlin Steel Corporation,* 301 U.S. 1 (1937).
[60] *Nebbia v. New York,* 291 U.S. 502.
[61] *West Coast Hotel Co. v. Parrish,* 300 U.S. 379.
[62] *Smyth v. Ames,* 169 U.S. 466.
[63] *F.P.C. et al. v. Hope Natural Gas Co.,* 320 U.S. 591. For further discussion, see pages 444–445.
[64] *Steward Machine Co. v. Davis,* 301 U.S. 548, 586–7; *Helvering v. Davis,* 301 U.S. 619.
[65] *Home Building & Loan Association v. Blaisdell,* 290 U.S. 398 (1934).
[66] *Norman v. Baltimore and Ohio R. Co.,* 294 U.S. 240 (1935).
[67] *Lincoln Federal Labor Union v. Northwestern Iron and Metal Co.,* 335 U.S. 525, 537 (1949).

picketing was a deprivation of the freedom of speech guaranteed by the Fourteenth Amendment,[68] but had come, by 1957, to recognize substantially complete regulatory power for the state.[69] Although the first decision erected a new constitutional guarantee for a party in interest, the later line of decisions on picketing has allowed the state legislature to make its own judgments with respect to the interests to be protected.

While the Court has withdrawn from its position of censor of legislation directly affecting economic interests, it has established new restraints on legislatures for the protection of civil rights. Such restraints often have economic aspects, or even substantial economic impact. Thus, civil-rights issues raised by anticommunist legislation has forced the Court to pass upon the constitutionality of laws affecting rights of employment of those who have been affiliated with Communist or Communist-front organizations, or who did not swear that they did not believe in overthrow of government by force or other illegal means.[70] More significant for the economy is the reinterpretation of the equal protection clause of the Fourteenth Amendment to give greater protection to minority groups. The reinterpretation has had a large effect on the movement in legislation and private industry toward removal of discriminations on the basis of race in employment and in choice of customers for service.

The new lines of decision show that the Court still sits and still finds room within general constitutional provisions for creative interpretations and for applying its view of "natural right and reason." They show also that there can be change in the economic and social interests protected by the Court. If, in one generation, judicial review can be an instrument for protection of vested rights in property, in another it can be an instrument for protection of minority racial groups. Although the decisions relate to civil rights, they have an impact upon the economy.

CONCLUSION

We have, as the more farsighted of our forefathers predicted, moved to universal suffrage; and the possessors of this suffrage, as Madison, Kent, Webster, and others foresaw, have used the power thus given as a means of counting tallies in their behalf. There has, moreover, been a great growth in the interests of man which could be protected or advanced by legislation. Ability to foresee this latter development would have compounded the fears of the Kents and the Websters.

On the other hand, as has been shown in Chapter 3, this is a pluralistic society, with a complex assortment of interests. Much more so than in the day when Madison wrote about the various ways men were split into fac-

---

[68] *Thornhill v. Alabama*, 310 U.S. 88 (1940).
[69] *International Brotherhood of Teamsters v. Vogt*, 354 U.S. 284 (1957).
[70] *American Communication Ass'n. v. Douds*, 339 U.S. 382 (1950).

tions, there are many kinds of interests. It is not alone the unequal division of property, but also the various kinds of economic interest—agricultural, industrial, labor—and the multiple splintering within these, which divide men into groups. In the face of this complexity, the older notions about protection of minority rights appear inadequate. An aristocratic upper house, and judicial review to protect vested property rights—the means favored by conservatives a hundred years ago—are inadequate as a social solution in the same way the Communist doctrine is false as a social diagnosis, for both assume a simple division of interests on a class basis.

Nevertheless, the belief of Madison and others that protection should be provided for the various interests in society is sound. In our day, this protection arises first out of the constitution of society itself. The different interests are organized, as has been shown in Chapter 3, for influence on Congress, the executive branch, and the public. The substantial interests find that organization and money provide means of asserting and defending their claims. Second, the protection arises out of the complexity of the process of policy formation and execution. The taking of a new step through legislation may involve participation of the President and his advisers, the two houses, their committees and their staffs, administrative agencies, and special study commissions. The carrying out of this legislation through steps in the administrative process will normally also involve the contribution of many experts within the agency of administration, opportunities for interests to present their views, and suggestions from the Congress. There is no assumption that issues can be determined on rationalistic, universal principles of jurisprudence and morality; rather, the process is partly a pragmatic one of finding what is workable and partly a free contest of groups to fulfill their objectives. Thus, the old ideal of protecting the separate interests of men and groups through the structure of government is carried into effect in a new way.

The other idea that certain rights are so important that they should have special protection through constitutional provision and judicial review remains. Some of these are protected by specific guarantees, but even here the Court interprets them (for example, the contract clause) according to its standard of reasonableness. Others, such as the modern guarantees under due process and equal protection, are vague and amount almost to a grant to the Court of a roving commission to determine the "received ideals" of the nation according to its own lights on what is "common right and reason." The Court is, therefore, another line of protection for the interests of men; but for which type of interests is a matter of uncertainty and change. In the long run it may follow, as Dooley said, the election returns or, as we would put it, the ideals of the nation; in the short run, it has its own ways of being creative.

Chapter 8. Powers of the National and State Governments

THE FACTORS which erased state lines and contributed to the development of a national economy have been noted: (1) the grand pattern of the Constitution and its interpreters; (2) the expansion of transportation and communication facilities; (3) the growth of giant corporate enterprise reaching for markets across the entire nation; (4) the reluctance of the states to use the powers they possessed to prevent out-of-state corporations from entering the several states for local business. The pervasive influences of war and threat of war, national defense, foreign trade, and foreign aid on the economy of the nation have also been noted.

It could be expected that the development of a national economy, and of international economic and political relations, would bring a concentration of the most meaningful powers of control and influence over the economy in the national government. This has indeed occurred. The states today possess important powers of regulation and service, but these are related, on the whole, to local matters. The expectations of the public for significant influence on the kind of results we get from the economy are concentrated on Washington.

What powers of control and influence exist in the national government? Conversely, what kinds of powers relating to the economy remain in the states?

A discussion of the specific powers of the national government should be preceded by reference to four facts about national powers. First, the national government, except for the area of foreign relations, has only delegated powers. The powers that are neither delegated to it nor prohibited to the states are, says the Tenth Amendment, reserved to the states or to the people. Second, the delegated powers are in part enumerated. The listing or enumeration in the Constitution includes reference to most of the basic functions of government affecting the economy: taxation and expenditures, money, commerce, war and defense, treaties. Third, the government has, in addition to the enumerated powers, implied powers. These are, as Marshall defined them for the Supreme Court in *McCulloch v. Maryland* in 1819, powers arising from the right to *choose any appropriate means* for carrying out enumerated powers. Thus, on the question as to whether Congress could establish a bank to aid the government in such functions as taxing and borrowing, Marshall's view was that it was no answer that

Congress could find other ways to borrow money or other places to put its tax revenues; it was sufficient that a bank was an appropriate means which Congress desired to use. Marshall found support for this view in the clause in the Constitution which gave Congress the power to pass laws that were "necessary and proper" to carry out enumerated powers; but in construing these words, he concluded that it could be implied that the Framers intended that Congress have a choice of means. The significance of the interpretation is that it has given elasticity and expansiveness to the enumerated powers. For example, Congress has been able, through the choice of means for carrying out a few money powers, to find the elasticity necessary to establish and regulate a national banking and currency system. Fourth, national supremacy, referred to in a preceding chapter, means that a provision of a state constitution or law which conflicts with a congressional law, *if the latter is in accord with the grants in the Constitution,* is null and void. National law, if in accord with those grants, is supreme.

NATIONAL POWERS

TAXING AND SPENDING. Perhaps the most pervasive of the national powers are the twin powers to tax and to spend. The power to spend is not separately granted, but comes from the taxing power and the borrowing power. There are no stated limits on the borrowing power, and the taxing power is given for broad purposes: to pay the debts, provide for the national defense, and *promote the general welfare.*

Money can be raised and spent, therefore, for the general welfare. The scope of the term "general welfare" was first argued in the processing-tax case in 1936.[1] Congress had set up the first agricultural adjustment program, to be paid for by a tax on processors. A processor against whom the tax was assessed contested its validity. The Supreme Court analyzed the scope of the phrase "general welfare," and quoted Justice Story's conclusion that the tax-and-appropriation power extended "only to matters of national, as distinguished from local welfare." The Court said that it was unnecessary to determine the scope of the phrase "general welfare," and held the statute invalid on the ground that it was a regulation of agriculture, which was beyond the delegated powers of the national government and was reserved to the states.

The decision is one of the museum pieces of constitutional law. In 1937 the Supreme Court upheld the taxes levied under the Social Security Act, taking note of the fact that it was too late to hold that legislation "to relieve the unemployed and their dependents is a use for any purpose narrower than the promotion of the general welfare." [2] Agriculture, and other

[1] *U.S. v. Butler,* 297 U.S. 1.
[2] *Steward Machine Co. v. Davis,* 301 U.S. 548, 586–587; *Helvering v. Davis,* 301 U.S. 619.

matters which the Court in 1936 would probably have regarded as local in nature, are now the subjects of national legislation. For example, national funds are expended in those local areas where natural disasters have occurred and in similar areas suffering from unemployment.

There was a time when courts in this country held that taxes spent for private benefit were not for a "public purpose," and thus were illegal. For example, loans for seed were held unconstitutional in the midwestern area,[3] and the Supreme Court held unconstitutional a grant by a city to a manufacturing concern for the purpose of encouraging it to locate in its borders.[4] But these decisions are museum pieces, too. The doctrine of "public purpose," like that of "national welfare" (asserted in the processing-tax case), seems no longer to be a real limit on the taxing power of Congress. It appears that the courts have accepted the idea that what may be proximately for a personal or local benefit may be in its ultimate effects for general welfare.

Moreover, there appears to be no effective means of contesting the constitutionality of most national taxes or expenditures on the ground of purpose. A taxpayer's suit, alleging illegality, has been the traditional means of contest. But it has been held that a taxpayer of the United States may not challenge in litigation expenditures from the treasury on the ground that an alleged unconstitutional purpose will increase the tax burden.[5] This was in 1923, and the decision still stands. Apparently, it is only when a special tax is levied for a special purpose, as in the processing-tax case, that an opportunity for challenge exists.

It can be concluded, therefore, that the purposes and amount of national taxes and expenditures are virtually free of constitutional limitation.[6]

The power to tax is granted in terms of purposes for which revenue may be used. It has, however, been used for purposes of regulation. In the Child Labor Tax Case (1922), the Supreme Court held that the power to tax could not be used to regulate a matter otherwise outside of national jurisdiction.[7] The decision is difficult to reconcile with some other uses of the power of taxation. For example, the tax on sale of narcotics is not levied on druggists and others for the purpose of raising money, but for the purpose of regulation.[8] The tariff has, of course, been used for a regulatory

---

[3] *State v. Osawkee Township*, 14 Kan. 418, 19 Am.Rep. 99 (1875); *Deering & Co. v. Peterson*, 75 Minn. 118, 77 N.W. 568 (1898); but upheld in *State v. Nelson*, 1 N.D. 88, 45 N.W. 33 (1890).

[4] *Loan Association v. Topeka*, 20 Wall. 655 (1875).

[5] *Massachusetts v. Mellon* and *Frothingham v. Mellon*, 262 U.S. 447 (1923).

[6] We do not overlook, of course, the fact that the taxing power is limited in certain ways—that is, to protect state governments, to prevent geographical discriminations in indirect taxes, to prevent taxation of exports, to require apportionment of direct taxes (except the income tax).

[7] *Bailey v. Drexel Furniture Co.*, 259 U.S. 20.

[8] Upheld in *U.S. v. Doremus*, 249 U.S. 86 (1919).

purpose.⁹ More significant, however, is the fact that today the scope of national jurisdiction under the commerce and other powers is so broad that the limitation of the child-labor tax case has lost its meaning.

MONEY. Congress' powers on money, in addition to taxing and borrowing, include those "to coin money and regulate the value thereof," and "to provide for the punishment of counterfeiting the securities and current coin of the United States." These fiscal and monetary powers have become the basis, through liberal construction, of our national banking and monetary system, as well as national control thereof. The constitutional basis for all this has been laid in a small number of cases. In *McCulloch v. Maryland* (1819) the power of the national government to establish a bank and branches thereof was upheld.¹⁰ In 1869 the Supreme Court held that Congress could levy a prohibitory tax on state bank notes.¹¹ After the Civil War, the power of Congress to authorize paper money and give it the quality of legal tender in the payment of debts was established.¹² Finally, in 1934, in the Gold Clause cases, the power of Congress to lower the metal content of the dollar was upheld, and thus the power to regulate " 'the value thereof' comes to mean 'value' in the sense of *purchasing power*." ¹³ It can be concluded that Congress' power over the medium of exchange and the banking system seems to be broad enough for any situation which might arise.

COMMERCE. *Gibbons v. Odgen* (1824) was the first important decision concerning the scope of the commerce clause.¹⁴ It had been argued in that case that "commerce" included traffic—that is, buying and selling—but not navigation. The Supreme Court held that commerce included "every species of intercourse," and thus navigation as well as buying and selling.

On the other hand, Marshall drew a distinction between that commerce which was "completely internal," and thus within the jurisdiction of the states, and that commerce which affected more than one state, and was thus within national jurisdiction. Also, a distinction developed between production (including agriculture, mining, and manufacturing) and commerce.

We have seen that the dichotomy between the fields of national and state power did not prevent the question from arising as to whether state regulations for local purposes could be, in effect, regulations of interstate and foreign commerce, and have seen that the courts said that under certain conditions the states could regulate such commerce.¹⁵ The question would

---

⁹ The constitutionality of protective tariffs was upheld in *Hampton & Co. v. U.S.*, 276 U.S. 394 (1928). On breadth of the taxing power for regulatory purposes, see especially *U.S. v. Kahriger*, 345 U.S. 22 (1953).
¹⁰ *McCulloch v. Maryland*, 4 Wheaton 316 (1819).
¹¹ *Veazie Bank v. Fenno*, 8 Wall. 533.
¹² Legal Tender Cases, 12 Wall. 457 (1871), 110 U.S. 421 (1884).
¹³ Edward S. Corwin, *The Constitution and What It Means Today*, 11th ed. (Princeton, N.J.: Princeton University Press, 1954), pp. 60–61. Corwin's italics.
¹⁴ See page 112.
¹⁵ Pages 112–114.

also arise as to whether the national government, through its power to regulate interstate and foreign commerce, could reach into the regulation of production and intrastate commerce. Except for the issue of the tariff, the question of the effect of the dichotomy on national power did not present itself as a large and troublesome issue until near the close of the nineteenth century.[16] Then the enactment of laws in Washington rapidly forced many issues concerning the scope of national power under the commerce clause.

The issues were first presented in antitrust cases. The first case to reach the Supreme Court under the Sherman Antitrust Act was the "Sugar Trust" case in 1895.[17] The government alleged that the American Sugar Refining Company refined 33 per cent of all sugar refined in the United States, and that it had made a contract with four other refining companies under which it exchanged its stock for the shares of stock of the other four companies, and that as a result the company had gained control over the refining of 98 per cent of the sugar refined in the country. The government alleged that the company monopolized the sale of sugar in the country and controlled its price, and that the purpose and intent was to restrain interstate and foreign commerce. It asked that the court order the stock exchanged to be returned, and enjoin further progress with the plan.

The Supreme Court ruled against the government. It said that the object was manifestly private gain in the manufacture of the commodity rather than control of commerce, and that commerce only helped manufacture to fulfill its function. In a key sentence, it declared, "The contracts and acts of the defendants related exclusively to the acquisition of the Philadelphia refineries and the business of sugar refining in Philadelphia, and bore no direct relation to commerce among the several states or with foreign nations." [18] This sentence implied that two things were outside the reach of the national government's power:

1. Agreements and acts relating to production. Here it was sugar refining, but in other instances it might be mining, fishing, agriculture, or diverse forms of manufacturing.

2. Agreements relating to acquisition of property. Here it was acquisition of refineries, and the question presented was whether purchase of corporate stock or corporate assets could be reached by national law.

It appears that the decision in this case presented a constitutional crisis more serious than any between the Dred Scott decision and the 1930's. Cleveland's attorney general reported in 1896 that it would be practically

---

[16] It was presented in *Daniel Ball v. U.S.*, 10 Wall. 557 (1871), the Supreme Court holding that the power of Congress extended to a navigable stream entirely within a single state on which interstate commerce moved.
[17] *U.S. v. E. C. Knight Co.*, 156 U.S. 1.
[18] At page 17.

impossible to apply the antitrust act to industrial corporations.[19] Some, however, refused to accept this answer. A constitutional amendment designed to give Congress power to reach such combinations passed the House of Representatives by a majority, though not by a two-thirds majority, in 1900. Thereafter, a drastic bill denying the privilege of interstate commerce to manufacturing firms committing proscribed offenses passed the House with one dissenting vote.[20]

But some noted that the Supreme Court had created a distinction in the "Sugar Trust" case between direct and indirect effects, and believed that it would be possible to prove direct effects upon commerce in antitrust cases relating to combinations of producers. And by 1900, the Supreme Court had begun to find, in the direct-effect doctrine, limits on the effects of the Knight Case. In 1899, in *Addyston Pipe and Steel Co. v. U.S.*,[21] it held an association of pipe manufacturers to be in violation of the Sherman Act. The defendants sold pipe to water and gas works. By their agreement, certain cities were assigned to each defendant. For these cities the association fixed the price of sale, the member who sold the pipe paid a bonus to the association, and the other members went through the pretense of competitive bidding to maintain the appearance of competition. For some other cities, the price of the low bid to be submitted was determined by the association, and the member who agreed to pay the highest bonus to the other members received the business. The object was clearly control over sales, and hence the Court could find a direct effect on interstate commerce. The contemporary significance of the case was that it showed that combinations of producers could be reached under the Sherman Act if their acts were directly related to sales in interstate commerce.

The implications of the Sugar Trust case with respect to corporate agreements for acquisition of property were removed by the decision of the Court in *Northern Securities Co. v. U.S.*[22] The Northern Securities Company was a holding company formed by the Morgan and Hill interests to hold stock in the Northern Pacific Railway and the Great Northern Railway —two parallel and competing trunk lines running from Duluth and St. Paul to Seattle and Portland. This combine was brought about, as was the sugar combination, by purchase of property rights. Four justices thought that if the power to regulate commerce could extend to changes in property ownership, the reserved powers of the state would be invaded, as well as the right of individuals and corporations to acquire property. But the majority held that this combination was within the reach of the national government, and was a violation of the Sherman Act.

---

[19] *Report of Attorney General* (Washington, D.C.: 1896), xxvii.
[20] Eliot Jones, *The Trust Problem in the United States* (New York: The Macmillan Company, 1922), pp. 325–326.
[21] 175 U.S. 211.
[22] *Northern Securities Co. v. U.S.*, 193 U.S. 197 (1904).

A third decision was significant in further establishing the authority of the national government. In the Swift Case, decided in 1905,[23] a number of meat-packing concerns were charged with having entered a combination to refrain from bidding against each other, to fix prices of sale, to restrict shipments of meat, and to perform other acts. The defendants' acts were not in interstate commerce, for the separate transactions in purchase and sale of meat were negotiated and consummated within a single state. The purchase of meat would be made in a stockyard within a single state. On the other hand, it was clear that purchases made in stockyards could affect shipments in interstate commerce, for prices could be bid up, causing ranchers to ship, after which prices could be run down. The Supreme Court looked at the scheme as a whole. It also gave birth to the concept of *the stream or current of commerce*. It concluded:

> commerce among the States is not a technical legal conception, but a practical one, drawn from the course of business. When cattle are sent for sale from a place in one State, with the expectation that they will end their transit, after purchase, in another, and when in effect they do so, with only the interruption necessary to find a purchaser at the stock yards, and when this is a typical, constantly recurring course, the current thus existing is a current of commerce among the States, and the purchase of the cattle is a part and incident of such commerce.[24]

The same would be true of sales of meat from slaughterhouses for shipment through the states.

It was now fixed by Court decisions that (1) combinations of producers, (2) acquisitions of property, and (3) intrastate sales which were part of a larger scheme could all be reached under the national authority over commerce if these things external to commerce itself had a sufficiently direct effect upon commerce among the States. The 1895 case had come to mean only that there had to be an effect on commerce of things done outside commerce if these were to be brought under national control. But the question of effect ceased to be an important constitutional problem in antitrust cases, for combinations of producers (whether through acquisition of property or through other means) which resulted in controls over a substantial portion of the product shipped in interstate commerce quite obviously had an effect on such commerce. What judges could not see in 1895 has long been accepted as self-evident. The lag of the judges in recognizing the self-evident produced a decade of doubt as to the authority of the national government to reach most large combinations, but since 1904, the problems in antitrust policy have not been those of power, but of wisdom and practical effect.

The power of the national government to reach activities outside interstate commerce which had an effect upon it was soon to be further substantiated in decisions on railroad-rate regulation. In 1914, the Shreveport

---

[23] *Swift & Co. v. U.S.*, 196 U.S. 375.
[24] *Ibid.*, pp. 398–399.

Rate case was decided. The origins of this case lay in an order of the Texas Railroad Commission, which fixed intrastate railroad rates so much lower than interstate rates that merchants in an East Texas city such as Marshall could buy more cheaply in Dallas and Houston than they could in Shreveport, which was less than one-third as far away. Upon complaint being brought to it, the Interstate Commerce Commission ordered the railroads to raise the intrastate rates so that they would not be discriminatory against interstate commerce, and the order was upheld by the Supreme Court.[25] In 1922, the Wisconsin Rate case was decided. The Intertate Commerce Commission, in order to see that the railroads would make a fair return, set a 3.6-cents-per-mile passenger rate. But Wisconsin set a 2-cent maximum for transportation within the state. It thus appeared that railroads, in order to make a fair return, would have to compensate for low intrastate rates by charging high interstate rates. To avoid this, the Interstate Commerce Commission ordered an increase in intrastate rates. Chief Justice Taft, for the Supreme Court, upheld the commission's order and made this significant statement:

Commerce is a unit and does not regard state lines, and while, under the Constitution, interstate and intrastate commerce are ordinarily subject to regulation by different sovereignties, yet when they are so mingled together that the supreme authority, the nation, cannot exercise complete effective control over interstate commerce without incidental regulation of intrastate commerce, such incidental regulation is not an invasion of state authority. . . .[26]

Further substantiation of national power came in two cases, decided in 1922 and 1923, under the stream doctrine of the Swift case. In one, the Supreme Court upheld the regulation of rates in stockyards, as provided in the Packers and Stockyards Act of 1921.[27] In the other, it upheld national regulation of sales on commodity exchanges, as provided in the Grain Futures Act of 1922.[28] In both cases it could be argued that the transactions themselves were purely local, but in both the Court could see that interstate trade was affected.

In the meantime, however, the power of the national government had been denied in another case. In 1916, Congress had passed an act prohibiting the transportation in interstate commerce of the products of mines and factories in which children had worked within the preceding thirty days. Congress had theretofore provided for many exclusions from commerce, such as lottery tickets, impure and adulterated foods and drugs, and uninspected meat. It had also passed the White Slave Act, prohibiting the transportation in interstate commerce of women and girls for immoral purposes. But in 1918, in the Child Labor case (*Hammer v. Dagenhart*), five of the nine

---

[25] *Houston, E & W.T.R. Co. v. U.S.*, 234 U.S. 342 (1914).
[26] *Wisconsin R. Comm. v. Chicago, B. & Q. R. Co.*, 257 U.S. 563, 588 (1922).
[27] *Stafford v. Wallace*, 258 U.S. 495 (1922).
[28] *Chicago Board of Trade v. Olsen*, 262 U.S. 1 (1923).

judges drew distinctions between the child-labor statute and these others, and held that the power to regulate the hours of labor of children in mines and factories was "a purely state authority." [29]

This decision in a closely divided court, and the decision in the Child Labor Tax case in 1922, fixed in many people's minds for some twenty years the idea that Congress could not, under any of its powers, exert positive power over labor or other conditions in production—that is, in mining, manufacturing, or agriculture. This opinion was confirmed by three decisions in 1935 and 1936. The court held, in the first that Congress had exceeded its power under the commerce clause in the National Industrial Recovery Act, in the second that agriculture was a local matter subject only to regulation by the states, and in the third that the provisions in the Guffey Act for regulation of conditions of labor in the coal-mining industry were unconstitutional.[30]

To some, this seemed to create another constitutional crisis. The argument had been presented to the Court, in *Hammer v. Dagenhart* in 1918, that Congress should be able to regulate commerce so as to prevent unfair competition from states with low labor standards. To this argument the Court majority replied, "The commerce clause was not intended to give to Congress a general authority to equalize such conditions." [31] There could be much argument over this question of intention of the Framers and what effect it should have on construction of the commerce clause in the twentieth century. More significant was the effect of the decision. It seemed to create a "no-man's land" in government power, an area in which neither government, national or state, could effectively operate. The states had the legal power, but they would be deterred by fear that standards prescribed in a particular state might be higher than those in other states, and thus penalize their producers in interstate competition. If this were true of hours of labor, it was also true with respect to unemployment insurance, regulation of agriculture, and many other matters. The alternative, therefore, to national power seemed to be *laissez faire*. If legal power was only in the states, this meant there was a vacuum in real governmental power. Such was the effect of the nationalization of the economy under the "grand pattern" upon the issue of the location of governmental power.

A similar issue had been raised by the antitrust statute. It was seen that if the legal power over combinations of large manufacturers rested only in the states, then freedom from control would be the result. The objective, of course, in the antitrust laws had been the negative one of keeping commerce free from restrictions. The Supreme Court had found ways of validating national power for such a purpose. Now Congress had begun to pass laws with positive regulatory effects, governing such things as the amount

---

[29] 247 U.S. 251, 276.
[30] *Schechter Corp. v. U.S.*, 295 U.S. 495 (1935); *United States v. Butler*, 297 U.S. 1 (1936); *Carter v. Carter Coal Co.*, 298 U.S. 238 (1936).
[31] 247 U.S. 251, 273 (1918).

of production in agriculture, the number of hours of work, and the minimum level of wages. What the Court was to do between 1937 and 1942 was to validate national power for positive regulatory ends in the same way it had validated national power some forty years earlier for the purpose of keeping commerce free from restrictions. And yet, the Court's decisions from 1937 to 1942 were not as revolutionary as this summary would indicate. For already the power of Congress to reach outside interstate or foreign commerce in order to carry into effect positive regulatory objectives had been upheld in the Wisconsin Rate case and the decisions concerning the Packers and Stockyards Act and the Grain Futures Act. True, these all related to extensions of national power to intrastate commerce. But on what logic could production be free of national power when intrastate commerce was not?

Decisions on three statutory programs spelled the difference between the pre-1937 and the post-1942 situation with respect to national power. First was the decision upholding the National Labor Relations Act. This act prohibited unfair labor practices "affecting interstate commerce." In *NLRB v. Jones and Laughlin Steel Corp.*, by a 5 to 4 decision, the Court upheld the act as applied to the corporation.[32] The Court said that "the fact that the employees here concerned were engaged in production" was "not determinative"; the question was "the effect upon interstate commerce of the labor practice involved."[33] It concluded, "When industries organize themselves on a national scale, making their relation to interstate commerce the dominant factor in their activities, how can it be maintained that their industrial labor relations constitute a forbidden field into which Congress may not enter when it is necessary to protect interstate commerce from the paralyzing consequences of industrial war?"[34] The act was held applicable on the same day to two relatively small manufacturing concerns.[35] It has also been held applicable to such things as gathering and distributing news to newspapers in the United States and foreign countries,[36] a privately owned public utility operating wholly within a single state,[37] and a small intrastate flour mill with few employees.[38]

The second statutory program was for agriculture. Congress passed the Agricultural Adjustment Act of 1938 to take the place of the act held unconstitutional in 1936.[39] For flue-cured tobacco, it provided that when the Secretary of Agriculture found there was an excess supply on hand, he could

---

[32] 301 U.S. 1 (1937).
[33] *Ibid.*, p. 40.
[34] *Ibid.*, p. 41. For further discussion, see page 311.
[35] *National Labor Relations Board v. Fruehauf Trailer Co.*, 301 U.S. 49 (1937); *National Labor Relations Board v. Friedman–Harry Marks Clothing Co.*, 301 U.S. 58 (1937).
[36] *Associated Press v. National Labor Relations Board*, 301 U.S. 103 (1937).
[37] *Amalgamated Ass'n of Street, Electric Railway and Motor Coach Employees of America, Division 998 v. Wisconsin Employment Relations Board*, 340 U.S. 383 (1951).
[38] *Stout v. Pratt*, 85 F 2d 172 (1936).
[39] See page 137.

establish a national marketing quota. If this action was approved in a referendum of producers, then the Secretary could apportion the national marketing quota among the states, after which the state quotas would be apportioned among individual farmers. Each farmer would thus get a marketing quota; if he marketed more than this through the warehouses, he would pay a 50-per-cent penalty on the excess above his quota. The Supreme Court upheld these provisions, the same justice (Roberts) writing the opinion who had written the opinion in the AAA case of 1936. The Court found that this was not a plan to control production; the plan did not limit the amount which could be planted or produced, but only penalized marketing of more than was allotted.[40]

The practical questions are clear: What would a farmer do with production he could not market? Why produce if you cannot market? Was this, in effect, a control of production? The framers of the 1938 act had been ingenious in finding a way of doing indirectly what the Court in 1936 had said they could not do directly. But if there was doubt about the similarities in effect, this was removed by the decision in *Wickard v. Filburn* in 1942.[41] As amended in 1941, the Agricultural Adjustment Act of 1938 provided for control of production even for use on the producer's farm. Acreage allotments for wheat production were to be given to farmers, and if these were exceeded and an excess amount of wheat produced, then the farmer paid a penalty or could store his excess or give it to the government. Filburn planted 23 acres instead of the 11.1 allotted, and consumed the wheat on his own farm. The Court took note of the old distinctions between production and commerce and between direct and indirect effects, and said that "questions of the power of Congress are not to be decided by reference to any formula which would give controlling force to nomenclature such as 'production' and 'indirect' and foreclose consideration of the actual effects of the activity in question upon interstate commerce." [42] It was immaterial whether the subject of regulation was "production," "consumption," or "marketing," or that "the appellee's activity be local," or whether the effect on commerce was "direct" or "indirect"; Congress could reach it if there was "a substantial effect on interstate commerce." [43] Moreover, the fact "that appellee's own contribution to the demand for wheat may be trivial by itself is not enough to remove him from the scope of federal regulation where, as here, his contribution, taken together with that of many others similarly situated, is far from trivial." [44]

The case can be compared with the Wisconsin Rate case. There Chief Justice Taft had said that "commerce is a unit," and thus that regulatory

---

[40] *Mulford v. Smith,* 307 U.S. 38 (1939).
[41] 317 U.S. 111.
[42] *Ibid.,* p. 120.
[43] *Ibid.,* pp. 124–125.
[44] *Ibid.,* pp. 127–128.

power over interstate commerce could extend to *intrastate commerce*.[45] Now the Court had virtually said that production and commerce were a unit, and that the power to regulate commerce could not be effective without control of *production* also.

In 1938, Congress provided for a third program in the Fair Labor Standards Act. This act set maximum hours and minimum wages, and outlawed child labor.[46] The act's application was different from that of the National Labor Relations Act. The latter extended to things "affecting" commerce, but the Fair Labor Standards Act applied to "production of goods for commerce." The Supreme Court unanimously upheld the statute,[47] and to do so stated that it was overruling *Hammer v. Dagenhart*. It said that Congress intended to prevent "the spread of substandard labor conditions through the use of the facilities of interstate commerce," and that the means adopted were "within the reach of the commerce power."

The statutory terminologies in the Agricultural Adjustment Act and the Fair Labor Standards Act were different. One regulated marketing and activities related thereto, including production; the other dealt directly with production of goods for commerce. But the practical effect of decisions upholding them is the same. These and other decisions of the Supreme Court have now established that through the "stream of commerce" doctrine, the "related to commerce" doctrine, and the prohibition of shipment in commerce, Congress can reach matters in intrastate commerce and production wherever this is "necesssary and proper" in order to carry into effect its policies for interstate or foreign commerce. What is now "completely internal," and thus outside the scope of congressional power, is indeed limited, and depends on decisions on what "effects" commerce.

WAR AND INTERNATIONAL RELATIONS. A broad over-all statement on the power of the national government to conduct war and international relations can be made: There can be doubt as to the origin and nature of the powers, but none as to the plenitude of power and the vast potential effects upon the economy.

The Supreme Court has said in regard to these powers:

It results that the investment of the federal government with the powers of external sovereignty did not depend upon the affirmative grants of the Constitution.

---

[45] Note the extent of the doctrine as applied in *United States v. Wrightwood Dairy Co.*, 315 U.S. 110 (1942), where the Agricultural Marketing Agreement Act of 1937, whose declared purpose was "to establish and maintain such orderly marketing conditions for agricultural commodities in interstate commerce . . . ," was held applicable to a dairy company *all of whose milk was produced and sold within the state* for which a marketing agreement had been adopted. The Court said: "The commerce power is not confined in its exercise to the regulation of commerce among the states. It extends to those activities intrastate which so effect interstate commerce, or the exertion of the power of Congress over it, as to make regulation of them appropriate means to the attainment of a legitimate end, the effective execution of the granted power to regulate interstate commerce" (p. 119).
[46] For further discussion of the act, see pages 287–288.
[47] *United States v. Darby*, 312 U.S. 100 (1941).

148   *The Constitution and the Economy*

The powers to declare and wage war, to conclude peace, to make treaties, to maintain diplomatic relations with other sovereignties, if they had never been mentioned in the Constitution, would have vested in the federal government as necessary concomitants of nationality. . . . As a member of the family of nations, the right and power of the United States in that field are equal to the right and power of the other members of the international family.[48]

This is the doctrine of inherent power—that is, that the government of the United States, as the representative of a sovereign nation, has, merely by virtue of this fact and not by reason of delegation in the Constitution, the power to act for the national interest in all matters relating to other nations.

This seemingly unorthodox constitutional doctrine would appear to be unnecessary insofar as the war powers of the national government are concerned. The Constitution grants an "aggregate of powers" to the Congress:

To lay and collect taxes . . . to pay the debts and to provide for the common defense;
To declare war, grant letters of marque and reprisal, and make rules concerning captures on land and water;
To raise and support armies . . . ;
To provide and maintain a navy;
To make rules for the government and regulation of the land and naval forces;
To provide for calling forth the militia to execute the laws of the union, suppress insurrections, and repel invasions;
To provide for organizing, arming, and disciplining the militia, and for governing such part of them as may be employed in the service of the United States. . . .

In addition, the President is made commander-in-chief of the armed forces, and the implied-powers clause gives authority to Congress to take all actions "necessary and proper" to carry out all powers delegated to it and other officers of the government.

The aggregate of war powers all center around the raising, supporting, and directing of the armed forces. Once this meant, on government's side, the conscription of men away from their jobs and businesses and the raising of money to buy equipment and supplies; it meant, on the side of the private entrepreneur, an adjustment of his operations to the changed conditions, but these adjustments were made on his own initiative and without a significant amount of public control. But in World War I, and even more so in World War II, supporting the armed forces necessitated public control over the economy. Modern war has become "total war" calling for the mobilization of the nation, including its economic resources. In World War II a number of laws created in the executive branch powers of centralized control over the economy. Thus, the President was authorized to allocate scarce supplies and materials,[49] and under this authorization the War Production Board made provision for conserving scarce items and channeling

---

[48] *U.S. v. Curtiss-Wright Export Corp.*, 299 U.S. 304, 318 (1936).
[49] 56 Stat. 236 (1941); 56 Stat. 176 (1942).

these to preferred uses, and the Office of Price Administration set up systems of consumer rationing. The Supreme Court even held that to deal in scarce commodities was a privilege rather than a right.[50] Congress authorized controls over prices, rents, and wages.[51] It authorized seizure of plants in case of strike,[52] and it provided for recovery of excessive profits.[53] The extensive program of economic mobilization was rationalized by the Supreme Court as being within the delegated powers of the government:

> With the advent of such warfare, mobilized property in the form of equipment and supplies became as essential as mobilized manpower. . . . The language of the Constitution authorizing such measures is broad rather than restrictive. . . . [It] places emphasis upon the supporting as well as upon the raising of armies. The power of Congress as to both is inescapably express, not merely implied.[54]

But this is not all. War powers may be exercised in time of peace: some will be exercised continuously; others may be called into effect in emergency situations—prior to war, for a period of adjustment after war, or for a sustained period of emergency. They may be exercised in long-range preparation for defense, as in the Atomic Energy Act [55] or the building of Wilson Dam in the T.V.A. area to produce nitrates.[56] They may be exercised for support of armies of allies or friendly nations, as in the lend-lease program for aid to Great Britain and Russia prior to and during World War II, or as in the recent military-aid programs. Even in time of peace, the exercise of the power to raise and support armed forces of this and other countries may affect the economy through a heavy burden of taxes, the expansion or contraction of government expenditures, or the imposition of controls. It is not too much to say that today the economy is constantly under the shadow of the war powers.

On types of conduct relating to other nations besides war and defense preparations, the grants of power in the Constitution are diverse and piecemeal. Congress is given the power to levy duties and other taxes, to regulate foreign commerce, to establish a uniform rule of naturalization, and "to define and punish piracies and felonies committed on the high seas and offenses against the law of nations"; the President is granted power to appoint ambassadors with the advice and consent of the Senate; the judiciary is given jurisdiction over cases affecting ambassadors and consuls, admiralty and maritime cases, and cases between a state or citizens thereof and foreign states, their citizens and subjects. The treaty-making power is also granted.

[50] *L. P. Steuart & Bro., Inc. v. Bowles*, 322 U.S. 398 (1944).
[51] Emergency Price Control Act, 56 Stat. 23 (1942) and amendments, 56 Stat. 765 (1942).
[52] War Labor Disputes Act, 57 Stat. 163 (1943).
[53] In a series of acts referred to as the Renegotiation Act. See *Lichter v. U.S.*, 334 U.S. 742, 745 (1948).
[54] *Ibid.*, pp. 755–756.
[55] 60 Stat. 755 (1946).
[56] Recognized as a constitutional basis for the building of the dam in *Ashwander v. Tennessee Valley Authority*, 297 U.S. 298 (1936).

These grants seem insufficient to cover all types of action taken by our government. Justice Sutherland, in the opinion from which the statement of inherent powers quoted at the beginning of this section was taken, noted three powers the Supreme Court had recognized as national, but which were not "expressly affirmed by the Constitution," existing only under "the conception of nationality." These were the power to acquire territory by discovery and occupation, the power to expel aliens, and the power to make international agreements which were not treaties.[57]

The treaty-making power is granted in terms different from the lawmaking power. Laws of the United States must be made "in pursuance" of the Constitution, treaties "under the authority of the United States." The Supreme Court has construed the treaty grant as being broader than the lawmaking grant. This was done in *Missouri v. Holland*.[58] A treaty to protect migratory birds had been made, and Congress had passed a law to carry this out. The Supreme Court took note of the fact that in district court decisions a former law (passed before the treaty was made) with the same aim in view had been held unconstitutional, but the treaty and the law enacted to carry it out were upheld.

This decision has raised much discussion as to the limits on the treaty-making power. It would appear that prohibitions of the Constitution cannot be violated by treaty, or that fundamental changes in the character or organs of government could not be made by treaty.[59] On the other hand, it appears that neither the doctrine of delegated powers nor the Tenth Amendment limits the treaty-making power. Treaties have been made which established reciprocal rights of American citizens and citizens of foreign countries on such matters as property ownership and engaging in business, on which Congress could obviously not have legislated in the absence of treaty.

This broad scope of the treaty-making power has led to proposals (chiefly, the Bricker Amendment) to amend the Constitution to restrict the treaty-making power. Proposals of this kind have narrowly missed submission to the states by the Congress. Advocates for limiting the power advance arguments in favor of states rights, and some fear the exercise of the treaty-making power on the subject of civil rights; opponents regard it as unwise to prevent the national government from having the same rights in regard to treaties that governments of other nations have.

This conclusion may be drawn: Whether from delegation or from inherent power as a nation, the government of the United States now exercises daily a variety of functions in foreign affairs which restrict or promote trade,

---

[57] *U.S. v. Curtiss-Wright Corp.*, 299 U.S. 304, 318 (1936), citing *Jones v. U.S.*, 137 U.S. 202, 212, *Fong Yue Ting v. U.S.*, 149 U.S. 698, 705 *et seq.*, *Altman & Co. v. U.S.*, 224 U.S. 583, 600–601.

[58] 252 U.S. 416 (1920).

[59] See Edward S. Corwin, *The Constitution and What It Means Today*, 11th ed. (Princeton, N.J.: Princeton University Press, 1954), pp. 107–109.

result in higher or lower taxes on the American economy, or which otherwise affect the economy. Perhaps it would be realistic to recognize that the growth of the industrial and military might of the nation, and its position of leadership among the free nations, has given the government power to perform whatever acts in foreign affairs appear to be in the national interest, insofar as these do not alter the structure of the government or violate the prohibitions of the Constitution.

STATE POWERS

It has recently been stated that "the policy-making authorities of the National Government are for most purposes the arbiters of the federal system." [60] The Constitution, as interpreted by the Congress, the President, and the Supreme Court, has given to the national government a vast aggregate of powers—taxing and borrowing, regulation of the monetary supply, regulation of commerce, national defense and conduct of relations with other countries, and others noted in Chapter 6—which seem to be sufficient for regulation, promotion, or stabilization of the economy to any extent Congress is likely to desire. Undoubtedly, the Constitution now subjects the economy to national politics.

But the same source quoted above has said that our federal system "has preserved a degree of local autonomy unmatched among the world's other great powers." [61] The states (and their subdivisions) still possess extensive powers of regulation and service to the economy. First, there are vast areas in which the states, either because of the constitutional reservation of power to them or because of the inaction of Congress,[62] possess original powers of legislation. Among these are the definition of the rights of ownership and of the rights and methods of transmission of property; the definition and punishment of ordinary crimes; the regulation of business, trades, professions, and labor in their local aspects (even though in some cases there may be some effect on interstate or foreign commerce); the supply of services, such as the construction and maintenance of roads; and the establishment of educational, recreational, corrective, and eleemosynary facilities. Some of these activities are expanding so rapidly that state and local budgets, taxes, and debts have for several years been increasing at a faster rate than at the national level.

Second, the national government has in many cases provided for state service or regulation. Thus, after the Supreme Court had held in 1944 that insurance was commerce,[63] the Congress passed legislation designed to

---

[60] The Commission on Intergovernmental Relations, *A Report to the President for Transmittal to the Congress* (Washington, D.C.: 1955), p. 59.
[61] *Ibid.*, p. 34.
[62] See pages 112–114.
[63] *U.S. v. South-Eastern Underwriters Association,* 322 U.S. 533.

152   *The Constitution and the Economy*

validate the continued regulation of the industry by the states.[64] Congress has power to regulate all interstate power and gas rates, but it has left the power to regulate interstate *retail* rates to the states. It provided in the Federal Power Act and the Natural Gas Act only for national regulation of wholesale rates, which the Supreme Court had held could not be regulated by the states. The Federal Power Act provides that national jurisdiction over security issues "shall not extend to a public utility organized and operating in a state under the laws of which its security issues are regulated by a state commission." National law requiring licensing of hydroelectric projects allows regulation of services, rates, and finances by the Federal Power Commission only in states which have no regulatory commission. Congress has exempted from the antitrust laws price maintenance agreements where these have been made lawful by the states. It has provided that the authorization of union security agreements in the National Labor Relations Act, as amended, shall not be applicable in states which prohibit such agreements, and has allowed states to exercise jurisdiction over labor disputes over which the National Labor Relations Board declines to assert jurisdiction.

Third, there is parallel action of the national and state governments in many areas of regulation and service. Both the national and state governments incorporate and supervise banks. Both levels of governments try to preserve honesty in the sale of securities. Both regulate railroads, utilities, labor relations, and seek to prevent sale of injurious commodities.

Finally, there is much cooperation between national and state levels in these and other areas. The national government has accepted state banks into the Federal Reserve and deposit-insurance systems, and a cooperative relationship has been established between the two levels of government on the examination of state banks. The national coal-mine inspection act of 1952 authorizes inspections jointly by national and state inspectors. The states have provided for creation of soil conservation districts to cooperate in the national soil conservation program. They have established unemployment-insurance programs to meet the standards of a national act, and they administer these programs in cooperation with a national agency. The Department of Justice, the Securities and Exchange Commission, and other national agencies cooperate with their counterparts in the states. State courts serve as courts of original jurisdiction for many types of cases arising within national jurisdiction, particularly those involving sums less than $10,000. These are examples of cooperative action by other means than the familiar grants-in-aid system, through which approximately 25 per cent of the costs of state government are met by grants from the national government, and approximately 30 per cent of the funds for expenditure by local governments are covered by grants from state and national governments.

In legislation on railroads, communications, power, natural gas, and mo-

---

[64] The McCarran Act, 59 Stat. 33 (1945).

tor carriers, Congress has made an especially strong effort to establish cooperative relationships. The Transportation Act of 1920 authorized the Interstate Commerce Commission to (1) confer with state authorities, (2) avail itself of their cooperation, and (3) hold joint hearings with them on any matter within the commission's jurisdiction and affecting the rate-making authority of the state. Similar provisions were contained in the Communications Act of 1934, the Federal Power Act of 1935, and the Natural Gas Act of 1938. In addition, the last three acts provided that the national regulatory commissions concerned could refer matters within their jurisdiction to joint state boards composed of members of state commissions from affected states. All of these authorizations were repeated in the Motor Carrier Act of 1935, but it went further and *required* decision by state boards where no more than three states were involved. Finally, the Federal Power Act and the Natural Gas Act—both of which provided for national regulation of *wholesale* interstate rates only—authorized the Federal Power Commission to assist the states by making studies on costs, supplying information, and loaning its rate or other experts.

Experience under these provisions has shown limitations and possibilities of national-state administrative cooperation. Joint hearings and joint boards are infrequently used, except where this is compulsory (in motor-carrier regulation). Even then, there are serious problems. There is much absenteeism on the part of board members, and the work of the boards is done substantially by examiners assigned by the Interstate Commerce Commission, with little contribution being made by the joint boards.[65] On the other hand, real and substantial results have been achieved from the continuous association of national and state officials in the National Association of Railroad and Utility Commissioners, through interchanges of data among regulatory agencies, through federal-state cooperation in developing uniform accounting requirements for firms subject both to state and national authority, and through assistance at times by the Federal Power Commission to state commissions.[66] Cooperation, to be effective, must be a means of assisting both parties to perform tasks for which they are separately or jointly responsible.

In addition to the activities of the states, there is much regulation and promotion of economic interests by political subdivisions of the states. Cities, for example, administer zoning plans (which limit the use of property), enact ordinances on health and safety, license trades (for example, electricians), grant special concessions to draw business to their locations, and do many other things affecting economic pursuits. Special districts are created for supplying power, water, and port facilities, or for other purposes.[67]

---

[65] See David Welborn, "National-State Cooperation in Regulatory Administration," *State Government*, **XXXIII** (Summer 1960), pp. 199–207, especially pp. 205–206.

[66] Welborn, *ibid., passim*. And see page 432 of this text.

[67] See page 608.

154 *The Constitution and the Economy*

In conclusion, it can be said that although the nationalization of the economy under the Grand Pattern of the Constitution has brought in its wake centralization of major economic controls in the national government, extensive regulatory and promotional functions are performed at state and local levels.

Part III. Policies Affecting the Economy Generally

Chapter 9. Monetary and Fiscal Policy

ECONOMIC ACTIVITY takes place within the framework of ideas and constitutional principles that have been described. These ideas and principles have implied different kinds of policies or activities for government. The mercantilist notions of the writers of the Constitution were followed by *laissez faire* notions in the late nineteenth and early twentieth centuries, and they in turn have been followed by notions that assign definite responsibilities to government in the economic arena. It has been amply clear that *laissez faire* notions have never been dominant in American policy, even though proponents of such views have always marched alongside proponents of governmental responsibilities. The purpose of this chapter is to examine the attitudes and policies that have sought to deal with economic fluctuations—that is the variations in the levels of use of economic resources.

POLICIES BEFORE THE GREAT DEPRESSION

Fluctuations in the quantity of economic activity have been characteristic of the American economy, as they have been of most industrial nations. The Panic of 1819 has been called "America's first great economic crisis and depression . . . [that] appeared to come mysteriously from within the economic system itself."[1] Another such event came in 1837, and there were major depressions in the 1870's and again in the 1890's. Interspersed between these major declines in output, with their attendant miseries, were minor variations—occurring irregularly, but with enough frequency to be called cycles.

In this century, the Panic of 1907 stimulated an elaborate investigation into the money and credit system.[2] The report led to a major reconstruction of the banking system through the creation of the Federal Reserve System

---

[1] M. N. Rothbard, *The Panic of 1819: Reactions and Policies* (New York: Columbia University Press, 1962).

[2] The Pujo Investigation, with the official title of *Report of the Committee Pursuant to House Resolutions 429 and 504 to Investigate the Concentration of Money and Credit* (Washington, D.C.: 1912–1913). The name comes from the Chairman of the Committee. An earlier comprehensive study had been made by the National Monetary Commission created by Congressional legislation in 1908. The study was published as *Report of the National Monetary Commission* (Washington, D.C.: 1912).

in 1913.[3] This major reform of the banking system was part of the New Freedom program of President Wilson. The reform postulated a relationship between the money-and-credit system and the performance of the economy, though the relationship was not spelled out in any detail. The money-and-credit system, it was clear, had important consequences, and the new banking law provided new tools that could be used to eliminate the shortcomings of the existing banking and money system.

Money issues had been important throughout our history, and the years preceding the Panic of 1907 were no exception. In the exercise of its authority "to coin money and regulate the value thereof," Congress had passed the Gold Standard Act of 1900, which required the Treasury to redeem United States and Treasury notes (existing paper money) in gold on demand. This act capped a macropolitical struggle that had endured through much of the nineteenth century. The silver-mining interests and their associates had pressed hard for bimetallism, and the 1896 presidential election was fought over this issue. William Jennings Bryan's famous "Cross of Gold" speech in the Democratic Convention of that year had been a plea for the free coinage of silver at a ratio of sixteen units of silver to one unit of gold. The so-called hard-money forces won with McKinley, the Republican nominee, and the 1900 legislation was the result. Despite the victory, the money issue continued to be bothersome, for the quantity of money was closely related to the size of the declining national debt, the backing for United States notes, and the supply of gold. The availability of credit at the banks furnished some additional equivalents of money, but the quantity was uncertain, and periodic strains or shortages occurred. The Panic of 1907 was an extreme instance. The existing banking system was composed of state and national banks that could extend bank credit, but private arrangements among the banks concentrated control of credit in major financial centers, with accompanying periodic shortages in many regions.

THE POLICY MODEL. The model of the economy on which the new currency and banking system was to be constructed implied a fairly stable set of activities, with minor fluctuations in demand for money and currency in different regions and at different periods of the year. The new system assumed that the demand for currency or credit fluctuated in different parts of the economy. Under the Federal Reserve System credit could be expanded or contracted as needed. Convertibility of currency and bank credit into gold was considered an absolute essential of public policy. According to the model, as demand for money and credit expanded to the limits of the legal reserves of banks, higher rates of interest constituted an automatic control that delimited expansion. Conversely, contractions in demand for credit or currency brought decline in interest costs. As demand for money and credit declined, the opportunity to make profits from lower costs

---

[3] 38 Stat. 251. This Act has been amended from time to time, with a major revision in 1935. Supervision of banking is described in Chapter 23.

could stimulate entrepreneurs to expand their activity. The assumption of full use of resources is implicit, although it was seldom stated to be an essential element in the model. That the quantity of activity could level off at less than full use of resources was considered to be an impossibility. Thus, the model in its refined form described a cycle with an upswing (the period of expansion of employment, investment, and rising prices), a turning point (the period of uncertainty, contraction of employment and investment, and declining prices), a downswing of continuing declines (declining employment and investment, and falling prices), and the lower turning point at which the low prices and declining inventories induced entrepreneurs to begin anew the investment and employing activities that generate the prosperity, or upswing, phase. As the expansion phase grew, the quantity of money and credit was to be limited in such a fashion that excess money and credit would not be available to develop inflation. On the downswing, money and credit were to be available to prevent deflation.

In this model, inflation occurs when the quantity of money and credit expands more rapidly than the productivity of the economy. That is, if capital and labor are fully utilized, additional money bidding for goods and services cannot increase output. Deflation, on the other hand, occurs when there are idle resources but inadequate money and credit in the hands of the government, businessmen, and consumers for purchasing output. The shortage of money and credit in the hands of buyers decreases the demand for labor, capital, and entrepreneurial capacity. As unemployment and unused resources increase, a further decline ensues, for it is no longer profitable to produce.

Characteristic of inflation is the full utilization of resources, with rising prices resulting from the efforts to trade money and credit for the limited goods and services. Rising prices also appear during the upswing of the business cycle, but rising prices are not inflationary until full utilization is reached, because until then, the unused resources will begin producing. On the other hand, falling prices occur on the downswing phase of the cycle, but these are not necessarily deflationary. In order for deflation to occur, the decline must be so general that the self-correcting actions cannot overcome the reinforcing downward movements. This condition is characteristic of a major depression.

It was assumed, in the economic analysis prior to World War I, that the resources of an economy would come to be used at their full capacity. Major deviations from such full use would occur only in the wake of natural catastrophes, serious disturbances such as war, or the pursuit of absurd governmental goals. Minor deviations could be attributed to temporary malfunctioning of the money-and-credit system. In order to prevent such a condition, the centralization of credit and currency controls through central banking was indicated, with responsibility in the central banking system for influencing the flow of economic activity in directions that would keep capital busy and labor employed. It was thought that a central banking system, with its capacity to advance credit in one direction and to check its movement in another, could offset the cyclical trends and keep the economy operating on a high level of activity. A central bank could have three tools. It could take over loans of banks at a discount or rediscount (that is, for an interest charge), thereby making money available to banks that were in short supply. Second, by controlling the reserve requirements of the banks dealing with depositors, the central bank could encourage or restrict expansion or contraction of loans. Finally, through its authority to engage in open-market operations by itself, entering the money markets to buy and sell short-term securities, the central bank could influence the amount of credit and currency that was available to commerce and business. In other words, the central bank had the duty of providing money and credit for business enterprises, thereby enabling the economy to function to the maximum advantage of all concerned.[4]

THE FEDERAL RESERVE SYSTEM. The Federal Reserve System, as it was created in the 1913 legislation, provided for a Federal Reserve Board appointed by the President with Senate approval, except that the Secretary of the Treasury and the Comptroller of the Currency (in the Treasury Department) would be members. It provided also for twelve regional bankers' banks that were owned by national banks in each of twelve regions. The twelve regional banks had their own boards of directors, and each was in some degree subordinate to the Federal Reserve Board. The Federal Reserve Board was the central governing body, with limited supervisory powers over the regional Reserve Banks and indirectly over banks that were members of the system. All national banks were members, and state-chartered banks were permitted to join. The concern here is with the system's supervision of the credit and currency supply and with the developments in the system.

The control devices available to the Reserve Board and its associated institutions are constantly in use. In order to ease credit conditions, the interest rate on rediscounted loans is reduced; in order to tighten credit conditions, the rate is raised. Similarly, a raise in reserve requirements reduces the loanable resources of the member banks; a lowering of such requirements increases the lendable resources. These requirements are fixed within the legal discretion authorized by the legislation. The regional Reserve banks administer the decisions through their member banks. Compliance with discount rates or reserve requirements were obligations that the member banks owed to the regional Reserve Bank. The controls can be fairly effective as checks on credit expansions, but they do not in themselves create a demand for credit.

The third instrument of control, open-market operations, has turned out

---

[4] Any text in economics will give the elements of the model. For an excellent discussion of central banking operations, see H. P. Willis, *The Theory and Practice of Central Banking, with Special Reference to American Experience, 1913–1935* (New York: Harper & Brothers, 1936).

to be the most important of the control devices. Each Federal Reserve bank, by buying securities in the open money market, increases the reserves available to the banks for lending. By selling to banks securities that it holds, it reduces their lendable resources.

The credit resources of the banks in the Federal Reserve System are thereby centralized under a common administrative control.[5] The centralization, however, was not adequate in the beginning. The 1913 legislation placed Open Market Operations in the hands of the Federal Reserve banks. These regional banks were not required to conform to the decisions of the Federal Reserve Board. Consequently, the regional interests of the banks were sometimes more influential than a model central system implied. Nonetheless, and despite fear of concentrated or centralized banking in Congress and among small bankers, a step had been taken toward effective controls.[6]

In the amended Federal Reserve Act of 1935, the composition of the Federal Reserve Board was changed by dropping the Secretary of the Treasury and the Controller of the Currency from ex-officio membership, and by creating a new Board of Governors of the Federal Reserve System of seven members. An open-market committee, which had emerged in 1922 to represent the Reserve banks and coordinate their open-market activities, was also reconstructed to consist of the seven board members plus five representatives of the Reserve banks. The new committee was empowered to require the banks to engage in operations in accord with its orders. The new committee exercises a more centralized control over credit controls, for the board can outvote the representatives of the Reserve banks.

The three controls can be used to reinforce one another, and ordinarily, policy decisions of the board all move in the same direction. The reserve requirement and the discount-rate controls are slow and often ineffectual, whereas the open-market operations have immediate consequences. As the Federal Reserve banks sell securities in the open market, the board is simultaneously reducing the reserves of the banks for extending credit. As the Reserve banks buy securities, they increase reserves in member banks for lending purposes. The desire of the member banks to maximize earnings will encourage lending or not, as the case may be. The board's policy aim of

[5] Formally the instruments of control are still not completely integrated. The board sets the reserve requirements; the directors of the Federal Reserve banks set discount requirements, but subject to the board's power of review and determination; the decisions on open-market negotiations are made in the Open Market Committee, but the board has a majority on the committee. In fact, the board maintains control, and much influence is exerted by its chairman. For full explanation, see Michael D. Reagan, "The Political Structure of the Federal Reserve System," *The American Political Science Review*, **LV** (March 1961), pp. 64–76.

[6] A description of the early period of the Federal Reserve System may be found in the following: Emanuel A. Goldenweiser, *Federal Reserve System in Operation* (New York: McGraw-Hill Company, Inc., 1925); *The Banking Situation in the United States* (New York: National Industrial Conference Board, 1932); E. Groseclose, *Money and Man: A Survey of Monetary Experience* (New York: Frederick Ungar Publishing Co., Inc., 1961), especially Book Ten; H. P. Willis, *The Theory and Practice of Central Banking, with Special Reference to American Experience, 1913–1935*, op. cit., passim.

restricting or expanding credit can be reinforced by the use of the instruments of control. In its essentials, the 1913 reforms still form the core of central banking activities.

RESERVE BOARD POLICY AND PROBLEMS. The granting of the controls did not, of course, determine the manner in which the Federal Reserve Board would use them. The 1913 legislation did not expressly formulate goals for the newly established system. The board has generally followed a policy of "accommodating commerce and business." The phrase is found in the legislative act, and provides a general standard concerning decisions *to expand or contract* credit. The policy makes the board's estimates of business needs the dominant element in decisions. The policy had a short run in the first years of the Reserve System. Then World War I generated new financial and monetary problems, and led to board consideration of the government's needs.

The board decided, in 1917, on a policy of assisting the Treasury in floating government securities. This was accomplished in substantial measure by discounting loans secured by United States obligations. The government was able to sell its bonds at low rates of interest through heavy extensions of credit by banks. The additional wartime controls on commodities and prices restrained the unstable situation, and the Reserve Board continued to support the low rates on government securities until 1920.

In an effort to regain control over the financial situation in 1920, the Federal Reserve authorities increased discount rates and maintained them at a high level for the next two years. There were, however, in this period large inflows of gold from abroad into the nation's banks, which enabled them to be immune to the System's controls over reserve requirements and discount rates. It was during this period that open-market operations were developed by the board as a significant means of influencing the money-and-credit situation. The board, with the assistance of the regional Reserve banks, began to use open-market operations as a means of managing the total credit reserves of the Reserve System as a single fund. This experience led to a conference of the governors of the regional banks in 1923. Goldenweiser sums up the situation in 1925 in the following way:

> The Federal Reserve Board's position in the matter was indicated by the adoption of the following principle with respect to open-market operations of the Federal Reserve banks: "That the time, manner, character, and volume of open-market investments purchased by Federal Reserve banks, be governed with primary regard to the accommodation of commerce and business and to the effect of such purchases or sales on the general credit situation." At the same time a committee of governors of the reserve banks was appointed to supervise, in conjunction with the Board, the open-market operations of all the reserve banks.[7]

[7] Emanuel A. Goldenweiser, *Federal Reserve System in Operation* (New York: McGraw-Hill Company, Inc., 1925), p. 61. This informal conference of governors marked the beginning of the regular meetings that have continued to the present. The banking reforms of 1933 and 1935 institutionalized the activity in the Federal Open Market Committee.

In the middle 1920's, the board became alarmed at the rate at which credit was moving into the securities market and the extent to which the commercial banks were entering into activities that bordered on investment banking, thereby implicating the Federal Reserve System in the potential consequences. The board sought to exercise "moral suasion" without great success. It soon became clear that the controls of the Reserve System were not comprehensive enough.

The model on which central banking controls had been established assumed the effectiveness of quantitative controls over money and credit. Now the issue of selective or specific controls over credit uses was posed. The flow of banking credit into security and real-estate transactions was increasing, and this seemed more akin to financing speculation than to accommodation of commerce and industry. The flow of credit into stock-market speculation posed the issue most sharply: If the bases for lending bank credit were to be decisions of businessmen and not central banking or political decisions, then it could be implied that central controls should not be exercised so long as adequate money and credit were available for business and industry. If, however, the extension of credit for security or real-estate speculation were unwise economic ventures because of their consequences for the economy as a whole, then the implication could be drawn that additional controls of a selective nature over the uses of credit should be applied.

The annual report of the Federal Reserve Board in 1923 formulated some guides for the administration of credit. It acknowledged the need to "accommodate commerce and industry," but it went on to find other guides in its basic legislation. Agriculture was entitled to accommodation, and, in general, credit was to be used for productive purposes. The generalization meant explicitly that the board did not look with favor on the use of the facilities of the System for speculation in business securities, either bonds or stocks. The means of detecting whether loans were being made for speculative purposes were admittedly not easy, but such selective controls were assumed by the board to be within the reach of its authority. The board implied that it could inquire into the loan policies of the banks requesting credit.[8] In 1929 the board showed itself seriously disturbed about the speculation in the stock markets:

> During the last year or more, however, the functioning of the Federal Reserve System has encountered interference by reason of the excessive amount of the country's credit absorbed in speculative security loans. . . . The Federal Reserve Board neither assumes the right nor has any disposition to set itself up as an arbiter of security speculation or values. It is, however, its business to see to it that the Federal Reserve Banks function as effectively as conditions will permit. When it finds that conditions are arising which obstruct Federal Reserve Banks in the effective discharge of their function of so managing the credit facilities of the

---

[8] The above account is based on the report in R. L. Weissman, *The New Federal Reserve System, The Board Assumes Control* (New York: Harper and Row, Publishers, Inc., 1936), pp. 280–293. The *Annual Report* of the board for 1923 has the discussion.

164 *Policies Affecting the Economy Generally*

Federal Reserve System as to accommodate commerce and business, it is its duty to inquire into them and to take such measures as may be deemed suitable and effective in the circumstances to correct them; which in the immediate situation, means to restrain the use either directly or indirectly, of Federal Reserve credit facilities in aid of the growth of speculative credit. . . .[9]

This was no more than a warning. It did nothing to prevent the later drastic decline in securities prices. A new stage in the money-and-credit situation was in the making. The 1929 stock market decline was followed by drastic general declines in economic activity. The consequences for money-and-credit policy were great, and in addition, a new theoretical account of the operation of a modern industrial economy was to be formulated—one that would lead to denial of monetary policy as a completely satisfactory solution for business cycles. The government was to become the central agency for maintaining stability of economic activity through the use of its capacity to spend, to levy taxes, and to manage its public debt. Fiscal policy, in short, was about to be born.

FISCAL POLICY DURING THE DEPRESSION

NEW CONDITIONS AND NEW POLICIES. The decade of the 1920's is usually called prosperous, and with justification, but the label did not apply to all segments of the economy in the United States. Agriculture endured depression throughout the decade. Congress, responding in the early part of the decade, set up new agricultural credit facilities. But neither these nor Federal Reserve policies could halt the agricultural depression, and Congress resorted in 1929 to price support for a few agricultural commodities. The agricultural legislation demonstrated that macropolitics would be substituted for the "natural" laws of economics whenever the latter were regarded as unsatisfactory.

The decline that agriculture had experienced now spread to all segments of economic life. Business firms could not continue to maintain existing levels of production when they were unable to dispose of their outputs, and hence discharged many of their workers. As unemployed workers increased in number, there was a simultaneous decrease in demand for goods, since the workers no longer had purchasing power. The decline in market prices of the securities that had been deposited for loans compelled the lenders, bankers or others, to call for more backing. The borrowers had to dispose of other assets in order to get additional resources to satisfy creditors. The general movement to dispose of securities and other assets reinforced the downward movement of prices. Banks found the security for their loans in-

---

[9] Weissman, *ibid.*, pp. 293–294. The quotation is from a statement that appeared in the *Federal Reserve Bulletin* for February 1929. See the discussion in Harold L. Reed, *Federal Reserve Policy, 1921–1930* (New York: McGraw-Hill Company, Inc., 1930), pp. 143–153, and Ch. V.

adequate, and were threatened by depositors who became frightened that their assets would disappear in the closing of the banks. The banking system was unprepared to meet a general demand for money and gold. The period was one in which those who had access to money or credit could write their own ticket; others simply had to readjust to the new marketing situation.

In these circumstances, the theory on which the Federal Reserve System was constructed called for easing credit and monetary conditions so that the entrepreneurs could and would begin to take advantages of the lower prices. The Federal Reserve System did provide "easy" money conditions. Reserve requirements were lowered, discount rates were reduced, and open-market operations increased the lendable resources of the banks. Despite these efforts, banks continued to fail, and employment continued to decline, as did prices of securities. The view that "prosperity was just around the corner" was whistling to keep up courage until the "natural laws" initiated the inevitable recuperation. The declining wages, interest, and rents failed to stimulate the expansion that theory described. It seemed that full use of resources was not automatic or even semi-automatic.

The macropolitical system did not tolerate this situation for long. The agricultural commodities on which the Farm Board had extented credit were taken over as security for the loans, and the wheat and cotton were made available for relief purposes. The decline in prices of securities led to the formation of the Reconstruction Finance Corporation early in 1932. The RFC, with the guarantee of government credit, was authorized to take corporate bonds and stocks as security for loans. It became a super bank. Instead of holders of securities having to take whatever the free market would offer, the RFC stood ready to make loans at "reasonable values" on the securities. The goal was to put a floor under the downward pressures on prices. As householders with mortgages on their homes lost their ability to maintain the payments on the mortgages, foreclosures by the creditors began to increase. The Home Owners Loan Corporation was formed, under government auspices, to lend money on such mortgages so as to reduce the number of foreclosures and their depressing consequences. Similar action was taken for agricultural mortgages. The Congress, acting under its authority in bankruptcy, limited the rights of creditors; and many states enacted modifications of insolvency laws. The Supreme Court was persuaded to revise some of its former holdings to enable the debtors to hold on to their assets.[10]

The Congress passed agricultural legislation in 1933 to broaden maintenance of prices, and it passed legislation to permit business to engage (under supervision) in combinations to restrain competition.[11] Appropria-

---

[10] For state legislation, see *Home Building & Loan Assn. v. Blaisdell*, 290 U.S. 398 (1934); Congress voided gold clauses in its own bonds, *Perry v. U.S.*, 294 U.S. 330 (1935); on private bonds *Norman v. B. & O. Ry.*, 294 U.S. 240 (1935); on restricted foreclosures on agricultural mortgages, *Wright v. Vinton Branch of Mountain Trust Bank*, 300 U.S. 440 (1937). Cf. with *Louisville Joint Stock Land Bank v. Radford*, 295 U.S. 555 (1935).

[11] See pages 240-241.

tions were also made to provide relief for needy and able-bodied persons seeking but unable to find work. A large public-works program was provided. Business was to be stimulated by national grants and loans to states and to local governments to encourage expenditures for needed public works. In sum, the New Deal administration loaned and spent money to "prime the pump" of the economy and, to support these activities, borrowed money on the credit of the United States. The theory was that the system would operate of its own momentum once it was started.

The large expenditure on public works and other programs meant deliberately unbalancing the national budget by spending more than was taken in by taxes. The step was not taken without misgivings, for it meant contradicting the Democratic criticism of the Hoover Administration for its failure to balance the national budget. For a brief period in 1933, President Roosevelt even tried to balance the budget.

A NEW THEORY. A theory on which to base a wide-ranging governmental program of assistance to the economy did not exist in 1932 and 1933. There had been one or two economists who suggested that governmental action could be used to keep an economy going. The socialists, of course, had a theory; but it involved transferring privately owned property into public ownership. To develop a theory that permitted both the direct governmental aid and the maintenance of private ownership of property seemed an ideological necessity. It was forthcoming from the English economist John Maynard Keynes. The core of his theory was that the output of an economy was the sum of the expenditures for consumption plus expenditures for investment. If Y equals output, and I equals investment in capital goods, and C equals consumption expenditures, the operation of an economy can be symbolized: I plus C equals Y. It makes no difference who makes the expenditures, but the amount is crucial. The maximum output of the economy is achieved when all income is spent for consumption and investment. The recipients of the income may be divided into two groups: (1) those who spend their income for consumption, or invest the remainder; and (2) those who withhold part of their income without investing or consuming it. The second group decreases the demand for output by the amount of the withholding, and the shortage of demand is transmitted back through the economy by decreased employment and failure to use productive resources. The level at which the productive resources of the economy are used will depend on the correspondence between I and C expenditures, and the productive capacity. High utilization of labor, capital, and entrepreneurial talent may be achieved by maintenance of proper adjustments, but there is no automatic achievement of such adjustments. However, failures of the private sector can be offset by government policies that increase or decrease the I and C as the situation indicates.[12]

[12] The original formulation of the theory is in John Maynard Keynes, *The General Theory of Employment, Interest and Money* (New York: Harcourt, Brace & World, Inc., 1936). The literature on the Keynesian analysis is enormous. The theory is sometimes

The theory explains the failure of the economy to use all of its resources by shortcomings in I or C. A substantial portion of C depends on the continuance of I, and the continuance of I depends on the demand for its output. Since technology constantly improves the efficiency of I (that is, decreases the amount of capital needed for the same output), a decline in C is to be expected unless countervailing forces are provided. In short, the new theory shows a built-in inability in the system to perpetuate itself at a high level of utilization and simultaneously suggests a way to that end.

The recognition that the economy could operate at less than maximum use of resources due to failures in I or C implies that the deficiency in the operation can be offset by proper or equivalent actions in one or both of those areas of activity. It implies that massive unemployment and unused resources, such as existed in the early 1930's, could be changed by massive increases in demand for labor and capital goods. The needed factor was the injection of a demand for both. Tentative actions in that direction had been taken with support for agricultural commodities, for the higher prices that the farmers received would create demand for the goods they wanted. Likewise, grants of relief to the unemployed created a demand that would consume goods and services. Governmental expenditures for capital goods such as roads, buildings, and public works would stimulate industry to produce and create employment both directly and indirectly. Such governmental expenditures should not be offset by taxes that decreased spending power in the hands of taxpayers, for then the action simply transferred money from one section of the economy to another with no net increase in demand. The great need was for creation of additional demand. Government was able to supply this by borrowing from the banking system, thereby creating new demand over and above that in the hands of consumers. Thus, the governmental debt could support both demand and bank credit. In order for the full productive resources of the economy to be used, it was necessary for the demand to be large enough to take up all the productive resources.

Two stages in theoretical formulation can be distinguished: first, the "pump priming" exemplified in the public-works program and such stabi-

---

called revolutionary, and it has been called many other less desirable things. See Dudley Dillard, *The Economics of John Maynard Keynes* (Englewood Cliffs, N.J.: Prentice-Hall, Inc., 1948). Almost any contemporary book on economics will discuss the theory. A prolific writer on the subject has been Alvin Hansen. See Harlan L. McCracken, *Keynesian Economics in the Stream of Economic Thought* (Baton Rouge, La.: University of Louisiana Press, 1961). For a recent detailed examination of the question of government spending, see F. M. Bator, *The Question of Government Spending* (New York: Harper and Row, Publishers, Inc., 1960).

The text does not describe the multiplier effect that is part of the theoretical analysis associated with fiscal policy. Briefly stated, the theory is that governmental spending or investment spending sets in motion demand in excess of the direct expenditure. The direct expenditures eventually are paid out in wages, returns on investments, and rents. These increase the total income available for expenditure by their recipients, and consequently increase demand in excess of the original direct expenditure.

lizing actions as those of the RFC and the HOLC. It became clear that this formulation was not adequate, for despite the drastic actions taken, unemployment and unused resources continued to exist.

The second stage centered on "maturity." An economy, it was thought, passed through stages over extended periods of time. Stages of growth and decline were suggested, as well as maturity. The economic habits that were successful in one stage would not necessarily be well adapted to other stages. In the growth stage heavy capital investments to increase output were desirable, but as the basic conditions moved toward maturity, less investment would be needed and larger portions of output could be devoted to consumption. Changes of this kind involved fundamental alterations in economic habits; in the movement from growth to maturity unstable conditions could be expected.

The economic discussions associated with the secular-stagnation theory led to the conclusion that monetary theory was inadequate to cope with major changes. The implied use of the budgetary surpluses and deficits, as well as taxation and management of the public debt, carried policy making into new fields. Fiscal policy is the name for policies in this area. Arguments for fiscal policy do not deny the need for monetary policies of the character previously described, but fiscal policy carries governmental intervention in economic matters to a point where the operation of the economy and the management of public finance become different facets of a common undertaking. The full implications of this development were not written into public law until 1946, but the Employment Act of that year had its forerunners in the discussions of the 1930's. The story of the Employment Act will be told later in this chapter, but it is now time to report on the events of the New Deal in the field of monetary policy.

REVISIONS AND EXPANSIONS IN MONEY-AND-CREDIT POLICY. The critical condition of the economy in 1931, 1932, and 1933 led to legislation that overhauled the monetary system. The runs on the banks had created very difficult conditions. Some state governors had even sought to close the banks in order to allow the situation to settle down. The new administration of President Roosevelt opened in March, 1933, with an executive order closing the banks for the period of March 6–9. Shortly thereafter, Congress amended the agricultural legislation with the Thomas Amendment,[13] which empowered the Treasury to issue currency with governmental securities as backing, and authorized the President to vary the weight of gold in the dollar up to 50 per cent and to fix the ratio of gold to silver. On April 5, 1933, the President ordered all persons to deliver their gold to the Federal Reserve banks, and on April 20 he placed an embargo on gold for all international transactions. In fact, no gold transactions could occur without special license from the Treasury. In June,

---

[13] 48 Stat. 31.

Congress enacted legislation voiding gold clauses in bonds and other contracts. As could be expected, these measures were challenged in the courts, but the legislation withstood the challenges.[14]

In the following year, Congress enacted the Gold Reserve Act, which denied the convertibility of paper money into gold. Through a series of actions in 1933, and culminating shortly after the passage of the Gold Reserve Act, the President fixed the price of gold at $35 per ounce, where it has remained until the present. The revaluation of gold netted the government a "profit," for its presently owned gold had been valued at $20.67 per ounce. With this legislation, the national government discarded the principle of currency convertibility within the country. The laws still require that there be a gold bullion reserve in support of currency. Legislation requires that the Federal Reserve banks maintain 25 per cent gold certificate backing for their deposits and their Federal Reserve notes outstanding. The remainder of the backing is acceptable discount paper. The country is now on a managed paper-money system with fractional reserves. One effect has been to reduce the probability of such bank runs as were common in the early 1930's, for the money is always available to meet depositor's demands. The country has, however, accepted the obligation of converting foreign-held dollars at the rate of $35 per ounce. Its participation in, and support of, the International Monetary Fund has obligated it internationally in a way that it is unwilling to accept domestically.

Reforms in the banking system were also adopted during this period. Among the objectives were greater stability for the banking system and more extensive and adequate controls for the Federal Reserve System over money and credit. Many proposals were made for reorganizing the System so as to obtain more centralization of controls and greater ability to cope with crises. The Glass-Steagall Act of 1932 [15] broadened the System's powers to make loans on the basis of government securities. The Banking Act of 1933 [16] brought most foreign transactions involving money and credit within the control of the Federal Reserve Board. Information on such dealings had to be given to the Federal Reserve Board. A Federal Deposit Insurance Corporation was created to insure bank deposits of $5,000 (now $10,000) or less. All national banks were compelled to become members and make insurance payments to the FDIC; state banks were permitted to join. In return for the insurance, the banks accepted some supervision of their policies and actions by the corporation. The result was to provide stability beyond that which existed before.[17] The act also separated commercial from investment banking.[18] Moreover, the Federal Reserve Board was given some authority to regulate the amount of bank

---

[14] *Perry v. U.S.*, 294 U.S. 330 (1935), and *Norman v. B. & O. Ry.*, 294 U.S. 240 1935).
[15] 47 Stat. 56.
[16] 48 Stat. 1.
[17] For further discussion of the FDIC, see pages 531–533.
[18] For the nature of investment banking, see page 537.

170 *Policies Affecting the Economy Generally*

loans that could be made on the security of bonds and stocks. The Banking Act of 1935, as noted earlier, reorganized the Federal Reserve Board. The new Board of Governors was given some additional powers, such as the power to approve or disapprove the selection of the chief executive officer of the Federal Reserve banks, and certain additional authorities to make its control over bank reserves more effective. As noted earlier, the board obtained a majority on the newly created Federal Open Market Committee (FOMC). The president of the Federal Reserve Bank of New York and the presidents of four other Reserve Banks also serve on that body. The presidents of the other member banks now rotate in service on the committee. Decisions are made by majority vote, and are carried into execution by staff members of the board and the New York bank.

The new legislation thus formalized a pattern of operations that had developed in previous years, with this marked difference: that the board was now in a position to outvote the banks, and moreover, the Reserve banks were bound to act in accord with the decisions reached in the FOMC. The Board of Governors and the Reserve banks share authority over discount operations, but reserve requirements are fixed by the Board of Governors. The FOMC is the major integrating mechanism in the System, and open-market operations are the principal control.[19] The new System increased the powers of the Board of Governors, and, by eliminating the representatives of the Treasury, potentially reduced the influence of that department in the decisions of the System. It must not be assumed, however, that the Treasury does not have substantial powers of a monetary character.

Congress also sought to bring within the control of the Federal Reserve System the use of credit on the stock exchanges. The 1934 legislation regulating the exchanges provided that the margin regulations should be made by the board. The extension of credit for stock purchases was limited to the banks that were members of the System, and the quantity of credit that could be extended on securities was restricted to the amount specified in the regulation issued by the Board of Governors. The purpose was to limit the amount of credit that moved into the stock markets. Hopefully, the extravagancies of the late 1920's would not occur again.[20]

This specific selective control of credit is a deviation from the usual

---

[19] A more detailed account can be found in any text on money and banking. The previously cited volumes of Weissman and Willis describe the situation in 1935. An excellent account of the internal operations of the System is found in G. L. Bach, *Federal Reserve Policy Making* (New York: Alfred A. Knopf, Inc., 1950).

[20] The proportion of the market price on which a bank could make a loan would be fixed by regulation. As the proportion approached 100 per cent, the regulation would restrict speculation; and as the proportion decreased, the same amount of credit would permit the purchase of more securities. This is a form of selective control. The lending bank has the responsibility to enforce the restriction. In 1963 there were suggestions that there was some laxity in the credit controls. These suggestions were associated with the broader investigations of the market operations that had been undertaken.

pattern of general controls. The Board of Governors has exercised other selective controls from time to time. Thus, it exercised temporary control over installment selling and real-estate transactions during World War II and the Korean incident. In general, it has opposed permanent use of such policies, although they would seem to be useful adjuncts of its general controls.[21]

Although selective credit controls have been sparingly used through the Federal Reserve System, they have been present in the United States through the use of special credit facilities. It has been pointed out that special banks and credit facilities were provided for agriculture prior to the Depression; these have been increased and expanded. Special credit facilities for other segments of the economy were created in the 1930's, and some of them still exist. The expansion of these facilities was another development in policy during the strains of the Depression period. They make a contribution to the economy, but their existence and independence from the controls of the Federal Reserve System create possibilities that they may operate with conflicting policies unless integration is secured in some manner.

The credit agencies that exist independently of the Federal Reserve System have been created for many purposes, but the outstanding purpose of the rapid expansion of these agencies was (1) to counteract the Depression. The other purposes that may be discerned are (2) "to provide needed credit services which are held to be unavailable, for one reason or another, through the private financial system"; (3) to meet emergencies such as war conditions or natural calamities; and (4) "to give preferential treatment to some group or industry"—for example, loans to veterans or loans to municipalities for low-rent housing.[22] Multiple purposes may be found in most of the agencies, and their creation and maintenance can be traced to the Depression. There were a few agencies before 1932, but most of these date from that year or later. In the case of the Veterans Administration, a new service was provided to a select group—a very large group after World War II. In a study for the Commission on Money and Credit, fifty-one lending programs are described, and these are divided into four classes. The total loans outstanding at the end of selected years are summarized in the following table:

---

[21] Arthur Smithies, "Uses of Selective Controls," in *United States Monetary Policy* (New York: The American Assembly, 1958). The other essays in this volume are useful for recent monetary history and general discussion.

[22] R. J. Saulnier, H. G. Halcrow, and Neil H. Jacoby, *Federal Lending and Loan Insurance* (Princeton, N.J.: Princeton University Press, 1958), pp. 23–25. Hereafter cited Saulnier, *et al.* This volume is a comprehensive summary of government and governmentally sponsored lending agencies. It is replete with tables and details on the multitude of agencies. Its data does not go beyond 1954. The study, *Federal Credit Programs* (Englewood Cliffs, N.J.: Prentice-Hall, Inc., 1963), prepared for the Commission on Money and Credit, usually brings the data to 1958. This volume is a collection of research studies by several authors.

SUMMARY OF LOANS OUTSTANDING*
(ALL FIFTY-ONE PROGRAMS AT YEAR'S END)

Type of Program	1929	1939	1949	1958
		(thousands of dollars)		
Agricultural loans	$1,947,745	4,779,776	6,080,540	12,244,210
Business loans	129,073	957,451	1,483,643	1,469,321
Housing loans		5,177,521	20,509,087	67,059,777
Miscellaneous	52,130	347,745	179,982	431,546
Total	2,128,948	11,262,493	28,253,252	81,204,854
Subtractions to eliminate double counting				
Agricultural loans		388,254	619,420	1,196,861
Housing loans		192,662	926,476	3,900,953
Total subtractions		580,916	1,545,896	5,097,814
Net total	2,128,948	10,681,577	26,707,356	76,107,040

* From Commission on Money and Credit, *Federal Credit Programs* (Englewood Cliffs, N.J.: Prentice-Hall, Inc., 1963), p. 3.

There is no single pattern of government participation in these special-credit institutions. In some cases, government has operated the institutions and made loans itself—as with the Reconstruction Finance Corporation, which made business loans, and the Home Owners Loan Corporation, which made loans to homeowners. In some cases it loans money directly to privately operated institutions, as in the case of the loans to rural electrification cooperatives. In some instances it has subscribed to the capital of lending institutions. Sometimes when this is done, an effort is made over a period of time to retire the government capital and leave the institutions "mutualized"—that is, under the ownership of the borrowers. Sometimes it has guaranteed the bonds of the credit institutions, thus providing for them a better standing in the securities markets. In some cases it has established a system of insurance for private credit, as in the Federal Housing Administration (FHA). For housing, the government has set up a system paralleling in many respects the one for commercial banking. Individual deposits in local savings-and-loan associations are insured through a government-sponsored agency, the Savings and Loan Insurance Corporation. These associations and various other types of loan organizations are eligible for membership in the Federal Home Loan Bank System. This system is organized similarly to the Federal Reserve System. There is a Home Loan Bank Board appointed by the President with the consent of the Senate. There are eleven Federal Home Loan banks operating in eleven regions. The banks and the system serve as a credit reservoir for the nation's home-loan institutions, issuing securities on the basis of the combined assets. They exercise controls over the home-loan institutions similar to those exercised by the Federal Reserve Board, the Comptroller of the Currency, and the FDIC over national banks.

Whatever the detailed arrangements, the credit institutions are organized under national law and are subjected to some amount of public control. They represent an adaptation of national credit policy to particular situations, and bring a considerable amount of selective promotion and controls over credit. Moreover, the expenditure program of the government may be involved in their operations. In the decade of the 1930's, the government provided substantial funds to these institutions; as a result, a budget imbalance was created, in the sense that its tax intake was not as large as the expenditure outflow. The difference between the intake and the outgo was a contribution to the demand for goods.[23]

THE NATIONAL BUDGET. The administrative budget accompanies the President's annual budget message, and it provides a plan of expenditures for the next fiscal year. The fiscal year ends on June 30, so that the message in January of each year is for the period beginning on the next July 1. The current fiscal year is then half-finished, and the message gives a report on the fiscal year that was completed on June 30. This administrative budget enables the Congress to control appropriations and to review the activities of the various agencies. The President's plans are open to approval or disapproval. The budget will estimate whether the income of the government from taxes will be adequate to pay for the planned expenditures. If the income is not large enough to meet the planned outgo, then cuts will have to be made in expenditures, or other sources of income must be found. If the income and outgo are in balance, then the budget may be thought of as neutral in its impact on the economy; that is, the payments of taxes that reduce incomes from one part of the population are paid out as appropriations to other parts of the population, with the result that the total money-and-credit situation is not altered.

If the income from taxes is less than the amount spent by the government, then it must borrow the needed amounts. If the borrowing is from the general public, the government competes with other borrowers. The net result may be the same as if the amounts had been raised by taxes. However, the government may borrow from the Reserve banks by exchanging its bills or other evidences of indebtedness for a deposit in the Reserve bank without an equivalent reduction in the incomes of individuals. The deposit may then be spent by the government, with the effect of increasing the total amount of money and credit and thereby increasing total demand. On the other hand, if the income from taxes exceeds the expenditures by government, the opposite may take place. The government simply reduces its debt to the banks, thereby decreasing the total demand for goods in the marketplace. A surplus in governmental tax income becomes a depressing influence. The government, it is evident, can increase or de-

[23] For more detailed discussion of credit and insurance mechanisms, see pages 603–606.

crease the total demand in the market and thereby influence the level of economic activity. This conclusion suggests that government may, through the management of its taxes and expenditures, be an extremely important element in the economy.

It will be noted that the preceding paragraph moved from the administrative budget to the impact on the economy. That progression is valid if all of the financial transactions of the government are included in the administrative budget. That this is not the case is apparent in the fact that the administrative budget does not include income and outgo connected with the social-insurance arrangements—for example, the OASDI, unemployment compensation, the railroad and other retirement systems, and some government corporations. The incomes to these funds or agencies are in separate accounts, and the outgo from these funds in any year may not equal the income. Any excess of income over outgo is loaned to the Treasury at fixed rates of interest. If the outgo exceeds income, the amount is borrowed from the Treasury. The financial operations of these agencies and funds must be counted into the total governmental operations to determine the economic impact of governmental finance. Thus, it is possible for the administrative budget to be in deficit and the cash budget of the government to show a surplus. The cash budget is a better economic indicator than the administrative budget, yet it is not a precise measure of governmental expenditures.

Since the end of the decade of the 1930's, the student of the national economy who wishes to evaluate the role of government must keep abreast of at least four aspects of activity: the Federal Reserve Board of Governors' monetary policies, the activities of the governmentally owned or sponsored lending agencies in agriculture, business, and housing; the condition of the cash budget; and the Treasury's management of the public debt.

POST-DEPRESSION DEVELOPMENTS

WAR AND ITS AFTERMATH. There was a considerable recovery of economic activity between 1933 and 1937. In the latter year, the Board of Governors resumed its traditional policy of accommodating business and industry, and indeed became so alarmed at the expansion of credit that it set in motion the restraining influences of raised reserve requirements.[24] At the same time, the other lending agencies began to contract their activities and to receive repayments on earlier loans. Whether as a result of these or other factors, there was a rapid decline in total economic activity. Before the nation had recovered fully from the low points of the Depression of 1933, a new recession of serious proportions set in. The

---

[24] E. A. Goldenweiser, "Federal Reserve Objectives and Policies: Retrospect and Prospect," *American Economic Review*, **XXXVII** (June 1947), pp. 320, 326.

taxes imposed by the social-security legislation of 1935 began to flow into the Treasury and on into the OASI and Unemployment Compensation funds, but the net flow of governmental funds outward into the market did not exceed the counterflow into the government. Among other features of decline, unemployment was again worsening. Inventories, too, were increasing beyond normal levels. Public expenditures, in order to take up some of the unused resources, were markedly increased the following year.[25]

The coming of World War II in 1939 brought enormous changes in the American economy. The European nations wanted the materials that could be produced here. The transfer of gold resulting from their purchases stimulated economic activity. Most important, the national government began intensive preparations for its own defense. The unemployed declined in numbers as the expansion got underway, and compulsory military service absorbed large numbers of young people. As full utilization of resources was achieved, inflationary pressures of great magnitude were created. Nevertheless, monetary policy could not be marshalled against inflation, because once again the Federal Reserve System undertook the support of the government in war-financing needs.

As early as 1937 the Board of Governors had introduced a "flexible portfolio policy," which involved the purchase of more long-term governmental securities and a reduction in the purchases of short-term securities. The new policy was " (1) to exert an influence toward orderly conditions in the money market, and (2) to facilitate the orderly adjustment of member banks to the increased reserve requirements effective May 1, 1937." [26] The immediate effect was to stop the decline in the prices of long-term governmental securities. The new policy involved no great activity prior to the outbreak of the war in Europe in 1939, which precipitated a decline in the price of governmental securities. The Open Market Committee decided to support the market for bonds by purchases, and it also announced that it stood ready to lend on governmental securities at par value at the going discount rate. The assurance was not limited to Federal Reserve member banks, but was extended to all banks, for obviously the purpose was to steady the market and to safeguard the portfolios of bonds held in the banks. Similar supporting actions were required in 1940 with the fall of the Low Countries, and again in 1941 following the attack on Pearl Harbor.

With the attack on Pearl Harbor, the United States became directly involved in the war. The Lend-Lease Act of March, 1941, had authorized

[25] For a contemporary discussion, see Alvin H. Hansen, *Full Recovery or Stagnation?* (New York: W. W. Norton & Company, Inc., 1938), especially Chapters 8, 9, 16, 17; and Arthur E. Burns and D. S. Watson, *Government Spending and Economic Expansion* (Washington, D.C.: American Council on Public Affairs, 1940). The latter volume provides an excellent account of the theories and policies of the period beginning in 1914.

[26] Lester V. Chandler, "Federal Reserve Policy and the Federal Debt," *American Economic Review*, **XXXIX** (March 1949), pp. 405, 406.

the President to provide extensive assistance to countries that were necessary for the defense of the United States. Now the United States was an ally and completely involved. Its own needs and those of its allies called for an all-out productive effort. The Board of Governors made the following statement on December 8, 1941:

> The existing supply of funds and of bank reserves is fully adequate to meet all present and prospective needs of the Government and of private activity. The Federal Reserve System has powers to add to these resources to whatever extent may be required in the future. The System is prepared to use its powers to assure that an ample supply of funds is available at all times for financing the war effort and to exert its influence toward maintaining conditions in the United States Government security market that are satisfactory from the standpoint of the Government's requirements.

As Professor Chandler remarks, "Thanks to a highly liberal Federal Reserve policy, the Treasury could get from the Reserve Banks or from commercial banks any funds that it needed beyond those secured by taxation and borrowing from non-bank sources. Of the $230 billion increase of the federal debt from June, 1940 to December, 1945, nearly $75 billion was taken by commercial banks and $22 billion by the Reserve banks." [27]

An "orderly market for government securities" was achieved through two main techniques: the maintenance of a low discount rate, and open-market operations. It was the System's policy to maintain existing interest rates on government securities. One consequence of that policy was the weakening of its control of money-and-credit conditions, for the governmental debt was "monetized," in the sense that it was exchangeable for money or its equivalent. The low interest cost to the government permeated the entire market, and inflation was restrained only by the development of counteracting influences. There were the persistent drives to encourage savings through purchases of government securities, including the Series E bonds; the use of price controls to hold down prices; the use of rationing to decrease demand for goods; the limitation of purchase of materials in short supply; the increase of taxes and the introduction of the withholding of income taxes. Moral suasion for cooperation with the war effort by reducing personal expenditures was exerted. The Board of Governors issued regulations restricting lending for housing and real estate, limiting consumer installment buying, and encouraging voluntary credit control. Such selective controls were acceptable for the emergency. Considerable success was achieved in these efforts, but the size of the war effort was enormous by any previous standards of the operation of the economy. The employable among the unemployed found jobs. Women were encouraged

---

[27] Lester V. Chandler, "Federal Reserve Policy and the Federal Debt," *American Economic Review*, **XXXIX**, pp. 405, 408. The quote from the Board of Governors is in Professor Chandler's article. It may also be found in the 1941 *Annual Report* of the board at p. 1.

to leave their households to aid in the effort. Full employment was achieved, labor shortages occurred, and controls were necessary to restrict competition for labor.

At the end of the war, it was apparent that if the Federal Reserve System was to regain its ability to control monetary policy, it would be necessary to obtain freedom from the financial needs of the Treasury. The Treasury was clearly interested in holding down the costs of the huge debt, but that meant low interest rates. These, in turn, meant inflationary conditions in the money markets, unless devices were developed to prevent the use of the debt as reserves in the banking system.

There were two conflicting views of the future. On the one side were those who feared the return of the depressed conditions of the prewar period. On the other were those standing with the System—who viewed the pent-up demands and large supplies of savings as the model condition for a highly inflationary situation. A decision between these two views was not made until "full accord" came between the Treasury and the Federal Reserve Board (March 1951). The Board and the Treasury had reached an agreement in 1947 under which the former withdrew support from some short-term bills. A further step to tighten money and credit was taken in 1948, when the discount rate was increased. Steps also were taken to reduce the reserves available to the banks, and then reserve requirements were increased. These moves to tighten the credit situation were halted with the 1949 recession, the trough of the first post–World War II depression. The board reversed its policy to counter the downswing.

The Korean Crisis in 1950 caused the government to increase expenditures, to reinstitute controls over prices, wages, and certain strategic materials, and to impose higher taxes. Still the upward pressures on prices caused the Reserve System to press for more extensive controls. Under the "full accord" finally reached in 1951, the System no longer was obligated to support the prices of governmental securities. However, the System agreed to smooth the transition to the free market in governmental securities, while at the same time steadily moving toward freeing itself from the shackles of price support.[28]

THE EMPLOYMENT ACT. As World War II neared its end in 1944, some members of Congress began to be concerned with the postwar

---

[28] The transition to the new situation was not accomplished without considerable notoriety and political struggle. Marriner Eccles, who had been associated with the Board of Governors of the Reserve System since its reorganization under the 1935 legislation, was not reappointed as chairman by Mr. Truman in 1948. Mr. Truman appointed Thomas B. McCabe to a vacancy on the board and to the chairmanship. Eccles had been identified with the tight-money policy, and the majority of the board was alleged to be in support of Eccles' views. In 1951 the Treasury, the board, and the President had a meeting on the issues. The President and the board were in disagreemnt as to what policies the board should follow. After several days of meetings, the "full accord" was negotiated in early March. Soon thereafter, McCabe resigned, and William McC. Martin, Jr., an Assistant Secretary of the Treasury, replaced him. Martin has been chairman to the present (1964).

economic situation. There were lingering doubts as to the ability of the economy to avert, of its own force, the staggering amounts of unemployment that had prevailed throughout the 1930's. It was conceded that there now existed a number of institutional brakes on an excessive downswing. The Unemployment Compensation System and other insurance schemes postponed demands and large savings from the war period, and the prospect of decreases in taxes gave further hope for sustained demand. Nonetheless, some Congressmen demanded additional assurances. In order to meet this demand, the Employment Act of 1946 was passed.[29] This Act declares a policy for the many agencies concerned with the operation of the economy. Section 2 of the Employment Act opens:

> The Congress hereby declares that it is the continuing policy and responsibility of the Federal Government to use all practicable means consistent with its needs and obligations and other essential considerations of national policy with the assistance and cooperation of industry, agriculture, labor and State and local governments, to coordinate and utilize all its plans, functions, and resources for the purpose of creating and maintaining, in a manner calculated to foster and promote free competitive enterprise and the general welfare, conditions under which there will be afforded useful employment opportunities, including self-employment, for those able, willing, and seeking to work, and to promote maximum employment, production, and purchasing power.

This complicated sentence is explained in great detail in the story that Stephen Bailey has told about the history of the act. For one thing, the statement is considerably at variance with the form in which it appeared in the bill introduced by Senator Murray (Democrat, Montana) in 1945. In its original version it called for "full employment," but the enacted version substitutes "maximum employment" as the objective. Niceties of language aside, the political parties, in their campaigns in 1940 and 1944, assured the nation that large-scale unemployment and depressions were events of the past, and that in the future the national government would take the responsibility of keeping able-bodied and willing persons at work. The monetary and fiscal programs now had a goal for their activities, and a measure of their success. The quantity of unemployment was the critical test. It is conceded that completely full employment is unattainable. Some unemployment will result from seasonal, technological, and sectional factors, and because of mobility and other factors affecting individual laborers.

In addition to other reasons for its passage, the act was a response to the concern that the full employment achieved in war should exist also in peace. The heroes of World War II ought not to return to breadlines and the WPA.

The new measure did not state specific policy approaches to accomplish

---

[29] The detailed story of its enactment is told in Stephen K. Bailey, *Congress Makes a Law: The Story Behind the Employment Act of 1946* (New York: Columbia University Press, 1950).

the legislative declaration of purpose. It did create machinery for policy study. A Council of Economic Advisers was to be appointed by the President to advise him. The council was to cooperate with the President in producing for Congress and the nation an annual Economic Report.[30] The Congress was to have a Joint Economic Committee to examine the Report of the President and to make comments on the policy recommendations. Coordination of private and governmental efforts toward a common goal was the key concept, and the means to the goal were to be "practicable." The council, it is clear, would have the prestige and the status that the President wished to give to it. The Bureau of the Budget was the central clearing house on the governmental budget, but the council conceivably could become the central clearing agency on all policies in their economic bearing.

The Presidents have all had a council. President Truman appointed his advisers promptly—two academic economists and one from the mixed world of government and business. Eisenhower appointed one member and seemed reluctant to appoint the other two, but he finally did. Again the academic world provided advisers, but with a distinctly different policy slant than that of Truman's advisers. President Kennedy followed the pattern of his predecessors, and to this time President Johnson has retained the same advisers. Their role has varied with their temperaments and with the wishes of the President. Controversies have developed within the council, and resignations are not infrequent. The council has maintained a small but competent staff, and has made use of the resources of the other administrative agencies.

The Congress has developed a staff for its own Joint Economic Committee. It has published a number of studies and has held hearings on a wide variety of problems. The quality of the staff work and the devotion of a number of the committee members have made the proceedings of this committee an important feature of policy making on general economic conditions.

The annual reports of the President go into the Congress early in each session, and they furnish elaborate analyses of the contemporary economic scene. Implications are drawn for policy decisions. The reports, in turn, are subjected to serious examination by the Joint Economic Committee and its staff. The two studies provide leads to governmental policies in a wide-ranging number of activities. Since the act envisages cooperation between private and governmental actions, business, labor, and agriculture are interested in the reports and in presenting their views to the committee in the hearings, which have become major annual events. The President obviously should relate his annual budget message to this eco-

---

[30] On the position of the Council, see Corinne Silverman, *The President's Economic Advisers* (University, Ala.: University of Alabama Press, 1959), reprinted in Edwin A. Bock and Alan K. Campbell, *Case Studies in American Government* (Englewood Cliffs, N.J.: Prentice-Hall, Inc., 1962), pp. 301–323.

nomic report, and indeed, occasionally a President combines the two messages into a single document.

The discussions of economic policy that grow out of these annual events have become important contributions to public policy. The conflicting views emerge in the discussions of whether to expand or contract governmental expenditures, to increase or decrease taxes, and on the importance of current wage agreements, inventory and investment decisions, and welfare programs. Business associations, labor organizations, members of the press concerned with business activity, the Committee for Economic Development, and many others participate in the elaborate dialogue on the implications of economic conditions for public policy. Rarely is the view expressed that such matters are none of the government's business. The interrelations between governmental and private economic decisions are now recognized as key phenomena in the level of total operations.

THE CONTEMPORARY SITUATION. Governmental concern with the level of economic activity has continued to be a matter of serious concern. There have been four detectable business cycles in the period since the war ended. The years immediately after the war were marked, as has been noted, by a continuously high level of activity, were followed in 1948–1949 by a trough and then by a pick-up which, with the advent of the Korean War, became an inflationary surge. Restrictive controls were imposed, subsequently government purchasing for military needs was reduced, and the trough of a second cycle came in 1953–1954. There was an easing of credit controls, a reduction of taxes in 1954, and the end of the trough. The upswing led into the boom of 1955–1957, and a downswing led to the third trough (1957–1958). Relaxed controls led again to a pick-up in economic activity that reached its peak in 1960. The trough of the fourth cycle lasted until 1961, and then the recovery got underway again. This has continued into 1964, the longest continued high level of activity in recent history. The Board of Governors in these years has acted according to the model explained earlier in this chapter. It has restrained credit in boom periods and eased credit in slack periods.

Beginning with the administration of President Eisenhower in 1953, there has been a marked change in policy toward the national debt. Steps have been taken to increase the proportion of the national debt in long-term securities. Since long-term securities bear higher rates of interest, this has meant a rise in interest costs. Usually these steps have been taken on the downswing of the cycle, so as to take advantage of lower interest rates. This policy coincided with the "hard money" policy that was to be expected with the accord of 1951. A heavy proportion of the debt has still been kept in short-term securities, for the conversion to long-term securities has not exceeded the amount of the deficits in the conventional and cash budgets.[31]

---

[31] See the discussion in B. Gross and W. Lumer, *The Hard Money Crusade* (Washington, D.C.: Public Affairs Institute, 1954). See also the discussions in *Staff Report on Employ-*

It seems doubtful that the policy on the debt has consistently followed the principles that the Keynesian formulation implies. The monetary and credit system is highly complex, with different consequences in different sectors of the economy. The reluctance of the Board of Governors to use selective controls restricts their effectiveness.[32]

The policies followed by the non-Reserve lending agencies, especially those concerned with housing, have tended to coincide with those of the monetary authorities, so that policy in one sector has reinforced policy in the other.[33] The credit agencies in housing have fostered low interest rates on mortgages at low points in the business cycles, and hence their roles have tended to be counter-cyclical. The low interest rates do not affect large business decisions greatly, but the state and local governments are apparently responsive.

The period since 1951 has been disturbing in two respects. There has been a persistent core of unemployed persons, with some sections of the country affected more than others by ongoing economic changes. The second phenomenon has been a low rate of growth in the economy as a whole. Again some sectors have displayed enormous increases in per-capita output, but the overall rate has been below the expected annual increase of approximately 3.5 per cent. Both problems have had consequences in public policy. The Congress has enacted, at the instigation of the President, programs for area redevelopment and retraining of workers. These programs are financed by direct grants from the Federal Treasury, and it is expected that workers in areas that have lost a source of economic strength (for example, the coal-mining regions), will develop other means of self-support. It is hoped, also, that workers whose skills are outmoded by technological improvements will be trained for new jobs.

The low rate of growth has been a puzzling phenomenon. Efforts have been made to encourage industry to improve its productive efficiency. Fiscal policy has allowed more rapid depreciation of equipment, with the expectation that firms would put more capital in newer machinery. These expenditures, presumably, would also expand the demand for goods.

The slowdown in the rate of growth, however, has overtones of the "maturity" thesis of the 1930's. In order to counteract the slowdown, the Kennedy Administration proposed in 1963 a cut in taxes in order to leave more resources in the hands of investors and consumers, whether corporate

---

ment, Growth, and Price Levels, prepared for consideration by the Joint Economic Committee (Washington, D.C.: Superintendent of Documents, 1959), especially Chapters 8, 9. For an interesting discussion of a conservative view of this period, see E. L. Dale, Jr., *Conservatives in Power, A Study in Frustration* (New York: Doubleday & Company, Inc., 1960).

[32] See Arthur Smithies, "Uses of Selective Controls," in *United States Monetary Policy* (New York: The American Assembly, 1958), and *Staff Report* cited in footnote 31 of this chapter.

[33] See Saulnier, et al., *Federal Lending and Loan Insurance* (Princeton, N.J.: Princeton University Press, 1958), p. 115; *Federal Credit Programs* (Englewood Cliffs, N.J.: Prentice-Hall, Inc., 1963), p. 272; and *Staff Report, op. cit.,* p. 393.

or individual. The same administration asked the Congress for legislation permitting the President to alter the rate of income taxation as a fiscal device to offset cyclical influences. The Congress gave little attention to the latter request, but President Kennedy and his successor President Johnson pressed hard for a significant reduction in both the corporate and the individual income-tax burden. The theory behind the request was that the low level of growth results from the absence of demand, and that the absence of demand, in turn, is traceable to the heavy cut that taxes take from personal and corporate incomes. The 88th Congress did not enact the reduction in taxes until President Johnson promised a cut in expenditures. (Since the Presidential demand was posited on a shortage in demand, it would be a contradiction to make an equivalent reduction in governmental expenditures. Tax policy and expenditures would have opposite effects on demand.) Congress approved the presidential proposal in February 1964; so the government has accepted the central position in the management of the level of economic activity, for the needs of the economy will now determine governmental policy.

THE MEANS OF INTEGRATION. The office of the President integrates the vast range of governmental activities into the order it possesses, but the Congress continues to wield the indispensable legislative authority for new programs or changes in existing programs. The President is elected in a national contest in which the urban and industrial sectors of the nation exert their main influence. The Congress is elected in constituencies within the separate states, and reflects their infinite varieties. The two national parties unify the latent cleavages with varying degrees of success, but division within both parties lies just below the surface unity in name, be it Democrat or Republican.

The President's office has two integrating devices: the administrative budget of expenditures and taxes, and the economic report with its policy implications. In the former, the office can and does compel the executive agencies to fit their proposals into the President's program, with the qualification that the independent boards and commissions (and occasionally a subdivision of an executive agency) may claim that their allegiance is to Congress. The expenses of the Federal Reserve Board of Governors are paid from the earnings of the Reserve banks; the board therefore escapes the disciplinary bond of the budget. The statutory obligations of the social-security funds, interest on the debt, pensions for veterans and retired employees, and appropriation commitments from previous years are also beyond budget discipline. Nonetheless, there is considerable flexibility in the annual budget request. The Bureau of the Budget, supervising the making of the administrative budget, has existed since 1921, and its importance as an aid to the President is well understood.

The second tool was made available to the President in the Employment Act of 1946, and consists in the previously described Council of Economic Advisers. The President may—and some presidents do—use this agency as a major economic policy integrator. The council receives policy proposals and examines them for their bearing on economic growth and the level of employment. The influence of the council's findings is dependent upon the President's willingness to support them.

The Congress has not developed effective integration within itself. Each house has a single Appropriations Committee, but the subcommittees have the dominant influence. Each house also has a single committee to consider revenue-producing proposals—called Ways and Means in the House of Representatives and Finance in the Senate. In response to the Employment Act of 1946, the Joint Committee was created to consider the President's Economic Report and to make studies of its own. This committee does not have authority to report legislation.

If legislation is needed for growth or employment, the matter is considered in the standing committees of the two houses having jurisdiction of the subject matter. If appropriations are needed, the Appropriations Committee must have its turn to examine the proposal after the subject-matter committees and the houses have passed the authorizing legislation. The decentralized character of Congress' operations has not been altered, despite the need for a more integrated policy-making process.[34]

There is, in addition, a lack of integration on money and fiscal policy within the Executive Branch. The Board of Governors and the Federal Home Loan Bank Board are regarded as independent agencies, though the responsiveness of each to the trend in policy of the administration in power is great. The Board of Governors itself lacks complete formal authority within the Reserve System. The Comptroller of the Currency, who supervises the national banks (and hence may effect their lending policies), is a semi-independent officer within the Treasury Department. Other agencies operate within circles of influence which condition their responsiveness to the President.

The absence of unity in the political system inevitably results in temporary adjustments and compromises in policy. These often seem much less firmly based than they are likely to be. The path to a compromise is initially strewn with obstacles, but once the compromise has been achieved, the route is likely to remain clear for future travel.

[34] For a brief review of some of the efforts to obtain more unity in congressional consideration of fiscal measures, see George B. Galloway, *Congressional Reorganization Revisited* (College Park, Md.: University of Maryland, 1956).

Chapter 10. The Sherman Act and Its Interpretation

WE HAVE ALREADY described the place of antitrust policy in the total pattern of American economic legislation.[1] The purpose is the maintenance of a competitive economy; stated differently, antitrust aims toward an economy in which the market is the effective instrument of social control. It restricts freedom of contract and combination, and freedom to monopolize; but it seeks to preserve the freedom of men to enter enterprise and to compete without unreasonable restraint from persons in positions of power. Its aims, in sum, are the freedom of men and the control of the economy by automatic, impersonal forces.

The basic antitrust act is the Sherman Act (the Antitrust Act) of 1890. Its meaning and significance will be discussed in this chapter. The succeeding chapter will analyze other antitrust legislation; and a third chapter will examine, against the background of knowledge of antitrust law and history, the problem of public policy toward modern industry.

THE MEANING OF WORDS

For clarification of the several words and phrases, the key provisions of the Sherman Act (the Antitrust Act) of 1890 are quoted in a graphic presentation:

Section 1

>*Every* contract,
>>combination in the form of trust or otherwise,
>>or conspiracy
>>>*in restraint of trade*
>>>>among the several states,
>>>>or with foreign nations,
>>>>>is hereby declared illegal. . . .

Section 2

>*Every* person who shall monopolize,
>>or attempt to monopolize,
>>or combine or conspire with any other person or persons to monopolize,

[1] See pages 94–95.

> *any part* of the trade or commerce
> among the several states,
> or with foreign nations,
> *shall be guilty of a misdemeanor....*

On their face these words and phrases appear comprehensive and definite. The "every" in both sentences is unqualified. "Contract, combination . . . or conspiracy" looks like a catch-all. To do or to conspire to do are both included. Likewise, attempts individually, or in combination or conspiracy with others, to monopolize are condemned equally with monopoly. And "any part" further broadens the prohibition. "Restraint of trade" seems to mean restrictions on, or impediments to, free trade.

But for several reasons these appearances are deceptive. First, some of these phrases had historic common law meanings which were more limited than dictionary definitions. Some judges thought that the words of a criminal statute should be given their strict and limited legal meanings; others believed that the words should be interpreted more broadly in the light of their popular meanings. Such differences have led to divisions on the Court—for example, in the Northern Securities Company case, in which the Court split 5 to 4 on the issue of whether the activities attacked by the government were really violations of the act.[2] Second, judges found the words too comprehensive, and tried to limit them so as to make them reasonable in their sight. Justice Holmes said that the act must be construed as though the question was whether two small exporting grocers should be sent to jail (that is, it must be applied the same for large and small traders); hence, it could not apply to every agreement or joint action that cut off previous competition. Some other judges thought the act was obviously directed at those who were powerful enough to restrict competition, and, in effect, sought to apply it only to "substantial" restraints of trade. Judge Taft, a circuit-court judge, thought, on the other hand, that to consider "how much restraint of competition is in the public interest" would be to "set sail on a sea of doubt." He would restrict the scope of the law on contracts in restraint of trade to those things which were null and void under the common law. To him, this meant determining whether the restraint was ancillary to a main and lawful purpose (that is, an agreement not to engage henceforth in a business in order to obtain a good price on sale of property), or whether its sole object was to limit competition.[3] Justice Holmes also would restrict the scope of the act—not, as some desired, by holding it applicable only to those gaining power to control competition, but by legalistic limitation of the words "contract . . . in restraint of trade" and "combination."[4] Chief Justice White thought the act was so comprehensive that to

---

[2] *Northern Securities Co. v. U.S.*, 193 U.S. 197 (1904).
[3] *U.S. v. Addyston Pipe and Steel Co.*, 85 F. 271 (1898); William Howard Taft, *The Supreme Court and the Sherman Act* (New York: Harper and Row, Publishers, Inc., 1914).
[4] *Northern Securities Co. v. U.S.*, 193 U.S. 197 (1904).

interpret it literally as extending to "every" restraint of trade would be "tantamount to an assertion that the act of Congress is itself unreasonable." [5] Third, judges differed in their views on intent and effect. Some viewed the act as just another criminal law designed to punish "bad" men or prevent them from doing evil things, and hence thought that persons should not be held guilty unless they had evil intent or purpose or had taken overt acts which injured competitors. Others viewed the act as a charter for a competitive economy, and were interested in the effects of men's acts in impairing the strength of competitors or in creating power to control the whole or a part of the market. These judges have thought that the existence of power, even though not immediately exercised in an evil way, could constitute a violation of the act.

As a result, there was much uncertainty in the beginning over the meaning of the two sentences. Forty-three years after the passage of the act, Chief Justice Hughes said that it had "a generality and adaptability comparable to that found to be desirable in constitutional provisions." [6] The Chief Justice regarded this "generality and adaptability" as an advantage, but many commentators have thought that uncertainties in the law have contributed to ineffectiveness in its enforcement.

In spite of the act's generality, some statements can be made initially about its effects:

1. Section 2 prohibits monopolizing. It does not prohibit every monopoly, for the word "monopolize" in the act is a verb. A person must *do* something, alone or with others, to be guilty of violation of the act. Section 2 prohibits such *action* as leads to *realized monopoly*—that is, *dominance* of a market by a single firm or a combination or conspiracy of separate firms. When monopoly is realized, dominance and intent (deliberateness or purpose) to monopolize are both necessary to create a violation, but the intent may be *inferred from a course of action* which produced the monopoly.

2. Section 2 also prohibits attempts to monopolize. In this case, achievement of monopoly is not necessary, but there must be proof of specific or subjective intent (not implied from a course of action).

3. Section 1 is a much broader provision. It deals with contracts, combinations, and conspiracies without respect to whether they create market dominance. It is directed against restraints upon competition. Its prohibition extends to such things as price-fixing (either directly or by controlling production), division of the market among parties participating in an agreement, and agreements and practices which exclude outsiders from a market.[7]

The act had an impact beyond that of the common law. The common

[5] *U.S. v. Trans-Missouri Freight Association*, 166 U.S. 290, 344 (1897).
[6] *Appalachian Coals, Inc. v. U.S.*, 288 U.S. 344, 360 (1933).
[7] See *Report of the Attorney General's National Committee to Study the Antitrust Laws* (Washington, D.C.: Superintendent of Documents, 1955), especially pp. 61, 389.

law had only made certain types of acts null and void—that is, unenforceable in the courts. The Sherman Act made acts illegal, and provided criminal penalties and civil remedies. Moreover, the Sherman Act was framed to meet, and was due to be applied to, situations very different from those covered by common law decisions.

THE RULE OF REASON

In 1897, in the second case to reach the Supreme Court under the Sherman Act, the Court split 5 to 4 on whether the act applied only to "unreasonable" restraints of trade. The majority held that it applied to all restraints, but Justice White argued otherwise for four dissenters, who believed that the combination to fix railroad rates, which was attacked in the case, was a reasonable response by railroad operators to prevailing competitive conditions.[8] In 1911, in the Standard Oil case, the Supreme Court, speaking through White (now Chief Justice), announced the rule of reason as the interpretation of the Sherman Act—with only Justice Harlan dissenting.[9]

The reactions to the decision varied. If big business was relieved, some parts of the public were alarmed. Harlan said it was judicial legislation.[10] Theodore Roosevelt, who, while President, had recommended legislation to distinguish between good and bad combinations, admitted that it was judicial legislation, but thought that since Congress had not acted to clarify the act, the Court had "had to" legislate.[11] One commentator has said: "the courts never did and never would enforce a prohibition of all direct and substantial restraints of interstate commerce. The recognition that a standard of reason shall be applied in the absence of any standard in the statute, tended to clarify the judicial process in subsequent cases. . . ."[12] But even if it clarified the nature of the judicial process, did it clarify the law? Taft argued in 1914 that the Court could find in the common law the guides for determining what was reasonable,[13] and years later the Supreme Court said the act was aimed only at restraints "comparable to those deemed illegal at common law."[14] But it has been noted that the situations dealt with under the common law were so different from those confronted in the modern economy that the precedents and guides of the common law are of little value.[15] And it was asserted in 1912 that the test of reasonable-

---

[8] *U.S. v. Trans-Missouri Freight Ass'n*, 166 U.S. 290.
[9] *Standard Oil Co. of New Jersey v. U.S.*, 221 U.S. 1.
[10] *Ibid.*, 90, 99, 104.
[11] *Outlook*, **XCIX**, p. 653 (November 1911).
[12] James Angell McLaughlin (ed.), *Cases on the Federal Antitrust Laws of the United States* (Cambridge, Mass.: published by editor, 1933), p. 215.
[13] William Howard Taft, *The Supreme Court and the Sherman Act* (New York: Harper and Row, Publishers, Inc., 1914).
[14] *Apex Hosiery Co. v. Leader*, 310 U.S. 469 (1940).
[15] Gerard C. Henderson, *The Federal Trade Commission: A Study in Administrative Law and Procedure* (New Haven, Conn.: Yale University Press, 1925), p. 6.

ness in the Court would not be what was applied under the common law, but what the Court would think should be applied.[16] Recently it has been pointed out that the rule of reason "makes it difficult to forecast how the courts will balance the pros and cons" in determining reasonableness, and that the requirements of proof are enlarged when unreasonableness must be demonstrated.[17]

Although the rule of reason still remains in effect, it is not necessary to show unreasonableness in all types of cases. Some types of agreement or action are regarded as illegal *per se*—that is, regarded as unreasonable in all instances. For other types of agreement or action, reasonableness must be determined by the facts in the case.

Today, after nearly a half-century under the rule of reason, it could hardly be contended that the Court had found it sufficient for giving clarity to the law. The Sherman Act has been construed differently in different periods, it has been construed inconsistently in the same period, and there is still uncertainty about its application in some types of cases. A distinguished judge has said: "And in connection with the Sherman Act, it is delusive to treat opinions written by different judges at different times as pieces of a jig-saw puzzle which can be, by effort, fitted correctly into a single pattern."[18] The point of this statement will become even clearer to the reader after the following analysis of the cases.

CLOSE COMBINATIONS AND SINGLE-FIRM POWER

A close combination is one by which previously independent firms are brought under common management. This may be achieved by *merger*, which is a fusion of two or more companies into one. Or it may be achieved by *purchase of stock*, either by one company buying stock in another or by an outside company buying stock in two or more concerns. This creates a so-called holding company—that is, a company holding stock in another. A close association could be formed also by a lease agreement, or by the trustee device—under which a trustee was designated to vote the stock of two or more companies.

What factors would make such combinations illegal? There were many problematic aspects to this question in the beginning. Would *intent* to monopolize be sufficient? Or would *achievement* of monopoly be required? What *percentage of market control* would amount to monopoly? Would the *formation* of a combination with substantial control of the market be illegal

---

[16] Herbert Pope, "The Reason for the Continued Uncertainty of the Sherman Act," *Ill. Law Rev.*, **VII**, p. 201 (1912).

[17] Louis B. Schwartz in *Report, op. cit.* (footnote 7 herein), pp. 391–392.

[18] J. Wyzanski in *United States v. United Shoe Machinery Corp.*, 110 F. Supp. 295, 342 (1953).

per se? Or would *unfair or coercive acts* toward outsiders be necessary for illegality? Were only *horizontal* combinations prohibited? Or could *vertical* combinations be illegal? The former would cut off competition between firms performing the same economic function (producing raw material, or processing such materials, or wholesaling, and so forth). The latter, by bringing successive stages of production and/or distribution under the same control, would limit the opportunities of sellers and buyers outside the combination.

Parallel questions arise with respect to the growth of a single corporation. Would mere growth to a dominating position be a monopoly under the Sherman Act? Or would coercive tactics or other illegal practices be necessary for illegality? And would intent to monopolize have to be shown?

The earliest close association case in the Supreme Court was the Sugar Trust case, decided in 1895. One company refining sugar had, by stock purchase, acquired control of four others and thus gained control of 98 per cent of domestic production. This combination escaped the antitrust act on constitutional grounds.[19] Next came the Northern Securities case (1904), in which the Supreme Court held illegal the holding-company purchase of two parallel and competing northwest railroads. This was a clear decision that a union of the two large competitors by the holding-company device was illegal; there were no additional circumstances, such as predatory acts towards competitors, to becloud the meaning of the case.[20]

Then came the decisions in 1911 that held illegal the Standard Oil and American Tobacco combinations. The opinion in the leading Standard Oil case [21] is long and confusing, and it leaves important questions unanswered. The Standard Oil Company was a holding company that had acquired a dominant position in the industry by *purchase of stock* of other companies. It had engaged in a variety of *predatory acts* toward outsiders. Its *intent to monopolize* seemed clear. The Court gathered all of these facts into an involved rationalization of reason for illegality. Evil intent was stressed as the thing which made the combination illegal; the evil intent was confirmed by the methods used. The unification of power and control gave rise "to the *prima facie* presumption of intent and purpose to maintain the dominancy over the oil industry, not as a result of normal methods of industrial development, but by new means of combination . . . "; [22] there was "intent and purpose to exclude others which was frequently manifested by acts and dealings wholly inconsistent with the theory that they were made with the single conception of advancing the development of business power by usual methods. . . ." [23]

This rationale left open some important questions: (1) Would obtaining

---

[19] See pages 140–141 for full discussion of the facts and the constitutional issue.
[20] See page 141 for fuller discussion of the case.
[21] *Standard Oil Co. of New Jersey v. U.S.*, 221 U.S. 1.
[22] *Ibid.*, p. 75.
[23] *Ibid.*, p. 76.

a predominant position without evil intent be legal? (2) Would there be a violation of the act if there was evil intent but failure to achieve the purpose? (3) What methods and practices would be sufficient to establish illegal purpose: the holding-company device alone? Or would unfair practices toward competitors be necessary? Obviously the accumulation of factors making for illegality in the Standard Oil case was so great that the Court was not called upon to clarify the law on these questions. And these questions were not resolved by the Tobacco case, for it too involved a plethora of considerations—evil intent, many methods of combination (not the holding-company device alone), and coercive acts toward outsiders.[24]

Some of these questions were involved in the unusually significant case against the United States Steel Corporation, decided in the Supreme Court in 1920.[25] The story of the steel industry from the nineties to 1911 is one of the most startling episodes in American finance and corporate concentration. There was competition in the steel industry in the middle nineties. From 1898 to 1900 a great combination movement brought into being large vertically integrated concerns. Then, with a new competitive struggle being threatened, U.S. Steel was formed in 1901. It was a holding company, "a combination of combinations," the largest industrial corporation the country had had, and in the beginning it controlled probably 60 to 70 per cent of the output of the industry. The rewards to owning interests were great. The Bureau of Corporations stated that all the common stock and a substantial proportion of the equal amount of preferred stock was "water" (represented no investment). Profits were high in the first decade, and served to "dehydrate" the concern. However, its percentage of total production declined between 1901 and 1911, when the government's suit was brought.[26]

The Supreme Court agreed "in the main" with one of the opinions in the lower court, which had found "illegal purpose from the very beginning" in the corporation. The Court took note of the Gary dinners, held from 1907 to 1911 by U.S. Steel and its competitors and used for price-control purposes. But it found no coercive acts toward competitors. And it found that the corporation had not achieved monopoly. It would not accept the government's contention that constancy of price levels indicated artificial influence. Its conclusions were pointedly stated: ". . . the law does not make mere size an offense or the existence of unexerted power an offense"; "It is against monopoly that the statute [Sherman Act] is directed, not against an expectation of it, but against its realization, and it is certain that it was not realized"; "Whatever there was of wrong intent could not be executed, whatever there was of evil effect, was discontinued before this suit was brought; and this, we think determines the decree"; dissolution

---

[24] *U.S. v. American Tobacco Co.,* 221 U.S. 106 (1911).
[25] *U.S. v. U.S. Steel Corp.,* 251 U.S. 447.
[26] On the combination movements in steel, see Eliot Jones, *The Trust Problem in the United States* (New York: The Macmillan Company, 1921), Chapter IX and p. 270.

would bring "a risk to the public interest, including a material disturbance of, and, it may be serious detriment to, the foreign trade. . . ."

The dissenting opinion by Justice Day was vigorous and lucid. To him there was illegality in the *formation* of the combination. He agreed that mere size was not an offense when obtained "by lawful means and development by natural growth." But he thought this combination had acquired a position of dominance, and that the purpose was to obtain greater profits through unified control. He considered a failure to dissolve a corporation because of risks to the public interest would be a "practical nullification of the act itself. . . ."

The decision of the Court may be summarized as follows. Although the main objective of a combination by ownership is elimination of competition, although its power position is great, although it engages with competitors in collusive price tactics, the combination is not illegal if its collusive practices have been discontinued, if it does not use coercive tactics toward outsiders, and if monopoly is not achieved. Evil intent in formation is not enough; unexerted power is not evil; the holding-company method is not itself illegal.

The decision was a close one (4 to 3) and almost certainly would have gone the other way if McReynolds and Brandeis had been participants; it was difficult to reconcile with the Anthracite Coal cases decided the same year; [27] it created a big gulf between the law on close and that on loose associations.[28] But it fitted the temper of the emerging twenties; and, combined with the emasculation of Section 7 of the Clayton Act,[29] it seemed to legalize the elimination of competitors by merger or stock ownership, provided only that monopoly was not actually achieved and that evil acts were not committed against competitors.

New attitudes were reflected in antitrust cases in the 1940's. Typical of the change is the case of *U.S. v. Aluminum Company of America*. Since a quorum for the case could not be formed in the Supreme Court, the case was sent from the trial court to the Circuit Court of Appeals in New York for final decision.[30] The case did not involve a combination, but the power of a single firm. The Court of Appeals found that the company had a monopoly of aluminum ingot production. It concluded that the company's percentage of production was over 90 per cent. It then made this significant statement on monopoly: "That percentage [90] is enough to constitute a monopoly; it is doubtful whether sixty or sixty-four per cent would be enough; and certainly thirty-three per cent is not." To the company's argu-

---

[27] *U.S. v. Reading Co.*, 253 U.S. 26; *U.S. v. Lehigh Valley Railroad Co.*, 254 U.S. 255. See the comments of Milton Handler, "Industrial Mergers and the Anti-Trust Laws," XXXII *Col.L.Rev.* p. 179 (1932).
[28] See pages 195ff.
[29] See pages 226–227.
[30] 148 F. 2d 416 (1945).

ment that it had not abused its position by charging unfair prices, the Court replied—in sharp contrast to the Steel case—that the issue of abuse of power was irrelevant. The company had a monopoly; the only issue was whether it had done anything itself which could be called "monopolizing"—that is, whether it had worked to bring about the monopoly. The Court noted that monopoly could be "thrust" upon persons so that they "unwittingly find themselves in possession of a monopoly"; but it found that the aluminum company had not been a "passive beneficiary of a monopoly." It had acted "progressively to embrace *each new opportunity* as it opened, and to face every newcomer with new capacity already geared into a great organization . . ." (Italics supplied). This was sufficient to establish violation by the company. It was unnecessary to show any specific illegal intent, for no "monopolist monopolizes unconscious of what he is doing."

In sum, the Aluminum case means that a company which achieves monopoly by seizing opportunities to expand, and thus excluding competitors, is guilty of violation of Section 2 of the Sherman Act, even though it does nothing to abuse its power. It has been said that this is "harsh doctrine," but "less harsh than at first blush might appear," because companies are not likely to obtain control, without patents or combinations, of as large a portion of the market as the Court indicated would be necessary for a monopoly.[31] The most significant aspect of the case is the potential effect of its doctrines on the illegality of *combinations:* existence of power without abuse of power, and achievement of monopoly without relation to specific intent, are illegal.

The logic in the Aluminum case was affirmed by the Supreme Court itself in a loose association case in 1946. American Tobacco Company, Liggett and Myers Tobacco Company, and R. J. Reynolds Tobacco Company had been convicted of violation of Sections 1 and 2 of the Sherman Act. The question considered by the Supreme Court [32] was whether exclusion of competitors was necessary to the crime of monopolization (Section 2). The Court held that it was not. It then took the opportunity to quote and endorse lengthy statements from the opinion of the Circuit Court of Appeals in the Aluminum case.

One may compare also the more recent United Shoe Machinery case.[33] The defendant company supplied more than 75 per cent of the types of shoe machinery it manufactured. The Court decided its monopoly was deliberate (not thrust upon it). This was determined by looking at its "business policies"—including especially leasing rather than selling.

Though deliberate expansion to a position of monopoly power without any abuse of such power is now illegal, it should not be forgotten that the

---

[31] George W. Stocking and Myron W. Watkins, *Monopoly and Free Enterprise* (New York: Twentieth Century Fund, 1951), p. 291.
[32] *American Tobacco Co. v. U.S.*, 328 U.S. 781.
[33] *United States v. United Shoe Machinery Corp.,* 110 F. Supp. 295 (D. Mass., 1953), affirmed *per curiam* 347 U.S. 521 (1954).

law may still be violated through abuses of power. An example is the A & P case,[34] in which the government insisted that it was not attacking size but abuse of power. In holding that A & P was guilty of conspiracy to restrain and to monopolize trade in violation of Sections 1 and 2 of the Sherman Act, the circuit court found that it had sought to maintain a two-price system—one for itself and one for its competitors; to accomplish this, it had threatened to boycott suppliers and place them on its blacklist, and had threatened to go into the manufacturing and processing business itself; it had set up ACCO, a buying-and-selling agency which, in buying for A & P, had received brokerage allowances from sellers and, in selling to competitors, had first skimmed off the best merchandise for A & P; it had forced suppliers to give it advantages not given to competitors, such as advertising and space allowances; with the gross profits accumulated by its buying and selling, it was able to undersell competitors and to "pick and choose" the retail outlets in which this advantage could be used. These and other practices established the abuse of power alleged by the government.

It is not necessary in a case such as this one to show the existence of monopoly power. Activities may be a restraint of trade in violation of Section 1, or an attempt to monopolize in violation of Section 2.

Significant decisions have been made by the Supreme Court in recent years on vertical integration. In the Yellow Cab case (1947)[35] the government charged that the Checker Cab Manufacturing Corporation (CCM) had acquired control over cab ownership in a number of cities, amounting to 86 per cent of the Chicago market, 15 per cent of the New York City market, 100 per cent of the Pittsburgh market, and 58 per cent of the Minneapolis market. The Supreme Court held that this kind of combination came within the ban of the Sherman Act. The vice of vertical integration was to limit the market for sales of taxicabs by other cab manufacturers and the freedom of the cab-operating concerns to purchase cabs from manufacturers other than CCM. Second, the Court said that *nationwide* obstacles to commerce were not necessary for violation of the Sherman Act; that act was "designed to sweep away all appreciable obstructions."

The implications of the decision in the Cab case were not clear. The case certainly could not mean that vertical integration was evil *per se*. It would be impossible to maintain such a position, in view of the recognized economic values in economic integration and its prevalence in American industry. The decision could be interpreted to mean that vertical integration was illegal if an appreciable amount of business was involved. That, too, would be drastic medicine for the economy. This was, however, the government's interpretation of the case. But in the Columbia Steel case in 1948, the Supreme Court rejected this simple interpretation of the Cab

[34] *U.S. v. New York Great A. & P. Co.*, 173 F. 2d 79 (Circuit Court of Appeals, 7th Circuit, 1949).
[35] *U.S. v. Yellow Cab Co.*, 332 U.S. 218. Decided only on the legal issues. Remanded for trial of facts. Dismissed, 80 F. Supp. 936 (1948); affirmed, 338 U.S. 338 (1949).

case, and decided the case before it by analysis of the total competitive situation.

In Columbia Steel the Court split 5 to 4 over the issue of vertical integration.[36] Columbia Steel, a subsidiary of U.S. Steel Corporation, was the largest producer of rolled-steel products in the Pacific Coast area. U.S. Steel owned over 51 per cent of the rolled-steel capacity of the Pacific Coast and approximately one-third of the capacity of the entire nation. The subsidiary, Columbia Steel, signed a contract for the purchase of Consolidated Steel Corporation, a buyer of rolled-steel products for use in steel fabrication. Consolidated's purchases of rolled-steel products amounted to a little more than 3 per cent of the total in the eleven states of the Far West and Southwest in which it operated. For "plates and shapes," its percentage of the market was 13 per cent. The majority thought the former figure was more important; the minority thought the latter was. The majority found the 3 per cent to be "a small part" of the consumption in the area, and held that the purchase of Consolidated by Columbia was not illegal, either because of the vertical integration described above, or because of the other charges by the government. It concluded that the effort to find a market for Columbia's products was "a normal business purpose."

The minority, speaking through Justice Douglas, said, "This is the most important antitrust case which has been before the Court in years. . . . Here we have the pattern of the evolution of the great trusts. Little, independent units are gobbled up by bigger ones." It thought the loss of Consolidated as a market by competitors of U.S. Steel was serious. It thought it might hold legal the purchase of Consolidated by an independent West Coast producer so as to form a unit which could compete with the giants, but U.S. Steel's percentage of production of rolled steel put it in a different position. A "company that has that tremendous leverage on our economy is big enough."

A few conclusions can be stated about the application of the Sherman Act to horizontal and vertical integration. Use of coercive tactics to force integration of firms or of evil practices toward outsiders shows intent to restrain trade or to monopolize, and may thus make integration illegal. Growth of a single firm through seizing opportunities and excluding competitors until a monopoly position is attained is illegal. But whether monopoly is 60 per cent or some higher proportion of the market is uncertain. Vertical integration is not evil *per se,* but may be illegal because of effects upon competition. Yet purchase of a market outlet with 3 per cent of the regional market by a company having 51 per cent of the regional output or 31 per cent of the national output is not illegal under the Sherman Act.

The word "combination" in Section 1 has not been used as effectively as other terms of the act. While Section 2 prohibits monopolizing or at-

---

[36] *U.S. v. Columbia Steel Co.,* 334 U.S. 495 (1948).

tempts to monopolize, Section 1 prohibits "combination . . . in restraint of trade." Might integration achieved by stock purchases or mergers, and resulting in a dominant position in an oligopolistic market (that is, short of monopoly), be illegal as "combination" in restraint of trade? In the Northern Securities case a combination was held illegal without respect to conduct toward competitors, but in the Steel case the issue of combination was evaded and the problem considered as one of monopoly, or of monopoly and restraint of trade combined. Though the decision in the Steel case "has been discredited, qualified, and ignored, and its incidental philosophy has been repudiated," the prohibition against combination has not yet been applied and construed in the new era of strength in antitrust law. But it has been said, "Any company whose history includes an episode of merger therefore faces the risk that it is a 'combination' for purposes of Section 1 of the Sherman Act, and a perpetual, standing, and incurable 'combination,' to boot. The mark of Cain is upon it." [37]

This issue, and others, under the Sherman Act may not now be as significant with respect to close combinations as those in the enforcement and interpretation of Section 7 of the Clayton Act. Its prohibitions against stock purchases and mergers whose effect "may be substantially to lessen competition, or to tend to create a monopoly," applying both to vertical and to horizontal combinations, will be discussed in the next chapter.

LOOSE-KNIT COMBINATIONS

A loose-knit combination is one achieved by agreement or understanding among parties under separate ownership. The Sherman Act has had a greater impact on such combinations than it has on close combinations.

EARLY CASES. The Sherman Act was successfully applied against several forms of loose association at an early date. In 1897 it was held that a rate-making association among western railroads was in violation of the act.[38] In 1899, in the first successful case in the Supreme Court against industrial combinations, it was held that an arrangement for division of sales was illegal.[39] This is the leading case for the doctrine that apportionment of territory or division of market is illegal under the Sherman Act. In 1905, agreements affecting prices by the leading packers were held invalid.[40] It was also held that actions of associations of laborers could be illegal under the act.[41]

[37] The words quoted here and earlier in the paragraph are from Eugene V. Rostow, *Planning for Freedom: The Public Law of American Capitalism* (New Haven, Conn.: Yale University Press, 1959), pp. 300 and 301.
[38] *U.S. v. Trans-Missouri Freight Ass'n.*, 166 U.S. 290.
[39] *Addyston Pipe and Steel Co. v. U.S.*, 175 U.S. 211.
[40] *Swift & Co. v. U.S.*, 196 U.S. 375.
[41] *Loewe v. Lawlor*, 208 U.S. 274 (1908).

PRICE AGREEMENTS. In 1927, in the Trenton Potteries case,[42] the Court held illegal an agreement of those controlling 82 per cent of the business of manufacturing and distributing sanitary pottery fixtures in the United States to fix and maintain uniform prices. The Court was asked to hold that a price agreement was bad only if there was an unreasonable restraint of trade. It answered, "the power to fix prices, whether reasonably exercised or not, involves power to control the market and to fix arbitrary and unreasonable prices. . . . Agreements which create such potential power may well be *in themselves* unreasonable or unlawful restraints" (Italics supplied). It did not regard reasonableness of the prices set an adequate criterion of legality: this was too "uncertain a test," and what is a reasonable price today may be an unreasonable price tomorrow.

This is the leading case for the rule that price-fixing agreements are not covered by the rule of reason, but are illegal *per se*—that is, in themselves unreasonable restraints. There have been only two cases in which the rule was not applied. The first was distinguished in the Pottery case, and is really not a significant exception to the rule. The Court had held in 1918 in *Chicago Board of Trade v. U.S.*[43] that it was legal for the members of a grain exchange to agree to maintain for a part of the day (from the closing of bids one day to the opening of the market the next) the prices that had been fixed by open competition on the market. The Court found sound reasons of convenience in the relations of buyers and sellers which led it to accept the reasonableness of the restraint.

The significant departure from the Trenton rule was in *Appalachian Coals, Inc., v. U.S.* in 1933.[44] One hundred and thirty-seven producers of bituminous coal, with 11.96 per cent of the production east of the Mississippi River and 74.4 per cent of the commercial production in the Appalachian Territory, had agreed to set up an exclusive selling agency to market their coal. However, they sold most of their coal outside Appalachian Territory and were faced with competition within it. The arrangement, of course, eliminated price competition among those who had entered the agreement. The Court said that the test to be applied was whether there were "undue restraints of interstate commerce," which was a clear departure from the Trenton case. In determining the question, the Court took note of the disorderly conditions and destructive practices in the marketing of coal: the surplus production; existence of distress coal pressing on the market; the pyramiding of coal, a device by which the same coal was offered for a producer by several sellers and thus competed with itself; and others. It also noted that there were no efforts to curtail production. It held the agreement to be legal, but instructed

[42] 273 U.S. 392.
[43] 246 U.S. 231.
[44] 288 U.S. 344.

the District Court to retain jurisdiction for further proceedings if future developments showed violation of the Sherman Act.

There had been much discussion of the wide difference in impact of the Antitrust Act between close and loose associations. The U.S. Steel decision had freed combinations by ownership where there was no monopoly and no unfair practices, but the Trenton case and the open-price association cases (see pages 198ff.) had shown that the Antitrust Act had real significance for loose combinations. In the Appalachian case the Court sought to close this gap, at least in part, by loosening the restraints on loose associations.[45]

The closing of the gap between the law on close and that on loose combinations by relaxing it on loose combinations was a hazardous step. Businessmen are more likely to be willing to form loose combinations to achieve common purposes than to sacrifice the independent existence of their firms by joining in a close combination. The danger, therefore, of removing the restraints of the law on formation of loose combinations is great. There was another way to close the gap, which was to tighten the law on close combinations.

The Appalachian case may be viewed as a realistic qualification of the law, in time of depression, for an industry which was in such distress that the government itself was soon to establish price stabilization for it. It has had no effect as precedent for other decisions, one reason probably being that the law on close combinations has been tightened since 1933. The Court, in its interpretation of the Sherman Act, was soon to reaffirm the doctrine of the Trenton case that price-fixing agreements were illegal *per se*. This came in the Socony-Vacuum case (1940).[46] Independent petroleum companies in the Mid-Continent and East Texas areas had surplus gasoline which they were unable to market except at distress prices. This distress gasoline amounted to about 17 per cent of the production in the area. The integrated companies and the independents had gentlemen's agreements that the former would purchase the surplus gasoline from the latter. They would thus be able to remove the depressing effect of this distress gasoline on the market and, in effect, maintain a floor on price. The Court held this combination illegal. It distinguished it from the Appalachian case: Both aimed to remove the distress production from the market, but in the oil case the purpose and effect was to raise and stabilize prices. It would be difficult, however, to avoid the conclusion that the important factor was the change in the times and the attitude of the Court. At any rate, the Court reasserted the rule of the Trenton case that price-fixing agreements were illegal *per se*, and, in effect, expanded the rule to include agreements which had a price-maintenance effect. It was immaterial whether the resulting prices

---

[45] See the statements in the Appalachian case at 288 U.S. 344, 376–377.
[46] *U.S. v. Socony-Vacuum Oil Company*, 310 U.S. 150.

were too high, nor could "genuine or fancied competitive abuses" legally justify agreements to maintain prices.

In the Paramount Pictures case in 1948 the Court unequivocally reaffirmed the Trenton rule. The District Court had found that the major defendants in the case had been guilty of horizontal and vertical price conspiracies. The Supreme Court upheld these findings and made the following statement: "We start, of course, from the premise that so far as the Sherman Act is concerned, a price-fixing agreement is illegal *per se*." [47]

OPEN-PRICE ASSOCIATIONS. One of the big developments in the twentieth century is the rise of trade associations. These perform many functions for their members, such as research, supply of information on legislative and other developments, and representation before public agencies. One type of activity is reporting to the members on market developments.

In 1921 the Supreme Court decided the first case relating to this type of activity. It was *American Column and Lumber Co. v. U.S.*[48] Three hundred and sixty-five members of the American Hardwood Manufacturers' Association, together controlling one-third of the hardwood production of the nation, had joined a "Plan" under which they would turn in daily sales and shipping reports (showing each sale, its terms, and so on), monthly production and stock reports, and price lists. The accuracy of the data was safeguarded by inspections of grades of lumber and audit of reports from members. A "Manager of Statistics" gave this data to the members in detailed weekly and monthly reports. One purpose of the "Plan" was stated to be "to keep prices at reasonably stable and normal levels." Market-report letters were distributed, and these and other reports discussed future market conditions. Monthly meetings were held, and suggestions that overproduction be avoided and prices maintained were made by the Manager of Statistics at these meetings and in letters and reports. With three justices dissenting, the Supreme Court held that the activities under the "Plan" violated the Antitrust Act.

The decision should be compared with two others made soon thereafter. In the Linseed Oil case,[49] the defendants had gone beyond the reporting of information such as in the above-discussed case; they had limited their freedom of action by agreeing to maintain price differentials among zones, had been given sales discounts agreed upon in meetings, and in other ways had evolved a tighter plan of operations than in the preceding case. The Court unanimously held that the combination was illegal. However, in the Maple Flooring case,[50] the Court, with three dissenters, upheld a *reporting plan* involving twenty-two firms producing about 70 per cent

[47] 334 U.S. 131, 143.
[48] 257 U.S. 377.
[49] *United States v. American Linseed Oil Co.*, 262 U.S. 371 (1923).
[50] *Maple Flooring Manufacturers' Association v. United States,* 268 U.S. 563 (1925).

of their type of flooring. The Court found that the data distributed to members related only to *past* transactions. It noted also that the data was made available to the government and the public.

After these three cases, one could have concluded that it was illegal to enter arrangements which restrain the freedom of the parties, that it was illegal to distribute information on future market conditions with advice as to action to be taken, but that it was not illegal to distribute information which related only to past transactions. But also, if one had looked at the line-up of judges, he would have seen that there had been changes in court composition between the American Column and Maple Flooring cases, and that only one justice had been with the majority in both cases.

The American Column decision may be compared with that in the U.S. Steel case the year before. Though the Court majority in the former stressed the danger of price stabilization, one may doubt whether reporting of information and advice on its significance to 367 firms producing one-third of the output would be sufficient to materially affect the market. It would be easy for individual firms to go their own way if it were to their advantage to do so. But in the Steel case, production and price could be firmly determined for half of the production of the industry. Was the Court overemphasizing danger in one case and overlooking it in the other?

The price cases brought a cleavage of opinion on the court. Justices Holmes and Brandeis wrote dissenting opinions in the American Column case, and the philosophy they stated was given expression in the majority opinion by Justice Stone in the Maple Flooring case. The main point was that the law should not frown on intelligent or rational competition based upon knowledge of the facts; there was, it was argued, advantage in having decisions of individual concerns made in accord with market conditions. Brandeis pointed out that large concerns could gather information needed for intelligent decisions by their own efforts, but that small concerns could not; he noted also that government agencies gathered and disseminated information in some cases.

If these arguments appear sound, it is also true that there are dangers in trade-association activity. The activities may go beyond dissemination of information and may lead to agreement on action. The NRA codes (1933–35) contained many provisions of this type. For example, a large number of them provided for notice of prices to a central code authority and a waiting period before these could be changed, and evidence showed that collusive and coercive action often followed to prevent recalcitrant members from cutting prices. Since that time, various types of agreements, such as on uniform discounts, basing points, or minimum prices, have been uncovered and prohibited in consent decrees issued in antitrust cases.

In 1936 the Supreme Court once again was called upon to determine the applicability of the Sherman Act to trade activities. The case was

Sugar Institute, Inc. v. U.S.[51] The argument in defense of the Institute was obviously based on the Appalachian Coals decision. It was argued that the Institute was a natural means of correcting the causes of a demoralized industry, including, among other things, secret concessions to buyers. The Supreme Court recognized the need for remedial measures. It held that in view of the past practices in the industry, advance reporting of future prices was not illegal. This appears to be a loosening of the proscription of law as established in the earlier cases. The Court held, however, that the defendants went too far in requiring "adherence to such announcements without the deviations which open and fair competition might require or justify." It also upheld a decree of the lower court that statistical information gathered by the Institute should, in the interests of competition, be distributed to the purchasing and distributing trade, though it did limit this to such information as would be of legitimate interest to such trade (not including information that could be legitimately treated as confidential).

THE SIGNIFICANCE OF SIZE. In the case just discussed, the Court said that "a fact of outstanding importance is the relative position of the defendants in the sugar industry.... They supply from 70 to 80 per cent of the sugar consumed."[52] In the Addyston case (1899) the defendants argued that their output did not exceed 30 per cent of the market, but the Circuit Court said that the fact that they might be subject to competition did not affect the illegality of the combination. In the American Column case (1921) the defendants produced one-third of the national supply, but the Supreme Court concluded that there had been an effect on prices. In the Socony-Vacuum case the Court said, "the power to fix prices exists if the combination has control of a substantial part of the commerce in the commodity," and might in some cases exist even without control of a substantial part.[53] But price-fixing, as contrasted with the power to fix prices, and some other practices are illegal without regard to size. In a bit of dictum in the Columbia case the Court said:

where a complaint charges that the defendants have engaged in price-fixing, or have concertedly refused to deal with non-members of an association, or have licensed a patented device on condition that unpatented materials be employed in conjunction with the patented device, then the amount of commerce involved is immaterial because such restraints are illegal *per se*.[54]

AN OMNIBUS CASE. One of the most discussed antitrust cases is the Paramount Pictures case.[55] It shows how a set of interconnected agreements, understandings, and practices of the leading firms can establish a planned pattern for an entire industry. The government's suit was against

---

[51] 297 U.S. 553.
[52] *Ibid.*, 600.
[53] 310 U.S. 150, 223–224.
[54] 334 U.S. 495, 522–523.
[55] *United States v. Paramount Pictures, Inc.*, 334 U.S. 131 (1948).

five major producers who, with their subsidiaries and affiliates, also distributed and exhibited films, and who are called the majors, or producer-exhibitors; two companies and their subsidiaries, which produced and distributed films but owned no theaters; and one company engaged only in distribution of films. The extent of restraint of trade as found by the courts was as follows: (1) There were two price-fixing conspiracies—a vertical one based on express agreements among various distributors and various exhibitors, and a horizontal one among all the defendants, which was not express but could be inferred from the pattern of price fixing disclosed in the record. (2) There was a conspiracy to restrain trade through *unreasonable* clearances—that is, unreasonable provisions for a time lag and a geographical distribution between first-run and subsequent runs of pictures in theaters. (3) There were unlawful pooling agreements for joint operation of a group of theaters and distribution of profits, and joint ownership by defendants of theaters, which in some cases was unlawful. (4) There were formula deals and master agreements, covering a number of theaters, which restrained competition. (5) There was block booking, under which a theater owner had to take a group of films, if he obtained any, and the Court held that defendants should not enter any license arrangement which made the exhibition of one film dependent upon the taking of another. (6) There were discriminatory actions against small independent exhibitors. In addition to restraints, there was the charge of monopoly based on the extensive ownership of theaters by the majors, particularly in the large cities and in the first-run showing of pictures. Though the district court found no monopoly, the Supreme Court held that its consideration of the issue had been too limited. It directed reconsideration of this issue. The lower court subsequently ordered the divorce of distribution from exhibition and prescribed a long list of remedies for the practices in restraint of trade which had been proven. In effect, this decree of the court provided for a restructuring of the pattern of distribution and exhibition.

EVIDENCE OF CONSPIRACIES. In the Tobacco case referred to heretofore [56] the verdict of the jury was that there was a conspiracy among the major tobacco companies to fix and control the prices and other conditions relating to the purchase of leaf tobacco for use in the manufacture of cigarettes, and also a conspiracy to fix and control prices and other conditions relating to the sale of cigarettes. Differently stated, the conspiracy reached backward to the raw materials and forward to the finished product. The jury found that there were intent and power to exclude competition to a substantial extent. The precise legal question presented in the Supreme Court has already been noted—that is, whether exclusion of competitors was necessary to the crime of monopolizing. The Court held that the power and intent to monopolize were sufficient to

---

[56] See page 192.

constitute the crime. The case, however, had an additional significance because of its treatment of the question concerning the kind of evidence that would be necessary to establish conspiracy. The jury's decision was not based upon any finding of actual agreements among the parties; it was based upon circumstantial evidence that a common course of action existed. The Supreme Court said:

The essential combination or conspiracy in violation of the Sherman Act may be found in a course of dealing or other circumstances as well as in an exchange of words. . . . Where the circumstances are such as to warrant a jury in finding that the conspirators had a unity of purpose or a common design and understanding, or a meeting of minds in an unlawful arrangement, the conclusion that the conspiracy is established is justified.[57]

This decision that illegality may arise from a common course of dealing which reflects common purpose and understanding was followed by a Federal Trade Commission case in which conscious parallelism of action appeared to be a sufficient basis for a holding of illegality under the Federal Trade Commission Act.[58] This idea was rejected by the Supreme Court in the Theater Enterprises case in 1954. It said that it had never held that "parallel business behavior . . . itself constitutes a Sherman Act offense."[59] A showing of conspiracy is still necessary, and something more than parallelism of conduct has been present in all cases. As yet, no case has been presented to the Court in which the record showed only that companies had functioned in an interdependent or parallel way. Apparently, it would be necessary to show more than parallelism—that is, intent, purpose, or plan to monopolize or to restrain trade.[60]

PATENTS AND THE ANTITRUST ACT

A patent grants a monopoly. The courts, therefore, are called upon "to make an adjustment between the lawful restraint on trade of the patent monopoly and the illegal restraint prohibited broadly by the Sherman Act."[61] The general guide for adjustment has been stated this way: "The owner of a patent cannot extend his statutory grant by contract or agreement. A patent affords no immunity for a monopoly not fairly or plainly within the grant."[62]

The patent grant has, nevertheless, been construed broadly in some very significant ways. It was decided half a century ago that nonuse of

---

[57] *American Tobacco Co. v. U.S.*, 328 U.S. 781, 809–810.
[58] The Steel Conduit case, discussed at p. 235.
[59] *Theater Enterprises, Inc. v. Paramount Film Distributing Corp.*, 346 U.S. 537.
[60] See *Report, op. cit.* (footnote 7 herein), pp. 36–42.
[61] *U.S. v. Line Material Co.*, 333 U.S. 287, 310 (1948).
[62] *U.S. v. Masonite Corporation*, 316 U.S. 265, 277 (1942).

a patent did not invalidate the grant.[63] Congress has authorized the patentee to assign his right to others, and the courts have recognized his right to split up his patent right by licenses to others. The patent holder who sells a patented article may not impose conditions on the resale of the article. His control vanishes with the sale. But he may impose conditions when he grants licenses to make and vend a patented article. And the patent holder has been allowed to grant licenses on condition that a cross-license to other patents be given him. These cross-licensing arrangements may result in a patent pool, in which the patents of each are made available to all those participating in the cross-licensing arrangement. Neither cross-licensing nor pools are illegal *per se.*

It has been said that the safeguards with which Congress had originally clothed the patent system had been so far modified that by "the first decade of the twentieth century the patent system had become a special sanctuary for trusts, pools, and trade confederacies." [64] The trend continued to the General Electric case of 1926. Not until about 1940 did the Supreme Court seem to be aware of the great threat to the competitive system posed by the actions of patent holders.

Patent holders have run afoul of the antitrust laws in various ways. First, patent holders may violate antitrust laws when they try to control unpatented articles or processes. The Court has held in many cases that the owner of a patent may not use its patent right to secure a limited monopoly of an unpatented material used in applying the invention. A well-known example is the decision in *International Salt Co., Inc. v. United States* in 1947.[65] It was held that International Salt could not legally condition leases of machines on which it held patents by a requirement that lessees use its unpatented salt. The same rule applies where the unpatented material is a part of the machine which embodies the patent.[66] Conditions restraining use of unpatented materials may violate the Sherman Act or Section 3 of the Clayton Act.[67]

---

[63] *Heaton-Peninsular Button Fastener Co. v. Eureka Specialty Co.*, 77 F. 288 (1896); *Continental Paper Bag Co. v. Eastern Paper Bag Co.*, 210 U.S. 405 (1908). As Justice Douglas says, this rule "came into the law over a century after the first patent act was passed." He and two other justices thought it was time "to be rid" of the rule—dissenting in *Special Equipment Co. v. Coe, Commissioner of Patents*, 324 U.S. 370 (1945). But note: "Contracts, combinations or conspiracies for nonuse of patented inventions to 'fence in' a technology or to 'block' a competing technology are clearly unreasonable *per se* antitrust violations. Similarly, for example, where there is substantial power arising from an aggregation of patents by a single owner in a given technological field, a decision not to use or license certain patented inventions may be evidence of monopolization or a specific intent to monopolize under Section 2 of the Sherman Act." *Report of the Attorney General's Committee to Study the Antitrust Laws* (Washington: Superintendent of Documents, 1955), pp. 230–231.

[64] George W. Stocking and Myron W. Watkins, *Monopoly and Free Enterprise* (New York: Twentieth Century Fund, 1951), p. 454.

[65] 332 U.S. 392.

[66] *Mercoid Corporation v. Mid-Continent Inv. Co.*, 320 U.S. 661 (1944).

[67] For fuller discussion of Section 3, see pages 222–225.

Another example of types of license restriction is package licensing. As was noted earlier, in *U.S. v. Paramount Pictures* [68] the Court held invalid "block booking" of copyrighted films. The decision, said the Court, applied only where the buyer was required to buy more than one film.[69] In *Ethyl Gasoline Corporation v. United States,* involving licenses by Ethyl (a subsidiary of Standard Oil of New Jersey) on use of a patented fluid to mix with gasoline to form a premium product, the Court condemned the licensing system of Ethyl and said, "The patent monopoly of one invention may no more be enlarged for the exploitation of a monopoly of another . . . than for the exploitation of an unpatented article . . . or for the exploitation or promotion of a business embraced within the patent." [70]

Second, license restrictions with respect to patented articles or processes may violate the Sherman Act. One kind of restriction is on price. A 1926 case construed broadly the rights of the patentee.[71] General Electric Company held patents on the process of manufacturing incandescent electric lights. Its percentage of the electric-light business in 1921 was 69 and that of its chief competitor (Westinghouse) 16. One issue was whether General Electric could set the resale price for two types of "agents"— large distributors and retailers. An agent does not acquire title to property, but acts for another in its sale. The Court held that since the distributors and retailers acted as agents of General Electric in their sales, the control of their prices by the latter was legal. A second issue was whether a license to Westinghouse to *make and vend* the lights could legally contain a provision for control by General Electric of the price of Westinghouse's sales. Though it was alleged that this was a device to eliminate competition in the *manufacture and sale* of lamps, the Court sustained the validity of the restriction.[72] The case has never been overruled, though four justices favored doing so in 1948.[73] It set up an important exception to the Trenton case rule that a price-fixing agreement is illegal *per se*.[74]

The import of the case has, however, been limited by later decisions. One outstanding case was *United States v. Masonite Corporation* (1942).[75] Masonite, holders of patents on the process of manufacturing hardboard, had entered into agreements with competitors under which, through a contract of *agency,* it authorized them to *market* Masonite's products, but at prices to be set by Masonite. The Supreme Court held that when a patentee by agency agreements makes use of the marketing system of

---

[68] 334 U.S. 131 (1948).
[69] *Ibid.*, 159.
[70] *Ethyl Gasoline Corporation v. United States,* 309 U.S. 436, 459 (1940).
[71] *United States v. General Electric Co.,* 272 U.S. 476.
[72] Affirming the decision in *Bement v. National Harrow Co.,* 186 U.S. 70 (1902).
[73] *United States v. Line Material Co.,* 333 U.S. 287 (1948).
[74] See above, page 196.
[75] 316 U.S. 265.

competitors with a purpose of fixing prices, there is an enlargement of the patent privilege and a violation of the Sherman Act.

How did the situation in this case differ from General Electric's licensing of Westinghouse? First, there was here only a license to vend, not a license to make and vend as in the General Electric case; and second, there were a number of agreements here with several competitors that had strong positions in the marketing of building materials. The Masonite decision limits the General Electric authorization for price fixing to a single licensee. Only where the patentee has one agent may he set the price of his product.

Third, patentees are restricted by the Sherman Act on cross-licensing and patent pools. Cross-licensing may have great advantages for the consumer. In the automobile industry the agreement of the manufacturers to allow common use of patents has generalized the benefits obtained by inventions. Cross-licensing agreements may enable a single machine to include all the best devices which have been discovered or a final product to reflect all the advances in technology. As for the holders of patent rights, these may often find that a cross-licensing arrangement is a means of avoiding a multiplicity of infringement suits between holders of rival patent claims. But in spite of their possible advantages for patentees and the public, cross-licensing arrangements may often be injurious to the public and be violations of the Sherman Act.

In an early case the Supreme Court held a patent-pooling plan to be in violation of the Sherman Act.[76] Two later cases illustrate the Court's position on such plans. In the Standard Oil of Indiana case in 1931,[77] the Supreme Court overruled the holding of a district court that a patent pool was illegal. To terminate conflict and litigation over rival patent rights, four holders of patents on the cracking process for increasing the gasoline yield from crude oil had agreed to pool their patents and fix and divide *royalty* charges thereon. The Court said that the illegality of the arrangements depended on whether there was power to dominate the industry so that the power to fix prices of the product (gasoline) would exist. The lower court thought that the control over royalties had a material and substantial effect on the price of the product; in its opinion, this was sufficient to make the agreements illegal.

One may compare the 1948 case of *United States v. Line Material Co.*,[78] in which the Court held a patent pool invalid. Here two firms, by a cross-licensing arrangement, placed in one of them the exclusive power to sublicense the patents and the power also to fix the sale price of the device which embodied the patents of the two companies; by supplementary contracts, those licensed to make and vend the device adhered to the prices

---

[76] *Standard Sanitary Manufacturing Co. v. United States*, 226 U.S. 20 (1912).
[77] *Standard Oil Co. et al. v. U.S.*, 283 U.S. 163 (1931).
[78] 333 U.S. 287.

set. The Court distinguished the case from the General Electric case, in which General Electric had controlled the prices of its licensees. "Where two or more patentees with competitive, non-infringing patents combine them and fix prices on all devices produced under any of the patents, competition is impeded to a greater degree than where a single patentee fixes prices for his licensees." [79] Of course, this could only be true because the single patentee already had a monopoly himself which he could retain or divide with others, whereas in case of agreement between two patentees, the patent monopolies would be broadened by being combined. The Court saw a difference between this and the Standard Oil of Indiana case, in which there was control over royalties instead of over the price of the product. It concluded that "when patentees join in an agreement as here to maintain prices on their several *products,* that agreement, however advantageous it may be to stimulate the broader use of patents, is unlawful *per se* under the Sherman Act" [80] (Italics supplied).

Probably the most sweeping recent decision on patent pooling, from the standpoint of effect on an industry, was that of the Court holding unanimously that the Hartford Empire-Owens patent combination in the glass industry was illegal.[81]

The Supreme Court's decisions after 1939 reveal a change in attitude toward patent restrictions and combinations. Stocking and Watkins showed that in a series of twelve cases after 1939 the Court "consistently outlawed the use of patents to monopolize or stifle competition." They conclude that in the twelve cases, the defendants were trying "to push to its logical extreme the doctrine of the cracking-patents case," but that "Though the General Electric and the Standard Oil Company of Indiana decisions have never been overruled, it is at least doubtful that either still represents a valid and binding precedent." [82]

CONCLUSION

There have been two two-way swings of the pendulum in Supreme Court decisions on the Sherman Act—two periods of weak followed by two periods of strong interpretation. In the beginning, the Sugar Trust case almost destroyed the act, except for railroads and labor. Then from 1899 (Addyston case) to 1911 the act was applied successfully to combinations of leading companies in some of the largest industries of the nation. After World War I the pendulum swung again. The Steel decision virtually liberated close combinations which used no predatory practices, the Gen-

---

[79] *Ibid.*
[80] *Ibid.*
[81] *Hartford Empire v. U.S.,* 323 U.S. 386 (1945).
[82] George W. Stocking and Myron W. Watkins, *Monopoly and Free Enterprise* (New York: Twentieth Century Fund, 1951), pp. 472–474.

eral Electric decision made possible the control of a product from manufacturer to consumer by a patentee, and the Appalachian Coals decision in 1933 seemed to limit the Trenton rule that price fixing was illegal *per se*. Only for associations for dissemination of information did the law seem to be tight, and this left questions as to whether the law was discriminatory against the small and middle-sized, as compared with the large firms. Then came the opposite swing. From about 1939 a new court in a new day put new vitality in the act. The Aluminum case took the place of the Steel case as a standard of judgment on monopoly, vertical integration could be illegal, the Trenton rule was reaffirmed, and the General Electric and Standard Oil of Indiana decisions were trimmed and brought into question as precedent. Tick-tock, tick-tock has gone the antitrust clock!

Will the clock go tick again? The pendulum may not swing that far again. First, there has been an accumulation of decisions, and second, there is now more consistency in the decisions as applied to different types of business acts. But a student who reads the next two chapters should keep in mind some parallels. He will note one tick-tock in the Clayton and Federal Trade Commission Act cases, paralleling the second tick-tock in Sherman Act cases. There is consistency in movement by the Court on different types of cases. More than this, he will note that there has been tick-tock, tick-tock in the enforcement effort of the government paralleling the tick-tock, tick-tock of the Court, and that these swings have paralleled swings in the temper and attitude of the nation. If this is true, the student may ponder what he learns about regulation of the economy from the perspective of history. Pendulums may still swing, even if not always in the same arc. The force of regulation may vary with the times. Courts may reflect the variations. About twenty-five years ago a scholarly study of judicial decisions in review of cases from the Interstate Commerce Commission and the Federal Trade Commission concluded that the courts will yield to a determined course of legislative-administrative policy.[83] Perhaps antitrust cases show that the courts move with the course of opinion in the other branches of the government and in the nation as a whole.

[83] Carl McFarland, *Judicial Control of the Federal Trade Commission and the Interstate Commerce Commission: 1920–1930* (Cambridge, Mass.: Harvard University Press, 1933), pp. 181–183 and 188.

Chapter 11. Additional Legislation on Combinations and Business Practices

THERE HAS BEEN much supplementary antitrust legislation passed since the Sherman Act. Some has provided for exemptions from the act, but the bulk of it has had the purpose of strengthening the antitrust policy. Though some legislation was passed earlier,[1] the biggest additions to the law were made in the Clayton Act and the Federal Trade Commission Act in 1914, and in further legislation passed between the middle thirties and 1950. There was a strong rising tide of sentiment in favor of further antitrust legislation from Theodore Roosevelt's administrations to 1914. The revelations of unfair practices by the nation's leaders in oil and tobacco in the cases in 1911 helped to focus attention on antitrust as a leading problem of the day. Democratic, Progressive, and Republican party platforms and presidential candidates vied with each other in 1912 in demands for further legislation.

The messages of the three presidents of this period are replete with suggestions for reform. Among the proposals advanced from 1903 to 1914 were the following:

1. Fact gathering on corporate activities and "pitiless publicity" of evil practices (an early Roosevelt idea).

2. An administrative commission to pass upon the reasonableness or unreasonableness of combinations (Roosevelt), or to aid the courts in framing dissolution decrees (Taft, then Wilson), or to advise businessmen without coming to terms with them (Wilson).

3. A federal incorporation act under which businesses operating in interstate commerce could voluntarily take out a federal charter (Taft).

4. Regulation of railroad security issues (Roosevelt, Wilson) and prevention of inflation of corporate stock (Roosevelt).

5. Prohibition of holding companies (Wilson, 1914) or advance government approval for one interstate corporation to hold stock in another (Roosevelt, 1907).

6. Explicit prohibition of unfair competitive practices (Roosevelt, Taft, and Wilson).[2]

[1] Particularly the establishment of the Bureau of Corporations in 1903.
[2] The names given in the text are only those first or chiefly associated with the proposals; there is no implication that others among the three did not make similar, perhaps even the same, suggestions. For the recommendations and ideas of these three presidents, see

The immediate precipitant for new legislation in 1914 was President Wilson's special antitrust message on January 20. He repeated the declaration included in several Democratic party platforms that "private monopoly is indefensible and intolerable," and offered a long list of suggestions which formed the background for the specific provisions of the two 1914 enactments. The legislation fell far short of the recommendations Wilson offered, but added considerably to antitrust law.

THE FEDERAL TRADE COMMISSION ACT, AS AMENDED

The Federal Trade Commission Act of 1914 (1) vested an investigatorial function in a new Federal Trade Commission (FTC), (2) gave this same commission enforcement functions, and (3) prohibited unfair methods of competition. Each of these will be discussed in turn.

THE INVESTIGATORIAL FUNCTION. In 1903 a Bureau of Corporations was established in the newly created Department of Commerce and Labor with power to investigate and publish data on corporations engaged in interstate commerce, except common carriers under the jurisdiction of the Interstate Commerce Commission.[3] In 1914 the investigatorial function was transferred to a five-man Federal Trade Commission. Section 6 of the act gave the commission power to gather and compile information, to require corporation reports, and to publish information obtained, excepting trade secrets and names of customers. These fact-gathering and corporate-reporting functions were broadly defined and extended to the organization, business, conduct, practices, and management of interstate corporations. In addition, Section 6 gave powers of investigation specifically related to enforcement of the antitrust law: (1) to investigate facts relating to any alleged violation of the antitrust acts upon the "direction of the President or either house of Congress"; (2) to investigate and make recommendations, upon request of the Attorney General, on readjustment of the business of any corporation alleged to be violating the antitrust laws, and (3) also upon the request of the Attorney General to investigate the manner in which decrees issued in antitrust cases were carried out.

---

particularly the following: For Roosevelt, 2 speeches recorded in *Congressional Record*, Dec. 3, 1907, and March 25, 1908, **XLII**, Pt. I, pp. 67ff, Pt. IV, pp. 3853ff, the Progressive Party platform of 1912 in Kirk H. Porter and Donald Bruce Johnson, *National Party Platforms, 1840–1960*, 2d ed. (Urbana, Ill.: University of Chicago Press, 1961), pp. 175–183, and the issues of his journal, the *Outlook*; for Taft, see messages to Congress on January 7, 1910, Dec. 6, 1911, *Congressional Record*, **XLV**, pp. 378ff, **XLVI**, p. 24, the Republican Party platform of 1912 in Porter and Johnson, pp. 183–188, and his book on *The Supreme Court and the Sherman Act* (New York: Harper and Row Publishers, Inc., 1914); for Wilson, see his *The New Freedom* (Garden City, N.Y.: Doubleday & Company, Inc., 1913) and his message to Congress on Jan. 20, 1914, *Congressional Record*, **LI**, pp. 1978ff.

[3] 32 Stat. 825, 827.

The functions in aid of the Attorney General have been minor in the history of the commission. The requests of the President and the Congress for investigation have not been confined solely to complaints of violation. Though the commission's investigations and recommendations have had a strong antitrust bias, they have not been confined to alleged antitrust violations. The chief significance of its work has been in the accumulation and reporting of data relating to corporation practices in general and their relation to the antitrust policy, rather than to particular violations and remedies therefor.

The commission had faith in the beginning in corporate reporting as one means of obtaining data. Efforts along this line for the iron and steel industry were, however, blocked by court action.[4] As a result, it was not until 1939 that the commission reinstituted the corporate phase of its investigatorial function. Except for a period of suspension during the war, this work has since been carried on without interruption and without court interference. The other phase of the commission's general investigatorial function, which might simply be called "economic investigations," also faced legal objections which frustrated the commission in its early history.[5] The legal issues related to the power of the commission to compel production of papers, and arose primarily under the Fourth Amendment. Today legal restraints do not seriously impede government in investigatorial, record-keeping, and reporting functions.[6]

The volume and range of economic investigation has been tremendous. Prior to 1932, over seventy investigations had been conducted. Of these, five were carried over from the Bureau of Corporations, fifteen were initiated by the commission, and forty-three, eight, five, and two, respectively, arose from direction or request from the Senate, House of Representatives, President, or Attorney General. Between 1932 and 1952 about forty-eight investigations were conducted. In this period there is a sharp decline in requests for investigation from Congress. Only thirteen began in this way, and only five and two with the President and Attorney General, respectively. The commission itself initiated the largest number.[7] In addition to its investigations, the commission in both world wars made cost or other

---

[4] *Claire Furnace Co. v. F.T.C.*, 285 F. 936 (1923). The ground of decision was that the information required did not relate to interstate commerce. Ultimately the Supreme Court reversed on jurisdictional grounds, leaving the substantive question undetermined. *F.T.C. v. Claire Furnace Co.*, 244 U.S. 160 (1927); followed in *F.T.C. v. Maynard Coal Co.*, 22 F. (2d) 873 (1927). Under present-day doctrines concerning national power over commerce, the obstacle raised in 1923 would not be significant.

[5] The most significant decision was *F.T.C. v. American Tobacco Co.*, 264 U.S. 298 (1924).

[6] For summary of present doctrines, see Redford, *Administration of National Economic Control* (New York: The Macmillan Company, 1952), pp. 156–163. But for restraints which still exist against arbitrary exercise of power, see *U.S. v. International Nickel Co. of Canada*, 203 F. Supp. 739 (1962).

[7] The facts in the above statistical summary are taken from the unpublished Ph.D. dissertation of Hugh M. Hall, Jr., *The Investigatory Function of the Federal Trade Commission, 1933–1952* (Austin: University of Texas Library, 1952).

studies for war agencies. The range of investigations has been wide. In many cases the same or related industries have been investigated more than once. Some of the notable investigations were the giant investigation of public-utility holding companies, initiated as the result of a Senate resolution in 1928; studies of distribution methods; basing-point pricing studies; and the postwar concentration and international cartel studies.

The effects of the investigatorial function in the early years were not large or significant. Judicial limitations led a leading observer to entitle a chapter, "The Commission Shorn of Power." [8] The unfavorable reception in the courts made the commission reluctant to pursue lines of inquiry that would raise further legal issues. Moreover, in the twenties the commission itself was affected by the soft attitude toward business practices and combinations which came to prevail in the nation and in the government. For more recent years Professor Hugh Hall has studied the function and concluded: [9]

1. The commission has been significant as a fact-gathering agency for Congress, the President, for war agencies, and to obtain information useful to those studying or having responsibility in development of economic policy. The revival of the corporate reporting function gives hope for even further utility for this fact-gathering function.

2. The investigatorial function has undoubtedly had some effect on legislation. In some cases its contribution has been to build a factual record which confirmed the need for legislation, as in the public-utility investigation; in some cases its investigation has added support to the demands of organized groups, as with respect to the Robinson-Patman Act; in some cases—though not often—it has developed recommendations for legislation which were adopted, the most notable being the amendment to Section 7 of the Clayton Act in 1950 after repeated recommendations by the commission in its annual and investigation reports.

3. The commission has not, however, been very constructive in preparing recommendations. It has often made recommendations within a traditional framework of antitrust or regulatory technique when a new and fresh approach in regulatory technique was needed. An example is found in the public-utility investigation. The commission gathered a stupendous amount of data, but its recommendations for action were unimaginative, and it was left to the later workers in the House Interstate Commerce Committee to evolve techniques of control particularly adapted to the situation revealed by the commission.[10]

4. In some cases, most notably in basing-point pricing, the investigatory

---

[8] Thomas C. Blaisdell, *The Federal Trade Commission: An Experiment in the Control of Business* (New York: Columbia University Press, 1932), Ch. 8.

[9] In his chapter in Emmette S. Redford (ed.), *Public Administration and Policy Formation: Oil, Gas, Banking, River Development and Corporate Investigations* (Austin, Tex.: University of Texas Press, 1956), pp. 302–305.

[10] see pages 435ff.

function has been an aid to the enforcement function of the commission. Except for a few areas, however, this effect is not clearly revealed.[11]

THE ENFORCEMENT FUNCTION OF THE FTC. In 1914, authority was vested in the FTC to enforce Section 5 of the Federal Trade Commission Act, which prohibited "unfair methods of competition," and Sections 2, 3, 7, and 8 of the Clayton Act, except where the provisions of this act were applicable to banks and common carriers.[12] A number of later acts have also provided for their enforcement by the commission. The enforcement technique set up in 1914 is the "cease and desist" order. The commission, after complaint and hearing, may order a violator to cease and desist from further violation. Appeals from such an order may be taken to a Court of Appeals, which is directed to uphold the order if it is based on "substantial evidence"; decisions of such courts are subject to review by certiorari by the Supreme Court.

The original acts provided no penalty for violation of an FTC order. If an order was not obeyed, the commission could appeal to a Court of Appeals; if it upheld the commission, any further violation would be contempt of court. This resulted in two weaknesses in enforcement: (1) the burden of moving to court was on the commission instead of on the party against whom the order was issued; (2) there was delay in obtaining compliance with an order. However, by an amendment to the Federal Trade Commission Act in 1938 (Wheeler-Lea Act), orders of the commission under Section 5 of the act become "final" when issued by the commission, unless and until set aside by a court; when an order becomes final, its violation is subject to "a civil penalty of not more than $5,000 for each violation." [13] By amendments to the Clayton Act in 1959, provisions of the same kind were made applicable to cease-and-desist orders issued by the commission in cases arising under that act.[14]

Under the cease-and-desist technique, violations occurring prior to issuance and finalization of an order are not penalized. The commission's function is to prevent further violation. However, violations of the Clayton and the Federal Trade Commission acts may be violations of the Sherman Act; also, violations of the Clayton Act are by that act made violations of the "antitrust" laws, and hence are subject to the same penalties as are violations of the Sherman Act. Where a violation of the 1914 acts is also a violation of the Sherman or "antitrust" acts, the government may proceed either through the FTC or through criminal or civil penalties initiated

[11] In 1961 the FTC reported that it had made a new use of its Section 6 (investigatorial powers). It had, in a concerted attack on brokerage payments to buyers in the citrus-fruit industry, demanded answers to mailed inquiries in an industry-wide investigation. *Annual Report of the Federal Trade Commission* (Washington, D.C.: 1961), pp. 2–3.

[12] Authority to enforce with respect to banks and covered common carriers was vested in the Federal Reserve Board and the Interstate Commerce Commission, respectively.

[13] 52 Stat. 111. Sections 5 (g) and (1).

[14] 73 Stat. 243.

and prosecuted by the Department of Justice, and private parties may sue for treble damages. Moreover, the Wheeler-Lea Act of 1938 contained supplementary provisions concerning the false advertisement of foods, drugs, devices (to cure disease or affect the structure of the body), and cosmetics. The commission need not wait for the completion of its proceedings in such cases. It may go at once to a court with a plea for an injunction or restraining order to stop the false advertising. Also, violations are, under certain specified conditions, subject to prescribed criminal penalties. Special protection has also been given to the public under other statutes. The Wool Products Labeling Act,[15] Fur Products Labeling Act,[16] and Textile Fiber Products Identification Act [17] require informative labelling on fabrics and furs, and the commission may apply to a court for a temporary injunction pending completion of cease-and-desist proceedings or, in the case of wool or furs, for seizure and condemnation of products in violation; civil and criminal penalties are also provided. Similar provisions for enforcement are contained in the Flammable Fabrics Act, which was passed to give the public special protection against apparel containing flammable fabric.[18]

It remains true, nevertheless, that the commission's chief implement for enforcement of the Federal Trade Commission and the Clayton acts is the cease-and-desist order. The commission has, however, developed supplementary methods of enforcement. One is in the arrangements for settlement of cases by consent order. Prior to issuance of a complaint, parties will ordinarily be given notice and an opportunity to agree, without admission of guilt, to desist from the practices about to be charged against the defendant. The second supplementary technique is the Trade Practice Conference. This is a conference of an industry held for the purposes of drawing up "rules" on what is illegal or undesired practice, and of securing voluntary compliance with the rules. The rules are classified now in two groups: Group I contains carefully prepared statements on existing statutory and decisional law; Group II contains rules deemed to be sound business practice.

The value of the trade practice conference has been much debated. Advantages claimed for the procedure are that it (1) clarifies the law, (2) promotes the purpose of the law by adding (in Group II) statements of practice deemed sound by the commission and the leaders in the industry, and (3) informs the trade and helps enlist its voluntary cooperation. On the other hand, it has been argued that (1) Group I formulations have no real value since they merely state the existing law, (2) Group II Rules may result in confusion rather than clarity,[19] and (3) the commission may place too

[15] 54 Stat. 1128 (1940).
[16] 65 Stat. 175 (1951).
[17] 72 Stat. 1717 (1958).
[18] 67 Stat. 111 (passed 1953, effective 1954).
[19] The first two objections were advanced by some members of the Attorney General's committee. See *Report of the Attorney General's National Committee to Study the Antitrust Laws* (Washington, D.C.: Superintendent of Documents, 1955), p. 370.

much reliance on trade conferences as an alternative to prosecution of cases. The commission was criticized for shifting too much to the trade practice conference in the twenties. Obviously, the trade practice conference should not be an alternative to enforcement proceedings. There is great value in having would-be violators realize that enforcement action is a possibility. There is also value in a legal process which results in a further definition of the meaning of the law. At the same time, administrators see advantage in efforts to obtain understanding of the proscriptions of law and voluntary compliance. It has even been suggested that the case-to-case approach—slow, piecemeal, with consideration of public interests in a setting of private litigation—is a poor approach to solution of the problem of trade practices, and that since the law cannot be evolved in detail by statutes, the legal definition of illegal practices through administrative rule-making would be advantageous.[20]

In 1955 the commission initiated an Industry Guide Program. It prepares "guides" that delineate what it believes to be illegal in a business practice, and conducts informational programs to obtain understanding of these. By 1961 it had prepared six "Guides," including one on cigarette advertising and one on advertising allowances.

Under the acts of 1914, the commission had enforcement duties with respect to two general types of practices: those involving fraud or dishonesty (deceptive acts), and those which restrained competition (monopolistic practices). In its early years the commission initiated cases against both types of practice. But adverse decisions in the court cases led it to virtually discontinue its efforts against monopolistic practices. By 1932 the commission initiated in an entire year only one Clayton Act case; it confined its efforts very largely to an attack on misbranding and false advertising.[21] By 1937 it had again entered the fray against so-called "monopolistic practices," and today it is active in investigation and prosecution of both deceptive and monopolistic practices.

Of course, there is overlapping in the jurisdiction of the commission and the Department of Justice in monopolistic-practice cases. Undoubtedly it had been the purpose of Congress, as stated by the Supreme Court, to supplement the Department of Justice's enforcement activity "through the administrative process of the new Trade Commission," and even "to permit the simultaneous use of both types of proceedings." [22] There is, therefore, a need for cooperation between the two, so that each may best deploy its own limited resources and so that the most effective remedy available to the

---

[20] See Milton Handler, "Unfair Competition," *Iowa Law Review*, **XXI** (1936), pp. 175, 259; F. F. Blachly and Miriam E. Oatman, *Federal Regulatory Action and Control* (Washington, D.C.: Brookings Institution, 1940), p. 51.

[21] *Annual Report of the Federal Trade Commission for the Fiscal Year Ended June 30, 1932* (Washington, D.C.), p. 64.

[22] *F.T.C. v. Cement Institute*, 333 U.S. 683, 693, 694–5 (1948).

two agencies may be employed. This cooperation is effected by regular and frequent conferences between representatives of the two agencies.

UNFAIR METHODS OF COMPETITION AND DECEPTIVE ACTS

Section 5 of the Federal Trade Commission Act prohibited "unfair methods of competition." In 1931, in the Raladam case, the Supreme Court ruled that there could be no "unfair method of competition" unless there was some competitor who could lose trade as a result of the practice under attack. The commission had entered an order against continuance of certain claims in advertising of an obesity cure. Though the false advertising could mislead the public, there was no evidence to show that competitors had been injured.[23] To correct this decision, the Federal Trade Commission Act was amended by the Wheeler-Lea Act to prohibit "unfair methods of competition in commerce, and unfair or deceptive acts or practices in commerce." This is the language of the provision today. The prohibition against "unfair methods of competition" protects competitors; the one against "unfair or deceptive acts or practices" protects consumers.[24]

There was a doctrine of "unfair competition" under the common law. Thus, one injured by a competitor simulating his trademark or trade name could bring action to stop the practice or to obtain damages.[25] The phrase "unfair methods of competition" has been construed to have a broader meaning,[26] as does, of course, the phrase added in the Wheeler-Lea Act. Some of the activities that fall under the interdiction of the Federal Trade Commission Act as amended are listed:

1. False advertising or misbranding of products.
2. Making false and disparaging statements respecting competitors' products and business.
3. Procuring the business or trade secrets of competitors by espionage, or by bribing their employees, or by similar means.
4. Various methods to create the impression that the customer is being offered an opportunity to make purchases under particularly favorable conditions when this is not the case.
5. Selling below cost or giving products without cost, with intent of hindering or suppressing competition.

[23] *Federal Trade Commission v. Raladam Co.,* 283 U.S. 643 (1931).
[24] The Wheeler-Lea Act was important. As has been noted in the discussion above, it not only broadened the substantive law, but made cease-and-desist orders issued in enforcement of the Federal Trade Commission Act "final" without court process, and added additional remedies for prevention of false advertising of foods, drugs, devices, and cosmetics.
[25] If there was a trademark, he also had a remedy under special statutory provisions in the Trade Mark Act.
[26] See, for example, *F.T.C. v. R. F. Keppel & Bro.,* 291 U.S. 304 (1934).

6. Buying up supplies for the purpose of hampering competitors and stifling or eliminating competition.

7. Threatening patent-infringement suits for the purpose of intimidating the trade and stifling competition.[27]

The largest number of the cases are against deceptive practices of various sorts. Recently, the commission reported that in a single year 292 complaints were issued and 272 orders to cease and desist were entered in deceptive-practice cases.[28] The most common type of case is against false advertising. The commission not only acts as a result of complaints received, but monitors advertising copy. In a recent year its staff reviewed 465,324 radio-television advertisements and 169,294 magazine and newspaper pages to discover violations.[29] At times, the commission has concentrated much attention on advertising of particular products, such as cigarettes and recently foods and drugs, wearing apparel, and textiles.

Yet antideceptive practices form only a part of the prosecutions under Section 5. Anticompetitive practices (called "antimonopoly" practices by the FTC) are also attacked under this provision. For example, an order was issued against a combination of manufacturers of women's garments and of textiles who sought to boycott outsiders' use of designs of their products.[30] Later discussion will show the use of Section 5 against basing-point pricing. Some practices that would constitute violation of the Clayton Act or the Sherman Act have been attacked as violations of Section 5.

THE CLAYTON ACT, AS AMENDED

SECTION 2. This section is designed to prevent price discriminations. The aim of the 1914 provision was to prevent firms that were operating over a large area from destroying rivals in particular communities by local price cutting.[31] The provision, as did certain other sections of the Clayton Act (Sections 3 and 7), added a new standard of illegality. In addition to the possibility of illegality under the Sherman Act or Section 5 of the Federal Trade Commission Act, price discriminations under this act would be illegal if the effect "may be to substantially lessen competition or tend to create a monopoly in any line of commerce." The purpose of the provision, like other sections of the Clayton Act, was *to prevent monopoly in its incipiency* by attacking practices through which monopoly power could be developed. It conformed, therefore, with the spirit and purpose of the Sherman Act and other antitrust provisions.

---

[27] For a more complete list, see *Annual Report of the Federal Trade Commission, 1953*, pp. 81–86.
[28] *Annual Report of the Federal Trade Commission, 1961*, p. 39.
[29] *Ibid.*, p. 30.
[30] *Fashion Originators Guild of America v. FTC*, 312 U.S. 457 (1941).
[31] See H. Rept. 627, 63rd Cong., 2nd Sess., p. 1960.

The section specifically exempted price discriminations between purchasers because of differences "in the grade, quality, or quantity" purchased. Subsequently there was much dissatisfaction among small retailers because of competition from chain stores and other mass-distribution outlets. An investigation of food chain stores was made by the Federal Trade Commission. It concluded that lower prices to chains by manufacturers than were granted to other buyers was "a most substantial, if not the chief, factor" in the lower selling prices of chain stores.[32] To restrict such quantity discounts, the Robinson-Patman amendments to Section 2 were passed in 1936.[33] They were passed, in other words, with protection of the small distributor in mind. Section 2, as amended, therefore, reflected the antitrust purpose of preserving a competitive system and the supplementary purpose of protecting the small competitor. These two purposes are not the same, and may run counter to each other. This is to say that the small competitor is to a degree protected from competition. Such protection is said to result in "soft competition."

The original Section 2 was complex and the Robinson-Patman amendments have made it the most intricate and controversial of the antitrust prohibitions. The Supreme Court has said that "Precision of expression is not an outstanding characteristic of the Robinson-Patman Act," [34] and Congressman Celler predicted "the courts will have the devil's own job to unravel the tangle. . . ." [35] In addition, Section 2 is a very difficult section to administer, and difficult for sellers to comply with. In fact, one question about the Robinson-Patman amendments is whether these go too far in the administrative burdens imposed on sellers and whether they are not, in fact, impossible to administer from either the private or government side.

The core of the price-discrimination section is now subsection 2(a). It makes it unlawful to:

discriminate in price
between different purchasers of commodities of like *grade* and *quality* . . .
where the effect *may* be *substantially to lessen competition* or *tend to create a monopoly* in *any line of commerce,*
or to *injure,* destroy, or prevent *competition* with any person who either grants or knowingly receives the benefit of such discrimination, or with customers of either of them.

The particular words of this provision should be carefully noted. First, "A price discrimination . . . is merely a price difference." [36] Second, although price differences according to grade and quality are still permitted, quantity discounts which have the stated effects are illegal. Third, the words

---

[32] Federal Trade Commission, *Final Report on the Chain Store Investigation* (Washington, D.C.: 1934), p. 53.
[33] 38 Stat. 730.
[34] *Automatic Canteen v. FTC,* 346 U.S. 661, 665.
[35] *Congressional Record,* **LXXX**, p. 9419 (1936).
[36] *FTC v. Anheuser-Busch, Inc.,* 363 U.S. 536, 549 (1960).

"may be" in this provision, though sometimes construed to mean a *reasonable probability*, were held by the Supreme Court in 1948 to mean a *possibility* of lessening competition or tending toward a monopoly.[37]

Fourth, a new test of illegality, unknown to other antitrust provisions, is added in the so-called "injury" provision at the end of the prohibition. The commission's initial effort under Section 2 had been scotched by court interpretation of the phrase "in any line of commerce." The commission had directed its effort toward differentials in price among different types of buyers, such as wholesalers, chains, cooperatives, and independent retailers. In the Mennen case, its complaint arose because Mennen refused to give its wholesale discount to a retail cooperative of druggists. The reviewing court found that the distributing organizations were in a different line of commerce from Mennen. In other words, the act was interpreted to apply only to the lessening of competition between the seller and those competing with him in the same type of trade. Adverse effect on competition among buyers was not affected by the act.[38] Though this interpretation stopped the commission's Section 2 program, a private suit (the Van Camp case) resulted in a reversal of the interpretation by the Supreme Court in 1929.[39] The injury provision of the present "2(a)," added by the Robinson-Patman Act, covers injuries to competition among buyers, and hence specifically provides for the same thing as was held in the Van Camp case.

The injury provision, however, does more than this. The "lessening of competition" and "tend to create a monopoly" phrases, to which it was added, require proof, as do other antitrust provisions, that the *vigor of competition* has been reduced. The injury provision, in contrast, apparently only requires proof of injury to *individual competitors*.[40] Even though active competition remained or the competition of a displaced seller or buyer was replaced by competition of another, the act could be violated. This is quite large protection for individual persons.

The Robinson-Patman Act provides for two main defenses against the prohibition in Section 2(a):

1. The "cost" defense: price differentials are allowed which "make only *due allowance* for differences in the cost of manufacture, sale, or delivery resulting from the *differing methods or quantities* in which such commodities are to such purchasers sold or delivered."

2. The "good faith" defense: a seller may rebut the prima-facie case against him

---

[37] *FTC v. Morton Salt Co.*, 334 U.S. 37 (1948).

[38] *Mennen Co. v. FTC*, 288 F. 774 (1923), certiorari denied, 262 U.S. 759 (1923); also, *National Biscuit Co. v. FTC*, 299 F. 733 (1924), certiorari denied, 266 U.S. 613 (1924).

[39] *Van Camp & Sons Co. v. American Can Co.*, 278 U.S. 245.

[40] See Stocking and Watkins, *Monopoly and Free Enterprise* (New York: Twentieth Century Fund, 1951), p. 367, including note 66. The majority of the Attorney General's Committee argued that the provision should be construed so as to be consistent with traditional antitrust policy; a minority disagreed, and thought this interpretation was in accord with neither statutory purposes nor Supreme Court pronouncements. *Report of the Attorney General's Committee to Study the Antitrust Laws*, op. cit., pp. 164–167.

by showing that his lower price (or extra services supplied) to a purchaser was made "in good faith to meet *an equally low price* of a competitor. . . ."[41]

The cost provision contains a proportionality rule. The original act was interpreted to allow *any* amount of reduction of price on large orders.[42] The amendments provide for reductions which make *only* "due allowance" for differences in cost of manufacture, sale, or delivery. But what constitutes "due allowances"? Section 2(b) puts the burden of proof in justifying a price differential on the seller against whom a complaint is issued. The commission has been strict in its requirements, and the difficulty of developing cost data which protect a price difference is exceedingly great. A study group has concluded that justification of differentials involves submission of accounting data which "only the most prosperous and patient business firm" may be able to afford,[43] and which may at best be inconclusive.

The cost provision allows justification on the basis of differences in *method*, as well as quantity, of sales. This means that so-called functional discounts may be made—that is, discounts to buyers who perform part of the function of distribution for the seller. The due-allowance provision applies, however, for functional as well as quantity discounts. The most difficult problem on functional discounts has arisen with respect to multiple-function distributors who perform different roles with respect to different sales. The commission's rule is that where a buyer performs double functions—for example, wholesaling and retailing—the supplier's functional discount can apply only to the portion of the sale which the buyer will sell at wholesale.[44]

The "good faith" provision allows a seller to reduce prices for some buyers without reducing for all, if this is done in good faith "to meet" (*not go lower than*) the price of a competitor. The provision has been construed by the Supreme Court to provide an absolute defense on a charge of price discrimination.[45] This means that a seller can meet a competitor's price even though the effect may be to injure competition. The limits on the good-faith defense have, however, been shown in two cases. In the Staley case a company had adopted a basing-point pricing system and made the claim that this was in good faith to meet competition. The Supreme Court held that the Staley Company could not use the good-faith defense to justify adoption of a competitor's patently *unlawful* pricing system by which price

---

[41] Also, it is stated that Section 2(a) does not prevent a seller from selection of his own customers or from making changes in his prices from time to time to meet changing conditions, such as deterioration of perishable commodities, obsolescence of seasonal goods, etc.

[42] *Goodyear Tire and Rubber Co. v. FTC*, 101 F 2d 620, certiorari denied, 308 U.S. 557.

[43] *Report of Attorney General's National Committee to Study the Antitrust Laws* (Washington, D.C.: Superintendent of Documents, 1955), p. 173.

[44] *Southgate Brokerage Co. v. FTC*, 150 F 2d 607 (1945). Also involved in the Standard Oil (Indiana) case.

[45] *Standard Oil Co. (Indiana) v. FTC*, 340 U.S. 231 (1951).

was raised rather than lowered.[46] More recently, it has been ruled that the good-faith defense could be used to justify price reductions only if made to meet individual competitive situations, not as an application of a seller's own pricing system.[47]

The Robinson-Patman Act buttressed the prohibitions of Section 2(a) with other rules, as follows:

1. Where discrimination (that is, difference) in price is shown, the burden of rebutting the prima-facie contention that this is a violation rests upon the accused seller (Section 2b).

2. Commissions, brokerage, or other compensation can be given only for services actually rendered (Section 2c). Seller and buyer are both made accountable for violations under this so-called "brokerage" provision.

3. Discriminations to buyers for services rendered to the seller *by the buyer* (for example, advertising of the product) or supply of services *by the seller* to the buyer are illegal unless made available to all "on proportionally equal terms" (Sections 2d and 2e).

4. The buyer, too, is in violation if he "knowingly" shall "induce or receive" an unlawful discrimination (Section f).

5. The FTC is authorized to fix quantity limits above which discounts shall not be allowed, "where it finds that available purchasers in greater quantities are so few as to render differentials on account thereof unjustly discriminatory or promotive of monopoly in any line of commerce" (Section 2a).

6. Criminal penalties are added for certain enumerated acts of discrimination.

The complications of the act are further increased by these provisions. The cost-defense test is not available in defense against charges of violation of the provisions.[48] Sections 2(d) and 2(e) introduce new tests of legality; that is, differences are allowable if made available to all "on proportionally equal terms." The good-faith defense is applicable to the three provisions—2(c), (d), and (e).[49]

Section 2 has been enforced, except for private suits, by the Federal Trade Commission exclusively. From 1936 to 1957 it had decided 430 cases and issued 311 cease-and-desist orders. Surprising, many would think, is the fact that 47 per cent of the cases have been brought under 2(c), the brokerage provision, solely, and it is ironic, many would also think, that some of

[46] *FTC v. Staley Mfg. Co.*, 324 U.S. 746 (1945).
[47] *Federal Trade Commission v. Standard Oil Co.*, 335 U.S. 396 (1958). This was a second decision in this case, and the Court upheld the lower court's reversal of the commission on issues of fact.
[48] See *FTC v. Simplicity Pattern Co.*, 360 U.S. 59 (1959).
[49] There has been some uncertainty about applicability of the good-faith defense to 2(d) cases, where the seller pays for the services rendered by the buyer. The FTC has thought the defense was not applicable; but for rejection of this view, see *Exquisite Form Brassiere v. FTC*, 301 F 2d 499 (D.C. Circuit, 1961), certiorari denied, 369 U.S. 888 (1962).

the most significant of these have been against voluntary associations or cooperatives representing the interests of small stores. The next largest number of cases (about 32 per cent) have been solely under 2(a). These have included, among other things, quantity (on single sales) and volume (quantity over a period of time) discounts, functional discounts, and territorial discrimination.[50] Only seven cases have been brought under 2(f)—that is, against buyers solely. The difficulties of proof that a buyer knowingly received an unlawful allowance or discount are, of course, great. One striking feature of these cases is that most of the orders have been issued without full legal contest. Only 45 of the 311 cases have ended in a full trial.[51] In only one instance, that of rubber tires sold in the replacement market, has the commission set quantity discounts; the commission's rule on the matter was set aside by a reviewing court.[52]

Controversy about the Robinson-Patman Act has extended from the discussions prior to its passage to the present day. Recently, a recognized authority, after exhaustive and thorough analysis, reached quite cautious conclusions.[53] Corwin Edwards concludes that the cases under the act have shown that there was a need for a statute against price discrimination. He thinks the statute "has afforded effective protection against the price-cutting activities of predatory would-be monopolists and that it has substantially reduced the discriminatory advantages in price enjoyed by large buyers." He concludes, nevertheless, that the statute "has only partly accomplished its purpose." Among other things, he points out that since the law strikes only at "manifestations of the power of the big buyer rather than at that power itself," buyers will often find ways of escaping from the effects of the statute. On the other hand, he points out that the law has been applied against the efforts of small buyers to obtain, through buying associations or cooperatives, the advantages of large chains, and states that his study shows no basis for a conclusion as to whether the legal protection given to the small buyer outweighs the damage done to his efforts at self-protection. He repeats the patently evident conclusion drawn by many that the commission has expended a considerable portion of its effort on proceedings, particularly under the brokerage provision, against small concerns. He thinks that the act may have encouraged efforts toward efficiency by forcing more careful analysis of costs by firms, but that it has also made business more expensive by requiring constant legal research relating to price decisions, and has made firms accept practices which were uneconomical. He finds that the act has had "no uniform effect of raising or lowering prices," but he thinks his

---

[50] See pages 232ff. for discussion of basing-point cases under Section 2(a). Basing-point pricing is one form of potential territorial price discrimination.
[51] For these and other data on enforcement, see Corwin D. Edwards, *The Price Discrimination Law* (Washington, D.C.: Brookings Institution, 1959), Chapter 4.
[52] For analysis of the proceedings, see Edwards, *ibid.*, Chapter 9.
[53] Edwards, *ibid.*, Chapters 19 and 20.

study strongly supports "the inference that the reduced pressure of buyers for concessions and the enhanced risk of the seller who makes concessions have tended to make sticky prices stickier and thus to reduce the flexibility and responsiveness of the price system." He concludes that "Excessive scope in the law has also tended to reduce the vigor of competition."

Edwards would amend the law with a more restricted view of purpose than the one behind the present statute. He thinks that the objective of preventing inequality among buyers has no place in a price-discrimination statute. This aim is now basic to many of the details of the present law, such as those protecting against injury to particular persons and the brokerage provision. This purpose, it is said, results in "an unfortunately pervasive control over price relationships." He would aim toward the preservation of market competition by restricting the discriminatory practices of powerful competitors. This is the objective of the Sherman Act and the prohibitions against lessening competition or tending to create a monopoly. He thinks the greatest danger is in the lessening of competition among sellers, although he sees also some danger in the lessening of competition as a result of the action of powerful buyers.

Edwards' analysis focuses attention on large issues and problems. What should be the objectives of legislation? Should law aim only toward preservation of a competitive system? Or should it aim also toward reduction of advantage to one buyer over another? If the latter is an objective, can it be best attained by fullest achievement of the first objective? Does more than this involve too deep a penetration into pricing policies? Or is the second objective important enough to justify additional administrative costs for government and business, and some additional stickiness in prices? Most professional commentators lean toward a single objective—the maintenance of competition; but there was in 1936, and there undoubtedly is now, strong popular appeal in the second objective.

SECTION 3. This section attacks tying clauses and exclusive dealing arrangements. A tying clause prevents use of an article by the buyer or lessee unless another is also *used* or, in its narrower sense, unless another is *used with it*. An exclusive dealing arrangement prevents *sale* of competitors' products. Section 3 forbids any person "to lease or make a sale or contract for sale of goods . . . or other merchandise, whether patented or unpatented" on condition that "the lessee or purchaser thereof shall not *use* or *deal* in the goods . . . of a competitor or competitors of the lessor or seller, where the effect" "may be to substantially lessen competition or tend to create a monopoly."

A seller or lessor who has a strong position with respect to one article may use a tying clause as leverage to force use or sale of one or more other articles. Or a large seller producing many products may use the tying clause to force distributors to take all of his products. This is known as "full-line forcing." In either case the buyer must take something he might not have taken in a free market. Also, the effect is to broaden the market control of the seller and to foreclose competitors from the range of products covered in the scheme. Tying clauses may have a particularly severe effect on sellers of specialty products or on small sellers. The exclusive dealing contract may take the form of a so-called "requirements contract," under which the purchaser agrees to take all of his requirements from the seller. Or it may take the form of a demand that the buyer handle no merchandise produced by other firms.

Section 3 does not cover contracts of agency, but only of lease or sale. Thus, where schoolboys delivered magazines for Curtis Publishing Company and the FTC found that there was an exclusive dealing restriction, the Supreme Court decided that there was no violation of Section 3, because the boys never acquired title to the magazines, but were agents for sale of magazines belonging to the company.[54] On the other hand, in the Standard Fashion Company case, in which a contract prohibited retailers from selling any patterns for women's and children's garments except those of the supplier, in which the claim was made that the contract was one of agency, the Supreme Court found that title had passed and that Section 3 was violated.[55]

One argument made to justify the tying clause is that of good will. In *International Business Machines Corp. v. U.S.*[56] an injunction was issued against the corporation's leasing its tabulating and other machines on the condition that the lessees use with such machines only tabulating cards made by the corporation. The corporation claimed that the condition was designed to protect its good will, in that it was essential for the successful operation of the machines that cards meeting certain specifications be used. The Supreme Court thought that this need could be met by the corporation's requiring in its leases that only cards with certain specifications should be used, but leaving it to the lessee to purchase such cards wherever he wished.

A tying clause or exclusive dealing arrangement may be a violation of the Sherman Act. But the standards set by the Clayton Act for determining illegality are tighter. The words "may be" (indicating reasonable probability rather than actual results), "substantial lessening," and "tend to" were new terms in statutory law in 1914. The major issue in Section 3 cases is whether the effect of leases or sales is to infringe these standards. The effect of the provision can be illustrated by a few cases. In 1922 the Supreme Court held illegal the requirement by United Shoe Machinery Company that lessees of its machines use with them only certain unpatented machines made by the company; the adverse effect on competition, or tendency to monopoly, was found in the Company's "dominant position in supplying shoe machinery of the classes involved."[57] In the

---

[54] *FTC v. Curtis Publishing Co.,* 260 U.S. 568 (1923).
[55] *Standard Fashion Co. v. Magrane-Houston Co.,* 258 U.S. 346 (1922).
[56] 298 U.S. 131 (1936).
[57] *United States Shoe Machinery Co. v. U.S.,* 258 U.S. 451 (1922).

Standard Fashion Company case, substantial effect on competition was found where 40 per cent of the pattern agencies were engaged in a scheme which limited sales to one pattern merchant in communities, thus shutting out competition entirely in many small communities and limiting competition even in large cities.[58]

In recent years the issue has been presented concerning whether a "quantitative test" of substantiality would be sufficient. Under this test, it would be sufficient to show that a substantial portion of commerce is affected; if so, the practice would be illegal *per se*. In the International Salt case in 1947, involving a tying contract, the Supreme Court said, "it is unreasonable, *per se,* to foreclose competitors from any *substantial* (italics supplied) market".[59] It was sufficient for the Court in this case that a substantial volume of business was affected. In an exclusive dealing case (the Standard Stations case) in 1949 the same decision was reached.[60] Standard Oil of California sold in seven western states 23 per cent of the gasoline— 6.8 per cent through its own stations, 6.7 per cent through independent stations with which it made exclusive dealing contracts on gasoline (and in some cases, on tires and other accessories), and the remainder directly to industrial users. The issue was over the exclusive dealing contracts. The Court was divided 5 to 4, but the majority held that it was enough that "the competition has been foreclosed in a *substantial* share of the line of commerce affected" (italics supplied).

The majority of the Attorney General's National Committee criticized the quantitative test, and thought that in exclusive dealing cases there should be *an analysis of market conditions* to determine effects on competition, and reasonable probability of economic harm. The minority would not disown entirely the "quantitative" test.[61] The issue thus drawn as to what would constitute proof of "substantial lessening" of competition was again considered by the Supreme Court in the Tampa Electric case in 1961.[62] Tampa had decided to burn coal in a new generating plant, and had contracted with Nashville Coal Company to supply the coal over a twenty-year period. The value of coal to be purchased was $128,000,000. The district court and the court of appeals had held that there was a substantial lessening of competition. To arrive at this conclusion, they seem to have considered that the relevant market in which competition was affected was the market for coal in "Peninsular Florida," in which the total use of coal was about equal to Tampa's estimated use for 1959. The Supreme Court overruled, basing its decision that there was no substantial lessening of competition on the conclusion that the

---

[58] *Standard Fashion Co. v. Magrane-Houston Co.,* 258 U.S. 346 (1922).
[59] *International Salt Co. v. U.S.,* 332 U.S. 392, 396.
[60] *Standard Oil Co. of California v. U.S.,* 337 U.S. 293.
[61] *Report of Attorney General's Committee to Study the Antitrust Laws* (Washington, D.C.: Superintendent of Documents, 1955), pp. 140–149.
[62] *Tampa Electric Co. v. Nashville Coal Co. et al.,* 365 U.S. 320.

relevant market was larger, including seven hundred competing sellers, and that the Tampa contract was only 1 per cent of this. On its face, the decision itself seems to turn on the quantity of the relevant market affected. Justice Clark, however, said that the high dollar value of the contract itself was not enough substantially to foreclose competition, for the annual trade in coal in the market was over a billion dollars. Also, in concluding his discussion of the Standard Stations case, he seemed to reject a simple test of "substantial share" of the market by referring to several things that must be considered in determining substantiality, such as the relative strength of the parties and the probable effect on "effective competition." It appears that Justice Clark's statements show the need now for the government, in making a case, to analyze other market factors besides the "substantial share" of the market referred to in the Standard Stations case.[63] This will increase the burden to be carried by the government in Section 3 cases, and will place a premium on high-quality economic analysis of market influences.

It should be noted, however, that the Supreme Court stated in 1962 that for an exclusive dealing contract to be held in violation of Section 3, "the market foreclosure must generally be significantly greater than if the arrangement is a tying contract." The reason, said the Court, was that the latter was "inherently anticompetitive," in that a buyer was forced to take something he didn't want, but that an exclusive dealing contract was not "inherently anticompetitive." [64]

SECTION 7. "We are all agreed, I take it, that holding companies should be prohibited," said President Wilson in his antitrust message to Congress in 1914. Beyond this, he suggested for consideration of Congress: "Shall we require the owners of stock, when their voting power in several companies which ought to be independent of one another would constitute actual control, to make election in which of them they will exercise their right to vote?" [65] These were far-reaching suggestions, growing out of the evidence of the day on how stock purchase could be made the means of monopolistic control. From the Sugar Trust case in 1895, through the Northern Securities case in 1904, to the Standard Oil case and the initiation of the government's suit in the U.S. Steel case in 1911, the

---

[63] What Justice Clark "did to *Standard Stations* is as neat a piece of judicial surgery as has been seen in some time." Milton Handler, "Recent Antitrust Developments," *Yale Law Journal,* **LXXI** (November 1961), pp. 74, 82.

[64] *Brown Shoe Co., Inc. v. U.S.*, 370 U.S. 294, 329–31. For further reference to tying agreements, see the discussion of patents, pages 202ff., and of the Paramount Pictures case, pages 200–201.

[65] *Congressional Record,* **LI,** p. 1979 (January 20, 1914). President Roosevelt, in 1907, had said to Congress: "The real owners of a corporation should be compelled to do business in their own name. The right to hold stock in other corporations should hereafter be denied to interstate corporations unless on approval by the proper governmental officials and a prerequisite to such approval should be the listing with the Government of all owners and stockholders, both by the corporation in which such stocks are owned." *Congressional Record,* **XLII,** Pt. I, p. 70.

226 Policies Affecting the Economy Generally

public had become increasingly aware of the threat to the competitive system by holding companies and stock purchase by one company in another. This method of growing to a dominating position was regarded as an unnatural one, in contrast to the normal growth of a corporation's business.

It is not surprising that Congress tempered the proposal of the President so as to prohibit only that which would be a threat to the competitive system. It took no action whatever on his proposal on individual voting of stock. As for intercorporate stock ownership, Section 7 of the Clayton Act provided that no corporation engaged in commerce should acquire stock in another corporation so engaged, and that no corporation should acquire stock in two or more corporations engaged in commerce, where the effect "may be to substantially lessen competition" between such corporations "or to restrain such commerce in any section or community or tend to create a monopoly." Purchase of stock solely for investment purposes and formation of subsidiary corporations to carry on the business of a corporation were specifically exempted, provided these did not result in substantially lessening competition.

It is surprising that the forceful recommendation of the President and the tight language of the new section ("may be," "substantially lessen," and "tend to create" were obviously more restrictive than the words in the Sherman Act) yielded such meager results over the succeeding quarter-century. It would be difficult to find an instance in American history where so little was achieved from legislation over so long a period. Six years after the Clayton Act, the decision of the Supreme Court in the U.S. Steel case went far toward removing the restrictions of the Sherman Act on acquisition of power through intercorporate stock ownership.[66] The 1920's was a period of formation of giant combinations, but only one of the sixty-three biggest industrial operating companies was formed from 1921 to 1928 (inclusive), while fourteen (or thirteen) of the twenty-one industrial holding companies were formed during this period.[67] Both the Sherman Act, under which the Steel case was brought, and Section 7 appeared to be inoperative as a preventive for the building of vast industrial empires through intercorporate stockholding.

The potential of Section 7 was largely destroyed by Supreme Court decisions in 1926 and 1934. In 1926 it overruled the commission on orders against Swift & Company and Thatcher Manufacturing Company. These two firms had acquired stock of competitors, and had used the control thus gained to consummate a purchase of the assets (a merger) of the firms acquired. In both cases the assets had been acquired prior to the initiation of FTC proceedings. The Court held that the commission had no authority to order the companies to divest themselves of the

---

[66] See pages 190–191.
[67] From James Angell McLaughlin, *Cases on the Federal Anti-Trust Laws of the United States* (Cambridge, Mass.: Harvard University Press, 1933), p. 287n.

acquired assets.[68] In the 1934 case, a holding company had acquired the stock of two companies that were alleged to be competitors. *After* the FTC had begun proceedings to undo this acquisition of stock, the holding company made arrangements, through its control of stock of the two companies, for the merger of the assets of the two. The Court held (5 to 4) that the commission had no power to order dissolution of the merger.[69] The lesson for those desiring to escape Section 7 was clear: acquire stock, sit still until the commission initiates proceedings, then arrange for merger of the companies whose stock is commonly held. Stock purchases could be illegal under Section 7, but mergers were not;[70] an illegal method could be used as the means of attaining a legal end.

For over twenty years the FTC urged repeatedly, in annual reports and reports on investigations, that Congress amend Section 7 so as to extend the prohibition against intercorporate stockholding to purchase of assets. After World War II there was another period of corporate mergers. Finally, the Celler-Kefauver Act of 1950 amended Section 7. The main change was to bring purchase of assets under the proscription of the section to the same extent that purchase of stock would be.[71]

This antimerger amendment is one of the most important provisions in present antitrust law. Both the FTC and the Antitrust Division have initiated extensive litigation involving mergers. In the first ten years of the effectiveness of the provision (1951–1960), 43 cases were filed by the FTC and 38 by the Antitrust Division for its enforcement, making a total of 81 cases. In 1961, 18 of the 60 cases filed by the Antitrust Division were Section 7 cases. Moreover, considerable success has been achieved in this litigation. By December 31, 1960, 30 cases had been terminated, with complete divestiture of assets of acquired firms in 12 (1 by court order, 4 by FTC order, 5 by consent decree, 1 by consent order, 1 being voluntary), with limited divestiture in 14 (1 by court order, 1 by FTC order, 6 by consent decree, 6 by consent order), and with denial of divestiture in 4 (by court decision). Some of the firms ordered by consent decree or otherwise to divest assets were Bethlehem Steel Corporation (of Youngstown Sheet and Tube Company, 1958), Pillsbury Mills, Inc. (of Ballard and Ballard Company and Duff's Baking Mix, 1960), Reynolds Metal Company (of Arrow Brands, Inc., 1960), Scott Paper Company (of three companies, 1960), A. G. Spalding Company & Bros., Inc. (of Rawlings Manufacturing Company, 1960), Anheuser-Busch, Inc. (of Miami Brewery and American Brewing Company, 1960), Gamble-Skogmo, Inc. (of Western Auto Supply Company, 1960), Gulf Oil Corporation (of Warren Petroleum Corporation, 1960). Moreover, the average time for settlement of these cases has not been extremely long: 15 months for Department

---

[68] *Swift & Co. v. FTC* and *Thatcher Mfg. Co. v. FTC*, 272 U.S. 554.
[69] *Arrow, Hart & Hegeman Electric Co. v. FTC*, 291 U.S. 587.
[70] They could, of course, be illegal under the Sherman Act.
[71] 64 Stat. 1125.

228 *Policies Affecting the Economy Generally*

of Justice consent decrees, 14 months for FTC consent orders, 27 months for Department of Justice court orders, and 45 months for FTC decisions.[72]

One of the most spectacular Section 7 decisions since 1950 did not arise under the merger amendment, but was a stock-purchase case initiated by the Antitrust Division in 1949. This was the du Pont case, involving the legality of du Pont's 23-per-cent stock-ownership interest in General Motors.[73] The government charged violation of Section 1 and 2 of the Sherman Act, and of Section 7 of the Clayton Act. Although the Clayton Act had not figured prominently in the contest of the parties, the Supreme Court based its decision entirely on Section 7.[74] The charge sustained by the Supreme Court was that du Pont, through its stock ownership, had an illegal advantage over competitors in the sale of automobile finishes and fabrics to General Motors—specifically that the effect of the acquisition was to "tend to create a monopoly" in a "line of commerce." Three issues were involved.[75] First, were the prohibitions of Paragraph 1 (against one corporation acquiring stock of another) applicable to vertical acquisition? In spite of the fact that neither the Department of Justice nor the FTC had brought any cases under the provision against vertical acquisitions in the 35 years between 1914 and 1949, and that the FTC had stated that the provision did not apply to such acquisitions, the Court said that vertical acquisitions were reached by the provision "whenever the reasonable likelihood appears that the acquisition will result in a restraint of commerce or in the creation of a monopoly in any line of commerce." Second, as of what date was legality to be determined? Again in a startling reversal of past assumptions, the Court held that the legality of the stock purchase was to be determined not on the basis of conditions existing at the time of purchase (1917 to 1919), but on those existing at the time of suit (1949). The dissent attacked this conclusion by pointing out that the prohibition of the statute was against *acquisition* of stock, not *use* of stock. The majority, however, referring to the purpose of Section 7 to prohibit acts in their "incipiency" that would produce the undesired effects, said, " 'Incipiency' in this context denotes not the time the stock was acquired, but the time when the acquisition threatens to ripen into a prohibited effect." It took note of the fact that the position of General Motors, and the significance of sales to it, in 1917 were quite different from those at the time of suit. It found

---

[72] All figures given in the paragraph in the text are from Charles F. Phillips, Jr., and George R. Hall, "Merger Litigation, 1951–1960," *Antitrust Bulletin*, **VI** (January–February 1961), pp. 19–41.

[73] *U.S. v. E. I. du Pont de Nemours*, 353 U.S. 586 (1957).

[74] "Only twenty of the seven hundred and fifty pages of the briefs of the Department of Justice, du Pont and General Motors were devoted to this issue." Milton Handler, "Annual Review of Recent Antitrust Developments," *The Record of the Association of the Bar of the City of New York*, **XII** (October 1957), pp. 411, 416.

[75] The decision was 4 (Warren, Black, Brennan, Douglas) to 2 (Burton, Frankfurter), with Brennan and Burton writing opinions. The dissent was on all three points.

that du Pont had "purposely used its stock to pry open the General Motors market. . . ." Third, what was the relevant market in which the tendency, or lack of tendency, toward monopoly was to be determined? Was it the total market of all purchases of finishes and fabrics? The General Motors brief stated "that in 1947 du Pont's finishes sales to General Motors constituted 3.5 per cent of all sales of finishes to industrial users, and that its fabrics sales to General Motors comprised 1.6 per cent of the total market for the type of fabric used by the automobile industry." Or was it the market for automotive finishes and fabrics? General Motors accounted for approximately two-fifths of the automobile sales in the nation, and "du Pont supplied 67 per cent of General Motors' requirements for finishes in 1946 and 68 per cent in 1947. In fabrics du Pont supplied 52.3 per cent of requirements in 1946, and 38.5 per cent in 1947." The Court concluded "that automotive finishes and fabrics have sufficient peculiar characteristics and uses to constitute them products sufficiently distinct from all other finishes and fabrics to make them a 'line of commerce' within the meaning of the Clayton Act."

This decision, like the one in the Steel case in 1921,[76] was made in a divided court; the decision might have gone the other way if the entire court had participated. Will its effects be as great as that of the earlier decision? The decision that Section 7 applies to vertical combinations is the kind that sets a clean precedent for the future.[77] Will the rule that illegality is to be determined as of the time of suit bring into question many stock acquisitions of the past, and hang as a continuing threat over all firms having made such acquisitions? Significant, perhaps, in this regard is that the court was here dealing with a substantial holding by the nation's fourth largest industrial concern in the second largest corporation in America. Will the government be as interested, or the courts as likely, to look retroactively on past stock acquisitions for companies of smaller size?[78] Finally, the Court in this case seemed to determine the effect on the market solely on quantitative factors. Will this be the trend in the future?[79]

---

[76] See pages 190–191.

[77] As to a change in the wording of the text to Paragraph 1 of Section 7 in 1950, the Supreme Court has said: "by the deletion of the 'acquiring-acquired' language in the original text, it [Congress] hoped to make plain that Section 7 applied not only to mergers between actual competitors, but also to vertical and conglomerate mergers whose effect may be to lessen competition in any line of commerce in any section of the country." *Brown Shoe Co. v. U.S.*, 370 U.S. 294, 317 (1962).

[78] The question is raised by Milton Handler in "Recent Antitrust Developments," *Yale Law Journal*, **LXXI** (November 1961), p. 424.

[79] Notice should be taken of the subsequent divestiture proceedings in the du Pont case. The Supreme Court remanded the case to the District Court to prepare a decree to carry out the Court's decision. The District Court, after taking evidence, declined to require du Pont to divest itself completely of General Motors stock, as urged by the government, but decreed that du Pont should transfer its voting rights in most of the General Motors stock to du Pont shareholders, and that additional measures should be taken to prevent du Pont control of General Motors. On appeal, the Supreme Court

The answer to this question at this moment is "No." In *Brown Shoe Co. v. United States* in 1962, the Supreme Court found that both in its vertical and horizontal aspects the acquisition by Brown Shoe of G. R. Kinney Company substantially lessened competition in violation of the antimerger amendment to Section 7. The Supreme Court said that though "the size of the share of the market foreclosed" was an "important consideration," "this factor will seldom be determinative." It noted the virtual identity of the language in Section 7 and Section 3. In the instant case, it took note of the historical trend toward concentration in the shoe industry. In a summary statement, it said:

> That is, whether the consolidation was to take place in an industry that was fragmented rather than concentrated, that had seen a recent trend toward domination by a few leaders or had remained fairly consistent in its distribution of market shares among the participating companies, that had experienced easy access to markets by suppliers and easy access to suppliers by buyers or had witnessed foreclosure of business, that had witnessed the ready entry of new competition or the erection of barriers to prospective entrants, all were aspects, varying in importance with the merger under consideration, which would properly be taken into account.[80]

Moreover, the Court said that the determination must be of the effect upon competition, not upon competitors.[81]

It has been noted that "three questions are crucial" in Section 7 cases,[82] as indeed in some other types of antitrust cases. First, what is the "line of commerce" or product market involved? Is the relevant market, for example, automotive finishes and fabrics, or all finishes and fabrics? Second, what is the section of the country or market area involved? Is it shoes for the nation as a whole, or shoes in regional or metropolitan areas that is significant? Third, what is the competitive impact of the merger or stock purchase in the relevant market? In determining the latter, it is competition, not competitors, which is significant. Also, quantitative factors—that is, "size of the share" of the market affected—may be important, and may even sometimes be determinative, but a showing of illegality will ordinarily require a full economic analysis of the effects on the market.

Discussion of issues of interpretation and of application of Section 7 have been supplemented by much discussion of increasing the effectiveness of the provision. This latter discussion has centered mainly on means

---

directed the District Court to enter a decree requiring divestiture of the stock, to commence within ninety days and be completed in no more than ten years from the effective date of the decree. *U.S. v. E. I. du Pont de Nemours & Co.*, 366 U.S. 316 (1961).

[80] For the references in the text, see pages 328, 329, and 322.

[81] *Ibid.*, p. 320.

[82] The questions are put in Charles F. Phillips, Jr., and George R. Hall, "Merger Litigation, 1951–1960," *Antitrust Bulletin*, **VI** (January–February 1961), pp. 25ff.

of getting better enforcement. The chief proposals will be dealt with in the following chapter.[83]

SECTION 8. In his special antitrust message to Congress in 1914, President Wilson recommended "laws which will effectually prohibit and prevent such interlockings of the personnel of the directorates of great corporations—banks and railroads, industrial, commercial, and public service bodies—as in effect result in making those who borrow and those who lend practically one and the same, those who sell and those who buy but the same persons trading with one another under different names and in different combinations. . . ." [84] These proposals were as sweeping as his proposals on holding companies. And yet the results were even more limited. Section 10 of the Clayton Act prohibited railroad contracts with interlocking firms for construction and maintenance above the value of $50,000, unless the contract was the most favorable available after competitive bidding. Section 8 prevented certain bank interlockings through joint directors or office holdings in two or more banks. It also prohibited a person from being a director of two or more corporations—other than corporations engaged in banking and railroad common-carrier service—under certain conditions.

There were large limitations on the scope of these provisions. First, there was no prohibition against a person's being a director of one industrial corporation and an officer or controlling stockholder in another, or against his serving as officer or controlling stockholder in more than one. Second, the application of the prohibition on interlockings in industrial corporations was dependent upon the condition that they had been "competitors, so that the elimination of competition by agreement between them would constitute a violation of the antitrust laws." This requirement of the Sherman Act test seriously limited the effect of Section 8 on persons or firms operating as competitors in any line of commerce. Moreover, the limitation to "competitors" meant that the prohibition did not, as recommended by Wilson, prevent those who buy and those who sell from being one and the same. Third, Section 8 did not prevent interlockings between banking and industrial corporations, and thus failed to prevent those who loan and those who borrow from being one and the same. Fourth, it did not prevent interlocking relationships among railroads and banks, or railroads and industrial corporations—except as limitation was contained in the competitive-bidding section. Fifth, it did

---

[83] At page 258. Restrictions on holding companies in banking are set forth in the Bank Holding Company Act of 1956; and approval for mergers by the Federal Reserve Board, the Comptroller of the Currency, or the Federal Deposit Insurance Corporation (depending on which has regulatory power—see page 531) is required by the Bank Merger Act of 1960. It has been held that Section 7 of the Clayton Act also applies to bank consolidations as distinct from acquisition of assets without consolidation. *U.S. v. Philadelphia National Bank,* 374 U.S. 321 (1963).

[84] *Congressional Record,* **LI,** p. 1978.

not prevent interlocking relations among state banks, although it did prevent a director in a state bank from being also a director in a national bank.

It is not surprising that a provision of such limited application should seldom have been the subject of enforcement action by the FTC or the Federal Reserve Board.[85] Nor is it surprising that large American business and financial concerns remain interlocked through directorships and offices, as well as by intercorporate stockholding.

A SPECIAL PROBLEM: BASING-POINT PRICING

Reference has been made to the possibility of the same set of acts being a violation of more than one of the laws relating to competition. This is illustrated by basing-point pricing. Basing-point pricing may be an unfair method of competition, a price discrimination prohibited by Section 2 of the Clayton Act, and/or a violation of the Sherman Act.

There are two types of geographical price structures: point-of-origin prices (usually called "f.o.b. mill" prices), and destination prices (usually called "delivered" prices).

Under the former, a buyer pays a mill price plus freight, and hence the price for buyers in different locations varies according to differences in freight costs; under the latter, the price is figured in some other way, and most buyers pay less or more than the mill price plus transportation. If the buyer pays more, the seller gets an excess called "phantom freight"; if he pays less, the seller must take the loss through freight absorption. In either case there is actual, even if not illegal, price discrimination among buyers, in that there are price differences among buyers not arising from differences in seller's costs.

So-called delivered pricing systems are of several types: (1) the postage-stamp system, under which prices are the same for the entire country; (2) zone pricing, under which prices are the same within each of a number of zones; (3) freight equalization, under which mill prices are reduced on distant sales, but nearby buyers buy on an f.o.b. mill basis; (4) basing-point pricing, under which prices are quoted as mill prices plus freight from one or more geographical points *irrespective of whether the shipment originates* at such points or somewhere else. There are two types of basing-point pricing: (1) the single basing-point system, under which prices are quoted from one geographical point, and (2) the multiple basing-point system, under which more than one basing point is set and the buyer may choose the quotation most favorable to him. To illustrate, when "Pittsburgh plus" was used in the steel industry, a buyer of steel

---

[85] There have been a few cases that tend to hold the line—for example, *U.S. v. Sears Roebuck & Co.*, 111 Fed. Sup. 614 (1953), 165 Fed. Sup. 356 (1958); *U.S. v. W. T. Grant Co.*, 345 U.S. 629 (1953).

paid the Pittsburgh price plus an amount equal to freight from Pittsburgh, even though he bought his steel from a mill much closer to him.

It is basing-point pricing that has aroused the concern of the F.T.C. and many economists. It is a system which is likely to be used in a market characterized by:

(1) a high degree of standardization of product, for example, steel and cement; (2) a low value per unit of weight, causing the freight rate to be a substantial portion of the delivered price of the commodity; (3) heavy overhead costs, making the efficient scale of manufacturing operations for a firm large; (4) production frequently below capacity; (5) specialized and long-lived production equipment; (6) market demand that is usually inelastic at and below prices which correspond to output considerably less than full capacity; (7) the prevalence of oligopoly, because of the small number of producers; and (8) production and markets that are both widely scattered.[86]

Economists attribute a number of disadvantages to basing-point pricing. It gives a competitive advantage to buyers located close to basing points, and conversely prevents the development of low-cost facilities in other areas. It thus restricts the decentralization of industry. Stocking concludes, in a recent study, that it has hampered the development of industry in southern locations.[87] It is argued also that the system has been accompanied, in industries such as steel and cement, by much unused capacity and higher prices and higher costs than would exist under strictly competitive conditions. Some economists believe that the system is a spontaneous development caused by conditions of imperfect competition; others that its existence indicates conspiracy among sellers.[88]

Agreement or conspiracy among sellers to use the basing-point system, like other collusive price arrangements, appears to be a violation of the Sherman Act. A lower court held that the concerted use of the basing-point system was an unreasonable restraint of trade in *Sugar Institute, Inc. v. U.S.*[89] However, the Department of Justice has not pressed cases under the Sherman Act. Rather, it has been the FTC, attacking the system first as an unfair method of competition and later also as a violation of the Robinson-Patman Act, that has fought the battle against basing-point pricing. In 1924 it issued a cease-and-desist order against the continued use of a single basing-point price system by U.S. Steel. The corporation, shortly after its formation in 1900, had set up the " Pittsburgh Plus" pricing system. After the FTC order, it set up two other basing

---

[86] Charles E. Landon, "Geographic Price Structures," *Law and Contemporary Problems,* **XV** (Spring 1950), pp. 125, 138.

[87] George W. Stocking, *Basing Point Pricing and Regional Development: A Case Study of the Iron and Steel Industry* (Chapel Hill, N.C.: University of North Carolina Press, 1954), pp. 191–192.

[88] See George W. Stocking, "The Economics of Basing Point Pricing," *Law and Contemporary Problems,* **XV** (Spring 1950), pp. 158–180.

[89] 297 U.S. 553 (1936).

234 Policies Affecting the Economy Generally

points—at Chicago and Birmingham—but set higher prices at these. The NRA code for the steel industry gave price-fixing authority to directors of the American Iron and Steel Institute, but this authority ended with the Supreme Court decision in 1935 holding the National Industrial Recovery Act unconstitutional. When, under the Wheeler-Lea Act (1938), FTC orders became final unless appealed in sixty days, U.S. Steel appealed. War and other causes put off a decision until 1948, when U.S. Steel signed a consent decree, which was signed by other steel producers in 1951.

In the meantime, the commission had attacked delivered pricing in other industries. By 1949 it had won in the courts, among others, four cases which elaborated the law and attracted much attention. The first two of these were novel, in that there was no charge of conspiracy. Both were brought under the Robinson-Patman Act. The Corn Products and Staley cases, decided by the Supreme Court on the same day in 1945, involved a single basing-point system for sellers of glucose (corn starch).[90] Glucose was manufactured by eight companies, all of whose plants were located within a radius of 400 miles from Chicago. All prices were quoted f.o.b. Chicago, so that the purchaser, wherever located, paid the Chicago price plus freight from Chicago. Corn Products Company produced about 45 per cent of the product. It had plants in Kansas City and in the Chicago rail-shipping area. Purchasers with a lower freight rate from Kansas City nevertheless paid Chicago prices plus the freight rate from Chicago to the place of delivery. Even Kansas City purchasers paid the phantom freight cost from Chicago. The evidence showed that this had caused several candy manufacturers (users of glucose) to move from Kansas City or neighboring cities to Chicago. The Supreme Court held that the system "results inevitably in systematic price discriminations, since the prices they receive upon deliveries from Kansas City bear relation to factors other than actual costs of products or delivery." It held that there was probable adverse effect upon competition among purchasers from Corn Products. In the Staley case the Court rejected the defendants' claim that their use of the basing-point system was a "good faith meeting of competition" in that they had adopted the pricing system of their competitors; the Court reasoned that the "meeting competition" phrase in the law allowed a seller to meet individual situations, but not to copy an unlawful pricing system of competitors which did not lower prices.

The third case was against the Cement Institute and its members. The Cement Institute has been referred to as "a system of private government" for an industry, for through it coordinated controls for the avoidance of competition were maintained. The "linchpin" of the "security system" for the industry [91] was an industry-wide multiple basing-point system. Com-

---

[90] *Corn Products Refining Co. v. FTC*, 324 U.S. 726; *FTC v. A. E. Staley Manufacturing Co.*, 324 U.S. 746.

[91] The quoted words are taken from, and the system of industry government is de-

plaint against the respondents was issued by the FTC in 1937, but the case was not decided by the Supreme Court until 1948.[92] As to the effects of the actions of defendants, the FTC alleged that the system resulted in quotation of identical prices and terms of sale by all of the defendants at any point in the United States. On the effects, the Supreme Court stated that multiple and single basing-point systems functioned in the same manner and produced the same consequences. The commission found that the multiple basing-point system in cement sales was maintained through understandings and agreements among members of the industry. The Supreme Court affirmed the commission's decision. It held that "concerted maintenance of the basing-point delivered price system is an unfair method of competition prohibited by the Federal Trade Commission Act. . . ." It also held that there was systematic price discrimination in violation of the Robinson-Patman Act.

The fourth case was the Rigid Steel Conduit case, decided in a Court of Appeals in 1948.[93] In this case the conspiracy doctrine, which had been applied in the cement case, was supplemented by what is customarily called the "conscious parallelism" doctrine. The court held that individual quotations of delivered prices was a violation of Section 5 of the Federal Trade Commission Act, when done independently and without collusion but with knowledge that one's rivals were using the same system. The Supreme Court in 1949 upheld this decision, without opinion, by a 4 to 4 vote.[94]

By 1948 it seemed to be clear that any industry-wide delivered pricing system that could be shown to have an injurious effect upon competition was illegal. Certain dicta in the Supreme Court's opinion in the cement case led some to fear that all prices not set f.o.b. mill were illegal, that freight absorption was therefore illegal, and that the individual seller would not be allowed to meet lower prices of a competitor on such matters. When U.S. Steel and the cement industries capitulated in 1948, the prices of steel and cement were set f.o.b. mill at levels which were higher than previous net mill prices, and many purchasers blamed the law rather than the companies. The result of these things was to draw the issue of basing-point pricing out of the limited arena of enforcement agencies and courts into that of macropolitics. A bitter fight over the issue ensued in Congress from 1948 to 1950.[95] It was a confused battle. Large sellers wanted a change in the law, but the battle for change was fought

---

scribed in, Earl Latham, *The Group Basis of Politics: A Study in Basing-Point Legislation* (Ithaca, N.Y.: Cornell University Press, 1952), Chapter 2.

[92] *FTC v. Cement Institute, et al.*, 333 U.S. 683 (1948).

[93] *Triangle Conduit & Cable Co. v. Federal Trade Commission*, 168 F 2d 175.

[94] 336 U.S. 956.

[95] The story is told in detail by Earl Latham in *The Group Basis of Politics: A Study in Basing-Point Legislation* (Ithaca, N.Y.: Cornell University Press, 1952), Chapters 3 to 6, inclusive, and by Corwin D. Edwards, in *The Price Discrimination Law: A Review of Experience* (Washington, D.C.: Brookings Institution, 1959), Chapter 12.

236 *Policies Affecting the Economy Generally*

also in behalf of purchasers believed to have been abused. There was confusion as to whether the purpose and effect of amendments was the clarification or the weakening of the law, and it seems clear that even many members of Congress were for a long time confused. Ultimately, after much jostling of bills between the houses, a bill was passed by both, only to be vetoed by the President. Congress could do no more than set up, by action of the Senate Committee on Interstate and Foreign Commerce, a watchdog subcommittee to keep its eye on the F.T.C.

It appears, however, that the appeal through macropolitics may have had effects. The FTC "has shown less zeal and persistence" since 1950 on basing-point pricing. This may conceivably be due to industry acceptance of the restrictions of law, but it may be due also to the macropolitics of new appointments to the commission or of threat from the Congress.[96]

It seems true, nevertheless, that the establishment of legal standards on basing-point pricing is among the most notable of the FTC achievements. The centerpiece of the law is conspiracy. Only in the corn-products cases has the FTC proceeded without the charge of conspiracy.[97] Conspiracy charges can be brought either under the Sherman Act or the Federal Trade Commission Act. Since this is true, there may be no real advantage in Section 2 of the Clayton Act in basing-point cases, particularly since the Supreme Court has held that FTC orders in conspiracy cases could apply to the practices of individual participating companies.[98]

EXEMPTIONS FROM ANTITRUST

It has been said that "Governments, apparently, have never been able to make up their minds as to which they dislike more, competition or monopoly."[99] At least in this country the legislation to strengthen the antitrust policy has been paralleled by many exemptions. Several types of exemptions exist.

EXPORT ASSOCIATIONS. The Webb-Pomerene Act of 1918 exempted from the Sherman Act associations formed exclusively to engage in export trade, provided such associations did not restrain the export trade of a domestic competitor, or restrain or enhance or depress prices within the United States. There was a similar exemption from Section 7. The associations were required to file documents on their organization and operation with the FTC. The commission could investigate such associations and make recommendations to them for readjustment of their affairs to bring them into compliance with the act, and if they refused to

---

[96] Edwards, *ibid.*, pp. 432–436.
[97] Edwards, *ibid.*, p. 437.
[98] *Federal Trade Commission v. National Lead Co.*, 352 U.S. 419 (1957).
[99] Fritz Machlup, *The Political Economy of Monopoly: Business, Labor and Government Policies* (Baltimore, Md.: Johns Hopkins Press, 1952), 182.

comply, it could refer its conclusions to the Attorney General. Though a much larger number have been formed, thirty-eight associations were registered with the FTC in 1960.[100] Some engage in selling operations, but most merely fix prices and allot quotas for their members. Some have joined cartel arrangements, but in a case in 1945 the Supreme Court held that participation with foreign concerns in cartel arrangements was illegal.[101]

Many believe that the Webb-Pomerene exemption is against the public interest. They believe that it is difficult for members of associations to keep their activities in foreign trade and domestic trade entirely separate. They question, moreover, the need of large American firms for alliance with others in promoting foreign sales. It has been suggested that the exemption be framed more narrowly so as to apply only to associations composed of firms of small size.[102]

RESALE PRICE MAINTENANCE. Exemption of resale price-maintenance agreements from the antitrust laws has been one of the goals of independent wholesalers and retailers in their battle with mass-distribution agencies, such as department stores, mail-order houses, and chain stores. It is another phase of the movement which led to the Robinson-Patman Act on price discrimination. The objective is to prevent price-cutting on products bearing a trademark or brand name. The movement gained force in the twenties, and led to the passage of the first modern, state retail-price-maintenance law in California in 1931. The statute authorized producers and owners of trademarked goods to contract with retailers or other resellers for maintenance of price. Two years later an amendment allowed contracts between a manufacturer and a single reseller to be binding on all resellers. By 1941 all jurisdictions except the District of Columbia, Missouri, Texas, and Vermont had laws legalizing resale price maintenance. In 1936 the Supreme Court upheld the legality of a state law, but the fact that such laws could not be applicable to interstate commerce led to the movement for a national act. Such an act was the Miller-Tydings Resale Price Maintenance Act of 1937.[103] It exempted from the Sherman Act and Section 5 of the Federal Trade Commission Act agreements between producers or distributors and resellers prescribing the minimum resale price of trademark or branded commodities, provided (1) that the commodities were sold in free and open competition with commodities produced or distributed by others, and (2) that such agreements would be lawful under state or territorial law as to intra-

---

[100] *Annual Report of the Federal Trade Commission, 1961*, p. 60.
[101] *U.S. v. Alkali Export Ass'n., Inc.*, 325 U.S. 196 (1945), affirming district court, 58 Fed. Sup. 785 (1944).
[102] See, for example, the recommendations of the Twentieth Century Fund's Special Committee on Cartels and Monopoly in George W. Stocking and Myron W. Watkins, *Cartels or Competition? The Economics of International Controls by Business and Government* (New York: Twentieth Century Fund, 1948), pp. 433–437.
[103] 50 Stat. 693.

state sales. Horizontal agreements between producers, distributors, or retailers were not allowed.

In 1951 the Supreme Court held that the Miller-Tydings Act did not legalize the binding of nonsigners in resale price-maintenance contracts.[104] Retailers who did not sign price-maintenance contracts could not be forced to maintain prices. This destroyed the effectiveness of the contracts. The blow to price maintenance was glamorized in New York when R. H. Macy and Company reduced prices on trademarked products and set off a price war of several weeks duration. Similar events occurred in other cities. Pressure on Congress mounted quickly from druggists and other small sellers, and it promptly (1952) passed the McGuire-Keogh Act, which specifically exempted from the antitrust laws contracts for price maintenance which were binding on nonsigners as well as signers, in any state in which such contracts were legal under state law.[105]

In spite of this victory in the Congress, the battle of the associations representing druggists and other small retailers for price maintenance was not won. Between 1952 and 1962, state courts in twenty-one states destroyed the effect of the McGuire-Keogh Act by holding invalid either the state fair-trade law or the nonsigner portion thereof. In 1960 the United States Supreme Court held that a manufacturer could not enlist the aid of a wholesaler or other retailers to prevent a noncomplying retailer from obtaining supplies.[106] And in 1961 it upheld a New Jersey decision that the state could deny a drug company the right to bring suit under the fair-trade law if it had not registered in the state.[107] On the other hand, manufacturers or distributors sometimes coerce retailers into maintaining prices by threatening to withhold the product, even when this is illegal under state law.

The battle for legalization of price-maintenance agreements has now come back to Congress. Dissatisfied with the impairment of fair-trade laws by court decisions, the advocates of legalization for price maintenance have pushed for national legislation which would provide this legalization without respect to state laws on the subject. Bills for this purpose were reported favorably from the House Committee on Interstate and Foreign Commerce in 1957 and 1963. Lately, such bills have been called "quality stabilization" bills.

The primary argument advanced in favor of such legislation is that discount and chain retailers are driving small, independent retailers out of business. It is argued, further, that the large stores use brand-name products as loss leaders or "bait advertising" to draw customers, that manufacturers should have the right to protect the integrity of their products,

---

[104] *Schwegmann Bros. v. Calvert Distillers Corp.*, 341 U.S. 384.
[105] 66 Stat. 693.
[106] *U.S. v. Parke, Davis & Co.*, 362 U.S. 29.
[107] *Ely Lilly & Co. v. Sav-on-Drugs, Inc.*, 366 U.S. 276.

that the consumer will have adequate protection through competition among manufacturers.

Those opposing the legislation argue that the consumer should be allowed to benefit from retail-price competition, that law should not aim toward "soft competition" for those who are engaged in the competitive struggle, that price-maintenance plans have the effect of preserving the *status quo* in distribution and preventing the consumer from obtaining the advantages of large-scale enterprise, and that there is no evidence that the reputation of products suffers from virile retail competition in their sale.

Concerning the practical effect of price maintenance schemes, it can be said that insofar as they are effective, they make the consumer pay a price to preserve the small retail outlet; on the other hand, manufacturers of some products will not try to restrict retail competition for sale of their products. The Federal Trade Commission has found evidence, however, that fair-trade acts have resulted in some coercion on manufacturers by retailers and wholesalers to force price-maintenance contracts, and in collusion between sellers on the same horizontal plane in an effort to generalize the effects of fair price-maintenance schemes.[108]

LABOR. In another chapter the struggle for exemption of labor from the antitrust laws is reviewed. In summary here, it may be said that the Supreme Court has liberally construed the exemption of labor to apply to pursuit by labor organizations of their legitimate objectives, but has held that labor organizations are subject to the antitrust act when they ally themselves with employers to maintain monopoly control over *commercial* competition in the marketing of goods and services.[109]

AGRICULTURAL COOPERATIVES. A provision in the Clayton Act, strengthened by amendment in the Capper-Volstead Act of 1922,[110] exempts from the antitrust laws the existence and operation of agricultural cooperatives. The latter contains a proviso that the Secretary of Agriculture shall order any group to cease-and-desist if he finds that it "monopolizes or restrains trade . . . to such an extent that the price of any agricultural product is unduly enhanced by reason thereof." The Cooperative Marketing Act of 1926 allows agricultural associations to gather and distribute "past, present, and prospective" production and marketing data.[111] It has been held, however, that farmer organizations, like labor organizations, cannot enter into price-fixing conspiracies with outsiders.[112] Nor can a cooperative use coercive tactics toward outsiders, nor combine

---

[108] See, on price maintenance, FTC, *Report on Resale Price Maintenance* (1945); House Select Committee on Small Business, *Fair Trade: The Problems and the Issues*, 82nd Cong., 2nd Sess., H. Rept. 1292 (1952); House Committee on Interstate and Foreign Commerce, *Minimum Resale Prices*, Hearings on H.R. 5767, 82nd Cong., 2nd Sess. (1952).
[109] See pages 308–309.
[110] 42 Stat. 388.
[111] Section 5, 44 Stat. 802, 803.
[112] *U.S. v. Borden Co.*, 308 U.S. 188 (1939).

with others to suppress competition by and among independent producers and distributors.[113]

The Robinson-Patman Act specifically exempts from price-discrimination provisions patronage refunds in proportion to purchases or sales to members of cooperative associations.

NIRA AND NRA. The antitrust laws were virtually suspended from 1933 to 1935 in the administration of the National Industrial Recovery Act (NIRA). NIRA was an omnibus measure, and its provisions relating to labor are summarized in Chapter 14. In its provisions concerning business, it was a response to businessmen's arguments that the downward trend of prices in the Depression should be counteracted by stabilization measures. It provided that "trade or industrial associations or groups" might propose codes of fair competition for their respective industries to the President, who would approve if he found that these groups were "truly representative" and imposed no "inequitable restrictions" on membership and that the proposed codes did not promote monopoly, eliminate or oppress, or discriminate against, small enterprises, and would tend to effectuate the policy of the act.[114] Any violation of standards in these codes would constitute violations of the "unfair methods of competition" provision of the Federal Trade Commission Act. The President set up the National Industrial Recovery Administration (NRA) to carry out his obligations under these provisions. Soon there was a code for each industry. The codes were administered by code authorities, representing, in the main, industrial groups which prepared the codes, though the public had a representative on each authority, and minority industrial groups and labor also had representation sometimes. This was a system of industrial self-regulation, with some overhead check from government. But the program developed so rapidly that the public checks proved inadequate.

Many of the codes contained provisions limiting production or allocating markets. Also, provisions for some form of limitation on price competition was quite general. These were some of the types of limitation: (1) prohibition against less-than-cost selling, as in the retail jewelry and retail food and grocery codes; (2) provision for filing of prices with the code authority, often accompanied by provision against change of prices without notice and a waiting period of some length, perhaps thirty days (such provisions were included in about 40 per cent of the first 280 codes); (3) provisions for uniform cost accounting and setting of prices on that basis, as in the cigar-container and malleable-iron codes; (4) complete definition of costs and setting of prices on that basis, as in the retail-lumber and building-materials code; (5) provision for free setting of prices—that is, without limitation to costs and accounting requirements, as in the cleaning-and-dying and bituminous-coal codes, and under certain condi-

---

[113] *Maryland and Virginia Milk Producers Ass'n., Inc. v. U.S.*, 362 U.S. 458 (1960).
[114] Title I, Sec. 3(a), 48 Stat. 195, 196.

tions the iron-and-steel code. Not only were business groups allowed jointly to limit production and fix prices, but evidence accumulated that there was coercion against those who did not want to go along.

The Roosevelt Administration was saved from a bad situation by the Supreme Court decision in May, 1935, holding the NRA unconstitutional. But the damage to the antitrust program was not so promptly liquidated. In some industries, forms of cooperation initiated during the NRA period were continued, and gave rise to antitrust prosecutions by the Antitrust Division.

REGULATORY ACTS. Few industries were subject to national regulation in 1914, and in no case had exemption from the antitrust laws been provided for an industry subject to national regulation. Limitation on entry existed only for banking, and on rate-making only for railroads. Today national regulatory agencies for many industries may limit entry, fix prices, or approve the elimination of existing competition. Many statutes allow merger, stock purchase, lease of facilities, or rate agreements subject to the approval of the regulatory agency. In some cases administrative approval gives full immunity from antitrust laws. This is true, for example, of approvals by the Interstate Commerce Commission. In vesting power of approval in regulatory agencies, the law usually requires that effects on competition be one of the factors to be considered in making the decision. Administrative discretion and supervision are substituted for the policy of enforced competition.[115]

Yet regulatory agencies cannot always grant immunity from the antitrust laws. Four recent cases indicate an attitude of strict construction of agency powers. It was held that the purchase of a dairy by a milk producers' cooperative was not protected from Section 7 of the Clayton Act by powers of the Secretary of Agriculture, for he had not been granted power to pass on such acquisitions.[116] Also, approval by the Federal Communications Commission of an agreement by the Radio Corporation of America to exchange its television station in Cleveland for one in Philadelphia did not prevent successful government action against the exchange as a violation of Section 1 of the Sherman Act.[117] Moreover, in a recent conflict of agencies, the Supreme Court limited the jurisdiction of the Federal Power Commission.[118] After the Antitrust Division had commenced action under Section 7 in a district court against a merger of El Paso Natural Gas Company and Pacific Northwest Pipeline Company, defendants filed an application with the FPC for approval of the merger. Al-

---

[115] See *Report of the Attorney General's Committee to Study the Antitrust Laws* (Washington, D.C.: Superintendent of Documents, 1955), pp. 261–313, and Walter Adams and Horace M. Gray, *Monopoly in America: The Government as Promoter* (New York: The Macmillan Company, 1955), especially Chapter 3.
[116] *Maryland and Virginia Milk Producers Ass'n., Inc. v. U.S.*, 362 U.S. 458 (1960).
[117] *U.S. v. Radio Corporation of America*, 358 U.S. 334 (1959).
[118] *California v. Federal Power Commission*, 369 U.S. 482 (1962).

though Section 7 exempted "transactions duly consummated pursuant to authority given by the . . . Federal Power Commission . . . under any statutory provision vesting such power in such Commission . . .," the Supreme Court held that there was no grant of authority to the commission to adjudicate antitrust cases. Finally, in another conflict of agencies —an injunction sought against a bank merger by the Antitrust Division the day after approval for the merger had been given by the Comptroller of the Currency—the Supreme Court held that the grant of power in the Bank Merger Act of 1960 to the Comptroller to approve bank mergers did not, in the absence of a specific exemption from the antitrust laws, immunize the merger from attack under these laws. This decision was rendered in spite of the fact that the Comptroller himself had been directed to consider the effect upon competition, along with other factors, in making his decision on a merger.[119] Clearly, the Court now regards antitrust as the nation's basic policy, and requires a strong showing of congressional intent for any exemptions by administrative decision from that policy.

SUMMARY AND CONCLUSIONS

Space limitations have prevented the description of all of the many additions and exceptions to American policy on combinations and business practices. The general results of supplementary legislation and administration can nevertheless be stated.

The antitrust policy has been strengthened in a variety of ways:

1. The concept of fair competition was added to that of free competition (Section 5 of the Federal Trade Commission Act).

2. The consumer's interest in fair and honest practices has been recognized (Wheeler-Lea Act).

3. Some specific types of acts or practices which would threaten competition have been attacked by legislation which sets standards ("substantially lessen competition," "tend to create a monopoly," "injure" competition) less rigid than those required under the Sherman Act (Sections 2, 3, and 7 of the Clayton Act).

4. Commission procedure has supplied additional techniques of enforcement which, though weak, have been of significance.

5. Investigation and corporate reporting provide information on corporate practices and economic trends.

6. Section 7 has been strengthened by the antimerger amendment, vigorous enforcement by the Antitrust Division and the FTC, and liberal judicial construction; and the conspiracy doctrine has been more firmly

---

[119] *U.S. v. Philadelphia National Bank*, 374 U.S. 321 (1963).

established through basing-point decisions. Both of these developments make antitrust more meaningful with respect to oligopolistic controls.[120]

On the other hand, some factors have made for weakness in the antitrust effort:

1. The 1914 acts failed in their scope to meet the high promise of President Wilson's special message, the wording of some sections left loopholes for escape from prohibitions, an unsympathetic judiciary broadened these loopholes (or created new ones), and an apathetic commission meekly accepted these results for more than a decade. The result was that twenty years after the great legislative effort of 1914, little more than a campaign against misbranding and false advertising had survived.

2. Though legislation has strengthened Section 5 of the Federal Trade Commission Act and Sections 2 and 7 of the Clayton Act, it has also softened competition (Miller-Tydings Act, in some respects the Robinson-Patman Act), suspended competition (NRA), or threatened competition (Webb-Pomerene Act, regulatory acts).

Overall, the recent tendencies parallel those noted for the Sherman Act. Antitrust has become more effective. The pendulum has swung toward strong enforcement. Yet new problems are faced. Will the softening of the quantitative test, and the issues concerning relevant markets and effects thereon, necessitate such intricate and exhaustive fact-finding and presentation as to seriously militate against effectiveness of the legal prohibitions?

[120] For further comment, see pages 253ff.

Chapter 12. Problems of Industrial Policy and Enforcement

To what extent should public policy aim toward a competitive economy? What are the means for attaining this objective? Should antitrust be supplemented or supplanted by other public policies? These are the key questions of industrial policy for government.

COMPETITION AS THE REGULATOR

Arguments on the need for competition as regulator of the economy are made from many approaches. First, the positive economic and social advantages of competition are stated. The arguments run approximately as follows: (1) Competition forces concerns to try to give the best deal to the purchaser. It forces the supplier to try to improve his quality and service or lower his price in order to retain or extend his patronage. (2) It eliminates the unfit, and concentrates production and distribution in the most efficient concerns. (3) It insures that resources—capital and labor—will be allocated to the uses most preferred by customers. (4) It keeps the economy fluid and adaptable. (5) It provides incentives to the broadest number of people—opportunities for new and challenges for old suppliers. Overall, it makes the consumer king, and thus is democratic and for the *general* or public interest.

Second, the dangers of private power are asserted. The antagonism to the monopolist reaches far back in Anglo-American legal history. It was reinforced on this continent by the hatred of special privilege to any in the grant of opportunities to develop resources. The anticorporationism and the antibigness complexes in the nineteenth and twentieth centuries have grown out of this tradition of the past. Private power is feared for many reasons: it may (1) create one-sided bargaining between buyers and sellers, (2) weaken the opportunities of competitors, (3) threaten dominance of government by special interests, or (4) even threaten the independent formation of public opinion. This fear of private power has been both an independent and a supplementary foundation for the argument that government power should seek to preserve competition as a regulator for the economy.

Third, the weaknesses of the alternatives to competition are emphasized. In the main, this is an argument: first, that if competition fails, government regulation must follow; and second, that such regulation cannot be as effective a regulator in the public interest as competition. Other alternatives, such as countervailing power and a business conscience, are not regarded as adequate safeguards. The alternatives to strict pursuit of a policy of enforced competition are to be considered fully in the next section. It is sufficient here to say that new arguments for alternatives to antitrust policy have added another dimension to the discussion of public policy.

In sum, the arguments for competition as a regulator are of several types. Some of the arguments are economic: they relate to efficiency in the production and distribution of goods and services. Some are political: they relate to the balances of power in the community. Some are based on considerations of feasibility: what are workable techniques of social control? The preference for competition rests in part on the neoliberal or conservative philosophy that automatic forces are superior to political decisions; in part on the reform liberalism that trusts in government to establish the conditions for a competitive order; in part on empirical considerations of alternatives of public policy.

It would be conceded by most that the arguments for competition would require qualification to be realistic. The ideal of impersonal regulation of the economy by market forces has always been something of a fiction—a concept of thought and analysis more than a description of realities. In this day the qualifications of competition arising from the changes noted in Chapter 2 are very large. The competition is not pure, but imperfect competition.[1] One form of this imperfect competition may be explained. Where a small number of concerns supply the market, and where each of these has a large fixed investment resulting in heavy overhead costs, each will find it beneficial to calculate carefully its price and output so as to render the maximum return on its capacity, whether used or unused. These calculations may be made with reference to long- or short-time spans, but with appreciation that any course of action which disturbs the effort to maintain prices in order to cover return on used and unused capacity may unstabilize the whole industry. The tendency is not to engage in price competition that eliminates excess capacity, but to calculate price so as to cover all costs, including the retention of excess capacity. Where demand is relatively inflexible and unused capacity is nontransferable to other profitable uses, then the tendency will be accentuated. Where there are a large number of sellers with nontransferable capacity, as in bituminous coal, then the urge of some sellers to recoup only a margin over direct costs may demoralize the industry; but where there are a few sellers, the common assumption that each

---

[1] The concept of imperfect or monopolistic competition was introduced by Joan Robinson, *The Economics of Imperfect Competition* (New York: The Macmillan Company, 1933) and E. H. Chamberlin, *The Theory of Monopolistic Competition: A Re-Orientation of the Theory of Value* (Cambridge, Mass.: Harvard University Press, 1933).

will carefully plan to avoid this result leads to action by all contrary to that assumed under the theory of pure competition. Such a common course of action may be facilitated by the leadership position of one firm. Other variations from the model of pure competition arise from factors different from those noted above, such as practices prevailing in bargaining between big sellers and big buyers, or the lack of arms-length relationships between buyers and sellers, or the ability of a producer of several commodities to use his position in one of these to advantage in the sale of another, or the use of brand names and advertising to differentiate the products of competing sellers.

Whether perfect or imperfect, competition will not be the sole regulator of the economy. In some instances the deleterious effects of competition are so great as to lead to public efforts to prevent the effects. Man refuses to accept the idea that he must be the victim of impersonal forces. Thus, conservation policies are established to limit too rapid exhaustion of resources, or unfair competition is prohibited, or levels of competition (for example, minimum wages) are established. For the economy as a whole, there is a substantial amount of central management to avoid deflation or inflation. Central management pulls the strings of credit and monetary supply, of public works, and of other compensatory devices to control, in part, the behavior of the dancing marionettes below. And for many areas in the economy, such as transportation, communication, household utilities, agriculture, labor, and others, the impact of competitive forces is modified to produce (it is hoped) a more beneficial economy. This is merely to repeat what we have brought out earlier: namely, that by the choice of men, this is a mixed economy—an economy governed in part by public decision and in part by other forces, the latter of which are themselves both market and organizational.

And yet it is widely believed that the place to be filled by the impersonal force of competition should be substantial. Public action to maintain competition continues, therefore, to be accepted as basic policy. But law and public opinion have frowned unequally on the several types of threat to competition. Coercive acts and predatory practices against competitors are condemned in the same way as unnecessary roughness in football. Fraud and deception, whether with adverse effects on competitors or consumers, are likewise condemned. Collusion and conspiracy—which, if effective, generally result in higher price levels, unused capacity, or other deleterious effects—are also condemned in law; but business groups have nevertheless often proposed that it would be good public policy to allow concerted action to fix prices or restrict output. Still more difference of opinion has existed over public policy with respect to growth of a single company to a position where even greater opportunities to control price and production would exist than through collusion among several competitors. Shall growth be a means by which competition can be destroyed or weakened? Should such growth be facilitated by corporation laws which allow pyramiding and interlocking of organizations? Should such growth be limited even where it is the result primarily of persistent seizing of opportunities? And should patent, export-trade, and tariff policies be reconsidered in terms of their effects on domestic competition?

These are crucial issues. They are issues not of private right, but of protection of the public interest. What are the means by which the public may have adequate protection? To this question a number of answers have been given which minimize the role of antitrust. What are these answers and how sufficient are they?

POLICY ANSWERS WHICH MINIMIZE THE ROLE OF ANTITRUST

BIGNESS IS GOOD. Justice Douglas restated the old fear of bigness (what Brandeis called "the curse of bigness") in his dissent in the Columbia Steel case:

> We have here the problem of bigness. Its lesson should by now have been burned into our memory by Brandeis. *The Curse of Bigness* shows how size can become a menace—both industrial and social. It can be an industrial menace because it creates gross inequalities against existing or putative competitors. It can be a social menace—because of its control of prices . . . size in steel is the measure of the power of a handful of men over our economy. That power can be utilized with lightning speed. It can be benign or it can be dangerous.[2]

David Lilienthal, formerly on the boards of directors of TVA and the Atomic Energy Commission, has called this "a frankly emotional antagonism to Bigness."[3] "Big Business," he says, "is basic to the very life of this country"; "Size is our greatest functional asset"; there is a "curse of smallness" in some industries—for example, coal and lumber; we should be concerned "with the establishment to the fullest of a *climate of opportunity for growth and attainment of size*. . . ."[4] He sets forth the "fruits of bigness": the great flow of armament and development of new scientific weapons, the greater ability than small business has to provide security for workers, the prodigious productivity, and the whittling of distribution costs.

Lilienthal does not, however, condemn competition. Rather, he argues that in place of the old competition of numerous small units, we have a "New Competition." The "crucial battleground of competition as to costs" has shifted to "improvement in management," "to better personnel practices," "and to new technological developments," in all of which bigness is superior to smallness. Beyond this, the New Competition provides for competition between alternative products; research for discovery of new and improved products; improvement of marketing; continuous creation of new

[2] *U.S. v. Columbia Steel Co.*, 334 U.S. 495, 535–536 (1948). Douglas' italics.
[3] David E. Lilienthal, *Big Business: A New Era* (New York: Harper and Row, Publishers, Inc., 1952), p. 4.
[4] Lilienthal, *ibid.*, pp. 3, 33, 143–144, 36. Lilienthal's italics.

areas of endeavor for newcomers to industry; an increase in the geographic area of competition to the "one Big Market"; competition between departments and between subsidiaries or affiliates of the same organization; and competition through advertising.

Likewise, he accepts the Sherman Antitrust Act as "a great feat of statesmanship."[5] There is need for a policeman to prevent coercive and deceitful acts and agreements to limit production, fix prices, divide markets, and other practices. But he condemns any attack through antitrust laws on bigness because of *potential* power to do wrong or because it is achieved by progressively embracing each new opportunity.[6]

Lilienthal has provided an up-to-date statement of an old point of view. Justice Holmes, President Theodore Roosevelt, and the Supreme Court in the U.S. Steel case were unwilling to accept the argument that bigness *per se* was evil. Not to this day has bigness alone been held illegal under the antitrust laws. Moreover, many have been unwilling to accept the idea that big management could not be efficient.

Today all must recognize that managerial science and art have enormously increased the capacity of man to direct efficiently large undertakings and large groups of men, and that big organization has been a material factor in the production and distribution of goods at low costs. But two questions remain: How big is big enough to obtain efficiency in a particular industry? How big is too big for safety? Bigness creates power. Power may be used beyond competitive contest on the plane of efficiency; it creates opportunities to win on other bases than efficiency. Is it sufficient to check its conduct after it arises? Or is it better to try to prevent power from developing which can compete on other bases than efficiency?

Are there adequate checks on big power in American industry without the enforcement of the antitrust laws in the way Lilienthal condemns? He thinks there is—in the conscience of corporate leaders, and in the checks and balances that exist. Each of these should be analyzed.

BUSINESS CONSCIENCE IS THE REMEDY. Lilienthal refers to a "new kind of 'top boss' of large business undertakings. He is a man with a strong and practical sense of responsibility to the public, and an awareness of the ethics of present-day business competition."[7] This idea that the conscience of business will be a great protection to the public is often repeated.

The idea has been considered most fully by A. A. Berle, Jr., law professor and former government official.[8] According to his rough estimate, 70 per cent of American industry is in what he christens "concentrates." These concentrates have become new centers of power; they seek to avoid competi-

---

[5] Lilienthal, *ibid.*, p. 42.
[6] Lilienthal, *ibid.*, chiefly Chapter 21.
[7] Lilienthal, *ibid.*, p. 27.
[8] Adolph A. Berle, Jr., *The 20th Century Capitalist Revolution* (New York: Harcourt, Brace & World, Inc., 1954).

tion by planning, and this increases their power; they are run by self-perpetuating oligarchies, and the legal controls are so limited that "the only real control which guides or limits their economic and social action is the real, though undefined and tacit, philosophy of the men who compose them." [9] ". . . the corporation, almost against its will, has been compelled to assume in appreciable part the role of conscience-carrier of twentieth-century American society." [10]

Berle has hope that philosophical premises—conceptions of conduct and responsibility—will come to dominate the leaders of American corporate industry. But Berle is too good a student of history to believe that such conceptions can fulfill their role without being embodied in law. He drew a parallel with the medieval-modern movement to control political power: "It may be said of the corporation as old Bracton said of the Crown: 'There is no king where the will and not the law prevails.'" [11]

It can be expected that standards of corporate conscience will continue to develop; it can be expected also that these will emerge in new rules of law. But big questions remain: What will be the source of this new law? What will its content be? As to its source, will it not arise in courts, legislatures, and public administration? If so, this is public regulation, even though in support of ideals held by much of the corporate community. The rules governing corporate practice have heretofore arisen in judicially created corporation law and legislative acts on sales of securities and unfair practices, and such rules have in recent years required administrative implementation. As to content, may the law not include antitrust as one of the regulators of size and corporate power and practice? Is corporate conscience, even when embodied in legal principle, only one hope, but not an all-sufficient hope for the problem of industrial power? [12]

COUNTERVAILING POWER IS THE REMEDY. Kenneth Galbraith, professor of economics at Harvard University, emphasizes not the inner conscience and the outer law, but the checks and balances operating within the economic system. In spite of the decline of competition, there is "the possibility that within the structure of the market shared by a few firms there are practical restraints on economic power. . . ." [13] He sets up the concepts of countervailing power and original power. Defining the latter,

---

[9] Berle, *ibid.*, p. 180.
[10] Berle, *ibid.*, p. 182.
[11] Berle, *ibid.*, p. 188.
[12] For appraisal and criticism of "corporate conscience" in the role Berle suggests for it, see Ben W. Lewis, "Economics by Admonition," *The American Economic Review*, XLIX (May 1959), pp. 384–398, and Michael D. Reagan's chapter on "Corporate Conscience or Corporate Arrogance" in his *The Managed Economy* (New York: Oxford University Press, 1963), Chapter 7. Lewis says cryptically, "It is not going to happen; if it did happen it would not work; and if it did work it would still be intolerable to free men" (p. 395).
[13] John Kenneth Galbraith, *American Capitalism: The Concept of Countervailing Power* (Boston, Mass.: Houghton Mifflin Company, 1952), p. 61.

he says, "When, anywhere in the course of producing, processing or distributing a particular product, one or a few firms first succeed in establishing a strong market position they may be considered to be the possessors of original market power." [14] Countervailing power is the opposing power of those who are subject to original power. It is the power exerted not by competitors, but by purchasers or suppliers to hold in check the possessors of original power. Original power "begets" countervailing power; countervailing power is "a self-generating force" on the buyer side to meet strong sellers, or on the seller side to meet strong buyers.[15] The result is "another regulatory mechanism" in the economy.[16]

Galbraith's regulatory mechanism is a vertical check-and-balance system. It is a supplement to the horizontal check-and-balance system supplied by competition. It revives the eighteenth-century ideal of automatic internal balances, common both to economic and political thought. Since it favors automaticity and limitation of government control, it is a new increment for neoliberal thought.

Galbraith gives examples of self-generated countervailing power. The original power of capital has been faced by the countervailing power of labor; the original power of strong sellers of consumers' goods by the countervailing power of food chains, variety chains, mail-order houses, department-store chains, and cooperative buying organizations; the original power of sellers of producers' goods by the countervailing power of buyers of these goods—for example, steel producers by automobile producers.[17]

From all this he draws a lesson for government. It should work with this regulatory instrument. First, it has a negative role of allowing the development of countervailing power. It should not oppose its development, as it has done in the Robinson-Patman Act and the A & P case. Where original power is not confronted with countervailing power, there is sound reason to apply the antitrust laws against it; where countervailing power is developing, there is no justification for attacking it while at the same time leaving original power untouched. Second, government has the positive role of strengthening countervailing power that is weak, as it did for "two previously disadvantaged groups"—workers and farmers. "Steps to strengthen countervailing power are not, in principle, different from steps to strengthen competition": both strengthen "the capacity of the economy for autonomous self-regulation." [18]

Galbraith has performed a useful function in pointing up a second type of regulator within the economy. The vertical confrontation of persons on

---

[14] Galbraith, *ibid.*, pp. 143–144.
[15] For this argument and the meaning of countervailing power, see Galbraith, *ibid.*, pp. 118–120.
[16] Galbraith, *ibid.*, p. 118.
[17] Galbraith, *ibid.*, pp. 123–129.
[18] Galbraith, *ibid.*, p. 155, and all of Chapter X on the role of the state.

opposite sides of the bargaining situation complements the lateral competition of persons performing the same function. But there are many large limits on the protection given by this second regulator. First, as Galbraith admits, it has not arisen in all cases where original power exists. Two examples are the farmer and the building-trade workers—the former not being able to organize countervailing power on his own initiative, the latter having a position of original power not met by countervailing power from the building industry. As a result, government is justified, Galbraith believes, in the first case in interposing its own support for the weak group, and in the second case in attacking the restrictive practices of some of the unions. Antitrust thus remains a needed remedy where countervailing power does not arise. Second, countervailing power may itself need control. For example, some will disagree with Galbraith on the A & P case, while others will think that the countervailing power of labor is now sometimes too big to be unregulated. Third, the existence of strong power in the hands of both buyers and sellers does not mean that they will oppose each other. Stocking has criticized the theory of countervailing power by reference to American Can Company and the U.S. Steel Corporation, two large corporations—one a buyer of tin plate for its cans from the other. He points out that for a quarter of a century, American Can Company received price discriminations that gave it advantage over competitors, and that, as price leader in the can industry, it tied the price of cans to that of tin plate to produce high prices for vegetable and fruit canners.[19]

Fourth, it does not follow from Galbraith's argument that there should be no limits on corporate concentration. Galbraith says "that it will be much easier for countervailing power to break into a position of market strength maintained by an imperfect coalition of three, four or a dozen firms than into a position held by one firm." [20] Fifth, the original power in an industry may have extended itself so far *vertically* that there is no opportunity for effective countervailing power to develop. Galbraith says that in some cases, "like the automobile and the oil industry" and to some extent the tobacco industry, the producers have integrated "their distribution through to the consumer" or "have an organization of small and dependent and therefore fairly powerless dealers." [21] In the automobile industry, government has passed legislation to protect dealers,[22] and in the oil and tobacco industries it has sought to use antitrust as a corrective. The student will find in the preceding discussion of the Paramount Pictures case

---

[19] Review of Galbraith's *American Capitalism* in *American Political Science Review*, XLVIII (March 1954), pp. 228–234.

[20] John Kenneth Galbraith, *American Capitalism: The Concept of Countervailing Power* (Cambridge, Mass.: Harvard University Press, 1952), p. 151.

[21] Galbraith, *ibid.*, pp. 127–128.

[22] By providing for suit by dealers against manufacturers who fail to act in good faith in compliance with terms of franchises or in termination, cancellation, or renewal thereof. 70 Stat. 1125 (1956).

an example of vertical controls which could be broken only by antitrust action.[23]

Sixth, the protections of countervailing powers break down in an inflationary period. Galbraith's own statement of this deficiency is as follows:

> When there is inflation, as noted, the self-regulatory mechanism based on countervailing power, ceases to be effective. It takes on, instead, a malignant form which becomes part of the dynamic of inflation itself. As demand for goods increases, and becomes increasingly inelastic, those who are exercising countervailing power on behalf of buyers are no longer able to make their power effective. The balance between those who are exercising it on behalf of sellers and their customers is upset. The consequences, especially in the labor market are profound. Employers who are faced with demand for higher wages can pay them and pass the added cost along in prices with impunity. They do. The higher wages become, in turn, the source of the higher income which helps sustain demand at the new prices.[24]

In other words, in inflation, original power and countervailing power do not effectively oppose each other, but together pass on costs to the public. Private power contributes a cost-push factor to inflation, and thus increases the magnitude thereof.

REGULATION IS THE REMEDY. Some believe that the only remedy for large private economic power is government regulation. This idea may be held by businessmen who fear regulation, or by public representatives who believe it cannot be successful; both may therefore desire to make antitrust effective. The idea may be held by others who accept giantism and great economic power, but who are willing also to take regulation as the remedy.

Three observations may be made concerning the prospect offered by this remedy. First, both history and reason indicate that overhead regulation by government will increase. In a constantly changing and increasingly interrelated economy, situations are bound to develop for which political correctives will be sought; concentration of power may be one of the factors which contributes to the development of these situations. Second, many who have studied the regulatory process are not too sanguine about the long-run effects of regulation. This problem of the beneficence of regulation has been discussed in theoretical terms; it will be presented for consideration in practical terms of accomplishment or lack of accomplishment in a number of industries on succeeding pages. One may draw his own conclusion as to whether regulation, or the alternative of government management, may be expected to be the best answer to the problem of private economic power. Third, many—probably most—will accept both the necessity of regulation (or government management) in some areas and the desirability of restricting the need for its use by maintaining or restoring automatic regulatory forces in the economy, whether of competition or of countervailing power.

---

[23] See page 200.
[24] *American Capitalism, op. cit.*, pp. 196–197.

EFFECTIVENESS IN ANTITRUST

In spite of the impossibility of perfect competition for much of American industry, and of the potential protections in the "New Competition," the conscience of business, countervailing power, and regulation, the central American policy for business is still the maintenance of competition. How effective is the policy? Could it be made more effective, and if so, how? There are no simple answers to these questions, and the answers are not definitive. Yet the questions introduce numerous and meaningful aspects of the problem of industrial policy.

ENFORCEMENT. The statutes provide a group of sanctions to be used in enforcement of the law on competition and trade practices. There are three types of sanctions for the Sherman Act. First, violations are misdemeanors, and the violator can be imprisoned for a term not exceeding one year, or fined in an amount not exceeding $50,000. Second, civil cases can be brought by the government to obtain injunctions or other remedies. Criminal and civil cases are brought by district attorneys and the Attorney General, and are now handled in the Antitrust Division of the Department of Justice. Third, suits can be brought by any injured party for triple the amount of damages caused by violations. By recent changes in the law, the national government itself may sue for damages when it is injured in its position as purchaser or proprietor. Sections 2, 3, 7, and 8 of the Clayton Act can be enforced by cease-and-desist orders of the FTC, civil suits by the government, and by suits for triple damages instituted by injured parties. Section 5 of the Federal Trade Commission Act can be enforced by cease-and-desist orders of the FTC; and Section 12 of that act, added in 1938 and relating to false advertising of foods, drugs, cosmetics, and mechanical devices affecting the human body, can be enforced by cease-and-desist orders of the FTC, restraining orders of courts, or under certain conditions by criminal action.

Consent orders will be issued by the FTC, and consent decrees by the courts, in both cases substantially reducing the time required for disposition of cases. A similar result occurs in criminal cases when the defendants, with the consent of the court, plead *nolo contendere,* which in effect reflects their unwillingness to contest the allegations. Also, both the FTC and the Antitrust Division have arrangements for advice or approval with respect to proposed activities. A merger plan, for example, may be submitted to the Antitrust Division, which—under a so-called railroad-release procedure—will review the plan and determine whether to waive the right to institute criminal proceedings with regard to the merger. However, it always reserves the right to institute civil proceedings if the plan eventually appears to be illegal.

When violations are determined by trial, or admitted or noncontested in consent orders or decrees or *nolo contendere* pleadings, appropriate remedies must be applied. Imprisonment is rare, and fines are often relatively small in terms of the size of the violations. Corrective, not punitive, action is normally desired, and is, of course, all that the FTC can provide. FTC orders and civil decrees of courts proscribe the illegal practices that were charged and substantiated. In order to insure that the parties may not have an opportunity to continue illegal practices, decrees may sometimes include prohibition of action which would not itself be illegal. It is sometimes charged that the Antitrust Division forces defendants, in order to avoid expense of trial, into acceptance of decrees which are too broad. Some protection, however, rests in the courts, which must approve the decrees. It is sometimes necessary, in order to provide a remedy, for the courts to decree some reorganization in an industry, as through divestiture of stock or assets acquired in violation of Section 7 of the Clayton Act, or through dissolution of a combination formed in violation of the Sherman Act.

There is no way of knowing just how much effect the existence of the antitrust laws has on the conduct of businessmen. The effect of law is measured in compliance, not in enforcement proceedings. Law may set new standards of morality that are accepted generally, or businessmen may be deterred from illegal action by the advice of their lawyers. The first line of enforcement is in the office of the private lawyer, where advice is given to the businessman. The number and the kinds of enforcement proceedings may, therefore, provide a poor index of compliance. As yet, no polling devices have been set up to gauge current voluntary compliance, and information on noncompliance is piecemeal.[25] Since, however, much business decision is secret, and since gross violations are nevertheless often revealed, it is evident that there is considerable violation and that enforcement proceedings are vital to the effectiveness of antitrust policy.

Private suits are an important means of enforcement, and occasionally, private suits, or suits of public agencies for damages, may be extremely significant. For example, hundreds of suits are now being pressed against electrical-equipment manufacturers for damages caused by identical bidding, and the sums are large. Yet a large burden of enforcement falls on the FTC and the Antitrust Division. These operate with limited public support. There are no large organized clienteles to support these agencies. They do have support from the committees on the Judiciary in the Congress and at times from other committees, and they are vigorously supported by a handful of strategically placed members of Congress. On the other hand, Congress may be the center of attack on vigorous enforcement, as has been shown, for example, in the basing-point dispute.[26] It appears that in efforts toward effective antitrust enforcement much depends on the zeal of administrative staffs and the support that can come to these from unor-

[25] For the view that the law has much effect, see Eugene V. Rostow, *Planning for Freedom: The Public Law of American Capitalism* (New Haven, Conn.: Yale University Press, 1959), pp. 307ff.

[26] See pages 232–236.

ganized community opinion and a small body of experts outside government. But much must depend also on support in political channels.[27] In the first period of vigor in enforcement—from 1901 to World War II—antitrust was a major component of the macropolitics of the time; presidents, backed by unorganized public opinion, generated strong enforcement. In the revival of antitrust enforcement in 1937, a zealous head of the new Antitrust Division had to find support in political channels for the greatly enlarged appropriations—theretofore niggardly—which Congress provided for enforcement activities.

The Antitrust Division operates on a budget of approximately five million dollars per annum and with a staff of about three hundred lawyers and some two dozen economists. The division, sometimes with the aid of the Federal Bureau of Investigation (FBI), makes preliminary investigations. For example, in 1961 the division received about a thousand notices, from various sources, of proposed mergers, and of these about one hundred and fifty were investigated. If, after preliminary investigation, it is deemed desirable to conduct a complete investigation, the division will use either a federal grand jury or the civil investigative demand. The grand jury is used when the choice is in favor of criminal action. Until 1962, the division found it difficult to obtain information for civil suits, due to its inability to compel production of information at the investigative stage of proceedings. It could, of course, use the grand jury as a means of obtaining information for criminal and civil proceedings with respect to the same set of practices. By the Antitrust Civil Process Act of 1962, the Department of Justice can, under carefully restricted procedure, now examine the books and records of corporations in cases under investigation through a compulsory process called the investigative demand.

There is a degree of awkwardness in some antitrust proceedings. Sometimes the real issue of interest for the public is what kind of economic policy or organization should prevail for an industry. This issue cannot be faced directly, for the proceedings are judicial rather than legislative or administrative. Attention must be centered on the question of violation of law; if violation is established, then the decree must be framed in terms of the offenses established. In spite of the framework, it can be assumed that judges will be influenced by their views on what kind of economic policy is in the public interest. Nevertheless, the process does not allow the freedom for revision of industry structure or practice that would be possible through legislative or administrative channels.[28]

A significant aspect of these proceedings are the requirements for proof. Normally, there will be a problem in anticompetitive (as contrasted with deceptive) practices cases of determining the market in which competitive ef-

---

[27] On this need for administrative agencies see pages 564–565, 577.
[28] It might prove fruitful to compare the direct process of industry reorganization in the Public Utility Holding Company Act, and the indirect process of court reorganization of the moving-picture industry.

fects are to be determined. There is no escape from this issue and the necessity of proof by the enforcement agency. Enforcement officials will tend to argue for a limited rather than broad definition of the affected market. There is the problem of effects on competition, of which there are various "indicators." [29] There are *structural* tests, such as the degree of concentration, the ease of entry, the independence of rivals, the amount of product differentiation, the potentials for competition, and others. There are tests on the *behavior* of participants, such as collusion, predatory practices, price discrimination, price leadership and followship, conscious parallelism in prices, frequency of price changes, and many others. There are questions of whether the market performs as it should (*market performance*), including such things as whether profits are excessively high, capacity is unused, cost savings are passed on to the consumer, innovation and progressiveness and growth exist, resources are wasted in selling activities, and others. In a particular case, only some of these criteria of competition will be involved. But which combination of them will be necessary to substantiate a charge of violation will often be crucial for the determination of the case. The discussion in the two preceding chapters will show that market-performance tests have not been materially significant in court opinions, and that the courts have been more interested in behavior of participants than in market structure. In recent years the Supreme Court, in interpreting the substantiality test in Clayton Act provisions, has tended to emphasize the need for looking at all the relevant market factors. This shows the necessity of thorough market analysis and presentation of different types of data, and hence points up the heavy requirements of proof. These requirements may be further increased by the necessity of tying the facts to the particular language of the antitrust provision under which the charge is brought.

The antitrust statutes have often been criticized for the uncertainty of the meaning of their provisions. This has probably had the several effects of leaving the businessman in uncertainty, of making him in some cases (as under the Robinson-Patman Act) overcautious, and of making him in other instances less careful than he should have been, of making the task of enforcement agencies more difficult, and of leading to softness of the courts toward violators. It appears now, however, that there is a large area of certainty in the laws, and that this certainty is cause for objection from some people.[30] Thus, some things are *per se* violations, and this causes criticism from those who want looser construction. The chief element of uncertainty which exists is in the interpretation of the facts with respect to non–*per se* violations.

---

[29] See Mark S. Massel, *Competition and Monopoly: Legal and Economic Issues* (Washington, D.C.: Brookings Institution, 1962), Chapter 7, where the term is used in the chapter heading and each of the tests described in our text is discussed.

[30] "There is much truth to the observation that it is easy to avoid violating the antitrust laws; what is difficult is to come as close as possible to doing what the law prohibits without violating it." Joel B. Dirlam and Alfred E. Kahn, *Fair Competition: The Law and Economics of Antitrust Policy* (Ithaca, N.Y.: Cornell University Press, 1954), p. 264.

For example, when there are two possible interpretations on the relevant market, which will be chosen?

When such questions are open, the validity of the decision will be largely dependent upon the quality of the economic analysis. The economics profession and the specialized bar dealing with antitrust cases have become quite sophisticated in analysis of market structure and behavior. The Antitrust Division, though weakened by frequent resignations, is strenghtened by an honors program for recruitment of top law graduates. Though district judges may handle antitrust cases infrequently, their perception is increased by the greater sophistication of the presentations of attorneys. On the side of factual analysis, therefore, more validity can be expected in antitrust decisions—and more good judgment in selection of cases to be prosecuted—than was true in earlier periods.

The big case is troublesome in a number of respects. A few such cases will absorb much staff time. One such case may run for months in a district court and for a decade, or thereabouts, in its progress from grand jury to final disposition. Similarly, an FTC case may run through a period of years.[31] Often, commentators contrast the small government staff of lawyers and the large staff of industry lawyers in a case, and a similar contrast could be drawn between the pay scales of the two. The case is tried also before the bar of public opinion, for the accused will run informational programs for public approval. Also, there is danger that big cases may have an undeserved influence on the law.[32] Yet there are some partial consolations for the public in the big case. Professional attention is now being given to the problem of obtaining expedition and efficiency in the trial of the large case, government lawyers may be quite able to hold their own against superior numbers and pay status, the trial before the public is for good will rather than influence on the judge, and, in something such as antitrust, perhaps the law made in the big case is the law that is most significant.

---

[31] Note the following example: Private complaint was brought to the FTC against major oil companies in the Detroit market on Sept. 29, 1939. After investigation, the FTC issued a complaint against Standard of Indiana and three other companies on Nov. 29, 1940. After involved proceedings, the FTC issued a cease-and-desist order against Standard on Oct. 9, 1945. After motion for rehearing, the FTC modified its order and denied rehearing on Aug. 9, 1946. Standard appealed, and on March 11, 1949, the appellate court upheld the FTC. Standard petitioned the Supreme Court for review, which granted the petition and upheld Standard's legal contention on "good faith" being a complete defense (Jan. 8, 1951). In the meantime, Congress had passed and the President vetoed a bill which included a provision on "good faith." The case went back to the FTC, which on Jan. 16, 1953, issued modified findings and order. After involved further proceedings, paralleled by further activity in Congress on the matter, the Court of Appeals vacated the FTC findings and order on May 3, 1955, and the Supreme Court upheld the Court of Appeals in a decision on Jan. 27, 1958. Eighteen years of bitter conflict were ended with a victory for the accused. See Joseph C. Palamountain, *The Federal Trade Commission and the Indiana Standard Case* (University, Ala.: University of Alabama Press, 1964).

[32] J. Holmes remarked that "Great cases like hard cases make bad law." *Northern Securities Co. v. U.S.*, 193 U.S. 197, 400 (1904).

258 *Policies Affecting the Economy Generally*

Over the past several years, discussion on the strengthening of enforcement has centered on three proposals. One was to give the Department of Justice authority to issue civil investigative demands, and this was finally done in legislation passed in 1962. The second proposal is for a premerger notification requirement, so that the FTC and the Antitrust Division would have advance notice of the intentions of parties to merge. The third proposal is that the FTC be granted the power, which the Antitrust Division has, to seek preliminary injunctions in merger cases, so that mergers under consideration by the commission could be delayed pending the completion of its proceedings. These last two proposals have been embodied repeatedly in bills introduced in Congress. Their enactment would strengthen materially the enforcement of Section 7.

METHODOLOGICAL APPROACHES. The problems in enforcement of the Sherman Act gave rise, at an early date, to one of the big debates in our history over methods of government. By 1914, three basic approaches in method had been advocated for antitrust. Though they accepted the other approaches to an extent, Presidents Taft, Theodore Roosevelt, and Wilson each placed emphasis on one of these. The first was a general statute to be given specific meaning through cases in the courts. Taft had faith in this method. He believed that the rule of reason provided a test through which the courts could give definite content to the general statute.[33] The second was specific legislation. Wilson desired "further and more explicit legislative definition of the policy and meaning of the existing antitrust law" so that "the law itself and the penalty" could be made plain.[34] The third was administrative supervision. Roosevelt believed that an administrative commission should be established to pass upon the reasonableness of combinations in advance of their formation, thus giving needed advice to businessmen and curbing injury to the public before it had developed.[35] Thus, each of the three placed his greatest faith in one of the three methods: judicial, legislative, or administrative.

Experience reveals that each of the three methods has its advantages and its limitations. Through the judicial method, some guidelines for business conduct have been developed. Some activities are illegal *per se;* others are known to be evil if prompted by evil purpose or causing certain known evil effects. In the judicial method, policy can be adjusted to concrete situations; decision can be more accurate, because all the circumstances are known, and the factors can be evaluated carefully under trusted procedure. The remedy also can be adjusted to the case. But the method has weaknesses: It is costly —too costly in money and time to be used in many cases; a single case may

---

[33] William Howard Taft, *The Anti-Trust Act and the Supreme Court* (New York: Harper and Row, Publishers, Inc., 1914).

[34] Address to Congress, January 20, 1914, *Congressional Record* (63rd Cong., 2nd Sess.), **LI,** p. 1979.

[35] See citations at page 208, note 2. For analysis of the historical conflicts, see James E. Anderson, *Emergence of the Modern Regulatory State* (Washington, D.C.: Public Affairs Press, 1962).

be in the courts for years; rules of law develop slowly; organization and business habits may have crystallized to an extent that an effective remedy is impossible; uncertainty as to legality leads to leniency in penalties. It is a clumsy and imperfect method for the purposes of antitrust, defensible only in terms of difficulties or dangers of other methods. The administrative method may be more expeditious. It can be preventive and thus effective. Discretion can be granted to the administrative agency to make decisions according to standards of desirable economic organization and policy, rather than on the basis of guilt of parties. But many dangers are seen in this approach. Businessmen have fears about the directions of decision and the uncertainties of discretionary judgments. Others fear that public interests will be sacrificed by premature decision, for all may not be revealed in the incipiency of plans which will occur in their unfolding; they fear also that public personnel will not be sufficiently precautionary and rigorous in the defense of the public interest. The legislative method offers the opportunity to establish new bridgeheads of policy. But vision is limited, and it is difficult to weave a rule that will fit the situations of the future. There is danger that loopholes will be left or rigidities created; and in this day of heavy congressional workload, it is difficult to obtain attention and time in the legislative process for needed amendments.

One approach not foreseen in 1914 was used effectively a generation later. In the Public Utility Holding Company Act,[36] Congress laid down a specific standard for the reorganization of the utility holding-company structure; and it gave a command, not merely an authorization, to an administrative agency to put the standard into effect. Thus, by legislative-administrative action, an industry was reorganized to fit the pattern deemed to be in the public interest. True, a similar effort, though with less force in the legislative directive to the administrative agency, failed in the Transportation Act of 1920, which contemplated the reorganization of the railway systems into a number of competing systems of comparable strength.[37]

A combination of the several approaches has been used in antitrust procedure. The general statute has remained the center of the program. But as Taft, Theodore Roosevelt and Wilson recommended, it has been supplemented by legislation proscribing specific acts and prescribing remedies. Likewise, it has been supplemented in practice by administrative advice to businessmen, by trade conferences, by an administrative tribunal—though the chief uses of the last of these has been in investigations and in adjudication, rather than in approval or disapproval of business plans. In the future, additional specific legislation and additional uses of administration may give further support to the basic antitrust statute. Antitrust—though conceived by many as an antidote to regulation—could become, much more than it already is, a complicated system of regulation in which legal proscrip-

[36] See pages 435–437.
[37] See pages 384–386.

POLICY. The effort to maintain competition was weakened in the beginning by policy on three other matters. First, the protective tariff set a floor under competition and sheltered the "monopolist" from competition below that floor. Second, the patent policy of Congress and the liberal construction of patent rights by the courts fostered large-scale monopoly and restrictions on competition. Third, the freedom of incorporation under state laws, and the lack of regulation of corporation finance, allowed opportunities for huge promoters' profits to influence materially the organization of some American industries. It is interesting to ponder whether different American policies on these matters might have been more effective than antitrust laws in maintaining a competitive system. Certainly, different policies in conjunction with antitrust would have made the effort more effective.

In addition to these factors, enactments which granted exemptions, refined the language of prohibitory clauses,[38] or contributed to soft competition have weakened the force of antitrust policy. There have also been aspects of judicial construction which weakened the policy. In the early days, emphasis on intent provided opportunities to escape penalty for anticompetitive results, the requirement of bad conduct (coercive and collusive tactics) allowed attainment of market power by stock acquisition and merger, and the restricted meaning given to provisions of the new legislation of 1914 virtually destroyed its impact on anticompetitive actions. These developments in judicial construction were followed by abandonment of antitrust and protection of anticompetitive practices through NRA codes in the first two years of the New Deal.

The revival of antitrust enforcement in 1937, and the subsequent changes in judicial construction which gave thrust to the effort, led to a counterattack, which has received some support from new economic doctrine. This counterattack on rigorous judicial policy is reflected in books, such as Lilienthal's, which expound the virtue of business performance and condemn an alleged judicial hostility toward big business. It was most clearly crystallized in 1952 in a lengthy analysis by a distinguished professor of antitrust law, S. Chesterfield Oppenheim.[39] Oppenheim condemned the *per se* violation doctrine, which he said "selects a particular fact—the restrictive agreement or, in industrial concentration cases, a particular market condition—as the decisive fact from which an irrebutable presumption of antitrust illegality is derived as an immutable rule of law." [40] He favored, rather,

---

[38] See the account of the framing of new legislation in 1914 in Gerard C. Henderson, *The Federal Trade Commission* (New Haven, Conn.: Yale University Press, 1925), Chapter 1.

[39] "Federal Antitrust Legislation: Guideposts to a Revised National Antitrust Policy," *Michigan Law Review*, L (June 1952), pp. 1139–1244.

[40] *Ibid.*, p. 1157.

a rule of reason which "draws the line between zones of legal and illegal conduct under the antitrust laws by consideration of all the factors and circumstances in any given situation." [41] He thought that in applying the rule of reason, the concept of "workable competition," recently developed by noted economists, should serve as the guide.

"Workable competition" is a term created in 1940 by Professor J. M. Clark.[42] The idea is that industry cannot be realistically described in terms of the dichotomy between pure competition and monopoly, but that the two are intermixed. The public interest will be served when the social benefits of the intermixture are as great as can be achieved under any alternative arrangement. This seems like down-to-earth realism, for it seems to say that the status quo of imperfect competition (now called "workable" or "effective" competition) should be accepted when nothing better can be achieved. The problem, however, is in determining when workable competition really does exist. The measure of this is uncertain, and particularly whether it is determined by market structure, business behavior, or market performance. The implication drawn by some commentators was that good or bad results in the market, such as fair prices and innovation and progress in the industry, would necessarily be the determining factor. Great emphasis would be placed on whether there was a high rate of innovation or progressiveness in the industry. Oppenheim himself argued that the three criteria of structure, business behavior, and market performance were related, and that workable competition could be determined only by "weighing all the salient economic variables in any specific industry or market factual situation." [43]

In addition to these ideas, there were condemnations of the Alcoa decision, the conspiracy doctrine as developed in the American Tobacco and the cement and steel-conduit basing-point-pricing cases, and the use of strictly structural standards such as the quantitative test in Standard Stations; and support for broad definitions of the relevant market and for looking at all the pertinent economic data.

Taken together, these various standards appear to add up to still another attempt to solve the problem of industrial policy by giving to antitrust a minimum role—in this case, by construing antitrust laws restrictively. Workable competition, market performance, and an unlimited rule of reason all work in the same directions: toward wider judicial discretion and broader permissiveness under the law. In fact, such standards would bestow judicial discretion of a scope hitherto not envisaged for courts in policy application. When is an industry operating with more social gain than would be achievable under any alternative arrangements? When is an industry sufficiently

---

[41] *Ibid.*, p. 1151.

[42] "Toward a Concept of Workable Competition," *American Economic Review*, **XXX** (June 1940), pp. 241–256. For history of the concept, see George W. Stocking, "On the Concept of Workable Competition as an Antitrust Guide," *Antitrust Bulletin*, **II** (September 1956), pp. 3–39.

[43] "Federal Antitrust Legislation: Guidepost to a Revised National Antitrust Policy," *Michigan Law Review*, **L** (June 1952), p. 1188.

progressive? When is it reasonable to allow or not to allow private control of the market? These questions may be appropriate ones for legislators trying to determine whether to place an industry under regulation, but enforcement agencies and courts need guidelines. The questions are not likely to be answered by an accumulation of all relevant facts, for facts without standards of decision do not provide guidelines for judgment. Clear guidelines may not be available in the present state of knowledge. It has been argued by economists, in fact, that "any over-all evaluation of performance" is "impossible"; [44] that such a broad standard would be "an invitation to nonenforcement"; [45] that "At best criteria of performance are instruments of diagnosis, not prognosis"; [46] that "total immersion in the rule of reason" would lead to "utter confusion"; [47] and even that "good performance can scarcely justify private monopolies in a society dedicated to private enterprise." [48]

The broad permissiveness of the suggested standards is obvious. Statute law now makes certain things illegal if they have adverse effects on competition, irrespective of argument on whether the effects are good or bad. Judicial construction establishing *per se* rules on certain types of conduct has added some additional definiteness to the law. This definiteness creates certainty for the businessman (though some may not like it) and a guide for enforcement to government agencies. Moreover, although economic facts and sophisticated analysis thereof are essential, standards of conduct which determine the relevance of data are essential for manageability of cases. The requirements for proof would become unbearable if law provided no definition of practices to be condemned.

While there has been counterattack against the vigorous and broadened antitrust policy of recent years, and answers thereto, there has also been discussion of ways of making antitrust fill a larger role than it now does. The most far-reaching proposal for an expanded role for antitrust is one which attacks head-on the problem of market power.

Carl Kaysen and Donald F. Turner believe that the dominant goal in antitrust policy should be "the protection of competitive processes by limiting market power." [49] "A firm possesses market power when it can behave persistently in a manner different from the behavior that a competitive market would enforce on a firm facing otherwise similar cost and demand

---

[44] Carl Kaysen and Donald F. Turner, *Antitrust Policy: An Economic and Legal Analysis* (Cambridge, Mass.: Harvard University Press, 1959), p. 82.

[45] Edward S. Mason in Kaysen and Turner, "Preface," xviii.

[46] Mark S. Massel, *Competition and Monopoly: Legal and Economic Issues* (Washington, D.C.: Brookings Institution, 1962), p. 221.

[47] Joel B. Dirlam and Alfred E. Kahn, *Fair Competition: The Law and Economics of Antitrust Policy* (Ithaca, N.Y.: Cornell University Press, 1954), p. 269.

[48] George W. Stocking, "Economic Tests of Monopoly and the Concept of the Relevant Market," *Antitrust Bulletin*, **II** (March 1957), p. 482.

[49] Carl Kaysen and Donald F. Turner, *Antitrust Policy: An Economic and Legal Analysis* (Cambridge, Mass.: Harvard University Press, 1959), p. 44.

conditions." [50] Market power is not effectively dealt with by antitrust laws, because the law does not proscribe large relative size unless it is associated with predatory conduct, is achieved by single firm monopolizing, or is supported by conspiracy.[51] The authors are obviously writing about *existing* aggregations of power, since *increases* in power can be attacked under Section 7 without respect to predatory conduct, monopoly, or conspiracy. Nevertheless, they conclude, "The principal defect of present antitrust law is its inability to cope with market power created by jointly acting oligopolists." [52]

Kaysen and Turner see several ways of attacking "undue" market power, for they would not think it realistic to attack all market power. One way would be to accept existing concentrations of power and devote attention to the "control of conduct, with a view to preventing any kinds of practices which sustain or increase market power. In particular, fairly stringent limitations on mergers would occupy a central place in policy." [53] The other ways would involve a retroactive attack on existing power. The model of the Public Utility Holding Company Act could be followed. This would mean the empowering of "an administrative agency to enforce the structural reorganization of firms or groups of firms possessing undue market power, all such processes to be commenced within a specified number of years." [54] Rather arbitrary cut-offs on size and significance of industries would be set for the guidance of the agency. The authors prefer, however, a permanent change in the law to prohibit "undue market power" and achievement of this objective through dissolution, divorcement, or divestiture. Arbitrary standards—for example, control by four or fewer companies of 80 per cent of the annual sales for five years—could be set, but they prefer "a fairly extensive economic inquiry for determination of each case." Although market power is primarily a matter of structure, they would look also at business behavior.[55]

Objections to the Kaysen-Turner proposals have rested primarily on two bases. Lawyers have thought that the standard of "undue market power" was too unclear for effective adjudication. Some economists have feared disincentive effects.[56] The authors themselves do not believe that the impairment of innovation or entrepreneurial vigor would be serious. They do recognize that there may be some conflict between such performance objectives and the destruction of undue market power, and they concede that if the scale of efficient operations in a market is such that only a few firms can attain it, so that increase in number of firms would bring "a substantial loss of efficiency," they would not favor action against the power

[50] Kaysen and Turner, *ibid.*, p. 75.
[51] Kaysen and Turner, *ibid.*, p. 106.
[52] Kaysen and Turner, *ibid.*, p. 110.
[53] Kaysen and Turner, *ibid.*, p. 95.
[54] Kaysen and Turner, *ibid.*, p. 97.
[55] See, in particular, Kaysen and Turner, *ibid.*, pp. 46 and 98.
[56] See Mason's "Preface" to Kaysen and Turner, *ibid.*, p. xix.

itself. They would also except from the policy power innocently thrust upon firms and power derived from "economies of scale, valid patents, or the introduction of new processes, products, or marketing techniques." [57]

The Kaysen-Turner proposal, like that of Oppenheim, focuses attention on large policy problems. It too, like Oppenheim's, points up difficulties in sweeping revision of statutes which have such complex effects as do the antitrust laws. A simple way to provide for the Kaysen-Turner policy would be to amend Section 2 of the Sherman Act to prohibit undue market power. This would meet directly the argument that the Sherman Act, by prohibiting monopolizing only in Section 2, misses the modern problem of oligopolistic power. But what exceptions would have to be made? Would the simple standard of "undue market power" be too unclear a standard? Could an arbitrary statutory standard, such as percentage of the market controlled by less than a stated number of firms, be devised that was realistic in terms of the necessary diversities in markets? How drastic a change would be anticipated—that is, how many industries would be affected, and to what extent would their reorganization be required? Beyond these questions of statute-framing and prognosis of effects is the larger issue of whether it would be politically feasible to make a sweeping change in antitrust law.

Probably a more effective approach would be to inhibit the further development of market power through policies available under existing statutes and now being followed, to an extent, by enforcement agencies. A vigorous enforcement of Section 7 would be the centerpiece of the policy. Enforcement could be made more effective by requirement for notice before mergers and by more ample means of preventing consummation of mergers pending study by the enforcement agencies. The construction of the section in the du Pont case even shows the possibility of using the statute to prevent enlargement of market power by the continued holding of stock acquired at an earlier period. The anticonspiracy doctrine offers further opportunities for attack on market power. The word "combination" in Section 1 of the Sherman Act might be resurrected from the limbo of the past and made the basis of attack on any company whose growth shows a record of mergers or stock purchases.[58] Close surveillance over all forms of coercive and collusive practice by those possessing market power could be part of a vigorous enforcement policy. The existence of market power could be the central test in surveillance of industries and selection of cases by the enforcement agencies.

There are other possibilities for more drastic antitrust policy, some of which have been noted earlier. Patent policy could be revised—cancelling patent rights in cases of nonuse over a stated period of years, making price-fixing clauses in patent licenses illegal *per se,* or restricting in other ways the terms of joint covenants on use of patents. The legalization of export

---

[57] See especially Kaysen and Turner, *ibid.,* pp. 45, 46, 90, 82ff.
[58] Suggested by Eugene V. Rostow, *Planning for Freedom* (New Haven, Conn.: Yale University Press, 1959), pp. 329–330, and see, above page 195, note 37.

trade agreements could be limited to firms of small size. Study could be given to the problem of conglomerate enterprises (that is, those engaged in many and diverse lines of commerce) to determine their effects on competition. Study could also be given to the interlockings of credit, investment, and insurance companies with industrial firms to see if it is desirable to broaden the prohibitions of Section 8 of the Clayton Act.

There are, it is clear, broad alternatives with respect to antitrust policy. Some regard the present course of policy as realistic in general, and desire that it be supported by vigorous enforcement, rigorous judicial construction, and piecemeal statutory changes. Others regard it as oversevere and as hazardous to efficiency, innovation, and progress. Others think there is need for a bolder and more concentrated attack on the existence of market power in modern oligopolistic markets.

THE ISSUES BROADENED AND SHARPENED: GOVERNMENT AND STEEL IN 1962

An episode in government-industry relations in April, 1962, may forecast new issues in consideration of industry policy. On April 10, Mr. Roger Blough of U.S. Steel handed the President a copy of a press release announcing the decision of U.S. Steel to raise its prices by approximately 3.5 per cent. Surprised and angered by the announcement, the President told the American people the next day that the price increase was a "wholly unjustifiable and irresponsible defiance of the public interest." After three days of pressure on the steel industry through numerous channels, U.S. Steel bowed and rescinded its price increase.[59]

The President's concern over this price increase was the result of developments which were basically political in nature, but which reflected also the organizational revolution within American industry. The end of the war and the release of wage-price controls set off a wage-price spiral that had continued through the succeeding years. Here was striking evidence of the weakness that Galbraith himself had seen in countervailing power. By 1960, moreover, the dollar deficit in American international balances had become alarming; in eight to nine years the gold reserve of the nation had dropped from about 23 to about 16.5 billion dollars. More favorable wage and price levels were drawing American investments abroad, resulting in American-produced foreign competition for American goods. In the face of an impending additional round of wage and price increases, the new administration had suggested policy guidelines for the economy, the heart of which was the principle that wage increases should not be demanded or granted which

---

[59] The facts in this summary of the events in April, 1962, are taken from the remarkable account, based on group reporting, by Wallace Carroll, *New York Times*, April 23, 1962, p. 1, columns 4–7, continued p. 25, column 1. A fuller account is contained in Grant McConnell, *Steel and the Presidency, 1962* (New York: W. W. Norton & Company, Inc., 1963).

exceeded increases in productivity in the economy as a whole. Such wage increases, it was argued, would be noninflationary, for they could be absorbed without price increases. The steel industry was of particular concern, because it could affect the economy through the increase of its own prices and also because it could set a pattern, as it had on other occasions, for wage-price developments in other industries. The Administration had succeeded in its efforts to avoid a steel-price increase in 1961, and had succeeded in getting labor to accept a settlement in 1962 which it considered to be in accord with its guidelines. It had thought that the cost increases provided in the labor contract would not be followed by a price increase.

Other companies immediately followed U.S. Steel's lead, so that the administration was promptly confronted with a price rise by producers of approximately 84 per cent of the nation's steel. The administration moved quickly on many fronts. The President sought to rally public opinion against the companies. On the antitrust front, the FBI promptly followed up on a lead that indicated possible collusion among companies, the Attorney General announced a grand jury investigation of their activities, the Chairman of the Federal Trade Commission said that his agency would investigate regarding possible violation of a 1951 consent decree binding companies to refrain from collusive price fixing or maintenance of identical prices, and chairmen of the House and Senate Antitrust subcommittees scheduled investigations. On another front, the Defense Department announced that steel purchases would be shifted to companies that had not raised prices, and promptly awarded a contract to a hold-out company. But the central front in the battle of the administration was persuasion. It used the channels of acquaintance and friendship to let Inland Steel and other hold-outs know that it would be pleased if they did not follow U.S. Steel's lead, and it also established contact with Blough to let him know that the President thought he had been double-crossed and to argue that U.S. Steel's action had been wrong. Seldom, if ever, has government moved with coordination of so many lines of attack on a domestic situation.

The outcome was that Inland Steel's board decided not to raise prices, and the increases which had been announced by most companies were revoked. Whether Inland Steel was influenced more by government influence than by conviction that the market was too weak to justify a price increase is uncertain. Corporate power bowed, but perhaps to the market and Pennsylvania Avenue combined.

The issues, however, were important for Main Street. Could there be a public interest in an increase in prices in an industry? It seems obvious that this could be true. If so, what protections could exist for this interest? Is the conscience and good judgment of industry leaders a sufficient, or at any rate the best, safeguard? Is it a dependable safeguard in an industry in which prices of different companies must be approximately the same, in which a leadership situation has weakened the horizontal checks and balances presumed to exist under competition, and in which the countervailing powers of industry against labor, and of buyers of the product against sellers, have been weakened? Is the answer affected by the position of the industry in the economy? Would a further break-up of the industry to destroy the leadership position of a firm give additional protection to the public? Is it desirable, in addition, to have public guidelines on policy, and to provide for some kind of government intervention to insure that these guidelines are followed, or at least seriously considered, in private decisions? It appears that the problems of inflation and world markets that lay behind the episode of 1962 have broadened the issues of industrial policy, and that the episode itself has sharpened them.

The broader issues had begun to have attention in Congress prior to the steel episode. There was some discussion of a policy for steel alone. Senator Gore, for example, had proposed that it be regulated like a public utility. Some basis was laid for consideration of steel separately by a study in 1959, in which it was concluded:

> If steel prices had behaved like other industrial prices, the total industrial price index would have risen by 40 percent less over the last decade and less by 52 percent since 1953. Finished-goods prices would have risen less by 23 and 38 percent, respectively.[60]

The main proposals, however, for legislation showed a belief that the problem to be faced was broader than steel. These proposals were for some form of fact-finding process with respect to potentially inflationary price increases that was similar to the fact-finding processes used in labor disputes. The proposal which received most attention was in a bill that provided for hearings by presidential appointees and for factual summaries and advisory statements by the hearing tribunals.[61] Ultimately, after the steel dispute, a bill was introduced which would have extended Taft-Hartley procedures—boards of inquiry and injunctions—to inflationary price increases.[62]

In the steel episode the President acted on his own responsibility. His position was similar to that of President Theodore Roosevelt, who intervened in a coal strike in 1902. President Roosevelt acted to get the two sides in the labor dispute to accept an arbitration commission; President Kennedy acted without an independent study. It could be argued that if action of this kind is to be taken, even occasionally, it should be regularized by statutory authorization and establishment of suitable procedures.

It would, of course, be ironic if the remedies applied against labor in cases of stoppage of industry, forty-three years (Taft-Hartley Act, 1947) after the pattern was shown in the action of President Roosevelt, should

---

[60] Otto Eckstein and Gary Fromm, "Steel and the Postwar Inflation," Study Paper No. 2, "Study of Employment, Growth, and Price Levels," Joint Economic Committee, 86th Cong., 1st Sess. (Nov. 6, 1959), p. 34.
[61] HR 6263, 86th Cong., 1st Sess., by Congressman Reuss.
[62] S. 3168, 87th Cong., 2nd Sess. (April 16, 1962), by Senator Gore.

now be applied against industry in cases of inflationary price increase. It is not likely to be so applied unless great need is apparent, nor without consideration of the many problems involved. One problem would be how to restrict government intervention to situations actually constituting serious threat to the economy. Regular and frequent interventions in price determinations would result in a substantial burden on government and a substantial departure from tradition. Another problem would be the development of standards or guidelines for decision. Would these arise in individual cases of intervention, or would guidelines be established in advance? Still another problem would be that of sanctions. Most of the recent proposals have contemplated that the proposals of fact-finding boards or other authorities would be only advisory to industry. Another problem is whether such interventions should be possible for wage increases as well as price increases.[63] Reference to this problem indicates that industrial policy merges with labor policy, which is the subject of discussion in the following two chapters. At this point it can be concluded that although the bills for regularized intervention themselves may appear now to be episodic, they show, nevertheless, the long-range potentials of policy if the safeguards of business judgment, countervailing power, and antitrust prove to be inadequate.

[63] For fuller discussion of the many problems, see Emmette S. Redford, "Potential Public Policies to Deal with Inflation Caused by Market Power," Study Paper No. 10, "Study of Employment, Growth, and Price Levels," Joint Economic Committee, 86th Cong., 1st Sess. (Dec. 11, 1959).

Chapter 13. Government Prescription of Conditions, Rights, and Benefits of Employment

GOVERNMENT REGULATES the labor market in two ways. First, it regulates the bargaining process by which employer and employee arrive at decisions. Such regulation extends to the determination of the rights that each will have in bargaining, the rules for conduct of bargaining, the limitations on the action of each party, and the ways the state will assist in trying to avoid conflict or bring the parties to an agreement. The feature which distinguishes this type of regulation is that the ultimate decision on labor benefits is left to the parties in contest. Second, government itself determines conditions of, rights to, and benefits from employment. The determinations range from simple requirements on safe and healthful working conditions to limitations on choice of employees and standards on wages and hours. The characteristic of this approach is that government takes certain matters out of the area of private bargaining, in whole or in part, and imposes its own decisions on them.

The distinction between the types of regulation of the labor market is not absolute. Some regulation of bargaining is not merely procedural. For example, national legislation outlawing the closed shop, and legislation permitting states to outlaw the union shop, relates to the substance of rights of persons and also to the strength of the parties in the bargaining process. Nevertheless, the distinction here made has real significance and, in addition, permits a division in the discussion of labor regulation by government. The second of these types of approach is discussed in this chapter, with the regulation of bargaining left for the succeeding one.

PREVENTION OF FRAUD

One of the early purposes of legislation by the states was to see that wages were honestly paid. Among such statutes were those providing that wages be paid in cash,[1] that employers redeem in cash store orders or other evidences of indebtedness issued in payment of wages,[2] and that where wages were fixed on the basis of weight of coal mined, the coal should not be screened before weighing.[3] Such statutes were challenged as violations of liberty of contract, but were upheld by the courts as reasonable regulations in the public interest. Today, provisions concerning time and method of payment of wages are common features of state labor legislation.

SAFETY, HEALTH, AND REHABILITATION

Legislation to insure safe and healthful working conditions began in the nineteenth century, but the movement for such legislation became strong only in the first decade of the twentieth. Many studies, such as those on phosphorus matches and white lead, aroused public interest in safety and health; and professional, labor, and industry groups, public agencies, and newly formed associations worked for legal proscriptions and standards. Congress and the state legislatures began the enactment of a great mass of safety and health legislation. Inspection by public authority became the accepted method of enforcement. The most significant development, however, was the delegation to administrative commissions of authority to develop safety and health codes. Leadership in this movement was taken by Professor John R. Commons in the State of Wisconsin, where an Industrial Commission, established in 1911, with the aid of advisory committees on which industry was represented set up inclusive and detailed safety rules to take the place of the mass of statutes which had already been enacted. In spite of these developments, many states still lag in the enactment of legislation and in the enforcement of legal standards.[4]

Paralleling the enactment of legislation has been the growth of interest in industry in the safety and health of its employees. Safety engineering is now an accepted responsibility of management, and in many industries is a highly specialized area of work. Sanitation, good lighting, rest rooms, and a multitude of other arrangements for healthful working conditions are prevalent in industrial and commercial concerns.

Safety and health protection has now been supplemented by public efforts to prepare for remunerative employment those who are vocationally handicapped by accident, disease, or congenital defect. The main public

---

[1] Upheld in *Erie R. Co. v. Williams*, 233 U.S. 685 (1914), in which the Court also upheld a requirement of semimonthly payment.
[2] Upheld in *Knoxville Iron Co. v. Harbison*, 183 U.S. 13 (1901), *Dayton Coal & I. Co. v. Barton*, 183 U.S. 23 (1901), and *Keokee Consol. Coke Co. v. Taylor*, 234 U.S. 224 (1914).
[3] Upheld in *McLean v. Arkansas*, 211 U.S. 539 (1909).
[4] On safety and health, see Don D. Leschohier, "Working Conditions," pp. 359–379, and Elizabeth Brandeis, "Labor Legislation," pp. 625–659, in *History of Labor in the United States, 1896–1932*, Vol. III (New York: The Macmillan Company, 1935).

program is the one provided in the Barden-La Follette Act of 1943,[5] which expanded the program set up under the Vocational Rehabilitation Act of 1920. The program is administered by the Office of Vocational Rehabilitation in the Department of Health, Education, and Welfare. This office makes grants to state boards of vocational rehabilitation, which are usually located in the state department of education. Services provided include physical examination to determine work capacity; necessary medical, surgical, psychiatric, and hospital treatment; prosthetic devices, such as artificial limbs and hearing aids; occupational counseling; training for jobs; maintenance during training; occupational tools, licenses, etc.; placement; adjustment aid after employment. An office in the Veterans Administration provides many vocational rehabilitation services to disabled veterans. Finally, public schools are now giving more and more attention to equipping the handicapped for some type of gainful employment.

FREEDOM OF LABOR[6]

FREEDOM FROM COMPULSORY LABOR. The Thirteenth Amendment prohibits slavery or involuntary servitude except as a punishment for crime. The prohibition of involuntary servitude makes peonage illegal. Peonage is a condition of enforced labor for liquidation of a debt or obligation. Thus, an Alabama statute which subjected to imprisonment farm workers or tenants who breached their contracts of employment and went to work for other persons in like employment was held unconstitutional,[7] as were similar statutes that had the effect of coercing the performance of labor for another. Congress, under its power to enforce the Thirteenth Amendment, has enacted an Anti-Peonage Statute that provides for punishment for those who impose, or aid in imposing, peonage.[8]

The prohibition of the amendment does not apply to contracts of seamen, which have long been regarded as involving exceptional obligations, nor to duties to the state, such as service in the army or on a jury. Draft laws have been upheld,[9] as were state work-or-fight laws in World War I and municipal requirements that indigents work for the municipality if they were to receive financial help.[10]

We have moved close to national compulsion of work in wartime. In World War II a work-or-fight order required all workers designated as "nondeferrable" (that is, in nonessential employment) to transfer to

[5] 57 Stat. 374.
[6] One aspect of labor's freedom—namely, the right to join or not to join unions is treated in the next chapter.
[7] *Peonage Cases,* 123 F. 671 (1903).
[8] 14 Stat. 546 (1867).
[9] *Arver v. U.S.,* 245 U.S. 366 (1918); *U.S. v. Brooks,* 147 F. 2d 134 (1945), certiorari denied 324 U.S. 878 (1945).
[10] *State v. McClure,* 105 Atl. 712 (1919); *Commonwealth v. Pouiliot,* 198 N.E. 256 (1935).

essential jobs or face induction into the armed services.[11] Also, efforts were made to prevent persons from leaving essential types of employment for other positions without the consent of their employers. On January 11, 1944, the President recommended a national service law "to make available for war purposes or any other essential services every able-bodied adult in the nation."[12] Others also have urged conscription of manpower in wartime, though during the last war additional labor was drawn into the market and to needed locations by inflation of wages. Since this means is expensive and of limited effect after the surplus manpower is absorbed, another war might lead to further proposals for conscription of labor. It may be that the preservation of the tradition of freedom of men to work or not work, or to choose their place of work, is dependent upon avoidance of emergencies of such serious nature as to lead to consideration of a labor draft.

FREEDOM AGAINST DISCRIMINATION. In 1915 the Supreme Court held invalid an Arizona law which required employers of five or more workers to hire not less than 80 per cent of these from qualified electors or native-born citizens. In the Court's opinion, Justice Hughes wrote, "It requires no argument to show that the right to work for a living in the common occupations of the community is of the very essence of the personal freedom and opportunity that it was the purpose of the Amendment [Fourteenth] to secure."[13]

Some laws which restricted economic opportunity for the alien have been upheld. For special reasons the Court upheld discrimination against aliens in employment on public works,[14] and prohibition of alien operation of pool halls.[15] Game, fish, and oysters are the property, according to long-standing decisions, of the citizens of a state, and hence their taking may be prohibited to aliens or citizens of other states. The most significant restriction on alien opportunity has been in state laws preventing aliens from owning real estate.[16]

The "right to work" has recently received attention in connection with the movement for fair employment practices laws. Such laws seek to prevent discrimination in employment because of race, color, creed, or national origin. It seems clear that there is a violation of the equal protection guaranteed in the Fourteenth Amendment when a state or any of its subdivisions or agents discriminates in hiring on any of these bases. On the other hand, as construed since the 1870's, there is nothing in the post–Civil War amendments to prevent discrimination in employment by private persons. Moreover, as the amendments have been construed, Congress is

---

11 8 Fed. Reg. 1996–1997 (Feb. 3, 1943).
12 *New York Times,* Jan. 12, 1944.
13 *Truax v. Raich,* 239 U.S. 33, 41 (1915).
14 *Heim v. McCall,* 239 U.S. 175 (1915).
15 *Ohio ex rel. Clarke v. Deckebach,* 274 U.S. 392 (1927).
16 *Oyama v. California,* 332 U.S. 633 (1948).

apparently without power to enact a law preventing all private discrimination, its power *under the amendments* being limited to enforcing the prohibitions on the states. Protection from private discrimination may be given, however, by the states under their police power or by Congress under its delegated powers. Thus Congress may outlaw discrimination by employers engaged in interstate commerce or operations affecting such commerce, or by employers receiving defense contracts. Since both the national and state governments have some authority over employment practices, the movement for enactments against discrimination has extended to both levels of government.

The origin of the national programs against discrimination was the executive order issued by President Roosevelt on June 25, 1941, which declared it "the duty of employers and of labor organizations . . . to provide for the full and equitable participation of all workers in defense industries, without discrimination because of race, creed, color or national origin." [17] Contracting agencies of the government were instructed to include provisions in contracts binding the contractor not to discriminate on these bases. It became the duty of two successive employment practice committees to try to obtain compliance with the basic policy stated in this and later executive orders. Though these committees issued "directives," they operated mainly through persuasion and education. The work of the committees became involved in much controversy, and though they seem to have obtained some results, they were hampered by unstable executive support, attack from within the Congress, doubt as to the scope of their authority, and other factors.[18]

After World War II there was a movement for a federal fair employment practices statute. Such a statute was passed by the House of Representatives on February 23, 1950. This statute would have given a Fair Employment Practice Commission the authority to use "conference, conciliation, and persuasion" to obtain compliance with the purpose of the act; it had been substituted, after much debate, for one which would have authorized a commission to issue cease-and-desist orders.[19]

Since 1948 there has been increasing effort in the executive branch to prevent discrimination in employment. This effort has been on three fronts. First, segregation in the armed services has been eliminated. Second, effort has been made to enforce the prohibitions against discrimination in employment in civil positions in the national government. Third, provisions against discrimination are included in government contracts, and effort has been made toward enforcement of these provisions. In addition to the responsibility placed on agencies, President Kennedy set up

---

[17] There had been previous isolated declarations, such as that against discrimination in the Unemployment Relief Act of 1933.

[18] For an analysis of the wartime experience, see Louis Ruchames, *Race, Jobs, and Politics: The Story of FEPC* (New York: Columbia University Press, 1953).

[19] 81st Cong., 2nd Sess., *Congressional Record*, **LXXXVI**, pp. 2162 (for original bill) and 2299–2301 (for bill passed and vote thereon).

a Committee on Equal Employment Opportunity, under the chairmanship of the Vice-President, to hear complaints, make compliance reviews, and take other steps to enforce the government's policy. Despite the efforts made, the Commission on Civil Rights concluded, after surveys, that there was no substantial difference in the patterns of federal employment and of private employment in cities over the country, and that there was "no appreciable difference" between federal contract and noncontract situations in the proportion of negroes employed or types of positions in which they were employed. The commission did think there had been progress toward the objectives, and looked with particular hopefulness on the efforts to stimulate training of negroes, on dissemination of information to negroes in colleges on the opportunities in federal service, and on recent efforts of the Committee on Equal Employment Opportunity to get firms to establish positive programs for employment of negroes. On a fourth front—grants-in-aid expenditures—the commission's studies showed that though some national agencies had antidiscrimination requirements, the efforts toward enforcement were in general either nonexistent or weak and ineffective.[20]

Beginning in 1945, a number of states and municipalities enacted fair-employment-practices acts. Typical of these is the New York statute, enacted in 1945. It makes it "an unlawful employment practice" for employers, labor unions, or employment exchanges to perform acts which would discriminate in employment "because of race, creed, color or national origin," and sets up a State Commission against Discrimination. This commission can create advisory agencies and conciliation councils at local, regional, and state levels, can make investigations, and can act against violations either by "conference, conciliation and persuasion" or by cease-and-desist orders.

In administration of the statute, the New York commission has placed emphasis on education and persuasion, and has seldom brought into action its compulsory powers. Some who have wanted more rapid progress than has been attained are critical of this failure to use the sanctions of the act, but the commission has believed that progress could best be made by educational efforts. There can be difference of judgment as to how much has been accomplished, but it appears that there has been an admission of minority groups to certain types of employment from which they were excluded and that the Commission may reasonably claim that some of this progress has been the result of its efforts.[21]

In 1963 negro demonstrations for removal of discriminations against their race quickly brought the issues of equal rights to a boiling point.

---

[20] Summary of experience of the national government on the several fronts is given in Wallace Mendelson, *Discrimination* (Englewood Cliffs, N.J.: Prentice-Hall, Inc., 1962), Chapter 3.

[21] See the analysis by Morroe Berger, *Equality by Statute: Legal Controls over Group Discrimination* (New York: Columbia University Press, 1952), Chapter IV.

President Kennedy, followed by President Johnson, pressed for a strong civil rights statute. The statute which was passed in 1964 defined a new offense—the "unlawful employment practice." This offense would be committed by any employer, employment agency, or labor organization that, in industries affecting commerce, discriminated in matters affecting employment against persons because of race, color, religion, sex, or national origin.

INSURANCE FOR WORKERS

WORKMEN'S COMPENSATION. Many more people were killed on the job (48,750) than in Korea (25,604 plus 8,529 missing) during the three years of that conflict.[22] Occupational casualties (killed, temporarily or permanently maimed, or ill) are one of the great costs of man's labor.

Under the common law the employer was not liable in case of death of a worker, for only the worker could sue. In case of injury, the employer's liability or nonliability was determined on the basis of whether he was at fault. Hence the worker had to prove that the injury was caused in the course of employment. And also the employer could set up one of the following so-called common law defenses to show that the injury was not his fault:

1. Fellow-servant doctrine, under which the employer was not liable if the injury was caused by another employee.
2. The doctrine of contributory negligence, under which the employer was absolved of liability if the injured worker contributed to the injury by his own negligence.
3. The doctrine of assumption of risk, under which the worker assumed the risks inherent in the job, of which he was presumed to have knowledge in advance.

Modification of these rules began in the nineteenth century, and by 1908 had been made in some way, at least for some industries, in most of the states. Modifications included right of suit in death cases, provision for ineffectiveness of employer-employee contracts under which the employer was relieved of liability as a condition of employment, and limitation of one or more of the common law defenses.[23] In 1908 the national government enacted the Federal Employers' Liability Act, which, as amended, is today applicable to railway workers whose duties are "in the furtherance of interstate commerce," and under which the assumption-of-risk and fel-

---

[22] Herman Miles Somers and Anne Ramsay Somers, *Workmen's Compensation: Prevention, Insurance, and Rehabilitation of Occupational Disability* (New York: John Wiley & Sons, Inc., 1954), p. 6.
[23] Somers and Somers, *ibid.*, p. 21; Walter F. Dodd, *Administration of Workmen's Compensation* (New York: Oxford University Press, 1936), pp. 11–16.

low-servant doctrines no longer apply and contributory negligence only reduces the amount of liability; with modifications, the protections of this act apply also to merchant seamen.

In the states, modification of the old system of liability on the basis of fault was not long regarded as a satisfactory solution. A wave of investigations across the country revealed many defects in the old system. These have been summarized as follows: [24] (1) Insufficient compensation. Figures such as the following were typical: "of 114 fatalities . . . in 1907 and 1908 the dependents received nothing in 38 cases, $100 or less in 9 cases, $101 to $500 in 34, $501 to $2,000 in 14, and over $2,000 in but 8 cases." (2) Wastefulness of the system. Insurance-company figures tended to show that only one-third to one-half of the payments of employers for protection came to workers, the remainder going to attorneys, claim agents, etc. (3) Delay. Court proceedings took months to years, during which the injured worker or his family were without benefits. (4) Antagonism between employer and employee.

As a result of the investigations, a radical departure from old concepts in employer-employee relations was introduced. This was the system of liability without fault, under which the employer was made liable for injuries in the course of employment irrespective of whether the fault could be attributed to him. The new system was called workmen's compensation. With it came other developments. Statutes prescribed the maximum liability for disability to which the employer would be subject. Insurance of this liability, either in state or private companies, became the rule. Most states set up special administrative agencies, usually boards, to administer workmen's compensation. If a trial is necessary to determine whether the injury occurred in the course of employment, and to determine the nature and amount of the injury, it is conducted, in most states, in the administrative tribunal, though appeal may go to the courts—sometimes, as in Texas, for a *de novo* (that is, completely new) hearing. In sum, the features of workmen's compensation are: liability of the employer, limitation of this liability by a definite schedule, insurance of his risk, and administration (in most cases) by special agency.

Once the new remedy was proposed, it spread rapidly through the states. Beginning with New York in 1910, workmen's compensation legislation had been passed in thirty states by 1915 and in forty-two by 1921. Ultimately it was adopted in all of the states. Congress has passed workmen's compensation statutes to cover its civil employees, public employees in the District of Columbia, and longshoremen and harbor workers.[25]

Though the movement for reform was not checked, the substance of workmen's compensation laws was affected by court decisions. In 1911 the

---

[24] Dodd, *ibid.*, pp. 19–26.
[25] For adoption of legislation see Somers and Somers, *op. cit.*, pp. 29–34, and Dodd, *ibid.*, pp. 27–29. A Maryland statute of 1902 and a Montana statute of 1909 were held unconstitutional. Dodd, *ibid.*, pp. 17–18.

New York Court of Appeals held that the compulsory statute of New York deprived employers of their property without due process of law.[26] This decision came just in advance of the wave of workmen's compensation statutes, and led to efforts by the states to limit statutory provisions in such a way as to avoid adverse court decision. The main effect of the decision was to lead to the enactment of optional plans, under which the employer could choose whether to come under workmen's compensation or stand on his common law rights. Only Washington, in the period of uncertain constitutionality, enacted a compulsory statute. In 1917, however, the issue of constitutionality was settled in three decisions of the Supreme Court of the United States in which it held constitutional a new New York statute, an Iowa statute which took away the employer's common law defenses if he did not come under the workmen's compensation statute, and the Washington compulsory statute.[27] Since that time, a majority of the states have shifted to the compulsory type of statute.

There has been a trend toward expansion of workmen's compensation to include more groups of workers, medical expenses, and some or all types of occupational disease. Statutes are also frequently amended to allow larger payments. Nevertheless, there are still many limits on the protection given to the worker. First, many workers are not covered by the system. While, in 1954, in some urban states 90 per cent or more of wage and salaried employees were covered, in twenty-one rural states less than 65 per cent were protected.[28] Among the causes of this limitation, the following provisions in particular state laws are especially significant: allowing employers to elect freedom from the system for all or some types of employment,[29] exemption of employers who have less than a stated number of employees, exemption of employers of farm labor and domestic labor.[30] Second, not all disability incurred in employment is covered. Some statutes apply only to hazardous occupations. In many states only enumerated occupational diseases are included.[31] Third, the payments are usually limited in three ways: to a percentage of wages, by a dollar maximum for weekly payments, and by a total maximum. A relatively good statute, for example, would be one providing, in case of total permanent disability, for medical expenses and cash payments of 66⅔ per cent of wages, with a maximum of $50 per week, with an absolute total of 15 to 20 thousand dollars.[32]

---

[26] *Ives v. South Buffalo Railway Co.*, 201 N.Y. 271.
[27] *White v. New York Central Rr. Co.*, 243 U.S. 188; *Hawkins v. Bleakley*, 243 U.S. 210; *Mountain Timber Co. v. Washington*, 243 U.S. 219.
[28] Somers and Somers, *op. cit.*, p. 38, taking figures from Dorothy McCamman and A. M. Skolnik, "Workmen's Compensation: Measures of Accomplishment," *Social Security Bulletin* (March 1954), p. 4.
[29] Somers and Somers, *op. cit.*, p. 39.
[30] See the table in Somers and Somers, *op. cit.*, pp. 40–43.
[31] Somers and Somers, *op. cit.*
[32] See the table in *The Book of the States, 1962–1963* (Chicago: Council of State Governments, 1962), pp. 498–499.

The low level and short duration of payments in many of the states is one of the present-day problems in workmen's compensation. The argument was sometimes made in the early days of the system that if the workman must suffer the pain and mental anguish of injuries, it was right for society to carry the financial cost. The statutes have fallen far short of this goal. Adjustment of maximums in statutes has not kept pace with the rise in income of labor. This lag in adjustment of rates of compensation has been paralleled by a more liberal attitude in the courts in cases of injuries not arising out of employment, or otherwise not covered by workmen's compensation statutes. As a result, some have wondered whether labor has not given up too much in its acceptance of fixed maxima and fixed percentages. Some have, in fact, looked for a complementary remedy, and have proposed that, as in England, the employee should have a right of suit for full recovery in cases of employer negligence.[33]

A second problem is the high operating costs, including insurance expenses, legal expenses of claimant and defender, and state administration and court costs. It has been estimated that these costs reach to 40 or 50 per cent of the amounts paid for workmen's compensation.[34] This is an improvement over the situation which existed prior to workmen's compensation, but leaves much to be desired, nevertheless.

A third problem concerns distribution of the cost. Merit-rating systems for determining employer contributions are used in some jurisdictions. These have the value of encouraging the employer to take all possible safety precautions, but also result in high cost to particular industries or concerns. Whether a wider spreading of costs should be an objective may be an arguable question.

Finally, workmen's compensation may need to be re-evaluated in terms of its relation to other forms of social insurance. It has now been supplemented by industry plans established by collective bargaining. Also, the national social insurance legislation provides payments to covered employees who are disabled to the extent that they cannot "engage in any substantial gainful activity," and state public assistance payments may be made to the permanently and totally disabled. Payments may be made to survivors of the injured under national social insurance and for dependent children under the state public assistance laws. A worker or his survivors may therefore be receiving compensation from two or three sources. Whether the benefits are adequate in case of accident will often depend on whether the worker was covered by more than one type of insurance.

The most recent exhaustive study of workmen's compensation, though recognizing the great progress made through the years, concludes as follows: "Once the pioneer trail blazer in social insurance, workmen's com-

---

[33] Including Samuel B. Horowitz, Arthur J. Altmeyer, and the American Federation of Labor. See Somers and Somers, *op. cit.*, pp. 191–193.

[34] See Somers and Somers, *op. cit.*, pp. 193–196, 279.

pensation has, like many other types of social legislation, not proved adaptable enough to keep abreast of a changing environment."[35] The authors suggest that there may not be enough difference between occupational and nonoccupational disability to justify their separation, or enough distinction between either or both of these and unemployment compensation to justify separation of disability and unemployment insurance. They also emphasize the tremendously significant contribution of industrial- and public-safety measures and, more lately, of rehabilitation programs. It was found that the cost of workmen's compensation was approximately 1 per cent of payroll, and that the injuries to workers incurred outside of employment were more than twice as numerous as those incurred in the course of employment. Prevention and rehabilitation, as well as compensation, are, therefore, necessary elements in the total approach to this problem.

UNEMPLOYMENT INSURANCE. During the Great Depression it was frequently said that the payment of insurance benefits to the unemployed in Great Britain helped put a floor to the depression in that country. Beyond this, unemployment, whether resulting from cyclical changes or not, was one of the obvious hazards of life, the effects of which could be mitigated by advance arrangements. Wisconsin enacted an unemployment insurance statute in 1932, and the national government followed with provisions in the Social Security Act of 1935 which practically forced all states to adopt such legislation.

The national statute provides for a 3.1 per cent payroll tax on employers engaged in such employment as is covered by the act, but the employer is exempted from all but four-tenths of 1 per cent of the tax if the state has an approved program. The four-tenths of 1 per cent goes into a national fund from which grants are made to the states for administrative expenses incurred in operating the insurance program. The standard set by national law for state taxes on employers is 2.7 per cent, but all states have adopted the merit-rating option, under which the rate of the individual employer's tax may be reduced on the basis of a record of low unemployment or low benefit costs. In three states (Alabama, Alaska, and New Jersey) additional taxes are levied on employees.

Benefits are paid to unemployed workers covered by the system. Most states prescribe a waiting period of one week of unemployment before benefits will be paid. To be eligible for benefits, one must be able to work and available for work, and must not be disqualified by such acts as leaving work without cause, discharge for misconduct, refusal to accept suitable employment. Disqualification may result also from the stoppage of work by a labor dispute, though the conditions of such disqualification vary among the states.

Many of the problems in unemployment insurance are similar to those

[35] Somers and Somers, *op. cit.*, p. 269.

in workmen's compensation. One is limitations on coverage. The national tax, and hence national requirements on state coverage, applied only until 1955 to firms employing eight or more persons, and since then to those with four or more. However, in many states the number has been lowered, and in 1962 employers of one or more were covered in twenty states. Following exclusions allowed in national tax law, the states commonly exclude from compulsory coverage: agricultural labor, domestic service, service for nonprofit organizations, and employment for state and local governments. Special national statutes provide for unemployment insurance for veterans, civilian employees of the national government, and seamen on certain vessels operated by the United States. Second, the level of benefits is not high in comparison with present wage levels and the cost of living.[36] Weekly benefits in the states and the District of Columbia varied in 1962 from minimums of $3 to $17 to maximums without dependents' allowances of $30 to $55 (median of $37). Some states allow dependency allowances, and this raises the range of maximums from $30 to $70.[37] Some argue that higher benefits would encourage persons to take advantage of opportunities for willful idleness, while others regard the inadequacy of benefits—particularly for high-wage employees—to sustain satisfactory living standards as a more serious evil. Third, as noted in the discussion of workmen's compensation, the coordination of unemployment insurance with other forms of social insurance is a problem which may merit consideration in the future. Fourth, there is the problem of duration of benefits. Although the period of payment varies among the states, and in most states according to the employment record of the individual, the most common maximum is 26 weeks. In two recent periods of high unemployment temporary national legislation provided for increased benefits to be paid by the states with funds provided by the national government.

The unemployment rate averaged 6 per cent in the five years following 1957, as compared with 4.3 per cent for the preceding ten years. Moreover, the average duration of unemployment in the later period was 14.3 weeks, as compared with 10.3 weeks in the earlier period.[38] This increase in the rate and duration of unemployment, the decline of state reserves in a period of high unemployment, and the need in such a period for national payments after state payments are exhausted indicate that some fundamental revisions in the system of unemployment insurance may be necessary in the future. Nevertheless, unemployment insurance is ameliorative, and not corrective, of the problem of unemployment. For avoidance or reduction of unemployment, other public programs exist. One is to

[36] All figures in this section are taken from *Comparison of State Unemployment Insurance Laws as of January 1, 1962*, Bulletin of Bureau of Employment Security, U.S. Department of Labor.

[37] *Ibid.*, p. 63. One state does not specify a maximum.

[38] *Annual Report of the Council of Economic Advisers*, transmitted to Congress, January 1963, with *Economic Report of the President*, p. 23.

improve the operation of the labor market. This is done by the counseling and placement activities of public employment offices, by study in the Department of Labor and the states to determine or to predict shortages and surpluses in geographical labor markets and in labor skills, and by distribution of information on these matters. Another is education and re-education of workers. Basically, this is the problem of the school system of the nation, but guidance to the schools and supplementary special programs appear to be necessary. The Manpower Development and Training Act of 1962 [39] was passed in an effort to meet some of these needs. It makes it the duty of the Secretary of Labor to develop and disseminate information on the impact of technological change, the mobility of workers, and other factors affecting the labor market. He is to make grants to states for approved training programs. The procedure is for the employment offices to make studies of shortages of skills, and following this, for plans to be developed for the schools or industries in the area to provide the needed training in the skills. Grants may be given to the unemployed for study in these programs.

Beyond all of these approaches, the primary solution for unemployment is job opportunities. The basic public policy regarding unemployment is the mandate in the Employment Act for the government to use its resources and techniques, in cooperation with private institutions and persons, to maintain maximum employment. This is the most urgent domestic need, and ability to meet the need is the severest and highest test on both public and private persons carrying responsibility in a mixed economy.

There is danger, however, that all the public responses to the unemployment problem will be outpaced by events. Automation, early retirement of employees, decline of opportunities for unskilled workers, obsolescence of old skills, an increasing supply of labor—all these threaten to destroy opportunity for those seeking the first job, those in the older age group, and those even in middle age who lose a job. Most people today are in a job-dependent status, many dependent upon a single job. Consequently, the cushioning of the effect of unemployment through unemployment insurance will be only one element in public policy which encompasses also education, assistance in locating jobs, and maintenance of an expanding economy.

OLD AGE, SURVIVORS AND DISABILITY INSURANCE. The most extended system of workers' insurance in this country is Old Age, Survivors and Disability Insurance (OASDI). OASDI is a national system instituted by the Social Security Act of 1935, and is commonly referred to as "social security." Initially it provided only for retirement benefits for workers, but it has been amended to provide benefits to their survivors and to disabled workers.

---

[39] 76 Stat. 23.

The arrangements for administration of the system are simple. The Social Security Administration of the Department of Health, Education, and Welfare is the administering agency. It keeps the records for each covered worker in a central location, but it provides information and assistance to employers and workers through field offices. Every worker included in the system is given a social security number, and a record of his wages is kept by name and number. To support the system a tax is levied on the first $4,800 of wages and salaries, one-half being paid by the employer and one-half by the employee. The tax rate in 1964 was $3\frac{5}{8}$ per cent for each. The employer deducts the employee's tax from his wages, adds his own tax, and transmits the tax payment. He also reports the amount of wages paid to each employee. From this latter report the figures are added to the worker's account so that a complete record of wages received by the employee in covered employment through his life can be maintained. When the employee retires, dies, or is disabled, a claim may be made for payment of monthly benefits.

The benefits to be received are computed on the basis of average wages received, though the alternative methods of calculation allow use of late and high-earnings years. In 1964 the minimum retirement benefit at age 65 or over is now $40 per month, and the maximum is $127. The disability benefit for a worker is the same amount as the retirement benefit. The amount of the benefit on an average income of $150 per month is approximately 50 per cent, and from this the percentage declines to where a person whose average wage was $400 or more would receive approximately 32 per cent of the $400. Additional payments are made for family members. Thus, additional payments would be made for a wife 62 or more years of age, a child under 18, or a dependent parent. However, the maximum payment for any worker, regardless of number of family dependents, may not exceed $254 per month. The scale of survivors' payments is also dependent on the wage record of the deceased worker. Thus, the wife, 65 years or older, of a deceased worker would receive $82\frac{1}{2}$ per cent of the benefit to which he would have been entitled on retirement. Provision is made for retirement at 62 with reduced benefits. Also, there are provisions regulating the amount of earnings from employment that one may make after 65 and still be entitled to benefits. One may earn from wages or salaries $1200 per year and still receive benefits, but $1 of benefits will be deducted for each $2 of salary between $1200 and $1700, and for each $1 of salary above $1700. One may, however, work some months and receive benefits for the months not worked; for example, a professor over 65 may receive social security benefits during summer months when he receives no income from wages.

The coverage under the original provisions of the Social Security Act was limited by many exemptions. Amendments to the act have now broadened its coverage until few groups are excluded. Employees of a religious, charitable, or educational organization may be included by decision of the organization and its employees. Employees of state and local governments may be included by action of their governments. A self-employed person, except those in the medical and dental professions (these groups have preferred to remain outside), may choose to come under the system and pay a tax equal to 1½ times the tax which would be levied on him if he were an employee. Domestic service for any employer for which $50 per quarter is paid, and farm labor for any employer for which $150 cash annually is paid or for whom twenty days work is performed, is included. Two large groups of excluded persons are federal government employees and railroad employees, for which separate programs have been established by national legislation. The consequence of the amendments is that an almost universal system of insurance is in existence to provide for retirees, survivors, and disabled, as defined in the act.

CHILD LABOR, MAXIMUM HOURS, AND MINIMUM WAGES

The earliest motivation for legislation against child labor, low wages for women, and excessive hours for children, women, and men was the humanitarian interest in the welfare of the person. The concern was primarily over safety, health, and morals. Later the idea developed, and was popularized in the Great Depression, that an employer who cut beneath the prevailing standards on hours, wages, and employment of children was an unfair competitor. This was a concept associated with the National Industrial Recovery Administration (1933-5), which sought to establish minimum labor standards. Other ideas have been of influence also, such as the prohibition of child labor to protect labor opportunities for adults, the reduction of hours of work to spread opportunity for employment, and the setting of minimum wages for men and women to sustain the economy by increasing purchasing power. Although the three types of legislation under this heading have been the subject of much controversy, all are now generally accepted elements in public regulation of the economy.

STATE REGULATION. *Child Labor.* It has been said that "Labor legislation in the United States as in England began with the regulation of child labor." [40] Such legislation began to be passed in the first half of the nineteenth century. "As early as 1879 there were already seven states which fixed a minimum age at which children might be employed and twelve which set maximum hours for children at work." [41] It was in the early part of the twentieth century, however, that the great volume of

[40] Elizabeth Sands Johnson, "Child Labor Legislation," in *History of Labor in the United States, 1896-1932* (New York: The Macmillan Company, 1935), Vol. III, p. 403.
[41] Johnson, *loc. cit.*

legislation began to be passed, and that the movement for state laws became universal, extending to the South, where large numbers of children were employed in textile mills.

Today child labor laws are in effect in all states, the District of Columbia, and Puerto Rico. Such laws are usually concerned primarily with the prevention of child labor in hazardous or unhealthful pursuits, the setting of minimum ages for employment, limitation of hours, and prohibition of night work. The most common method of enforcement is the employment certificate, on which age must be certified as a condition of employment. Of even more significance in obtaining compliance with child labor laws are the compulsory school attendance statutes. Significant also in meeting the problem of child labor are the programs of social insurance and public assistance. Under OASDI payments for support of children are made to retirees or survivors—for example, to a widow with children under 18. In addition, the Aid to Dependent Children program, administered by the states with grants-in-aid from the national government, has provided payments for support of approximately $3\frac{1}{2}$ per cent of the child population of the nation for many years. Thus, widow's aid, initiated on a spotty basis in some of the states more than a half-century ago, set the pattern for a substitute for child labor in needy families.

Maximum Hours. Legislation limiting the hours of work for women was passed in several states before the Civil War. It has been said, however, that the first effective law was passed in Massachusetts in 1874. This act was passed after approximately thirty years of agitation on the part of laborers in textile mills. By 1896 thirteen states had laws on hours of labor for women. The ten-hour day was the usual standard, though a few set a lower figure—including Illinois, which enacted the first effective eight-hour statute in 1893.[42]

In 1908 the Supreme Court of the United States upheld state limitation of women's work hours.[43] Whether because of this decision or not, the next decade was a period of rapid progress in women's working-hour legislation.[44] Statutes have continued to be passed and standards raised in old laws since that time. Today laws limiting working hours of women in one or more industries are a standard part of labor legislation in the states and the District of Columbia. There is, of course, variation in the definition of industries to which the limitations apply.

Legislation on hours of work for men came later, and less universally than for women. The earliest type of such legislation was for public works. State and federal action to try to limit hours on such projects began before the Civil War. Near the end of the nineteenth century statutes limiting the hours that men could work in mining began to be

---

[42] For a fuller account, see Elizabeth Brandeis' chapter on "Women's Hour Legislation" in *History of Labor in the United States, 1896–1932, op. cit.*, pp. 457–466.

[43] *Muller v. Oregon*, 208 U.S. 412.

[44] See Elizabeth Brandeis, *op. cit.*, pp. 474–495.

passed, and the constitutionality of such legislation was upheld by the Supreme Court of the United States in 1898.[45] The Court took note of the injurious effects on men's health of long hours in mining. Maximum duty limitations for railroads began about the same time, with Congress passing such a law in 1907. Around the turn of the century, also, laws were passed limiting hours in certain other industries. Such legislation was, however, inhibited by the decision of the Supreme Court in 1905 that held invalid the New York statute which limited the hours that men could work in bakeries and confectioneries.[46] Apparently, hours could be limited in particular industries only if there was an unusual threat to the safety and health of the worker or safety of the public. In 1917, however, a general limitation of the hours of work in mills and factories was upheld by the Supreme Court.[47] But such legislation remained exceptional until the New Deal period, when the movement for limitation of hours of labor shifted to the national government.[48]

Wages. There had been little regulation of wages by government in this country prior to 1933. The earliest type of regulation was minimum wages for women. The first law of this type in the United States was passed in Massachusetts in 1912. This statute authorized a board to set minimum wages, taking into account both the financial condition of the industry and the cost of living; the wages set were not mandatory, enforcement being dependent on publicity and public opinion. In 1913 eight other states passed minimum wage laws, and in the next decade laws were passed for several other states, the District of Columbia, and Puerto Rico. In most states the authority to set the rates was vested in a board; in some, wages were to be set only on the basis of the cost of living; some also provided for penalties for violation.[49]

By a 4 to 4 vote in 1917 the U.S. Supreme Court allowed minimum-wage legislation for women to stand,[50] but in 1923 it held invalid the District of Columbia act by a 5-to-3 majority.[51] After this decision no further minimum wage laws were passed until 1933, when seven state laws started the movement anew. The Supreme Court, by a 5 to 4 decision, held invalid a statute of the State of New York in 1936;[52] but in 1937 it reversed, by a 5 to 4 decision, the holding of 1923 and established the constitutionality of state minimum wage legislation for women.[53]

There was little additional history regarding wage regulation prior to

[45] *Holden v. Hardy,* 169 U.S. 366.
[46] *Lochner v. New York,* 198 U.S. 45.
[47] *Bunting v. Oregon,* 243 U.S. 426.
[48] For a summary of laws prior to 1932, see Elizabeth Brandeis' chapter on "Hour Laws for Men" in *History of Labor in the United States, 1896–1932, op. cit.,* pp. 540–563.
[49] See Elizabeth Brandeis' chapter on "Minimum Wage Legislation" in *History of Labor in the United States, 1896–1932, op. cit.,* pp. 501–539, particularly pp. 502–503.
[50] *Stettler v. O'Hara,* 243 U.S. 629.
[51] *Adkins v. Children's Hospital,* 261 U.S. 255.
[52] *Morehead v. N.Y. ex rel. Tipaldo,* 298 U.S. 587.
[53] *West Coast Hotel Co. v. Parrish,* 300 U.S. 379.

the beginning of national legislation. A provision of a state statute providing for overtime pay at higher rates was upheld by the Supreme Court in 1917 as an arrangement to make hours regulation effective.[54] The Court also upheld a national statute of 1916 (the Adamson Act) which provided for shorter hours and the payment of the same total wages pending investigation, but four of the five justices in the majority did so on the ground that there was an emergency.[55] But in 1923 the Court held invalid the plan of the State of Kansas, as applied to wages in food industries, for compulsory settlement by a state board of labor disputes where necessary to maintain industrial peace.[56]

NATIONAL REGULATION. Except for the Adamson Act and maximum-duty limitations on railroads, the earliest effort of the national government to regulate hours, wages, or child labor was in the child labor statutes of 1916 and 1919. The lag in this type of legislation in many states had led to a movement for a national statute, through which the objectives of the movement could be attained quickly and universally. In 1916, Congress, by a topheavy majority, passed an act which prohibited the shipment in interstate commerce of products of mines and factories where the labor of children was used in violation of the standards set in the act. This act was held unconstitutional by a 5 to 4 decision of the Supreme Court in 1918.[57] Thereafter, a new act based upon the taxing power was passed, and it, too, was held unconstitutional.[58] Congress then, in 1924, submitted a constitutional amendment to the states which would have given Congress power to regulate or prohibit labor of persons under 18 years of age.

In spite of the earlier court decisions, which seemed to show that the national government had no power to regulate labor conditions in industrial establishments, the national government quickly embarked on an extensive program of labor regulation in 1933. With unemployment causing widespread suffering and despair, a thirty-hour labor law was being advocated by some. Others favored a floor under wages to prevent further decline in wage levels and competitive advantage to low-wage concerns and sections, and to maintain purchasing power. It is not surprising, therefore, that the President's Re-employment Agreement (which employers were asked to sign) and codes of fair competition framed under the sponsorship of the National Recovery Administration (NRA) contained provisions outlawing child labor and prescribing floors for wages and ceilings for hours. Quite suddenly, the scope and the objectives of labor legislation had been broadened. Minimum wages were set for men

---

[54] *Bunting v. Oregon*, 243 U.S. 426.
[55] *Wilson v. New*, 243 U.S. 332.
[56] *Wolff Packing Co. v. Industrial Court*, 267 U.S. 552.
[57] *Hammer v. Dagenhart*, 247 U.S. 251.
[58] *Bailey v. Drexel Furniture Co.*, 259 U.S. 20 (1922).

as well as women; and spreading of labor opportunities, and the maintenance of mass purchasing power and of fair competitive practice, took the place of health and morals as the justification for labor legislation.

Though this whole program fell with the Supreme Court decision of 1935 that held the National Industrial Recovery Act unconstitutional, the pieces of the program described above were picked up and embodied in a new act—the Fair Labor Standards Act of 1938. This act was upheld by the Supreme Court in a complete reversal of its 5 to 4 decision in 1918 on the scope of the commerce power, and it is today, as amended, one of the pillars of national labor legislation.

The Act contains three types of standards: [59]

1. Child Labor. It created the offense of "oppressive child labor," which was defined to include employment of persons (1) under 16 years of age in any occupation (except by a parent in an occupation other than manufacturing and mining, or an occupation found by the Secretary of Labor not to be detrimental to their health or well-being), or (2) between 16 and 18 years of age in any occupation which the Secretary of Labor finds and declares "to be particularly hazardous for the employment of children between such ages or detrimental to their health or welfare."

2. Maximum hours. It sets forty hours as the maximum number of hours per week, unless payment is made at one and one-half the regular rate of compensation for the hours of employment above forty.[60]

3. Minimum wages. It sets $1.25 as the minimum compensation per hour to any employee.[61]

These standards have not been applicable to all employees. Prior to 1961 approximately 24 million workers were covered, and legislation at that time brought in approximately 3.6 million more. The act is applicable, in general, to employees engaged in commerce or in production of goods for commerce, or to processes or occupations closely related to such production. But there have been many exemptions. The child labor prohibition does not apply to the following: agriculture (if the employment is outside school hours); delivery of newspapers; acting in motion picture, theatrical, radio, or television productions. Also, the Secretary of Labor is directed to make exemptions from the prohibition of labor between ages 14 and 16 in occupations other than manufacturing and mining if confined to periods not interfering with

---

[59] 52 Stat. 1060, amended 63 Stat. 910 (1949), 69 Stat. 711 (1955), 75 Stat. 65 (1961).

[60] This was forty-four for the first year, forty-two for the second year, and forty thereafter.

[61] Under the 1938 provisions, this was 25 cents for the first year, 30 cents for the next six years, 40 cents thereafter, subject to adjustment upward to 40 cents at an earlier date under prescribed procedure, including the recommendation of an industry committee. The minimum was changed to 75 cents in 1949, $1.00 in 1955, $1.15 in 1961, $1.25 in 1963. For establishments first brought under the law in 1961, the minimum of $1.25 will not be reached until 1965.

schooling and under conditions not detrimental to the child's health and well-being. The hour and wage provisions do not apply to many groups, including, among others, public employees and employees of nonprofit organizations; employees in agriculture and fishing, and in processing of agricultural products within the "area of production"; employees in bona-fide executive, administrative, or professional work; employees engaged in publication of newspapers with less than 4,000 circulation having primarily a local market; outside salesmen; and taxicab drivers.

There was a big battle over exemptions in Congress in the Eighty-sixth Congress (1959–60), when the two houses passed widely different bills, and again in 1961, when a compromise bill was passed. The biggest conflict was over the inclusion of employees in retail and service occupations. The compromise bill extended the coverage of the Fair Labor Standards Act to include retail or service establishments with annual sales of $1,000,000 (provided they receive $250,000 of merchandise from across state lines), local trolley or bus carriers with sales of $1,000,000, construction companies with sales of $350,000, and gasoline service stations with sales of $250,000. The act was also made applicable to any other type of establishment with annual sales of $1,000,000 which had employees engaged in commerce or production of goods for commerce. Exempted, however, were restaurants, hotels, and laundries.

The experience in the Fair Labor Standards Act is exceptional in the long period of time which elapsed (1938–1961) before substantial amendments were made in coverage. Ordinarily, legislation setting minimum standards starts with limited coverage and is gradually expanded to include additional groups. Now that the issue of coverage has been debated, and since many members of Congress are dissatisfied with the exemptions allowed in the compromise of 1961, it is probable that the battle over some remaining exemptions will be renewed in later Congresses.

In addition to the Fair Labor Standards Act, the national government has passed legislation governing hours and wages when work is done under contract for the national government. As for construction of national public works, the requirement of an eight-hour day goes back to 1892;[62] overtime pay is allowed under the present statute if wages are paid at the rate of time-and-a-half.[63] The Davis-Bacon Act, as amended, requires all contractors on public works costing $2,000 or more to pay the prevailing rates of pay in the locality.[64] The Secretary of Labor determines the prevailing rates. As to goods produced for the government under contract, the important Public Contracts Act of 1936 (Walsh-Healey Act) applies. It provides for the eight-hour day or forty-hour week, but the Secretary of Labor has, under delegated authority, authorized work beyond this if time-and-a-half wages are paid.

[62] 27 Stat. 340.
[63] 54 Stat. 884.
[64] 46 Stat. 1494 (1931).

Contractors must pay the prevailing minimum wage in the area of production, as determined by the Secretary of Labor.[65]

COMMENTS. What conclusions can be reached about the function of government in prescription of minimum labor standards such as those discussed in this section? It would undoubtedly be generally agreed that law has not been the chief factor in raising labor standards and establishing a high level of purchasing power. For these results, the increase in production, the high level of employment, and the power of unions have undoubtedly been of more significance. As for child labor, public action to enforce school attendance and to provide insurance and assistance payments supplement work-prohibition statutes. There are also difficulties of enforcement, and in many states enforcement of labor laws has been notoriously weak.

This does not mean that proscriptive statutes will have no effect. They must, of course, operate within realistic limits, and the national statute of 1938, with its gradual approach in raising minimum wages and lowering maximum hours, is an example of such an effort. They may, on the other hand, lag behind developments in the economy: inflation may destroy the significance of minimums in wage laws, or movements in industry for shortening hours may outstep the provisions in law. But assuming realistic limits and amendments in requirements with changing conditions, proscriptive law may have the effect of raising labor standards and of limiting the effect of competition from low-wage areas in those situations where the bargaining power of labor is weak. These situations may not always be those in which labor is most unskilled, though this will often be true.

In addition to raising wages for a substantial number of persons, what are the effects of minimum wage legislation? It may be assumed that virtually all of this increase is readily spent and virtually none saved (except for social insurance deductions). Minimum wage legislation may, therefore, increase expenditures for those types of goods which can be bought by persons with wages at the minimum level. It may, by forcing an increase in price, decrease expenditures for some other products or services—that is, for items with elastic demand theretofore produced by labor that was paid less than the new minimum, and purchased by those with wages above the minimum. Some general increase in price level may result, but this will be absorbed by the population in general, and thus only to a small extent by those at the lower wage level. There would thus be some transfer of income from those with incomes above the minimum to those who had previously made less than the new minimum. The effects on employment may parallel those on purchasing. Production, and hence employment, may be stimulated in markets where low-income buyers spend their money. Yet any wage increase has some tendency to raise costs and stimulate use of labor-saving devices and, to the extent the market is elastic, to reduce buying of the

---

[65] 49 Stat. 2036. Exemptions from all or part of the act are made in the law and by the Secretary of Labor.

product produced by the labor receiving the increase. Also, an increase may divert some employment from geographical areas with low wages to competing areas with higher wages.

The disparity in results of such legislation for different groups in the population leads to conflict among groups. There is some class conflict, for the immediate interests of workers receiving wages below a new minimum conflict with those of buyers of products or services supplied by low-cost labor. There is some sectional conflict between those in low-wage areas seeking to attract industry, and those in high-wage areas seeking to resist its movement to low-wage areas. There is some conflict on functional lines, for employers who will be faced with the necessity of adjusting their wage scales upward will be opposed by representatives of labor interested in raising the wage scale. There are also ideological conflicts. Some with a conservative or neoliberal attitude will object to the substitution of legislative for market decisions. Others will favor such legislation because of belief that an increase in the purchasing power of low-income groups will stimulate growth in the economy, or that greater social justice can be achieved by altering the flow of income to underprivileged groups, or that distress will be relieved and the severity of social problems reduced.

In a market economy the minimums in wages would be determined by impersonal, market factors. In a mixed economy, market influences remain. These influences set feasibility limits on the level of minimum wages to be set by legislators, and they determine the adjustments in wages above the minimum, in labor-saving arrangements, and in buying habits resulting from the legislative prescription. The public decisions are made for the purpose of overriding the strictly market conditions which prevail immediately. These public decisions may be made in part on economic conditions, for it may be believed that by overriding immediate market conditions, better market conditions will ultimately prevail. But the public decisions are made in part on the basis of noneconomic considerations, such as men's ideas on fair play, amelioration of social evils, or even so vague a thing as the kind of society they would like to see exist. No type of legislation illustrates more completely the mixture of special interests and shared ideals, and the diversity of considerations in the matrix of public decision.

CONCLUSIONS

The most obvious conclusion to be drawn from this chapter is that the role of government has been to set minimum labor standards. Minimum wages, maximum hours, and prohibition of child labor set a floor of labor standards; safety and health legislation prescribe minimum standards; social insurance legislation gives a minimum amount of protection; but employees are free to seek, and employers to grant, higher wages, shorter hours, additional protection for health and safety, and additional security against the hazards of life. Legislation, except for the emergencies of World War II and the Korean period, has built floors, not ceilings.[66]

Labor, like other groups in the population, will benefit from social expenditures, such as those for education, and social programs, such as urban renewal and conservation of scarce resources. Beyond the floors and the general social benefits, the welfare of labor will depend upon the operation of forces in the private market, including collective bargaining, the level of demand, and many other factors. Even this area is affected by political forces, for the level of demand is affected by government, and the instrument of collective bargaining, as will be shown in the next chapter, is regulated. Politics, therefore, is a vital element in labor welfare.

For a long time labor unions were concerned primarily with legislation to protect their interest in unionization. Beginning with the Great Depression they became interested also in minimum labor standards, and have actively pushed for improvement of these standards. They have also, in the postwar years, become interested in the macro-economic effects of government's fiscal and monetary policies and in the social programs of government.

Minimum labor standards are particularly helpful to those who have a weak bargaining position in the private economy. Yet, with approximately 40 per cent of the American people not voting, and with the poor having weak political influence beyond the ballot, it may be assumed that those with weak bargaining positions in the economy are also weakly represented in the political process. Legislation of the type considered here is most likely, therefore, to be passed when the interests of the weak coincide with the interests of other groups. Hours limitation or prevention of child labor may be helpful to the whole working population; minimum wage legislation may derive support from employers in high-wage areas seeking protection against diversion of industry to low-wage areas. Also, on such matters, the general moral consensus of the community may be of more than usual significance. The ideals of fair play, justice, and opportunity for all are brought into the arena of influences when minimum standards are being considered.

One effect of minimum-standards legislation is to lift the troughs. Yet they may do more than this. They may set new standards of *general* applicability, as when an unemployment compensation act is passed. Or they may set standards for the future toward which tendency will move, as when law proscribes racial discrimination. Beyond this, they may stimulate new developments in the private sector, as when safety legislation emphasized the need for safety engineering in industry, or as when social security spurred the general movement toward provision for retirement in industry plans

[66] For discussion of emergency action, see pages 350–352.

and private insurance. In many ways, it appears, law is a schoolmaster which, when expressing the dominant moral consensus of the nation, leads toward goals larger than those fulfilled in its provisions.

There are many problems that will persist through time in minimum-standards legislation. One is that of the appropriate level of the standard. When it is a social-insurance payment or a minimum-wage standard, then adjustments through time may be called for, either because inflation has eroded the standard, or because of a general productivity increase in labor, or because society's measure of what is appropriate has changed. If the standard is set too low, then either misery is preserved for the low-wage earner and his family, or payments on the basis of need will have to be provided out of the social income of society. This is, of course, a part of the explanation for the continuance of the aid for the dependent aged, blind, and childen. If the payments are too high, they may generate habits of work shirking, or create excessive cost to the economy. Heretofore, the problem has been mainly one of correcting the lag in benefit payments in an inflationary period. For other types of programs the problems may be different, but persistent nevertheless. Thus, the level of the hours of work limitation raises peculiar problems, and these are being discussed now, as they were in the thirties. The issue of further reduction of the level may become a crucial one in politics if unemployment levels remain high.

It appears that there are some problems that will not be solved by standing, inflexible rules in a dynamic economy. Up to now, the forty-hour standard has exhibited a high degree of permanence. On the other hand, levels of social insurance payments have been amended repeatedly.

Another problem is breadth of coverage. Years ago an American scholar described the Russian problem of the mid-twenties as a "scissors crisis." He meant that the Russians had been finding ways of bringing some measure of the promised new society to the industrialized segment of the economy, but had made no progress on the agricultural front.[67] Similar problems on a lesser scale have been presented in this country in minimum-standards legislation. Such standards are, with some exemptions, applied to the organized sector of the economy, but many exceptions may be made for those working for small companies, for agriculture or agricultural processors, or for other groups. For this there are many explanations. One has been the administrative problem. Laws are difficult to enforce on multitudes of small producers and distributors. But this problem is no longer of serious dimensions, for much social legislation now is applicable almost universally. Another cause has been the political strength of the small producer, particularly in agriculture. Finally, there has been a reluctance to impose burdens for the benefit of the necessitous on those thought to be themselves necessitous or facing the possibility of extinction by economic forces. Basic

---

[67] Maurice Dobb, *Soviet Economic Development since 1917* (New York: International Publishers Co., Inc., 1928), Chapters 8 and 9.

economic considerations may be seldom considered. For example, to merely raise the question of whether the small farmer or the small grocer is not primarily a laborer, and his return fixed to a large extent by the level of wages in agricultural or distributive employment, would run counter to the folkways of thinking about the position of the small entrepreneur.

The tendency with respect to coverage is clear. More persons are being brought under coverage because employment is increasing in covered occupations or industries. Also, exemptions have been trimmed in amendments to basic legislation. It may reasonably be expected that both of these tendencies will continue.

Another problem is correlation among the several programs of legislation. The adequacy of benefits will sometimes be dependent upon whether a person is under two public systems or one. It has been stated earlier that full consistency cannot be expected in legislation in a pluralistic society. This is particularly true in cases where the national and state governments are both active—often cooperatively, but sometimes independently. Nevertheless, the suggestion made earlier in this chapter that it may be time for a national study commission to take a look at this problem deserves consideration.

Still another problem is the relation of public and private effort in meeting some of the basic problems that have arisen. This is, to a large extent, the question of levels put in a different way. A pertinent example is provision of income for retirement years. Present law provides a retirement benefit of approximately 32 per cent of the first $400 of a salary of $400 or more per month. This is merely a cushion for one who makes, for example, $700 or $1,000 per month, and hence the public program is supplemented by many private industrial plans or by personal savings. This illustrates the mixed nature of the American economy, the pluralistic nature of solutions to problems faced by people, and the emphasis on minimum standards only in government programs. But the question will always exist as to whether the lines drawn between public and private are the appropriate ones. Since different persons fare differently under different approaches, the questions are likely to recur in the politics of the nation.

There is the additional problem of to what extent the costs of men's needs should be met out of the employment relation. In general, the ideal will be that employed persons shall have a living wage, so that they live out of their wage rather than out of the wage plus supplemental payments from government. Many of the costs of nonworking periods—due to unemployment, injuries in the course of employment, retirement—are also carried in the employment bill of the nation. The alternative is payment out of the general tax revenues. The issue between the two methods forms a complicated problem and involves the question as to what part of the costs of the life of men should be paid out of the employment relation.

In minimum-standards legislation men are not merely trying to make the market effective, as in antitrust, or to regulate and make operative the bargaining of persons, as in legislation on labor-management relations, or to sustain the conditions for economic growth and stability, as in fiscal and monetary policy; they are directly and purposely rearranging and ordering the distribution of benefits from the economy. In no other area of public policy except taxation is this distributive function of government legislation so obvious. The public has become interested in spreading opportunity and relieving misery, and this has resulted in political interest in the allocation of benefits. Political decisions override the circumstances which allocate misery to the injured, the aged, the unemployed, the poorly paid, and the minority racial groups. The motives undoubtedly lie in the shared interests of all in minimum safeguards, in the shared moral sentiments of the community, and to an extent also in the interests of special groups pressing for legislation for their benefit, in opposition to other special groups pressing for legislation for their benefit. The phenomena are political. The market is one of the factors operating above the level of social protection for the elementary needs of man; all that is beneath that level is part of the public sector of the economy, and is in the domain of politics.

Chapter 14. Government Policy on Employer-Employee Relations

REGULATION OF employer-employee relations has become one of the most persistent problems of government. Each party in the labor market battles for law that will operate on its side, and the public is concerned about discovery of means for protecting its interests.

The battle between the parties for the support of government began in the first half of the nineteenth century and became more intense near the close of the century. Labor first wanted recognition by courts for the legality of unionization, while employers wanted unionization to be held to be illegal conspiracy. Labor has wanted freedom to use the strike, the boycott, and picketing, while the employer has wanted restrictions on these and has favored use of the injunction as a means of counterattack against labor's weapons. Also, the battle over whether union membership should be protected, or even be a requirement for employment, has been recurrent in the twentieth century as, for example, on the issues concerning yellow-dog contracts, the union shop, and the closed shop.[1]

In recent years a third interest, that of the public at large, has been considered. The components of the public interest in labor-management relations are obvious and can be simply stated. Initially the public had an interest in rules which would be fair to the parties and in preservation of peace at the site of the labor dispute. Later, attention was focused on continuation of economic operations. Prevention of the "interruption of the flow of commerce" or of "the stoppage of industry" became the touchstones of the public interest. Recently, the interest of the public in the terms of settlement themselves has been recognized. The public interest in "noninflationary" settlements—in avoidance of "cost-push" inflation—is now asserted.

At first, the issues in employer-employee relations were fought and settled in the courts. The twentieth century has been characterized by the emergence of legislative policy; and beginning in 1926, legislation with admin-

---

[1] For definition of the last two terms, see page 314. A yellow-dog contract is one made by a laborer with his employer in which he agrees not to join a labor union.

istrative enforcement has become the dominant method in the regulation of labor-management relations.

American labor policy is built on the freedom of the contesting parties and the desire to withhold government intervention. This is in sharp contrast to policy in most other industrialized nations. In some nations the freedom of labor to organize its own unions, independent of state or employer control, has been denied. In fascist nations the impetus for such denial comes from employer interests, while in communist nations it comes from those presumably interested in labor's benefit. In practice, however, both systems result in a denial of freedom to all parties, and labor policy becomes one element in totalitarian controls. In many other nations, where the freedom of the parties to organize is preserved, the freedom and scope of private bargaining are limited. In European countries the following factors may work toward less freedom for private parties than exists in the United States (and in Canada): (1) many matters on which there is bargaining in this country may be enacted into law; (2) grievances may be taken out of the hands of unions and handled by work councils set up under statutory schemes; and (3) bargaining may be between national associations of employers and national associations of employees with government, by law or understanding, reserving the right of approval or disapproval of the bargain.

The search for a balanced system with freedom and rights to both parties is a sound instinct of a democratic society. It is possible to think of all wages, hours, and other benefits being determined by government, but this would involve a stupendous, perhaps unworkable, administrative burden and a limitation on freedom which neither of the parties involved desires. American labor policy shows, therefore, a central motive: *to preserve the system of collective bargaining between the parties and to reserve government intervention for the necessary regulation of this relationship, and beyond that for only the setting of minimum standards or for intervention in emergencies.*

GOVERNMENT ACTION PRIOR TO 1926

A combination of laborers for the purpose of improving their earnings was a conspiracy under English law until well into the nineteenth century. Some American courts followed this English doctrine. But in 1842, in the case of *Commonwealth v. Hunt*,[2] Chief Justice Shaw of the highest Massachusetts court held that a union was not illegal *per se*, and that a strike for a closed shop was not a criminal conspiracy. This became the leading case in American courts on the legality of unionization. Unionization was not a conspiracy, and the legality of the acts of unions was to depend on

[2] 4 Metcalf 111.

whether these were lawful means of pursuing lawful ends. The courts became an instrument not of prohibition of all union effort, but of regulation, through their determinations of what were lawful ends and lawful means. On this a prolific new body of common law doctrine developed.

A further step, favorable to the other side, was taken when the injunction began to be used against labor. Apparently the first labor injunction was issued in this country in 1875.[3] It was soon issued from other courts, and in 1895 wide public attention was given to the device through a decision of the U.S. Supreme Court upholding the use of the injunction in the famous Chicago strike of Pullman workers.[4] By 1900 the application for the labor injunction was a customary procedure of employers in fighting a strike or other labor action. The injunction came to be used to break strikes and secondary boycotts, to limit picketing, and even, in 1917, to forbid union officials from attempting to organize laborers who had signed yellow-dog contracts.[5]

Another occurrence which assisted the employer was the decision of the Supreme Court in the first Coronado Coal Company case in 1922, holding that an *unincorporated* union could be sued for damages for which it was responsible.[6] This made union treasuries subject to court levy in case of damage to property or injury to persons as a result of official union action.

Recognizing that the individual laborer was at a disadvantage in dealing with a large corporate employer, states and the national government (for railroads operating in interstate commerce) passed legislation to protect laborers who joined, or wished to join, unions. These acts met an unfavorable response in the Supreme Court. In 1908 the Court held invalid an act of Congress which prohibited discharge of a laborer by a railway company because of union membership.[7] An act which made the yellow-dog contract illegal was held unconstitutional by the court in 1915.[8] In this case, however, the dissents foretold the development of the law after 1930. Justice Holmes argued that the aim of the statute was to provide that "equality of position between the parties in which liberty of contract begins"; and Justice Day, in a dissent for himself and Justice Hughes, argued that laborers, like others, had a right to join associations, and that the act of Kansas was designed to protect the right of the laborer rather than interfere with the right of the employer.

To an extent the issues concerning rights of parties in labor disputes became engulfed in interpretation of the antitrust laws. Whether the Antitrust Act of 1890 was entended to apply to labor combinations and their

---

[3] Paul F. Brissenden, "The Labor Injunction," *Political Science Quarterly*, **XLVIII** (September 1933), p. 414.
[4] *In re Debs,* 158 U.S. 564 (1895).
[5] *Hitchman Coal and Coke Co. v. Mitchell,* 254 U.S. 229.
[6] *United Mine Workers v. Coronado Coal Co.,* 259 U.S. 344 (1922).
[7] *Adair v. U.S.,* 208 U.S. 161.
[8] *Coppage v. Kansas,* 236 U.S. 1.

activities seems uncertain,[9] but it was applied against labor by lower courts almost immediately, and in 1908 the Supreme Court held that it was applicable to labor.[10] A hatter's union, in support of its effort to unionize a manufacturing company, had sought the aid of its friends within and outside labor in a boycott against purchase of the company's hats. The court held that secondary boycotts (that is, reaching to those not involved immediately in the particular conflict) affecting interstate commerce were illegal under the Sherman Act, and that the union was liable for treble damages under the act. The case was finally settled by a payment of $234,000 by the union and the AF of L.

Following this decision labor began agitation for exemption from the Sherman Act, and this agitation was not abated by the decisions in 1911 holding that the Sherman Act would be construed by a "rule of reason." As a result of this agitation and labor's dissatisfaction with the use of the injunction in labor disputes, the Clayton Act of 1914 contained several provisions relating to the labor injunction and labor's position under the antitrust laws. In regard to the latter, Section 6 provided:

> That the labor of a human being is not a commodity or article of commerce. Nothing contained in the antitrust laws shall be construed to forbid the existence and operation of labor, agricultural, or horticultural organizations, instituted for the purposes of mutual help, and not having capital stock or conducted for profit, or to forbid or restrain individual members of such organizations from lawfully carrying out the legitimate objects thereof; nor shall such organizations, or the members thereof be held or construed to be illegal combinations or conspiracies in restraint of trade under the antitrust laws.

Samuel Gompers, top official of the AF of L, hailed this as labor's "Magna Carta." But a careful reading of the provision fails to reveal a reason for this praise. The first sentence is a glittering generality. The long sentence that follows says only that it is not illegal under the antitrust laws to form and operate unions, and that the antitrust laws shall not be construed to prevent their members from "lawfully carrying out the legitimate objects thereof." But the courts could still, as previously under the common law, determine what was "lawful" and what was "legitimate." For example, would the secondary boycott, held illegal in 1908, now be "lawful"?

Another provision of the Clayton Act worked to labor's disadvantage. Section 16 added a new means of enforcement for antitrust laws—namely, injunction suits brought by private parties. It was noted in 1930 that of sixty-four cases brought against labor under the Sherman Act after the

---

[9] See the summary of the argument on this point in Edward Berman, *Labor and the Sherman Act* (New York: Harper and Row, Publishers, Inc., 1930), Ch. III, and the literature there cited.

[10] *Loewe v. Lawlor* (Danbury Hatter's case), 208 U.S. 274.

passage of the Clayton Act, thirty-four had been brought under this provision.[11]

But under what conditions could the injunction be used against labor in antitrust cases? The Clayton Act, in Section 20, seemed to limit the use of the injunction in labor cases. It provided that no restraining order or injunction should be issued in any court of the United States in any case between one or more employers and employees involving conditions of employment, unless issuance were necessary to prevent irreparable injury to property for which there was no other adequate remedy. It listed categories of acts against which no such injunction could be issued. Included were peaceful cessations of work, peaceful picketing, refusing to patronize, and "peaceful and lawful persuasion" of others not to patronize (secondary boycott). But Section 20 proved to be no help to labor. In the Duplex case in 1921 the Supreme Court, by a 6 to 3 decision, found that a secondary boycott was not "peaceful and lawful persuasion," and that the provision against issuance of an injunction applied only "to parties affected in a proximate and substantial . . . sense by the cause of dispute." Thus, the doctrine of the Danbury Hatter's case that secondary boycotts were a violation of the Sherman Act remained intact in spite of the Clayton Act, even though it could be argued, as it was by the dissenters on the Supreme Court in the Duplex case, that the parties engaged in a boycott actually had a common interest.[12]

During the next few years the antitrust laws were applied against labor in a significant number of cases. Outstanding were the decisions in three cases. In the Coronado Coal cases it was held that when a non-union mine was struck to prevent competition of its goods in interstate commerce with goods from union mines, and when this was shown to be the intent of the union, then it was liable for damages.[13] This decision threatened the success of organizational strikes. The railroad shopmen's strike of 1922 was broken by an unusually sweeping injunction in which even peaceful acts were prohibited on the ground that they were inseparable parts of a conspiracy to restrain interstate commerce.[14] And in the Bedford Stone case in 1927 the Supreme Court gave a very broad construction to the secondary-boycott rule, which apparently ruled out any use of the "rule of reason" in such cases. Justices Brandeis and Holmes argued in a dissent that the reasonableness of the action of the laborers could "hardly be doubted by one who believes in the organization of labor." [15]

---

[11] Edward Berman, *Labor and the Sherman Act* (New York: Harper and Row, Publishers, Inc., 1930), p. 103.
[12] *Duplex v. Deering*, 254 U.S. 443, quotation from p. 472.
[13] *United Mine Workers v. Coronado Coal Co.*, 259 U.S. 344 (1922), 268 U.S. 295 (1925).
[14] See Edward Berman, *Labor Disputes and the President of the United States* (New York: Columbia University Press, 1924).
[15] *Bedford Stone Co. v. Journeymen Stone Cutters' Assn.*, 274 U.S. 37, 58 (1927).

At the end of the 1920's Professor Felix Frankfurter could conclude, with respect to the Sherman Act, that "There can be no doubt of its potency as a restraint upon the activities of organized labor," and with respect to labor's attitudes, that "labor passionately believes that the courts' meaning is unduly restrictive of labor's right of association." [16]

Some more general conclusions can be added. By the end of the first quarter of the twentieth century, there was a considerable body of law regulating labor-management relations. Second, this regulatory law was court-evolved and court-administered. Legislative enactments had been held unconstitutional, or were mill for almost limitless judicial construction. In labor-management relations, as in public-utility pricing,[17] regulation of conflicting economic interests was centered in the courts. Third, the decisions of the courts "tilted the scales" to the side of the employer.

LEGISLATION ON RAILWAY LABOR

Judicial regulation in favor of the employer was to be only the first stage in the evolution of American policy. Labor-management relations broke into the arena of macropolitics, the Congress stepped to the center of the stage, the Supreme Court accepted its policies, and the scales were tilted by government in the other direction. In this second stage, four large events shaped one of the most revolutionary developments in the role of government in American history. These were the Railway Labor Act of 1926, the Norris-LaGuardia Act of 1932, the National Labor Relations Act of 1935, and the Supreme Court decisions on application of antitrust to labor in 1940–41.

Present-day national legislative policy on employer-employee disputes was first crystallized in railway labor legislation. The basic policy is set forth in the Railway Labor Act of 1926, as amended in 1934.[18] That act was the culmination of nearly forty years of national effort to find a pattern for peaceful settlement of railway labor disputes. Congress had passed acts in 1888, 1898, 1913, 1920,[19] and in 1916 had avoided a railway strike by prescribing for a temporary period the full terms of settlement (Adamson Act).[20] The legislation of 1926 was based on the hope that collective bargaining, supplemented by legislative requirements as to rights and duties of parties and by government aid and influence toward settlement, would provide the most satisfactory means of maintaining industrial peace and the continuity of commerce.

---

[16] Foreword to Edward Berman, *Labor and the Sherman Act* (New York: Harper and Row, Publishers, Inc., 1930), pp. xiv, xv.
[17] See Chapter 19.
[18] 44 Stat. 577 (1926); 48 Stat. 1185 (1934).
[19] 25 Stat. 501 (1888); 30 Stat. 424 (1898); 38 Stat. 103 (1913); 41 Stat. 469 (1920).
[20] 39 Stat. 721.

The act declares that it "shall be the duty" of carriers and employees "to exert every reasonable effort to make and maintain agreements . . . and to settle all disputes . . . in order to avoid any interruption to commerce. . . ." It provides that the parties shall have the right to designate representatives for this purpose "without interference, influence, or coercion" by the other. If either the carriers or the representatives of the employees intend any change in existing agreements, they shall give at least thirty days' notice to the other. It then becomes the duty of the parties to confer with each other and try to reach an agreement. A board was created (called, since 1934, the National Mediation Board, and having three members appointed by the President with approval of the Senate) which shall use its best efforts to mediate disputes and, if this fails, to try to get the parties to agree to arbitrate. If all such efforts fail and a dispute shall "threaten substantially to interrupt commerce," the board shall notify the President, who may, in his discretion, create a board to investigate and report concerning the dispute. This fact-finding board shall report to the President within thirty days, and during that time and for thirty days thereafter, no change shall be made, except by agreement of the parties, in the conditions giving rise to the dispute.

Some important amendments of the Railway Labor Act were enacted in 1934. First, the rights of employees were further defined. This was the year after passage of the National Industrial Recovery Act, and provisions included in Section 7(a) of that act [21] were now inserted in the Railway Labor Act. It declared, "Employees shall have the right to organize and bargain collectively through representatives of their own choosing," and prohibited the yellow-dog contract. These provisions only elaborated the provision of the original act against "interference, influence, or coercion" by either party in choice of representatives of the other. Second, the National Mediation Board was given the function of determining, upon request of either party, the individuals or organization authorized to represent the employees. To make such determinations, the board was authorized to conduct elections by secret ballot among the employees. Third, for deciding on grievances or disputes arising out of *existing contracts,* there was created a National Railroad Adjustment Board, with eighteen members selected and paid by the carriers and eighteen selected and paid by labor. The board would function in divisions with equal representation of each party, and would use a neutral referee when there was deadlock on a division; awards of the board could be reviewed and enforced in court. In 1936 the act was further amended to include persons and concerns engaged in air transportation.[22] An amendment in 1951 permitted the negotiation of the union shop and checkoff of union dues.[23]

There are, since the 1934 amendments, two main aspects of the Railway

[21] See page 309.
[22] 40 Stat. 1180.
[23] 64 Stat. 1238.

Labor Act. One relates to disputes on matters of rights (that is, arising under contracts), which are handled—as noted above—by the National Railroad Adjustment Board. The policy here is compulsory settlement of disputes through an administrative system established by law. This part of railway labor policy has not been followed in subsequent legislation relating to industrial labor. The Taft-Hartley Act (1947) provides for the use of the common law procedure of suit in court by either party alleging violation of a labor contract, with one modification from the common law: the suit could be brought by the employer against the union itself. There has been a trend, however, toward voluntary arbitration of such disputes, with such arbitration provided for in collective labor contracts. The arbitral awards have been held to be enforceable in the courts,[24] and recently the scope and finality of the decisions of the private arbiters has been liberally defined in the Steelworkers' Trilogy cases.[25] In other words, while, for railway-labor disputes on issues of right, legislation provides for compulsory arbitration and for administrative arrangements for effecting it, for disputes on matters of right in industry the law provides for suit, but the Supreme Court has reinforced voluntary arbitration as developed by the parties in labor contracts.

The other part of the Railway Labor Act relates to disputes over matters of interest (that is, over what is to go in the labor contract). It is on this that the act set the pattern for American labor policy, to be followed later in general outline in industrial labor legislation. It is this aspect of policy which is to be developed in the subsequent discussion.

The pattern of public policy embodied in this act is outlined on the chart on page 303. Public policy has set up a framework for peaceful settlement. The heart of the policy is collective bargaining ending in a written contract. The employees have the right to choose their own representatives. The action phases are notice, conference (bargaining), mediation and suggestion of voluntary arbitration, and fact finding by an independent board, followed by still more conferences. The act does not say what will happen if all this procedure of collective bargaining, assisted by the National Mediation Board and a fact-finding board, fails to bring agreement between the parties and the national interest is seriously threatened as a result. The uncertainties of the future—the action to be taken in particular situations, or the possibility of additions in public policy—can only be registered by a question mark. Nor does the act say anything concerning management and labor attitudes and policies regarding the employment relationship, but it is obvious that if the policy of collective bargaining is to bring industrial peace, there must be attitudes of willingness to confer in good faith,

---

[24] *Textile Workers Union of America v. Lincoln Mills of Alabama,* 353 U.S. 448 (1957).
[25] *United Steelworkers of America v. American Manufacturing Co.,* 363 U.S. 564 (1960); *United Steelworkers of America v. Warrior & Gulf Navigation Co.,* 363 U.S. 574 (1960); *United Steelworkers of America v. Enterprise Wheel and Car Corp.,* 363 U.S. 593 (1960).

THE PATTERN OF PUBLIC POLICY ON
EMPLOYER-EMPLOYEE DISPUTES

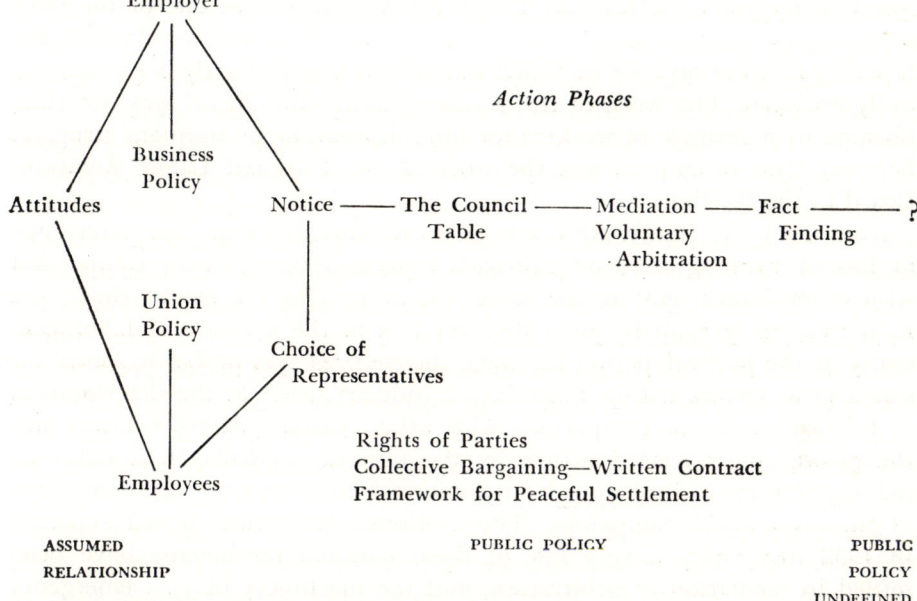

and policies which narrow the range of disputes to be settled by bargaining.

The Railway Labor Act was upheld in a decision in 1930 which may be viewed as a watershed in Supreme Court decisions on labor legislation. The case was *Texas and New Orleans Railroad Co. v. Brotherhood of Railway and Steamship Clerks*.[26] The Brotherhood sought an injunction to restrain the company from interfering with employees in organization and in choice of representatives, and the company claimed that the prohibition on such interference in the Labor Act was unconstitutional. The Court, speaking through Chief Justice Hughes, noted the congressional purpose to provide for the amicable settlement of disputes which threaten interstate transportation, and said, "Freedom of choice in the selection of representatives on each side of the dispute is the essential foundation of the statutory scheme." In reasoning reminiscent of that of Day and Hughes in their dissent in *Coppage v. Kansas*,[27] the Court noted that labor had the right to organize and that Congress could safeguard this right. It concluded, "The Railway Labor Act of 1926 does not interfere with the normal exercise of the right of the carrier to select its employees or to discharge them. The statute is not aimed at this right of the employers but at the interference with the right of employees to have representatives of their own choosing." This decision was followed by one in 1937 which held that the provisions

[26] 281 U.S. 548.
[27] See page 297.

of the act requiring employers to "treat with" employees and exert every reasonable effort to reach an agreement were enforceable obligations and did not violate the Constitution.[28]

For many years the Railway Labor Act was viewed as one of the most successful of national laws. Contributing to the favorable results was the fact that this was an area in which unionization had already been substantially achieved. The work of the National Mediation Board was not complicated by a struggle of workers for unionization, or by frequent struggles between rival unions, as was the work of the National Labor Relations Board in the thirties.

After 1941 the results were not as satisfactory. Though the percentage of loss of working time on railroads remained very low in comparison with other industries,[29] strikes were not averted to the extent they were in the earlier period. In part, this was due to the pressure of labor generally in the postwar period for wage increases. It was probably somewhat due also to factors within the railroad industry, such as the deterioration of railroad wages in comparison with other wages.[30] Another factor was the growth of concerted action by the unions, resulting in a tendency for negotiations to be handled on a national basis between representatives of unions and of companies. The National Mediation Board reported in 1952 that "only a very few of these national movements have been settled in mediation or arbitration, and the machinery of . . . emergency boards has grown increasingly ineffective in the settlement of such disputes." [31]

It was, in fact, the actions of the chief executive which kept the railroads running in the postwar period. "In 1943, 1946, 1948, and 1950, Government seizure and operation of the railroads followed the failure of emergency boards to end disputes. Strikes preceded the seizures in 1946 and 1950." [32] Thus it was concluded: "The President's intervention in nationwide disputes already closely approximated compulsory settlement. In 1943, 1946, and 1948, the President had proposed the terms on which agreement was reached." [33]

Furthermore, the railroads were kept running in 1963 and 1964 by emergency action of Congress and the President. In 1963 long-standing disputes, especially over retention of certain types of labor the railroads regarded as unnecessary, came to a head. With a strike impending and

---

[28] *Virginia Railway Co. v. System Federation No. 40*, 300 U.S. 515.

[29] See the table at p. 130 of Wayne L. McNaughton and Joseph Lazar, *Industrial Relations and the Government* (New York: McGraw-Hill Company, Inc., 1954).

[30] See report of the Senate Committee on Labor and Public Welfare, S. Rept. 496. 82nd Cong., 1st Sess. (June 27, 1951), p. 16.

[31] National Mediation Board, *Eighteenth Annual Report* (fiscal year ended June 30, 1952), p. 24.

[32] Leonard A. Lecht, *Experience Under Railway Labor Legislation* (New York: Columbia University Press, 1955), p. 232.

[33] Lecht, *ibid.*, p. 233.

all other means of settlement having been exhausted, Congress enacted the first compulsory settlement statute since the Adamson Act. It prohibited a strike for six months and provided for a special arbitration panel to settle the two main issues in dispute. In the following April the hour of a strike on other issues was at hand, and President Johnson called the representatives of the roads and unions to White House offices and kept them in negotiation until a settlement was reached. Collective bargaining was preserved, but under arrangements which cannot be repeated frequently.

The substantial achievements under the railway labor act should not be overlooked. In addition to the low rate of work stoppage, the record of the National Mediation Board is impressive. Its election procedure solves jurisdictional conflicts, and it normally handles a few hundred mediation cases and a number of arbitration proceedings each year. The board's own interpretation of the effectiveness of emergency boards was reported in 1962:

During the 28 years the National Mediation Board has been in existence 134 Emergency Boards have been created. In most instances the recommendations of the boards have been accepted by the parties as a basis for resolving their disputes without resorting to a final test of economic strength. In other instances, the period of conflict has been shortened by the recommendations of the boards which narrowed the area of disagreement between the parties and clarified the issues in dispute.[34]

THE LABOR INJUNCTION:
THE NORRIS-LAGUARDIA ACT, 1932

Labor's antagonism to judicial regulation of labor disputes was focused on the labor injunction. This is easily understandable. In the first place, the injunction was the most effective of all remedies against labor. Damage suits and criminal prosecutions operate slowly and with uncertain results, but injunctive relief could come quickly and immediately throttle labor's efforts. And second, the abuses or excesses in the use of the labor injunction by the courts were sometimes enormous. The use of the instrument was poorly regulated by the conventional restraints upon errant or excessive judicial action.

The injunction is an equitable remedy and is normally issuable upon a showing that irreparable damage is threatened for which the remedies at law (that is, nonequitable remedies) are inadequate. The writs of injunction are of three types:

. . . first, the temporary restraining order or injunction *ad interim*, which in ordinary course issues *ex parte*, without notice or hearing; second, the temporary

[34] National Mediation Board, *Twenty-eighth Annual Report*, p. 7.

306 *Policies Affecting the Economy Generally*

injunction or injunction *pendente lite,* issuing after an opportunity to be heard; third, the permanent injunction, based on a full hearing and enforcing the final decision on its merits. Hearings on motions to continue or dissolve a restraining order or temporary injunction are intervening stages in this process.[35]

Violation of an injunction subjects the violator to punishment for contempt of court, which traditionally has been without jury trial, though after the Clayton Act jury trial existed under certain defined conditions.

The opportunity for error or excess in the issuance of injunctions was great. Restraining orders were issued without hearing. Sometimes they were issued on the basis of vague and ambiguous complaints. The injunctions themselves were often exceedingly broad. An example has been given above of the railway shopmen's strike, in which peaceful activities were enjoined along with lawless ones. Sometimes the orders were general and vague, leaving the parties uncertain as to the restrictions imposed, but afraid to act because of the danger of contempt proceedings. Anxious to protect property from possible damage, judges frequently moved quickly and with broad orders. "Government by injunction" came inevitably under suspicion because of the absence of safeguards against abuse.[36]

The Norris-LaGuardia Act [37] achieved for labor what it had failed to obtain through the injunction provision of the Clayton Act. It prohibited issuance of restraining orders or injunctions in any U.S. court except in "strict conformity" with provisions of the act. It declared it to be the public policy of the United States that labor should have full freedom of self-organization without "interference, restraint, or coercion" by employers. It declared that yellow-dog contracts should be unenforceable in U.S. courts, and should not afford any basis for granting any legal or equitable relief in such courts. On the injunction it included in the main these provisions:

As to procedure. (1) No temporary or permanent injunction should be issued except after personal notice to all known persons against whom relief was sought, after hearing of witnesses in open court, and after findings of fact by the court; (2) no restraining order should be issued except "upon testimony under oath, sufficient, if sustained, to justify the court in issuing a temporary injunction upon a hearing after notice," and such orders should be effective for no longer than five days; (3) no restraining order or temporary injunction should be issued unless security was provided to insure payment for injury due to erroneous issuance of the order or injunction; (4) restraining orders or injunctions should prohibit only such specific acts as were expressly complained of in the com-

---

[35] Felix Frankfurter and Nathan Greene, *The Labor Injunction* (New York: The Macmillan Company, 1930), p. 54.

[36] For full discussion, see Frankfurter and Greene, *ibid.,* Chapters II and III. For its period, the labor injuction was a problem of due process similar to that of congressional investigations in the past 25 years.

[37] 47 Stat. 70 (1932).

plaint and were expressly included in findings of fact; (5) trial by jury was guaranteed in cases of contempt.

As to substance. (1) Restraining orders and injunctions could be issued only where there was a showing that the local police forces were unwilling or unable to maintain order; (2) they could be issued only to avoid substantial and irreparable injury to complainant's property; (3) they could not, in any case arise from a "labor dispute," prohibit any person singly or in concert from doing any of a long list of acts, including, among others, ceasing to work, becoming or remaining a member of a labor organization, paying strike benefits, giving publicity to the facts of a labor dispute in any way not involving fraud or violence, and assembling peaceably to act or organize; (4) the terms of the act were defined broadly with the effect of broadening the protections of the act. Thus, "labor dispute" was defined to include disputes concerning terms of employment "regardless of whether or not the disputants stand in the proximate relation of employer and employee"—a definition which seems to reverse the position of the Supreme Court in the Duplex case. And other definitions made legitimate participants out of those "engaged in the same industry, trade, craft, or occupation," or having "direct or indirect interests therein."

The effect of this act, with respect to government's relationship to the economy, should be noted. On the one hand, it is part of the legislative trend from the Railway Labor Act to the National Labor Relations Act to give protection to labor in self-organization and collective bargaining. In this sense, it can be correctly regarded as pro-labor legislation. At the same time, this legislation is the furthest extention in the history of labor relations in this country of a "hands off" policy. It pulled the federal courts out of labor controversies to a very considerable extent, for they were restricted in the use of their most effective instrument. It has, therefore, been correctly referred to as a policy of *laissez faire,* or economic free enterprise.[38]

There are, however, important limitations on the effect of the act. First, it does not prevent federal court injunctions in labor cases, but only regulates the procedure and limits the purposes. A second limitation grew out of a coal strike in 1946. The government seized the mines involved and later obtained a temporary restraining order to prevent a threatened walkout of the mine workers. The miners violated the order on the advice of their leaders that the restraining order was illegal because of the Norris-LaGuardia Act. The court fined John L. Lewis, the union leader, $10,000 and the miners' union $3,500,000 for contempt of court. The Supreme Court upheld the lower court, although it reduced the fine on the union to $700,000. The Supreme Court held that the Norris-LaGuardia Act was not intended to apply to a suit brought by the

[38] Charles O. Gregory, *Labor and the Law,* rev. ed. (New York: W. W. Norton & Company, Inc., 1949), p. 192.

308 *Policies Affecting the Economy Generally*

government.[39] Third, Congressional enactments of 1947 and 1959 specify uses of the injunction to protect certain employer and employee rights, and to prevent strikes in national emergencies for eighty days.[40] The result is that the injunction now serves as a means of implementing national labor policy. In some cases it can be obtained by private parties; in others, by the government. Though abuses have been corrected, the labor injunction is back for new and important uses.[41]

THE ANTITRUST ACT IN A NEW PERIOD

What Congress did in rejecting the past concerning labor injunctions the Supreme Court itself was to do several years later concerning the Sherman Antitrust Act. The change in position was made in two cases in 1940 and 1941.

The first arose out of the attempt of the hosiery workers to organize non-union shops in the industry. A strike was called against the Apex Hosiery Company, and its plant was seized and held by the strikers in a so-called sit-down strike. Property was destroyed and the company prevented from shipping hosiery, much of which would have moved in interstate commerce. The trial court awarded damages to the company under the Sherman Act, and the Supreme Court reversed. Justice Stone, for the majority, recognized that the Sherman Act applied to labor and that interstate commerce was affected, but he interpreted the act to apply to restraints "upon commercial competition in the marketing of goods or services," and not to efforts of union members to "eliminate the competition from non-union made goods."[42] This case should be compared with the Coronado Coal cases, summarized at page 299. The Apex Hosiery case set a new rule of judicial interpretation based upon the distinction between direct suppression of *commercial* competition and promotion of the legitimate objectives of union activity.

The second case arose out of a jurisdictional dispute between carpenters and machinists at the Anheuser-Busch plant in St. Louis. The machinists having been awarded the work, the carpenters went on strike. They also requested friends to quit buying Anheuser-Busch beer, thus attempting a secondary boycott. The Antitrust Division of the Department of Justice, as part of its vigorous campaign under Thurman Arnold's direction to eliminate alleged abuses in the union movement through the instrumentality of the antitrust laws, brought a criminal case against leaders of the union. When the case reached the Supreme Court,[43] Justice Frank-

[39] *U.S. v. United Mine Workers*, 330 U.S. 258 (1947).
[40] See pages 318–319.
[41] For a summary of present-day uses, see Benjamin Aaron, "The Labor Injunction Reappraised," *Labor Law Journal* **XIV** (January 1963), pp. 41–81.
[42] *Apex Hosiery Co. v. Leader*, 310 U.S. 469 (1940). Quotations from pp. 495 and 503.
[43] *U.S. v. Hutcheson*, 312 U.S. 219 (1941).

furter interpreted the Norris-LaGuardia Act in such a way as to make it applicable to all forms of antitrust proceedings, not just injunction cases. He reasoned that Congress' statement of policy in Norris-LaGuardia governed the interpretation of Section 20 of the Clayton Act, which in turn was applicable in all antitrust cases affecting labor. Hence, the secondary boycott, protected against injunction by the Norris-LaGuardia Act, was protected also against other types of action to enforce the Antitrust Act. Congress, according to the Court, had expressed a policy which overruled the Duplex case.

The Supreme Court's opinions in the Apex and Hutcheson cases did not mean that the Antitrust Act had no application to labor activities. The Court was soon to apply the act against collusive action between employers and laborers to exclude outsiders from a local market.[44] In this, the Allen-Bradley case, there were agreements binding electrical workers, contractors, and manufacturers in New York City in a program to monopolize all the business in the city. In such a case, the union was held to be subject to the Sherman Act.

In sum, the antitrust laws are now interpreted to deal with the commercial rather than the labor market. They do not restrain unions in the usual activities that they engage in for promotion of unionization and for obtaining benefits from employers. They do make it illegal for unions to join with manufacturers or others in schemes to monopolize or restrain trade in commercial markets.

It will be seen in the subsequent discussion that many of the matters that used to be or might be covered by antitrust law are now covered by labor law. The provisions of the National Labor Relations Act, as amended, cover such matters as secondary boycotts, organizational picketing, and hot cargo. Unions are restricted, but by a body of legislation related specifically to labor-management relations.

NATIONAL LEGISLATION ON INDUSTRIAL LABOR: LABOR'S RIGHTS

The omnibus National Industrial Recovery Act of 1933, in its famous Section 7(a), made it mandatory that every code contain these conditions: (1) that employees shall have the right to organize and bargain collectively through representatives of their own choosing, and shall be free from interference by employers in designating representatives or in other concerted activities for collective bargaining; (2) that no employee shall be required, as a condition of employment, to join any company union or to refrain from joining or assisting a union of his choice. Except for the limitations on

---

[44] *Allen-Bradley Co. v. International Brotherhood of Electrical Workers*, 325 U.S. 797 (1945).

federal courts in the Norris-LaGuardia Act, this was the first effort of the national government to protect *industrial* laborers against employer interference in the choice of representatives. Under existing decisions of the Supreme Court, it had been assumed that such protection would have to come from state governments. This extension of national policy went down with the remainder of the NIRA when the act was held unconstitutional in 1935.

But the substance of 7(a) got a new life in the National Labor Relations Act of 1935 (the NLRA). That act, as amended, is (with the Fair Labor Standards Act, the Walsh-Healey Act, the Norris-LaGuardia Act, the Railway Labor Act, the Labor-Management Relations (Taft-Hartley) Act, and the Labor-Management Reporting and Disclosure Act) one of the seven major labor acts of the national government.

The philosophy of the act is largely that of the Railway Labor Act, and the techniques are those of that act and the Federal Trade Commission Act. Section 1 states two reasons for the act: (1) bargaining power between unorganized employees and employers is unequal; (2) protection of the right of employees to organize and bargain collectively prevents strikes and interruptions in the flow of commerce. It is the latter which is emphasized, and thus the act borrows the justification of the Railway Labor Act, as summarized in Chief Justice Hughes' opinion. Section 7 states that employees shall have the right to join labor organizations, to bargain collectively through representatives of their choosing, and to engage in concerted activities for the purpose of collective bargaining or other mutual aid or protection. Section 8 strengthens this general statement of right by making it an "unfair labor practice" for an employer to do any one of five specific things: (1) to interfere with, restrain, or coerce employees in the exercise of the rights guaranteed in Section 7; (2) to interfere with the formation or administration of any labor organization or give financial or other aid to it; (3) to discriminate in hire or tenure in such a way as to encourage or discourage membership in any labor organization (except that he could sign a closed-shop contract with the legitimate representatives of employees); (4) to discharge or otherwise discriminate against an employee because he filed charges or gave testimony under the act; (5) to refuse to bargain collectively with the representatives of his employees.

The act provided for a National Labor Relations Board of three members, appointed by the President with consent of the Senate, to perform two functions: (1) like the National Mediation Board, it would determine and certify the representatives of the employees; (2) like the Federal Trade Commission in cases of unfair trade practices, it would investigate charges of "unfair labor practices," issue complaints, hear and determine the cases, and issue cease-and-desist orders.

Both the act and its administration became involved in fierce controversy. For this there appear to be three main reasons. First, the act obviously had as its purpose the encouragement of unionization. This purpose, of course, was not palatable to employers. Many violently objected to the act: for example, one said, "All hell would freeze over" before he would sit at the conference table with labor representatives. It should be recalled that whereas unionization had been achieved by railway labor on an extensive scale, many large industrial companies had not yet been unionized. There were then only about one-fourth as many union members as today. This very fact indicates the significance of the Wagner Act in history, and explains the objection of employers to its policy. At first the attack was on its constitutionality. In 1937, however, the majority of the Supreme Court, speaking through Chief Justice Hughes, upheld the act and also held that it could be applied to manufacturing concerns.[45] It used language similar to that in the Texas and New Orleans case: the right to join unions was "a fundamental right," unions were "essential to give laborers opportunity to deal on an equality with their employer," experience has shown that recognition of the right of employees to choose their representatives for collective bargaining "is often an essential condition of industrial peace." The only addition to the 1930 case that was needed was to recognize the close connection between production and commerce.[46] After this decision, the antagonism of employers was directed against what they considered one-sided administration and one-sided provisions of the act.

The second cause of controversy was the parallel rise of the conflict between craft and industrial unionism. In the same year that the Wagner Act was passed a Committee for Industrial Organization was formed, and in the next few years the unions that were to form the nucleus of CIO were first suspended and then expelled from AF of L. This schism in the labor movement made NLRB's task of determining the appropriate unit for collective bargaining one of the most difficult and controversial ever handed to an administrative agency. It found it necessary to determine, in case after case, whether a craft or industrial unit was the appropriate one for collective bargaining and, in addition to this, whether the plant, the company, or the industry was the appropriate unit. For such decisions it had no definite guidelines in the act, and it had to make its decisions on a case-to-case basis, with little opportunity afforded to develop guides for decision. Thus, it became inescapably the arbiter of conflicting claims between warring groups. Employers in general sided with AF of L, accusing the board of being pro-CIO, and also objected to decisions which favored intercompany bargaining, while the CIO itself found some objectionable decisions.

A third cause of controversy was the conviction among employers that the board was going too far in its interpretation of the act. Thus, in the

---

[45] *National Labor Relations Board v. Jones and Laughlin Steel Corp.*, 301 U.S. 1.
[46] See pages 140ff. for discussion of judicial doctrines on this relationship.

Mackay case the board held that employees who had been on strike were protected by the act,[47] in the Packard case that supervisory employees were entitled to all the benefits of the act,[48] and in a number of cases that the employer had interfered with free choice of representatives by way of presenting his views on labor-union organization or activities. Such interpretations by the board seemed to employers to go too far. On the other hand, the board had a record of approval in the courts which would have been the envy of most administrative agencies.

In part, the controversy over the board was inevitable, for the act itself stated a pro-union policy. In addition, the board was aggressive in enforcement of the act. For this it could hardly be condemned; on the other hand, an exhaustive committee investigation of the board revealed some instances in which excessive zeal of employees of the board led them into inappropriate activities.[49]

NATIONAL LEGISLATION ON INDUSTRIAL LABOR: COMPREHENSIVE POLICY

The years 1932 (Norris-LaGuardia Act) to 1941 (Hutcheson case) were labor's decade. The period after World War II was a third phase in American labor policy. There was to be no reversal of the revolution from judicial to legislative-administrative regulation; this change was only part of the general movement in society toward the dominance of macropolitics, and toward legislation and administration as its instruments. The new phase had two characteristics: (1) the pro-labor policy was supplanted by one in which employer interests were given greater protection than in the prewar years; (2) the regulation of rights of parties, initiated for industrial labor in the National Labor Relations Act, was to be absorbed into a comprehensive policy on labor-management relations, following in essence—though not in all details—the pattern of the Railway Labor Act.

Special arrangements were made during World War II to prevent impairment of the war effort by industrial strife:

1. The leaders of AF of L and CIO gave a no-strike pledge. This pledge was kept to a remarkable extent, though some strikes did occur. The major labor disturbances occurred, however, in the coal industry, in which the leaders of labor had not joined in the no-strike pledge.

2. The War Labor Disputes (Smith-Connally) Act of 1943,[50] sometimes called the "Anti-Strike Act," prohibited a strike unless there had been

---

[47] Upheld by the Supreme Court, *National Labor Relations Board v. Mackay Radio and Telegraph Co.,* 304 U.S. 333 (1938).

[48] *Matter of Packard Motor Car Co.,* 61 NLRB 4 (1945).

[49] Special Committee to Investigate National Labor Relations Board, H. Res. 258. 76th Cong., 2nd Sess. (1940).

[50] 57 Stat. 163.

notice of a dispute to government agencies, a thirty day "cooling off" or delay period, and a ballot of employees; it also authorized the President to take possession and operate ("seize") plants whenever labor conflict threatened production needed for the war effort. This legislation was to be in effect until six months after the end of the war.

3. After earlier steps had proved inadequate, a National War Labor Board was created with powers of mediation, to settle disputes (compulsory settlement), and to set maximum wages (a regulatory function). This board was succeeded in 1945 by the National Wage Stabilization Board, which had similar functions for a temporary period.

Labor-management conflicts flared quickly after the end of the war. Continuation of such conflicts, dissatisfaction among employers with the National Labor Relations Act and its administration, and the desire to forge a new labor policy to take the place of the temporary war expedients led to introduction of a number of measures in Congress. Finally, an omnibus act—the Labor Management Relations (hereafter referred to as Taft-Hartley) Act of 1947—was passed over the President's veto. It had four titles, of which Title I, amending the National Labor Relations Act, and Title II, dealing with conciliation and national emergencies, are the most significant. After a Senate Committee investigation had revealed racketeering and corruption in unions, another omnibus act—the Labor-Management Reporting and Disclosure Act—was passed in 1959. It amended the Taft-Hartley Act in many details, and added new provisions on internal management and responsibility in unions.

The Taft-Hartley Act was the most controversial of postwar measures. Labor leaders and President Truman demanded its repeal, and the latter called it a "slave labor" act. Because of this criticism, it is worthwhile to keep in mind the extent to which the act contains provisions which:

1. seem to be in the normal current of long-run labor legislation;
2. deal with matters on which compromise between the positions of employers and employees is difficult;
3. would especially irritate labor, perhaps unnecessarily.

The act will be discussed in three parts: (1) rights of parties, (2) settlement of labor disputes, and (3) miscellaneous provisions. Amendments to the act in the 1959 legislation will be included in the discussion.

RIGHTS OF PARTIES: AMENDMENTS TO THE NATIONAL LABOR RELATIONS ACT. Whereas the NLRA defined and protected only labor's rights, the Declaration of Policy in the act of 1947 states its purpose "to provide orderly and peaceful procedures for preventing the interference by either [employer or employee] with the legitimate rights of the other." It states the further purpose of protecting "the rights of individual employees in their relations with labor organizations." To carry out these purposes, many amendments were made to the NLRA, of which the following are of particular significance:

1. Section 7 is amended to include a statement of the individual laborer's right to refrain from joining a union except where a union-shop contract exists.

2. The old Section 8, which defined the unfair practices of employers, became Section 8(a), and includes this major change: it is now an unfair labor practice for the employer to sign a closed-shop contract, but he may sign a union-shop contract. The difference is this: under a closed-shop contract, the employer may hire only those who are already members of the union; in a union-shop contract, those whom he employs must become members of the union if they are not already members. The act allows such contracts only if the only conditions for the new employees to become or remain union members are payment of usual dues and initiation fees. The effects of a union-shop contract are (1) to give the employer a free choice of employees, but (2) at the same time to prevent employees from having a "free ride"—that is, to obtain the benefits of union efforts without paying their part of the cost.[51]

These provisions carry the national government into regulation of the *substance* of the labor-management bargain, in contrast to the purely procedural regulation in the act of 1935. In other words, these provisions regulate the content of the bargain, not just the process by which parties bargain.

There is an important exception to the union-shop provisions. Where state law prohibits union-membership agreements, these are, by specific provision of the Taft-Hartley Act, to be controlling. A considerable number of the states now have legislation—called "right to work" laws—which bars all or some union-shop contracts.

3. A new Section 8(b) is added which defines acts that constitute unfair labor practices of *labor organizations or their agents*. In the main, these are the unfair labor practices: (1) to coerce employees with respect to rights guaranteed in Section 7 (that is, to self-organization and collective bargaining, or to refrain from doing these things); (2) to try to get an employer to sign a closed-shop contract; (3) to refuse, if it is the legitimate representative of the employees, to bargain collectively with an employer; (4) to try to get an employer to make a payment for services not rendered (called "featherbedding");[52] (5) to engage in, or induce employees to engage in, a secondary boycott; (6) or to force employer action in certain types of jurisdictional disputes, such as forcing him to bargain with one union when another has been certified as the representative of employees.

[51] A provision requiring a majority vote of all eligible employees before signing a union-shop contract was removed by amendment in 65 Stat. 601 (1951).
[52] Not all "featherbedding" is prohibited. See *American Newspaper Publishers Association v. NLRB*, 345 U.S. 100 (1953); *NLRB v. Gamble Enterprises, Inc.*, 345 U.S. 117 (1953).

4. Freedom of speech is guaranteed as follows: "The expressing of any views, argument, or opinion, or the dissemination thereof, whether in written, printed, graphic, or visual form, shall not constitute or be evidence of an unfair labor practice under any of the provisions of this Act, if such expression contains no threat of reprisal or force or promise of benefit." The objective was to protect employers' speech, but the provision applies to all parties, and has played a significant role with respect to union speech in some situations.

5. Persons employed as supervisors are exempt from the definition of "employee." Hence, although supervisors may join unions and engage in collective bargaining, they do so without the protections of the act.

6. The board is directed not to include professional employees in a bargaining unit with other employees unless the professional employees favor this by majority vote, or to put plant guards in a bargaining unit with other employees, or to deny separate representation to a craft unit merely because an industrial union had already been certified by the board as the appropriate unit.

7. Whereas, under the act of 1935, the board allowed striking employees to vote in elections to determine the bargaining unit, the new act prohibits this, except where the striker can show that he has not been permanently replaced, or where the strike is caused by an unfair labor practice of the employer.

Many changes are made in the arrangements for administrative enforcement. A general counsel, appointed by the President with consent of the Senate, is given the functions of preliminary investigation and of prosecution which had previously belonged to the board in unfair labor practice cases. The board itself is increased in size to five members, and its function in unfair labor practice cases is governed by rules more similar to those governing courts. The board is now allowed, upon issuance of a complaint, to go to a court for a temporary restraining order. Priority is to be given to the investigation of charges of secondary boycott, and where there was "reasonable cause to believe" such a charge was true, it was made mandatory on the officer handling the matter to take the case to a district court for consideration of the issuance of an injunction.[53]

Clearly, the provisions concerning rights of parties gave employers a victory on some matters on which there is deep difference of opinion and interest between organized labor and management. These differences resulted in the introduction of numerous bills to amend the Taft-Hartley Act, and in repeated hearings on the proposals. No amendments resulted until the consideration of legislation on corruption in unions provided new opportunities for the rival parties to seek to better their position. Congressmen responsive to labor's sentiments sought to get "sweeteners"

[53] This provision has been qualified somewhat by amendment in the Labor-Management Reporting and Disclosure Act.

for labor into the legislation, while congressmen responsive to employer views tried to take advantage of the tide of opinion on labor "corruption." In the end there were some "sweeteners," but the main thrust of the amendments was to tighten further the restrictions on labor. Additionally, the legislative law on labor relations, which, in its provisions and the judicial interpretation thereof, had become exceedingly complex with the Taft-Hartley Act, now became even more so. There is wide scope for administrative (through the NLRB) and judicial construction, through which the provisions of law may be tailored to the practicalities and immediacies of the labor market. And there is still dissatisfaction in labor and management with resolutions of the conflict between them in the law.

One point of difference has been over the union-shop provisions. Many employers object to the provision of the act that allows contracts for union membership. Having succeeded in outlawing such agreements in many states, they would like to outlaw them by national legislation also. Thus, for example, the representatives of the National Association of Manufacturers have said, 'We recommend that the union shop and every other form of compulsory unionism be . . . prohibited." [54] On the other hand, organized labor has objected strongly to the anti-closed-shop provision. The objection has been pressed particularly on behalf of the typographical, maritime, and construction unions. The typographical unions have long operated under closed-shop conditions; it is claimed that the maritime unions, through their hiring halls, have eliminated many of the worst evils in hiring employees for maritime service; and it has been asserted that the conditions of casual employment in the building trades, maritime, and certain other industries reduced the protective effect of the Taft-Hartley Act, which did not allow a union-shop contract to require union membership in less than thirty days. Many have recognized the unreality of the thirty-day provision, and President Eisenhower recommended that for the construction, amusement, and maritime industries this time provision be changed to seven days.[55] In the amendments of 1959 this change and certain other relaxations of the union-shop provisions of the law were made with respect to the building industry. Also, recent Supreme Court decision has widened the use of referrals to employers by a union from hiring halls, while at the same time seeking to maintain safeguards against the development of the closed shop prohibited by the Taft-Hartley Act.[56]

[54] "Proposed Revisions of the Labor-Management Relations Act of 1947," *Hearings* before the Committee on Labor and Public Welfare, U.S. Sen. 83rd Cong., 1st Sess. (1953), Part I, p. 245. For similar recommendation for the U.S. Chamber of Commerce, see p. 137.

[55] Message from the President of the United States Transmitting Legislative Recommendations Affecting Labor-Management Relations, *Congressional Record*, 83rd Cong., 2nd Sess., C:1 (January 11, 1954), pp. 128-130.

[56] Upholding an agreement which provided for referral of casual workers by the union on the basis of seniority. *Local 537, International Brotherhood of Teamsters, etc. v. NLRB*, 365 U.S. 667 (1961).

The differences over the secondary boycott are persistent. The subject is so complicated that it can only be understood thoroughly by extensive study of particular fact situations. Even if it were agreed that the secondary boycott was in principle undesirable, there would still be questions as to when an activity was so closely associated with the labor dispute as to be, in effect, "primary" rather than "secondary." For example, it has been recognized by the courts that an employer who takes over and performs "struck work" can be an economic ally of the employer immediately involved in a labor dispute, and hence that the secondary boycott provision did not prevent a union from trying to induce employees to strike against the employer taking over the work.[57] On the other hand, work at a common site or on a common project does not by itself remove the secondary position of the employer; hence, it was held that a strike to force a general contractor to terminate a contract with a subcontractor by employing nonunion labor, was illegal under the Taft-Hartley prohibition.[58]

There were amendments to the secondary-boycott provision in the 1959 act, primarily in order to close certain loopholes in the prohibition. To close one gap, it was provided that, with exceptions for the building and "apparel and clothing" industries, it would be an unfair labor practice for a union and an employer to enter into a "hot cargo" agreement—that is, one in which an employer agrees not to transport, handle, use, or sell the product of another employer.

The act of 1959 contained still other amendments to Taft-Hartley. One added a new section which makes picketing to force an employer to recognize or bargain with a union an unfair labor practice under certain circumstances. One sweetener for labor was a provision permitting the NLRB to make rules allowing strikers "not entitled to reinstatement" to vote in elections conducted within twelve months after the beginning of a strike.

One of the most important provisions removed a no-man's land in labor law. The NLRB had, first on an *ad hoc* basis and later through the issuance of "jurisdictional yardsticks," declined to take jurisdiction over small businesses. Concurrently, the Supreme Court was evolving the pre-emption doctrine for labor relations. According to this doctrine, the enactment of national legislation pre-empted jurisdiction over most labor matters affected by the legislation, and hence state laws could not apply even though the NLRB declined to assert its jurisdiction.[59] To some parties, NLRB's failure to assert jurisdiction appeared to be a sacrifice of

---

[57] *Douds v. Metropolitan Federation of Architects*, 75 F. Supp. 672 (S.D.N.Y., 1948).
[58] *NLRB v. Denver Building & Construction Trades Council*, 341 U.S. 675 (1951). It may be noted that the exception of building trades from the "hot cargo" amendment, discussed in the next paragraph of the text, would allow a contract to be signed in a situation such as that in the case here cited; however, the decision is still good law, because it is still illegal to strike to get such a provision in the contract.
[59] *Guss v. Utah Labor Relations Board*, 353 U.S. 1 (1957).

interests protected by the NLRA, particularly the protections for labor's right to organize; to others, especially those favoring state laws less favorable to labor, the exclusion of the states from small cases was an unjustified limitation of state jurisdiction. The 1959 act resolved the issue with a compromise. On the main issue, it declared that the states could take jurisdiction over labor disputes which the NLRB had by rule or decision exempted from its jurisdiction. On the other hand, the board was prohibited from expanding (though it could contract) its exemptions. The compromise leaves uncertainties: What law will be applied by the states—that in the NLRA, or their own law? How will it be determined which disputes are exempted by NLRB's various standards—by the state courts, or by NLRB? [60] It appears probable that state laws will be applied in such cases, and that clearer guidance, either by rule or advisory opinion, will be given by the NLRA on exemptions from its jurisdiction.

SETTLEMENT OF LABOR DISPUTES. The Taft-Hartley Act contains provisions designed to facilitate the settlement of labor disputes through collective bargaining and fact finding. The main outlines of the statutory plan are similar to those in the Railway Labor Act, but there are nevertheless some significant differences.

Already it has been noted that the NLRA of 1935 made it an unfair labor practice for an employer to refuse to bargain collectively with representatives of his employees, and that the amendments thereto in the Taft-Hartley Act made it an unfair labor practice for an employee organization to refuse to bargain collectively with an employer. The act defines the obligation "to bargain collectively." It includes:

1. Notice. Where there is a collective-bargaining contract in existence, it shall not be terminated or modified without sixty days' written notice to the other party and thirty days' notice to the Federal Mediation and Conciliation Service. All terms of the existing contract shall remain in effect, without any strike or lockout, for sixty days after the notice or until the expiration of the contract, whichever occurs later.

2. Conference. The parties must "meet at reasonable times and confer in good faith."

3. Written contract. The execution of a written contract on matters agreed upon, if requested by the other party, is required.

The act creates an independent agency, called the Federal Mediation and Conciliation Service (successor to the Conciliation Service of the Department of Labor), to assist in settlement of disputes through conciliation and mediation.

The act authorizes a procedure for "national emergencies." "Whenever in the opinion of the President . . . a threatened or actual strike or lockout affecting an entire industry or a substantial part thereof . . . will

---

[60] See Elvis C. Stephens, "The No Man's Land of Labor Relations Remains Unoccupied," *Labor Law Journal*, **XIV** (February 1963), pp. 192–200.

... imperil the national health or safety, he may appoint a board of inquiry . . . ." The board's report will include a statement of facts and of each party's position, but "shall not contain any recommendations." When the President receives the board's report, he may direct the Attorney General to petition a district court for an injunction to prevent a strike or lockout. This injunction may remain in effect for eighty days. Its issuance places the parties under obligation to try to agree. The Conciliation and Mediation Service shall offer its assistance. Also, the board of inquiry will be reconvened and make a report by the end of the first sixty days. After this sixty days, if the dispute is still unsettled, the NLRB will take a ballot of the employees within fifteen days to determine whether they wish to accept the employer's last offer, and shall count the result within five more days. If the dispute is still not settled, the President shall submit a full report to Congress.

The pattern of public policy shown on the chart on page 303 is again adopted: settlement by the bargaining of parties is the objective; right of parties to choose their own representatives, notice, conference, aid of a mediatory agency, and fact finding are the elements of the plan. But there are big differences from the Railway Labor Act: an injunction may be issued to maintain the status quo, there is a ballot on the employee's last offer, and fact-finding boards cannot make recommendations.

There has been much controversy and difference of opinion about these provisions. The fairness and the effectiveness of the provisions have been questioned.[61]

Judgment on these or any other emergency provisions must probably be made on three bases: (1) will they facilitate or interfere with the process of collective bargaining, on which the nation has placed its dependence for ultimate settlement; (2) will they tilt the scales unfairly toward either party in the bargaining process; (3) will they protect the public against a stoppage of operations which would seriously threaten the public welfare? As is usual on social questions, experience does not provide a certain answer, and judgments will differ according to interest and other factors.

Labor leaders attack the provision for the injunction. In part this is emotional—the result of the long struggle against the hated anti-labor injunction. The objection goes deeper, however. Labor objects to limitations on the right to strike. In this instance the argument that the law is framed to apply equally to strikes or lockouts appears to labor to be specious. The lockout is an unused device, while the strike is labor's basic weapon. The injunction, therefore, is regarded as unfair. By preventing the strike, it reduces the pressure on the employer, may enable him to save money by delaying concessions, and may tend to fix in the public mind the at-

---

[61] The hearings heretofore cited are a useful source of information. A very helpful analysis is Irving Bernstein, Harold L. Enarson, and R. W. Fleming (eds.), *Emergency Disputes and National Policy* (New York: Harper and Row, Publishers, Inc., 1955).

titude that labor—against whom the injunction is issued—is the cause of the failure to reach agreement.

But what about the public interest in nonstoppage of operations? Labor leaders generally would probably agree with the statement of an experienced labor mediator that "A good case can be made for the statement that the nation has never really suffered seriously from a strike," [62] or with the position of Walter Reuther that if a real emergency arose, Congress could take care of the matter.[63] But others believe that emergencies do occur, and that the nation should have a policy to meet them.

Actually the emergency procedure of the Taft-Hartley Act has been used sparingly. During the first sixteen years under the act (1948–1963 inclusive) the emergency provisions were used 23 times—10 by President Truman, 7 by President Eisenhower, and 6 by President Kennedy. In 19 of these the injunction was issued; in only 11 of these were settlements reached during the period of the injunction, though a strike for all or a substantial portion of the workers followed in only 4 of the cases.

It is unlikely now that the nation will give up the effort it has carried on for years to find a policy to deal with real or reputed emergencies. On the other hand, proposals have been made which would attain the objectives of policy without issuance of an injunction against labor. Thus, it has been proposed that, instead of the Taft-Hartley procedure, the President be allowed to appoint fact-finding boards, and at the time of their appointment call upon the parties to continue or resume work. This would accord with railway labor policy. A modification of the proposal is that the law should provide that on appointment of a fact-finding board, and until its report, the strike or lockout should be illegal.[64]

Beyond dropping the word "injunction," either of these changes would have a further advantage. At present, fact-finding boards normally make a hurried study and a report, after which the injunction may be issued. The changed procedure would remove the pressure on the boards to do a hasty job. It would give them more time for a thorough analysis.

Labor regards the ballot on the employer's last offer as an unfair attempt to separate the union members from their leaders. The provision grew out of a widespread belief that the rank-and-file union members did not agree with the positions their leaders took. Actually, no last-offer ballot had, by the end of 1963, gone in favor of the employer's last offer; and in every case where a last-offer ballot was involved, the ultimate solution was more favorable to the union than the so-called "last offer."

---

[62] Cyrus S. Ching, *Review and Reflection: A Half-Century of Labor Relations* (New York: B. C. Forbes, 1953), p. 103.

[63] See, for example, testimony of Reuther, "Proposed Revisions of the Labor-Management Relations Act of 1947," *Hearings* before the Committee on Labor and Public Welfare, U.S. Sen. 83rd Cong., 1st Sess. (1953), Part I, p. 368.

[64] See, for examples of the two proposals, the bills printed in "Proposed Revisions of the Labor-Management Relations Act of 1947," *ibid.*, Part I, pp. 9–10. S. 1026, 83d Cong., 1st Sess. and S. 1075, 83d Cong., 1st Sess.

Union members have backed their leaders, and the statutory provision has not achieved the purpose that those favoring it had in mind.[65]

The prohibition against fact-finding boards making recommendations has been the subject of re-analysis. Senator Taft himself changed his mind on the prohibition and proposed an amendment to remove it, which the Senate passed.[66] President Eisenhower recommended that the boards be allowed to make recommendations at the final stage, though not before.[67] The major objection to the present prohibition is that it puts an element of inflexibility in the approach toward solution of a dispute. In some cases a recommendation would perhaps have no effect; in others it might be effective in bringing the dispute to an end. It is now generally recognized that some flexibility in approach should be allowed to meet the different situations presented.

MISCELLANEOUS PROVISIONS. *Labor Organization Reports.* The benefits of the National Labor Relations Act were denied to any labor organization unless it and its affiliates filed with the Secretary of Labor a statement of its constitution, officers, fees, internal administration, and finances. The information was to be kept up to date annually, and the reports on finances sent to all the members of the union. Labor ceased to object to the filing requirements, though it did argue that rights of unions should not be forfeited because of some defect in filing.[68] In the Act of 1959 the reporting requirements were expanded; but for enforcement of these, criminal and civil sanctions were substituted for loss of union rights.

Communist Associations. The Taft-Hartley Act also imposed a very stringent noncommunist oath on union officials, and denied the benefits of the NLRA to unions whose officials failed to take the oath. Unions regarded this as unfair because of their own efforts to eliminate communists from officeholding, and of the failure to require a nonfascist employer oath. The provision was repealed in 1959, and a new provision, enforced by a criminal sanction, prohibited any person from serving as an officer who had been a member of the Communist Party during the previous five years.

Labor Organization Contributions. The provisions of the Federal Corrupt Practices Act applicable to corporations, and prohibiting them from making campaign contributions in connection with nomination and election of presidential electors and members of Congress, are made applicable to labor organizations. The term "labor organization" is defined to

---

[65] Senator Taft recommended the repeal of the provision. *Congressional Record,* 81st Cong., 1st Sess., **XCV**:6 (June 16, 1949), p. 7802.

[66] *Congressional Record,* 81st Cong., 1st Sess., **XCV**:7 (June 30, 1949), p. 8717.

[67] Message from the President of the United States Transmitting Legislative Recommendations Affecting Labor-Mangement Relations, *Congressional Record,* 83rd Cong., 2nd Sess., **C**:1 (January 11, 1954), p. 129.

[68] See testimony of Walter Reuther, "Proposed Revisions of the Labor-Management Relations Act of 1947," *op. cit.,* Part I, p. 372.

include only organizations which deal with employers, and hence labor leaders, like corporate executives, have been free to organize other associations to receive contributions of money from individuals and to use these in elections.

A Policy Addition: Internal Union Operations. Although courts had developed some law—enforceable by worker's suit—with respect to rights of members of unincorporated unions, the concern of government with the internal operation of unions had been minimal prior to 1959. The Reporting and Disclosure Act moves the government into the business of policing the internal management of unions. Why did this expansion of government functions come about? Because, as is so frequently found in the background of legislation, gross abuses had been revealed. Racketeering, corruption, and abuse of power were unearthed in a Senate investigation conducted by Senator McClellan.

The section is a hodgepodge of provisions, in part the result of conference-committee compromises, the interpretation of which will be open to the courts and the application of which will raise many problems. In general, they relate to four subjects. First, the law sets forth requirements for democratic process in union government. It states equal rights of members in nominations, voting, and attendance at meetings; rights of expression of opinion in union affairs; and details of the election process, such as maximum terms of officers, secret ballot, and union distribution of campaign literature. There is an implicit assumption that democracy in unions will reduce abuses of labor power, perhaps also an assumption by some that it will reduce the power of leaders—neither of which may be true. Second, the law provides a "bill of rights" for union members, including, in addition to the democratic-process freedoms, rights with respect to suit and due process in disciplinary actions. Interesting questions on rights of unions to make reasonable rules for the orderly conduct of their meetings, on what will be due process in disciplinary actions, and on other matters are left open, but these may not be rapidly pushed, because the bill of rights is to be enforced solely by individual-member action. Third, reports to be submitted to the Secretary of Labor extend generally to the constitutions, organization, and finances of unions, and also to the security ownership and transactions of officers which might involve them in a conflict of interest between personal gain and union responsibility. Fourth, the act imposes fiduciary standards on officers of unions, and sets forth regulations on such things as the bonding of officers and the making of loans to them from union treasuries. All in all, the Reporting and Disclosure Act marks a new substitution of legislative for judicial policy making, of federal for state responsibility, and an enlargement of government regulation of a type of private association which has become quasi-public.

PROBLEMS FOR THE FUTURE

The long contest over the rights of employees and employers may be expected to continue. The center of the contest has moved from courts to legislatures. The main features of policy are determined by Congress, and certain principles seem to be fixed. Among these are the right of labor to organize for collective bargaining, the duty of each party to negotiate in good faith, the right of employers to express their opinions in a noncoercive way to their employees, the liability of labor organizations to suit, the recognition of the distinctiveness of the supervisor's position, determination of questions of representation by election, and prohibition of political contributions from corporate or union funds. On other points, policy questions may be less fixed. The secondary boycott, held illegal under the Antitrust Act in the Danbury Hatters, Duplex, and Bedford Stone cases, then protected by the Norris-LaGuardia Act and the Hutchinson case, then prohibited by the Taft-Hartley Act, will probably remain on the proscribed list; but the adjustments in the line separating the illegal from the legal will still be in controversy. There will continue to be contests over picketing—in legislatures, courts, and at strike scenes.[69] In the states policy is not fixed in any common pattern. In some states labor-relations acts have followed the policy of national law. But on many policy matters, such as mass picketing and the union shop, states have followed their varied courses. Moreover, the extent to which national policy will govern small businesses is left uncertain by the 1959 statute.

More significant than these issues are the questions concerning interests of a third party—the public as a whole. Collective bargaining has now been accepted. It is conducted often between giants on both sides of the bargaining table. These giants are agents of large groups, and they bargain with objectives in mind which are only partly economic, but which involve also their own prestige and power and the values of the communities they represent. A few of these opposing agents may occupy, at a given moment, a strategic position so that agreements reached will, like precedents in the judiciary, fix a new trend in labor contracts. Thus, agreements of a few may affect labor and capital communities larger than those to which they are responsible, and indeed affect the interests of the whole public. The problem of private power and public interest is presented in a new way.

For some citizens, the solution of the problem lies in an attack on so-called "labor monopoly." This would involve something different from an attack on the closed or the union shop, which brings all workers in one category into one union. The latter is an issue affecting the power of the two parties, but does not go to the heart of the issue of modern

[69] On picketing, see pages 133–134.

labor power. The issues involved are those of the breadth of bargaining and the breadth of union membership. The first is the question of industry-wide bargaining, the latter of a union so broad in membership that it can make a pattern-setting agreement with one employer which would then be offered to other employees in the same industry.

Such issues did not arise under the Antitrust Act. Decisions under that act related to methods of labor—for example, to secondary boycotts and the strike to cut off competition of non-union goods—not to existence of labor monopoly. Since about 1940, even these matters have been exempt from antitrust. Yet the argument is frequently made that labor monopoly should be prohibited. This could not be done by simple amendment of the antitrust laws declaring that unions, like corporations, should be subject to these, for the law and the decisions on antitrust have been framed with the facts of industry in mind. A statute making labor subject to the antitrust laws would have no clear meaning. But should antitrust or labor statutes be amended to limit in specific terms the breadth of bargaining and of union membership and understandings among unions on a common course of action? This would be drastic medicine, similar to a statute limiting the size and breadth of activities of industrial companies sufficient to make competition the effective regulator in every industry. Ideas such as these point up the heavy stakes of power in union-management relations—stakes for labor, management, and community. They raise questions, too, as to what is politically feasible given the present power of unions. These may be issues of macropolitics, but a consensus strong enough for a decision to apply the sweeping remedy just mentioned is unlikely. It is more likely that the power of the parties will continue to be regulated through rules on secondary boycotts, picketing, and other matters close to the firing line in the union-management battle.

If strong power positions remain, so that conflict or determinations at particular centers of labor-management confrontation may have serious consequences for the community, then two large problems of public policy rise like a precipice before policy makers. The first is, what shall be the public policy in case of failure of bargaining? When bargaining, mediation, and emergency action have all failed and cessation of work is threatened, then what policy content shall be put in the place of the question mark on the chart on page 303?

One suggestion is that no legislation be passed, but that action be improvised by Congress or the President when and if necessary. This suggestion is actually based on the view that a real emergency is not likely to exist, or will occur seldom, or that legal provision for emergency settlement would lead to unnecessary interventions.

Another suggestion is government seizure and operation until agreement can be reached by the parties. Seizure, as we have seen, was used by the government in World War II. It is authorized by existing statutes in some of the states. Seizure has differed from fact finding with a request for no strike concurrently, and from the injunctive remedy of Taft-Hartley, in that it was more flexible. It could be continued indefinitely, and the government could maintain the status quo or make changes with respect to the conditions under dispute.

Where seizure has been used, there have been uncertainties on legal questions. Normally, the government left the managers in charge of operations without significant change, except where change was made in the conditions under dispute. In 1951 the Supreme Court held that a company could recover from the government that portion of operating losses attributable to government operation of a seized mine.[70]

It has been argued that the advantages of seizure were in the flexibility and in the uncertainties, for the uncertainties make government reluctant to overuse it and the parties doubtful as to who would benefit. One author holds that if a law relating to seizure, or experience in its use, clarified the uncertainties, it would be a "wasting asset."[71] Seizure does not, of course, provide a final settlement, but like the injunction, it is a means of preventing interruption of operations pending settlement.

Another suggestion is for settlement by government—called compulsory settlement or compulsory arbitration. This amount of government intervention is not desired by either management or labor, for it takes away the freedom of decision allowed under present arrangements. If used often, it would result in a radical decrease in the amount of economic freedom allowed to labor and management. The proposal raises many questions. After careful analysis, a competent authority has summarized his conclusions concerning these:

(1) There are in fact not many "emergency" disputes which can be said to endanger the public health and safety sufficiently to warrant the imposition of compulsory controls in a free society; yet public sentiment favors enactment of legislation designed to resolve such disputes. (2) Resolving labor disputes through a quasi-judicial procedure is not as analogous to our civilian court disputes as some would argue, but it is sufficiently like the work of existing administrative agencies to be feasible. (3) Compulsory arbitration will unquestionably adversely affect collective bargaining, though in varying degrees, and perhaps never to the point of bringing the whole economy under regulation. (4) "Politics" in connection with the act cannot be avoided in the United States, and there will always be a tendency to seek both favorable legislation and administration, which will in turn impair collective bargaining. (5) Compulsory arbitration will not eliminate labor disputes, but it may reduce them. (6) Enforcement of an award which is unacceptable to labor will be extremely difficult no matter what the sanctions are.[72]

---

[70] *U.S. v. Pewee Coal Co.*, 341 U.S. 114.
[71] Archibald Cox in Irving Bernstein, Harold L. Enarson, and R. W. Fleming (eds.), *Emergency Disputes and National Policy* (New York: Harper and Row, Publishers, Inc., 1955), p. 242.
[72] R. W. Fleming in *Emergency Disputes and National Policy, op. cit.*, p. 216. Fleming's careful discussion on the six points is recommended.

A bit of elaboration is needed on two of the above points. The question in point 2 is whether there would be any criteria the deciding authority could use. One suggestion is to use the comparable wage in other industries. Labor, of course, would object to this on the ground that it would prevent the lead from being taken toward a general increase in compensation in industries covered by the compulsory-settlement system. The comparable wage would not be a satisfactory criterion if the system were extended to a considerable number of industries. In the latter event, it is difficult to see how a discretionary judgment by the deciding authority could be avoided. And such a judgment would be inappropriate for a court, and would necessarily devolve upon some part of the executive branch or upon *ad hoc* committees. The point made above with respect to politics (point 4) is well taken. It may be added that if compulsory settlement were extended to a number of industries, the issues concerning labor benefits, like those concerning agricultural benefits, would be deep in politics. The political struggle between groups would be intensified, and politics would absorb a larger part of the area of conflict in society than might be desirable or safe.

There seems to be one point on which most authorities are agreed: whatever provisions are made for handling emergencies, whether fact finding, injunction, seizure, or compulsory settlement, they should be sparingly used. It may be better for the public to suffer some real and occasional hardships than to get into the habit of prompt intervention in real or fancied emergencies. Either much patience must prevail in public officials and the public itself, or the nation will find it has moved the decision of one of the most vital of matters—a man's daily wage—into politics and administration.

On the other hand, there are some areas where the public is not likely to tolerate the strike, at least if protracted. This is true, for example, for schools, hospitals, local utility service, defense and space projects, transportation, and communication services. There are other industries in which the toleration of the public would be dependent upon the extent to which the supply of commodity or service was curtailed. It may be, therefore, that Congress will ultimately be led by some series of events to put something in place of the question mark on the chart on page 303—that is, will declare a policy for handling serious emergencies when the processes of bargaining and fact finding seem to have been exhausted.

The second problem of public policy is whether the public can leave the determination of some issues to private parties whose jurisdiction is industry-wide, or whose decisions are pattern-setting. These decisions may have such large consequences toward inflation, impairment of the American competitive position abroad, increase of unemployment, or other results as to raise a question whether they should be made in a forum where only private parties, under constraint to represent their limited clienteles, participate in the decision. The issue, as presented with respect to prices, has been discussed at the end of Chapter 11. With respect to the labor settlement, what are the ways in which public control or influence could be exerted? This is a question of growing prominence in exploratory congressional and public deliberation.

A common objective in these explorations for solution is the desire to avoid substitution and public decision for collective bargaining. At the same time, there appears to be an awareness of a present drift toward public intervention and a desire to avoid settlements by mere imposition of unregularized presidential power on an *ad hoc* basis.

One step was taken in 1962 which may form the kernel of a future policy. The Council of Economic Advisers offered "guideposts for non-inflationary wage and price behavior" for companies and unions.[73] One was that "the rate of increase in wage rates (including fringe benefits) in each industry be equal to the trend rate of over-all productivity increase," [74] which the President accepted as his standard for recommendation to industry and labor. It may be that setting guideposts will become a permanent policy. If so, it can be expected that Congress will set guidelines in legislation for the President to follow in his determination of guideposts, and that the Council of Economic Advisers, or some other organ, will have responsibility for making studies and recommendations on guideposts.

The setting of guideposts over a period of time would not be a simple task. Inevitably, there would be more than one guide, because of both the complexities of the problems and the diverse pressures in the world of macropolitics. Where a type of labor has been at a disadvantage in the past, the simple test of average increase in productivity would be inappropriate. The test would ultimately be objectionable to labor, on the ground that it would freeze the existing distribution of income. Moreover, greater wage increases would be needed in special situations, such as the attraction of labor to an undermanned industry. World War II experience shows that standards are refined, new standards are added, and regulation becomes complex over a span of time.[75]

Apart from the declaration of guideposts, how can the public interest be represented in settlements? One suggestion has been for management and labor to co-opt neutrals to serve on tripartite pre-negotiation study groups. The neutrals would contribute to the study of technical issues and mediate their solution.[76] The suggestion contemplated such study groups for the different companies or industries in which the bargaining was to be conducted, but their work could be supplemented by a study center in the national government. A further means of public participa-

---

[73] *Annual Report of the Council of Economic Advisers* (Washington, D.C.: 1962), p. 185.
[74] *Ibid.*, p. 189.
[75] See the discussion at pages 350–352.
[76] George H. Hildebrand, "The Use of Tripartite Bodies to Supplement Collective Bargaining," *Labor Law Journal*, XII (July 1961), pp. 655–664.

tion is through mediation. Present-day public mediators are often very skilled, and they could use their influence toward decisions in line with public guideposts. A further possibility under discussion recently is for authorization by Congress of presidential fact-finding boards in cases where economic stability is seriously threatened by an impending settlement in a key industry or in a pattern-setting situation. The proposal has received most attention with respect to price increases (see page 267), but it has been recognized also as a possibility for wage increases.

We have come in the end, as in the discussion on antitrust, to the hard issues of the future. Collective bargaining, like freedom of the firm to set prices, is a valued tradition. Nevertheless, if internal checks in the economy—whether competition, countervailing power, or publicly responsive conscience—do not function adequately, or if high-priority goals for the economy are threatened, then consideration may be given to new ventures in public policy and technique. The ultimate decisions will be dependent upon the mixture of public need, party interest, and cherished ideals which prevails in the macropolitics of the nation.

Chapter 15. Economic Controls in Wartime

IT IS NOT POSSIBLE to foresee what kinds of emergencies will face the United States in the future, and hence how the economy and government's relationship to it will be affected. Nuclear devastation may be suffered and may be followed by measures to sustain life and industry, and to rebuild the economy and rehabilitate persons, while military operations are simultaneously conducted. Sustained conflict without nuclear attack, similar to the Korean War, may exist in areas of the world, and may lead to the necessity of reorienting production to meet military needs. Similarly, a build-up of military power in anticipation of military conflict may require a diversion of production from civilian to national purposes. Famine or plague, or wars of friendly nations, may make huge portions of the world dependent upon American help for a temporary period, again calling for redirection of American productive resources in accord with national goals. Finally, domestic peacetime conditions may lead to specific bottlenecks in production or general inflationary pressures which will call into use some of the types of control heretofore employed in mobilization periods.

The kind of emergencies referred to are those which create, or arise with, an imbalance between demand and supply, with shortage on the supply side. The shortage may be sufficiently severe to dictate new patterns of control, even an elaborate system of economy management, by government.

Although the shape of such emergencies is unforeseeable, it is useful to know the relevant experience from which the nation can draw in confronting them. In World War I, World War II, and the Korean War, experience was acquired in managing an economy with shortages, and particularly in redirecting production and limiting use, in accord with national objectives. The experience is indicative of the flexibility of a mixed economy, of the feasibility of combining private production and government management on a temporary basis, and of the possibilities for preserving traditional institutions and values within a circle of governmental requirement and limitation. It reveals also a multitude of techniques for managing the economy to achieve overriding national objectives. The lessons of the experience and the techniques of control are a part of the reservoir of national competence for future emergencies.

The extent of controls will be influenced by the degree of imbalance

330 *Policies Affecting the Economy Generally*

which exists or is anticipated. In all-out mobilization for war, the shortages, actual or anticipated, may be so serious that a fully managed economy will be essential. In a limited war, or in a limited build-up of military preparedness in anticipation of the possibility of war, the necessity for controls may be more limited. There is danger that delay in establishing controls will impede the necessary development of new production and will generate inflationary forces that will be difficult to bring under control. On the other hand, precipitate or unwise use of controls would cause unnecessary hardships to individuals. It is important that a substantial body of persons within the nation know the forms and uses of controls and the problems in their use, so that sound judgments will be possible in their selection and in the timing of their use.

In the discussion in this chapter of the nation's experience, primary attention will be devoted to World War II. The controls in World War I were less developed, and those in World War II set the patterns for the Korean War.

THE CHANGE TO A WARTIME ECONOMY

It is difficult for one who did not live through the experience to grasp the extent, pace, and manifold directions of the changes in the economy when the nation moved into World War II. New and large goals were set for the production of war materials. Production was shifted almost overnight from peacetime to military purposes. New plants were built, and old ones were expanded and converted. Within hours, calls began to go to millions of men for the armed services. Other millions were drawn into war plants. Shortages developed—shortages of materials, and shortages of men who had the skills needed in defense production. Consumers anticipated shortages of goods and began buying beyond immediate needs. Producers also sought to meet future needs by advance purchases. Some shortages were critical, and some goods previously in plentiful supply were no longer available at all. Government expenditures leaped quickly to new high levels, and full employment and overtime wages put more money in the hands of millions of people. New money for workers and new contracts for business, shortages, and advance buying all combined to create inflationary pressures. The lives of people were disrupted: they moved to new jobs or into military service, their businesses declined or advanced, their skills became useless or valuable depending upon new utilities, their purchases were curbed by government, and their income was increased or decreased by circumstances beyond their control.

These events in the conversion from a peacetime to a wartime economy led to a new control system operated by government. The dominant factor in the new situation was military requirements. Government demands for manpower, facilities, materials, and finished goods were large, and these demands had priority over all other claims, except for what was needed to meet essential consumer needs.

To meet military requirements, an economic control system with three elements was evolved. The first element was *production programming*. Programming is the advance planning of needs to be met and the scheduling of use of the productive resources of the nation to fulfill these needs. Government requirements are broken down into specific end products—for example, airplanes and tanks, and then into components thereof, such as steel and copper. The schedules of production of finished goods and components growing out of production programming become priorities for the economic system.

Because the production schedules to meet military requirements and essential consumer needs created shortages, the second element in the control system was *allocation of scarce resources* to essential uses. Acute shortages of materials, facilities, and skills of particular kinds became bottlenecks in the production program. There was also a general insufficiency of manpower, facilities, and materials to meet all war needs and all civilian demands. In such a situation, controls were adapted to the particular types of shortage situations. Some of the controls allocated facilities for production and distribution, materials, or manpower among producers and suppliers of goods, while others allocated finished goods among consumers by a system of rationing.

The large military requirements increased demand so greatly that inflationary pressures were created. One way to minimize these was to increase production so as to bring supply more in line with demand. Also, the allocation system held in check new demand pressures by legally limiting purchases or excluding some buyers from the market for scarce goods. These devices were not by themselves adequate to prevent inflation in a wartime economy, and hence there was a third element in the economic control system. This was *stabilization* controls, of which there were two types. Indirect controls limited the amount of purchasing power in the hands of consumers, and included such things as tax increases and sale of war bonds to consumers. Yet these controls left a surplus of purchasing power over available supply. This was the inflationary gap—that is, a gap between demand and supply, with the overage on the demand side. Direct controls were imposed to restrict the effects of this inflationary gap, and included such things as price, rent, and wage controls.

The effect of military requirements, bringing in their wake production programming, allocation, and stabilization measures, was a radical transformation of the economy. The government was so large a buyer that the market as a whole became virtually monopsonistic. A new standard of essentiality governed production and distribution, which meant merely that when scarcities existed, essential uses had to be met first. The means of determining resource use were changed. In peacetime, custom determines much of the pattern of resource use, slight changes being made from year to year;

and beyond this, the pattern is determined by millions of decisions of buyers and sellers in a multitude of separate markets. But in a wartime economy, decisions on resource use are centralized in government. A wartime economy is a planned economy, with whatever amount of centralization of decision making in government is required to mobilize the economic resources of the nation for victory. Yet, in spite of the centralized direction, it may be (and was in this country in World War II) still a mixed economy. Private production, though for government account, was retained; private decisions, though restricted, supplemented those of government; and the private economy, though temporarily functioning under centralized direction, was preserved for resumption of normal peacetime operations after the war. Moreover, the political system continued to function very much as in peacetime, which meant that economic groups still had access to government in ways which would enable them to assert and obtain consideration of their interests.

PRODUCTION PROGRAMMING

"Production programming means determining feasible production goals on a timetable for planes, tanks, guns, shells, trucks, tires, railroad cars, army jackets, field ration units and other finished products; and for the aluminum, steel, copper, electronics, plastics, rubber, textiles and other materials going into them." [1]

The same author added that production programming involves three things: preparation of tentative production schedules or statements of requirements for munitions and other finished goods; conversion of these end-product requirements into requirements for materials and manpower; and comparison of supplies and manpower available with the estimates of requirements to determine what cutbacks will be necessary. To illustrate with a specific example, at the first stage it is determined that 100,000 planes are needed in a period of twelve months, in the second stage that this will require a certain amount of aluminum, rubber, and other products, and in the third stage whether there will be any bottlenecks in supply of any material or production of any part which will prevent realization of the goal of 100,000 planes.

The crucial nature of production programming was patently revealed in the military build-up of World War II. The build-up of American production was restrained by uncertainties as to the future role of the United States in the global war developing after September, 1939, but it was accelerated as time passed and certain events occurred. On the President's suggestion, in 1939 Congress revised the Neutrality Act to permit sale of

---

[1] Donald H. Wallace, *Economic Controls and Defense* (New York: Twentieth Century Fund, 1953), p. 98.

military supplies to friendly nations on a cash basis; also, a draft law was passed in 1940 and other steps taken to build up the nation's "short-of-war" preparedness. In March, 1941, the United States initiated the Lend-Lease program, through which it transferred military supplies without cash to nations opposing Germany, and the attack of Germany on Russia in June added Russia to the recipients of such aid. The scale of American involvement was not finally determined, however, until the attack on Pearl Harbor on December 7, 1941. Soon after the passage of the Lend-Lease Act, a summary of the combined requirements of the chief military claimants—the Army, Navy, Maritime Commission, the British—and of Lend-Lease had been developed. It was, however, a loose set of program goals heterogeneously compiled and stated in aggregates. In the central organization established to mobilize production (National Defense Advisory Commission in 1940, then the Office of Production Management in 1941, and then the War Production Board in 1942), the economist Stacy May headed a statistical bureau in which he was assisted by such other able economists as Robert R. Nathan and Simon Kuznets. May was pioneering in the development of statistical tools through which the feasibility of production goals could be determined. In late 1940 Jean Monnet, a Frenchman who had been assisting the British supply authorities, came to the United States to urge much larger production goals. May, on the basis of preliminary studies, reached the conclusion that it was feasible to increase production goals. Moreover, a Production Planning Board was created within the production authority to anticipate future problems and propose means of meeting defense objectives. In the summer the President took a big step toward an all-out effort by directing the Secretary of War to determine the munitions and equipment needed to give the nation superiority over its potential enemies; he followed this with creation of a Supply, Priorities and Allocation Board (SPAB) to determine total requirements for defense and civilian needs. It worked with the military departments and other major claimants to obtain data for a consolidated balance sheet of production. The result was the development, by November, 1941, of a Victory Program of production.

This was but a first step toward the development of goals for 1942 and 1943. Stacy May, upon analyzing the Victory Program, determined that it could not only be met, but that the United States could double its committed program. Donald Nelson, head of the production agency, submitted to the President, on the basis of the Victory Program and the economists' analysis, a recommendation for a vastly increased program. Following the Pearl Harbor attack a few days later, and upon the urging of Lord Beaverbrook and Prime Minister Churchill on a visit to the President at Christmas, President Roosevelt set goals for military equipment. In a dramatic presentation to Congress, he went beyond recommendations made to him and set such hitherto undreamed-of goals as production of 45,000 tanks and 60,000 planes in 1942, and 75,000 tanks and 125,000 planes for 1943. The production planning group had been recommending larger goals to the Army, which now proceeded to raise requirements for other items not included in the President's list.

The economists' position was now reversed; they reached the conclusion that the new goals could not be achieved. They also concluded that if goals were set too high, then allocations of component materials to producers would be excessive and beyond what could be supplied; the priorities system would thus be strained. Moreover, some components would come through on time and others would not; airframes could be produced without engines to go with them, or tank guns without the tanks. As a result of these conclusions by the economists and also by Nelson, an effort was made to get the President and the services to reduce their goals, but with no success. Accordingly, Kuznets developed a much more careful study in the summer of 1942. Using national-income analysis as a tool, he sought an estimate of what the nation could produce and what portion of it could be used for military production. In addition, he pursued three other lines of study: the raw-materials situation, requirements and supply of industrial equipment, and requirements and supply of labor. He concluded that the plans for 1942 and 1943 could not be realized, and that one effect of pursuing them without reduction would be to create bottlenecks, particularly in critical materials. Again Nelson sought reduction of goals and again met resistance, but by the end of the year the Services, primarily the Army, had reduced their statement of requirements by approximately 10 per cent.

This summary of what came to be called the feasibility dispute [2] shows some of the problems in production programming. There is a problem of coordination in the three phases of planning dealing with strategy, logistics, and production. By the end of 1942 Nelson had worked out an agreement with the Army and Navy on the respective responsibilities of the War Production Board and the Services. He recognized the authority of the latter to plan strategy and hence to determine end-product schedules, but the latter were to be within the limits of feasibility determined by the board. Moreover, the scheduling of production would be the responsibility of the production agency, and it would have the authority to direct the logistics branches of the Services on the preparation of schedules and other information needed. There is, in addition to the problem of division of responsibilities, the technical problem of developing the statistical data and the practical problem of obtaining the compliance of all parties concerned with dates set for supply of the needed information. These problems are all subsidiary, nevertheless, to that of getting a statement of goals which will guide effort and which will be realistic in terms of what can be achieved.

After 1942 goals and capabilities were more nearly matched. Revisions in production goals were made as need required. Thus, in 1943, successive downward revisions in plane-production schedules were made. Moreover, new needs were stated, and these sometimes called for top priorities. In

---

[2] The summary comes from John E. Brigante, *The Feasibility Dispute* (University, Ala.: University of Alabama Press, 1950).

late 1942, for example, the President put four programs on a top-priority list: destroyer escorts, aircraft, high-octane gasoline, and rubber. Since all of these made calls on the same short materials, the War Production Board had to establish preferences among them; and when it put rubber production at the head of the list, a conflict arose with the War Department, which desired that aviation gasoline head the list. This conflict, like many others, erupted into politics, the Truman Committee making an investigation and upholding the authority of the War Production Board.

The methods of production programming—involving organization, procedure, and statistical technique—evolved between 1941 and 1943. They could be applied in another military build-up. In the Korean War the pattern was as follows: [3]

1. Procurement sections of the three armed services prepared production schedules of 600 products representing about 75 per cent of the dollar value of military "hard goods" to be produced on a two-year timetable.

2. Each procurement section broke down these end-product schedules into requirements of component materials—some on a monthly basis, others on a quarterly basis.

3. The schedules for end products and component materials were sent to the Munitions Board, which developed an integrated program for the Department of Defense as a whole. This step was an advance over procedure in World War II, at which time the Army and Navy presented their estimates independently.

4. The schedules from the Department of Defense went to the Defense Production Administration (the production agency corresponding to the War Production Board in World War II).

5. The Defense Production Administration also received schedules from the Atomic Energy Commission, the Maritime Commission, and the several governmental agencies which were responsible for presenting the claims on behalf of the civilian economy.

6. The Defense Production Administration gathered information concerning available supplies and compared them with the requirements submitted from the military and other claimants.

7. The Defense Production Administration decided on the feasibility of the proposals and on cutbacks in requested allocation of materials, after which claimant agencies revised their estimates to accord with any cutbacks applicable to them.

[3] Taken substantially from Donald H. Wallace, *Economic Controls and Defense* (New York: Twentieth Century Fund, 1953), pp. 101–104.

ALLOCATION

As noted earlier, allocation may be of facilities, materials, or of manpower, and materials may be allocated by producer controls or by consumer rationing.

FACILITIES. From 1940 to 1943 there was a tremendous push toward new construction and conversion of existing facilities. Some of the construction for commodities in extreme shortage, such as rubber and aluminum, was by government, but most of it was by private companies under government contract. Encouragement to private enterprise was provided by allowing certificated facilities to be totally depreciated for tax purposes over a five-year period. This stimulus to essential production was accompanied by restrictions on the nonessential. Limitation orders prohibited or limited the production of specified end products. The immediate prohibition of the manufacture of automobiles and other consumer durable goods after Pearl Harbor opened the way for a very large conversion of facilities to war production. Priority orders on materials were denied for nonessential production. Somewhat later, approval was required for any new private construction above specified dollar amounts, and still later, limitations were put on nonmilitary government construction and procedures established for review of all government plans for construction.

MATERIALS ALLOCATIONS. The term "allocation" came to be used only for industry controls, the more restricted term "rationing" being used for controls over consumer purchasing. Allocation of materials was the most crucial of all wartime controls, for it—rather than facilities and manpower controls—was the chief means of implementing production scheduling. The allocation system moved through stages, and in general the movement was from particular to general controls, but for certain critical materials it was toward strict budgetary control of specific items.[4]

The initial technique was the priority order or preference-rating certificate. The producer obtained from the production agency (ultimately the War Production Board) a certificate of priority for production of an end product which he could then serve on a supplier, and the latter, in turn, would be required to push production on this order ahead of any others not having a similar rating. Priority orders themselves came to be rated by their relative urgency, carrying the symbols A-1, A-2, B-1, B-2, and so on,

---

[4] For fuller analysis, see James W. Fesler and Associates, "Allocating Materials," in Lester V. Chandler and Donald H. Wallace, *Economic Mobilization and Stabilization: Selected Materials on the Economics of War and Defense* (New York: Holt, Rinehart & Winston, Inc., 1951), pp. 107–135; Donald H. Wallace, *op. cit.*, Chapter 6; and John Lord O'Brian and Manly Fleischmann, "The War Production Board Administrative Policies and Procedures," *George Washington Law Review*, XIII (December 1944), pp. 1–60. For still fuller analysis, one may turn to the official history: *Industrial Mobilization for War: History of the War Production Board and Predecessor Agencies, 1940–1945* (Washington, D.C.: Superintendent of Document, 1947).

so that the value of a priority order in areas of critical shortages was dependent upon its own rating.

This system had serious disadvantages. For one thing, it swamped the production agency with a burden of paper work which the agency was unable to carry. Applications for preference ratings sometimes exceeded 10,000 per day. Moreover, the ratings were qualitative only, and set no limits on the amount of production which could be demanded through their use. The constituent units of the production agency gave out priorities separately, manufacturers could use them for any amount their consciences allowed, and the result was an inflation of priority paper. In the language of the day, they were referred to as "hunting licenses."

The first improvement of the system was the issuance of blanket preference-rating orders, which assigned preferences to whole categories of end products. This reduced the work load on the production agency, but did not solve the problem of lack of quantitative control.

Other techniques were soon developed. One was the conservation order. The earliest of these, issued in October, 1941, forbade the use of copper in the manufacture of certain listed articles; a modification came in the aluminum order which prohibited manufacture of any articles except those on a prescribed list. Another technique introduced after Pearl Harbor consisted of limitation orders, referred to in the preceding section on "Facilities." There were also simplification orders, which sought to cut down on frills and production of expensive models, and to standardize products. For example, in the men's-clothing industry, a cooperating industry committee agreed upon reductions in use of material in men's clothing, including such things as elimination of trouser cuffs and double-breasted coats. There were also set-aside orders, which required that all production, or a certain proportion of it, be set aside for prescribed uses. By the beginning of 1942 there was also a Production Requirements Plan, under which manufacturers could elect to submit each quarter a statement of their requirements for materials; under this plan the total requirements of a manufacturer were allocated to him on a quarterly basis. Finally, there were Production Scheduling Orders. These were especially designed to see that all capacity, of small as well as large producers, was used. Under the system the manufacturers of the scarcest components presented their order books to the War Production Board for approval before production was commenced. In this way production could be scheduled so as to make use of all plants.

The several techniques used in combination with one another sufficed for most materials. For three critical items—steel, copper, and aluminum—a tighter program called "Controlled Materials Plan" (CMP) was developed and used both in World War II and the Korean War. CMP operated much like the budgeting of expenditures in governments. Claimants for these controlled materials submitted statements of requirements, broken down by months and by specific forms and shapes of the materials in accordance with a CMP Materials List. The submittals were studied in the steel, copper, and aluminum divisions of the War Production Board, conferences were held with claimants when there were issues about their requests, and ultimately each claimant was given an allotment. It could then revise its production plans and initiate a vertical allocation of its supply, through which prime contractors would receive allotments and in turn divide these among their subcontractors, and so on down the line. Allotment numbers were given to prime contractors, and the possession of an allotment number was insurance that supplies would be provided. CMP was the ultimate perfection of the control system, and set a pattern which could be used in another emergency for any critical shortage materials.

The War Production Board worked out administrative methods for handling the difficult task of materials allocation. Required for effective administration were arrangements for coordination of the divisions within the agency, for liaison and cooperation with claimant agencies and for review and approval, or veto, of their demands, for considering appeals of manufacturers, and for dealing promptly and effectively with violators of regulations.

CONSUMER RATIONING. Rationing burst upon the American people suddenly and surprisingly after the outbreak of World War II. Following the loss of American vessels in the Far East and the accompanying revelation that the natural rubber supply of the nation was cut off, sale of tires was frozen at all retail outlets three days after the war began, and tire rationing was initiated at some 7,000 quickly constituted local boards less than four weeks later. During 1942 a total of ten rationing programs were initiated, and others followed in 1943. For varying periods the following commodities were rationed: tires, automobiles, gasoline, bicycles, fuel oil and kerosene, stoves, solid fuels (Pacific Northwest only), sugar, coffee, processed foods (canned fruits and vegetables), meats and fats, rubber footwear, shoes, and typewriters.[5] The common feature of all these programs was that some form of ration "currency"—certificate, coupon, or stamp—given by government was necessary to purchase a rationed commodity. The buyer paid for the commodity in dollars and cents, but had to offer also the ration certificate, coupon, or stamp.

There were two chief purposes for which rationing was instituted. One was to insure that supplies would be available for essential uses. When, for example, tires were not available for all automobile users, it was necessary to see that those who were performing services essential to the war effort and to the maintenance of essential community services would get the tires available. The second purpose was to provide equitable distribution among the people of commodities in short supply. When gasoline, food, or shoes were in short supply, both the principles of a democratic society

[5] For a summary of wartime experience, see Harvey C. Mansfield and Associates, *A Short History of OPA* (Washington, D.C.: Superintendent of Documents, 1947), Chapters 5 and 7 particularly. A more specialized treatment will be found in Emmette S. Redford, *Field Administration of Wartime Rationing* (Washington, D.C.: 1947).

and the necessity of maintaining the morale of the people required fair sharing of the available supply.

There are other purposes which can be served by a rationing program, but which were of less importance in World War II. One is conservation of resources. Thus, rationing of used typewriters during World War II enabled typewriter manufacturers to convert to ordnance production. Still another purpose would be support for the stabilization program. No rationing program was instituted in World War II for the purpose of aiding price control, but the curtailment of demand through rationing had the incidental effect of reducing price pressures. In an emergency that created shortages more severe than those in World War II, a fuller correlation of all the several controls for allocation and stabilization to support the purposes of each would probably be necessary.

Two general types of rationing were employed during the war. In the certificate type, the regulations required that applicants meet certain standards of eligibility before they could receive rations. The applicant filled out a form, designated local authorities determined whether it showed eligibility for a ration, and if so, the applicant was granted a certificate which became a one-time authorization to buy. Certificate rationing was adopted for tires, automobiles, bicycles, typewriters, rubber footwear, and stoves. In the second type, called stamp or coupon rationing, consumers were given a block of coupons which could be used for recurrent purchases, within the quantities and in the time frequencies allowed by the regulations. This type was used for foods, fuel oil, gasoline, and shoes. Sometimes the principle of equal sharing was applied, as when all automobile users got a basic ration of gasoline or all persons got an allotment of sugar, shoes, or meat; in other cases, special needs were recognized, as when additional amounts were allowed for designated types of essential automobile use or when coffee was granted only to persons age 16 or over. Sometimes the coupons were for a family of items (for example, canned fruits and vegetables); these were given values in number of points which would be varied from time to time as the supply changed; this form of coupon rationing is called "point" rationing.

Since the war another form of rationing—namely, general expenditure rationing—has been the subject of some discussion. In expenditure rationing the consumer is limited in the total amount he may spend for all purposes in a given period. In a plan developed some years ago it was suggested that all currency could be withdrawn from circulation and consumers could be allotted dollars by banks only in the amount allowed under rationing regulations.[6]

Returning to the experience of World War II, reference may be made

---

[6] See T. Scitovsky, E. S. Shaw, and L. Tarshis, *Mobilizing Resources for War* (New York: McGraw-Hill Company, Inc., 1951); or for a shorter treatment, Shaw and Tarshis, "A Program for Economic Mobilization," *American Economic Review*, **XLI** (March 1951), pp. 30–50.

to the techniques used in rationing. In the beginning, each dealer reported his inventory, and from then on he was accountable for his supply. When he sold commodities, he obtained certificates or coupons from the purchaser, which he in turn passed on to his supplier in payment for his own purchases. This upward flow of currency to match the downward flow of commodities was called the "flowback" system. Ultimately, the ration currency reached a throat in the distribution system, at which point the accounts were audited. Inventory accountability, flowback of currency, and audit of primary distributors were the elements in the scheme.

There were many problems in administration of rationing, some of which can be described in quite general terms. One was the problem of determining "who gets how much." The Office of Price Administration, which administered rationing, was given an allocation (a paper figure) by the War Food Administration, the Petroleum Administration for War, or other "supply" agency of an amount which it could, in a stated period, allocate to consumers. It then had to work out rules on eligibility and quantities to be allocated to eligible persons. The quantity figures were adjusted frequently, as the allocations of supply for consumer use were altered by the supply agencies. These decisions in Washington had to be administered in the field. Whenever the regulations made the grant of rations dependent upon a showing of eligibility, then a decision had to be made on whether an applicant was eligible and, if so, for what amount. These decisions were in most instances made by local, unpaid board members. In the year 1945 they processed 133,000,000 individual applications for gasoline, tires, and home canning sugar alone.

A second problem was the provision of a medium for payment for rationed commodities. War rationing books, containing stamps, were issued periodically to each person. Community resources were mobilized for the task of distributing books to all persons. Other currency was given either at local boards or through issuance centers to persons found to be eligible for it. A ration banking system was established which allowed dealers to deposit ration coupons in banks and write checks to their suppliers. Central currency-issuance centers were established to mail rations to individuals in order to cure the problem of theft of ration currency from local boards, and a large program of verification of stamps accepted by gasoline dealers was set up to defeat the counterfeiter of stamps. Rationing operations were the largest of the government's wartime administrative undertakings, and involved tens of thousands of volunteer workers and thousands of paid workers.

Another problem was to obtain understanding and compliance. Rationing touched every person in the nation, and the solvency of the system of control depended upon its acceptance by people. Local boards would be too lenient in granting rations, individuals would find ways of evasion, black markets would develop if a spirit of cooperation did not exist. The administrators of the program spent much time and effort in obtaining understanding of the reasons for rationing and of the restrictions which went with it. They also devised ways of avoiding leaks in the system, the most effective of all of these being the quota system. For example, after grant by the local boards of about 50 per cent more home canning sugar in 1944 than had been allocated to OPA for the purpose, and after many local boards, in the first few weeks of the home canning season in 1945, had granted more rations than the year before, OPA divided the national quota among local boards and gave them stamps only in amounts equal to their quotas. On the other hand, in contrast to its successes, when the agency validated more food-rationing currency than it could allow to be spent and, as a corrective, imposed a Christmas cancellation of stamps, it suffered a severe setback in its effort to obtain understanding and acceptance.[7]

MANPOWER. When World War II started in Europe there was still slack in the American economy and about 9 million unemployed persons in the country. By drawing into the working force about 8 million of these, some 5 million previously unemployed women, and other millions from persons reaching the working age for the first time, the United States added about 15 million persons to its wartime manpower pool. Even though some 12 million persons were added to the armed services, the labor force was greatly expanded.

As a consequence of the manpower reserve at the beginning of the war, shortages in the work force, except for specific skills, did not become threatening until 1943, and were never serious enough to require stringent controls. The nation does not, for this reason, have experience in manpower controls comparable to that gained for materials allocation from 1941 to 1945. The chief controls may be quite briefly noted. The central machinery was the public-employment office, which during the war sought to direct workers to essential jobs. Through their referral policies, they could do much to place workers where they were urgently needed. The employment offices were nationalized for the duration of the war, and operated under the direction of the War Manpower Commission. This commission instructed the local offices to give priority to plants in the order of their importance. The commission sought the cooperation of employers through agreements on their part not to hire a worker previously employed unless he presented a certificate of availability from his previous employer. This was a somewhat feeble effort to meet the problem of workers moving from one job to another, creating a tremendous turnover—at a rate, in fact, of about 100 per cent per year in 1943. Acute shortages developed in some areas, particularly on the West Coast. To meet these, the commission set up voluntary control plans, which encompassed committee establishment of priorities among labor claims, setting of employ-

[7] See Martin Kriesberg, *Cancellation of the Ration Stamps* (University, Ala.: University of Alabama Press, 1952), reprinted in Harold Stein, *Public Administration and Policy Formation: A Case Book* (New York: Harcourt, Brace & World, Inc., 1952), pp. 761–774.

ment ceilings for plants, and controlled referral by the employment offices. Such voluntary programs could have only a quite limited effect in an area of acute shortage where employers were seeking employees to enable them to fulfill their contracts. The Manpower Commission also sought to get war contracts awarded to contractors in areas of less acute manpower shortage, but its pressure on the War Production Board and the military departments—which were seeking the maximum use of plants wherever located—was quite ineffective. Deferral policies of the Selective Service System (administering the draft for armed services) were not based primarily on essentiality of work performed rather than on existence of dependents, but deferrals were made for certain categories of essential employment, and the President's "work or fight" order was aimed toward maximum use of manpower.

There were suggestions prior to World War II for a labor draft in case of an all-out war. The administrative difficulties of successfully directing the use of the civilian manpower of the nation through a labor draft would be immensely greater than those in administering a military draft. The size of the work force, the diversity of the skills required, the limitations on mobility of family heads, and many other factors would make a labor draft a difficult, if not impossible, undertaking. Moreover, a labor draft would be the most severe of all wartime measures, and would run so strongly against the traditions of the nation that its use in any except the most extreme emergency would be avoided by wartime policy makers. There are many alternative policies which could be adopted and, if placed high on the agenda of central administrative organizations, could accomplish much more than was necessary in World War II. One would be a vigorous campaign to draw more labor into the work force. A second would be longer hours of work. Deferment policy in draft boards could be based in large measure on essentiality of occupation. Incentives could be offered to labor, such as provision of adequate housing in areas of labor shortage. Incentives through wage increases would, however, raise serious issues of stabilization policy. Retraining of workers for new skills required in a war effort could be vigorously pushed. The employment offices could be given strong directives on priorities in placement. Broad use of limitation and conservation orders with respect to things to be produced would close nonessential enterprise and force workers into other occupations. Through such means, the necessity for stronger manpower controls might be avoided.

STABILIZATION

There are three reasons why prevention of inflation will be a part of the objectives of policy makers in a mobilization economy. First, inflation impairs the efficiency of mobilization. Chandler and Wallace have summarized the effects:

> Rapid increases of prices and wages can evoke widespread strikes and other industrial disputes, make fixed-price contracts infeasible and enhance greatly the degree of risk and uncertainty in economic transactions, induce private hoarding of materials and finished products, divert an excessive amount of attention away from production and into speculative activities, decrease the willingness of people to save, and, in general, lower national morale and create dissatisfaction, unrest, and disunity.[8]

Second, inflation distributes inequitably the burden of mobilization on the population. The accumulated savings of individuals in the form of bonds, notes, and insurance diminish in value. Those who depend on these savings for their livelihood suffer greatly. Salaried groups will suffer also because of the lag in salary increases behind price increases. On the other hand, other groups in the population reap huge benefits from the mobilization through increases in their property values and their profits. Third, inflation threatens the tranquillity of the society and the stability of social and political institutions. Inflation such as could be produced in a mobilization economy if controls to avoid it were not imposed could lead to revolutionary shifts in the relationships among groups in the society and to such severe hardships for many people that discontent would spread and perhaps lead to demands for radical changes in public policies and political institutions. Inflation is a breeding ground for radical, antidemocratic movements.

Inflation develops in wartime because of deficit financing of mobilization expenditures. Knowing that in previous wars inflationary pressures had given rise to large price increases and to bust-boom cycles, many economists favored financing the major part of government expenditures in World War II through taxes, or through taxes and forced savings. Others recognized the inherent difficulty of attaining this objective without destroying production incentives or imposing inequitable burdens on portions of the population, and also the political difficulties of achieving these several results. Taxes were substantially raised, and sale of government bonds to the public vigorously pushed. Nevertheless, the funds obtained by these methods did not meet the rapid growth of government expenditures. Prior to 1940 national expenditures were running at an annual rate of 8 billion dollars, and by the second quarter of 1945 the annual rate was 101 billion dollars. In the six fiscal years following June, 1940, almost 49 per cent of national expenditures was met by taxes, and about 60 per cent of the deficit was met by sale of bonds to nonbank

---

[8] Lester V. Chandler and Donald H. Wallace, *Economic Mobilization and Stabilization: Selected Materials on the Economics of War and Defense* (New York: Holt, Rinehart & Winston, Inc., 1951), pp. 180–181.

purchasers. The remainder—close to 90 billion dollars—was borrowed from the banking system. The banks paid for the bonds by creating new deposits, which resulted in an increase in the money supply.[9] Moreover, cashable bonds sold to the public were mere deferments of purchasing power which could be released during the immediate postwar period. The result of the financing policies of the government was to create a huge inflationary gap—the gap between money available for expenditure and goods available for purchase. To prevent this gap and the greater gap between demand and supply of particular commodities in acute shortage from producing a runaway inflation, direct controls were imposed on prices, rents, and wages.

PRICE CONTROL. *Methods and Policies.* Two general types of price control to combat inflation may be distinguished. In selective price control, ceilings are placed only on selected products, and perhaps only at some stages of production and distribution. Selection will be made of those products which are essential for war production and community needs, and for which increased demand leads to a threat of major price increases. The effort will be mainly directed toward the source of the production process, and at points where the product moves through few channels. It will be primarily or exclusively imposed on raw-materials suppliers, primary producers, and possibly first distributors. Selective control has the advantage of enabling the price-control authorities to concentrate their attention on major areas of threat to the price structure and to tailor their regulations to the marketing practices of specific industries. It may be inadequate because the increases in demand generate pressures on the price structure generally, or because of the administrative difficulties of imposing controls on many separate industries. In the second type of control, which is general price control, price ceilings are placed on nearly all commodities and services. Some exemptions may be made because of administrative difficulties or for other reasons. General price control will be effected by regulations of broad applicability, but these will be supplemented by special regulations tailored to the conditions in particular industries.

There are three techniques for setting maximum prices. The first is the price freeze, which merely means that regulations prohibit a seller from charging more than he charged under the same conditions during a named base period. It has two main virtues: it can be imposed quickly and over as broad an area as is desired, and it allows each seller to keep the prices established by his own practice. Its main defect is that it is difficult to enforce, because the buyer will lack information on what the ceiling prices are, and even the seller may not have adequate records to show all of his prices in the base period. A freeze may be a good beginning

---

[9] The figures are taken from Lester V. Chandler, "The Nature of War Finance Problems," in *ibid.*, pp. 181–190.

but a poor type of regulation to live with over a period of time. The second technique is formula pricing. There are many types of formulas, but the most common is a percentage of mark-up over cost. Through formula pricing, uniform maximum mark-ups can be prescribed for distinct categories of merchandise. It may simplify price control both for the government and the seller. On the other hand, it will normally create some inflation of prices, because the price-control authority will feel that it cannot successfully impose a ceiling which is not somewhat above the average or median price charged in the industry. The third technique is dollars-and-cents pricing. In this type of control the specific price which can be charged for a commodity or service is prescribed. This price can be publicized, usually through a requirement that the price be marked on the commodity—perhaps by the manufacturer; hence the consumer's cooperation in enforcement may be obtained. The deficiencies of the technique are the administrative difficulties in establishing dollars-and-cents prices for many types of commodity and sale, and the inflationary effect of allowing all sellers in a category to come up to a ceiling which will probably be somewhat higher than the average or median price hitherto charged. Both margin pricing and dollars-and-cents pricing sacrifice a bit on the line of control to obtain a holding point.

Some large decisions on policy standards will be required in any price-control program. In World War II the first decision was that the profit motive should be retained. Following this, the major pricing standard was the "over-all industry earnings standard." According to this standard, prices would not be raised for an industry unless it could be shown that the industry as a whole was not operating as profitably as it was during a normal peacetime "base" period. Under this standard the insuperable administrative burdens and the threat to the price structure in price adjustments for individual companies were avoided. It was a tight standard, and was attacked as being profit control rather than price control, to which the reply was made that no standard for determining when price increases should be made could avoid the profit reference. Another pricing standard was the product standard, according to which the prices for an individual product line in a multiproduct industry would not be raised if they covered out-of-pocket costs for the bulk of the production. This, too, was a tight standard, and was relaxed in the less serious inflationary threat which existed during the Korean War, when price controls were re-established. There were, during World War II, some special circumstances which led to departure from general pricing standards. For example, differential pricing, under which the high-cost producer was allowed a higher price than others, was adopted for copper in order to ensure urgently needed production.

One method used in World War II to encourage production and to hold down living costs was the payment of subsidy to producers. To encourage production, nonferrous-metals producers, for example, were paid a premium for output above a normal quota. To hold down the cost of living, subsidies were made to agricultural producers. Particularly large were the subsidies designed to keep down the price of meat and bread. Subsidies to prevent increases in consumers' prices were widely criticized, but they had many advantages. They prevented price increases which would have been far larger than the subsidies (because of the cumulation of distributor mark-ups between producer and consumer), helped prevent demands for increased wages, and avoided the tremendous administrative burden of amending price regulations to allow for increased prices at successive distribution stages.

Development of Price Control in World War II. Except for some quite limited experience in World War I, the nation faced World War II without any real experience in price control to curb the effects of an inflationary gap. Although Bernard Baruch, who had administered selective controls in World War I, advised a general freeze of prices, a start was made with selective controls. The first price "schedule" was issued for second-hand machine tools in February, 1941, and fourteen months later over one hundred schedules or regulations had been issued. In April, 1942, a general freeze order for all commodities and services not exempted was issued. It froze all prices to the highest levels charged by sellers in March.

In the meantime a price-control act had been passed. The early schedules were issued with only whatever legal authority the President possessed, and contained no penalties. They could be enforced only by action of production authorities in withholding priorities, or by threats—called "jawbone control." The Price Control Act of February, 1942, vested in an Office of Price Administration the power to set prices which were "generally fair and equitable." Although, because of experience already acquired, the act served as an admirable charter of operations, it left serious gaps in stabilization. The two significant gaps were the omission of any authority to control wages and the requirement that prices should reflect 110 per cent of parity to agricultural producers, or meet other equally high standards. As a result of the parity provision, the General Maximum Price Regulation issued in April could protect the consumer on only about 60 per cent of his food dollar. Not until the Stabilization Act of October, 1942, was the President authorized to regulate wages, and the parity provision amended to enable control to be exercised over most of the remaining food products.

In the year following the issuance of the general freeze order, the Office of Price Administration faced tremendous problems. By the time the order was issued imbalances had been created in the price structure. One kind of imbalance created what was called the "price squeeze." When, after a period of rapidly accelerating prices, a freeze is placed on all prices of all sellers on a single base period, then retailers will find that they are squeezed, because wholesale prices will have gone up in the base period, but will not then have been reflected in increased retail prices;

and similarly, wholesalers will find that their prices do not reflect increases made by their suppliers, and so on backward through the marketing channels. OPA officials talked about rolling back the prices of sellers in the early stages of production and distribution so as to remove the downstage squeezes, but this proved to be impossible. This meant a roll upward of prices at the later stages of distribution. One way to get out of the difficulty was to issue margin regulations under which, in place of freeze prices, the retailer or other distributor would be given a margin over his merchandise cost. As a result of squeezes and other imbalances created in the period before controls were imposed, the OPA staff was under pressure to get out corrective amendments of the general regulation and additional special regulations adapted to the situations in specific industries. It was a burdensome task, extending over many months. The result ultimately was to restore a balance in price relationships which the agency could "live with," but with this came some yielding on the price line which existed in April, 1942.

In April, 1943, there was a threatened coal strike which brought to official attention the widespread discontent over the failure of the government to hold the price line. Labor leaders argued that an increase in the price level of about 23 per cent from the beginning of the mobilization build-up justified demands for wage increases beyond those allowed by government policy. Recognizing the need for tighter control, the President issued the "hold the line" order, which gave new directives to the OPA, the War Labor Board, and the Secretary of Agriculture, and prohibited any upward revision in prices, above those required by law, which would increase the cost of living without the consent of the Economic Stabilization Director. Following this order, there was phenomenal success in holding the price line for a two-year period, the consumer price index registering only a 2 per cent rise in the price level. Contributing to this result were many factors other than the hold-the-line order. OPA had restored the internal balance in the price structure. It had been able to bring 90 per cent of food purchases under control after the Stabilization Act of 1942, and in the following spring it rationed canned fruits and vegetables and placed price ceilings on fresh fruits and vegetables. It developed effective dollars-and-cents pricing at the retail level for a major portion of the food basket. By April, 1942, a balance of labor, agriculture, and business interests had been achieved which could be retained until the end of the war. Subsidies on agricultural prices shifted increased cost of foods from the price ticket to the government budget.

Although the inflationary gap still existed, and although the great rise in prices after the end of World War I warned of the danger of premature removal of controls, the discontent of powerful groups with price control led to a rapid relaxation of controls and the collapse, in 1946, of the price-control program. Discontent with controls was accompanied by belief that purchasing power would have to be stimulated to avoid a postwar deflation. Group political pressure for advantage had continued during the war, but now that the war was over, there was a release of group pressures in the macropolitical arena with such force that restraints of reason seemed to be without effect. Wage controls were substantially withdrawn immediately after V-J day, and virtually destroyed in a steel wage settlement in February, 1946. The abandonment of food rationing, except for sugar, in November, 1945, was in large measure a concession to agricultural interests, and the pressure of these interests for removal of price controls was unrelenting. Business groups pressed for relaxation of the strict pricing standards of the war period. While the OPA staff struggled to develop prompt reconversion pricing policies to selectively decontrol prices, and to frame rules for pricing of commodities not in production during the war, the pressures for the lifting or loosening of controls mounted. In June, 1946, when the price-control act came up for renewal, the Congress, reacting to group demands, placed so many amendments in the act for protection of particular interests, business and agricultural, that the President vetoed the act. Before Congress passed a renewal act there was a hiatus of twenty-five days without legal price control. When the twenty-five days were over wholesale prices had risen 10 per cent, with food prices leading at 24 per cent, and Congress had provided an act which allowed recontrol of many items only after waiting periods and under conditions. The amendments to the act required so many adjustments in price schedules that an impossible burden was imposed on the OPA staff. The collapse of price control followed, leaving controls at the end of the year only on rent, rice, and sugar. The inflationary pressures that had been held in restraint during the war were now released, and the price advances initiated in the twenty-five summer days continued.

Of the many conclusions that could be drawn from the wartime experience in price control, a few are of special significance. A group of young economists, lawyers, and political scientists worked out the methodology of price control so that in a future emergency the ways of doing the the job would be known from the beginning. Second, once the balances among prices and among wages are broken, then time will be required to restore the balances, and some inflation of prices will have resulted. Third, price and wage controls are so distasteful to the groups subjected to them that when dire necessity seems no longer to require their subjection to control, their resort to political pressure to obtain their normal freedom appears to be inevitable.

The Korean War. Two things are worthy of note about price control during the Korean War (1950–53). First, there was a delay of several months before controls were imposed. There was no act authorizing controls until about three months after the beginning of the war. President Truman, undoubtedly remembering the unpopularity of his defense of controls after the end of World War II, and facing a congressional election in November, was in no hurry to impose controls. The agencies of administration moved reluctantly and with indecision. They favored selective controls, but a rapid upsurge of prices at the end of 1950 led to the imposition of general controls, both of prices and of wages. By the time price controls were established in January, 1951, a substantial amount of price inflation had occurred, and some imbalances in the price structure had been created. Second, since the mobilization was a limited one and the exigencies of the situation did not seem to be as great as in a complete mobilization, the standards set and administered in both wage and price control were less stringent than in World War II.

RENT CONTROL.[10] Rent increases, which began to occur around military and industrial installations as early as 1940, were of particular concern to those in government responsible for production and stabilization in World War II. If housing were not available on reasonable terms, or if rent increases caused frequent moves, there would be labor unrest and impairment of morale in the population generally. Consequently, attention was given to methods of preventing increases as early as 1940.

Early efforts were directed toward getting voluntary cooperation of landlords, obtaining community assistance through establishment of fair-rent committees, and securing state or local rent laws or regulations. As all of these efforts offered little promise for the kind of emergency which was developing, Congress was asked to pass rent-control statutes. It did this for the District of Columbia in December, 1941; and in February, 1942, it included in the Emergency Price Control Act authorization to the Office of Price Administration to set up rent control in other areas. The act authorized only rent control for residential accommodations, and no controls were established at any time during the war for commercial rents or for the sale price of rental units.

Rent controls were never established for the entire country, but were set up area by area. The enabling legislation authorized the Price Administrator to designate defense-rental areas and to recommend local action for stabilization of rents in such areas. If after sixty days he found that rents had not been stabilized, he could set maximum rents. The usual procedure was to make a survey of an area prior to giving notice for the purpose of determining the need for control. By 1947 there were about 650 rent-control areas, including more than 75 per cent of the country's population.

The technique of control was to freeze rents to a base-period date. Frequently there was a rollback to a date at least as early as the beginning of the rent survey for an area. Area rent offices were set up to carry the regulations into effect.

Rent control was a large administrative task, and brought with it some

---

[10] For full discussion of this subject, see Harvey C. Mansfield and Associates, *A Short History of OPA* (Washington, D.C.: Office of Temporary Controls, 1947), Chapter 4.

tough administrative problems. The task of administration and of enforcement was simplified by a decision to require registration of all rental units at the beginning of control in an area. The registration gave essential facts about the rental unit, such as number of rooms and rental price on the ceiling date. The forms were made in triplicate so that one could be retained by the landlord, one kept by the rental office, and one given to the renter. The large task of adjusting rents for various reasons is reflected in the fact that rents were adjusted for about one out of twenty units during the period of controls. There was also a problem of setting rents for new units—that is, units on which there was no rental experience. The method used was to allow the owner and the tenant to agree on a fair rent, and file this with the area rent office for approval or amendment. The biggest problem, however, was to prevent evasion of rent ceilings. The devices of evasion were numerous, and included such things as security deposits, tie-in sales of furniture, and eviction of a tenant to obtain another who would be willing to make illegal payments. Rent regulations came to be framed in such a way as to make illegal many of the common forms of evasion. The most serious technique of evasion was through sale of the property. Since real-estate prices were uncontrolled, there was a temptation to the renter and the landlord to arrange for sale of the property. If such action became widespread, persons unable to buy or living only temporarily in a location would find it difficult to obtain accommodations. To meet the problem OPA required relatively large down-payments on sales, and prohibited eviction of a tenant without a period of notice and a showing that the purchaser intended to occupy the house himself.

The shortage of housing after the war to meet the needs of workers and others who moved from one location to another, of returnees from the armed services, of college students swarming the campuses, and of others, was so great that rent control was continued into 1947. In the closing days of the program there was much complaint and allegation by owners of unfairness in retention of strict controls, and as a consequence, adjustment provisions were liberalized.

Rent control did not meet the same degree of antagonism in Congress that price controls did. No serious charge would have been made that they did not, for their duration, give real protection to the renter. In the five years preceding November, 1945, the rent component of the Bureau of Labor Statistics' cost-of-living index rose less than four points, though the median rent payment had increased 23 per cent. Surveys also showed that owner net profits had increased materially, partly because of a higher occupancy rate, and partly also, no doubt, because smaller sums were spent to maintain the properties than in normal periods.

WAGE CONTROL. In a mobilization economy the power of employers to countervail the demands of labor for wage increases is weakened. Labor shortage will make it necessary for the employer to grant concessions in order to retain a labor supply, and the cost may be transferable to the government or to other purchasers of his production. In World War II the pressure for increased wages was moderated and delayed by the general labor surplus which existed at the beginning of the war. Nevertheless, wages were bid up by employers to attract laborers to new plants requiring increased amounts of certain types of labor, shortages of specific types of labor developed almost immediately, and the general labor supply tightened quickly.

The earliest interest of the government was in settlement of labor disputes.[11] Even in March, 1941, a National Defense Mediation Board was established to try to settle disputes through mediatory efforts. Its purpose was to prevent interruption of work that would interfere with defense production. It was succeeded in 1942 by the National War Labor Board. Later in 1942 the dispute-settlement function was merged with the function of wage stabilization in the operations of the War Labor Board. In the Stabilization Act of October, 1942, the President was finally given authority to stabilize wages, and he promptly directed the War Labor Board to carry out the task. Stabilization of salaries over $5,000 was made the responsibility of the Bureau of Internal Revenue.

For dispute settlement and wage stabilization the agency of administration was a tripartite board composed of persons appointed to represent the employer interest, the labor interest, and the public interest. To assist in carrying out its responsibilities, the board set up thirteen regional offices, each headed by a board, and seventeen industry agencies. In some cases wage settlements could be approved only after consideration of their effects on prices by the Director of Economic Stabilization.

The technique of a freeze of all wages was never employed. By the time stabilization of wages was introduced there was acceptance of the need for allowing some increase in wages above those at the beginning of the defense program in order to compensate for increases in prices. Increases within certain limits were permitted, and this allowed some flexibility and some scope for employer-employee negotiation when the limits had not been exceeded.

Standards were evolved by the board for determining what increases would be allowed. First, prior to the enactment of the Stabilization Act, it had laid down the Little Steel Formula, according to which wage increases of 15 per cent above those prevailing in January, 1941, would be allowed. This was supposed at the time (July, 1942) to correspond with

[11] For summaries of the wartime experience, see Harold W. Metz, *Labor Policy of the Federal Government* (Washington, D.C.: Brookings Institution, 1945), pp. 183–194; Abraham L. Gitlow, *Wage Determination Under National Boards* (New York: Prentice-Hall, Inc., 1953), pp. 112–179; and H. M. Douty, "The Development of Wage-Price Policies," and W. Ellison Chalmers, Milton Derber, and William H. McPherson, "Problems and Policies of Dispute Settlement and Wage Stabilization in World War II," in Chandler and Wallace, *Economic Mobilization and Stabilization* (New York: Holt, Rinehart & Winston, Inc., 1951), Chapters 16 and 17.

the increase in cost of living which had occurred. While the standard was not always followed precisely, it remained the basic standard for determining wage increases until the end of the war. Second, wage increases were allowed because of inequalities and inequities. These were of two types—interplant and intraplant. For determining allowable interplant increases, the board set up rate brackets—that is, the range of wages from minimum to maximum for a given occupation in a given labor market. Many inequalities between plants were corrected, but after the hold-the-line order in 1943, the requirements for adjustment of wages on the basis of claims of interplant inequality were more stringent. Third, wage increases were allowed to correct substandard wages. The meaning of substandard was never precisely defined. After a time the board came to accept increases to bring wages up to 50 cents per hour without petition to it, but it also made decisions that wages higher than this were substandard. Since wages in some industries, such as the laundry and cleaning industry, were often less than 25 cents per hour at the beginning of the war, substantial increases occurred in the substandard category, calling, in turn, for substantial price increases. Fourth, the board allowed some increases to aid in the prosecution of war. Occasionally, a wage increase would be a means of correcting an acute shortage of a specific category of labor.

This review of major standards does not reveal the enormous complexity and difficulty of the task of wage stabilization. The board could not always follow precisely these general standards. It was pushed to make fringe adjustments—that is, to allow gains for labor which would not be reflected in the basic wage rate. Examples were vacation pay, travel time (portal-to-portal pay in coal mining), and union maintenance provisions.

At the end of the war labor leaders pressed the arguments that increases in the basic wage rate had been much less than the increase in the cost of living, that overtime wages characteristic of the war period would disappear, and that increases in purchasing power were needed to prevent a postwar depression as war plants closed. As has been noted, controls on labor benefits were removed, which contributed to the demand of industry and agriculture that controls on them be removed also.

The quick inflation of prices during the Korean War led to the revival of wage stabilization, which existed from January, 1951, to the spring of 1953. Again, a national board and regional boards were established. Again, a general standard for increases (this time 10 per cent) to match the increase in prices was established. Again, other standards were set. An extensive set of regulations was issued to govern all types of collateral means of raising compensation, such as increases in bonus payments and employer contributions to retirement funds.

PROBLEMS OF ORGANIZATION AND COORDINATION

Mobilization and stabilization in World War II brought new tasks different from the peacetime functions of the executive departments. Although in some cases the new tasks were delegated to existing departments and agencies, most of the larger ones were assigned to new organizations. Sometimes these organizations were linked to departments in some way or other. Thus, the War Food Administration was headed by the Secretary of Agriculture, and the Petroleum Administrator for War served under the Secretary of the Department of Interior. Also, department heads served on boards established for the direction of new programs. On the other hand, large new organizations—such as the War Production Board, the National War Labor Board, and the Office of Price Administration—were responsible directly to the President.

In the discussions after the beginning of the Korean War the view came to prevail that for the limited mobilization anticipated new functions should be assigned, insofar as possible, to existing departments and agencies of the government. Hence, the production scheduling and allocation functions which, in World War II, were assigned to the independent War Production Board were delegated to a Defense Production Administration within the Department of Commerce. Direct stabilization controls, however, were placed in new organizations—namely, the Office of Price Stabilization, the Wage Stabilization Board, and the Salary Stabilization Board. Even for these new organizations, however, old-line agencies rendered assistance on a much greater scale than during World War II. The management agencies of the government helped in the establishment of field offices of the new organizations, and the Wage and Hour Administration of the Department of Labor itself performed some field functions for the Wage Stabilization Board. It may be assumed that in any emergency of the future the competence of the established agencies to perform many mobilization functions would be much greater than at the beginning of World War II, and hence that there would be a probability of their greater use.

In World War II the vast new machinery was organized on two conflicting principles. Some organizations were set up on the basis of function to be performed, others on the basis of the commodities or industries to be dealt with. Among the former were the War Production Board for production scheduling and allocation of materials, the War Manpower Commission for manpower controls, the National War Labor Board for wage stabilization, and the Office of Price Administration for price and rent controls and consumer rationing. Among the latter were the War Food Administration, the Petroleum Administrator for War, and the Office of

Defense Transportation. There was almost constant conflict between the organizations responsible for functions and those responsible for commodities. These conflicts were in part jurisdictional, but they arose basically from different foci of interest. While some agencies were forced by their assignments to think in terms of general purposes, such as allocation or stabilization, the commodity agencies thought in terms of particular industries and became, to an extent, claimants for and protectors of these.

These conflicts were only part of the reason for a problem of coordination among agencies. Goals could only be achieved by collaboration among agencies carrying responsibility for different assignments. At almost every major step there was need for coordination—between the armed forces and the production authority, the wage-control and the price-control authorities, the manpower and the production and stabilization authorities—indeed, between almost any two of the agencies, and often among several of them. Coordination was achieved in the main through interagency liaison conferences and committees, and was based on awareness by each agency of the nature and urgency of the functions of the others. Nevertheless, a structure of coordination appeared to be essential, and this was achieved with two steps. In October, 1942, just after the Congress had passed the Stabilization Act, the President created an Office of Economic Stabilization (OES) to "formulate and develop a comprehensive national economic policy relating to the control of civilian purchasing power, prices, rents, wages, salaries, profits, rationing, subsidies, and all related matters." [12] When the hold-the-line order was issued the following year the functions of the office were greatly expanded. In May, 1943, the President created the Office of War Mobilization (OWM) [13]—later the Office of War Mobilization and Reconversion (OWMR)—which had a much more comprehensive jurisdiction. It was given jurisdiction, in effect, over the whole economic mobilization and stabilization program. These two layers of coordinative authority, particularly the OWM, functioned as the special agents of the President, who had become deeply engulfed in problems of military strategy and international negotiation.

The heads of these offices worked through small staffs who acquired expertness in resolving differences among the agencies. The agencies had authority to issue directives binding other agencies, and in some cases did so. On the whole, however, their main role was to resolve conflicts and to negotiate cooperative arrangements as such action became necessary.[14] The war experience in coordination was regarded as sufficiently satisfactory to be copied in the Korean War. While in World War II the means of coordination were developed after the need arose, in the Korean

[12] Executive Order 9250, October 3, 1942.
[13] Executive Order 9347, May 27, 1943.
[14] See Herman M. Somers, *Presidential Agency: The Office of War Mobilization and Reconversion* (Cambridge, Mass.: Harvard University Press, 1950).

War the two levels of coordinators were established within months after the beginning of the conflict.

PLANNING FOR FUTURE EMERGENCIES

Since shortly after World War II there has been in the Executive Office of the President some agency responsible for planning for economic mobilization and stabilization in future emergencies. At the present time, the responsibility for coordinating government planning along these lines is in the Office of Emergency Planning. Each agency of the government has been directed to make plans for performing functions related to its responsibilities. Strategic and critical materials have been acquired and retained (stockpiled) in government inventories under the authorization of a series of acts. Studies are conducted on the needs for such materials in conventional and nuclear war, so that adequate supplies of these may be on hand. Stand-by authorities are vested in the President under provisions of the Defense Production Act which are still in force. Among such authorities are those to require that priority be given by manufacturers to defense contracts, to allocate materials and facilities as necessary and appropriate for national defense, to prevent hoarding of scarce materials, and to guarantee or make loans for the purpose of expanding production and supply. In addition, each agency of national administration has stand-by plans for emergencies that may occur.

While it is assumed that economic controls necessitated by an accelerated build-up of defenses or a limited war would be developed and administered by the national government, plans for a post-nuclear attack situation call for state and local governments to assume responsibilities in resource management and economic stabilization in undamaged areas until the national government is able to undertake the responsibilities. It is assumed that some of these areas would be isolated from the rest of the country, and that except for field offices, the functioning of national or even state agencies for these areas would be interrupted. It is assumed also that extreme shortages would exist, and that stringent controls to conserve scarce supplies would be needed. Hence, the national government has asked each state to designate an Emergency Planning Director, establish an Emergency Resource Planning Committee, and to set up task groups to develop plans for state and local action in several fields of activity related to resource use, including, among others, production, construction and housing, economic stabilization, food, and manpower. The state organizations are expected to develop operating organization and capacity at the local level in the several fields. For price control, rent control, and rationing, plans are based on the assumption that an order of the President would immediately freeze prices and rents and authorize rationing, and that the state and/or local authorities would be prepared, without the aid of national officials, to apply the controls within their jurisdictions in accordance with guidelines developed for them in advance by the Office of Emergency Planning. Although there is much variation among the states in the progress made for post-attack emergencies, it is probably not too much to say that at present (1964) they are ill-prepared for these and other resource-management and stabilization functions.

Part IV. Regulation and Promotion of Industries

Chapter 16. Industry Regulation and Promotion: A Preview

THERE IS DISCUSSION in the preceding chapters of those elements of policy which apply to the whole economic front—that is, which affect the actions of men in the diverse fields of employment of labor and capital. This part will treat the regulation and promotion of particular industries. The two areas of policy are not fully distinct from each other. Credit control through the banking system has been considered as part of the controls affecting the economy as a whole, but banking regulation will be viewed also as regulation of a particular industry. Transportation regulation, conversely, is treated as regulation of a particular industry or set of industries, though transportation is, of course, a service to the entire economy, and promotion and regulation thereof may be a service to shippers of all types of commodities. Yet the distinction, as applied to the set of things discussed in the preceding part and in this part, has validity and significance. We are to deal now with the policies and methods of government when it decides to set up a separate system of policy and administration for one of our major industries.

PANORAMA OF INDUSTRY REGULATION AND PROMOTION

It is possible to present a panoramic view of national activity with respect to particular industries. The chart on pages 362–364 shows major industries concerning which the national government has been most active. These include banking, transportation, communications, securities, household utilities, agriculture, housing, and atomic energy. It is instructive to study the chart historically. It can be seen that the accumulation of national interest has been gradual and continuous. Banking was the first industry to be regulated (1863) and railroads the second (1887), and these were the only major industries regulated nationally prior to the twentieth century. In the first decade of the new century (1901 to 1910), the two major developments were the strengthening of railroad regulation (1903, 1906, 1910) and the beginning of quality protection to the buyer of meat (1906) and of foods and drugs generally (1906). Statutes provided for regulation of oil pipelines and wire communication, but administrative control of these was not significant immediately. It has already been shown that in the second decade there was establishment of the Federal Reserve System and extension of antitrust legislation and establishment of the Federal Trade Commission. In addition, railroad regulation was vastly extended in the Transportation Act of 1920, a comprehensive policy for development of merchant shipping through a U.S. Shipping Board was initiated (1916), national grants to states for highway construction were authorized (1916), and a government-organized system of long-term farm credit was started (1916). In the twenties, often regarded as a dormant period, national regulation was extended to packers and stockyards (1922), grain-futures trading (1922), air transportation (1926), and radio (1927). Then came the bulge of the thirties. In addition to the new thrusts in labor legislation, already discussed, this—the period of the New Deal—was the decade in which bank deposit insurance (1933) and motor-carrier regulation (1935) were initiated, a more complete transportation policy was stated (1940), regulation of air transportation (1938) and communication industries (1934) were rounded out, and new programs of action with respect to securities (1933), securities exchanges (1934), electric utilities (1935), gas utilities (1938), agriculture (1933), and housing (1933–1937) were launched. The following decade was largely one of war controls and their liquidation, but after this came new developments of lasting significance. Two of these—the Labor-Management Relations Act (Taft-Hartley) and Employment Act—have already been discussed; a third was the Atomic Energy Act (1946). The decade of 1951 to 1960 was a relatively static period insofar as new advances in national action on the economic front were concerned. One notable exception was the inauguration in 1956 of the soil-bank program. Since 1960, the major new venture has been the telstar program (1962).

In the states the industry that has been subjected to regulation for the longest period is banking. The history of regulation of this industry runs back to the early part of the nineteenth century. Railroads have been regulated by the states in some way from the beginning of the industry, and the present-day system of regulation dates from the 1870's. Public-utility regulation followed very quickly. In the first decade of the twentieth century the attention of state governments was directed to the evils in the insurance industry, and regulation of a stringent nature was initiated. So-called "blue-sky laws," designed to prevent fraud in the sale of securities, were passed in the second decade. Economic regulation of trucks and buses began in the third decade. Though conservation measures for oil had been in effect for some years, proration of production was introduced in the late twenties and became significant with its use in the East Texas field in 1931. The states have always been active in passage of laws to protect health, morals, and safety, and these have affected the operation of industries within their borders. They have passed laws on agriculture and labor, and on monopolies and business practices. They have, through court decisions and legislation, defined water rights and provided, through legislation and administration, for conservation and allocation of water. They have also set up requirements for licensing of professions and service trades. In sum, since the Civil War, there has been in the states, as in the nation, an expansion in the number of industries regulated and in the variety of regulations imposed.

SUBSTANTIVE TYPES OF REGULATORY ACTION

Five major types of regulatory action with respect to industries can be distinguished. The first is prescription of standards of conduct, operation, or service. Much of such regulation is designed to protect health, morals, or safety. There was a vast increase in such legislation from the late nineteenth century onward. But much of such legislation prescribes standards with purely economic objectives. Examples are the requirements in regard to service to be rendered by transportation and utility industries, and those relating to prudence in loans by banks. Standards are frequently enforced by an extensive system of inspections and examinations.

A second type of regulation is licensing. The essence of licensing is that government consent must be obtained before action is taken. Professor Freund called this the "enabling power" of government, and recently it has been called "governmental preconditions to business action."[1] However called, licensing is done under a number of names which describe a requirement for government consent. Thus, a "certificate of public convenience and necessity" is generally required for entry into regulated transportation or household utility service. A franchise is required by cities for municipal utility service. A permit is required in Texas to drill an oil well. "Incorporation" is the word used for granting permission to use the corporate form of organization. "Approval," "registration," "consent," and "certification" are other terms used. But the word "licensing" is itself the most commonly used—for example, for many learned professions, occupations, and service trades; to sell insurance as insurer, agent, or broker; to operate radio stations. The word is commonly used, however, in a generic sense to cover all types of requirement for government approval before action is taken.

Licensing is one of the most persistent forms of government control. It was widely used in the states in the early part of our history.[2] It was the core of the first national act for regulation of a major industry—chartering being required for national bank status in the act of 1863.

The stringency of licensing requirements and the impact upon indus-

---

[1] Ernst Freund, *Administrative Powers Over Persons and Property* (Chicago: University of Chicago Press, 1928), especially Chapter VII; Melvin Anshen and Francis D. Wormuth, *Private Enterprise and Public Policy* (New York: The Macmillan Company, 1954), p. 136.

[2] See page 9.

MAJOR AREAS OF NATIONAL INDUSTRY REGULATION AND PROMOTION

Area of Regulation and Promotion: Significant Policy or Administrative Change*

Dates	Banking	Transportation - Railroads	Transportation - Water	Transportation - Motor Carriers	Transportation - Air	Oil Pipelines	Communications	Securities	Utilities	Agriculture	Housing	Atomic Energy	Oil	New Agency Established	Chief Present Agency of Administration
1863	National Bank Act													Comptroller of the Currency	Comptroller of the Currency
1887		Act to Regulate Commerce	Joint Rail & Water Rates											Interstate Commerce Commission	Interstate Commerce Commission
1903		Elkins Act													Interstate Commerce Commission
1906		Hepburn Act[1]				Hepburn Act[1]				Meat Inspection[2] Food and Drug Act[2]					1. Interstate Commerce Commission 2. Department of Agriculture
1910		Mann-Elkins Act[1]					Amendment to the Act to Regulate Commerce[2]								1. Interstate Commerce Commission 2. Federal Communications Commission
1913	Federal Reserve Act[1]	Valuation Act[2]												Federal Reserve Board	1. Federal Reserve Board 2. Interstate Commerce Commission
1916			Shipping Board Act[1]	Highway Subsidies[2]						Federal Farm Loan Act[3]				U.S. Shipping Board Federal Land Banks	1. Federal Maritime Commission and Administration 2. Bureau of Public Roads 3. Federal Land Banks, Farm Credit Administration, Department of Agriculture
1920		Transportation Act[1]							Water Power Act[2]					Federal Power Commission	1. Interstate Commerce Commission 2. Federal Power Commission
1921										Packers & Stockyards Act					Department of Agriculture
1922										Grain Futures Act					Department of Agriculture
1923										Agricultural Credits Act				Federal Intermediate Credit Banks	Federal Intermediate Credit Banks, Farm Credit Administration, Department of Agriculture
1926					Air Commerce Act										

362

Year	Acts								Federal Radio Commission	Federal Communications Commission
1927				Radio Act						
1932	Deposit Insurance[1]	Emergency R.R. Transportation Act					Fed. Home Loan Bank System			Federal Home Loan Banks, Home Loan Bank Board, Housing and Home Finance Agency
1933					Securities Act[2]	Tenn. Valley Authority Act[3]	Production Control[4] Marketing Agreements & Orders[4] Extension of Farm Credit[4]		Federal Deposit Insurance Corporation, Tennessee Valley Authority, Agricultural Adjustment Commission	1. Federal Deposit Insurance Corporation 2. Securities Exchange Commission 3. Tennessee Valley Authority 4. Department of Agriculture
1934				Communications Act[1]	Securities Exchange Act[2]		National Housing Act[3]		Federal Communications Commission, Securities Exchange Commission	1. Federal Communications Commission 2. Securities Exchange Commission 3. Federal Housing Administration, Housing and Home Finance Agency
1935	Amendment of Federal Reserve Act		Motor Carrier Act[1]			Public Utility Holding Company Act[2], Federal Power Act[3]	Rural Electrification[4]	Contraband Oil Act[5] Interstate Oil Compact	Rural Electrification Administration	1. Interstate Commerce Commission 2. Securities Exchange Commission 3. Federal Power Commission 4. Rural Electrification Administration, Department of Agriculture 5. Department of Interior
1936		Merchant Marine Act[1]					Soil Conservation & Domestic Allotment Act[2] Commodity Exchange Act[2]			1. Federal Maritime Commission 2. Department of Agriculture
1937							Agricultural Marketing Act[1]	U.S. Housing Act[2]	Public Housing Administration	1. Department of Agriculture 2. Public Housing Administration, Housing and Home Finance Agency
1938				Civil Aeronautics Act[1]	Malony Act[2]	Natural Gas Act[3]	Agricultural Adjustment Act[4] Federal Crop Insurance Act[4]		Civil Aeronautics Board	1. Civil Aeronautics Board Federal Aviation Agency 2. Securities Exchange Commission 3. Federal Power Commission 4. Department of Agriculture

(continued on next page)

MAJOR AREAS OF NATIONAL INDUSTRY REGULATION AND PROMOTION (Cont.)

Area of Regulation and Promotion: Significant Policy or Administrative Change*

Dates	Banking	Transportation — Railroads	Water	Motor Carriers	Air	Oil Pipelines	Communications	Securities	Utilities	Agriculture	Housing	Atomic Energy	Oil	New Agency Established	Chief Present Agency of Administration
1940		Transportation Act													Interstate Commerce Commission; Civil Aeronautics Board
1946										Farmers Home Administration Act†		Atomic Energy Act[2]		Atomic Energy Commission	1. Department of Agriculture 2. Atomic Energy Commission
1948		Reed-Bulwinkle Act													Interstate Commerce Commission; Civil Aeronautics Board
1949										Agricultural Act of 1949[1]	Housing Act of 1949[2]				1. Department of Agriculture 2. Urban Renewal Administration, Housing and Home Finance Agency
1954										Agricultural Act of 1954,[1] Agricultural Trade Development & Assistance Act[1]		Atomic Energy Act[2]			1. Department of Agriculture 2. Atomic Energy Commission
1956	Bank Holding Company Act														Federal Reserve Board
1958					Federal Aviation Act										Federal Aviation Agency
1959													Import‡ Control		Department of Interior
1960	Bank Merger Act														Comptroller of the Currency; Federal Reserve Board; Federal Deposit Insurance Corporation
1962							Satellite Act							Communications Satellite Corporation**	Communications Satellite Corporation; Federal Communication Commission; National Aeronautics and Space Administration

* Numerals following act refer to chief present agency of administration listed in last column. ** Nongovernmental agency.
† Giving statutory foundation to a program inaugurated in previous decade.
‡ Compulsory control initiated by Presidential order.

tries varies considerably. On the one hand, licenses may be granted routinely upon compliance with formal requirements, and they may be permanent or renewable automatically if law has not been violated. On the other hand, licenses may be granted under rigid requirements which only a portion of the applicants can meet; the licensee may be subject to continuous supervision as a condition of retention of his license; the license may be subject to amendment or revocation; and the agency which grants, supervises, and revokes may have vast discretionary power over the licensee.

A third type of regulatory action is price control. In the eighteenth century prices were set in the states for many products, seemingly without regard to the kind of industry or product. In the nineteenth century price setting by the state declined. There was a revival of price control in the last thirty years of the century, but this was largely restricted to transportation and household utilities. Price control was regarded by the courts as an exceptional control which could be used in only a few industries. Liberty of contract between buyer and seller and between employer and employee came to be recognized as part of the liberty and property right protected by the due process clause of the Fourteenth Amendment. But at the same time the courts allowed price control in industries said to be "affected with a public interest." Two kinds of rationalization favorable to price control appear in the cases. First, it was said that there were certain industries which, because they stood in the "throat of commerce," or held out to serve all the public (as railroads and public utilities did), or received privileges (such as the right of eminent domain), were under a constructive obligation to deal reasonably with the public. Second, "virtual monopoly" was sometimes recognized as sufficient justification for price control. In 1876 the Supreme Court upheld the constitutionality of state regulation of prices of grain warehouses by use of both kinds of rationalization.[3] In 1913 it upheld regulation of insurance rates on the ground that prices were not fixed in "the higgling of the market but in the councils of the underwriters."[4] In 1921 it upheld temporary regulation of rents on the basis of an emergency situation,[5] as it had regulation of wages in an emergency in 1917.[6] It seemed to be allowing price control in response to situations where the buyer was at a competitive disadvantage in bargaining with the seller. This was sociological jurisprudence. But from 1923 to 1928 the Court swung around to the position that price control could be justified, except in emergencies, only in those industries (such as transportation) which had been subject

---

[3] *Munn v. Illinois,* 94 U.S. 113.
[4] *German Alliance Insurance Co. v. Lewis,* 233 U.S. 389 (1913).
[5] *Block v. Hirsh,* 256 U.S. 135 (1921).
[6] *Wilson v. New,* 243 U.S. 322.

to price regulation in the past.⁷ This was a jurisprudence of historical analogy.

It has been shown in an earlier chapter that Justice Stone protested this turn in the jurisprudence affecting price control, arguing for sociological jurisprudence, and that Justice Holmes protested also, arguing, however, for unlimited state sovereignty on the matter.⁸ Holmes' view, which seemed extreme in the 1920's, was accepted in the 1930's. By that time the push for price control had come from the disadvantaged seller. Under NRA code provisions prices were propped in many industries. The Agricultural Adjustment Administration supported agricultural prices in general by indirect means; and for the milk industry in particular, national and state governments embarked on direct price-support measures. In 1934 the Supreme Court rejected the idea that price fixing was possible only in a special category of industries said to be "affected with a public interest," and somersaulted to the view that price control was within the discretion of legislative bodies.⁹

Legislation may provide for price control to protect the buyer, as it has in the following industries: transportation, household utilities, insurance, banking (interest rates), warehousing, and stockyards. During World War II and the Korean situation ceiling prices were set on most commodities and services to protect the buyer and to safeguard the economy from inflation. Or legislatures may have in mind the protection of sellers, as in the milk industry, the coal industry during the late thirties, NRA codes, fair-trade laws, and minimum price regulation for transportation and utility industries. In addition to direct maintenance of prices, legislatures may seek to maintain prices by indirect means, as through the tariff, proration of oil production, and the various methods used to maintain prices of agricultural commodities.

The fourth major type of regulatory action is limitation of production. Limitation of production, in its broadest sense, includes any action to restrict entry for economic reasons, to restrict expansion, or to allocate production. Limitation of entry for economic reasons is a familiar form of action in transportation and utility industries. Similar is limitation of licenses for banking institutions on the basis of community need. In 1932, when Oklahoma had sought to restrict entry into the ice business, the Supreme Court held that this was a violation of due process, since the ice business was not "affected with a public interest." ¹⁰ The junking of this concept in 1934 and the expansion of production controls during the past

---

⁷ Held invalid: compulsory arbitration in meat-packing industry, *Wolff Packing Co. v. Industrial Court,* 262 U.S. 522 (1923); limitation of mark-up of theater-ticket agencies, *Tyson v. Banton,* 273 U.S. 418 (1927); regulation of employment-agency charges, *Ribnik v. McBride,* 277 U.S. 350 (1928); setting minimum wages for women, *Adkins v. Children's Hospital,* 261 U.S. 525 (1923).

⁸ See pages 78–79.

⁹ *Nebbia v. New York,* 291 U.S. 502 (1934).

¹⁰ *New State Ice Co. v. Liebmann,* 285 U.S. 262 (1932).

twenty-five years show that the decision on whether to impose production controls in an industry, like that on price control, is one which lies within the discretion of legislatures.

Production controls were established for many industries in NRA codes between 1933 and 1935. Today, except for limitations on entry and expansion in transportation, utility, and banking industries, and the output limitations resulting automatically from the various licensing statutes, the main fields of production control are agriculture and crude oil.

The fifth type of regulatory action is financial control. The financial institutions—banking and insurance—are subjected to rather stringent supervision to insure solvency and to prevent fraud. In addition, financial control has been provided for transportation and utility industries in national legislation and in the legislation of many of the states. Financial supervision in such industries typically extends to security issues and limitation and supervision of intercorporate financial relations.

SUBSTANTIVE TYPES OF PROMOTION

There are six main types of promotion of particular industries which are significant in today's economy. The first is subsidy. Subsidy once took the form of directing the flow of resources to preferred users. Thus, land was granted in large amounts to stimulate the construction of railways so that agriculture, industry, and commerce could expand. It now takes the form of directing the flow of money income to publicly determined purposes. It is, in reality, though perhaps unrealized by most persons, a public decision on budgeting of national income. It is allocation directly in contrast to indirect allocations through regulatory devices such as the setting of minimum prices, limitation of entry, and control of production. The largest subsidies are for agriculture, these now running to several billions of dollars every year. But there are others: for example, to the airline transport industries directly through subsidies to airlines and indirectly through public construction of airports and airway facilities, and to the housing-construction industry through grants for public housing and urban-renewal projects.

A similar method of industry aid is tax exemption or benefit. Tax favoritism is also a form of budgeting of national income to purposes which have obtained a preferred position in the macropolitical contest. The most familiar tax benefit for a particular industry is the depletion allowance on national income-tax payments for various resource industries. On oil it can be as high as 27.5 per cent of gross income. The tariff is a form of tax aid when used for protection and promotion of home industry rather than as a means of raising revenue. States and cities compete with each other in the offering of tax advantages for location of industry in their borders, and some today offer subsidies for the same purpose.

A third form of government promotion is loans to private firms. Loans may be made directly by government or through quasi-public organizations set up for this purpose. Illustrative of the latter is the system of Federal Land Banks set up in 1916 for making loans to farmers. Loans may be accompanied by some subsidy, as when they are made at a lower rate of interest than that paid by the government for its funds. The most extensive system of government credit is that for agriculture, but at one time or another government has made loans for assistance to many of our industries.

A fourth method of industry promotion is insurance. Bank-deposit insurance, instituted in the depression, may be regarded as more protection for the depositor than as promotion for an industry; but it has effect, nevertheless, in promoting bank stability and security. In housing, the elaborate system established by national legislation for socialization of risks has helped the individual obtain low-rate, high-percentage loans, but it has also supported the construction and the home-financing industries.

The fifth method is government contract for construction or production. The immediate objective in such instances may be stimulation and support of industry, as when public works are expanded in depression, or public expenditures are directed toward industry revival in depressed areas. Usually, the industry-promotion objective is subsidiary to other public objectives, such as defense and education, but the promotional effect on industry may be large nevertheless.

A final form of government promotion is research. Lately this author listened to the story of the screw-worm eradication program. Some years back ranchers in Southwest Texas were convinced that the research of Department of Agriculture employees on the sex habits of screw worms indicated that there was a "screw loose" in somebody's head in the department. Today, as a result of that research, the ranchers of Texas have arranged for a factory to produce millions of sterile male screw worms for distribution in the air so that they may mate with females and bring death to the whole screw-worm family. It is estimated that the saving from loss of animals to the cattlemen of the Southwest will be about $100,000,000 per year. This example illustrates the great boon to agriculture and industry in the research program of government, which started for agriculture in the nineteenth century, and has now burgeoned into billions of dollars of expenditure dropping benefits on drug, electronics, and perhaps most other industries.

GENERAL QUALITIES OF GOVERNMENT ACTION

Many industries are now subject to regulation, or regulation and promotion, which is so broad that it may be referred to as comprehensive regulation, or comprehensive regulation and promotion. Comprehensive regulation and promotion may be said to exist when it extends to a wide range of actions or decisions with respect to an industry. When regulation has moved beyond the making of decisions with respect to a few matters to decisions on many matters of conduct, and is continuous rather than occasional or intermittent, it has become comprehensive. Regulation of the medical profession, for example, is not comprehensive, for it includes only initial licensing, judicial rules respecting suits for malpractice, occasional cancellation of a license, and a variety of minor rules—such as those on prescription of narcotics. In contrast, regulation of airlines is comprehensive, for it operates continuously over such matters as safety, amount of service, and rate of charge. In comprehensive regulation two or several of the substantive forms of regulation will normally be employed, and a number of objectives will be sought. In its most complete development, comprehensive regulation stretches beyond specific and limited objectives to the broad and general purpose of maintaining a healthy and publicly responsible industry. This, it will be seen in the next chapter, was the transition made in railroad regulation in the Transportation Act of 1920.

Regulation, and possibly some accompanying promotion, may also acquire the feature of intimacy. By intimacy is meant the penetration of public controls toward the central core of private managerial responsibility. This concept is one relating to depth of regulation. Obviously, regulation which extends to close supervision of the conduct of a licensee, with possibility of alterations of the terms of his license, as in airline regulation, has penetrated more intimately into conduct than regulation that is limited in ordinary cases to the granting of an initial license, as in medicine.

Regulation may be conducted according to strict legal standards. Or it may be carried out by administrators with vast discretion to apply general, perhaps multiple, perhaps even conflicting, guides set in law. The former is legal regulation, the latter discretionary regulation, though any system of regulation is likely to show some measure of both. Similarly, promotional activities may be conducted under strict legal standards, as in tax exemptions or benefits, or with vast discretion in administrators, as in loan operations.[11]

It was once customary to make a distinction between regulation and management. The Supreme Court once said, "It must never be forgotten that while the state may regulate with a view to enforcing reasonable rates and charges, it is not the owner of the property of public utility companies, and it is not clothed with the general power of management incident to ownership." [12] This distinction has quite limited significance in some fields of industry regulation. Public decisions on alteration of terms of licenses, on rates, on consolidations, on contract terms may penetrate deeply toward the heart of management. Moreover, these decisions must be made with an eye on wisdom as well as on law. They must be made in consideration of what

[11] On law and discretion in public administration, see Emmette S. Redford, *Ideal and Practice in Public Administration* (University, Ala.: University of Alabama Press, 1958), Chapter II, and *Administration of National Economic Control* (New York: The Macmillan Company, 1952), Chapter 4.

[12] *State of Missouri ex rel. Southwestern Bell Telephone Co. v. Public Service Commission of Missouri*, 262 U.S. 276, 288 (1923).

will be sound policy for an industry. When regulation, or regulation and promotion, is comprehensive and intimate, the discretionary judgment of the public regulator, if wisely exercised, will be made for the industry on considerations similar to those governing the decision of the corporate executive for his company. There will, of course, be some difference, for the public regulator is under larger constraint from law, and presumably under greater constraint to think in public terms, than is the private administrator. Yet the fact remains that regulation and promotion of an industry may create a public board of directors for an industry which has what two authors have called "policy and managerial" responsibility for the industry.[13]

In conclusion, it can be said that the mixes between regulation and promotion, between public and private responsibility in industries, between legal and discretionary action, will vary in the different systems of industry regulation and promotion. The variations, along with the patterns and problems of control and service for the separate industries, will be revealed in the chapters which follow.

[13] Frederick F. Blachly and Miriam E. Oatman, *Federal Regulatory Action and Control* (Washington, D.C.: Brookings Institution, 1940). See their discussion at pages 18–25.

Chapter 17. Railroad Regulation

RAILWAY REGULATION appropriately comes first in the discussion of regulation of particular industries, for not only has it been the field of regulation of longest experience in this country, except for banking regulation, but its historical development had great influence in development of patterns of regulation of American industries. This is true of two features of railroad regulation. The first is that of administrative methods, for it was in railroad regulation, to a considerable extent, that the organization and operating techniques used in regulation of particular industries had their origins. The second is that of policy, including rates, services, finance, and industry integration. The statutory terms, administrative methods, and judicial decisions in railroad regulation have helped shape the mold of regulation for transportation and other utilities. Those who frame regulatory statutes today usually borrow heavily, consciously or unconsciously, from the experience of the nation in regulating railroads. This chapter emphasizes, therefore, the evolution of the pattern of railroad regulation.

BACKGROUND OF INTERSTATE COMMERCE ACT

STAGES IN PUBLIC POLICY. Public policy on railways moved quickly in the nineteenth century into new stages: from state ownership in some states to private ownership; from encouragement through subsidy to hostility reflected in new measures of control; from legislative to administrative control; from state to national regulation.

In addition to the slight controls by the judiciary over the railroads as common carriers, initial public control was attempted through charter provisions. As abuses in obtaining special charter privileges from legislatures were revealed, the legislatures passed general laws governing incorporation which contained much detail on the rights and obligations of railways. The inadequacy of these methods led quickly to the establishment of commissions which served as agents of the legislature in gathering facts and in performance of administrative tasks, such as safety inspection and supervision of the carrying out of charter provisions. But though such temporary or permanent commissions were established between 1832 and the Civil War, the modern commission movement really began after the Civil War. Postwar agricultural discontent with railway rate discriminations and rate levels led to the Granger movement, which had the objective of correcting the existing railroad abuses. As a result, commissions of two types were established. One was the advisory type, of which the Massachusetts commission created in 1869 was the model. This type of commission could investigate and report, but its determinations on rates were recommendatory only, and depended for their acceptance by the railroads on publicity and the pressure of public opinion. The second type was the "strong" or "Western" type of commission, which had authority to set rates. Illinois created the first such commission in 1871, and its action was followed quickly in a number of other states.[1]

The Granger legislation was promptly given a clean bill of health by the Supreme Court of the United States. In 1876 it upheld the power of the state to regulate rates, and even held that a state could, in the absence of legislation by Congress, prescribe the maximum charges for transportation of persons and property into the state from outside, or from the state to points outside.[2] In 1886, however, the Court, in the famous Wabash decision, reversed the part of the decision relating to state regulation of interstate commerce, holding that interstate rates must be subject to uniform national regulation.[3]

There had long been discussion of railroad legislation in Congress, and in 1886 the Cullom Committee of the Senate reported a long list of abuses in the railroad industry. The decision in the Wabash case made national regulation imperative, and the Interstate Commerce Act of 1887 followed quickly.

ECONOMIC FACTORS. The railroad industry is one with high capital investment with relation to gross annual income. It is, therefore, an industry with high constant cost—that is, costs which remain the same irrespective of the volume of traffic moved. The result is a strong effort to obtain a high volume of traffic over which the constant costs can be apportioned. If facilities are unused, the natural tendency is to reach for all traffic which will cover variable costs and an appreciable portion of the fixed constant cost. To obtain such traffic, managers may resort to competitive rate cutting. This may bring loss of earnings, perhaps even threat of bankruptcy, for concerns in the industry, and can also lead to poor service to the public. Where the number of concerns is small, there is a strong tendency for them to avoid these unsavory results by combined action.

This was, indeed, the course of events in the 1870's and 1880's. The railway network had been expanded rapidly into new and partially developed areas. Cutthroat competition for traffic was followed by arrangements to pool traffic or earnings and, when this practice was prohibited in 1887, by formation of rate-fixing associations.

---

[1] For fuller summary of the development of regulation in the states, see Robert E. Cushman, *The Independent Regulatory Commissions* (New York: Oxford University Press, 1941), pp. 19–41, and the Cullom Committee Report, Senate Report No. 46, 49th Cong., 1st Sess. (January 18, 1886).
[2] *Peik v. Chicago & N.W.R. Co.*, 94 U.S. 164 (1876).
[3] *Wabash, St. L. & P.R. Co. v. Illinois*, 118 U.S. 557 (1886).

The undesirable results were accentuated by the unevenness of competition. There was actual monopoly of rail transportation for a large proportion of intercommunity connections. Rate cutting occurred only where there was water or rail competition, and hence some localities were favored over others. The struggle for traffic also led to discrimination among particular shippers, for railroads sought by rate reductions to entice shipments from large shippers.

The Granger movement was motivated mainly by a belief that rates were excessive. Intensive competition among the railroads soon led to reduction in rates, but the evils of discrimination in rates and the threat to the public interest in railway agreements remained unabated. It is not surprising, therefore, that the first national regulatory act was aimed at a fair level of rates, elimination of discrimination, and the prevention of existing methods of combination.

THE INTERSTATE COMMERCE ACT OF 1887[4]

THE STATUTORY BEGINNINGS. The act of 1887 applied to rail transportation, or joint rail-water transportation under the same management or control. It brought under regulation these forms of transportation in interstate and foreign commerce. It contained provisions on rates, on pooling, and on methods of administration.

On rates, the act did three important things. First, it set the general standard that all rates should be just and reasonable. Second, it prohibited various forms of discrimination. It prohibited personal discriminations—that is, special rates and rebates for particular persons. It forbade also the giving of any undue or unreasonable preference or advantage to any person, concern, locality, or type of traffic. A so-called long-and-short-haul provision (Section 4) struck at the discrimination involved in charging more from Jonestown to Smithstown than from Jonestown to Williamsburg when Smithstown was between the two. It made it unlawful to charge "greater compensation in the aggregate for the transportation of passengers or of like kind of property, under substantially similar circumstances and conditions, for a shorter than for a longer distance over the same line, in the same direction, the shorter being included within the longer distance." Relief from this provision could be granted by the commission established by the act. Third, the act prescribed publicity of rates. It required carriers to print and post rate schedules and to file these with the commission. Advances in rates could be made only after ten days' notice. An amendment in 1889 required three days' notice before rate reductions.

The anti-pooling provision of the act was included as another means of preventing unjust rates, though it reflected also the policy of enforced

[4] 24 Stat. 379.

competition which Congress was shortly to adopt for all foreign and interstate commerce in the Sherman Antitrust Act. It prohibited the pooling either of freight or of earnings.

For administration, the act provided for the first federal regulatory commission, the Interstate Commerce Commission. It was to be composed of five members—no more than three from one party—appointed by the President with the advice and consent of the Senate, serving overlapping terms of six years, and removable by the President only "for inefficiency, neglect of duty, or malfeasance in office." The commission could hear complaints, investigate upon its own motion, require production of papers and testimony of witnesses, make findings and reports and issue orders, and appeal to circuit courts if carriers failed to comply with its orders or requirements.

WEAKNESSES IN REGULATION. This first national regulatory measure for railroads proved to be inadequate, due in part to weaknesses in the act and in part to narrow construction of its provisions by the courts. First, the act itself provided no penalties for violation of a rate order of the commission. If a carrier failed to obey an order, the burden was on the commission to go to a circuit court for enforcement. The average length of time required for final court disposal of appeals was about four years.[5] Second, reduction of rates below those published were not punished, except possibly by a nominal fine, if there was no discrimination among shippers. The act failed, therefore, to relieve the pressure on railroads to make quick, general rate reductions in order to obtain competitive business.[6] Revenues so lost could, of course, be compensated for only by higher rates on other transportation. Third, the courts held that the power exercised by the commission, for the first ten years of its existence, to set future maximum rates to correct abuses was not granted by the act.[7] This meant that the commission's rate-making power was limited to decision on the legality of existing or past charges. It could not, when it found existing rates to be in violation of the act, set the rates for the future. Fourth, the courts allowed new evidence to be introduced in the trial of cases on appeal. The effects were summarized by the Interstate Commerce Commission: "The same case is not tried before the court which is tried before the Commission. The trial before the Commission, therefore, with all its attendant expense and consumption of time, goes practically for nothing. . . . A procedure like the present one tends to bring the body into disrepute and is grossly unfair to it and to the complainants who appear before it."[8] Fifth, the commission's interpretation of the long-and-short-haul provision was overruled by the courts. The commission allowed relief from the provision whenever the railroad had to meet water competition for the long haul, because it could do nothing to

---

[5] Interstate Commerce Commission, *Annual Report*, 1897, p. 32.
[6] See *Annual Report*, 1901, p. 8.
[7] *Cin., N.O. & Tex. Pac. Ry. v. I.C.C.* (Social Circle Case), 162 U.S. 184 (1896); *I.C.C. v. Cin. N.O. & Tex. Pac. Ry. Co.*, 167 U.S. 479 (1897).
[8] *Annual Report*, 1897, pp. 31–32.

correct this situation (having no jurisdiction over water transportation). However, it refused to grant relief in cases of competition on the long haul from other railroads, viewing its power over these rates as a sufficient corrective. In 1897 the Supreme Court ruled that such rail competition could create dissimilar conditions and hence justify departure from the rule in Section 4.[9] Not only did this weaken the rule, but it increased the load of work on the I.C.C., which now had to pass on a much larger number of petitions for relief.[10]

In addition to these deficiencies, there was question as to the wisdom of an outright prohibition of pooling. The commission recognized that some kind of joint arrangements were necessary in regard to traffic handled jointly by two or more railroads, and hence questioned the wisdom of the antipooling provision. It suggested at an early date that Congress consider authorization of pooling subject to approval and regulation by the commission.[11] Furthermore, the act of 1887 provided for only one-handed regulation. It allowed rate regulation, albeit weakly, but it did not provide for regulation of service or of finance.

THE STRENGTHENING OF RATE REGULATION

The pooling provision was not changed prior to a broad revision of railway policy in 1920. The weaknesses in the rate provisions of the act were corrected in acts passed in 1903, 1906, and 1910, and by a more favorable judicial attitude.[12]

THE ELKINS ACT OF 1903.[13] The Elkins Act corrected the second weakness in rate making listed above. It made the published rate the standard of lawfulness. Any charge different from a published rate was a violation of the act, for which criminal penalties could be imposed.

The railroads themselves desired the enactment of this legislation, for it protected them from pressures from large shippers for general rate reductions for their immediate benefit.

THE HEPBURN ACT OF 1906.[14] The Hepburn Act marked the beginning of a second stage in national regulation of railroads. It laid the

[9] *I.C.C. v. Alabama Midland Ry. Co.*, 168 U.S. 144 (1897).
[10] For summary of the judicial interpretation of the act of 1887, see Carl McFarland, *Judicial Control of the Federal Trade Commission and the Interstate Commerce Commission* (Cambridge, Mass.: Harvard University Press, 1933), pp. 102–114.
[11] See particularly *Annual Report*, 1893, p. 9; 1894, p. 63; 1897, p. 49.
[12] Also significant was the Expediting Act of 1903 (32 Stat. 823), which empowered the Attorney General to request expedition in the courts of ICC cases of "general public importance," and the Compulsory Testimony Act of 1893 (27 Stat. 443) which remedied the unconstitutional effect of original sections of the act of 1887 providing for compulsory testimony.
[13] 32 Stat. 847.
[14] 34 Stat. 584.

basis for strong administrative regulation. In contrast to the Elkins Act, it was vigorously fought by the railroads.

The act extended the jurisdiction of the commission to (1) express companies, sleeping-car companies, and oil pipelines, and (2) such facilities of rail transportation as switches, spurs, tracks, terminals, freight depots, yards and grounds, cars, and such services in connection with transportation as refrigeration and storage. It struck at the evil of granting passes by prohibiting them, with certain exceptions. It strengthened the publicity provisions by changing the period of notice required to change rates from ten to thirty days, except where departures were authorized by the commission.

But the main changes were the following two—one substantive and the other a set of means for implementing the substantive provisions of the regulatory act. First, the commission was given the authority to prescribe maximum future rates. This included the authority to set joint rates (for hauls by more than one railroad) and to determine the apportionment of such rates among railroads handling the traffic. Second, the decisions of the commission became authoritative decisions; that is, violation of valid administrative orders subjected the roads to penalty. Stated differently, administrative orders had legal force and effect unless set aside by a reviewing court. The Hepburn Act provided:

All orders of the Commission, except orders for the payment of money [reparation orders], shall take effect within such reasonable time, not less than thirty days, and shall continue in force for such period of time, not exceeding two years, as shall be prescribed by order of the Commission, unless the same shall be suspended or modified or set aside by the Commission or be suspended or set aside by a court of competent jurisdiction.

Penalties provided by the act applied from the date of effectiveness of an order. Except for reparation orders (for repayment of excess charges in the past), the appropriate court, upon petition of the commission or the Attorney General, was to enforce such order if "regularly made and duly served." Moreover, injunctions could not be issued suspending or restraining the effect of an order except upon notice to the commission and decision, after hearing, by a three-judge court.

These changes altered significantly the nature of the regulatory system. Real power of a legislative nature (setting rates for the future), which the courts had been reluctant to recognize in the act of 1887,[15] was now unmistakably granted to the commission in the provision authorizing the setting of future maximum rates.[16] And a system of authoritative administrative control was initiated by the provisions which made the commission's orders effective.

[15] See the reasoning in the Maximum Freight Rate case, 167 U.S. 479, 506–511.
[16] "The establishment of a rate is the making of a rule for the future, and therefore is an act legislative, not judicial, in kind. . . ." *Prentis v. Atlantic Coast Line Co.*, 211 U.S. 210, 226 (1908).

The courts responded quickly and sympathetically to the new declarations of purpose of Congress.[17] First, it was held by the Supreme Court—in apparent contradiction of certain provisions of the act, but in line with the broad purpose of Congress to strengthen the system of administrative control [18]—that exclusive original jurisdiction (sometimes called the doctrine of primary jurisdiction) rested with the Interstate Commerce Commission.[19] This doctrine, though not applied in all types of cases, means, when applied, that parties cannot go to the courts instead of the commission for initial determination of the reasonableness of rates. The commission must make the first decision. Second, the courts on appeal decided the cases on the record made before the commission (that is, new evidence was not allowed at the court stage), and upheld the commission if its decision was based on substantial evidence.

THE MANN-ELKINS ACT OF 1910.[20] Two changes of significance were made in rate provisions of the Interstate Commerce Act in 1910. First, the Mann-Elkins Act flatly prohibited carriers to charge more in the aggregate for a short haul than for a long haul, the former being within the latter, unless commission consent was given. The commission itself could determine whether there were competitive conditions to justify the price differences. Second, this act gave the commission the authority to suspend changes in rates, pending its investigation of their reasonableness. It could suspend increases for four months and, if more time for investigation were needed, for an additional six months. The power to suspend rates resulted from a choice of Congress on the degree of public control over rates. Some had desired that the commission pass on all rates. The commission itself recommended in 1916 that it pass on all changes, and for a brief time after 1917 this was the requirement of law.[21] But the decision in 1910 was for a more moderate type of control—one that placed less burden on the commission and allowed changes in rates upon the initiative of railway management without delays which might be caused by administrative bottlenecks. The power given to the commission is, in effect, one of roving intervention and veto: all proposed changes are filed with it; those which, upon preliminary study, appear to raise questions needing further study are suspended; and these can then be studied further and set for hearing if veto of the changes is to be seriously considered.

The effect of the Acts of 1903, 1906, and 1910 was to establish extensive and authoritative control over rates, including the following:

[17] See Carl McFarland, *Judicial Control of the Federal Trade Commission and the Interstate Commerce Commission, 1920–1930* (Cambridge, Mass.: Harvard University Press, 1933), pp. 114–125.
[18] See I. L. Sharfman, *The Interstate Commerce Commission* (New York: Commonwealth Fund, 1931–1937), II, pp. 393ff.
[19] *Texas & Pac. Ry. v. Abilene Cotton Oil Co.*, 204 U.S. 426 (1907).
[20] 36 Stat. 539.
[21] See Sharfman, *op. cit.*, I, p. 59n.

1. The railroads were required to publish rates and file these with the ICC, and could make changes only after thirty days' notice.

2. The commission could set future maximum rates, hear cases on award of damages for excess charges in the past (reparation cases), suspend proposed changes in rates pending investigation, act upon complaint or upon its own initiative, and issue orders which became effective unless set aside by a court.

COMPREHENSIVE REGULATION: THE TRANSPORTATION ACT OF 1920

New Conditions and New Purpose.

By 1920 great changes had occurred in the conditions affecting railroads. The enlarged transportation requirements resulting from United States participation in World War I called for arrangements for coordination in the use of all cars, tracks, and other railroad facilities, and this end was finally achieved through government operation with a standard return guaranteed to the railroads. In meeting war needs the condition of railway properties was severely depleted. Consequently, at the end of the war the railroads were in need of substantial investment to restore and improve the condition of properties, so that satisfactory service could be provided to the nation; this investment could only be made if railroad credit could be rehabilitated, and this in turn required the prospect of reasonable earnings.

Under these conditions a tremendous shift in public policy was made in the Transportation Act of 1920. Theretofore, the objectives in railroad regulation had been primarily negative; the aim of Congress had been to prevent abuses, particularly discriminatory and excessive rates. Though the positive power to fix maximum future rates was granted to the commission in 1906, the underlying purpose was still the correction or prevention of abuses. In essence, the Interstate Commerce Commission was conceived to be a guardian of public interests against the excesses of private railroad interests. In 1920 the objectives became positive. Congress imposed upon the commission the affirmative duty of maintaining adequate railway service for the nation. To attain this end the commission's regulatory power was extended beyond rate regulation to organization, service, and finance—indeed, to almost every important aspect of railway management except labor relations.[22] Rate regulation was now a part of a larger regulatory pattern, in which the primary objective was to insure a healthy industry. Under the new concept of purpose the commission's relationship to the industry changed from one of presumed antagonism to one of guardianship. The purpose of guardianship was to build a sound industry capable of rendering good service to the public.

[22] Provisions on labor were included in the act, but were not administered by the ICC. For discussion on railway labor, see page 300.

RATES. Two modifications in old rate-making powers were made in the act. First, the maximum period of suspension of rates by the commission was reduced from ten to five months.[23] This was thought to be fairer to the railroads, and at the same time the shipper was deemed to be adequately protected by the provision in combination with his right to sue for reparation for excess past charges. Second, the commission's discretion in long-short-haul cases was reduced in several ways.

Two new provisions were related to the objective of insuring adequate revenues so that the railroads could attract new capital and provide good service. The first authorized the commission to set minimum rates. It would thus be able to prevent the loss of revenues from competitive rate cutting. Protection against competitive rate cutting had been sought before 1920 in the provision that railroads could not change rates without thirty days' notice; now the power of the commission could back up the resistance of the roads to pressures for rate cutting. This new authority gave the commission power similar to that usually given in present-day statutes to agencies regulating utility rates, which customarily now have power to prescribe "maximum and/or minimum" rates.

The other change initiated a new experiment in rate regulation. It prescribed a so-called rule for rate making. Theretofore the commission had been guided by such general standards as "fair" or "reasonable." The new statute contained a rule which seemed to provide a quantitative or mathematical formula. Its basic aim was to provide for an adequate return so that railroad credit could be rehabilitated. The commission was to set rates so that

> carriers as a whole (or as a whole in each of such rate groups or territories as the Commission may from time to time designate) will, under honest, efficient, and economical management and reasonable expenditures for maintenance of way, structures and equipment, earn an aggregate annual net railway operating income equal, as nearly as may be, to a fair return upon the aggregate value of the railway property of such carriers held for and used in the service of transportation.

If allowance is made for the qualification "as nearly as may be," and for commission discretion on rate groups, economical management, and reasonable railroad expenditures, it can be seen that this statutory provision provides the basic standard of "annual . . . fair return upon the aggregate value."

RECAPTURE CLAUSE. An integral part of the new rate policy was the "recapture clause" of the Transportation Act. It was part of the attempt to deal with the coexistence of weak and of strong railroads. The act stated that uniform rates for competitive carriers which would sustain all the indispensable carriers would enable some to receive an income in excess of a fair return upon the value of their property. It provided, therefore, that any carrier which received in any year a net railway operating income in

---

[23] The period is seven months, at the time of this writing.

excess of 6 per cent of the value of its railway property should (1) place one-half of the excess in a reserve fund, which could be drawn upon for dividends and other purposes in years when it made less than 6 per cent, and could only be used freely by the railroad when the fund reached 5 per cent of the value of its railway properties, and (2) surrender the other one-half into a general railroad contingent fund, from which the commission could make loans to railroads for stated purposes, or could purchase equipment and facilities for lease to railroads.[24]

COOPERATION AND CONSOLIDATION. Prior to 1920 the national policy of enforced competition was applicable to the railroad industry in the same way that it was to other industries. Popular indignation over pooling led to its prohibition in 1887. The Sherman Antitrust Act was held applicable to railroads in 1897.[25] In that year rate agreements were held illegal, and in 1904 the elimination of competition between two parallel railroads by the device of a holding company was held illegal.[26] The Sherman Act was applied against railroads in many cases in the succeeding years, and is still applicable to them. Section 7 of the Clayton Act applies to railroads, and the same act required competitive bidding in railroad dealings relative to securities, supplies, and construction where more than $50,000 was involved and where the railroad and the supplier had interlocking officials.

Yet the policy of enforced competition was criticized from the beginning. Senate acceptance of the prohibition on pooling was a compromise by which the Senate got a commission, and the House the prohibition on pooling.[27] Only a few years after its creation the ICC recommended allowance of pooling under the commission's supervision.[28] Four justices of the Supreme Court thought, in 1897, that rate agreements were not unreasonable restraints of trade.[29] President Roosevelt, in 1906 and 1907, recommended authorization of agreements among railroads with approval of the ICC.[30]

The Transportation Act of 1920 adopted a new policy, allowed today for many regulated industries, of cooperation and combination subject to administrative supervision. Practically all forms of combination and cooperation, except rate agreements, were allowed. Competition was not forsaken, but it was qualified by the new policy of regulated cooperation and consolidation.

The act, first, allowed pooling if approved by the ICC. Second, it allowed acquisition of control by one carrier of another through lease, stock purchase, or any other method not involving consolidation into a single system,

[24] Constitutionality of the recapture provisions was upheld by the Supreme Court in *Dayton-Goose Creek Ry. v. U.S.*, 263 U.S. 456 (1924).
[25] *U.S. v. Trans-Missouri Freight Ass'n.*, 166 U.S. 290.
[26] *Northern Securities Co. v. U.S.*, 193 U.S. 197.
[27] Robert E. Cushman, *The Independent Regulatory Commissions* (New York: Oxford University Press, 1941), p. 44.
[28] Note 11, supra.
[29] *U.S. v. Trans-Missouri Freight Ass'n.*, 166 U.S. 290, 343–374.
[30] *Congressional Record*, **XLI**, p. 27; **XLII**, p. 69.

if approved by the commission. Third, the commission was directed to "prepare and adopt" a plan for consolidation of railway properties into a limited number of systems. This would be the long-run solution to the weak-strong railroad problem, just as the recapture provision was the short-run solution. The plan was to preserve competition as fully as possible, and was to produce systems which would "so far as practicable" have equal costs. Railroads could voluntarily, subject to approval of the commission, consolidate properties in accordance with the consolidation plan. Finally, no one could serve as an officer or director of more than one railroad without approval of the ICC; and since officers and directors were prohibited from profiting from such things as sale of securities, representatives of banking houses were excluded from railroad directorships unless they acted solely as representatives of stockholders.[31]

SECURITIES. Presidents Roosevelt and Wilson had both recommended regulation of financial transactions of railroads. Finally, in the Transportation Act, railroads were prohibited from issuing securities (except short-term notes within prescribed limits) or assuming financial obligations without approval of the ICC. The state governments, some of which had regulated railroad security issues, were to be notified by the ICC of pending applications. Financial regulation was necessary to prevent financial scandals and dissipation of railroad credit, and hence to promote the policy of rehabilitating railroad credit and maintaining a sound railway system.

SERVICE. The Transportation Act also extended the commission's power in the field of railroad service. First, whereas an earlier act (The Esch Car Service Act of 1917 [32]) had given the commission some power over "car service," strictly defined, the act of 1920 defined "car service" to include all the rolling stock—locomotives, cars, etc.—of railroads. It was made the duty of the railroads to supply adequate car service and to establish reasonable rules with respect thereto. The commission could require carriers to file car-service rules with it, and could itself, after hearing, on complaint or its own initiative, make car-service rules. Second, the commission was granted power to require common use of terminals and appurtenant trackage, subject to the condition that the ability of a carrier to handle its own business would not be impaired. Third, the commission could, in an emergency, exercise controls over car service and terminals without hearing. It could, in other words, act summarily. Through these controls, coordinated use of the railway facilities, which in World War I required government management, might be achieved by private management under commission regulation. Fourth, no railroad could extend a line, or construct a new line, or abandon all or any part of a line, or operation thereof, without a certificate of public convenience and necessity from the commission.

SAFETY. The accretion of legislation on safety has not been sum-

---

[31] See Sharfman, *op. cit.*, **I**, p. 195.
[32] 40 Stat. 101.

marized in this discussion. It should be noted at this point, however, that the ICC had accumulated powers over safety, primarily powers of inspection; and that the act of 1920 extended these powers to the prevention of railway accidents by prescription of requirements for installation of automatic train-stop, train-control, or other safety devices.[33]

CONCLUSIONS. The almost exclusive preoccupation with rates, except for safety, in the regulatory pattern prior to 1920 would not, it may be assumed, have continued even if the conditions in railway transportation had been different after World War I. Modern industry regulation normally does not stop with rate regulation. In industries most similar to railroads—namely, the utilities and other transportation industries—regulation has extended to such matters as entry, finance, and consolidation. There had, in fact, been proposals prior to World War I for extending railroad regulation, particularly to finance and joint action by railroad managers. Yet it was the immediate plight of the railroads, and the new purpose of insuring a healthy railroad transportation system, which moved the Congress in 1920 to a broader system of railway regulation. Regulation became comprehensive. In fact, there is in this country no system of regulation more comprehensive than that which has existed for railroads since 1920.

REGULATORY LEGISLATION SINCE 1920

Three things have led to changes in legislative policy since 1920. Some features of the pattern of 1920 proved to be unworkable, and were abandoned. New conditions, particularly the rise of competing forms of transportation, brought new problems. And sectional and group pressures have been exerted toward certain changes. Nevertheless, the modifications in the pattern of regulation of 1920 have been piecemeal and amendatory, and have not altered much of the basic framework of comprehensive regulation established at that time. The modifications have been made in a number of acts, but many of them were included in the miscellaneous provisions of the Emergency Railroad Transportation Act of 1933 and the Transportation Act of 1940.

RULE FOR RATE MAKING. The effort to provide for quantitative rate making under the rule of "annual . . . fair return upon the aggregate value" in the Transportation Act of 1920 had failed, mainly for two reasons. First, the statute contained no guide for determining "aggregate value." By the Valuation Act of 1913, the Interstate Commerce Commission had been directed to obtain data on the value of the railroads. It had been told to get various kinds of data. Thus, it was told to get for "each piece of property, other than land," such things as the original cost, the cost of reproduction new, the cost of reproduction less depreciation. It was told to get other

---

[33] On safety legislation, see Sharfman, *op. cit.*, **I**, Ch. 6 (1931).

information, relating to the value of land—both original cost and present value, to the corporate history and financial structure (stocks, bonds, etc.), and other matters. But it was not told how to put these separate items of information together into a statement of "aggregate value." From what columns of figures—original cost, reproduction cost, reproduction cost less depreciation—would the commission add? Or how would it make compromises between the several columns? Or what weight would it give to the value of stocks and bonds outstanding? On these and other questions there was no statutory guide for the commission. It made an effort to get a single-sum statement of value for a short railroad, but the Supreme Court of the United States decided that it had erred in failing to give attention to the reproduction-cost item.[34]

Second, the 1920 rule for rate making failed because it was not always possible to raise earnings by raising rates. The ICC stated the purpose of the rule as follows: "Both the present rate-making rule and the recapture provisions were founded upon the theory that the rates charged by the railroads could be so adjusted—moved up and down from time to time—as to maintain a comparatively stable level of aggregate earnings." [35] The commission noted that this would require lowering rates in prosperity and raising them in depression. The latter could have the effect of decreasing the amount of goods hauled, and thus defeat its purpose. The commission found it necessary to consider the effect of rates on traffic in determining whether to raise rates. This led to recommendations on its part for a new guide for rate making.[36]

A new guide was adopted by Congress in the Emergency Transportation Act of 1933. The guide read as follows:

> In the exercise of its power to prescribe just and reasonable rates the Commission shall give due consideration, among other factors, to the effect of rates on the movement of traffic; to the need, in the public interest, of adequate and efficient railway transportation service at the lowest cost consistent with the furnishing of such service; and to the need of revenues sufficient to enable the carriers, under honest, economical, and efficient management, to provide such service.[37]

This guide, in effect, says to the ICC that it shall consider the need for low rates that will not drive away traffic, and of high rates that will provide sufficient revenue to enable the carriers to provide good service. This means that the ICC must make a judgment based upon opposed factors. The judgment is based upon factors which an intelligent railroad executive would consider —though it should be possible to assume that the regulatory commission would give somewhat more attention than the railroad executive to the lowest level of rates which would be necessary to bring in the needed revenue.

---

[34] *St. Louis & O'Fallon R. Co. v. U.S.,* 279 U.S. 461 (1929).
[35] *Annual Report,* 1932, p. 16.
[36] *Annual Report* for 1930, p. 96; for 1931, pp. 107–110, 347–367; for 1932, pp. 16–18.
[37] 48 Stat. 211, 220.

384 *Regulation and Promotion of Industries*

The new guide asks for an informed business judgment, not for application of a quantitative formula. It recognizes that rate making in the complex railway transportation system must be a judgment of men, rather than the mere application of rule.

RECAPTURE CLAUSE. The commission also recommended the repeal of the recapture provisions. It noted the practical difficulties in collecting the money and the fact that even if collected, the funds would be no answer to the strong-weak railroad problem.[38] Taking profits from the strong and loaning the money to the weak would not produce systems of equal competitive strength. With the change in the rule for rate making, any logic behind the provisions for recapture collapsed. The provisions were repealed in the act of 1933.

CONSOLIDATION OF RAILWAY PROPERTIES. The revision of the rule for rate making and the repeal of the recapture provision marked the failure of one kind of overall planning for the railroad industry. The 1920 scheme for safeguarding the returns of railroads in good and bad times by rate adjustments, and for balancing the return of strong and weak systems by recapture and reassignment of earnings, failed because it was unrealistic. An industry's need for money cannot be met merely by adjusting its prices, and the imbalance in earning power among its companies cannot be corrected merely by taking the returns of the strong and loaning them to the weak. Yet this latter was not really expected. It was a palliative, and it was hoped that for the long run the imbalance in strength of the companies would be corrected by the second kind of industry planning provided for in the Transportation Act of 1920. What was the history of this second kind of planning, and why did it fail?

The history can be recorded quite briefly. Directed by the act to develop a consolidation plan, the commission promptly employed Professor William Z. Ripley, a recognized transportation authority, to develop a consolidation plan; and it issued in 1921 a tentative plan. After extensive hearings and much delay, the commission finally issued its plan for nineteen railway systems in 1929. In the meantime, however, the commission's majority had lost faith in the wisdom and practicality of a consolidation plan, and had recommended to Congress repeatedly that the directive to it to develop a plan be repealed. Instead, Congress sought to give the consolidation plan a more important place in railway integration. Whereas the Transportation Act of 1920 had allowed stock purchases and leases to be consummated without concordance with the consolidation plan, Congress provided in the emergency legislation of 1933 that all forms of railway integration were to be subject to the requirement of conformity with the consolidation plan. This capstone on the edifice of 1920 had no real effect; and in the Trans-

---

[38] See especially, *Annual Report*, 1931, pp. 107–110 and Appendix G, and *Annual Report*, 1932, pp. 16–18.

portation Act of 1940, Congress repealed the provisions for a consolidation plan and left the roads free to adopt any methods of combination, subject only to the approval of the commission.

The reasons for the failure of the plan for planning are, in part at least, easily discernible. Overall planning, and action in accord therewith, is alien to the methods of the ICC. It is fixed firmly in a tradition of case-to-case decision characteristic of a quasi-judicial tribunal. It found that the task put upon it of developing a plan was hard, it saw the practical difficulties in the way of realization of benefits from such a plan, and hence it went unenthusiastically through merely formal compliance with its responsibility. The practical difficulties created serious obstacles. At the heart of these was the understandable objection of strong railroads to taking on weak systems, which would be one of the needs if the design for systems of equal competitive strength was to be consummated. There was some sentiment in Congress for a compulsory plan, but it is obvious that this would raise issues of property rights. Unification by this route may be feasible only under government ownership. There were many miscellaneous obstacles: lack of interest among railroad managers, opposition of labor and of local interests, difficulties of completing negotiations among the systems, certain impediments in the law.

In 1933 Congress enacted additional legislation for railroad coordination. The railroads were in serious financial condition. The growth of water and motor transportation in the years following World War I had produced an excess of transportation facilities. The decline of shipping during the depression had accentuated the difficulties arising from the surplus. A severe decline of railroad earnings led to a series of studies and recommendations for action. The outcome was the passage of the Emergency Railroad Transportation Act of 1933. It created a Federal Coordinator of Transportation, a position held by the universally respected member of the ICC, Joseph B. Eastman. The purpose of the act was to achieve economies, financial reorganization, and study of means of improving transportation regulation The provisions were to be effective for one year only, but were kept alive by subsequent legislation until 1936.

The results under the act were disappointing. It contained limitations on the coordinator, particularly an interdiction against actions which would have the effect of reducing employment, except such as resulted from attrition. The coordinator sought to attain the objectives of the act through consultation, committees, and voluntary cooperation of the interested groups. He met intransigence in railroad management, and antagonism from labor. Although he possessed the power to issue orders, the power was virtually unexercised. Whether a bolder assault upon the problems by an administrator who was willing to exercise power and garner political support would have produced substantially greater results in the setting of conflicting

386 *Regulation and Promotion of Industries*

interests and antagonisms remains, as the leading commentator has said, "history in the conditional mood." [39]

To some persons, the foregoing history may indicate inability of government to develop and execute plans for the reorganization of an industry. To others it may only be a revelation of problems which are still to be confronted. Railroad merger is again a problem of public policy. The objective of mergers would be to effect economies and to strengthen the railroads for performance of that part of the transportation function for which they have inherent advantages. Some experts believe that a quick step-up in mergers is essential for survival of the railway transportation needed for commerce, the postal system, and the defense of the nation. This may require facilitation through a variety of means: financial support through government loans and guarantees, ease in abandonment of trackage and facilities, speed-up of consideration of merger cases. Moreover, the old issue of consolidation piecemeal or according to plan may be urgent. Can a piecemeal approach meet the needs, unless there is some guiding pattern for regional and national consolidation? Can such a pattern be developed under a system of regulation of private enterprise? What kind of combination of public and private contribution to the objective should be sought? Should the roads be given the duty to develop regional plans for approval by the commission? If so, should public goals be set for such industry planning? What policies should prevail with respect to displacement of labor? Can private and public initiative really be generated for prompt adjustment of a declining industry to the new dimensions required of it? [40]

RAILROAD HOLDING COMPANIES. The regulatory act applied to "carriers," which was held not to include companies owning stock in, but not operating, railroads. This left a loophole in regulation, particularly since the holding company could be a device for uniting railroads and a means of manipulation of their financial assets. The Emergency Railroad Transportation Act brought holding companies under the relevant provisions of the Interstate Commerce Act. They were subjected to the provisions concerning reports, accounting, and securities. Also, the provisions concerning consolidations of railroads were made applicable to holding companies.

REGIONAL DISCRIMINATIONS. For many years there was a rising crescendo of complaint from the South and the West that railroad rates favored the northeastern portion ("Official" Territory) of the country, and that this had the effect of encouraging location of industry in that section and discouraging its location in other sections. The mounting criticism of this situation brought a commission investigation of regional rate relationships. Ultimately, an order was issued by the commission for an increase in

---

[39] Earl Latham tells the story in *The Politics of Railroad Coordination, 1933–1936* (Cambridge, Mass.: Harvard University Press, 1959), quotation from p. 271.

[40] For further discussion of railroad consolidation, see *National Transportation Policy*, Report of the Committee on Commerce, U.S. Senate, by its Special Study Group on Transportation Policies in the United States. 87th Cong., 1st Sess., 1961.

rates in Official Territory by 10 per cent, and an equal percentage decrease in all other parts of the country, except "Mountain-Pacific Territory," and between these points of the country and Official Territory.[41] In the meantime, the Transportation Act of 1940 had amended the antidiscrimination provisions of the Interstate Commerce Act to include the words "region," "district," and "territory," thus assuring the ICC of power to remove regional discriminations.

RATE AGREEMENTS. It will be recalled that the reversal of policy on cooperation among carriers in the Transportation Act of 1920 did not extend to rate agreements. These remained under the interdiction of the Sherman Antitrust Act. Yet rate agreements were made, in effect, through the activities of the rate bureaus, which had been organized by the carriers. New rates were ordinarily not fixed by the carriers individually, but by bureaus after an elaborate procedural process. Both the state of Georgia, under the leadership of Governor Arnall, and the Department of Justice attacked the legality of the activities of rate bureaus in court suits. The railroads and the ICC argued that the activities of the rate bureaus were reasonable and indeed necessary, at least with relation to the setting of rates for joint hauls. The battle lines were drawn in a fierce struggle between two departments of the national government and between the two sets of interests—the railroads and those favorable to the Georgia and Department of Justice suits.

The railroads and the ICC won. The Reed-Bulwinkle Act[42] exempts agreements concerning rates, classifications, division of rates, and similar matters, from the antitrust laws, if in conformity with the ICC's approval. A number of provisions in the act were aimed toward protection of the shipper and any railroad desiring to act independently: (1) ICC approval could be given only after hearing, and it could impose conditions and maintain continuous supervision over rate bureaus. (2) Every agreement should allow freedom of independent action, either before or after action of a bureau, to each railroad. (3) Rate agreements could not be made among carriers of different classes (railroads, express, and sleeping-car companies are one class, while pipelines, motor vehicles, water carriers, and freight forwarders are each a different class).

The act legalized what had been past practice; but, as in the case of other forms of cooperative action or consolidation, it sought to protect the public by administrative supervision. Whether abuses will exist in the practice of the rate bureaus depends materially upon the effectiveness of the commission's oversight over the bureaus and over the rate structure in general.

A TRANSPORTATION POLICY. An important milestone in the history of transportation regulation is the Transportation Act of 1940.[43] Already

---

[41] *Class Rate Investigation, 1939*, 262 ICC 447 (1945), upheld in *N.Y. v. U.S.*, 331 U.S. 284 (1947).
[42] 62 Stat. 472 (1948).
[43] 54 Stat. 898.

its provisions on consolidation and regional rate discriminations have been noted. Another change of significance was the placement of responsibility for regulation of all interstate water carriers in the ICC. The Motor Carrier Act of 1935 had given the commission the authority to regulate interstate motor-carrier activities. These extensions of authority of the ICC to motor and water carriers, and the growing consciousness of the interrelationship of the several modes of transportation, led to a new statement of policy to guide the ICC in the regulation of the four modes of competition subject to its jurisdiction (railroads, oil pipelines, motor carriers, water carriers). The 1940 act declared it to be "the national transportation policy of the Congress":

to provide for fair and impartial regulation of all modes of transportation subject to the provisions of the Act, so administered as to recognize and preserve the inherent advantages of each; to promote safe, adequate, economical, and efficient service and foster sound economic conditions in transportation and among the several carriers; . . . all to the end of developing, coordinating, and preserving a national transportation system by water, highway, and rail, as well as other means, adequate to meet the needs of the commerce of the United States, and of the Postal Service, and of the national defense.

There were important directives in this statement of policy: to preserve the "inherent advantages" of each mode of transportation, to promote service and foster sound conditions, and to develop "a national transportation system." These are key objectives in the relationships of the modes of transportation and regulatory action with respect thereto—matters which will be discussed in the next chapter.

FINANCIAL DIFFICULTIES. Additional steps beyond the Emergency Railway Transportation Act of 1933 were taken during the depression of the thirties to relieve the financial plight of the roads. They were allowed to borrow from the Reconstruction Finance Corporation, a government corporation. The Bankruptcy Act of the national government was amended by the addition of Section 77, applicable to railroads. This section sought to facilitate railroad reorganizations during bankruptcy proceedings, and to insure that management during the process was at reduced cost and in the interest of the interested parties. It provided for participation by the ICC in the development of reorganization plans, and required that such plans should have the approval both of the court and of the commission.

After World War II there was an upward trend in railroad earnings until 1955, after which a marked decline occurred. As a result, a Transportation Act of 1958 employed a technique which had become familiar in national legislation. It authorized the ICC to guarantee loans to railroads for additions and betterments or for maintenance, with the aggregate not to exceed $500,000,000, and the authority to terminate in 1961. This authority was extended to 1963. The same act gave the railroads the option of seeking ICC, rather than state, approval for discontinuance of trains. The

ICC had possessed jurisdiction over complete abandonment of a line, but not over discontinuance or change of schedules, and it was thought that some of the state commissions had been unsympathetic to the railroads' pleas for discontinuance. Finally, the act of 1958 announced a policy on minimum rates which should give the railroads more freedom in meeting motor-carrier competition. This change is explained in the next chapter (see pages 403 and 421).

COMMENTS ON RAILROAD REGULATION

While governments sought, in the beginning, to promote railroad transportation, regulation soon came to dominate government actions. And although there has been some promotional purpose in railroad regulation, regulatory objectives, regulatory terminology, and regulatory methodology have characterized government legislation and administration for almost a century. The railroad industry is less promoted and more regulated than many industries now covered by special legislation.

The system of railroad regulation is the product of a long accumulation of legislative enactments. It is an evolved system resulting from legislative effort to adapt and expand regulation to meet revealed needs over a span of some seventy years—from the initial act in 1887 to the last major amendment in 1958. It has been built block by block, with some tearing down and rebuilding in the process.

In the beginning the aim was negative, in that it was to prevent rail owners from harming shippers. Though positive power was given to the commission in 1906, the purpose of regulation remained negative until the "about face" of 1920, when attention was concentrated on the health of the railroad industry. This new purpose has led to a certain railroad-mindedness on the part of the commission, described by a commissioner with long service as "protective guardianship" of the roads.[44]

For the first thirty-three years, regulation was restricted to rates, except for safety requirements and a simple prohibition of pooling. In 1920 the jurisdiction of the ICC became comprehensive. It suddenly covered almost all aspects of railroad operation except labor-management relations, which were subjected to regulation, but under other agencies. Railway service, finance, and organization were included in the broad plan of regulation set up in the Transportation Act of 1920.

Regulation also penetrated more deeply toward the central core of management decisions. It is true, of course, that rate regulation in any form reaches toward the heart of business decisions; but when rate regulation

---

[44] Clyde B. Aitchison stated this as the purpose of the Transportation Act of 1920. *Hearings* before a Subcommittee of the Committee on Interstate and Foreign Commerce, House of Representatives, 79th Cong., 1st Sess., pursuant to H.R. 2536 (October 1945), p. 13.

extends to the veto or to the setting of maximum and/or minimum rates in the myriad complexities of railroad-rate structure, and when this is accompanied by meticulous controls over finance, service, and consolidations, then regulation encompasses the heart and the blood flow in and out. Railroad regulation since 1920 has been not only comprehensive, but intimate.

Despite the comprehensive jurisdiction of the ICC and the intimacy of its controls, railroad management is still allowed wide latitude for initiative and freedom of action. On rates, the pattern of 1910 was for a roving power of intervention rather than approval or disapproval of all rates. The Reed-Bulwinkle Act, confirming the practice of the past among the railroads, even allows railroad managements to make arrangements for joint setting of rates, and this is done in practice by rate bureaus. Most of the commission's powers over service, finance, and organization are exercised upon petition of railroad management. Yet the withholding or veto power of the commission is great indeed.

Although the jurisdiction of the ICC is comprehensive with respect to the subjects of railroad management, it is nevertheless not comprehensive with respect to the transportation market within which the railroads operate. The next chapter will show the extent to which transportation of commodities on certain types of common carriers (water and motor) is exempt from rate regulation, the extent to which passengers and freight move on unregulated, private facilities, and the extent to which jurisdiction over transportation facilities is divided in the government. The existence of the exempt commodities and the unregulated private carriers, and the division of jurisdiction, means that the ICC's comprehensive and intimate control operates over only a portion of the transportation market. In 1920 a complete system of railroad regulation was substantially a complete system of transportation regulation; but even with the added controls exercised today over water and motor transportation, the ICC operates over only part of the transportation market.

The Transportation Act of 1920 was the most ambitious piece of industry planning in the history of this country. It showed great faith in the ability of men to order an industry according to plan. Rates were to be set according to a mathematical formula, the imperfections of the method were to be corrected by recapture and wise use of the recaptured funds, and a long-run solution to the uncoordinated and planless railway structure was to be effected through a plan for consolidation. These results were not attained. Chief among the reasons was the hard core of irresistible facts which made both rate-fixing according to formula and recapture unfeasible, as well as consolidation in the absence of use of tremendous overhead compulsion.

Except for these diversions from the long-run path of regulation, railroad regulation has been pragmatic in nature. This is the way Professor Sharfman has characterized railroad regulation. He has referred to the "relatively minor role played by precedent," the absence of "any controlling degree of finality" in decisions, the use of "trial-and-error methods," the frequent recourse to modification and supplementary action, the fact that "the Commission's rulings" are "predominantly a matter of informed judgment, flexibly adjusted to changing circumstances and conditions, with the pressure of legal necessity emerging only on relatively rare occasions." [45] Professor Sharfman has said that the ICC's "task is not primarily to achieve a goal, but to maintain a moving balance between ideal ends and immediate practical considerations." [46]

To some extent, the aims of planning have been met in recent years through the comprehensive rate proceeding. This type of proceeding provides an opportunity for broader rate determinations and more extensive effects than is possible through piecemeal consideration of smaller petitions.

The regulatory powers are exercised by a commission now composed of eleven members serving overlapping terms of seven years. They are appointed by the President with the consent of the Senate, and removable by the President for "inefficiency, neglect of duty, or malfeasance in office." It is regarded as an "independent" commission—that is, independent of policy control by the President. Its administrative activities are in the hands primarily of a number of bureaus, some of which are functional and some of which handle special problems related to motor carriers, water carriers, and freight forwarders, respectively. It has delegated decisional authority (subject to appeal to the commission) to several divisions, composed of members of the commission, and to a number of employee boards.

It has been called the "Supreme Court of the Transportation World." The description is inappropriate, first, because its decisions can be appealed to courts, but chiefly because its functions are not primarily judicial. It has extensive legislative and also executive functions, such as inspection powers to enforce the safety laws. But rather than characterize its functions in terms of the traditional separation of powers as executive, judicial, or legislative, it is more realistic to say that in addition to certain routine functions, it must make policy and managerial decisions on railroad matters.

In part, these decisions are made on the same considerations the railroad executives would take into account. For example, will an increase in rates bring in more revenue and stabilize the earnings of the roads, or will it decrease traffic and increase the difficulties of the railroads? In part, the decision is based on consideration of other and broader interests— those of shippers and other carriers—and upon a close regard for the directives in the governing legislation. All of this makes for complexity in the decisional process. To insure that there is fair consideration of all interests, and that its decisions will stand up in the courts, the commission

---

[45] Sharfman, *op. cit.*, Vol. II, pp. 367–384.
[46] Sharfman, *op. cit.*, Vol. III-B, p. 766.

operates behind a heavy façade of judicial procedure; and the record in a case will include all the kinds of expert testimony that the roads, other interests, and the commission staff can bring to bear on the issue at hand. The process is necessarily slow, and contributes to inflexibility in railroad matters. This has its disadvantages, but it is part of the process of protecting the full scale of interests involved.

The commission's work has had such great significance for the group and regional interests of the nation that it is not surprising that politics has swirled around it. A long controversy over lake cargo rates became the dominating factor in appointments to the commission for many years.[47] The agricultural interests were once able to get a resolution through Congress directing the ICC to give what was, in effect, special consideration to the influences of rates upon movement of agricultural products.[48] The South demanded, and finally received, consideration of what it regarded as unfair rate discriminations.

Yet the commission has been a viable institution. It has been influential as an aid to Congress in shaping the developing pattern of regulation. Sharfman has concluded that "While the Congressional response has often been tardy, it has seldom swerved, in essence from the direction of the Commission's recommendations." [49] It has long since won a favorable attitude from the courts. It has been able, to a quite remarkable extent, to retain for itself the decisional power on matters subject to its jurisdiction, and without frequent or substantial reversal either from courts or the Congress.

Carrying forward the distinctions made in Chapter 3, it can be said that railroad regulation exemplifies politics on the intermediate level. There is the triangular relationship among the interests immediately affected, the commission, and the commerce committees of the Congress. The centerpiece is the commission. Only occasionally do the conflicts burst into macropolitics, and even then the compromises are usually adjusted within the established subsystem for railroads within the government. Seldom, even, does the power of the presidency have any significant bearing on this ongoing, traditional system.

Some would say that the viability of the administrative agency was due to its success in balancing the interests of the nation. Others would say that it is due to the acquisition by the commission of railroad-mindedness. Typifying this viewpoint was an elaborate article in 1952 which argued that, whereas railroad regulation resulted from farmer demand, and whereas the commission derived its support prior to World War I from shipper groups, the commission had looked for support from the railroads since

---

[47] See Harvey C. Mansfield, *The Lake Cargo Rate Controversy* (New York: Columbia University Press, 1932), pp. 161–194.
[48] Hoch-Smith Resolution, 43 Stat. 802 (1925).
[49] Sharfman, *op. cit.*, Vol. I, 290 (1931).

the Transportation Act of 1920.⁵⁰ It was argued that railroad interests had been pleased with the ICC, for it had been lenient in adjustment upward of railroad rates, had lent its support to monopoly developments in the industry, and had favored railroads against motor and water carriers. It was concluded that the ICC, by its own limitation of viewpoint, had been enfeebled for the new adjustments to change required for the transportation world.

These charges were vigorously denied by a member of the commission's staff. It may be impossible for anyone except a close student of decisions, written opinions, and other sources to form a sound judgment on the truth of the charges. It can be said that the railroads are not always entirely pleased with the effects of the regulatory system, and that the ICC is under the necessity today of balancing a wide variety of transportation and shipping interests. To be viable, to maintain its position as the centerpiece, to avoid eruption of conflict into macropolitics or reversals in the courts, it must be moderately successful in giving attention to the "inherent advantages" of each mode of transportation under its jurisdiction, as required by the Transportation Act of 1920.

A more prevalent criticism, and one which has come from higher sources, is that regulation has become too strict and should now be relaxed in certain respects. A presidential advisory committee chaired by Secretary of Commerce Weeks recommended in 1955 that in view of the fact that the monopoly element in transportation which existed in 1920 had been eliminated by the growth of competition among transport facilities, common carriers should "be permitted greater freedom, short of discriminatory practices, to utilize their economic capabilities in the competitive pricing of their service. . . ." ⁵¹ President Kennedy, in 1962, said to Congress that he was "convinced that less federal regulation and subsidization is in the long run a prime prerequisite of a healthy intercity transportation network." ⁵²

Yet it is by no means certain that the direction of movement will be toward less, rather than more, government action. President Kennedy noted the possibility that Congress could extend rate control to water and motor transportation of exempt commodities rather than remove control over

---

⁵⁰ Samuel P. Huntington, "The Marasmus of the ICC: The Commission, the Railroads, and the Public Interest," *Yale L. J.*, **LXI**, pp. 467–509 (April 1952). A reply to this article by an instructor at Harvard University was written by a member of the commission's staff: Charles S. Morgan, "A Critique of 'The Marasmus of the ICC: The Commission, the Railroads, and the Public Interest,'" *Yale L. J.*, **LXII**, pp. 171–225 (December 1952). See also Samuel P. Huntington, Charles S. Morgan, and C. Dickerman Williams, "The ICC Re-Examined: A Colloquy," *Yale L. J.*, **LXIII**, pp. 44–63 (November 1953).

⁵¹ *Revision of Federal Transportation Policy,* A Report to the President Prepared by the Presidential Advisory Committee on Transportation Policy and Organization, April 1955, especially p. 7.

⁵² "The Transportation System of Our Nation," Message from the President, House Document 384. 87th Cong., 2d Sess.

rail transportation of these. The decline in earnings of railroads—which has already led to temporary loan guarantees by government, a reactivation of the merger movement within the railroad industry, and pressure within it toward reduction of labor costs—may lead to more positive government action for promotion of a healthy railroad industry. And the problems of transportation in general may lead to supplementation of the pragmatic approach of the ICC with new adventures in policy development for the transportation industries.

All these questions about the future directions of government action with respect to the railroads merge into the conditions and issues of transportation as a whole. Railroad regulation is now unavoidably what it was not in 1920—namely, an aspect of government's policies toward various transportation industries. It will be discussed further in the concluding section of the following chapter.

Chapter 18. Government and the Transportation Network

TRANSPORTATION, like power, credit, and communications, is one of the common servants of the economy. Like these others, it is a matter of great public interest. The great public need for it, and the tremendous opportunities for increasing the benefits from it, have attracted public attention to transportation in this country and made it a matter of both business and political concern.

ELEMENTS IN THE TRANSPORTATION NETWORK

Transportation service is now offered to the public by a group of transportation industries. Each has peculiar characteristics and offers distinct advantages, and regulation and promotion have been tailored in each industry to the characteristics of the industry and the opportunities for development of its service. In addition, each of these industries is part of the nation's transportation network, as is also the transportation of persons in private automobiles, and of freight by the owners of the freight. The interrelations among the components of the transportation network complicates the task of policy development. This chapter presents the response of government to the several transportation industries, other than railroads, and directs attention to the problems arising from the coexistence of multiple elements in the transportation network.

The domestic, intercity transportation system has five major components. The first is rail transportation. It is the most important component in freight transportation. Railroads still carried in 1959 more than 45 per cent of our intercity freight traffic. Their great advantage is for large shipments of carload (or greater) quantities over considerable distances. Their share of passenger transportation has, however, rapidly declined, as the private automobile, bus, and airplane have come into extensive use. The coming of the rails had tremendous effects on the development of the nation, for it allowed the great development of inland centers of commerce, thus surmounting the limitations of a coast- and river-bound economy; it also facilitated the national use of regional resources, made for diversification in regional agricultural and industrial development, and at the same time was a bond of unity for the nation.

Water transportation has the great advantage of being cheap, but also the disadvantages of being slow, undependable as to schedule, and frequently carrying only one-way cargo. It is therefore advantageous primarily for commodities of great bulk and imperishability. It is, for this reason, an important part of our transportation network. The domestic system includes (1) the Mississippi River–Illinois Canal (connecting the Mississippi River and Lake Michigan)–Ohio River (including transportation on its feeders, the Monongahela and Allegheny Rivers)–Tennessee River system, altogether providing an extensive, inland, nine-foot channel; (2) the Great Lake–St. Lawrence system, with its unusually low transportation cost; (3) the Atlantic and Gulf Coastal system; (4) the intercoastal transport through the Panama Canal Zone and around Cape Horn; and (5) river-to-coast transport (other than the Mississippi River and its tributaries) and inland canals, such as the New York Barge Canal (the old Erie Canal).

Highway transport has in two generations substantially transformed the American transportation system. It includes the private automobile, the bus, and the truck. Among the different forms of transportation, the private automobile is the largest volume carrier of passengers, and the bus is a competitor of railroads and airlines. The truck has been supplementary to and competitor of railroads. Truck use prevails for short and small hauls, and trucks are also competitors on much long-haul traffic. Among the advantages of motor transport—buses and trucks—are accessibility to communities not reached by rails, flexibility as to schedules, and a general adaptability to the needs of shippers and communities.

Air transport invaded the field of transportation a decade or two behind motor transport. Its primary utility has been for fast, distance passenger movement, and for light, nonbulky freight items. Further expansion seems certain, due to many factors, including technical improvements in air equipment, development of cargo facilities, and increasing dependence on fast travel and cargo delivery. The main encumbrance is time required for getting to and from terminal facilities.

The fifth form of transport is the oil and gas pipeline. The oil pipeline has long been used for transportation of crude oil, and in recent years for transportation of gasoline also. The oil pipeline and the coastal tanker provide the most economical forms of transportation for crude oil, and the gas pipeline is the technological means of moving natural gas.

The proportions of the nation's transportation load carried by these several modes of transport shifted radically in the postwar years. The table following shows the picture for 1946 and 1959.[1]

---

[1] Figures from *National Transportation Policy,* Report by Special Study Group on

		1946	1959
Freight:			
Billions of Ton-miles	Railroads	602.1	582.0
	Motor carriers	82.0	275.0
	Inland waterways	124.0	195.0
	Oil pipelines	95.7	225.0
	Air carriers	.093	.67
Passenger:			
Billions of Passenger-miles	Railroads	66.3	22.1
	Buses	26.9	20.4
	Inland waterways	2.3	2.3
	Air carriers	5.9	29.1
	Private automobiles	253.6	670.0

In freight transport there has been a large growth in motor-carrier and oil-pipeline transportation. The railroads have suffered only a slight decline in volume of traffic, but have lost heavily in the percentage of traffic hauled. In passenger transport the notable facts are the sharp tendency toward disappearance of railroad transportation, the rapid increase of air transportation, and the tremendous expansion of private automobile travel. Approximately 90 per cent of intercity movement of persons in 1959 was by private automobile.

These several forms of transportation complement each other in meeting diverse economic and social needs. Three general introductory statements can be made about government's relation to them. First, it has promoted the development of each of the five forms. It gave large subsidies of land to railroads. It began early in our history to give aid to water transportation through harbor improvements, removal of obstructions in rivers, and building canals; and in the twentieth century there has been a revival of interest in waterways, with enormous expenditures on river and harbor improvements. It has built highways for the aid of motor transport. It has subsidized air transport through air-mail subsidies, operation of an air-traffic management system, and construction of airport facilities. It has authorized the use of the sovereign power of eminent domain for obtaining rights-of-way for pipelines. Communities of the nation and the various economic interests have been so interested in rapid development of transportation service that they have pressed government for help for each of these forms of transportation as it became significant. Second, all the forms of transportation are regulated. Regulation has usually followed after an initial period of promotion, but in air transport it has existed in some forms from the beginning of the development of the industry. Third, the national government has had an important part in the regulation of all of these forms of transportation. Transportation in-

Transportation Policies in the United States, Committee on Commerce, U.S. Senate. 87th Cong., 1st Sess., Senate Report 445 (1961), Tables VI and VII, pp. 59 and 61.

dustries are to a great extent interstate industries, and their interstate activities and some of their intrastate activities have become matters of national concern.

There are two other vital parts of the transportation facilities. One is intracity and intra-metropolitan-area facilities, such as surface and underground railways, buses, taxis, and private transportation—all of which, except the latter, are subject to regulation. The other is maritime transportation, which is supported and controlled by government. These two groups of facilities—one local and the other international in scope—are so different and so distinct from the intercity transportation system that they are not discussed in this chapter.

MOTOR CARRIERS

As had been true of railroads, regulation of motor carriers began in the states. Much of the state regulation has been designed to promote public safety and conservation of highways. Although state laws vary, typical standards are vehicle registration, vehicle inspection to enforce mechanical requirements, driver licensing, rest periods or limitation of work periods for drivers, and limitation of size and weight of trucks. But the states also initiated economic regulation of motor carriers. The states began to regulate rates and require certificates of public convenience and necessity for commercial carriers.

The states quickly ran into two major problems. One was the problem of the contract carrier. The scope of service and the legal status of such a carrier are different from those of the common carrier. A common carrier is one which offers service to the public generally; such carriers have been recognized to be subject to economic regulation in England from an early date, and in this country since *Munn v. Illinois* in 1876.[2] A contract carrier is one which offers service only to customers with which it desires to contract. The states sought to give them a status similar to that of common carriers. For this there were some good reasons. Common carriers are essential, especially for small shippers, but also for industry in general. If contract carriers were not regulated, they could undercut the rates of common carriers and threaten their financial soundness and the adequacy of their service. Also, common carriers could seek to escape regulation by the subterfuge of acting as contract carriers. Nevertheless, the state laws which sought to regulate contract carriers as common carriers were held unconstitutional by the Supreme Court of the United States.[3] The State of Texas discovered a means of meeting the situation by setting

[2] See pages 365–366.
[3] *Michigan Public Utilities Commission v. Duke* (1925), 266 U.S. 570; *Frost Trucking Co. v. Rr. Commission of Cal.* (1926), 271 U.S. 583; *Smith v. Cahoon* (1931), 283 U.S. 527.

up a separate system of regulation for contract carriers. Common carriers were subjected to the requirement of a certificate of public convenience and necessity, and to maximum- and minimum-rate regulation; contract carriers were required to get permits, and were subjected only to minimum-rate regulation, forms of regulation which were reasonably adapted to the protection of the common carriers of the state. The Texas system was upheld by the Supreme Court in *Stephenson v. Binford*,[4] and set the pattern for future regulation by the states and the national government.

The other problem was that of interstate operations. In 1925 the Supreme Court held that a state could not require a certificate to operate a motor carrier in interstate commerce.[5] This created a situation similar to that existing in regard to railroads after the Wabash decision: Congress only could provide for regulation of interstate traffic. The result was that the states, as represented in the National Association of Railroad and Utilities Commissioners, joined with certain other interests in a demand for national regulation.

Although bills for national regulation followed immediately after the 1925 decision, legislation was not passed until 1935. In the meantime, the excess of transportation facilities and the depression had brought intense competition for traffic. Motor carriers with small investment were able to undercut the railroads on rates. The competition was particularly effective on short hauls, but the motor carriers were also able to skim the cream on long-haul transportation of some commodities. The railroads, in serious plight, sought economies in their own operations, and also pushed for regulation of motor carriers. They were especially interested in minimum-rate regulation. The motor-carrier industry itself was unstable as a result of ease of entry and exit, and of imprudence or lack of experience among operators. Some of the larger motor carriers came to favor regulation. Also, many shippers preferred a more stable transportation industry, with dependability of continuous service, rate structures, and joint haul arrangements. The juncture of these various private interests and of the state regulatory authorities led to the Motor Carrier Act of 1935.[6]

The two dominant themes in exposition of the new legislation were contained in reports of Mr. Joseph B. Eastman, Coordinator of Transportation and respected member of the ICC, and were repeated in reports from congressional committees. The first was that competition "must be held within reasonable limits and kept from assuming destructive and wasteful forms."[7] The second was that "a complete and coordinated system of

---

[4] 287 U.S. 251 (1932).
[5] *Buck v. Kuykendall*, 267 U.S. 307 (1925).
[6] 49 Stat. 543. Part II of the Act to Regulate Commerce, as amended.
[7] Report of Federal Coordinator of Transportation, *Regulation of Transportation Agencies* (1934), Sen. Doc. 152, 73rd Cong., 2nd Sess., 24. See also *Report of the Federal Coordinator of Transportation*, 1934, H. Doc., 89 (74th Cong., 1st Sess.), and S. Rept. 482 (74th Cong., 1st Sess.).

legislation touching all forms of transportation" should be established so that the objective of a coordinated transportation system for the nation could be achieved.[8]

In line with the latter objective the Motor Carrier Act subjected motor carriers to the supervision of the ICC. It provided for regulation of four classes of business concerns: brokers, private carriers, common carriers, and contract carriers. Brokers are persons who sell or arrange for transportation service. Their financial responsibility was deemed to be of public concern. Hence they must obtain licenses, and are subject to commission requirements on accounts and reports and financial responsibility. Private carriers are those who transport in connection with their business or occupation. The act makes these subject to safety regulations which may be prescribed for them by the ICC. Common carriers are subjected to the conventional types of regulation for such carriers. The commission may prescribe accounting forms and require reports from them. They have obligations in regard to filing, publishing, and adhering to published rates similar to those of railroads, and the commission's powers over rates include suspension and setting of maximum and/or minimum rates. Common carriers are in general subjected to the same requirements in regard to security issues, and to consolidations or other methods of combination, as apply to railroads. They must also obtain certificates of public convenience and necessity to render service or extend service. These certificates are for indeterminate periods and may be suspended, changed, or revoked. The commission may make safety rules, including qualifications of employees, hours of service, safety of operation, and standards of equipment. It may also require bonds, insurance, or other evidence of financial responsibility in regard to injuries, death, or loss or damage of shipments.

Contract carriers are subjected to the same provisions of law regarding accounts and reports, security issues, consolidations, safety, and financial responsibility (except the provisions on loss or damage to shipments). Following the Texas pattern, there are, however, two differences for contract carriers. They are regulated only as to minimum rates, and they must obtain permits rather than certificates of public convenience and necessity. The requirements for the permit and the certificate are stated somewhat differently.

The primary purposes of the regulatory provisions were safety, financial responsibility of carriers, and prevention of excessive and destructive competition. Although the provisions of the act for the attainment of these purposes appear to be rather comprehensive, there are a number of elements of looseness in the regulatory scheme. First, under a so-called "grandfather clause," common and contract carriers already in operation were to be granted certificates or permits. This accorded with the usual practice

[8] Quoting from S. Rept. 482, *op. cit.,* p. 3.

in regulatory statutes of beginning with the situation as it has developed at the time of the initiation of regulation. Second, there were a number of exemptions from all provisions of the act, except those relating to safety, the most significant of which were motor vehicles used exclusively in distribution of newspapers, and those used exclusively in carrying livestock, fish (including shell fish), or agricultural commodities (not including the manufactured products thereof). This, as will be seen in the subsequent discussion, constituted a wide rent in the regulatory scheme. Third, the commission's authority is expressly restricted to interstate and foreign commerce, thus preventing the exercise of jurisdiction over intrastate matters having an effect on interstate commerce, as in the regulation of railroads. There were even provisions for mandatory use of joint state boards on certain matters affecting three or fewer states, and for optional use of joint boards on most important matters.[9] Fourth, a number of provisions allow freedom for small-scale operations or transactions. Consent for consolidations is not required where no more than twenty vehicles are involved, nor for security issues where the par value of the securities to be issued, together with those outstanding, does not exceed $500,000; and the act preserves the freedom of the common carrier to add to facilities over the routes, or between the termini, or otherwise within the areas it is authorized to serve, and the freedom of the contract carrier to add new contracts and new facilities within the scope of its permit. Finally, the commission cannot award reparation for excess charges in the past, nor can it prevent the abandonment of operations of a motor carrier which discontinues all its operations, nor can it require motor carriers to establish through routes and joint rates with other motor carriers. Thus, a combination of factors—including agricultural interests, the pre-existence of motor-carrier facilities and state regulation, and the peculiarities of an industry with many small operators—led to a looser system of regulation than that which had evolved for railroads.

There has been a wide range of problems in administration of the regulatory scheme. For the first time the government was regulating small carriers. Regulation of railroads was regulation of a relatively small number of big business units, but regulation of motor carriers was for a multitude of small operators. This meant a large volume of work for the commission. Approximately 90,000 grandfather applications were filed immediately after passage of the act, and it took the commission several years to dispose of this first load of work. Since then it has been administering a system of competition controls and safety and financial requirements for numerous operators. It has been difficult to administer the load of work and obtain compliance from all operators. Moreover, the complexity

[9] On ICC jurisdiction over interstate railroad rates, see pages 142–143; and on joint boards, see page 153.

of the task is increased by the many types of motor-carrier operators. In addition to the types defined in the law, there are various degrees of specialization among the freight carriers. Yet the most significant addition to responsibility was that of balancing a wider diversity of interests than had been required under railroad regulation. The commission was now an intermediary between railroads and motor carriers, common and contract carriers, carriers and shippers, and in myriad confrontations of carriers of the same type seeking operating rights or other benefits under the statute.

Its largest function under the act is that of management of competition. The commission restricts and supervises competition. The first means of doing this is by control of operating rights through powers over entry and consolidation. The key power is "control over entry"—a broad term used to include initial certification and extensions of operating authority. Initially the commission sought to hold in bounds the operating rights of carriers by strictness in determination of grandfather rights. The carriers at this time operated in diverse ways, and their applications since have called for various kinds of service rights. The commission has granted the rights through certificates and permits limited to commodities, routes or territories, or classes of service. Route grants may be limited to service through named cities. Common carriers may be limited to haul in one direction. The result is that motor-carrier operating rights are chopped up into pieces, in contrast to the rights of general service that railroads possess.

These restrictions on operating rights have grown out of, first, the grandfather base, and second, the commission's *ad hoc* determinations on whether the conditions for new entry or expansion meet the requirements of the act. In the case of common carriers, the act provides that the applicant must be "fit, willing, and able properly to perform the service proposed and to conform to the provisions of the Act and the requirements, rules, and regulations of the Commission thereunder. . . ." This includes such things as personal qualifications, financial stability, and compliance with regulations. The more important requirement is that the applicant show that the added service is required for the "public convenience and necessity." Certain general statements may be made about the kind of showing that must be made to establish "public convenience and necessity." In general, the applicant must show that the existing service is inadequate to meet the needs of shippers. Shippers' support on an application may be important, though it is not conclusive of the need for the additional service. The commission will grant applications to meet a demonstrated public need, but it will protect existing carriers where their service is economical, efficient, and adequate. The adequacy of existing rail service, as well as that of motor-carrier service, may be considered, but the Supreme Court has reminded the commission that it must assess the "inherent advantages" of each form of transportation before rejecting a motor-carrier application on the ground that rail service is adequate.[10] The Court has also said that rate advantage "is precisely the sort of 'inherent advantage' that congressional policy requires the Commission to recognize." [11]

The commission is now the moderator in a tight system of control of fragmented operating rights. There is reason to believe this fragmentation of rights has led to some inefficient use of facilities. In 1959 the commission initiated a broad proceeding designed to ease many of the effects of fragmented operating grants.[12] Objection came from many carriers. Carriers may be restive under restrictions on their operating rights, but they may also be fearful that broad modifications in the system will operate to the advantage of their competitors. The commission is, to a substantial extent, restricted by the interests arising out of the established system, and may find that any liberalization of operating rights must come in case-to-case determinations over a period of time.

Another instrument in the management of competition is control over minimum rates. In motor-carrier regulation there has been much more interest in minimum rates than in maximum rates. The purpose has been to avoid destructive rate competition. The destructive effects to be avoided may be on motor carriers, and the commission at an early date in five territorial rate cases moved to avoid financial failures among motor carriers by setting minimum rates. The destructive effects may be on the railroads. This being true, lively differences of opinion have developed over public policy. Motor-carrier interests have sometimes objected to efforts to protect railroads through setting minimum rates on motor transport. On the other hand, railroad interests have objected to decisions which appeared to hold an umbrella of protection over motor carriers that transport products which railroads could carry at a cost advantage. The position of the ICC appeared to be somewhat uncertain on the problem, and in the decade of the fifties there was much discussion of public policy. The railroads desired a freer policy on rate reductions. In 1958 Congress amended the rate-making standards to limit umbrella-holding over one form of transportation to protect another. The amendment, in words of which the precise meaning will require judicial construction, said:

... the Commission, in determining whether a rate is lower than a reasonable minimum rate, shall consider the facts and circumstances attending the movement of the traffic by the carrier or carriers to which the rate is applicable. Rates of a carrier shall not be held up to a particular level to protect the traffic of any other mode of transportation, giving due consideration to the objectives of the national transportation policy declared in this Act.[13]

---

[10] *Schaffer Transportation Co. v. U.S.*, 355 U.S. 83, 89–90 (1957).
[11] *Ibid.*, p. 91. Standards as well as procedures are discussed in David M. Welborn, *The Certification of Motor Common Carriers of Property: A Study in National Regulatory Administration* (Ph.D. Dissertation, University of Texas, 1961).
[12] Ex Parte No. MC-55.
[13] Transportation Act of 1958, 72 Stat. 568.

One further problem in the relationship of rail and motor-carrier transportation has been the conditions under which the railroads should be allowed to engage in motor transport themselves. In general, the ICC has taken the position that railroads should be allowed to engage only in trucking operations which are auxiliary to rail service, and should not be allowed to set up new competing truck competition or extend motor transport outside their own territory.

The management of competition, though tight and detailed over a set of things, disappears or withers with respect to others. Because of three exempted or partially controlled matters, only about one-third of motor-carrier freight moves on common carriers.[14] The first of the three gaps in control is the exemption of trucks carrying agricultural and fisheries products. The category of exempt items was being expanded by court interpretation and ICC action in accord therewith until Congress in the Transportation Act of 1958 declared that certain items added by interpretation should no longer be exempt, and otherwise froze the exemption to those items which had been listed by the Bureau of Motor Carriers of the ICC.[15] The second gap is the exemption of private carriers from economic control. This, too, is a big gap, and one which could be enlarged by subterfuge. Carriers actually engaged in what was essentially a transportation operation could try to avoid minimum-rate control through the subterfuge of having a firm buy and sell the product they hauled. In 1958 Congress sought to prevent this by an amendment which, in effect, prevents private carriage except where it is a furtherance of "a primary business enterprise" other than transportation.[16] The third gap is the partial exemption of contract carriage. Here, too, carriers may seek to evade the requirements of the law. They may become common carriers in fact, even though they have only contract-carrier permits. On this matter, too, a tightening amendment was adopted.[17] Thus, although Congress has acted to prevent the broadening of the substantial exemptions from common-carrier controls, these exemptions remain. For private and contract carriers, the exemptions are necessary because of the nature of their businesses; for carriers of agricultural and fisheries products, the exemption is a special one unrelated to the nature of the carrier itself.

AIR CARRIERS

ORIGIN AND PURPOSES OF PUBLIC POLICY. The air-transport industry was fathered and nurtured by the Post Office Department. "Without the assistance of the mail, the industry would not have been built up,"

[14] *National Transportation Policy, op. cit.*, Table I, p. 50.
[15] 72 Stat. 568.
[16] *Ibid.*
[17] 71 Stat. 411 (1957).

commented the President of the private Air Transport Association in 1937.[18] The Post Office Department initiated the carriage of mail in its own planes in 1916. In the Air Mail Act of 1925 Congress authorized the Postmaster General to arrange with private companies for airmail carriage, and by 1928 the transfer to private transportation was complete. Development of an air-transport industry was encouraged by a requirement of the Post Office Department that the carriers transport passengers. In 1934, following charges of fraud in letting of mail contracts to private carriers, army planes carried the mails for a brief period.[19] A series of accidents led quickly to a return to private industry. The series of events fixed one point in air-transport development: air transport, in most countries a public enterprise, would be in this country a private industry.

A general aviation statute had been passed in 1926.[20] This was primarily a safety-regulation measure, and its administration was placed in the Department of Commerce. Economic regulation resulted from a series of enactments concerning the mails, and was carried out by the Post Office Department. It had control over mail routes and the awarding of mail contracts. Mail contracts were awarded on the basis of competitive bidding, but after 1934, the ICC had authority to review and fix mail pay rates.

In 1938 the incomplete and fragmented system of control was replaced by a comprehensive statute containing the nation's long-range aviation policy. The statute was the Civil Aeronautics Act.[21] It was replaced in 1958 by the Federal Aviation Act,[22] but the new act contained no substantial modifications of the system of economic regulation established in 1938; however, it built upon and expanded the safety regulation features of that act. The two acts may be treated as one, except for certain features of safety control. At present, with exceptions to be noted, safety regulation is conducted by the Federal Aviation Agency, headed by an administrator appointed by the President with the Senate's approval, and located outside the executive departments. Economic regulation has been, since 1938, under the Civil Aeronautics Board, which is composed of five members appointed by the President with consent of the Senate. Under another statute—the Federal Airport Act of 1946—grants are made to states for airport construction.[23] This statute is administered by the Federal Aviation Agency.

In the basic legislation of 1938 and 1958 there were three main objectives. One, of course, was safety. The safety legislation is applicable to

[18] Testimony of Colonel Edgar S. Gorrell, *Hearing* before the Committee on Interstate and Foreign Commerce, House of Representatives (75th Cong., 1st Sess.), on H.R. 5234 and H.R. 4652 (March 31, 1937), p. 79.

[19] See Paul D. Tillett, *The Army Flies the Mails* (University, Ala.: University of Alabama Press, 1954).

[20] 44 Stat. 568.
[21] 52 Stat. 973.
[22] 72 Stat. 811.
[23] 60 Stat. 170.

aviation generally, not just to commercial airlines. The other two objectives were those of economic regulation, and they applied only to the air-transport industry. The first of these was promotion of air transport "to meet the needs of the foreign and domestic commerce of the United States, of the Postal Service, and of the national defense." These words, and such others as "encouragement and development" and "promotion of adequate, economical, and efficient service," appear in the preamble of the governing legislation. Although the pattern of regulation is in general that of conventional public utility legislation, the promotional objective is strongly emphasized. The second objective of economic regulation was, as stated in the preamble, "sound economic conditions" in the transportation industry.

The hearings, reports, and debates on a regulatory measure [before the 1938 act] are replete with condemnations of "unbridled," "cut-throat," "disastrous," "destructive," "wasteful," "unregulated" competition and of "chaotic conditions," "unsound ventures," "haphazard growth," "blind economic chaos," and industry sowing of "wild oats." What was favored was "orderly and sound growth," "orderly planning," "a measure of stability," "financial stability." [24]

The president of the Air Transport Association pointed out that only 60 of the 125 million dollars invested in the industry remained; and Mr. Joseph Eastman, prominent in the background of the act, found in the facts of railroad history and the techniques of railroad regulation a pattern of regulated competition that should be adopted for air transportation.[25] In sum, safety for passengers and aviation personnel, promotion of air transportation, and stability of an industry were the dominant objectives.

The emphasis on promotion and sound economic conditions is one of the peculiarities of economic regulation of airlines. Another is that the pattern of regulation and promotion was set, as in radio and television regulation, prior to the flush growth of the industry. Still another is that control is centered almost exclusively in the national government, in contrast to the divided control which exists for most regulated industries. Similarly, in contrast with regulation for many other industries, the number of units under economic regulation has always been small. Some of these factors have simplified the task of regulation, and the last of them has led to intensive concern with each company in the industry.

SAFETY. Safety on the airways is promoted by licensing, safety rules, and air-traffic management. The licenses are called certificates. Certificates are required for airmen (pilots, mechanics, members of crews), for air carriers to insure "safe operation," and for planes and their equipment to assure that only airworthy equipment is flown. These are issued, suspended, or revoked by the Administrator of the Federal Aviation Agency, with certain

---

[24] From Emmette S. Redford, "The Significance of Belief Patterns in Economic Regulation," *Western Political Quarterly*, **XIV** (September 1961), p. 17.

[25] Redford, *ibid.*, for citation of sources.

rights of appeal to the board (CAB). The administrator also issues safety rules to govern flying, and these have become quite elaborate. Also, air traffic is subject to the traffic management system, maintained by the Federal Aviation Agency. Controls over take-off, flying on the airways, and landing are maintained by controllers in the traffic towers at airports. The agency's authority extends, with limitations to safeguard military responsibilities, to military as well as civil air traffic. The air-traffic control system incorporates the use of electronic devices to correct the hazards of traditional see-and-be-seen flying. The air-traffic control system cost approximately $600 million in the fiscal year 1963.

This system of safety controls is similar to that for highways, for the latter includes licensing of drivers, inspection of vehicles, driving rules, and policing of the roads. It is peculiar only in that it is much more elaborate, much more expensive, and is a national function. The results are reflected in the safety record of commercial airlines. Neither in 1961 nor in 1962 was there a single fatal accident on international traffic of American flagships flying regular passenger schedules, and in 1962 the casualty rate on domestic service of airlines flying regular schedules was 0.26 per 100 million passenger-miles flown.

ECONOMIC REGULATION. While safety regulations apply to all who use the air for flight, economic regulation is designed only for the commercial segment of aviation. The legal features of regulation follow the evolved pattern for transportation and utility industries. Certificates are required for domestic and foreign air transportation. These, as in motor-carrier regulation, are to be issued if the applicant is "fit, willing, and able" to perform the service properly, and if "such transportation is required by the public convenience and necessity." Foreign carriers obtain permits for foreign air transportation upon a showing that they are "fit, willing, and able" to perform the service properly, and that the transportation will be in the "public interest." Certificates for overseas or foreign transportation and permits to foreign carriers must be approved by the President. Requirements of other countries must also be met. As for rates, carriers must file schedules with the board and must publish them, give notice to the board of proposed changes, and establish and observe "just and reasonable rates"; the board may suspend rates and prescribe maximum and/or minimum rates. The board is also directed to set mail pay rates. Mergers and means of acquisition of control or of joint operation must be approved. Pooling arrangements may be disapproved. But the usual power to regulate security issues is not granted. Also, the board is prohibited from exercising controls over scheduling or changes in equipment and facilities, though it may determine that service is inadequate.

The Certificate System. The heart of regulation of air carriers, as of motor carriers, is the management of the certificate system. Initial grants were made under requirements of a grandfather clause; but even though the board started with existing rights, it has had ample discretion in shaping the air-transport industry. In its administration of the certificate system it has accepted the opinion of the framers of the regulatory act that there should be regulated competition—a system under which "air carriers and the public are safeguarded against uneconomic, destructive competition and wasteful duplication of services. . . ."[26] It has respected the mandate of the act to seek "sound economic conditions" and to promote air transportation, though perhaps with some sacrifice of the latter for the former objective.

It has established categories of service to be certificated. The chief of these is domestic trunkline service, which is the scheduled service between major traffic centers. This service has been restricted to and allocated among the grandfather carriers. Although the board has never ruled out the possibility of certification of additional trunklines, it has never shown disagreement with its statement in the Delta case in 1941 that the number of carriers was sufficient to prevent monopoly and to afford the competition contemplated by the act.[27] Initially there were nineteen domestic trunkline carriers, but the number has now been reduced by attrition to eleven. These eleven recently did approximately 97 per cent of the domestic airline passenger business and four (American, Eastern, TWA, and United) had about 70 per cent of this business.

The soundness of these concerns is of prime importance to the board. It has protected them from outside competition and from entry of new companies. In apportionment of opportunities among them balanced competition has been an objective. To meet this objective, an elaborate set of rights and restrictions are couched in certificate terminology dealing with stopover, through, turnabout, and other forms of service. Yet balanced competition is compromised with other objectives in route cases. New certification may be granted to the carrier which is best equipped to render the service. In spite of the board's efforts, the result of the grandfather certifications and of subsequent route grants has always been a weak-strong carrier situation.

The board has always been under pressure to expand service to communities, and has sometimes been criticized for failure to authorize more competition. One cause for its reluctance to make additional route awards was its desire to hold down subsidy costs, which did not disappear for the domestic trunklines until the fifties. In 1955, in three major route cases, the board made new awards which very substantially increased the amount of competition among many major traffic centers. Critics have questioned the timing of this increase in competition, arguing that it should have come earlier, or that it should not have come in 1955.[28] The expansion in operating rights was made just prior to the increase in costs and seat capacity through introduction of jet transport.

A second type of scheduled domestic service has been rendered by local-

[26] *Annual Report of the Civil Aeronautics Authority, 1939*, p. 2.
[27] Delta Air Lines *et al.*, Service to Atlanta and Birmingham, 2 CAB Reports 447, 480.
[28] See, for example, Richard E. Caves, *Air Transport and Its Regulators: An Industry Study* (Cambridge, Mass.: Harvard University Press, 1962), p. 439.

service carriers. The authorization of scheduled carriage of persons, property, and mail between smaller cities began in 1946. Over four hundred applications were filed for the service; twenty-two local-service companies were certificated. The number is now thirteen. They were given temporary certificates, and each had obtained one or more renewals prior to an act of Congress in 1955 providing for their permanent certification.[29] They are confined to geographical regions and normally operate without competition. The board's policy has been to keep the trunklines out of local-service operations and the local-service lines out of trunkline business. The local-service carriers are feeders to the trunklines, and they broaden airline service to small and medium-size cities. Their operations are heavily subsidized, about 31 per cent of their gross revenues being from direct subsidy in the year ending September 30, 1963. Community desires and the motive of promoting air transport lead toward expansion of local service; the desire to hold down the amount of subsidy operates as a countervailing pressure. The CAB has now adopted a "use it or lose it" policy, under which it will terminate authorization of service unless, excepting unusual circumstances, individual points enplane an average of five or more passengers daily and route segments show an average of seven or more passengers per plane-mile.

Other types of certificated service are all-cargo, helicopter, international, and supplemental. The last of these has been a threat to the trunklines and a thorny problem for the board. They have offered nonscheduled and irregular service, but have wanted certification for scheduled service. The board, at an early date, exempted them substantially from economic regulation. After the war, many new companies or persons inaugurated new call-and-demand service. Some of these pioneered in the development of coach service, and were therefore a major influence in the transition from luxury to mass air-transportation service. The board thought they were interested only in the most profitable traffic ("cream-skimming"), and sought to prevent them from setting up regular or scheduled service. Ultimately, the board authorized them to engage in unlimited charter operations, and to make up to ten flights per month between any two points. This was regarded by the trunklines as too generous, but it prevented the "nonskeds" from being a serious threat to the trunks. In 1962 Congress authorized the board to issue permanent certificates to these carriers, and gave the board certain powers of control to insure that they would perform their contractual, and meet their financial, obligations to the public.[30]

Rates. One can observe certain peculiarities in the historical record of regulation of airline rates. One is that the board had a double function: setting rates to be charged to the public, and determining the mail pay and subsidy element in revenues. Subsidy through mail pay was one of the means

---

[29] 69 Stat. 49.
[30] Public Law 87-528, July 10, 1962.

of promoting air transportation. The act directs the board, in setting mail rates, to consider, among other things, the need of each carrier for mail pay sufficient to insure the performance of the mail service and, together with other revenues, "to maintain and continue the development of air transportation to the extent and of the character and quality required for the commerce of the United States, the Postal Service, and the national defense." With this directive, the board began setting mail pay rates on a need basis. However, when it became apparent in 1942 that some of the stronger carriers might be self-sufficient, the board began a shift to figuring rates on a compensatory basis for the service rendered. By the middle fifties most of the trunklines were receiving no subsidy. Today the act provides for separate calculation of the service compensation and the subsidy supplement, the former being paid by the Post Office Department and the latter by the board. The subsidy supplement has ceased to be of significance to the trunkline industry generally,[31] but is a prop for the local-service carriers.

Airline rate regulation has been peculiar, moreover, in the extent to which the board has been engrossed in determinations with respect to a minor portion of the traffic, and has given relatively little attention to the major component in revenues. Mail pay and subsidy determinations were necessary, and hence were a constant element in the commission's business. Likewise, there has been a flow of decisions of the type generally made in regulatory agencies on public charges—that is, decisions on discrimination in rates and on applications for rate increases or decreases. Nevertheless, no general investigation of rate levels on passenger business was carried to completion until 1960, and standards for rate making were not determined until that time. The board had initiated a general investigation of passenger rates in 1943, when wartime prosperity raised airline earnings; but the investigation was dropped when compromise reductions of about 10 per cent were made for most carriers. Nearly two years later the board again initiated, and subsequently dropped, a general investigation after certain reductions were made. In 1947 the board, now concerned with the financial difficulties of the carriers, proposed to and obtained from the carriers a formal agreement to raise rates 10 per cent. In 1948 similar discussions were held, but these resulted in no agreement. In 1948 a threat of a rate war led the board to set minimum cargo rates. Following a revival of airline earnings, the board in 1952 initiated a general passenger fare investigation, but dropped it in 1953.

With carrier earnings still high, the board yielded to congressional pressure for a general investigation. The General Passenger Fare Investigation (GPFI) began in 1956 and was concluded in 1960. It had two purposes: to determine standards for rate making, and to determine what the rates should be. Although the board concluded, at the end of the lengthy investigation,

---

[31] After all trunklines had been off subsidy for years, Northeast Airlines, on October 4, 1963, was allowed subsidy on its New England business.

that it still did not have the facts it needed to determine specific rates, it did determine some standards for rate making. The issues presented showed some of the peculiar problems of rate fixing for airlines. Some of the carriers argued that the profit margin should be figured as a percentage of sales (margin-of-return on sales), but the board rejected this for the traditional rate of return on a rate base. Valuation problems presented little difficulty, though there were some other issues on the rate base. To determine the appropriate rate of return, the cost-of-capital approach was used. This meant a determination of the proportions of debt and equity capital, and the rate on each which would be necessary to attract capital to the industry. One of the problems was the difference in financial strength of the several carriers—a typical problem in regulation of oligopolistic markets. The board took the two groups of carriers—the Big Four and the others, determined the return needed for each, and then took the weighted average of the two figures. Since there is volatility in airline earnings, the question was raised in the course of the proceedings as to whether some rule for automatic adjustment of rates could be adopted, but this was not found to be feasible. This question serves to focus attention on one problem in rate making for a volatile industry. Rate-making proceedings are so lengthy that conditions in the industry change during their pendency. This was true in the GPFR. The most important factor affecting airline earnings is the use of seat capacity, and the introduction of jets had brought a decline in percentage of seat use and earnings. The investigation, in part conducted to determine whether rates were too high, had lost much of its significance by the time it was concluded. In the meantime, the board had raised rates without completion of the investigation, and in two instances had done this by the informal method of announcing to the airlines that it would approve certain stated increases if they would ask for them. The problem of finding a method of prompt adjustment of rates to changed conditions remains unsolved.[32]

Issues on the rate level may not be as important as those on the structure of rates. By "structure" is meant the internal relationships in the pattern of rates—the amounts to be derived from long and short hauls, from coach and first-class tickets, the relationship of family rates to other rates, and similar questions. On the first of these the board has faced the problem of the taper—that is, an additional per-ticket charge of one dollar or more to compensate for extra costs in short hauls. The biggest issue has been coach-fare rates. Many critics have believed that the goal for airlines should have been a mass transportation system, and that the board and the industry have been dilatory and unimaginative in efforts to develop low-cost transportation. Family and other forms of promotional pricing present the same kinds of issues as coach fares. The express responsibility of the board for promoting airline transportation gives peculiar significance to these questions of struc-

---

[32] For fuller analysis, see Emmette S. Redford, *The General Passenger Fare Investigation* (University, Ala.: University of Alabama Press, 1959).

ture in airline pricing. Members of the board have often differed among themselves on the extent to which promotional pricing to reach for a wider market should be encouraged or permitted.[33]

COMMENTS ON THE SYSTEM OF REGULATION AND PROMOTION. Airline transportation presents an example of macropolitical decision on basic policy for an emerging industry, and subsequent development and application of that policy in a subsystem of intermediate politics. The Congress and the President became involved in decisions for an industry, resulting in the act of 1938. The basic policy decisions emerging in the formative period were that air transport should be a private industry, that regulated competition should be the structural pattern, that traditional utility techniques should be employed in regulation, and that safety, promotion, and stability should be the dominant objectives. As these policies have been applied the usual triangular subsystem in interconnected centers of influence has developed. The administrative elements in the subsystem are the Civil Aeronautics Board and the Federal Aviation Agency. The congressional elements are the Senate and House Committees on Interstate and Foreign Commerce, the Subcommittee on Aviation of the former and the Subcommittee on Transportation and Communication of the latter, the House and Senate subcommittees on the Department of Commerce and Related Agencies of the committees on Appropriations, and certain other committees which, from time to time, are able to work themselves temporarily into positions of influence. The industry elements are the associations, chiefly the Air Transport Association and the Air Line Pilots Association. Within these organizational centers are a few persons who are strategically placed for influence: members of the board, administrator of the FAA, chairman of the Senate Subcommittee on Aviation, chairman of the House Committee on Interstate and Foreign Commerce and of its Subcommittee on Transportation and Communication, chairmen of the appropriations subcommittees, and executive heads of the leading associations. These and the executives and attorneys of the companies are strategically located for influence on the decisions with respect to commercial aviation.[34]

Reference may be made to the two tests of a politico-economic system set forth in Chapter 3—expertness and responsiveness. Undoubtedly, there is much expertness on the details of airline affairs in the staffs which back up the persons in strategic positions. Airline policy is strongly responsive to the community pressures for service, to the interests of the companies supply-

---

[33] More complete discussion of airline pricing policies may be found in Richard E. Caves, *Air Transport and Its Regulators: An Industry Study* (Cambridge, Mass.: Harvard University Press, 1962), Chapters 7 and 17, and in Paul M. Cherington, *Airline Price Policy: A Study of Domestic Airline Passenger Fares* (Boston: Harvard Business School, 1958).

[34] For full discussion of the interrelations in the aviation subsystem, see Emmette S. Redford, "A Case Analysis of Congressional Activity: Civil Aviation, 1957-58," *Journal of Politics*, **XXII** (May 1960), pp. 228-258. For distinction between macropolitics and subsystem (or intermediate) politics see page 58.

ing the service, and to the policies of promotion and industry stability enunciated in the regulatory act. Many other interests are brought into the arena of influences, usually on a more occasional basis than those cited. Sometimes, therefore, the interaction within the subsystem of administrative, legislative, and industry centers is supplemented by concerted action with, or compromises with, leaders representing additional interests. This has been true, for example, in the decisions respecting the relations between commercial and military air transport.[35] Sometimes also the decisions have to be made in the forum of macropolitics. Illustrative was the resolution of a major conflict between military and civilian interests by an amendment presented on the floor of the Senate during consideration of the Federal Aviation Act.[36]

While airline regulation illustrates possible organizational relationships and political features of a system of industry control,[37] it also offers opportunity for analysis of economic and other benefits or losses from a system of regulated oligopoly. Such an analysis for the trunkline industry was undertaken recently by Richard E. Caves. He found that the "major standing policies" of CAB "do not coincide with the economist's usual criteria of efficiency. The Board aims at more than a normal amount of resources in the air-transport industry, service in more city-pair markets than can sustain it commercially, and probably a faster rate of development of new aircraft than unrestricted market forces would produce."[38] He finds that "the airlines have a market structure which makes them more workably competitive than some unregulated industries in the economy."[39] From this it would appear that public regulation has been undesirable; but on the other hand, some may feel uncertainty as to the way the industry would have functioned without regulation. There is no history of unregulated air transport under similar conditions to those of 1938 to the present by which tests can be made of the findings from economic logic. Also, Caves points out that there must be consideration of whether there are other objectives which repay the losses from misallocation of economic resources. He notes the following objectives, which lie outside "the usual norms of economic welfare":

1. Contribution to military potential.
2. Maintenance of a regular network of air routes uniting the nation's cities and towns.
3. Speeding the development of transport aircraft.
4. Maximizing the safety of air transport.
5. Keeping fares as stable as possible, and restricting use of price discrimination.[40]

[35] *Ibid.*, pp. 237–240.
[36] See Emmette S. Redford, *Congress Passes the Federal Aviation Act of 1958* (University, Ala.: University of Alabama Press, 1961), pp. 30–32.
[37] It illustrates also some legal-administrative problems. See pages 558–559.
[38] Richard E. Caves, *Air Transport and Its Regulators: An Industry Study* (Cambridge, Mass.: Harvard University Press, 1962), p. 433.
[39] Caves, *ibid.*, pp. 448–449.
[40] Summarized from Caves, *ibid.*, p. 434.

He finds that none of these "special objectives seems very compelling," but that "not all of them can be dismissed as worthless." [41] He concludes that "the decision ultimately is a political one." [42]

This final conclusion by Caves coincides with the theme of this book from Chapter 2 forward. Politics is the final court of appeal. Decisions in this court are not based entirely on economist's tests. Indeed, we have pointed out that in the economy of organizations, private decisions may not be based entirely on economist's tests. But what political decision should be made? As Caves says, an economist may feel that the sacrifices of his values are hardly worth the gain; on the other hand, there may be others who will feel that the political decision on allocation of resources is more valid—by virtue of whatever degree of expertness and responsiveness exists—than an allocation made in a private oligopolistic market.

WATER CARRIERS

Water transportation conducted under common control with rail transportation has been subject to regulation by the ICC since 1887. The powers of the commission were extended in 1906 and in the Panama Canal Act of 1912. Independent water carriers were given some protection by the long-short-haul provision. Legislation relating to independent, port-to-port transportation was passed in 1916, 1933, and 1938; but such legislation was limited in objective and scope. Since small investment was required to enter water transportation, and the investment was nontransferable to other uses, instability and excessive rate cutting were prevalent. The conditions were similar to those in water and air transport prior to their regulation, and it is not surprising that Congress adopted the same methods of regulation. The legislation was enacted in 1940,[43] and became Part III of the Interstate Commerce Act, Part I of which deals with railroads and pipelines, and Part II with motor carriers. The provisions of Part III were to be carried out by the ICC.

The regulation extends to common and contract carriers, and includes two types of control for each. The provisions on these matters parallel closely those in the Motor Carrier Act. Common carriers obtain certificates of public convenience and necessity upon a showing that they are "fit, willing and able properly to perform the service," and that the service will be for public convenience and necessity. Contract carriers obtain permits if "fit, willing, and able," and if the operation will be consistent with the public interest and the national transportation policy. Grandfather clauses preserved existing rights. Contract carriers were subject to minimum-rate control, common carriers to the comprehensive rate controls to which

---

[41] Caves, *ibid.*, p. 438.
[42] Caves, *ibid.*, p. 449.
[43] 54 Stat. 898.

common carriers by rail, motor carrier, and air had previously been subjected. There were no additional provisions concerning such things as security issues and consolidations. There was a duty imposed upon common carriers to establish through routes with other water carriers and with rail carriers, and they were permitted to form through routes with motor carriers.

The most distinctive feature of this regulatory act is the vastness of the exemptions. The main exemption is of all transport in bulk (that is, not in containers) when the cargo space of the vessel is being used for the carrying of not more than three such commodities. This provision is applicable to all water transport except that covered at the time by the Intercoastal Shipping Act of 1933, which applied controls to intercoastal common and contract service via the Panama Canal and to coastwise and Great Lakes common carriers. There are other exemptions for such things as ferries, vessels transporting no more than sixteen passengers, defined types of small crafts, and for liquid cargoes in bulk in tank vessels designed for use exclusively in such service.

PIPELINES

The Hepburn Act of 1906 made the provisions of the Interstate Commerce Act applicable to common carriers engaged in "transportation of oil or other commodity, except water and except natural or artificial gas, by means of pipelines, or partly by pipelines and partly by railroad, or partly by pipelines and partly by water." [44] At that time the commodity subjected to regulation was crude oil; since 1930 some gasoline and other refined products have also been transported in pipelines. Natural gas pipelines were not subject to national regulation until 1938, and were then placed under the jurisdiction of the Federal Power Commission.

Crude-oil transportation has always been controlled in substantial degree by the major oil companies. In recent years approximately 75 per cent of the crude oil has moved in pipelines, and of this, 80 to 90 per cent has moved in lines owned by about nineteen companies. The ownership of the transportation facilities by the major companies has placed the independent producer and marketer at a great disadvantage, and it was this fact that led to the provision for pipeline regulation.

The act provided for common-carrier status for pipelines. The pipeline owners, including Standard of New Jersey, the dominant company, sought to avoid this status by transporting only after purchase. The Supreme Court, in the Pipeline Cases in 1914, held that all except one of the pipeline companies were, in fact common carriers, in spite of this evasive tactic.[45]

[44] 34 Stat. 584.
[45] The Pipeline Cases, 234 U.S. 548.

This did not fully correct the plight of the independent. The major companies required tender of the product in large quantities. The ICC has held that a requirement of more than 10,000 barrels is unreasonable,[46] but the largest producing state (Texas) has set a 500-barrel minimum. The independent could also be discriminated against by high rates. However, there have been relatively few complaints on rates to the commission, and it was slow in exercising its jurisdiction. Not until 1934 did it institute a valuation of pipelines and a general investigation of pipeline rates. In its decision it allowed a rather high return of 8 per cent on fair value.[47] It was also alleged that the owners of lines could be favored through rebates in the form of dividends. A consent decree fixed 7 per cent as the maximum allowable dividend.[48] The independent operator will often lack connection to a pipeline; he may be forced, therefore, to use other forms of transportation, to build refining facilities at the crude-oil source, or to go without a market for his oil.

There have been proposals for separating the business of oil refining and transportation. There was an effort to get a commodities clause for pipelines included in the Hepburn Act. The commodities clause, as applied to railroads, prevents them from owning commodities which they transport, though court decisions have established some qualifications of the principle. The Federal Trade Commission in 1917 recommended separation of ownership of pipelines from the other parts of the petroleum industry,[49] and this suggestion has been vigorously debated. Some writers have considered the step essential for a competitive oil industry; others have argued that the incentive to build needed lines would be impaired, and that the independent would not benefit to the extent anticipated.[50]

PROBLEMS IN TRANSPORTATION POLICY

THE COMPLEX OF INTERESTS. The diversity of interests in the transportation system of the nation is almost incomprehensible. There are shippers' interests, community interests, carriers' interests, national interests, and a multitude of conflicting interests within each of these categories.

[46] *Brundred Bros. v. Prairie Pipe Line Co.*, 68 ICC 458 (1922); Reduced Pipe Line Rates and Gathering Charges, 243 ICC 115 (1940).
[47] *Ibid.*, p. 143.
[48] *U.S. v. Atlantic Refining Co.*, Civil Action 14060, D. Col. (1941).
[49] Federal Trade Commission, *Report on the Price of Gasoline* (Washington, D.C., 1917), pp. 161 and 164.
[50] See William Beard, *Regulation of Pipe Lines as Common Carriers* (New York: Columbia University Press, 1941), pp. 120ff; Eugene V. Rostow, *A National Policy for the Oil Industry* (New Haven, Conn.: Yale University Press, 1948); G. S. Wolbert, *American Pipe Lines* (Norman, Okla.: University of Oklahoma Press, 1952); and Leslie Cookenboo, Jr., *Crude Oil Pipe Lines and Competition in the Oil Industry* (Cambridge, Mass.: Harvard University Press, 1955).

As a consequence, all three kinds of politics described in Chapter 3 influence public policy and administration.

A view backward over the span of history will show clearly that the most basic desire of the American people and their governments with respect to transportation has been promotion, and that regulation, in spite of the attention given it, has been a less impelling objective. Communities, and the shippers within them, have wanted governments to promote railroad development, to build highways, to dredge harbors and make rivers navigable, to subsidize commercial airlines directly and to aid air transport generally by airport construction and air-traffic management. Out of this grows micropolitics, which is the game of pressure for attainment of the particular objectives of individuals, groups, or sections. Dallas and Fort Worth build separate airports fifteen miles apart, and Dallas seeks the navigability of the Trinity River, and in both of these situations the promotion or protection of interests leads to the national capital; the examples only illustrate the involvement of enterprising communities in the micropolitics of transportation.

With the establishment of government programs of activity, political subsystems develop within which the game of intermediate politics is played. There are the Bureau of Public Roads, the state highway departments, corresponding committee centers in Congress and state legislatures, and a vast group of contractors and supply companies, shippers and carriers forming a subsystem of political interaction and of influence on decisions on appropriations for highway development. There is another subsystem composed of the Army Engineers, the committees on public works in the Congress, the private Rivers and Harbors Congress, and other interests which influence the development of waterways. There is a rather distinct subsystem for commercial air transportation, though this one overlaps with the subsystems for rail and motor transportation in the committee organization of Congress. These subsystems are the primary arenas of conflict and adjustment of transportation interests.

Transportation questions also move into the arena of macropolitics as the support of the President, congressmen outside the subsystems, and the public are sought. Yet the subsystems operate continuously, and the interventions from macropolitics are occasional. Moreover, the instruments of macropolitics are weak. The Bureau of the Budget provides a focus for overall consideration of government's investment policy in transportation, but it handles this function along with a multitude of others. An effort was made to make the ICC a center for an enlarged subsystem when it was given jurisdiction over regulated motor and water carriers. But the general executive and legislative organization is broken into pieces forming parts of separate subsystems, and there are probably no private organizations with strong influence prepared to give continuous attention to overall transportation policy.

In such a setting, it is too much to hope for consistency, orderliness, and rationality in public policy and administration. Micropolitics is checked in many ways through the resistances in the political and administrative system, but it makes for ragged pieces in the quilt of policy. Much rationality may be attained through the subsystems, but they are not organized for promotion of a unified transportation program for the nation. It can never be hoped that anything as pluralistic as transportation, existing in a pluralistic economy and in pluralistic politics, could evolve according to neat patterns, but it will be helpful at a later point to raise the question whether the instruments of overall planning and coordination should be strengthened.

THE CENTER AND THE PERIPHERY. Regulation of transportation has been comprehensive in two respects. It has been extended to all modes of transportation service, the major dates being: for railroads 1887, 1906, and 1920; for oil pipelines 1906; for motor carriers 1935; for air carriers 1938; and for water carriers 1940. It has been extended, insofar as common carriers are concerned, to many elements of policy and managerial decision. Rate regulation extends both to minimum and maximum rates and to the actual rate. For railroads, motor carriers, and airlines, regulation extends also to entry, expansion, and exit; to consolidations and other steps toward single or joint management; to adequacy of service; to safety; to security issues (except for airlines).

Within the area of regulation there is a tendency toward detailed control. Rate controls extend to the specific rate to be charged. In motor-carrier and airline regulation the grants of operating rights are meticulously refined.

Yet the transportation system as a whole is neither comprehensively nor intimately controlled. Private carriage is, of course, not subject to economic regulation. The controls over contract carriers are much looser than those over common carriers. Broad exemptions of common-carrier transport are made, the chief of these being the agricultural-commodities exemption from motor-carrier regulation, and the bulk-commodities exemption from water-carrier regulation. Regulation extends to a relatively small segment of passenger transportation, for approximately 90 per cent of intercity passenger traffic is by private automobile. Comprehensive and detailed regulation extends to only a portion of freight traffic, for in 1959 only 67 per cent of the intercity freight was regulated common-carrier transport, a decline from 79 per cent in 1946. The figures for particular modes of transportation in 1958 were: railroads, 100 per cent; motor carriers, 32 per cent; oil pipelines, 78 per cent; inland waterways, 6 per cent.[51]

Regulation is primarily of the common-carrier center, with some supporting control over contract carriage. The periphery of unregulated pri-

[51] *National Transportation Policy*, Report by Special Study Group on Transportation Policies in the United States, Committee on Commerce, U.S. Senate (87th Cong., 1st Sess., 1961), pp. 49–50.

vate and exempt carriage, and of partly regulated contract carriage, is large. The result is that common-carrier transport is subjected to much unregulated competition.

Regulation at the center is itself limited in stringency by the relationship between public and private responsibility. Initiative rests substantially with private parties. There are opportunities for public planning and for public initiation of proceedings, but most actions of public agencies are taken on petition. Moreover, compulsory powers over organization of the transportation industries are limited, and may necessarily be so. Also, the complexities of the transportation system have led to private arrangements for cooperative development of rate structures and for joint fares; public control over these matters is supervisory and interventionist, not comprehensive and not continuous with respect to particular schedules and rates. The regulatory system is to a substantial extent a veto system. It may be hoped that it will also yield some general policy and guidance for the private operator.

These comments indicate that there are inherent limitations on what can be accomplished through regulation. There are many of these, but in transportation regulation the two suggested above are of particular significance. Regulation can deal with only a portion, not the whole, problem of transportation. And applied to the complexities of shipping in a diversified economy and large country, it will be limited by the necessities of private initiative and responsibility. The expectations from regulation should not be placed too high, nor the failures in transportation attributed to it too readily.

THE HEALTH OF THE COMMON CARRIERS. Although contract and private carriage offer alternative facilities to shippers, the common carriers are the essential core of the transportation system. It is upon them that shippers must depend for regular, dependable, and adequate service. Moreover, the railroads remain a necessary element in the system, both in normal peacetime conditions and for the flexible expansion of service which may be required in a national emergency. Hence, while public policy promotes highway, water, and air facilities which can be used for private and contract carriage, it necessarily must reflect concern for the health of the common-carrier network and for the railway component thereof.

The setting to which regulatory policy must respond has undergone a revolutionary change. Where once the railroads had a monopoly for much intercity transportation, there is now competition among modes of transportation service and for common carriers from private, contract, and exempt carriers. It is this fact of competition which sets the problem of present-day transportation policy.

Some responses have been made to the changed setting. The Transportation Act of 1940 directed that consideration be given by the ICC to the "inherent advantages" of the modes of competition subject to its jurisdiction, and a similar directive was given to the CAB in 1938. In 1957 and 1958 Congress tightened the restrictions on exempt, private, and contract motor-carrier operations to give more protection to the common carrier. It also gave a new directive relating to rate competition between different modes of carriers.

The response of the future may in some ways lead toward expanded regulation. Fair and Williams have said, "it is desirable to empower the Commission to require the establishment of through routes between several types of carriers, as it may now do in respect to connecting railroads." [52] They suggest also that if large-scale consolidation of railroads is to be achieved within a reasonable time, "it appears that government must assume leadership and force the issue," and further that government leadership will be required to work out an integrated nationwide small-shipment service.[53] These proposals regarding coordination and integration undoubtedly assume leadership with a minimum of coercion,[54] but they do look toward expanded public responsibility. It is possible, also, that the exemptions of motor carriers of agricultural and fisheries products, and of water carriers of bulk products, will be narrowed. President Kennedy suggested to Congress in 1962 that it might want to consider removing the exemption of bulk commodities, though he preferred the other course mentioned below in discussion of minimum rates.[55]

On the other hand, the response may be toward relaxation of some forms of control and more reliance upon competition as the regulator. The two methods of regulating competition are control of entry, consolidation, and exit, and control of rates. Control over entry has produced a complex system of detailed regulation couched in a special terminology of rights and restrictions. The effects are hard to measure, but some of the general trends or effects may be noted. For the administrative agencies this task of managing competition through regulation of entry rights has resulted in a heavy burden of detail. In air transport a history of tight restrictions on extension of service by the existing trunklines was reversed in 1955. By 1958, among the leading 100 city-pairs served, 89 were served by two or more carriers, 63 by three or more, and 33 by four or more. In motor-carrier regulation, the trend has been toward restriction, so that a recognized authority could conclude that "many important routes such as the transcontinental are now served by two to five carriers and often, because of gateway and other restrictions, there is only one effective competitor or none at all except for private carriers, exempt carriers, or carriers

---

[52] Marvin L. Fair and Ernest W. Williams, Jr., *Economics of Transportation,* rev. ed. (New York: Harper and Brothers, Publishers, 1959), p. 673.

[53] Fair and Williams, *ibid.,* p. 672.

[54] See the remarks on limitations on government action on these matters in Ernest W. Williams, Jr., and David W. Bluestone, *Rationale of Federal Transportation Policy,* Appendix to *Federal Transportation Policy and Program* (Washington, D.C.: U.S. Department of Agriculture, 1960), pp. 66ff.

[55] "The Transportation System of Our Nation," Message of the President to Congress, House Doc. No. 384 (87th Cong., 2d Sess.).

of other types."[56] Also, flexibilities in motor-carrier service are impeded by the restrictiveness of grants. As for the railroads, controls on entry have restricted their development of truck, bus, or other alternative modes of transport, though piggyback transport and joint-rate agreements between railroads and truck lines offer opportunities to the rails under the existing system.

The unsatisfactory load factors (unfilled seats) on the airlines make it unlikely that there will be in the near future any further extension of service rights on any significant scale, and the question is whether attrition through abandonments of service or consolidation will reduce competition. On the other hand, it has been forcefully argued that there should be a gradual relaxation of the restrictions on surface-transport service.[57] The initiation of the proceedings in Ex Parte No. MC-55 shows that the ICC is conscious of the problems of detailed supervision; but whether there can be any back-up of consequence from the detailed system of control, in view of the many interests involved, is uncertain.

While there has been much professional argument for relaxations on entry controls, there has been even more professional judgment for, and more official interest in, allowing a freer play of competitive forces on rates. The discussion centers on minimum rates, for competition has made the protection given to carriers against uneconomic rate cutting a much more important problem than protection of the public against excessive charges. Among other things, it is argued that minimum-rate controls prevent realization of the cost advantages of railroads[58] and divert traffic to unregulated carriers.[59] The former has been referred to as umbrella-holding over motor-carrier rates. Congress in 1958 sought to correct this situation by providing that rates of one mode of carrier should not be held up to protect those of another. To prevent the diversion of traffic to unregulated carriers, President Kennedy recommended to Congress that the exemption from minimum-rate controls for bulk commodities, now applicable to water carriers, and for agricultural and fishery products, now applicable to motor carriers, be extended to all carriers. He also recommended that Congress pass legislation which would eventually remove minimum-rate controls on passenger transport.[60]

Congress has, however, not repealed minimum-rate controls for traffic other than bulk commodities and agricultural and fishery products. There is a dilemma on the matter of minimum rates: on the one hand, a fear that regulation will produce uneconomic rate levels and rate relationships; and on the other, a fear that the absence of regulation would create destructive rate cutting, instability in the finances of common car-

[56] Williams and Bluestone, *op. cit.*, p. 13.
[57] Williams and Bluestone, *ibid.*, pp. 22–32.
[58] See Ernest W. Williams, Jr., *The Regulation of Rail-Motor Rate Competition* (New York: Harper and Row, Publishers, Inc., 1958), pp. 221–222.
[59] See *National Transportation Policy, op. cit.*, p. 427.
[60] Message on "The Transportation System of Our Nation," *op. cit.*

riers, and shipper dissatisfaction with unstable rate structures. The problem is not one of abandonment or retention of controls, but of steerage between Scylla and Charybdis. The problem is complicated by the fact that accurate intermodal cost computations are not available, and that there are different ways of figuring costs. Thus, determining whether a railroad rate was unreasonably low on the basis of out-of-pocket cost alone would give advantage to railroads because of the much larger investment in fixed assets than exists in motor carriers. But to prevent a railroad from meeting any competitive rate by reducing its rate below full allocation of all costs would operate disadvantageously for the railroads, and would impose excessive rigidity on railroad rate making.[61] To say that rates should be set on the basis of cost only drives one back to another position between Scylla and Charybdis.

There is, it may be concluded, no easy or final set of answers to the problems of common-carrier regulation. It is sometimes said that it is desirable to allocate resources as nearly like a free market would allocate them as possible, but that free market is an ideal "laid up in heaven" rather than an achievable condition. The actual condition of the 1870's and 1880's, and of the thirties on transportation matters, was not regarded as satisfactory. Neither will the results of regulation. But it is unlikely that the great risks of returning to a pre-regulatory situation will be taken. Corrections, however, may be made in the operation of the evolved institutional system, and some of these may operate in the direction of looser controls.

The special problem of the health of the railroad industry is likely to plague the industry and its regulators in future years. Some of the directions of movement are indicated: public leadership and private initiative on consolidation, freedom to the railroads to abandon unremunerative passenger transport, public support for the railroads in removal of uneconomic labor requirements, relief from grade-crossing costs redounding to the benefit of competing traffic, cost-reducing measures by railroad management, and perhaps more freedom to adjust rates to meet competition. It is not likely that the health of the railroads will be sought by curtailing the promotion of other forms of transportation, though the railroads may be aided by placing some greater proportion of the costs of alternative forms of competition on the users thereof.

INTEGRATION OF TRANSPORTATION POLICY. The nation has never had a structure through which a unified transportation program could be developed. For a brief time the Federal Coordinator of Transportation supplied a central planning center, but the office disappeared after having provided only the outlines of regulatory policy. Since 1950 there has been an Under Secretary for Transportation in the Department

---

[61] For the ICC's response, see Marvin L. Fair and Ernest W. Williams, Jr., *Economics of Transportation*, rev. ed. (New York: Harper and Row, Publishers, Inc., 1959), pp. 602–604.

of Commerce, but the power and influence of the position bear no resemblance to what would be necessary to develop an integrated transportation program.

To achieve this objective, there have been recommendations for a department of transportation. The latest official recommendation for a department was made by President Eisenhower in his last State-of-the-Union message to Congress. There had been plans in the Eisenhower Administration to push for the establishment of a department, but the introduction of the bill in 1958 for a separate federal aviation agency diverted attention to this proposal.

If a department were established, what kinds of function might be given to it? First, it would absorb the functions of the Federal Aviation Agency, and could be given the executive and promotional tasks now placed in the separate transportation agencies. The Bureau of Public Roads could be placed in the department. Less likely—indeed, hardly conceivable—would be the placement of the Army Engineers in the department; for although they are engaged in river navigation projects, their work is also related to flood control and other objectives, which lead most authorities to think that they should be located in a department concerned with conservation of water resources. Second, it could be given the task of planning the investment policy of the nation in the several modes of transportation and the extent and ways of recovering all or a portion of the costs from the users of transportation service. Investment policy includes such matters as expenditures for highway construction and for river navigation, subsidies to airlines, and loan guarantees for railroad and airline companies. User charges would include transportation taxes and taxes on fuel used by carriers, including in either case any charges to be collected for benefits from use of the expensive air traffic-management system. Third, a department could be given responsibility for planning steps to be taken to achieve more effectively the objectives of the national transportation policy. Such planning could extend to such matters as the role for which each type of carrier was adapted, and the ways that regulatory and promotional policies could be adjusted toward fulfillment of the role by each mode of carrier. It may be assumed that the regulatory functions would remain in the present agencies, or that these functions would be combined in a single regulatory commission.

The limitations on results achievable from such a department have frequently been overlooked. It could not be expected to include within it all the administrative components of the subsystems affecting transportation. Certainly, it could be anticipated that the Army Engineers would not be included. The congressional components of the subsystems would remain undisturbed. As a result of these things, the department's ability to obtain an overall view of transportation, and to act as an effective agent for resolution of conflicting interests, would be limited. Moreover, unless present views of the independence of the regulatory function were revised,

424 *Regulation and Promotion of Industries*

it would lack means of carrying its policy objectives into effect, other than recommendation to Congress or the influence its plans would have on the regulatory commission or commissions.

Yet almost every study of transportation emphasizes the need for coordination in government activities. There are some alternatives to a department of transportation, though these might not be as effective. The Department of Commerce could be strengthened for the study-and-planning function. Or the President's staff resources could be strengthened. Or some gain might be made by consolidation of regulatory agencies. The persistent facts are, first, that there is need for coordination in the government's policies, and second, that the size of the task, the diversity of interests affected, and the number of administrative, congressional, and industry agents which must participate place limitations on the ability to achieve the objective.

Chapter 19. Public Utility Regulation

THE TERM "public utility" is a commonly used one. It is difficult, however, if not quite impossible, to define precisely its meaning.

There is not even full agreement as to what industries should be included in the category. There is a first group of industries which can be called household utilities. They serve also industrial and commercial establishments, but they have in common the supply of essential household needs. Included are electricity, gas, telephone, water, and sewage-disposal industries. All commentators would include these, and perhaps also local transit facilities offered to the public, in the hard core of the public-utility classification. A second group of industries which are commonly, although not always, included in the category are those offering transportation services to the public. These are the common carriers by rail, motor, water, and air, and auxiliary public services such as those supplied by express companies and freight forwarders. Third, there is a miscellaneous group of industries which seem to belong in the category of public utilities, including those supplying telegraph, stockyard, and grain-elevator service, and taxis, cotton gins, and grist mills.

For a period these industries were said to be "affected with a public interest." But use of the phrase brought confusion when it came to be applied also to certain industries which had characteristics unlike those of utilities. The phrase "affected with a public interest" was applied to any industry whose price could be constitutionally regulated. When the Supreme Court decided, in 1934, that legislatures could provide for price regulation for any commodity or service, the phrase ceased to have any legal significance.[1] It can now be dismissed from all discussion of public utilities.

Utility industries are sometimes described in terms of the types of regulation imposed upon them. The usual types of regulation are control of service and of rates of charge. But there are variations in the kinds of regulation enacted for utilities, and the same kinds of regulation may be imposed on other industries which would not be called public utilities.

The traditional explanation of public utilities which seemed most uni-

---

[1] See page 366.

versally applicable, and seemed to distinguish the group most clearly, was a legal one. Certain businesses have been under a legal obligation to serve all persons who demanded service. The industries were susceptible to regulation in ways which would insure that they dealt fairly with those who were forced to rely upon their services. But suddenly the proposals in civil-rights legislation for requiring restaurants, hotels, and other industries to offer service to all, or virtually all, without discrimination showed that the legal obligation to serve all may be imposed by legislation upon almost any industry.

The obligation to serve all was initially a common law obligation imposed by the courts. The courts also said that the supplier was under an obligation to serve at reasonable rates. Why should the courts have held that certain industries were under these obligations? The answer seems to be that a tendency toward monopoly was recognized to be characteristic of these industries. If a man had the only ferry at a crossing, it was reasonable to impose upon him the obligation to serve anyone who came, and to do so at a fair price.

Under the conditions of the twentieth century, other definitions of utilities are given. Utilities are referred to as natural monopolies. The economist explains this in terms of the economics of overhead costs. The capital investment in a utility system is so large that it cannot be duplicated in competitive systems with the prospect that these systems will be able to make returns on the capital outlay. Stating the proposition differently, it can be said that the public benefits from the spread of capital costs of an enterprise over as many units of consumer service as possible, and hence from service by a single firm to all persons in the area of supply. This condition is not true for all utilities; it has been seen that, for transportation, the public has desired competition and that there has been much professional opinion in favor of using competition as a regulator. Moreover, the economics of overhead cost applies in many non-utility industries. This is merely to say that the economic characteristics of all utilities are not the same, and that the economic characteristics of all utilities are not distinct from the economic characteristics of all other industries. For example, the argument on overhead costs does not have the same applicability to airlines as it does to water and electric utilities, and will have less applicability to motor carriers than to steel.

In the case of several of the utilities there are physical reasons for monopoly which are as important as the economic reasons. A modern city cannot grant rights-of-way to competing electric, gas, and telephone companies, as it could not at an earlier date make such grants to competing street-railway systems. Nor could it tolerate two or three gas companies tearing up city streets whenever needs for repair or for extension of service arose.

In the telephone industry there is the additional reason of public convenience. The writer recalls that in his boyhood two telephone companies competed in his community of four hundred people. Customers paid a nickle transfer charge for a call to a person on the opposing line. This absurd situation illustrates, in an extreme way, the public convenience as well as the economic advantage of monopolistic telephone service.

Essentiality of the service has often been stated as a characteristic of utilities. In answer, it can be said that food, shelter, and clothes are even more essential. Moreover, one can sometimes take an alternative service, such as coal or oil rather than gas for heating, or electricity rather than gas for cooking. In reality, the essentiality factor is an aspect of the monopoly factor: the customer finds that the service of a particular supplier is essential if the use of that commodity is to be obtained.

Utilities are usually granted certain legal privileges. First, they get a franchise, or certificate of public convenience and necessity, which often grants them a monopoly. Second, certain types of utilities have been given the right of eminent domain.

In summary, it may be said that the concept of the public utility may include these factors:

1. Legal: obligation to serve all who are willing to pay, franchise rights, right of eminent domain.
2. Economic: natural monopoly resulting from high overhead costs.
3. Physical: necessity of avoiding public rights to multiple suppliers.

Not all of these, however, appertain to every utility, and some of them are applicable to other industries.

This chapter concentrates attention on the hard core of monopolistic, privately owned utilities. Transportation has been discussed separately because of its peculiar history and problems; it is especially distinct today from the household utilities in the extent of intermodal and intramodal competition. We are dealing in this chapter with regulation of monopoly in its most distinctive aspects in American experience. To a considerable extent this experience is common for electric, gas, and telephone utilities. Water is more generally supplied by publicly owned enterprises than by regulated private monopolies. We shall deal in this chapter with that part of regulatory experience which is common to all three of the major privately owned, monopolistic utilities, or which is common to electric and gas utilities. Certain special problems for the telephone industry, the peculiar problem of field pricing for natural gas, and the influence of public promotional policies on electric-power development will be reserved for treatment in chapters on Communications, Oil and Gas, and Public Enterprise, respectively.

Three distinct historical periods are discernible. The first is the municipal or pre-commission period, ending in 1907. The second is the state-regulation period of 1907 to 1933. The third is the state-national period, characterized by three features: state action to strengthen legislation, national participation in regulation, and revision of rate-regulation practices following a decision of the Supreme Court in 1944. It will be seen that there has been a long period of public travail in the evolution toward the relatively stabilized regulatory pattern which now exists.

MUNICIPAL CONTROL

In the nineteenth century state powers concerning water, gas, power, telephone, and street railways were delegated to municipalities. For these the instrument of promotion and control was the franchise. The franchise granted rights of operation within the city and the use of city streets. In their anxiety to obtain services many cities granted rights in franchises which were later regretted. Some franchises granted exclusive rights in perpetuity without reservation of adequate control powers. In time there was a trend toward term franchises and the inclusion of regulatory provisions—that is, provisions concerning rates and services.

Defects in this system of control were quickly revealed. First, the city franchise, like the state charter for the railroad, proved to be too inflexible for regulatory purposes. Franchises were contracts, and provisions either were not subject to change, or required action by city council or voters. Second, consolidation and expansion of utility companies led to operations extending beyond city boundaries. Third, franchise grants became engulfed in corruption in many cities. Utilities saw opportunities for great gain in favorable franchise grants, and politicians were tempted to share in these gains. In New York State, for example, an investigating commission, headed by Charles Evans Hughes, reported gross abuses in the local gas company, which led promptly (1906) to the establishment of a state commission to regulate gas and electric companies in New York City.

There are still some states which vest regulatory powers over some local utilities in municipalities. In Texas, for example, electric and telephone utilities are regulated by cities rather than by the state. The typical sequence of events is a petition for a rate increase from a utility, a contract by the city with some concern to study the utility's finances, a period of higgling and of threatening from both sides, and a grant of an increase substantially less than that requested. It is government by threat and compromise.

In most states the function of the city government is different. It is the representative of the community's interests before the state and national regulatory agencies. Cities commonly intervene in rate-making proceedings, and often initiate rate cases in state and national jurisdictions.

STATE REGULATION

The movement for state regulation swept rapidly across the country, and led quickly to the establishment of commissions. New York's 1906 statute for New York City was followed in 1907 by a public-service law for the whole state. In the same year Wisconsin adopted a much more comprehensive statute, including water and telephone utilities as well as gas and electric companies, and providing for extensive authority over the latter. Georgia passed a regulatory statute in the same year; six years later half the states had commissions; and in a short time thereafter all states except Delaware had established a state agency to regulate some utilities. Today most states have provided for regulation of all or most utilities by a state regulatory agency.

Most of the early statutes, however, provided for incomplete regulation. They required certificates of public convenience and necessity, and provided for rate regulation, but they seldom included provisions for control over such matters as accounting, security issues, consolidations, and intercorporate relationships. Over the years additions have been made to the authority of most regulatory commissions, both as to the utilities included and the matters brought within the jurisdiction of the regulatory agencies. Especially around 1930, a new movement for strengthening state regulation was generated by dissatisfaction with inadequate control. A number of states that had been leaders in development of state regulation established investigating commissions and enacted new legislation. A particular objective was to meet the problem created by the complexities of intercorporate structure and utility finance.

There has always been much variation among the states with respect to the scope of the laws, the vigor of their application, and the standards and methods of application. Though there has been a tendency to round out the jurisdiction of commissions, there are still many gaps. One of the notable developments has been the more adequate requirements on the keeping of utility accounts. Uniformity on this and some other matters has been facilitated by the existence of the National Association of Railroad and Utilities Commissioners, and also by leadership of the national regulatory commissions. The state commissions are sometimes poorly financed for the tasks committed to them, and also often lack the political support and public interest required for effective performance. In spite of the decisions on rate making by the Supreme Court of the United States prior to 1944, there was considerable variation among the states in policies of rate making. The change by the Court in 1944 has left the states with much freedom to adopt their own standards and methods in rate making.

The primary responsibility for regulation of service and charges to the consumer still rests with the states. Local telephone service and the distribution of electricity and gas to consumers are subject now, as they have been since the years following 1907, to regulation by commissions in most states.

NATIONAL REGULATION:
ELECTRIC AND GAS UTILITIES

In 1920 a Federal Power Act vested in a Federal Power Commission the functions of issuing licenses for construction of hydroelectric projects on waters and lands subject to federal jurisdiction, and of regulating the rates of these licensees. The interstate transmission of electricity remained unregulated by the national government. Today, interstate transmission of electricity, interstate transportation of natural gas, and wholesaling of electricity and natural gas are regulated by the Federal Power Commission (FPC) and electric and gas utility holding companies by the Securities and Exchange Commission (SEC). The most important statutes are the Public Utility Act of 1935,[2] which contained the Public Utility Holding Company Act and the Federal Power Act, and the Natural Gas Act of 1938.[3] The Federal Power Act set up a new Federal Power Commission to continue the licensing and rate-making functions of the old commission, and to assume the new powers over interstate power facilities; the Natural Gas Act extended the jurisdiction of the commission to interstate wholesale sales of natural gas.

The need for national regulation became urgent because of the rapid growth in interstate sales of electricity and natural gas, and because of the parallel development of the interstate holding company. It will be interesting to the student to observe how national regulation of these two industries was designed to fill gaps in the state regulatory system and to make state regulation more effective.

REGULATION OF INTERSTATE GAS AND ELECTRICITY RATES. The natural gas industry is now divided into three parts. At one end is production, which is a non-utility enterprise and is regulated by states in ways unrelated to utility regulation. At the other end is distribution, which is a traditional utility enterprise and is regulated by states. In the middle is transportation, done through pipelines; this, too, is a utility enterprise, and was to become the subject of national regulation. Formerly, the pipeline companies were also heavily engaged in gas production, but today the three aspects of production, transportation, and distribution are substantially separated into three distinct industries. Pipeline companies buy gas from producers and sell it at wholesale prices to retail distributing companies. They sell also directly to companies for industrial use. The electric utility industry, on the other hand, is one in which there is usually integration of generation, transportation, and distribution in the same company. There is, however, some separation of wholesale and retail busi-

[2] 49 Stat. 838.
[3] 52 Stat. 821.

ness, with one company generating and transporting the energy, another distributing it to consumers.

A series of Supreme Court decisions fixed the powers and limitations of the states in regulation of interstate electric and gas rates. Three questions were presented and answered. First, could a state at the receiving end regulate intrastate retail rates of a distributing company which purchased from an interstate wholesale company? The answer was "yes." The Court held in 1918 that gas ceased to be in interstate commerce when it passed into the mains of the local company, and that the establishment of retail rates by the receiving state was not an interference with interstate commerce.[4] Second, could a receiving state regulate interstate retail rates—that is, rates charged by a company which itself transported the supply across state lines? The answer was "yes." The Pennsylvania Gas Company transported gas by pipeline from a source of supply in Pennsylvania, and delivered it directly to consumers in Jamestown, New York. The Court held that though this was a sale in interstate commerce, "general and uniform regulation" was not required by the Constitution; the states could regulate as long as Congress did not legislate on the subject.[5] Third, could a state, either at the receiving or the dispatching end, regulate interstate wholesale rates? The answer was "no." The Kansas Natural Gas Company produced and bought gas, mostly in Oklahoma but some in Kansas, and transported it into Kansas and from Kansas to Missouri, and in each state sold it to distributing companies. The Court held that Missouri and Kansas could not regulate the charges of the wholesale company to distributing companies. The predominant interest was national, in the Court's opinion, and the states could not regulate even in the absence of congressional legislation.[6] In another case the Court held that a state at the dispatching end could not regulate an interstate wholesale rate in order to prevent discrimination against consumers in its jurisdiction through lower rates in the adjoining state.[7]

In the Federal Power Act and the Natural Gas Act Congress left to the states the regulation of interstate retail rates, which the Court had held they could regulate in the absence of congressional legislation; Congress authorized FPC regulation of wholesale (sales for resale) rates, over which the Court had said the states had no jurisdiction. There was an exception for natural gas: the FPC could not regulate sales for resale for industrial use only. The FPC has recommended that this gap in regulation be closed. Congress has not concurred.

Though the states had authority to regulate interstate retail rates, they

---

[4] *Public Utilities Commission for the State of Kansas v. Landon*, 249 U.S. 236 (1918).
[5] *Pennsylvania Gas Co. v. Public Service Commission*, 252 U.S. 23 (1920).
[6] *Missouri v. Kansas Natural Gas Co.*, 265 U.S. 298 (1924).
[7] *Public Utilities Commission of Rhode Island v. Attleboro Steam and Electric Co.*, 273 U.S. 83 (1927).

faced administrative difficulties in their efforts to do so. How could a state commission obtain the information necessary to determine the rate base when a portion of the properties were located outside the state—perhaps in several states? A study in 1931 on electric transmission showed that generally a choice was made between two methods.[8] Some states attempted to set rates so as to yield a reasonable return on property used and useful in the state, excluding all property located outside the state. This could lead to ridiculous results: where only transmission lines were located in the state, failure to include outside generating properties led to an unreasonably low rate; but where major generating facilities existed within the state and much power was exported, then local rates set to yield a return on the whole were too high. Some states tried to avoid these difficulties by considering the interstate system as a whole and determining what portion of it was used and useful for the state, but this still left the problem of determining value on the system as a whole and making an allocation of the portion which served the state. The difficulties faced by a state were insuperable, particularly because of variation in accounting methods and lack of supervisory controls in many states. It was stated in 1934 that for electric utilities, eighteen states had no controls over security issues for purposes of capitalization, twenty-six had none over depreciation, and six had none over rates and services. Ten states in 1935 exercised no control over accounting.[9]

These difficulties could have been met by granting the FPC authority to regulate interstate retail rates. Congress chose instead to provide for national assistance to the states. The FPC was authorized to (1) investigate and determine, upon its own notion or request of a state commission, the cost of production or transmission of electric energy in interstate commerce in cases (retail sales) where the commission had no authority to set rates; (2) make available to the states information and reports; and (3) make available to a state, upon its request, its trained experts. The commission has aided states in these ways. More significant, however, were two other things: (1) the agreement with the states, through the National Association of Railroad and Utilities Commissioners, on a uniform system of utility accounts, and also the requirement by the commission that interstate utilities keep such accounts, and (2) the determination of original cost of interstate utilities, frequently with the cooperation of the state commissions. Through these means the difficulties of the states were reduced, though not eliminated. In the same ways the FPC aided the states in regulation of interstate retail gas rates, under authority granted by the Natural Gas Act.

[8] Hugh Langdon Elsbree, *Interstate Transmission of Electric Power: A Study in the Conflict of State and Federal Jurisdiction* (Cambridge, Mass.: Harvard University Press, 1931), Chapter IV.
[9] *Hearings* on H.R. 5423, House Committee on Interstate and Foreign Commerce (74th Cong., 1st Sess.), pp. 496–497.

OTHER TYPES OF REGULATION OF OPERATING COMPANIES. On wholesale rates the Federal Power Act contained the provisions normally included in regulatory acts: requirement that rates be just and reasonable, that they not be discriminatory, that they be filed with the commission, and that changes not be made without notice; authorization to the commission to suspend rates pending their consideration, to initiate consideration of rate schedules, to deny rate-change petitions, and upon finding that rates are unreasonable or discriminatory, to set the rates. The commission was not given the power to issue or deny certificates, this being left to the states. The FPC could upon petition of a state determine and order adequate service. It could regulate security issues, but only where no such regulation was provided by a state in which the utility was organized and operating. It could prescribe accounts to be kept. It could fix depreciation rates. Acquisitions of control through merger or other means required approval of the commission, as did disposal of facilities. Being officer or director of more than one utility, or serving as officer or director of a utility and also of a finance company or electric supply company supplying utilities, was prohibited unless authorized by the commission.

The commission was directed to set up regional districts for interconnection and coordination of power facilities, and to promote voluntary coordination within and between such districts. It was delegated limited power to order physical interconnections and quite complete powers of this kind in a war or other emergency. These provisions anticipated the development of grid systems for interchange of electricity among companies.

Much of the Natural Gas Act follows the pattern of the Federal Power Act, and contains identical or similar language. This is true of accounting controls, the power of the commission to fix rates of depreciation, and powers over rates, except that the commission cannot raise a gas rate above that contained in a schedule which is filed. There are, however, some substantial differences. Since wholesale service in natural gas is so largely distinct from the distributing service regulated by the states, companies subject to the act are required to obtain certificates of public convenience and necessity as a condition of service or extension of service. Abandonments also require the approval of the commission. The limited power to require physical interconnections is granted, but no broad emergency power such as that contained in the Federal Power Act. Moreover, no power is granted to the commission to control security issues. Nor is there any prohibition of interlocking offices or directorships.

REGULATION OF HOLDING COMPANIES. The student of regulation will do well to ponder two startling things about the history of utility regulation in this country. First, the most fantastic and speculative growth of the holding company occurred in an industry which was presumably subject to regulation—the electric utility industry. Second, regulation of the holding company, when it did come, was drastically purgative.

The facts about the development and status of electric and gas utility holding companies were revealed by the most stupendous investigation ever conducted by the Federal Trade Commission. The investigation was reported in over ninety volumes. Other studies of the problems created by holding companies were made in the states, the most significant being that of the New York State Commission on Revision of the Public Service Commissions Law.

The utility holding company, in the form in which it developed, was largely a post-World War development. The development was rapid both in the electric and gas utility industries. By 1928–32 a small number of holding-company groups controlled three-fourths or more of the privately owned electric-power industry. Three groups controlled approximately 44 per cent of the industry. In the less-developed gas industry the major portion of pipeline transportation was under the control of a small number of holding companies.

What were the features of the holding company systems? These may be described for the electric power industry particularly. First, there was much pyramiding—that is, layering of holding company on top of holding company. In one system "there were ten companies in one line of control from the top to the bottom of the pyramid." [10] In this way many companies could be brought under a centralized control. There were between three and four hundred corporations in the group controlled by the Associated Gas and Electric Company of New York.[11] Second, pyramiding small investments in stock could be the means of controlling vast empires. Thus, in the company just referred to, a majority ownership of stock with a book value of $8,000,000 gave practical control over companies with book values of nearly one billion dollars.[12] Third, some of the systems controlled operating companies scattered from coast to coast. Fourth, the holding-company systems were usually connected closely with banking and underwriting groups. Fifth, the holding companies or their affiliates, at charges prescribed by them, supplied the operating companies with various types of services—managerial, engineering, legal, financial, central purchasing.

There was much discussion of the relative advantages and disadvantages of holding companies. On the advantage side, the value of central services for operating companies was asserted. Particularly emphasized were the advantages in financing resulting from diversified risks, better access to underwriters and money markets, and ability to market securities in

[10] Temporary National Economic Committee, *Hearings*, Part V-A (1939), 2414, quoted by Hugh M. Hall, *The Investigatory Function of the Federal Trade Commission, 1933–1952* (Ph.D. Dissertation, University of Texas, 1953), p. 112.

[11] N. Y. State Commission on Revision of the Public Service Commissions Law, *Hearings*, Vol. III, 2752, cited by William E. Mosher and Finla G. Crawford, *Public Utility Regulation* (New York: Harper and Row, Publishers, Inc., 1933), p. 334.

[12] New York State Commission, *ibid.*, Vol. III, 2773, Exhibit 205, cited by Mosher and Crawford, *ibid.*, p. 335.

large quantities. The opportunity afforded to combine small plants into one operating system with use of central generating facilities was also stressed. On the other hand, a long list of disadvantages was set forth in studies:

(1) excessive charges to operating companies for services rendered; (2) write-up of book values during the purchase, merger, and expansion of companies; (3) overcentralization of control; (4) excessive profits for stockholders of controlling companies; (5) abuses, such as manipulation of accounting, concealment of assets, diversion of income from operating companies to controlling financial groups; (6) the difficulty, if not impossibility, of public control.

The last disadvantage merits emphasis in this discussion. The states and cities were confronted with a labyrinth of changing intercompany affiliations and transactions which was beyond comprehension unless followed minutely and continuously. They lacked facts necessary to determine the appropriate level of charges by holding-company affiliates to operating companies. Their efforts to regulate rates were complicated by the excessive book values resulting from write-ups. They lacked jurisdiction and practical means to control the nationwide systems.

Disastrous effects of the use of holding companies primarily as a means of quick financial gain rather than as a means of developing a sound utility structure were patently revealed in the late twenties. The giant Insull system collapsed, bringing the receivership of a number of companies. The stock of Cities Service Company, another utility holding company, after a 4 to 1 split in the summer of 1929, moved rapidly upward to 68 in October, and then dropped precipitously, going in 1932 to $1\frac{1}{4}$.

It was an era of dizzy finance, and perhaps the dizziest dance on the speculative floor was utility finance. The developments in finance made public control almost a mockery.

There were suggestions for state control of the utility holding companies, and legislation on the subject was enacted in some states. Nevertheless, the fundamental solutions were sought in national legislation. They were worked out under the leadership of Chairman Rayburn of the House Committee on Foreign and Interstate Commerce, with the expert assistance of Walter M. W. Splawn of the Interstate Commerce Commission and two young staff lawyers named Thomas Corcoran and Benjamin Cohen.

The solutions can be best understood if they are considered in three parts. The first requirement was registration with the SEC. No electric or gas utility holding company could make use of the mails or the facilities of interstate commerce unless it was registered. Registration was accomplished by filing a registration statement which included a complete disclosure of the relevant facts on the financial structure and operations of the company and on all the associate companies in its system. Registration statements provided the basic information needed by the SEC for discharge of the responsibilities imposed upon it. The constitutionality of the act was attacked by challenges to the registration requirements, but these were upheld in 1938,[13] and the commission proceeded with its work.

The central objective of the act was simplification of holding-company systems. The SEC was directed to examine the corporate structure of every registered holding company and subsidiary to determine the extent to which the structure could be simplified, the unnecessary complexities eliminated, the voting power equitably distributed among security holders, and the ways the properties and business of companies could be confined to form in each case an integrated public-utility system. The commission had several means of achieving the objective of simplification, and all were used. One was to use its control over security issues. The SEC could require simplifications of corporate financial structure when petitions were made for refunding of old, or issuance of new, securities. Another weapon was its control over reorganizations. With many concerns in bankruptcy, the requirement of the act that no reorganization plan of a holding company or subsidiary thereof should be approved by a court without the approval of the commission bolstered the SEC's administration of corporate simplification. Most important, however, was the famous "death sentence" in Section 11(b). The section made it the duty of the commission to require by order every holding-company system to limit its operations to a "single integrated public utility system." This was the key provision of the act. It represented the congressional judgment that if a holding company were to offer any advantages, it would be because it was a means of operating an economically and geographical integrated system. The corporate system must be simple, and the area it served must be unified. There were exceptions and additions. A system might be allowed to keep auxiliary businesses necessary or appropriate for operation of a utility system. But hotels and many of the other businesses formerly operated would have to go. Under tightly prescribed conditions, a system might be allowed to keep a second integrated system, but there could not be more than two levels of holding companies in any system. Companies were allowed, under the act, to submit their own plans for revision of their structures, and the Commission invited them to do so. If no plans were submitted, the SEC could devise its own.

The third part of the plan of the act was the set of provisions for continuing regulation of holding companies and their affiliated interests. The SEC could regulate their security issues and intercompany transactions. With respect to the latter, the act contained strict provisions on service, sales, and construction contracts to insure that funds were not drained away from operating companies to the holding companies and their affiliated service companies.

A peculiarity of the commission's responsibilities was that its permanent task of regulation would be relatively simple if the immediate job were done

---

[13] *Electric Bond and Share Co. v. Securities and Exchange Commission*, 303 U.S. 419.

successfully.[14] Its big job was to undo what had been done, to establish a simplified structure, and thus to liquidate a problem for itself and the state commissions. It was hampered by delay in the final determination of the constitutionality of the act as a whole, this not coming until 1946.[15] But it moved with vigor far beyond that usually characteristic of administrative agencies. In approximately two decades after the passage of the act it forced a drastic reorganization of the holding-company structure. It required separation of oil and gas companies, under the single integrated-system standard. It eliminated oil companies as public-utility holding companies. Some of the largest holding-company systems—for example, Electric Bond and Share Company, with four subsidiary holding companies, 131 domestic subsidiaries, and consolidated assets of $3.6 billion dollars; and Cities Service Company, with 125 member companies and consolidated assets of over $1 billion— have now ceased to be utility holding companies. Nine hundred and twenty-six companies, with assets of approximately $13 billion, have been separated from their respective parent companies. The number of holding companies which have been subject to the act is 224, but by 1961 the number had been reduced to 18 main and 4 small systems. These had met the requirements of the act for integration and simplification. The percentage of the privately owned electric and gas utility industry within holding-company systems had declined from four-fifths to one-fifth.[16]

The commission moved on other fronts. Thus it sought to increase the safety of utility investments by forcing increase of equity financing. In 1935 it was not uncommon for 70 to 80 per cent of the capital to be in bonds, and the SEC aimed at a 50–50 division between equity and debt capital. It attacked the problem of equitable allocation of salaries where the same person was a director or officer in operating, holding, and service companies in the same system. It made rules on charges by service companies. All in all, the reorganization and establishment of regulation of holding companies has been one of the most successful ventures in American regulatory experience.

One further feature of the act should be mentioned. Conflicts over utility regulation had spilled over into macropolitics, the utilities had spent vast sums directed toward influencing public policy, and they had fought vigorously the enactment of the regulatory legislation of 1935. The act included, therefore, a provision on disclosure of political activities. It became unlawful for persons employed by holding companies or their subsidiaries to present matters affecting such companies before Congress, its members, the SEC or FPC (or their members or employees), except under requirements of disclosure prescribed in rules of the SEC.

[14] The story of the commission's accomplishments during the first ten years is given by Ralph K. Huitt, *National Regulation of the Natural Gas Industry* (Ph.D. Dissertation, Austin, Tex.: University of Texas, 1950), Chapters V and VI.
[15] *North American Company v. SEC*, 327 U.S. 686.
[16] Most of the details in the text are from Securities and Exchange Commission, *Twenty-Seventh Annual Report* (1961).

REGULATION OF RATES

Without doubt, Americans have struggled more, and suffered more frustration, in regulation of utility rates than in any other effort in economic regulation. The story is a long one, reaching back to 1876; it is a complicated one, for it deals with economic purposes, engineering and accounting data, judicial doctrines, conflicting interests, and political struggle; it is a revealing one, for it shows a big gap between clear popular objective and the operations of the governmental system.

THE LOCATION OF RESPONSIBILITY. The story begins with a struggle over the location of responsibility, a struggle which undoubtedly is not even yet concluded. The rate issue was presented to the Supreme Court in *Munn v. Illinois* in 1876. The Illinois legislature had set maximum rates for grain elevators. Could the decision on the level of rates be reviewed in the courts? The Supreme Court answered with a definite and sweeping statement: "For protection against abuses by legislatures, the people must resort to the polls, not to the courts." [17] The answer was given, however, in a closely divided court.

This decision that rates fixed by the legislature were conclusive and non-reviewable by courts was followed by persistent effort of litigants to win a reversal. This led, in turn, to expressions of judicial uncertainty. In 1884 the Supreme Court said: "What may be done if the municipal authorities do not exercise an honest judgment, or if they fix upon a price which is manifestly unreasonable, need not now be considered, for that proposition is not presented by this record." [18] In 1886 the Court said: "This power to regulate is not a power to destroy, and limitation is not the equivalent of confiscation." [19] The ugly word "confiscation" was now extended beyond its traditional legal meaning of actual taking of physical assets to include effects of regulatory action on the earning power of property. The doubts of the 1880's were followed in the nineties by reversal of the position of the seventies. By 1894 all doubts were removed when the Court definitely stated judicial responsibility to determine reasonableness, and held rates set by the Texas Railroad Commission to be unreasonable.[20]

For this assumption of judicial responsibility the explanation must be found in the trends of the period. Due process had not been given a substantive meaning in 1876; it had been by 1894. Property rights were getting an expanded meaning in court decisions.[21] The courts had moved into a

---

[17] 94 U.S. 113, 134.
[18] *Spring Valley Water Works v. Schottler*, 110 U.S. 347, 354.
[19] *Stone v. Farmers' Loan and Trust Company*, 116 U.S. 307, 331.
[20] *Reagan v. Farmers' Loan and Trust Co.*, 154 U.S. 362.
[21] See for general treatment John R. Commons, *Legal Foundations of Capitalism* (New York: University of Wisconsin Press, 1924).

period of sympathetic construction of property rights which was to extend to the 1930's.[22]

The claim of judicial responsibility still stands. The first point in the discussion of rates is fixed: the courts will review rates to determine whether they are so low as to constitute a deprivation of property without due process of law. Statutes now provide that rates shall be reasonable and just, which means that they cannot be excessively low or high. The courts may, therefore, say that utility rates set by commissions are too high. There is a zone of reasonableness between the constitutional floor of confiscation and the statutory ceiling of excessive charge. The courts have only rarely been a forum for consideration of claims that rates were too high; they have been constantly a forum to which the utilities could appeal, alleging that rates were too low—either because in violation of statutory standards, or because in violation of the constitutional interpretation that rates shall not be "confiscatory."

ELEMENTS IN A REASONABLE RATE. What is the test of the constitutionality of rates? The test is "reasonableness." How determine reasonableness of rates?

The first step in the answer is that rates must be high enough to cover the following:

1. Operating costs, including salaries, repairs, billing of customers, and other items.
2. Depreciation on the property.
3. Taxes.
4. Return for the investor.

Most of these have created difficult problems for regulatory agencies. Commissions may inquire into the justification for operating expenses and refuse to allow unjustified items to be recovered in the rates. But practical difficulties have been encountered: (1) commissions may not have sufficient personnel, or sufficiently expert personnel, to review operating costs; (2) management must be allowed a wide scope of discretion on such matters—both for efficiency, and to maintain the legal balances between public and private responsibility; (3) supplies or services may be purchased from affiliated interests. Normally it may be assumed that prices paid to firms in an arms-length relationship are reasonable, but the same assumption would be dangerous if the purchases were from affiliated interests. Depreciation is itself an expense item, and has given rise to distinct and troublesome issues. Utilities, on the one hand, have wanted generous allowance of annual depreciation rates in operating expenses, and on the other, a low total charge of depreciation against the sum on which a return was to be allowed—a way of eating the cake of capital and still retaining it. The courts have been slow

[22] See Chapter 7.

in accepting doctrines under which the consumer does not make double payments on capital. Moreover, in the early period of regulation accounting methods were so undeveloped in utility practice that reliable estimates of depreciation were often impossible. The opportunities for broad difference of opinion are not as large today, but there are still some issues of depreciation in most utility cases.

Fair Value. All the other problems were minor in comparison with the problem of determining the value of the property on which the investor should have a fair return. The general rule on valuation followed by the national courts from 1898 to 1944 was stated in *Smyth v. Ames:* fair return on fair value. "We hold," said the Court, "that the basis of all calculations as to the reasonableness of rates . . . must be the fair value of the property being used by it for the convenience of the public." [23]

How was the regulator to determine the fair value of utility property in use? Could the general guide of "fair value" be given specific content? The Court in 1898 had no definite answer. It did not prescribe a single test of value; on the contrary, it listed a number of factors which were "to be given such weight as may be just and right in each case." Three main types of factors were listed.[24]

One was market value of stocks and bonds. This obviously could not, by itself, be the standard of value. Since any change in rates would alter earnings capacity, and thereby the market values of securities, this test would mean maintenance of the *status quo,* whatever it might be. This would deny the right to regulate. Market value of securities is a factor which might influence a regulatory decision, for too abrupt or drastic a change in rates, if downward, might impair the ability of a utility to obtain new finance capital. Yet "what is" as a test of "what should be" is so inadequate that this standard of value was never regarded as primary.

Another test was the actual cost of the property, referred to as "original cost."

A third test was "present as compared with the original cost of construction." Present cost later came to be interchangeable with "reproduction cost," and meant what it would cost to reproduce the property under present prices.

Either of the latter two sums, with adjustments downward for depreciation, could be a statement of value. Hence, the actual cost of the property less depreciation, and the estimated cost of reproducing the property at current prices minus depreciation, were rival tests of value. At first, some defenders of consumer interests were antagonistic to original cost because they did not want the consumer to be saddled with payment of a return on extravagant and wasteful expenditures, which so commonly accompanied the early development of utilities. Later, however, the "actual cost" test

---

[23] *Smyth v. Ames,* 169 U.S. 466, 546 (1898).
[24] *Ibid.,* p. 547.

was revised to "actual legitimate cost," and this test was given wide currency as a result of its forceful advocacy under the name of "prudent investment" in a dissenting opinion by Justice Brandeis in 1923.[25] According to this theory the consumer should pay a return only for what was prudently invested in the utility enterprise. By this time, however, the rising price level had led to demands by utilities that value be based on the cost of reproduction.

Reproduction Cost. Although the Supreme Court did not reject the dictum in *Smyth v. Ames* that there were multiple types of evidence of value, it did lean heavily toward reproduction cost as the primary evidence of value. This trend was evident prior to World War I, but was more clearly revealed in a series of decisions dating from 1923. These decisions made the judiciary appear to be prejudiced toward higher returns for utilities. A protracted period of depression could, however, reverse the benefits of reproduction cost to the consumer; and it is not surprising, therefore, that some advocates of reproduction cost should, during the Depression, express doubts as to its universal applicability.

Although arguments were made for and against reproduction cost, the general result was to erect insuperable barriers to effective rate regulation. The controversy and the experience illustrate the intermingling of economic and administrative factors in regulation of industries. One element in the controversy was the conflict of opinion over the nature of a regulated industry. In an unregulated industry, such as real estate, it is expected that values will move up and down with the ebb and flow of the business cycle. It was argued, however, that in regulation of a monopoly the purpose should be to bring service to the consumer at the lowest cost consistent with the attraction of capital to the industry and rendition of efficient service. This could be accomplished, it was argued, most effectively with maximum elimination of risks, such as would result from a stable return on a stable investment. The conflict, however, centered on the issue of economic justice for the investor. Some believed that it was essential for fairness that the investor in utilities, like the investor in nonregulated industries, have the benefit of a rise in values in an inflationary period. Others believed that those who put their money in a regulated industry did so with protections against competition and other market forces, and hence had no legitimate claim for speculative returns due to inflation. This argument still goes on today, though those who argue for variability in the investor return may seek to accomplish the objective in other ways than through use of the reproduction-cost method.

The economic arguments against reproduction cost were especially forceful because of the general practice of figuring the overall return on total value without consideration of the capital structure of the firm. If a large propor-

---

[25] *Southwestern Bell Telephone Co. v. Public Service Commission of Missouri,* 262 U.S. 276.

tion of the investment of a utility firm is in securities with a fixed return (bonds, debentures, preferred stock), and the return on the total value of properties is adjusted upward, then the effect on the common-stock return is pyramided. Only the common-stock holder gets the benefit, and his benefit is a disproportionate amount with relation to the overall increase in value of property. The common stock may appreciate in value at an enormous rate, the stockholder gaining a very large unearned increment. Conversely, a decline in the price level brings the reverse effect on stocks. If the decline is great enough, a threat to the security of fixed-return investments may develop. Hence, reproduction cost with an overall rate of return without consideration of capital structure may lead to speculation in common stocks, insecurity for bond holders, and because of these things, to higher costs for capital and consequently to higher costs to consumers. While these results may be acceptable in unregulated industry as concomitants of market controls, they can be considered as inappropriate when regulation seeks low cost for consumers in monopolistic industries. It is not surprising, therefore, that some commissions rejected use of an overall return figure, and tried to keep the variations in return for common stock proportional to the changes in the reproduction cost of the properties.

The greatest weakness of reproduction cost as a test of value is that it is difficult, if not impossible, to apply. The usual method of determining reproduction cost has been to inventory the property in use, determine the cost of reproduction of each item, and subtract an item for depreciation. It is difficult to grasp the sheer magnitude of the task as it was undertaken in the second, third, and fourth decades of this century. It has been estimated that the valuation of railway properties up to 1930, under the Valuation Act of 1913, cost the companies $138,000,000 and the ICC $45,000,000.[26] An estimate for the New York Telephone Company valuation in the twenties placed the cost for the company at $5,000,000.[27] The large cost of inventorying would today be substantially reduced by the existence of more adequate inventory records. Yet the difficulty of determining the cost of reproducing the items remains. Technological improvements bring substitutes or improvements in facilities; hence, many items in the inventory may no longer be manufactured, at least in their precise form. Determination of a reproduction cost in such cases is an estimate of something that does not exist. Also, items in the inventory may, at the time of reappraisal, be produced under conditions substantially different from those existing at the time of construction. Sometimes it would be unreasonable to value on the basis of present costs; for example, where gas utility mains were laid before street paving, it would not be reasonable to charge the public with costs of tearing up the pavement and replacing it. In other situations, it only leads to un-

---

[26] John Bauer and Nathaniel Gold, *Public Utility Valuation for Purposes of Rate Control* (New York: The Macmillan Company, 1934), p. 120.

[27] William E. Mosher and Finla G. Crawford, *Public Utility Regulation* (New York: Harper and Row, Publishers, Inc., 1933), p. 205.

certainty to seek to estimate what it would cost to produce something under conditions which did not exist when the construction was done. The problem is further complicated by the need for determining whether "spot" (that is, current) or normal prices shall be used. Since the rates are to be applicable for a future period, the utility of the valuation will depend on its accord with future reproduction costs, but the level of future prices is a subject for economists' guesses and lawyers' arguments thereafter.

The result of these difficulties of ascertaining reproduction cost is to produce wide disparity of estimates on the total value of a utility. This was well-illustrated by the following estimates of value of the New York Telephone Company on its intrastate business as of July 1, 1926:

ESTIMATES OF FAIR PROFITS FOR NEW YORK TELEPHONE COMPANY*

(on intrastate business as of July 1, 1926)

	Fair Value	Rate	Fair Return
Majority of Public Service Commission	$366,915,493	7%	$25,635,000
Federal Court	397,207,925	7%	27,804,555
Minority of Public Service Commission	405,502,993	8%	32,480,000
Special Master's Report	518,109,584	8%	41,448,777
Company claim based on Whittemore appraisal	528,753,738	8%	42,300,299
Company claim based on Stone & Webster	615,000,000	8%	49,200,000

* N.Y. State Commission on Revision of the Public Service Commissions Law, Report of Commissioners (1930), p. 38, reproduced in Felix Frankfurter, *The Public and Its Government* (New Haven, Conn.: Yale University Press, 1930), p. 105.

A theory which produces such conflicting results is bound to lead to prolonged contests before commissions and appeals to courts for more favorable consideration. Under the separation-of-powers doctrine the courts of the United States, and of many states, cannot decide the proper rate, but can only remand to commissions for reconsideration. The result can be a march upward and downward between courts and commissions.

The evils of reproduction-cost valuation are compounded by the fact that nothing can be settled for long. By the time the process is completed, price levels will have changed and new reproduction-cost figures will be needed. As a result, public regulation is kept on a constant run on the same treadmill.

The need for revaluations led the Maryland commission years ago to attempt a different method of bringing valuations up to date. The commission had a starting point in a valuation approved by a district court in 1923. Instead of making a physical revaluation of the property, it trended the 1923 figures by use of price indices to bring the valuation up to date as of 1932. It used sixteen different price indices, giving each a weight of 1 to 4.

The method was disapproved by the Supreme Court. It was willing only to accept price indices as evidence "to be considered with all other relevant factors."[28] This left the commission with the task of making revaluations of the separate components of the physical assets.

It is not too much to say that reproduction-cost theory was not carried out in practice. In view of the accounting deficiencies, interlocking company relationships, and the gaps in regulation, it is probable that no theory of rate making would have worked with even moderate success for the nation as a whole during the first thirty years following the introduction of commission regulation in 1907, though reasonable success was achieved in some jurisdictions. Reproduction cost, however, had its own infirmities. It was too time-consuming to be universally applied, could only be arrived at by approximation, and gave rise to conflict between the utilities and the public. Moreover, the expense and difficulties of revaluations, and the contests over estimates, prevented regulation from keeping abreast with changes in the price level. One effect, therefore, was to accentuate the time lag in regulation. Furthermore, commissions sometimes sought to avoid the full results of application of the theory. In a period either of rapid decline or rise of prices, commissions would seek to resist the extreme effects on consumer costs and on investors' income. Finally, the Supreme Court was not consistent in its requirements. It sometimes looked beyond theory to practical results, and moderated doctrine to fit the situation.[29]

Judicial Reversal. Reproduction-cost valuation means a fluctuating rate base. From a multitude of sources—judges, commissions, investigating committees, scholars—there came recommendations in the twenties and thirties for a fixed rate base. A fixed rate base would be determined according to a formula, and thereafter additions and subtractions would be made.

The Federal Power Act of 1935 authorized the FPC to "investigate and ascertain the actual legitimate cost of the property" of electrical utilities, and the same authorization was given to the commission for natural-gas utilities in 1938. As a result of complaints, filed with the FPC by the cities of Akron and Cleveland and the Public Utility Commission of Pennsylvania, that rates charged by the Hope Natural Gas Company to local distributing companies were unreasonable, the commission initiated an investigation. After hearings, it ordered a substantial reduction in rates, based on its findings of actual legitimate investment. The Supreme Court upheld the commission.[30] In doing so, it junked the *Smyth v. Ames* rule and set up new principles with respect to rate regulation. The majority of the Court concluded that the method of fixing a rate was unimportant so long as the end result was satisfactory: "It is not theory but impact of the rate which counts. If the total effect of the rate order cannot be said to be unjust and unreason-

---

[28] *West v. Chesapeake & Potomac Telephone Co. of Baltimore City,* 295 U.S. 662 (1935).
[29] See Irston R. Barnes, *The Economics of Public Utility Regulation* (New York: Appleton-Century-Crofts, Inc., 1942), pp. 386–387.
[30] *Federal Power Commission v. Hope Natural Gas Co.,* 320 U.S. 591 (1944).

able, judicial inquiry under the Act is at an end. The fact that the method employed to reach that result may contain infirmities is not then important.[31]

This is pure pragmatism from the pen of a pragmatic judge—Justice Douglas. It left no rule for rate making—either present cost or actual investment. The result—not how one got there—was important.

But how would a pragmatist determine whether the end result was good? In this case, Justice Douglas, who had been a member of SEC, found the answer in the facts of corporate finance. He said that the rate-making process "involves a balancing of the investor and the consumer interests."[32] The investor had a legitimate concern in the financial soundness of the utility. Douglas took a look at the financial history of the company and found that the investor had done exceedingly well, and that in terms of the relevant financial factors would do well under the rates set by the commission. He concluded:

Rates which enable the company to operate successfully, to maintain its financial integrity, to attract capital, and to compensate its investors for the risks assumed certainly cannot be condemned as invalid, even though they might produce only a meager return on the so-called "fair value" rate base.[33]

PRESENT-DAY RATE MAKING. The Hope case was a turning point in rate making. It marked, for one thing, the end of supervision by the federal judiciary over the details of the rate-making process. From *Smyth v. Ames* to the Hope case the federal judiciary imposed its requirements on rate making. The Supreme Court overruled state commissions and state supreme courts, and prior to 1934 the federal district courts intervened by injunction. The latter practice was stopped by the Johnson Act of 1934, in which Congress virtually excluded federal district court intervention in state rate cases.[34] Then the Supreme Court in the Hope case freed federal courts and state commissions alike from the necessity of following a single method in rate making.

It was not clear at the time what the effect of the decision in the Hope case would be. For the vagaries of reproduction cost there was now substituted the uncertainties of "end result." If vagaries in the first had given opportunities for judicial reversals, so likewise might the uncertainties of the second. Justice Frankfurter, who had heaped more labels of discredit on reproduction cost than perhaps anyone in the country, and had made the greatest pitches for judicial deference to the expert, could not accept the apparent open-endedness of pragmatism. "Expertness is a rational process and a rational process implies expressed reasons for judgment."[35] He still

---

[31] *Ibid.*, p. 602.
[32] *Ibid.*, p. 603.
[33] *Ibid.*, p. 605.
[34] 48 Stat. 775.
[35] 320 U.S. 591, 627. Justice Jackson also believed that the Court "should for the guidance of the regulators and the regulated reveal something of the philosophy, be it legal or economic or social, which guides us" (p. 645).

wanted the Court to perform its traditional function of offering a standard. But Justice Douglas, for a majority of the Court, had offered discretion to the commissions, comparable to that which legislatures had invested in them, and averred that "a presumption of validity" should accompany a commission's "product of expert judgment." [36] This is standing judicial language, of course, and may not mirror the realities of judicial decision. But in this instance withdrawal of the Supreme Court was foretold. The quest for efficiency and justice in rate making went to the national and state commissions and to the state courts.

The second consequence of the Hope case has been that commissions exercised their freedom toward development of new methods of rate making. There is variety in the methods employed, and some commissions—either by choice or because the state statutes or courts required it—have stuck to the traditional method of fair return on a changing rate base. The general trend, however, has been toward building on the foundations suggested by Justice Brandeis in his famous dissent in the Southwestern Bell case in 1923.

What are the methods used? It should be noted, first, that the commissions today have a large advantage over the early commissions in the existence of accounting data which is generally adequate for rate-making purposes. Federal income-tax requirements and the regulations of national and state commissions have led to cost records which are more complete.

Second, the basic shift has been away from property evaluations and toward investment accounts. The amount prudently or legitimately invested in a utility is the amount on which it is assumed a return should be made. And actual investment is generally assumed to be prudent investment. With accounting records more complete, and with a historical record of supervision over utilities in a state, it can usually be assumed that the investment accounts are an accurate reflection of the legitimate property cost. This basic shift simplifies enormously the task of regulation. There are no revaluations to be made, and the one standing record of the amount on which a return is to be made is in the investment accounts.

Third, the rate of return to be allowed to the investor is determined by capital cost. To determine capital cost, it is first necessary to look at the capital structure—that is, to determine the amount of the capital which is debt (evidenced by bonds) with a fixed return, and the amount which is equity (evidenced by common stocks) without a fixed return.[37] For the bonds, the cost is determined by the actual record. If bonds actually were sold at a par value of $100 with an interest rate of 4 per cent, then the amount the utility should be allowed to make on that $100 of investment is 4 per cent. This is the imbedded cost. When, however, rates are being set for the future, and it is anticipated that new debt will be incurred, a prediction has to be made on the interest which will have to be paid. This calls for analysis of

[36] *Ibid.*, p. 602.
[37] For simplification, only two types of securities are assumed in the discussion. There is, in fact, a tendency toward disappearance of preferred stocks.

costs of capital in the capital markets. For stocks, the amount of return is determined by this latter method. A determination is made of what would be the current cost of obtaining equity capital for industries with corresponding risks. The Supreme Court said in the Hope case that "the return of the equity owner should be commensurate with returns on investments in other enterprises having corresponding risks." [38] The current cost of obtaining equity capital is, of course, the amount which must be paid if capital is to be attracted to the industry. There are various types of evidence which may be used to indicate what the investor will expect to get on his money. The most commonly used evidence is earnings-price ratios. An analysis is made of the percentage of earnings to market price of stocks in industries with corresponding risks.

After it is determined what the proportions of bonds and stocks are, what the return on bonds is or will be, and what the return on stocks should be, then a statement of overall return can be made. An example is given:

Bonds:	$100,000,000 outstanding	4% interest	$4,000,000 cost
Stocks:	$100,000,000 outstanding	8% return	8,000,000 cost
Overall return:	$200,000,000		$12,000,000

In this instance the $12,000,000 capital cost can be figured as a 6-per-cent return on $200,000,000 capital. Actually, this latter figure is of significance only as a result and not as a guide, if the method is applied as indicated.

Depreciation, of course, has to be figured from the property accounts. At present, there is controversy in rate cases over depreciation. Utilities may desire to use for rate making the accelerated depreciation allowed in income-tax reports. This would theoretically be of no consequence, except for allocation of cost between present and future rate payers, for no more than total actual property cost should be recoverable over a period of years. Actually, utilities will seek maximum reductions now and hope for non-application of theory tomorrow.

It will be apparent that the current methods in use by many commissions are much simpler than the old method of determining overall return on reproduction cost. The methods rely on accounting data and the facts of corporate finance. In summary, it involves adding operating expenses, depreciation, debt charges, taxes (including the corporate income), and an additional sum sufficient to yield the stockholder a return equal to that received by investors in other firms with similar risks. This total figure is the amount which should be brought in by rates.

One of the special issues which arises is that of capital structure—that is,

---

[38] 320 U.S. 591, 603.

of how much of the capital should be in bonds. On the one hand, it is recognized that debt should not be so large as to raise the threat that the company's income may not cover it in depressed periods. On the other hand, it is in the consumer's interest to have the maximum amount of debt in the capital account consistent with safety. This is true for two reasons: a prospective debt cost of 4 per cent is only half of a prospective equity cost of 8 per cent; federal corporate-income taxes do not have to be paid on the debt cost, but they double the equity cost. Hence, the difference in cost in the example given is between 4 per cent and approximately 16 per cent. Some commissions strive to obtain a debt proportion of 50 per cent or more, and it has been suggested that the SEC should use its controls over security issues to force utilities toward capital structures which give maximum protection to consumer interests consistent with safety.[39] This is an argument for adaptation of policy to new conditions, for while once the SEC battled to reduce the excessively high debt-stock ratios, the suggestion now is for correction of excessively low ratios.

It is still argued by some, and pressed in many rate cases, that there should be some upward adjustment in the stockholders' returns when inflation has occurred since the investment was made. The argument is not one of necessity, for with the cost of capital approach, the return is large enough to attract capital. The argument is made on the basis of economic justice. Its weaknesses are, first, that there seems to be no reason why the consumer should pay more than is necessary to get the investor to put his money in the enterprise, and second, that a large proportion of investments—evidenced by government and corporate bonds, mortgage notes, savings accounts, insurance policies—are made with the understanding that there may be attrition of capital by inflation. Years ago, Professor Irving Fisher proposed that returns on fixed-income securities be adjusted according to changes in the price index, but the failure of this idea to take hold shows that there are investors who prefer fixed return on a fixed amount.

Nevertheless, commissions still may provide some compensation for the attrition of capital. Those which still follow fair return on present cost do so automatically. Other commissions may make some adjustment upward in the rate of return (for example, from 6 to 6.5 per cent), either in acceptance of the argument of fairness, or to reduce the possibility of appeals to the courts by the utilities affected.

The foregoing discussion of rate making has been based on the assumption that the utility would still be attracting sufficient customers to make it possible to earn a return. This is generally true in electric, gas, and telephone utilities, for increasing population and expanding use of service have made these dynamic growth industries. But where a utility—for example, the street railway in many cities—is a declining industry, there is no alchemy in regula-

---

[39] Donald C. Cook and Herbert B. Cohn, "Capital Structures of Electric Utilities under the Public Utility Holding Company Act," *Va. Law Rev.*, **XLV** (1959), pp. 981–1006.

tion which can compensate for lack of customers. In this situation the courts may uphold an order of a commission which contemplates returns far below what would be a reasonable return on either the cost of reproduction or the actual legitimate investment.[40] Also, the foregoing discussion has dealt with the level of rates, not with their structure. Structuring of rates is a technical task. In the electrical-power industry, for example, it involves such things as whether to have a flat minimum charge, what reductions shall be made for successively large blocks of electricity used, what differences shall be made between domestic and commercial rates, and what adjustments shall be made to encourage use at off-peak hours when the capacity of the utility is not being used. Involved with decisions on these matters is the question of use of promotional rate policies. The foregoing discussion has not encompassed the possibilities of promotional rate cutting for the purpose of increasing use. This will be touched upon in the later discussion of public enterprise. Finally, it will bear repeating that the appropriateness of utility rate-making methods for the setting of field prices of natural gas is left for later discussion.

CONCLUDING COMMENTS

Experience in utility regulation shows that regulation moves to governmental jurisdictions that are as wide as the industries regulated. Utility industries grew beyond localities and then beyond states, and in the wake of these trends, regulation moved to the state and then to the national government. Yet a role for each level of government may be retained. National intervention has had the effect of strengthening state regulation, so that the national and state governments perform complementary roles. Cities may still exert a strong influence by initiating cases for the protection of their citizens in state and national regulatory agencies.

Experience also shows that rate regulation in monopolistic industries will not be an effective means of protecting public interests unless it is supported by other forms of control. Supervision of accounting methods, approval of security issues, and control of intercorporate relations are essentials for effective rate regulation.

Finally, experience shows that there may be a long interval between recognition of the need to regulate and establishment of adequate means to accomplish it. A half-century after *Munn v. Illinois* sanctioned the power to regulate (1876) the utility entrepreneurs were far beyond the reach of the regulators—extending service across state lines, gripping operating companies in centralized and irresponsible financial maneuvering, contesting for returns on capital figures which did not represent costs, and working in the macropolitical arena to protect the financial houses which had been erected.

[40] See, for illustration, *Market Street Railway Co. v. Railroad Commission of California*, 324 U.S. 548 (1945).

450 Regulation and Promotion of Industries

Remedies were sought and the foundations for adequate and effective controls laid in the Congress, the legislatures of the states, and a decision of the Supreme Court. Even today, however, there are gaps in the system of regulation.

There has been a decline of interest in utility regulation. It is not often a significant aspect of macropolitics. The journals of law, economics, and political science give relatively little attention to it. This great change from the tempest of the past may be due to the absorption of the public and the scholars in new problems. It may be also that a reasonable degree of efficiency has been attained in regulation. On the other hand, it may be that macropolitics feeds only on the spectacular and the gross, and that there are problems on the technical level and problems of evaluation of results which should once again attract the attention of the independent student of government's methods, and of its achievements and failures.

Chapter 20. The Regulation of Communications

To COMMUNICATE is to transmit a message from one person to another. The message may be private, or it may be intended for the public at large. The distance may be great or small. A conversation, a public lecture, a telephone call, a telegram, or a cablegram qualifies as a communication. Governmental policies have, at different times, impeded or encouraged communications. The first amendment to the Constitution states a policy toward the transmission of messages through speech and the press, and judicial interpretation has applied the policy to various techniques of communication. There are also laws that regulate communication. These range from the prohibition of pornography and the release of privileged information and information on security matters to the subsidizing of distribution through the mails of newspapers and periodicals. Books, personal interchanges, movies, radio broadcasts, and other forms of communication are affected in many ways by the laws of the nation and the states.

The concern here is with those communication industries that are regulated for economic considerations. The industries that qualify are the telegraph, the telephone, the international cable, and radio and television broadcasting. The first three are public utilities, and are subject to the usual controls of such industries. The national government regulates the interstate and international facets, and the states control, to the extent that they desire, the intrastate features. Radio and television broadcasting is subject to the exclusive control of the national government, and since these are not designated utilities, the controls over them differ from the controls applied to the utilities.

THE TELEGRAPH[1]

This was the first form of electrical communication. Samuel F. B. Morse demonstrated the feasibility of sending messages by wire in 1835, and gave a public demonstration of the process in 1838. At first, little attention was given to the invention, but activity increased in the 1840's and 1850's. A transcontinental service accompanying the expansion of railroads came in 1861. The two industries have been closely associated, for the telegraph

---

[1] For a general treatment, see *Telecommunications: A Program for Progress*. A Report of the President's Communication Policy Board (Washington, D.C.: Superintendent of Documents, 1951).

needed rights of way from the railroads for its wires, and the railroads began very early to use the new service. The service expanded rapidly in the late nineteenth century, so that all parts of the country were interconnected by wires. The Western Union Telegraph Company began business in 1851, adopting in 1856 the present corporate name. Postal Telegraph began a competitive telegraph service in 1881. The merger of the two companies in 1943 ended the competition between them. As will be seen, there are services that compete with the surviving Western Union.

The national government encouraged expansion of telegraph service by legislation in 1866, which granted to telegraph companies rights-of-way over public lands. In 1888, when regulation originated, Congress empowered the Interstate Commerce Commission (ICC) to require telegraph lines that had received subsidies from the national government to interconnect their lines. The rates and practices of interstate communication carriers were brought under ICC supervision in the Mann-Elkins Act of 1910; they remained there until Congress, in the Communications Act of 1934, transferred the regulatory authority to the Federal Communications Commission (FCC).

The Communications Act [2] exempts intrastate telegraphic activities and intrastate communications carriers that only connect with interstate or international carriers. An interstate telegraphic carrier is obliged to provide service and to establish interconnections with other such carriers. The charges must be just and reasonable. Discriminatory practices, charges, and services are illegal. Tariffs of rates must be on file. New rate proposals may be suspended, and the FCC may prescribe the maximum and minimum charges. Interlocking directors of regulated companies are prohibited without FCC approval. Acquisitions of additional lines or companies of an interstate character are subject to approval. The FCC prescribes the kind of accounts and records that must be kept, and may require reports. In short, a comprehensive set of regulatory controls exist.

These controls prohibit the merger or consolidation of companies without approval, and since the statute reflects in many ways an attitude favoring competition between telegraph companies and between kinds of interstate service, the FCC sought Congressional approval of the merger of Postal Telegraph with Western Union when the two companies were in financial difficulties in the late 1930's and early 1940's. The Congress enacted a statute granting permission, and required the Bell System to sell its TWX service to the new combination if a satisfactory price could be negotiated. The successor company was unable to negotiate a satisfactory purchase price, and the TWX acquisition was dropped. The Western Union has since developed its own Telex service to compete with the TWX, and the Bell System has continued to provide the TWX service.

The greatest use of the telegraphic service has been in interstate commerce and by the national government, especially for military uses. The states

[2] 48 Stat. 1105.

have exercised little control, although some of them have sought to control racing information by telephone and telegraph. At the national level, routine regulatory actions have been carried out. There has been little controversy, except over antimonopoly actions.

Western Union has developed and expanded its services in recent years through development of electronic communications, computer services, inventory controls, and centralized record-keeping services. In addition to its own lines and services, Western Union operates wires leased from the Bell System.

The regulated activities include a wide variety of rates and services. To the traditional personal message with regulated rates have been added night rates, telephone service, leased wires, private wires, facsimile-reproduction services, newswire services, and, last but not least, the variety of services that are supplied to the many governmental agencies. The communications system provided by the telegraph company, of which the national government is the largest single customer, is considered an essential feature of the defense system of the United States.

The FCC has the responsibility of valuing properties used for service, but thus far there has been little activity of this type. There has, however, been enough competition between the forms of communication to prevent Western Union from taking unreasonable advantage of its customers. The United States negotiates directly with Western Union for its use of the facilities. The states rarely show interest, presumably for the reason that there has been little demand for state regulation on the part of the consumers.

THE TELEPHONE[3]

The invention of the telephone came in 1875, and the patent was issued the following year. Alexander Graham Bell is credited with the invention of the device, by which the voice is transformed into electric waves and the waves sent over a wire, at the end of which the waves are converted back into the equivalent of a voice. The telephone, in contrast to the telegraph, was quickly put to commercial use. By the end of 1880 there were 47,900 telephones in service in the United States, and expansion has not yet stopped.

There are about 2,100 telephone companies in the United States, but the largest company is the American Telephone and Telegraph Company (AT&T). The AT&T was incorporated in 1885, and it is now a holding

---

[3] See generally Noobar R. Danielian, *American Telephone and Telegraph* (New York: Vanguard Press, 1939); FCC, *Investigation of the Telephone Industry of the United States*, H. Doc. 340 (76th Cong., 1st Sess., 1939); "Direct Regulation of American Telephone and Telegraph Company," *Yale Law Journal*, **XLVIII**, p. 1015 (1939); Charles B. Hagan, "The Bell System and a Decade of Regulation," *Current Economic Comment*, **XVII** (1955), p. 38, and *Telecommunications, op. cit.*

company for the twenty operating telephone companies that own most of the telephones in the United States. The AT&T also owns the Western Electric Manufacturing Company and Bell Laboratories. This combination of companies is widely know as the Bell System. AT&T also operates the Long Lines Department over which long-distance telephone calls (over forty miles) are carried. The subsidiaries of the System provide telephone service in the various parts of the United States; they purchase their equipment from the Western Electric Manufacturing Company, and AT&T provides financial advice and other services to them. The system was built up over the years by the acquisition of many local companies. The independent companies are interconnected with the Bell companies, making nationwide telephone service readily available.

The telephone is a public utility; thus, it may be subjected to the controls imposed on other utilities. The authority over the telephone is divided between the states and the nation. Intrastate telephony is subject to regulation by the states, and interstate service is regulated by the FCC. As was stated in the previous section, interstate communications carriers were first brought within ICC control in 1910. The ICC exercised control until interstate activities of telephone common carriers became subject to the FCC in 1934.

Most of the states, but not all, have brought intrastate telephone service under the supervision of the state regulatory agency for utilities. A few states have no regulation of telephony, and a few others authorize the cities to regulate the service. A state faces many novel problems in regulating a subsidiary of a nationwide holding-company system. Since many of the Bell companies serve more than one state, capital equipment and other common expenses must be divided among the states in order to reach a legal basis for calculating a fair return. This entails cooperation among the states. A committee of the National Association of Railroad and Utilities Commissioners (NARUC), an organization of state regulatory commissions, has undertaken the study of common problems. The committee has now worked for many years on valuations of the Bell System and on the distribution of the common assets among the states that a subsidiary company serves. The NARUC Committee on Telephone Regulation has used the records of the FCC and has kept abreast of the current investments and financial practices of the Bell companies. Most of the state regulatory agencies use the findings of the committee in rate proceedings within their states. Despite cooperation in the NARUC, the Telephone Committee is seldom satisfied with its results. The complexity of the AT&T arrangements, and its skill in maneuvering rate proceedings, deprive many of the state regulatory authorities of satisfaction in their efforts. Some of the problems will be described below.

The FCC has regulatory authority over interstate charges and services. In order to exercise effective control, the FCC has authority to investigate the telephone carriers, to value their property for rate-making purposes, to supervise intercorporate relations, and to require reports of various kinds. The FCC has the duty to require that charges be just, reasonable, and nondiscriminatory. It requires interstate tariffs to be filed. Charges other than those filed are illegal. Reparations procedures are established. The commission is instructed to supervise interlocking directorates, and to maintain control over extensions of service as well as over new services. It may inquire into management, prescribe accounts and depreciation, and approve or disapprove the terms of consolidation. In short, the commission has authority to oversee quality of the service and charges. The information that FCC acquires in its regulatory role may also be used to assist the states in their own regulatory actions.

Despite statutory instruction, a valuation of the properties of the Bell System has not been completed. On several occasions the FCC has instituted motions looking toward a reduction in interstate long-distance rates, and in every instance the AT&T Long Lines Department has negotiated a new set of rates, usually a reduction. The result is that the FCC has not been very helpful to the states in their regulatory operations. The Bell System has, however, established physical interconnections with the smaller companies, discontinuing a former practice of asserting that the facilities of the smaller companies were of too poor a quality for interconnection with AT&T equipment.

In rate proceedings before the state regulatory agencies operating companies present their own cases, but they are assisted by a special staff of experts from AT&T. The agencies are often less skilled than the officials of the Bell System, with results often favoring victory for the system. Telephone rates have increased steadily in the post–World II period. It is difficult to isolate the causal relations of this increase apart from a general rise in prices. However, several problems have arisen in most of the rate cases.

The telephone business is alleged to be an increasing cost enterprise by virtue of the need for additional lines as additional customers are connected into the exchanges. The growing complexity of the exchanges, and the additional lines also, it is argued, increase the value of the service. The system has expanded its capital investment in very large amounts since World War II, so that the additional capital cost is a charge that must be included in the rates. The added customers share some part of the added costs, of course, so that the tendency has been for the rates to rise at a slower rate than that of expansion of capital investment. The financing of the Bell System is arranged through AT&T. That company owns most of the stock in the operating telephone companies, and thereby controls their boards of directors. In a few instances, AT&T's control is by contract or other devices. The operating company expands in accord with the general program of AT&T, and each state agency approves expansion programs. The needed capital for the expansion is obtained from AT&T in exchange for operating company securities, usually common stocks. The operating companies do not sell their securities to the general public. The AT&T raises the capital that it needs through sale of its securities (bonds or stocks) to the general public. Since AT&T is not an operating company in the states, the latter have no regulatory power over it. This financing plan is quite likely to increase the costs to be recovered from the rate-payers through higher rates, for a corporation with a capital structure composed of stocks will demand a larger return than a corporation that has a portion of its capital represented in stocks and the remainder in bonds. State regulatory agencies are not obligated to accept the capital structure of the operating company, and some have required a set of capital accounts that are different from the actual structure—a complicated procedure that has nevertheless been managed successfully.

Capital investment creates still another problem for the regulatory authorities. Many of the Bell System companies operate in more than one state, and the Long Lines Department used for intrastate service creates a proper charge for the rate-payers of that state. On the other hand, the proportions of the intrastate capital equipment used to perform interstate service creates a proper charge against that service. The multiple services from the same equipment impose the duty of allocating some proportion of the capital costs to the respective services. The NARUC committee, described earlier, has been important in these allocations. It is also necessary to allocate the other costs of service—for example, taxes, labor, interest, etc.—among the respective services. Again complex problems are posed for state agencies that in many instances are ill-equipped to grapple with them.

The interstate long-distance call service provides a special complication. The regulation of these rates is a duty of the FCC, but that agency has as yet not completed the valuation of the assets of the system. The rate reductions in interstate long-distance service have not been paralleled by similar reductions in intrastate long-distance calls, and hence there may have been some transfer of capital costs from interstate to intrastate service. It is impossible at this time to demonstrate that the intrastate services have had to absorb the costs of the reduced interstate rates, but the possibility exists.

In addition to the business and domestic service of a local and long-distance character, the Bell System has cables and wires that provide telephonic and telegraphic services to the press, to radio and television, to business firms for various kinds of service, to its competitor (Western Union), and to the various governmental agencies. The capital and operating costs of these services must be allocated by the proper regulatory authority among the services.

Not the least of the problems of regulating the system arises from the intercorporate relations between the Western Electric Manufacturing Company and the operating companies. The equipment for telephonic service used by the operating companies is purchased exclusively from Western. Since the Bell System purchases much more equipment than all the other phone companies combined, the market situation is monopsonistic. As a result, the prices that Western charges the operating companies may be higher than they would be in a competitive market. Western's prices, the system argues, are the market prices, and should be entered into the accounts of the companies for rate-making purposes. The NARUC has not found a satisfactory means of determining reasonable prices for the equipment. In 1949 the Antitrust Division of the Department of Justice instituted proceedings under the Sherman Act to separate Western from the AT&T system. The eventual negotiated decree of 1956 did not, however, require separation, although some limitations were imposed on patents held by AT&T. Regulatory authorities are still seeking to reduce the costs of equipment, but there is as yet no adequate means available to them.

Depreciation is a continuing problem of regulation, as it is for all utilities that have a large capital investment. The accounts for telephone companies that were specified by the ICC uses the straight-line method of depreciating property. Under this method, the life of the capital equipment is estimated, and the investing company is entitled to recover in earnings over that period an amount that is equal to the original outlay. Each year the company is entitled to earn an equal contribution to a fund that will, at the end of the life of the equipment, equal the original investment. As the years proceed, the fund accumulates. It may be spent by the company, but the accounts enable the regulatory authority to write off the outlay at the end of the period. The expended fund, of course, increases the capital investment in the enterprise. Alternatively, the fund may be returned to the investors with no increase in capital resulting. The principle of depreciation is an accepted practice in utility regulation.

The outcome of the first stage in the regulatory process is the determination of the total earnings that the regulated company is entitled to receive. The next stage is to determine the manner in which the necessary charges will be distributed among the users of the service. It has been pointed out that the allocations of the costs of the services will assign to types of service the requirement of producing the necessary income. In each of these types there will be different types of users and different services. The final rate schedules embody the detailed rate patterns. Attention will be given here only to the rate patterns for local business and domestic telephonic service. The charges for the other types of telephonic service, such as the press' photographic leased circuits, will not be described.

The company is authorized to earn the necessary amounts from the area that it serves, and in many instances the Bell companies provide statewide service. If the area is less than the state, the earnings must come from the area served. In a large state the company will provide local service through exchanges, and these exchanges in turn connect with the other exchanges, either through the lines of the company (up to forty miles) or through the Long Lines Department for greater distances. An exchange provides interconnections between the lines that reach the customers of the service. The customer dials through the exchange to reach the recipient on another line. Through the exchange, the number of lines necessary for communication between many customers is enormously reduced.

Each community within a state has an exchange that varies in the number of locally interconnected phones. As the number of phones that are interconnected within an exchange increase, it is customary for the basic charge for service to increase. The justification for the increase is based on the higher costs, and also on the value of service, for it is argued that the larger the number of interconnected phones, the greater the value of the service to the subscribers. Another uniform pattern in rate structure is for charges on business phones to be substantially greater than for domestic service. A line may serve more than one subscriber. If it does, subscribers pay less than for a single party line. Charges for other variations in services are filed separately. Variation in exchange rates according to size of the exchange may be carried to such an extreme that some of the very small exchanges are hardly self-supporting, while the larger exchanges more than earn their costs and a reasonable return. Some states, as a matter of regulatory policy, do not permit one exchange to subsidize another, but ordinarily the regulatory agency allows the phone company to file a schedule of rates that will enable the company to obtain the needed income. Unless the proposed rates are unjust and/or discriminatory, they are allowed to become effective.

Telephone companies that serve areas not serviced by the Bell System have substantially the same mode of operation that has been described above. In recent years there has been a trend to combine the independent companies into large enterprises, but no striking changes are to be anticipated on that account. The General Telephone Company is acquiring many of the existing smaller companies. It also has acquired a manufacturing subsidiary for supplying equipment to the operating telephone companies. Since the Bell System is spread so widely over the country, the size that General can attain is limited, unless dual telephone service is again permitted.

Rural areas often have cooperative telephone systems. Congress has in recent years provided a loan fund administered by the Rural Electrification Administration to enable thinly populated communities to develop telephonic communications. In areas with electrical cooperatives, experimentation with using the electrical lines for telephone purposes has gone forward and with considerable success, but the cooperative telephone undertaking is very small in comparison with the volume of service provided by the independent companies and the Bell System.

INTERNATIONAL CABLES

The telegraph was based on electrical impulses sent through wires on land. Samuel F. B. Morse also experimented with sending similar impulses over a wire under water. His experiments of 1842 were crowned with success in New York Harbor. The next step was the development of cables under the ocean so as to establish connections among major nations. An unsuccessful effort of 1857 to lay a cable across the Atlantic was followed up successfully in 1866. In 1881 and 1882 AT&T laid two cables across the Atlantic and leased them to Western Union, which thus entered the business of transmitting international telegraphic messages. Cables to other points around the world followed, and several companies now have cables or leased cables that serve the various parts of the world either directly or by interconnections.[4]

The permission to land a cable in the United States is governed by the Submarine Cable Act of 1921.[5] That act continued certain policies that had previously been followed by the President. The permits are conditioned by clauses that prohibit monopolistic practices and preserve competition between the companies that maintain the international communications facilities. The FCC advises the President on granting the permits. It has been public policy to preserve competition between the American companies that have cables, and also to influence the rates of foreign companies that are granted landing permits. Controls are imposed for protection of shipping and harbor facilities.

There are ample cable (and radiotelegraph) circuits to most parts of the world. There are also many international treaties dealing with the problems that have arisen. The United States is a member of the International Telecommunications Union, the general agency concerned with cooperation in the common concerns of the member nations. There are international agreements on the rules for using these communications services. The agreements relate to such things as safety of life at sea, international air-transport controls, and weather reporting, and insure that the actions of the various nations do not conflict.

BROADCASTING

EMERGENCE AND CONTENT OF REGULATION. The ability to send electronic signals without wires suggested the possibility that the signals could be adapted to transmit aural and visual signals. This possibility became a reality for aural signals immediately following the First World War. Visual images were not achieved before the Second World War. With these technological developments came the possibility of sending out signals for general reception—that is, broadcasting of signals for reception by members of the public who possessed the requisite receiving apparatus.

The first important broadcast of general news was made in 1920, when

---

[4] International communication is also carried on by radio waves. Successful radio telegraphy or wireless telegraphy was accomplished in the 1890's. The technology improved to the point where it was widely used for intership and ship-to-shore communications. In 1912, transocean radio telegraph service was established between San Francisco and Honolulu. The service has developed in subsequent years to provide communications among most parts of the world.

[5] 42 Stat. 9.

radio station KDKA in Pittsburgh, Pennsylvania, broadcast the presidential election returns of that year. Immediately, there was a rapid expansion of stations broadcasting programs for general reception. The increase in number of stations posed problems for the Secretary of Commerce, who had been authorized by 1912 legislation to grant radio licenses. That legislation had been primarily concerned with licensing equipment for safety at sea, and it was ill-adapted to cope with the new situation. The Secretary of Commerce, Herbert Hoover, sought the cooperation of the radio industry to prevent licensees from broadcasting on the same wave lengths, and he also issued regulations to classify stations so as to prevent interference. These steps were frustrated by court decisions that denied his authority to impose restrictions on licensees.[6]

The aftermath of the judicial rulings was hectic, for there was no official means of preventing licensees from using whatever part of the broadcast band they wished, with whatever power they wished, and at the hours they chose. The radio industry responded by organizing and developing a set of controls, and then requesting the Congress to enact them. Congress responded favorably with the Radio Act of 1927.[7] This legislation created the Federal Radio Commission to administer the granted authority to license radio stations and to classify stations and impose auxiliary controls. The new commission sought to impose order on the situation by dividing the existing 732 licensed stations over the 90 available channels so as to reduce interference and overlapping. A considerable measure of success was achieved, but the situation needed still more rigorous controls to bring satisfactory order. Since the Congress was unclear as to what it wished to accomplish, the act was allowed to run for only one year. It was extended in 1928, but permanent legislation was enacted in the Communications Act of 1934. That legislation has remained the basic statement of policy. Modifications of the legislation have been made from time to time, but the basic grants of power have prevailed to the present. The administrative provisions were amended substantially in 1952.[8] Especially significant also was another set of amendments added in 1960.[9] These, like the 1952 Amendments, were primarily concerned with procedural problems, but new and more detailed powers

---

[6] In *Hoover v. Intercity Radio*, 286 Fed. 1003 (1923), the Secretary was denied discretion in the issuance of licenses; in *U.S. v. Zenith Radio Corporation*, 12 Fed. (2d) 616 (1926), he was denied authority to issue regulations beyond the specific terms of the statute. The effect of these two rulings was to remove any official control. See L. White, *The American Radio* (Chicago: University of Chicago Press, 1947) and Gleason L. Archer, *Big Business and Radio* (New York: American Historical Company, Inc., 1939). An excellent brief account may be found in *Regulation of Broadcasting*, a study made for the House of Representatives Committee on Interstate and Foreign Commerce, 85th Cong., 1st Sess. (Washington, D.C.: Government Printing Office, 1958). Hereafter this study is cited as *Regulation of Broadcasting*.

[7] 44 Stat. 1162.

[8] 66 Stat. 71. See the comments in T. H. Wall, and J. B. Jacob, "Communications Act Amendments 1952—Clarity or Ambiguity," *Georgetown Law Journal*, **XLI** (1953), p. 135.

[9] 74 Stat. 889.

were made available to the Federal Communications Commission (FCC), the main regulatory agency created in 1934.

The fundamental grant of regulatory authority to the FCC is the authority to license persons to engage in the broadcasting of electronic signals. The grant of authority includes control of equipment and communications. The concern here is primarily with the rules governing commercial broadcasting, although the grant of control includes other communication services, as well as experimentation and research to develop new services and to improve existing services. The legislation makes it clear that broadcasting licenses are granted for limited periods of time, that property rights do not exist in a license or a portion of the broadcast band, and that the holders of licenses owe duties to the public.

FCC is authorized to classify stations, to prescribe the nature of the service they should provide, to assign the bands of frequencies, to determine the location of stations, and to regulate the kinds of apparatus to be used. The sanctions that the FCC has over licensees are of three kinds: (1) the applications for renewal are periodically made to the FCC, and at each renewal the FCC may refuse to renew the license; (2) the FCC may issue orders to a licensee to cease and desist from a practice that is contrary to the policy of the legislation and the commission; and (3) forfeitures or fines up to $1,000 may be ordered for failure of the licensee to act in the proper manner. The FCC may also revoke a license for violations of the act. Revocation usually has been considered too strong a penalty, and the FCC has rarely resorted to it. On a few occasions renewals have been refused to holders of a license. The other two sanctions were first given to the commission in 1952, and have not been much used; all are subject to review in the courts.

THE TYPES OF BROADCAST SERVICE. There are three distinct broadcast services licensed for commercial purposes. The first to appear was the Standard Broadcast Service, which dates from a Federal Radio Commission order of 1928. This service, amplitude modulation (AM), occupies a band of frequencies from 540 to 1600 kilocycles. The band makes 107 frequencies for AM stations. The frequencies have been classified to provide powerful, clear-channel stations that can cover wide areas, regional clear channels with less power, and local stations with still less. Some of these stations are also authorized to operate only during daylight hours in order to protect clear channels for night-time broadcasting. The classes of stations compete with one another, but the goal of equal listener service cannot always be achieved by local stations alone. The clear-channel stations are expected to provide some service to all areas. The allocations have been modified in details through the years as the technical skill in controlling interference has improved.[10] The goal of substantially equal listener service

---

[10] The Radio Act of 1927, as amended on the floor of Congress, included the Davis Amendment. This amendment specified that the nation should be divided into five equal population areas. The areas were specified in the legislation. Each area was to be entitled to an equal number of broadcast stations and equal broadcast service. As a consequence,

in all areas has not been achieved; but in many areas, especially in and near metropolitan areas, listeners are provided with many choices.[11]

The second commercial broadcasting service was first licensed by the FCC in 1940, and is known as frequency modulation (FM). This type of electronic signal follows a straight line, and consequently the signal may not be received beyond the horizon of the station from which the signal is emitted. This service occupies the frequencies between 88 and 108 megacycles. FM is not subject to the kinds of electrical interferences that disturb the reception of AM broadcasts, and it has a special ability to transmit musical sounds with high fidelity. The two qualities led the FCC to develop a table of allocation of frequencies to preserve them. The same requirement of equality of listener service was applicable to this form of broadcasting, and the new service also posed the question of common ownership of both AM and FM licenses. This issue will be examined below.

The commercial broadcast service that has generated the greatest regulatory difficulties has been television. It was first licensed in 1941, but World War II postponed immediate expansion. In the postwar period the demand for licenses rapidly expanded. In 1945 the FCC issued an allocation table for TV stations consisting of thirteen very high frequency channels (VHF) between 44 and 216 megacycles. Channel 1 was subsequently withdrawn, so that only twelve channels were available for licensing. Licenses were granted for these channels, and many stations began broadcasting. In 1948 the FCC issued its famous "freeze" order, providing that it would not issue more licenses until technical problems were clarified. The order was lifted in 1952 in a new table of allocations. In the new table the FCC opened to license seventy additional channels in ultra high frequencies (UHF)—from 470 to 890 megacycles. At that time there were 108 stations in operation from the licenses granted prior to the freeze. The total number of stations that were possible within the twelve VHF channels was 400 in the nation. The new UHF channels made possible an additional 2,000 stations in 1,200 different communities. In the new table of allocations the FCC also reserved 275 licenses for educational institutions.

There were two problems of a technical nature resolved in the 1952 table of allocations. The earlier table had been based on the assumption that only the VHF channels could be then used for transmission and reception of

---

the five areas were equal in population and unequal in the space to be served. Each region had the same number of broadcast outlets assigned, but it was not financially profitable to serve some of the large western areas with small populations. The amendment remained in the Communications Act of 1934, but it was repealed in 1936. The requirement of substantially equal listener service has been the goal in recent years. It should be noted that an allocations table does not guarantee that there will be stations broadcasting at the designated locations.

[11] There have been persistent controversies over the allocations and classifications. The daytime licensees have sought greater freedom, and there have also been demands for redesigning the clear channels. The proceedings have lingered on the dockets of the FCC for many years. For an excellent discussion, see *Daytime Radio Stations,* Report of the Select Committee on Small Business, Sen. Rept. No. 1168 (85th Cong., 1st. Sess., 1957).

qualified signals, and that it was better to make the service available in the limited number of channels than to await the development of qualified service in other channels. The new table provided for an immensely larger number of stations, but the earlier start of the stations in the VHF frequencies made it extremely difficult for the UHF stations to succeed financially. The VHF stations were located in thickly populated areas, and were scattered thinly elsewhere. The new UHF stations were allocated to the same areas. Moreover, the existing receiving sets were seldom equipped to receive the UHF signals. Financial success was rare for these stations, and most of the licenses were returned to the FCC.

The FCC had "intermixed" the UHF stations among the VHF stations; that is, licenses in both frequencies were granted to the same communities. The hoped-for competition did not develop, and the commission was vigorously criticized for its failure to develop an adequate policy. Obviously, the successful VHF stations were well-satisfied, for their number was limited, and a rich harvest in advertising income could be reaped, especially in the metropolitan regions. The large number of new frequencies did not alleviate the oligopolistic condition, and could not until there were substantially equal numbers of sets capable of receiving the UHF signals in areas of competition. The existing millions of receiving sets could be qualified to receive the UHF signals, but that required expenditures for new equipment. All-channel sets were being manufactured, but they were more expensive. The unregulated manufacturers of VHF sets were content with their profits.

The FCC sought a way out of the cul-de-sac. One way was to "de-intermix" —that is, to license all the broadcasting stations in a single broadcasting area on one or the other frequency. That solution would provide economic justification for production of UHF receiving sets, and also make for competitive broadcasting within the area from a larger number of stations. It was opposed by the existing licensees, who would perforce have to make their facilities conform to the new requirements, and by the existing set owners, who did not demonstrate any strong desire to change their existing sets. Another route would be to compel set manufacturers to make and sell sets capable of receiving all channels. The FCC, caught in these conflicting pressures, postponed any immediate changes, and it was not until 1961 that the commission threatened to go ahead on de-intermixture if legislation were not enacted to compel the manufacture of all-channel sets. In 1962 Congress finally passed legislation prohibiting the shipment in interstate commerce of sets that could not receive all channels. The way was now open to a better future for the UHF licensees, but it would take time for the number of sets to increase to the point where the licensees could reach audiences equal in size to the VHF stations.

The other aspect of the VHF-UHF controversy involved educational TV. The smaller number of frequencies on the VHF allocation left few frequencies for that kind of station, so that the solution of the UHF set matter provided a greater opportunity for educational television. The educational licensees have increased in number and have formed a network to assist one another in the development of programs and in other ways. Congress has also come to their assistance through appropriation of funds to assist such stations in providing a wider range of television service and to experiment with teaching by TV. Educational TV has a bright future.

LICENSING POLICIES. The AM frequencies were first in appearing and the number of licensees rapidly increased. Usually there were more applicants than there were channels, especially in the thickly populated parts of the country. The result was that the FCC and its predecessor, the FRC, had to make choices from the applicants. Since the frequency was public property and the statute denied private ownership, the FCC was in the position of granting permission to use public domain for private gain. The FM service, with its special qualities, was envisaged as a strong competitor with the AM stations, but it has not in fact become one. The development of TV opened for license a national resource of great financial value. The FCC has been subjected to vast pressures in the exercise of its authority to assign frequencies, and while the statute provides a few guides, enormous discretion was vested in the commission.

The statute prohibits licenses to aliens, to foreign governments, to corporations organized under the laws of a foreign government, to any corporation of which more than one-fifth of the capital stock is owned or voted by aliens, or to corporations directly or indirectly controlled by foreigners.

Those who seek a license must file an application with the commission that specifies citizenship, character references, and financial and technical qualifications. The application also specifies the frequency desired, the power wanted, the hours and days of operation intended, and the characteristics of the programs to be broadcast. The commission has no obligation to seek out applicants. These specific characteristics can be met so easily that they furnish inadequate grounds on which the FCC can justify the grant of a license to one applicant rather than another. The commission is instructed also to take into account the public interest, convenience, and necessity when it grants the license. It is the large generality of these qualifications that make the selection of the successful applicant open to controversy.

In the face of multiple applications the FCC has had to develop more specific guides in the granting of licenses. An early example is provided in *FCC v. Pottsville Broadcasting Co.*[12] In 1936 Pottsville Broadcasting Company applied for a permit to construct a broadcasting station at Pottsville, Pennsylvania. The FCC denied the permit on the grounds that (1) the applicant was financially disqualified, and (2) he did not sufficiently represent local interests in the community the station was to serve. On review in the Court of Appeals, the commission was reversed on the first ground, the Court finding that the commission had erroneously construed the laws of

[12] 309 U.S. 134 (1940).

Pennsylvania to reach its conclusion. The Court did not pass on the second count, and remanded the case to the commission. The commission did not issue the license immediately, but ordered Pottsville's application to be considered along with two other new applicants. Pottsville then asked the Court of Appeals for mandamus to compel the FCC to consider its original application without comparing it with the two new applicants. The Court granted the writ, and the commission asked for review in the Supreme Court, which was granted. The Supreme Court dissolved the mandamus, thereby upholding the administrative practice of the commission. The Court's discussion of the FCC's role in the granting of licenses merits quotation, for it states the rule governing one facet of FCC practice to the present day. Justice Frankfurter, for the unanimous Court, stated:

> The Commission's responsibility at all times is to measure applications by the standard of "public convenience, interest and necessity." The Commission originally found respondent's application inconsistent with the public interest because of an erroneous view of the law of Pennsylvania. The Court of Appeals laid bare that error, and, in compelling obedience to its correction, exhausted the only power which Congress gave it. At this point the Commission was again charged with the duty of judging the application in the light of "public convenience, interest and necessity." The fact that in its first disposition the Commission had committed a legal error did not create rights of priority in the respondent, as against later applicants, which it would not have otherwise possessed. Only Congress could confer such a priority. It has not done so. The Court of Appeals cannot write the principle of priority into the statute as an indirect result of its power to scrutinize legal errors in the first of an allowable series of administrative actions. Such an implication from the curtailed review allowed by the Communications Act is at war with the basic policy underlying the statute. It would mean that for practical purposes the contingencies of judicial review and of litigation, rather than the public interest, would be decisive factors in determining which of several pending applications was to be granted.

The grant of wide discretion to the commission was acknowledged when the Supreme Court allowed the FCC to reopen a similar type of proceeding in order to take new evidence.[13]

The commission was also successful, in the same term of the Supreme Court, in another aspect of the licensing power. The FCC received an application from a newspaper in Dubuque, Iowa, for a license. An existing licensee in East Dubuque, Illinois, intervened to object to the granting of the applicant's request for the reason that there was inadequate advertising revenue to support a second broadcasting station in the area. Sanders, the existing licensee, also requested permission to transfer his station to Dubuque. The commission granted a license to the applicant newspaper, and also granted Sanders permission to move across the river. Sanders then asked that the commission's new license be set aside for failure to consider the allegation of economic injury, thereby acting capriciously and arbitrarily.

[13] *Fly v. Heitmeyer*, 309 U.S. 146 (1940).

He was supported in the Circuit Court of Appeals of the District of Columbia. The Supreme Court granted certiorari, and reversed the lower court's ruling. The main issue for present purposes was the claim that the commission was obligated to take into account the possibility of economic injury in the granting of licenses. Justice Roberts, for the Court, said:

> We hold that resulting economic injury to a rival station is not in and of itself, and apart from considerations of public convenience, interest or necessity, an element the petitioner must weigh and as to which it must make findings in passing on an application for a broadcasting license. . . . The Act recognizes that the field of broadcasting is one of free competition. . . .[14]

The competitive philosophy embodied in the legislation and the administration of the act is also manifested in the provisions (1) prohibiting those persons engaged in telephone, telegraph, or cable businesses from exercising controls in radio where the effect is substantially to lessen competition or restrain commerce; (2) making the antitrust laws applicable to manufacturers or sellers of radio apparatus; and (3) authorizing the FCC to refuse a license to applicants who have been convicted of violations of the antitrust laws. The opinions of the Supreme Court in the previously quoted cases, *Pottsville* and *Sanders,* implement the same philosophy.

The Communications Act authorizes the FCC to "make special regulations applicable to radio stations engaged in chain broadcasting," which is defined as "simultaneous broadcasting of an identical program by two or more connected stations." The chain network broadcasting a common program had appeared early in radio history, and several networks (or chains) existed when Congress passed the legislation of 1934. It is composed usually of several stations which have a common owner, who in turn enters into contracts with independent licensees to buy time on their stations. The program originates in the network or in a firm that has purchased network time. The other stations are connected through telegraph or telephone wires in a way that permits the single program to appear simultaneously on the several network stations. The rapid expansion of networks (there were four national and thirteen regional networks by the late 1930's) seemed to threaten monopoly, and the FCC conducted an investigation that resulted in the general order of 1941. The findings were that the networks exercised too much authority over the independent licensees, threatening local control as well as independence. The outcome was a commission order in 1941 stating (1) that it would not license AM stations holding contracts with a network that prohibited them from broadcasting programs of another network; (2) that it would refuse licenses to stations that were contractually unable to broadcast programs that other local network stations refused to broadcast; (3) that it would refuse licenses if the network contracts were for a period longer than a year; (4) that it would refuse licenses if the network contract

---

[14] *FCC v. Sanders Bros. Radio Station,* 309 U.S. 470 (1940).

denied the local station freedom to make its own programs, either by making its own program or by denying a network program on the ground of the public interest; (5) that it would refuse licenses in order to prevent a single network from owning two outlets in the same area; and (6) that it would refuse licenses if the independently licensed station was not free to fix the prices for sale of its time for non-network programs.[15]

The two major national chains challenged the legality of the regulation, and were successful in winning the right to have the regulation reviewed.[16] On review, the Supreme Court supported the FCC and the general competitive principle for radio. Justice Frankfurter, speaking for the majority of the Court, said:

The Act itself establishes that the Commission's powers are not limited to the engineering and technical aspects of regulation of radio communication. Yet we are asked to regard the Commission as a kind of traffic officer, policing the wave lengths to prevent stations from interfering with each other. But the Act does not restrict the Commission merely to supervision of the traffic. It puts upon the Commission the burden of determining the composition of that traffic. The facilities of radio are not large enough to accommodate all who wish to use them. Methods must be devised for choosing from among the many who apply. And since Congress itself could not do this, it committed the task to the Commission. In essence the Chain Broadcasting Regulations represent a particularization of the Commission's conception of the "public interest" sought to be safeguarded by Congress in enacting the Communications Act of 1934. The basic consideration of policy underlying the Regulations is succinctly stated in its Report: "With the number of radio channels limited by natural factors, the public interest demands that those who are entrusted with the available channels shall make the fullest and most effective use of them. If a licensee enters into a contract with a network organization which limits his ability to make the best use of the radio facility assigned to him, he is not serving the public interest. . . . The net effect (of the practices disclosed by the investigation) has been that broadcasting service has been maintained at a level below that possible under a system of free competition. Having so found, we would be remiss in our statutory duty of encouraging 'the large and more effective use of radio in the public interest' if we were to grant licenses to persons who persist in the practices."

The Chain Regulations have remained substantially the same over the intervening years, but they did not succeed in avoiding a great deal of control by the networks. In 1956 Congress appropriated money for an extensive study that extended over a two-year period. Other studies have been made. The conclusion of the Antitrust Subcommittee of the House of Representatives Judiciary Committee in a recent report is a fair statement of the present situation:

[15] *Report on Chain Broadcasting,* by Federal Communications Commission, 1941. The *Report* is a thorough study of the situation. The Order is at pp. 91–92. See also T. P. Robinson, *Radio Networks and the Federal Government* (New York: Columbia University Press, 1943).

[16] *Columbia Broadcasting System v. U.S.,* 316 U.S. 407 (1942); the same issue involving the National Broadcasting System is found at 316 U.S. 447 (1942).

The networks have performed an outstanding service in bringing to the American public, on a simultaneous, nation-wide basis, public service, cultural and entertainment programs of national interest. . . . At the same time, it is clear that CBS and NBC have a dominant position in the industry, and therefore exercise vast influence over television broadcasting and determine in large measure what the American people may hear and see over their television sets. . . . No single factor accounts for the concentration of influence and power in these networks. . . . These factors include . . . faulty frequency allocations by the Federal Communications Commission. . . .[17]

The networks usually have at their center a group of stations that form the core of a financial interest, and the affiliated stations—independent licensed stations associated by contract with the central core—contribute to an enhancement of the influence that the financial or control group may exercise. The FCC has issued regulations limiting the ownership of station licenses in the same person or group. In the standard frequency and FM, a maximum total of seven stations in each is permitted. In television the maximum number of stations that may be owned by the same group is also seven, but not more than five may be VHF. There is no rule prohibiting the ownership of the maximum number in the separate services. The rationale of the commission's policy is that more concentration of control than the maximum limits is not consistent with the public interest, convenience, or necessity. The rule limiting the number of stations that may be owned by a single group provides an opportunity for an applicant to seek more than the number of stations, but he must prove to the commission that the public interest requires the waiver of the rule. The authority to issue the rule has been sustained.[18]

A single interest is prohibited from owning more than one outlet in each of the services in a single broadcasting community. It is not uncommon for a licensee to own both an AM and FM station in the same city, and an additional holding of a TV station is often to be found in the big networks. Where common ownership exists, each of the services is expected to provide a program for part of the broadcast period that may not be included on the other services. In the case of FM and AM ownerships, at least two hours of individual programming is required.

The existence of these restrictions and limitations has not prevented a demand for a tighter control of the networks, including direct control by the commission. The Congress has not agreed to this demand up to the present writing. However, there are many studies by committees of Congress that urge such a step. The influence that the network can wield over the independent licensee, through a threat of withholding programs and/or favoring

---

[17] *The Television Broadcasting Industry*—H. Rept. 607 (85th Cong., 1st Sess.), p. 140. Similar views may be found in many places. Cf. T. P. Robinson, *op. cit.* and *Network Broadcasting*, Report of the House Committee on Interstate and Foreign Commerce (85th Cong., 2d Sess.). This report is also known as the Barrow Report.

[18] *U.S. v. Storer Broadcasting Co.*, 351 U.S. 192 (1956).

competitive stations, has deprived the legally responsible license-holder of effective control of his privilege.

In support of the commission's plan to encourage the independent licensee are several auxiliary guides to granting licenses. The minimum standards for a license can be met by many applicants, and these auxiliary rules assist in reaching decisions in situations where other things are equal. Thus, if an applicant for a license is a newspaper or movie exhibitor and another is not, the latter will be favored. Local ownership is a favorable consideration. As a broadcasting area increases in population and has more stations, the commission tolerates more specialization in the individual stations. If the listeners have the choice of local stations, regional stations, or clear-channel stations, the commission's view seems to be that the entire number of broadcast stations is regarded as a common program undertaking. In some large cities the listener has the choice of seven or eight stations. In the smaller communities, on the other hand, each broadcaster is expected to provide a wider variety of program content within his single station. The dominant theme in commission practice is to compare the applicants and what they promise with one another. The license goes to the applicant who, in the judgment of the FCC, best meets the needs of the local situation. Since there are many qualities regarded as desirable, and since these are distributed in unequal quantities, the final choice of licensee in a particular instance may often seem arbitrary. Moreover, consistency in the weighing of the qualities has not been a dominant characteristic of the commission. The issues involved are complicated enough when the service in a single community is involved, but they are compounded when applicants from two communities are seeking the same frequency and it is not technically possible to allow each community to have the outlet. The comparison then is between the broadcast services in different communities.[19]

Competition for the frequencies is common in the settled urban communities; but the table of allocations shows that in many instances there have been no applicants, or only a single applicant, for some available frequencies. Until recent years it has been the practice of the commission to grant the license if an applicant could qualify on the minimum grounds stated in the law. There have been a few instances recently in which the FCC has denied the license despite the absence of competition for it. The ground has been that the broadcasting service proposed by the applicant was inadequate, and hence that the public interest would not be served. The denials have not been challenged in the courts, and they have been associated with the wide-ranging criticism of the extremely poor quality of radio programs of many licensees, especially some of the small and poorly financed stations.

It was pointed out earlier that the licenses are granted for limited periods

---

[19] *FCC v. Allentown Broadcasting Corporation,* 350 U.S. 1015 (1955). For an excellent discussion of the problems and conflicts in the competition for a major TV channel, see Victor G. Rosenblum, "How to Get into TV: The FCC and Miami's Channel 10," in Alan F. Westin (ed.), *The Uses of Power* (New York: Harcourt, Brace & World, Inc., 1962).

of time, and that the holder does not gain a vested right in the privilege of using the frequency. The consequence is that the licensees periodically have to return to the commission for their authority to use the public domain. The act permits the grants for commercial broadcasting to run for three years, and they have been made for that period of time in recent years. The application for renewal permits the commission to examine the manner in which the holder has performed on his promises, and to decide whether to renew his license. It has been rare for the commission to refuse renewals for failure to execute the promises made. The commission has lectured license-holders for their shortcomings, but seldom has it failed to renew a license.

The holders of licenses are permitted to transfer them to others with the permission of the commission. The statute does not specify that the transferee of a licensee must have the qualifications of the original applicant. This curious feature has enabled qualified persons to gain the license and then to transfer it, usually for a price, to another. The commission has treated the process as a rather routine one. The holders of licenses in the metropolitan communities have often been able to realize handsome gains with little more effort than applying and receiving the license and then immediately selling it. However, in 1960, at the request of the commission, Congress enacted legislation requiring commission approval of arrangements made between competing applicants for the same frequency when the grant of one application is inconsistent with the grant of the other. The commission has often had the experience of reviewing several applicants apparently filing for the same frequency, only to find later that all had disappeared except one. The new legislation enables the FCC to learn the terms under which the applicants withdrew from active competition. The grounds for the legislation were that mergers or other consolidations may have been accomplished, or pay-offs made for withdrawing applications. The commission is entitled to know of such arrangements, and may approve them, but failure to disclose the information may later become grounds for revocation of license because of erroneous statements in the application.[20]

PROGRAM CONTENT. The considerations the commission must take into account in granting licenses include the proposed program, but consideration of program content borders on censorship. Censorship by the commission is specifically interdicted by the act; nor may the commission interfere with the right of free speech by means of radio communication. Somewhat inconsistently, persons are prohibited from uttering "any obscene, indecent, or profane language by means of radio communication." The licensee, as owner, is responsible for what takes place on his broadcasts; hence, libel and slander suits may be entered against him in the regular courts. The exception for political broadcasts will be described below. Here

---

[20] In *U.S. v. R.C.A.*, 358 U.S. 334 (1959), the Supreme Court held that FCC approval an exchange of TV licenses did not prevent the Department of Justice from instituting proceedings under the Sherman Act.

the concern is with the connections between program control, censorship, and licensing.

Lotteries and other schemes dependent on chance are prohibited. The legislation has always required that paid programs and items be announced. The revelations in the 1950's of "payola," "door prizes," and many other forms of unrevealed contributions that supported "plugs" on broadcasts led to the issuance of a public notice by the FCC which specified in great detail the kinds of items that required announcement as paid items. The Congress also enacted legislation in that year making it a criminal offense to fail to reveal payments or other valuable considerations related to programs. It was also made a criminal offense to engage in deception in contests of intellectual knowledge or skills. This legislative action also resulted from the findings of congressional committees and public revelations of rigged contests.

The reporting of news events has been a public-service feature of both radio and television. It was early recognized that the owners of radio stations occupied important positions in their ability to influence the outcome of public controversies. The earliest commission discussion of the matter occurred in the announcement of the *Mayflower* doctrine in 1941. In the course of a proceeding on the renewal of a license, whose owner had favored one set of candidates and refused time to their opponents, the FCC renewed the license but expressed the view that owners of licenses should not editorialize over the air. The opinion was severely criticized, and in 1949 the commission issued a *Report on Editorializing by Broadcast Licensees,* which included some guidelines for station owners. The policy outlined in this *Report* permitted the licensee to present candidates and public issues favorably, but it was obligated to allow a fair opportunity to opposing views on substantially equal terms. This policy, usually called the "fairness" principle, prevails today. It allows a considerable discretion to the local station owner, and distinctions are made between news reporting and analysis on the one hand and editorializing on the other. On the latter the station owner has the obligation of granting fair opportunities to opposing views.

The "fairness" rule approaches the obligation imposed on stations in election contests. In the latter situation, the station owner is not obligated to make broadcast time available in such contests; but if he does make time available to one "legally qualified candidate," he must provide "equal time to all other such candidates for that office." The broad requirement was modified in 1959 to exempt the station owner from an obligation to provide equal time for legally qualified candidates on bona-fide newscasts, interviews, documentaries, and on-the-spot news coverage of events.[21] In 1960 the section

[21] 73 Stat. 557. Sen. Rept. 562 (86th Cong., 1st Sess.), explains the origins of the measure and its implications. The FCC had been rigorous in its interpretation of the section, and in one instance advised Chicago stations that equal time would have to be given Lar Daly, a perennial candidate for public offices in Chicago, for news clips that had been used of other candidates.

was amended to exempt stations from the equal-time requirement for presidential candidates in that year.[22] In 1963 a similar exemption passed the House of Representatives.[23]

The station licensee is prohibited from censoring political broadcasts, yet the national legislation does not expressly remove the licensee's liability under state legislation for libel or slander. The Supreme Court has corrected that omission by interpretation.[24]

These limitations on program leave most of the time and selection of content to the licensee's discretion. This has not satisfied all listeners and viewers, and great controversy has raged about both the quantity of identical programs and their low quality. The Blue Book Report in 1946 was the commission's first full-scale review of its role in programming. It concluded:

Primary responsibility for the American system of broadcasting rests with the licensee of broadcast stations, including the network organizations. It is to the stations and networks rather than to federal regulation that listeners must primarily turn for improved standards of program service. . . .

While much of the responsibility for improved program service lies with the broadcasting industry and with the public, the Commission has a statutory responsibility for the public interest, of which it cannot divest itself. . . .

In issuing and in renewing licenses of broadcast stations the Commission proposes to give particular consideration to four program service factors relevant to the public interest. These are: (1) the carrying of sustaining programs, including network sustaining programs, with particular reference to the retention by licensees of a proper discretion and responsibility for maintaining a well-balanced program structure; (2) the carrying of local live programs; (3) the carrying of programs devoted to the discussion of public issues, and (4) the elimination of advertising excesses.[25]

These principles have continued to guide the commission, but the critics have not been satisfied. Indeed, the new chairman of the FCC spoke in 1961 of the "vast wastelands" of programs. It is clear that the commission is pressed on one side by broadcasters who are satisfied with the quality and quantity of existing programs, and on the other by some segments of their audiences who do not always find the fare equal to their standards. However, from the size of the listening audience, the willingness of advertisers to pay the costs, and the earnings of the broadcasters, it is difficult to deny the existence of satisfaction in the current policy-making process. It is also difficult to deny the fact that the broadcasting services have, on many occa-

[22] 74 Stat. 554. See Sen. Rept. 1539 (86th Cong., 2nd Sess.). The Senate Committee on Commerce conducted an extensive inquiry into the 1960 election under the title *Freedom of Communications,* Sen. Rept. 994 (87th Cong., 2nd Sess.), 6 volumes.

[23] The Senate had not acted by July 1964.

[24] *Farmer's Educational and Cooperative Union v. WDAY,* 360 U.S. 525 (1959).

[25] The official title of the Blue Book Report is *Public Service Responsibility of Broadcast Licensees* (Washington, D.C., 1946). The quotations are to be found on pp. 54 and 55. The *Report* provides an elaborate summary of the program situation and problems at that time. A later private study is summarized in D. W. Smythe, "What TV Programming is Like," *Quarterly of Film Radio and Television,* **VII** (1952), pp. 25–31.

sions, provided great and highly desirable programs for those who would observe them.

CONCLUSION

The communications industries surveyed in this chapter are in one sense a closely knit group. The telephone, the telegraph, the cables, and the radio have been closely associated in their technological developments. The firms have usually found that their services and technology reached into neighboring fields. Combinations have been made and broken apart at the behest of public policy.

The policies described show a persistent effort on the part of government to prevent a consolidation that embraces the entire electronic field. The telephone companies have been kept out of the telegraph business, unless the latter was incidental to telephone service and not of a character to overcome the telegraph service. The same principle can be seen operating in cables. The highly interrelated technology led to the potentiality of monopoly in the development of radio, but public policy has opposed that development.

The common-carrier status of all the communications services, with the exception of radio broadcasting, has been maintained through both state and national regulations. The Federal Communications Commission has been the major national agency regulating privately owned services. The commission wields the usual public-utility type of regulations, except for radio broadcasting, for which a different type of regulation has been developed.

The rapid technological developments in radio broadcasting have obligated the FCC to concern itself with a novel set of problems, and it has not always acquitted itself with brilliance. In retrospect, the strength of the conflicting forces and lack of clarity as to goals suggest that it had an impossible task from the outset. The persistent interest of Congress in a new industry that had such potentials for the nation's political life, and industry's drive for the large profits from advertising, brought many values into confrontation. It cannot be said that a clear resolution of the relative importance of the values has yet been won, but it is inevitable, in a constitutional democracy such as this one, that efforts toward a viable compromise must continue.

Chapter 21. Oil and Gas: Production, Producers' Prices, and National Policy

ALTHOUGH MARKETED in different ways, oil and gas are often joint products from common reservoirs, and are in the production phase parts of a single industry. The distinctive problems for government with respect to oil and gas arise out of the peculiarities of the production phase and the first stages of marketing thereafter.

The petroleum industry has been involved in many types of relationship with government. Oil marketing arrangements have been a recurrent subject of antitrust suits. Oil transportation by pipeline can be regulated as a public utility by the Interstate Commerce Commission. The movement and sale of natural gas is subjected, in its transportation and distribution phases, to conventional public utility regulation—the transportation phase primarily by the national government, the distribution phase by the states. These several aspects of public policy toward oil and gas have been discussed already; this chapter is devoted, except for some broader concluding comments, to those distinctive aspects of policy which are closely related to the production phase.

There are some peculiarities in public regulation of oil and gas production. The regulation of production is by the states. Moreover, since between one-third and one-half of the petroleum production in this country has for more than thirty years been in Texas, the policy of that state has been crucial. The Railroad Commission of Texas, composed of three popularly elected members, probably has had a much greater impact on an industry and on the public welfare than any other state regulatory agency; it is probable also that its task of "accomodation of conflicting private interests" has been more "beset with perplexities" and its problems more "thorny" than those of any other permanent regulatory agency in this country.[1]

---

[1] The borrowed words in the conclusion are those of the Supreme Court in *Railroad Commission v. Rowan and Nichols Co.*, 310 U.S. 573, 579 (1940), 311 U.S. 570, 573–574 (1941).

PETROLEUM PRODUCTION AND ITS REGULATION

PHYSICAL CONDITIONS.[2] Petroleum ranges from gases to light or heavy liquids, and even to solids such as asphalt and petroleum coke. The liquid and the gas lie entrapped in reservoirs beneath the earth's surface, varying in depth from a few hundred feet to several miles. The reservoirs, though often referred to as "pools," are not underground lakes; they are porous strata of rock. In these porous strata the liquid oil and the gas are mixed, with varying amounts of each in the different reservoirs. Since the gas is lighter, there may also be a gas cap at the top of the reservoir. These minerals are trapped in an immobile condition by the geologic structure. When, however, the mineral bed is pierced by a drill, action is induced among the elements in the reservoir. There may be an explosion of oil or gas upward, or a lesser degree of upward movement, and there will be a rearrangement or stirring of the elements in the reservoir.

The sticky oil is pushed to the surface by underground pressures. It may be moved by gas drive. The gas drive may be the pressure downward from a gas cap. Or it may be dissolved-gas pressure—that is, pressure induced by the movement of the gas particles in mixture with the oil. Or the oil may be pushed upward by water drive—that is, by pressure of water surrounding the oil reservoir. These pressures may be dissipated in various ways: the gas in the cap may blow off, the gas in mixture with the oil may escape, the water may penetrate the oil in fingers or channels. In such ways the pressure which lifts the oil is diminished, and the oil remains unrecovered in the sands. When the natural drives are exhausted the mechanical process of pumping may be used to extract a portion of the remaining oil. Or secondary recovery processes may be employed. By this is meant that underground pressures are increased by injection of gas or water into the sands.

In this kind of setting the primary objective of conservation will be to recover, or preserve for later recovery, as large a portion of the petroleum resources as production techniques permit. This means the application of engineering knowledge to the efficient utilization of gas and water drives provided by nature, or to their artificial creation by fluid injection. Such an objective may run counter to economic objectives. Some or all of the owners of the rights in the deposits may want to withdraw the deposits at a rate or in ways which will rapidly exhaust the reservoir pressures. One of the concepts in petroleum engineering is maximum efficient rate (MER), which is the highest rate of producing oil and gas which does not cause physical waste or reduce ultimate recovery.

---

[2] The most useful recent discussion of the factors relating to production of oil and gas and to their conservation is Erich W. Zimmermann, *Conservation in the Production of Petroleum: A Study in Industrial Control* (New Haven, Conn.: Yale University Press, 1957).

The gas component in the petroleum mix has its own special qualities. Some gas is produced from gas wells—that is, wells that produce gas only. Other gas, called casing-head gas, is produced with oil. The name arose to describe the gas associated with oil in the subsurface which was separated from the oil at the head of the well casing. Another distinction is between wet and dry gas: wet gas contains a sufficient amount of liquid content to justify its separation. Also, gas is distinguished as sweet or sour, the latter being characterized by its high sulphur content.

There are production aspects peculiar to natural gas only. In the early days there was no market for much of the gas produced or producible, and gas wells were capped pending development of a market. However, when gas was produced in conjunction with oil, it was blown into the air or used for the manufacture of carbon black. Both the blowing into the air and the use of large quantities of gas to manufacture carbon black were regarded as inordinate waste, but producers of oil were willing to waste the unwanted gas, a by-product of the oil, since there was a good market for oil. This is a peculiar example of the inability of the market to govern the supply of a product.

Through the years uses for the gas have been developed. Liquids are stripped from wet gas, and technological advances have increased the productivity of such stripping. Dry gas can be returned to the reservoir to improve gas drive pressure on oil. Sulphuric content can be removed from most sour gas to make it acceptable for use. The market for gas itself has enormously expanded.

CORRELATIVE RIGHTS. While the physical conditions appertaining to oil and gas distinguish these resources from all others, so likewise does the law with respect to their ownership and recovery. And while the production from many fields was virtually exhausted before engineering knowledge about recovery and uses had developed, so also legal principles were established before their consequences could be foreseen.

There is some kind of right of ownership by the surface owner in the subsurface deposits. It is defined differently in different states, some recognizing ownership when the oil is reduced to possession, others while it is in place. There is also the rule or law of capture, according to which the owner of the surface has the right to drill wells on his land and take as his own all the oil and gas obtained through such wells. The courts probably saw two advantages in the rule of capture: to hold that a man had a legal right to what he captured was a feasible escape from the difficult, if not impossible, alternative of determining what oil or gas was beneath each man's property; also, the rule appeared to have the social advantage of favoring the man who wished to produce over the one who did not. But under this rule, how could owners of adjoining property protect themselves? A judge said, "Nothing; only go and do likewise." [3] This has the advantage of encouraging produc-

---

[3] *Barnard v. Monongahela Natural Gas Co.*, 216 Pa. 362, 365, 65 Atl. 801, 803 (1907).

tion. It also has other consequences, however. It compels a race in drilling and toward rapid withdrawal of the oil and gas. It leads to drilling according to the division of property lines, rather than according to the objective of obtaining the greatest ultimate recovery. It can lead to a spurt in production far beyond any market demand for the product at the time.

An oil reservoir is a unit. Planned development of the unit under single ownership could lead to avoidance of physical and economic waste—the economic waste of excessive drilling and servicing of wells, the physical waste resulting from inability to space wells so as to obtain maximum recovery, the physical waste from inability to apply techniques for reinjection of gas and water, and the economic wastes of production of a product for which there is no market or economical means of storage. But with multiple ownership and correlative rights of the owners under the law of capture, the difficulties of avoiding exceedingly large wastes are great, and may sometimes be insuperable.

THE COMPLEX OF INTERESTS. Although it is impossible to review the full variety of interests in petroleum production, a sketch of some of these will add a third dimension to the complexities produced by physical conditions and legal doctrines, and illustrate how the search for public policy must be made within a complex of diverse factors. There are the interests of innumerable landowners. Normally they lease their property for oil development, and agree to a flat sum for the lease and a royalty— one-eighth, or greater, of the sums obtained from sale of product from the lease. If oil is discovered on any part of the block of leases obtained from the owners, then the lessee is obligated to drill offset wells on other pieces of property for the benefit of the lessors. The leases may be obtained for the benefit of majors or independents. The majors in the oil industry are the companies with vertical integration from production to distribution; all other developers are independents, and they may be small or large individual operators or companies. The independents in the gas industry are those not owned by the pipeline companies, and includes some of the major oil companies. There are a host of surrounding interests, including drilling contractors, supply companies, lease developers, attorneys. Then there are the interests of the states and the local governments in the producing areas, for these find a source of revenue in oil and gas production. More remote, but still of great significance, are the consumers and would-be consumers, with their interest in supply and favorable price. Included is the interest of future generations if oil and gas remain needed resources. Finally, there is the interest of the nation in the resources needed for national defense.

THE ADVENT OF REGULATION. Regulation of the oil industry was precipitated by a dramatic event. On October 3, 1930, the wildcatter "Dad" Joiner brought in a gusher in East Texas. He had discovered the largest single oil reservoir known to man, a reservoir lying underneath a finger of earth some eight miles wide and forty-two miles long. By January there were three more wells; by June there were seven hundred; by August a million barrels of oil were produced on three successive days (in a nation whose daily production the year before was about two million); and by July the price of crude oil had dropped from over $1 to 10 cents per barrel. This affluence of black gold created another set of problems for government.[4]

The problems were shaped by the combination of the three factors of legal rights, physical conditions, and economic interests. Because land ownership over the reservoir was divided among small farmers and town lot holders, rights of capture existed in many persons. Because the discovery was unanticipated, the majors had not gained control through leasing rights. The reservoir was relatively shallow, and therefore the cost of drilling a well was relatively low. A mad scramble for leases and a fast race in drilling resulted. The pressure which lifted the oil was water pressure, and the engineers soon learned that flush production reduced the pressure. Uneven drilling, causing the water to channel into the reservoir, accentuated the reduction. New interests were created. Farmers and some of the independent drillers and leaseholders wanted to get as much money as quickly as they could. Small refineries were constructed around the edges of the field. Their owners, in debt and seeing that their opportunities for gain might be temporary, also wanted oil to flow freely. The majors began to lease properties and drill. The position of the interests in the struggle over controls of production was affected by their inability to foresee the rapidity and extent of the development which was occurring. In this struggle, neither the independents nor the majors were united, and the positions of many contenders changed as the full effects of events were unfolded.

By the summer of 1931 utmost confusion prevailed. The State of Texas had a conservation statute which had been strengthened materially in 1919. The law attacked the initial forms of waste and hazard in the industry, requiring abandoned wells to be plugged, and prohibiting the burning of gas in flambeau lights or allowing gas to escape from a gas well, and similar acts. It also vested administration in the Railroad Commission, which under its authority issued rules—such as the famed Rule 37—to regulate the spacing of wells. In 1929, however, the definition of waste which the commission was to prevent was changed so as specifically to exclude "economic waste" from the definition. This cast doubt on the commission's authority. Were its orders to limit production designed to prevent physical waste of the resource, or economic waste in the form of production beyond market demand? Was limitation in order to prevent the need for overground storage in earthen tanks, from which some oil would evaporate, prevention of physical waste, or an effort to maintain price? The com-

---

[4] The data in this section are taken, in the main, from Warner E. Mills, Jr., *Martial Law in East Texas* (University, Ala.: University of Alabama Press, 1960).

mission issued orders, producers obtained injunctions, the commission issued new orders, and both the statutory authority of the commission and the constitutional power of the state were uncertain. In the legal contests the federal courts participated alongside the state courts. The governor, standing in the middle of the conflicts over control, illustrated the confusion which arises when a devotee of *laissez faire* faces chaos in an industry whose welfare is critical for the economy of his state. Governor Ross Sterling—a self-made man reputedly worth $80,000,000, an organizer and former president of Humble Oil Company, a practical man with very limited education, an appointed state highway commissioner who was elected to his first public office one month after Dad Joiner's discovery—believed strongly in freedom of enterprise from the hand of government. Yet a decline of nine-tenths in the value of one of the state's leading products lifted immediate need above theory in his thinking. He thought the Railroad Commission was inefficient, and fought unsuccessfully for a new commission. He wanted controls, but he thought prevention of physical waste would bring the situation under control, and opposed, as price fixing, authorization to the commission to adjust production to market demand. The legislature, facing the issues presented, was as confused and split as were the interests on the outside. In East Texas itself confusion and disorder were heaped on top of feverish activity in drilling and marketing. Railroad Commission orders were violated. An effort to put into effect a voluntary program of production control failed quickly. The governor, led to believe that the step was necessary to avoid violence, proclaimed martial law and ruled the field with troops until the Supreme Court of the United States said this was unconstitutional.[5] In the end, the legislature amended the statute to allow proration to reasonable market demand, the governor accepted, and the policy of the state was fixed.

This case summary not only shows the background of a new policy, but also draws attention to some aspects of, and questions about, political intervention in the economy. Conditions are the controlling force. They give rise to interests. The interests have access to the political forum. In that forum the policy of the nation is determined. One may raise the question as to whether there is not in many situations a kind of political determinism at work. Would it have made any difference if another man had been governor, or if other men had been in the legislature? With the oil industry being as important to the economy and to state and local budgets as it was in Texas, was it not inevitable that Texas would adopt a policy of holding production down to market demand? And one may raise the further question as to whether the decision on policy would have been different if it had been made in the larger forum of national politics? Perhaps there is doubt, and if so, the judgment on political determinism will be qualified to take account of the forum in which decision is made;

[5] *Sterling v. Constantin,* 287 U.S. 378 (1932).

but perhaps the change in forum would have made no difference. At any rate, it seems clear that one can understand a political economy only by looking at conditions, interests, and the forum of decision.

He will have to look also at other factors. There were belief patterns that made the issue difficult. Men who believed in a free market would accept control only in extreme exigency. They wanted, however, an answer which would reconcile the economic interest in price and the economic belief that government should have nothing to do with price. They wanted avoidance of physical waste, but many accepted with great reluctance proration to market demand in order to avoid economic waste. Perhaps the great contribution of men to the policy adopted was not from the politicians, but from the experts—the petroleum engineers. A long-time member of the Railroad Commission once remarked that the most notable discovery ever made for regulators was that bottomhole pressure was declining in the East Texas field. Hence, proration avoided physical waste at the same time that it maintained price. This conjunction of engineering science and economic desire was convenient for regulators. And it illustrates the double motivations which may often exist in public policy. Proration may contribute to avoidance of physical waste and to solution of the problem of correlative rights; it may also contribute to stabilization of an industry.

THE PRESENT-DAY SYSTEM OF REGULATION. Oil and gas production is regulated by the separate states, and each state maintains its freedom to frame its policies. This freedom exists in conjunction with an Interstate Oil Compact, approved by Congress in 1935, under which each member state commits itself to maintain laws for the prevention of physical waste. Initially there were six members, and twenty years later there were thirty. Their laws vary, especially with respect to curtailment of production to meet market demand. The advantage of the compact has been that through the Interstate Oil Compact Commission created by it, there could be fact-finding studies, discussions, and recommendations to the member states. But there are no sanctions to force state action. General Ernest O. Thompson, long-time member of the Railroad Commission of Texas, has asserted that it was "a restatement of rights of the sovereign states to each run its own affairs," and "served as an effective roadblock against the federal encroachment on state sovereignty." [6]

From the beginning until the present men have inquired into, debated about, and made assertions on the purposes and effects of the system of regulation. There is one clear answer. There are three purposes and three effects: prevention of physical waste, protection of correlative rights, and stabilization of an industry. The first of these places control of production

---

[6] Quoted by Erich W. Zimmermann, *Conservation in the Production of Petroleum: A Study in Industrial Control* (New Haven, Conn.: Yale University Press, 1957), p. 209, from a paper presented to the Interstate Oil Compact Commission in Houston, Texas, December 12, 1950.

in the chain of conservation measures to which the nation was first aroused in the first decade of the century; the second places it in the family of zoning laws, allocation of water rights, regulation of the various rights of ownership in corporations, and other measures to define or apportion joint interests; and the third aligns it with limitation of agricultural production, minimum price fixing, and other measures for managing supply or underpinning price.

Whether men would have embarked on an effective program of conservation without the interest in price may be doubted; also, the possibility that protection of correlative rights or stabilization may impede the most effective use of conservation measures is unquestioned. Different purposes are served by the same measures of regulation, or different purposes get in the way of each other. Nevertheless, all three of the cited objectives are compulsions for action, and the correlation of objectives leads men to accept measures they would not accept for a single purpose.

The laws of the major producing states have long contained quite extensive prohibitions or regulations which prevent physical waste. They seek in part to prevent outright dissipation of the mineral resource, in part to ensure greater recovery of the resource imbedded in the sands. They cover a wide variety of things, but illustrative are rules requiring proper casing of wells, prohibiting the dissipation of gas into the air, requiring maintenance of proper gas-oil ratios, limiting the rate of flow to maintain pressures, requiring or encouraging re-injection of gas or water, and preventing storage in earthen tanks. On such matters, regulation and engineering science move hand in hand with the support of an industry which has become more conservation conscious as costs of exploration and drilling have increased and markets have expanded.

Proration to market demand, whatever its relations to prevention of physical waste and protection of correlative rights, undoubtedly is aimed at stabilization. The Bureau of Mines of the United States government issues monthly estimates of market demand, and breaks this down for the several states. California and Illinois, among the major producing states, do not provide in their laws for proration to market demand. But California oil is sold largely in five Western states, and the Illinois production is insufficient to destroy the efforts of other states. The other major producing states regularly prorate production to meet market demand. The methods of Texas are illustrative of state practice. The Railroad Commission has before it the Bureau of Mines figures, the estimates from the major oil purchasers of their anticipated purchases (called "nominations"), figures on storage, and other data from which it can make its determination on a statewide oil production figure. This figure is divided among fields, and within fields allocations are made to particular wells. Until recently, the chief means of adjusting production from month to month was to change the number of days of production, and in recent years this figure was often as low as eight to nine days per month. Nowadays, the

Railroad Commission converts the per-day allocations into a monthly allowable by multiplying them by the number of calendar days in the month; it then determines the percentage of its monthly allowable that each will be permitted to produce during the ensuing month. The change from days of production to percentage of monthly allowable makes for more precise control. Irrespective of the technique, under the proration system production may be considerably less than MER. There is obviously no complete correlation between the physical waste and the stabilization components in the system of regulation.

One means of protecting correlative rights has been through well-spacing rules. Typically well-spacing regulations limit the number of wells by prescription of minimum distances from property lines and from other wells. Nowadays they are supplemented by density orders, which specify, for example, that the density shall not be greater than one well per forty acres. In the absence of a unitization plan for a field, the rules must be designed to meet two needs which may conflict: to prevent excessive drilling and to preserve the rights of each owner. The Texas commission adopted, in 1919, Rule 37 to regulate well spacing, which, as amended and adapted by special field rules, still stands. The biggest burden of work on the commission has been the granting of exceptions to Rule 37 in quasi-judicial proceedings. These exceptions sometimes can have a snowballing effect. Made to protect rights of specific owners, they may increase density of drilling so that exceptions have to be made for other owners. In the East Texas field the number of wells ultimately reached over 27,000. With the large number of wells, the commission lost ability to adjust well quotas to the subsurface conditions. With a state statute prescribing a minimum well quota of twenty barrels a day per well, there was little surplus to award to the owners of wells in the rich "fairway" of the field. Under the conditions existing in East Texas there was only approximate justice among the persons having correlative rights.[7]

Freedom to drill wells with restriction only by well-spacing rules may lead to enormous wastes. It may lead to physical waste of the underground resource; it leads to the economic wastes of excessive drilling, a competent authority estimating in 1952 that this waste could be conservatively estimated for Texas as $100,000,000 annually, on the average, for the preceding five and one-half years.[8] Individual drilling may also impede full protection of correlative rights. The solution adopted by many of the producing states has been compulsory pooling laws. Pooling means *the combination of small tracts for the drilling of one well*. Texas does not have a compulsory pooling statute, and the ease of obtaining exceptions from

---

[7] See the review of facts in *Railroad Commission v. Rowan and Nichols Co.*, 310 U.S. 573 (1940), 311 U.S. 570 (1941).

[8] Robert E. Hardwicke, "Oil Well Spacing Regulations and the Protection of Property Rights in Texas," *Texas Law Review*, **XXXI** (1952), pp. 99–127, at p. 111.

well-spacing rules has minimized the incentives for voluntary pooling. The constitutionality of a compulsory pooling law was upheld long ago.[9]

The correlative rights of owners are also protected by proration formulas. These have not always provided completely equitable allocation among producers, the chief reason being that minimum allowables for small tracts have left an insufficient remainder for proration to other tracts. In the last few years, however, the Supreme Court of Texas has moved to put an end to discrimination. Recent decisions have held invalid the proration of the field allowable among producers on the basis of number of wells and acreage (one-third on the basis of number of wells, and two-thirds on the basis of acreage) where this resulted in unfair apportionment to wells on small tracts.[10] Such decisions will encourage, or even compel, pooling by owners whose individual allowables would be so low as to make it unprofitable to drill separately.

The most comprehensive means of preventing waste and protecting correlative rights is unitization. "Unitization" means *the development of an entire reservoir as a unit.* It involves a plan for integrating the separately owned tracts of land overlying a common reservoir into a single producing unit, and distributing to each owner that share of the income attributable to his ownership. Unitization can achieve much more than pooling; it allows maximum benefit to be obtained from recycling and other pressure-maintenance operations. Although unit development was forcefully recommended as long ago as 1924 by H. L. Doherty, executive of the Cities Service Company, it has been slow in developing. Many states have passed legislation permitting voluntary unitization, with accompanying immunity from prosecution under state antitrust laws. In the first fourteen years following the adoption of the Texas statute in 1949, the Railroad Commission approved 394 unitization plans, almost one-half in the last three years. In the large SACROC Unit Agreement, owners of interests in 47,450 acres joined in an agreement, as a result of which it was anticipated that an estimated 720 million additional barrels of oil would be recovered.[11]

The advantages of unitization are so great that from Doherty's statement in 1924 to the present there have been arguments for cumpulsory unitization. Louisiana adopted the first statute in this direction in 1940, but the statute related only to recycling. Oklahoma adopted a comprehensive compulsory unitization law in 1945, and its constitutionality has been upheld.[12] About a dozen states now have some form of compulsory unitiza-

---

[9] An Oklahoma statute was upheld in *Patterson v. Stanolind Oil and Gas Co.*, 182 Okla. 155, 77 Pacific 2d 83 (1938), appeal dismissed, 305 U.S. 276 (1939).

[10] *Atlantic Refining Co. v. Railroad Commission*, 346 S.W. 2d 801 (1961); *Halbouty v. Railroad Commission*, 357 S.W. 2d 364 (1962).

[11] Railroad Commission of Texas, Oil and Gas Docket No. 126-#8-25,412, January 30, 1953.

[12] *Palmer Oil Corp. v. Phillips Petroleum Co.*, 204 Okla. 543, 231 Pac. 2d 997 (1951), appeal dismissed in *Palmer Oil Corp. v. Amerada Petroleum Corp.*, 343 U.S. 390 (1952).

tion statute. Texas is not included, but the Railroad Commission has sometimes used indirect compulsion toward unit operation—as in threats to close down fields if casing-head gas was not conserved. The compulsory unitization statutes themselves usually allow much voluntarism. The plans must be acceptable to a majority of the interest holders, and the coercion is on the minority. It is not a simple operation to arrange or administer, for there are problems of defining the reservoir, determining the share of income for each interest, and supervising the implementation of the unitization plan.

One final aspect of the system of regulation deserves mention. This is the problem of compliance with regulatory orders. This was another problem which had to be solved in the East Texas field. The rewards for producing "hot oil"—that is, oil in excess of the amount allowed by state orders—were so great and the spirit of independence among producers so strong that the state found it impossible at first to enforce its regulations. A band of well testers and other enforcement personnel was by itself insufficient. Ultimately, the problem was solved by three moves. First, the national government prohibited the shipment in interstate commerce of oil produced in violation of state law. This support for the states has existed continuously since 1935.[13] Second, the tender system was developed. Under this system it was illegal to move or sell oil or its products, except in the last stages of distribution, without a permit from the commission in the form of a tender. A "manifest" moved with the oil from owner to owner. Third, the Courts finally gave support to the commission, and hence its orders came to have permanence and to be accepted as valid. Colonel Thompson has said that for years the Railroad Commission "lived in the courthouse"; but for more than a generation now, the legality of the state systems of control has been established. Recently, one more threat to the control system was discovered. It was learned that there had been a large amount of slant drilling in the East Texas field, through which owners were able to steal from the underground deposits of other owners. The state authorities immediately initiated prosecution against the alleged violators.

SOME COMMENTS ON ADMINISTRATION. Government in this country has seldom been confronted with situations as chaotic as that which existed in East Texas following the discovery well of 1930. When order had been established a pattern of control for oil production was in effect. The pattern has been amplified by legislation in the several producing states, but a few comments on administration as it developed in Texas will be of interest to students of regulation. There are a number of factors that contributed to the order and pattern which developed. The heart of the control system is the Railroad Commission. The tendency of the voters

[13] An order of the President prohibiting shipment of contraband oil was held invalid in *Panama Refining Co. v. Ryan*, 293 U.S. 388 (1935), after which Congress passed the statute prohibiting shipment, 49 Stat. 30.

to re-elect commissioners has brought continuity of membership. General Thompson has been (as of 1964) on the commission since 1933. Other members have served in that period for twenty and sixteen years. In general, the membership has had the respect of the oil industry. There has been much continuity of a staff serving commissioners with long tenure. An important role has been played by the courts. In the beginning and for several years, the commission was in almost every federal and state courthouse where jurisdiction could be asserted. Ultimately, the Supreme Court of the United States said that the problems were too complex for "judges who are called upon to intervene at fitful intervals," and that the federal courts should assume that the Railroad Commission had the expertness needed for the solution of these problems.[14] But the law of Texas now provided for appeals from the commission to the district courts in the capitol city, and from there to the Court of Civil Appeals in the same city. The latter court became a kind of specialized court on oil and gas cases. Here, too, there was continuity and also ability, for three of Texas' ablest judges sat on the court continuously for about a quarter of a century, during which oil and gas law was being made. A factor of great importance was the attitude of the oil industry. The industry in general, and particularly that portion of it which looked for stability and business over a long period, supported the system of regulation. It is impossible to conceive of a state commission operating a control system over production of a resource so important to the state's economy as oil has been in Texas without the support of the industry. Next, the creation of the Interstate Oil Compact Commission provided a forum for influence on the policies of other states and toward uniformity in these policies. This is, as is apparent from the preceding pages, only a limited uniformity, but the degree of it is important nevertheless. Finally, the national government has made significant contributions to the system of control. Statements of market demand and prohibition of shipment of "hot" oil have been important supports for state control.

York Willbern has commented on the anomaly of a state commission, elected by the people under a long ballot and not required to select personnel from civil service lists, that exercises control over a national industry. Its methods of administration would not meet all the standards of "purists" in the study of administrative law—though it has successfully adapted its procedural techniques to the requirements of diverse types of situations.[15] Its administration of the well-spacing rules may have been defective, and the law under which it operates may need changes with respect to pooling and unitization. There will be great differences of opinion over stabilization as an objective paralleling, and at times conflicting with, those of

---

[14] *Railroad Commission v. Rowan and Nichols Co.,* 310 U.S. 573 (1940), 311 U.S. 370 (1941).

[15] See Kenneth Culp Davis and York Y. Willbern, "Administrative Control of Oil Production in Texas," *Texas Law Review,* **XXII** (1944), pp. 149–193.

prevention of waste and protection of correlative rights. But though he recognizes all of these things, Willbern concludes:

Actually, a remarkably effective mechanism has been developed for discovering and reconciling the views and needs of those within the industry and for carrying them out. It has perhaps been largely fortuitous that the wider public interest has generally been in the same direction as these views and needs. So long as no great divergence develops, it seems likely that administrative control of petroleum production will continue to be exercised in much the same pattern as that which has been pioneered by the Texas Railroad Commission.[16]

PRODUCERS' PRICES

There have been two questions with respect to producers' prices for natural gas that moves in interstate commerce: Should the national government set the prices of producers and gatherers of gas? How could a fair price for producers and gatherers be determined? The first was a question of jurisdiction; the second, one of method.

THE ISSUE OF JURISDICTION. No politico-economic issue has loomed larger or been fought more vigorously in the macropolitics of the nation since World War II than the issue of whether the national government should exercise jurisdiction over the prices paid by pipelines to the producers and gatherers of natural gas. The setting for the conflict lay in the ambiguity of a provision of the Natural Gas Act. The act stated that its provisions would apply "to the sale in interstate commerce of natural gas for resale," but would not apply "to the production or gathering of natural gas." It appeared to be conclusive that a sale anywhere from the well head on down the stream of commerce would be a sale in interstate commerce of the gas moved across state lines. Certainly a producers' sale to a pipeline was a sale for resale. The question was: What was exempted by "the production or gathering" proviso? Did "production or gathering" include only the physical acts of drilling, lifting, and assembling the gas? Or did it include also the commercial act of sale of the gas? What was Congress' intention? Did it intend only to regulate pipeline transportation and sales? Or did it intend to close all the gaps in state regulation? The states regulated the physical act of production, but not the sale price of producers. Congress certainly intended to close the gap at the distribution end, specifically to provide for the regulation of the wholesale rates of pipeline companies which the Supreme Court had held the

---

[16] York Y. Willbern, "Administrative Control of Petroleum Production in Texas," in Emmette S. Redford (ed.), *Public Administration and Policy Formation: Studies in Oil, Gas, Banking, River Development, and Corporate Investigations* (Austin, Tex.: University of Texas Press, 1956), pp. 2–50, particularly pp. 49–50.

states could not regulate. Had it intended also to close any gap prior to pipeline transportation of gas?

The Federal Power Commission did not claim jurisdiction over sales by independent producers and gatherers to pipeline companies. Nevertheless, two things disturbed the natural gas industry. Since the pipeline companies owned producing wells, or owned companies which produced gas and sold it to them, it would be necessary for the commission, when it set rates for pipeline sales, to include a sum for gas the pipeline company produced or bought from its subsidiaries. In the Hope case the Supreme Court upheld the commission's use of "actual legitimate cost" as the test of the value of company-produced gas. Nothing could be more foreign to a gas producer's way of thinking. He has the mood of a speculator, often suffering large losses and always gambling on a big return. To attempt to chain him to a utility method of pricing, to fair return on actual cost, was tantamount to waving the red banner in the eyes of an ungovernable bull in the arena. He wanted a market price, not a utility price, for his gas. The other thing was that some language used by the commission in the Interstate case in 1943 [17] led the industry to fear that the commission might be reversing its earlier conclusion that it did not have jurisdiction over sales by independent producers to pipelines.

There was another factor of importance to the producer, and important also to the other side in the conflict that was to develop. Gas had long been an unwanted product—blown into the air as oil was produced, or capped in wells for lack of a market. At the time the Natural Gas Act was passed it was priced at around 2 cents per thousand cubic feet (MCF) at the well head. But the building of pipelines in the forties foretold a new period for the gas producer. Growing demand in the fifteen years after the war was to raise the price to above 20 cents. The producer wanted the fruits from the new demand, and the consumer wanted protection against excessive increases.

The conflict was basically one between producer interests and consumer interests. The producer interests included some of the nation's large oil and gas companies (Humble, Gulf, Shell, Texas, and Phillips) which sold to gas pipelines. It included also some thousands of small independents. The oil and gas industry, including the pipeline companies, was substantially united in opposition to commission jurisdiction. Prominent among the representatives of the consumer interests were mayors of Eastern cities, municipal organizations, labor unions, and gas utility (distributing) companies. Among the points pushed in the debate by the industry was that competition in producer sales would be an adequate protection for the consumer, and that the imposition of controls would dangerously diminish incentives to continue exploration for natural gas. These points were con-

---

[17] Docket Nos. G-149 and 132, 3 FPC 416, affirmed *Interstate Natural Gas Co. v. Federal Power Commission,* 156 F. (2d) 949 (1946) and 330 U.S. 852 (1947).

tested by the consumer representatives, who believed that control was necessary to ensure fair prices for the consumer.[18]

The conflict over jurisdiction took the form of a six-round battle. The first round was fought in the Congress. The initiative was taken by representatives of producing states who wanted to lift the threat of utility regulation of producers' prices. Bills were introduced which proposed to limit the commission to the setting of a "reasonable market price" at the producer stage of commerce. Ultimately these bills came to be referred to as the Kerr Bill, after Senator Kerr, a sponsor from the producing state of Oklahoma. In 1948 and 1949 the bills passed the House by large majorities, but were not reported by the Senate Committee on Interstate and Foreign Commerce.

The second round was fought in the Senate. Commissioner Leland Olds, who had been a member of the commission for ten years and had been widely hailed as a leader in commission policies, was renominated in 1949. By this time Olds had changed his mind about the jurisdiction of the FPC over producers' prices. He had also opposed the enactment of the Kerr Bill. The industry, therefore, fought his confirmation. The attack upon him before a Senate subcommittee, led by a member of the House of Representatives from an oil-producing state, sought to establish from his writings that he had held Communist ideas in his early manhood. In spite of President Truman's intervention in his behalf, Olds' renomination was rejected in the Senate by a 53 to 15 vote.[19]

The third round was fought also in the Senate. The FPC was now divided on the issue of whether it had jurisdiction. In the absence of new legislation it appeared that the issue would be decided by the new chairman of the commission. To avoid the uncertainties the opponents of jurisdiction pushed for the passage of the Kerr Bill. The bill passed the Senate by a vote of 44 to 36; the House concurred in Senate amendments and passed the bill by the narrow margin of 176 to 174. Nevertheless, the bill was vetoed, and the veto was not overruled.

The fourth round was in the commission. The issue there was whether Phillips Petroleum Company, the largest independent seller to pipelines, was subject to the act. The issue of jurisdiction was finally cleanly joined in the commission. The commission held, by a divided vote, that it did not have jurisdiction. Commissioner Draper, who voted with the majority, was confirmed by the Senate for a new term; Commissioner Buchanan, who dissented, was rejected when his reappointment was considered.

The next round was before the courts. The Court of Appeals reversed

---

[18] For a case study on the contest, see Edith T. Carper, *Lobbying and the Natural Gas Bill* (University, Ala.: University of Alabama Press, 1962), reprinted in Edwin A. Bock and Alan K. Campbell, *Case Studies in American Government* (Englewood Cliffs, N.J.: Prentice-Hall, Inc., 1962).

[19] See Joseph P. Harris, "The Senatorial Rejection of Leland Olds: A Case Study," *The American Political Science Review*, **XLV** (September 1951), pp. 674–692.

the commission, and its decision was affirmed by the Supreme Court.[20] Thus, finally, the Supreme Court in 1954, by a majority of 5 to 3, handed the commission the jurisdiction it had declined. The main opinion of the Court, written by Justice Minton, rested on the two points that "production or gathering" included only the physical acts, and that the congressional purpose was to plug the gaps in state regulation at both ends of the interstate transmission systems.

The Phillips decision led to a final round of conflict in the Congress. The industry, now having its fears confirmed, organized for a massive campaign to win public and congressional support. Although some people in the industry wanted complete exemption of producers' prices, the industry bent its effort in support of a report of a presidential advisory committee in favor of allowing the commission to determine "reasonable market price." The opposing forces also developed organization for the fight in Congress. The forces representing the producing states won in the houses, but the end result was determined in an unusual way. Senator Case of South Dakota announced that he had been offered a payment of $2,500 to influence his vote, and President Eisenhower vetoed the bill with a statement approving the purpose of the bill but disapproving efforts in its behalf which were "arrogant" and "in defiance of acceptable standards of propriety." [21]

Thus ended, for the time being and perhaps for all time, the contest over jurisdiction. The contest illustrates the point that interests which are sufficiently threatened by a policy (or proposed policy) of government will shop from one counter to another in government to obtain a favorable decision. It illustrates that appeal will be made from administrative substructures, and even from the judiciary, to macropolitics when the issues appear to be really vital. There is no escape from politics when the stakes are worth the cost.

THE METHOD OF PRICING. The Phillips decision resulted in something unusual in American regulation—price control at three stages to protect the consumer. First distributor rates, then pipeline rates, then producer prices were regulated. Countervailing power of distributing companies had been regarded as insufficient protection in 1938 against monopolistic pipelines. After World War II the power of the great pipeline purchaser against producers was regarded as inadequate by consumer spokesmen. Nor did they regard competition among producers as adequate protection. Support for these views seemed to be evidenced in the trends of the day, for large firms were coming to dominate at the producer end, and the rapidly increasing demand had shifted the competitive advantage to the seller.

Regulation has not yet been an effective supplement to countervailing

---

[20] *State of Wisconsin v. Phillips Petroleum Co.*, 205 F. (2d) 707 (1953); *Phillips Petroleum Co. v. Wisconsin*, 347 U.S. 672 (1954).
[21] *Congressional Record,* **CII**, Part 2, 2793.

power of buyers and competition among sellers. The complexities of price fixing for producers are tremendous. First, a large volume of work was created for the regulatory agency. Producers were now subject to the provisions of the Natural Gas Act regarding certificates and rates. In a single year independent producers filed 6,047 certificate applications and, in the same time span, almost 11,000 rate applications. Although many of the filings were of the routine type required with the initiation of regulation, the commission announced in 1959 that it would take thirteen years with its existing staff to clear the docket of producer rate cases already filed, and that with the filings contemplated for the next thirteen years, it could not become current before 2043 A.D. even if its staff were tripled. This cry of despair came from a commission which had contributed to the bad situation by its own delays, for it had continued to hope, until President Eisenhower's veto, that it would be relieved of a task it did not want.

A second factor is the complexity of procedure. Section 5 of the Natural Gas Act allows the commission, on its own motion or upon complaint, to institute a rate proceeding. But the burden of making a case is on the initiator, and due process requirements prevent orders to decrease rates without hearings and supporting data. The commission has neither the time nor the resources for such a procedure. Section 4 allows the commission to suspend for five months producers' filings for increases. The burden of making a case is on the applicant. Hence, the commission, swamped by the rate-making burden, waits for Section 4 cases, thus taking advantage of the applicants' disadvantages under the procedure. Section 7 allows the commission to impose conditions at the time it grants certificates. The commission held, in the Signal Oil case in 1955, that it could condition its grant of a certificate with a requirement for a lower initial rate than was proposed.[22] This, however, presented the commission with a problem. It had to determine the reasonable initial rate, and do this without the delays which would be involved in a full-scale rate case. Ultimately, the commission virtually abandoned the effort. Then the Supreme Court, in the Catco case (in which the commission had initially sought to impose a condition and had withdrawn in the face of the sellers' threat not to sell), said that the commission should give "careful scrutiny" to rates in Section 7 cases.[23]

Third, the commission's responsibility is complicated by the practices which have existed in producer-pipeline contracts. Producers selling on a rising market have signed contracts with pipelines with a most-favored-nation clause included. Under such a clause the pipeline company is committed to raise its price to the producer if it pays higher prices on later contracts with other producers. Hence, a price rise allowed to a

[22] *Signal Oil and Gas Co.*, 14 FPC 134 (1955), affirmed 238 F. (2d) 771 (1956), certiorari denied, 353 U.S. 923 (1957).
[23] *Atlantic Refining Co. v. Public Service Commission*, 360 U.S. 378 (1959).

producer in a certificate or a Section 4 case can "trigger" a round of most-favored-nation increases.

Finally, and most important, is the problem of finding a formula for rate making. It has been noted that producers regard return on cost as an inappropriate formula. There are, moreover, administrative difficulties in determining costs for a large number of producers. Justice Jackson, dissenting in the Hope case, argued that it would be illogical to pay a fictitious Roe five times as much for his gas as was paid to Doe just because Roe had to spend five times as much to get his out of the ground.

> The service one renders to society in the gas business is rendered by what he gets out of the ground, not what he puts into it, and there is little more relation between the investment and the results than in a game of poker.[24]

He thought, in effect, that a "fresh eye" ought to be given to producers' prices, and suggested a field price—that is, a single price for a field—rather than a separate price for each producer. Yet shift from cost to field pricing would not solve all problems. There would still be the question of how to determine the reasonable field price. Consumers would fear that such a price would be derived from averages or market conditions, and would be on the high side. The commission, in the City of Detroit proceeding, used the dominant field price in an integrated pipeline-producer case; the allowance to be paid on its own production was determined by what the pipeline would have had to pay an independent producer for gas in the same field. The commission was reversed in the courts, which held that it could not disregard costs.[25] Legally, here the matter stands: the commission, under the Hope doctrine, need not follow any particular method, but under the Detroit doctrine it must give some attention to costs.

What is the way out of the difficulties of regulating producers' prices? Some suggestions were made in the Landis report to the President-elect on regulatory agencies.[26] Landis noted that Senator Paul Douglas had pointed out that an exemption for producers of natural gas of sales for resale in interstate commerce of less than 2 billion cubic feet per year would remove 4,191 producers, whose total production of natural gas was only 9.26 per cent of the volume purchased by interstate pipelines in 1953, from the jurisdiction of the commission. He noted also that if the commission would make use of the authority in Section 7(f) to define service areas and allow expansions without new authorizations in such service areas, thousands of authorizations for service could be eliminated. The commission itself has sought to simplify its problem by adopting area

---

[24] *FPC v. Hope Natural Gas Co.*, 320 U.S. 591, 649 (1944).
[25] *City of Detroit v. FPC*, 230 F. (2d) 810 (1955), certiorari denied, 352 U.S. 829 (1956).
[26] James M. Landis, *Report on Regulatory Agencies to the President-Elect,* printed by the Subcommittee on Administrative Practice and Procedure, Committee on Judiciary, U.S. Senate (86th Cong., 2nd Sess., Committee Print, December 1960), pp. 54–58.

pricing. Acting on the Phillips case,[27] which had been remanded to it in 1954, it abandoned the rate base method and individual pricing in favor of area pricing. It issued a policy statement and two lists of ceiling prices for each area—one for new contracts, and a lower one for increases in old contract terms. These price lists were to be for the purpose of guidance. Since then the commission has commenced area-price proceedings.[28]

Area pricing, a new name for field pricing, though expected to make the work load more manageable, brings its own problems. There may sometimes be difficulty in defining areas. There is the problem of balance among high- and low-cost producers. Will many exceptions have to be made for high-cost producers? Or will the commission's area rates be set high enough to reduce the burden which would fall on it in setting special rates? What kinds of data will be used in setting area rates: costs of representative producers? market history? demand-supply factors? value of gas as compared with other fuels?

It may be expected that this problem will be solved with results intermediary between those desired by the contending parties. The consumer has a law and a court ruling, and gains something out of the commission's jurisdiction. The producer has two gains: the delays have put off the regulation he feared, during which time prices have advanced; the area-price technique must mean some use of averages (toward the high side) and hence a looser control than is sought in regulation of monopolistic utilities. It has been said that the commission is making progress. It "is freely using rate conditions, its area rate hearings are nearing completion, and it is making a genuine effort to simplify organization, procedures, and forms." [29] In 1962 there was an entirely new commission; all members had been appointed by a new administration. It will be instructive to observe how successfully a new group of men, coming to office after it was clear that regulation was here to stay, will handle the problems. It may be expected that regulation, as supplementary to countervailing power and competition, will work no miracles, but that a pattern of control, somewhat on the loose side, will ultimately evolve.

NATIONAL POLICY

SUMMARY OF POLICIES. In addition to the development of national policy with respect to producers' prices for gas, there have been a

[27] 35 P.U.R. 3d 199 (1960).

[28] The Supreme Court has said, "We share the Commission's hopes that the area approach may prove to be the ultimate solution." *Wisconsin v. Federal Power Commission*, 373 U.S. 294 (1963).

[29] Nicholas Johnson, "Producer Rate Regulation in Natural Gas Certification Proceedings: CATCO in Context," *Columbia Law Review*, **LXII** (May 1962), pp. 773–820, 796. This article and the following contain good summaries of existing problems: "FPC Regulation of Independent Producers of Natural Gas" (unsigned note), *Harvard Law Review*, **LXXV** (January 1962), pp. 549–568.

variety of other moves in the national forum which have had an effect on the oil and gas industry and its supply of commodities to the public. Some of these have not been encompassed in the discussions in the earlier chapters on antitrust and public utilities.

The national government itself is the owner of substantial oil reserves underneath the Western lands from which came, at a recent date, approximately 5 per cent of the nation's oil production. It has also been steward of Indian properties. In general, the national government has followed policies on development and conservation similar to those in the states. Under the Mineral Leasing Act of 1920 the Secretary of Interior has leased lands to private developers, receiving in payment annual rentals and royalties. The Secretary has authority to issue rules and regulations with respect to conservation matters, and amendments to the 1920 act have vested authority in him to compel unit development. In order to provide a reserve supply for national emergency, certain areas of the public domain have been set aside as Naval Reserves, and, under the administration of the Secretary of the Navy, exploratory and developmental activities have created a readiness reserve of petroleum supply.

The even administration of national statutes has been disturbed by some unusual events. In the twenties President Harding's Secretary of the Interior, Albert B. Fall, was convicted of accepting a bribe in connection with the leasing of naval reserves, and oilman Harry Sinclair of contempt in the course of the investigations of the leases.[30] Also, President Hoover in 1932 suspended leasing until a review of conservation measures could be made.

As has been noted, the national government has given support to the conservation-stabilization policies of the states. National policy on this matter developed in the decade from 1925 to 1935. In December, 1924, President Coolidge created a Federal Oil Conservation Board, noting the need for prevention of waste and that "The proper adjustment of supply to demand was . . . not merely a method of preventing physical waste of oil and gas but also a matter of economic concern to the industry and of vital concern to the nation." [31] The board, in its first report in 1926, declared the right of the states to prevent physical waste and to protect correlative rights, and that the national government's jurisdiction over production was limited to the national domain. In its fifth report, in 1930, it outlined a plan for an interstate oil compact. In the meantime, in 1930, the Secretary of the Interior began the issuance of market forecasts. The National Industrial Recovery Administration pursued stabilization policies for the petroleum industry similar to those for other industries. By 1935 state control of production was accepted, an interstate compact

---

[30] See Burl Noggle, *Teapot Dome: Oil and Politics in the 1920's* (Baton Rouge, La.: Louisiana State University Press, 1962).

[31] Quoted in Erich W. Zimmermann, *Conservation in the Production of Petroleum: A Study in Industrial Control* (New Haven, Conn.: Yale University Press, 1957), p. 125.

had been formed, shipment in interstate commerce of oil produced in violation of state proration orders was a national crime, and monthly forecasts of market demand by the Bureau of Mines were customary. The policy in the national forum paralleled that which evolved at the same time in the State of Texas.

Special encouragement to the petroleum industry has been included in the income tax law. In production of a mineral the capital asset itself is used up. For this reason, a depletion allowance is accepted on income obtained from production of minerals. In the case of petroleum, the amount of the depletion allowance is 27.5 per cent of gross income from petroleum production, provided it does not exceed 50 per cent of net income. In the industry it is argued that this high allowance is justified because of the fact of depletion and because of the need for encouraging discovery and development of petroleum reserves. In opposition, it is believed by many that the allowance is excessively large. The conflict of opinion and interest creates one of the tender spots in national politics, with the interests associated with oil striving to keep the issue submerged and the opposed interests often trying to bring it into open and active reconsideration.

Another matter which became engulfed in politics was the issue of ownership of tideland oil resources. The Supreme Court decided that the soil beneath the three-mile marginal belt did not belong to the original states, and hence not to the states later admitted.[32] A special claim made by Texas, on the basis of its assertion of title prior to admission as a state to soil three leagues out (ten and a half miles), was rejected by the Court.[33] In 1953 Congress passed the Submerged Land Act, which quit-claimed the soils, including the minerals thereunder, within the three-mile zone to the coastal states.[34] The act was vague about claims beyond the three-mile limit, and the United States brought action to settle the issue. The Court rejected the claims of Louisiana, Mississippi, and Alabama, but upheld those of Texas and Florida to ownership three leagues out.[35]

A new development in national policy, and one which substantially alters the roles of the national and state governments in regulation of the oil industry, is the import control program. After World War II there was a constantly increasing flow of imported oil into the country, the volume of the imports being approximately tripled between 1945 and 1953. Because of fear of domestic shortage in the future, in the postwar period there were official statements approving of the increase in importation and the development of foreign resources by American companies. Beginning about 1955 there was a change in official attitude. Reporting in that year, a cabinet committee on Energy Supplies and Resources Policy suggested that importing companies restrict, voluntarily and on an individual basis, imports to 1954

---

[32] *U.S. v. California*, 332 U.S. 19 (1947).
[33] *U.S. v. Texas*, 339 U.S. 707 (1950), 340 U.S. 848 (1950).
[34] 67 Stat. 29.
[35] *U.S. v. Louisiana, Texas, Mississippi, Alabama, and Florida*, 363 U.S. 1, 121 (1960).

totals. Following this, major companies announced voluntary restriction policies. Upon advice from the Director of the Office of Defense Mobilization and a cabinet committee that imports threatened national security, the President himself in 1957 appealed for a voluntary reduction program of approximately 20 per cent. In 1959 the President, as a result of a certification from the Director of the Office of Civil Defense, proclaimed that imports of crude oil and its derivatives were threatening security, and instituted a compulsory control program. The Secretary of Interior sets quotas for companies.

As a result of these developments the national government now has the new function of determining the amount of crude oil and petroleum products to be imported, and of allocating the amount among companies.

The decisions on the national interest with respect to imports are not made in a political vacuum. On the contrary, the interest conflicts are so complex and intense that one may wonder whether official judgments can be made on national security considerations alone. Even on national security there are rival considerations to be balanced. Threat of ultimate shortage of domestic supply, and maintenance of friendship with the Middle East and South American producing countries, are factors which suggest caution in restriction of imports, while the encouragement of the continued exploration for and development of a domestic supply is a factor which supports restriction. But resolution of these conflicting considerations is complicated by the pressure of interests for solutions favorable to them. The major oil companies which have production abroad, from which a cheaper supply of crude can be obtained than from domestic fields, oppose a policy of severe restriction. Independents that have gone into Venezuela or other foreign countries desire free importation, and so do refiners supplied by them. On the other hand, the independent producers and all the interests allied with them see in importation a threat to their security and prosperity. The producing states see a threat of the withering of tax sources and of the decline of home industry. The coal industry is affected by the competition of imported heavy fuel oil. The problem of policy is complicated further by the product mix. The impact on interests is affected by the fact that a large portion of the importation is heavy fuel oil. The position of the various interested parties will be influenced by their own position with respect to crude oil production and the production of particular oil products.

For the student of regulation there are two aspects of the new policy which are of particular significance. First, this new function of setting import limits and company quotas for oil and oil products illustrates the new intertwining of private and national security interests, and of domestic and international considerations of policy. There are national interests, which are one kind of public interest; protection of these is an imperative beyond economic considerations; but this protection is difficult, because an expert decision on the national interest would at best be an uncertain judgment and, under the actual conditions, will be made within a context of private pressures. Second, the new function of controlling imports places the national government in the dominant position in the regulation of the oil industry. Stabilization of the oil industry may now be affected more by national import controls than by state production controls. State production quotas themselves must be limited by the size of the nationally protected market. The politics of oil shifts from the state to the nation.

SUGGESTIONS OF NEW POLICY. There have been suggestions for radical change in national policy affecting the petroleum industry. Some of these relate to this industry alone, others to a policy for all fuels industries.

The leading suggestions with respect to the oil industry alone have been pulled together in a little book by Eugene V. Rostow.[36] His first suggestion, a repetition of one made some forty years ago by Henry L. Doherty, is compulsory unitization of oil fields under national law. By this means the evils of the rule of capture would be evaded. The trend now is toward unit development, the producing states providing generally either for voluntary or compulsory unitization. It is not likely, however, that a strong move will be made for a national statute. Such a move would arise only if there were new evidences of great waste or a development of shortage of supply, and in either of these events the producing states would probably tighten their controls so as to avoid national control.

Rostow believes that with unitization the advantages of conservation could be obtained without prorationing. He joins the company of professional critics who have condemned prorationing to equate supply with demand. The correlation, or lack of correlation, between prorationing and conservation and the merits and demerits of stabilization have long been debated. Whatever the balance in the facts, it cannot be anticipated that an industry in which the supply factor is so volatile, having gained a workable control system, will willingly accept its abandonment. It may be that there is a kind of law of response to volatility, according to which either a private monopolistic control or a public system of regulation attuned to industry needs will be sought when the unstabilizing factors in an industry become excessive. At any rate, the stabilization objective has been confirmed in state and national forums for approximately thirty years.

Rostow also joins the company of those who have argued that the oil industry should have a more competitive structure. His primary suggestion for making it more competitive is vertical and horizontal division of the major companies, the vertical division being designed to separate the industry into four parts: production, refining, transportation, and distribution. He suggests that the approach toward this objective could be made through Section 2 of the Sherman Act, building on the doctrines in the American Tobacco decision of 1946.[37] Whether the objective, if deemed desirable, would be attainable under the Sherman Act is, of course, uncertain.

[36] Eugene V. Rostow, *A National Policy for the Oil Industry* (New Haven, Conn.: Yale University Press, 1948).
[37] See pages 192, 201–202.

It can be expected, however, that the industry will be under continual surveillance by the antitrust enforcement agencies, and it will not be surprising to most observers if it is the subject of future antitrust suits, as it has been so often in the past.

Although not so specifically set forth or forcefully advanced, there have been suggestions of the need for a national fuel policy. Two episodes will illustrate to some extent the issues and problems involved. The first was the Natural Gas Investigation of the Federal Power Commission in 1945 and 1946.[38] The commission, delegated the power to grant or withhold certificates of public convenience and necessity, had exercised the power in conventional public-utility fashion. In determining whether to issue certificates to pipelines, it had looked at the adequacy of supply, physical facilities, financial resources, and market demand. But there were arguments that in determining authorizations for use of natural gas consideration should be given to three other factors: (1) the effect that substitution of natural gas for coal would have on employment in coal mining and railroad transportation; (2) the need for retaining gas for industrial uses in the producing states in the South and Southwest, where industry was then relatively undeveloped; (3) the superior values of natural gas as fuel for home consumption, as a raw material for chemical industries, and perhaps for conversion to liquid fuel, and the more ready substitutability of coal for boiler fuel and other industrial uses. Assuming that it had no authority to consider such broad issues, the commission held an exploratory investigation to unfold the facts needed for a national policy. The main result of the investigation was to reveal the variety of interests and views on use of a single energy resource. In the background, as in all discussions of conservation and use of oil and gas, was the uncertainty as to the period over which natural gas would be available, and hence over the degree of prudence to be exercised in its use. Yet this was only one of the factors influencing opinions about policy. The industry favored a free-trade policy—one which would allow it to grow without restriction. This position was supported by the official representatives of most of the producing states. Representatives of the State of Louisiana, however, argued that regional need for a mineral resource for industrial development was sound basis for restricting outside uses. Railroad, coal, and labor groups also opposed extension of natural gas uses in coal burning territory. In the face of these and other expressions of opinion and interest, it is not surprising that the commission split 2 to 2 in its conclusions on the desirability of restricting use.

The other episode was the report of the Paley Commission. In its report to the President in 1952 it took a look forward to 1975.[39] It tried to estimate

---

[38] Natural Gas Investigation, Docket No. G-580. The summary which follows is condensed from Ralph K. Huitt, "Federal Regulation of the Uses of Natural Gas," *American Political Science Review*, **XLVI** (June 1952), pp. 455–469.

[39] *Resources for Freedom: A Report to the President by the President's Materials Policy Commission* (Washington, D.C.: 1952), Vols. I–V.

the demand for energy resources under various conditions of supply, including price. It assumed that in considerations of policy to be adopted resources would have to be grouped in terms of their end uses, and that it was "well-nigh impossible to consider petroleum policy without giving attention to competing sources of energy—coal, natural gas, and hydroelectric power." [40]

The two episodes point toward certain conclusions. The Natural Gas Investigation shows that policy must be developed in a matrix of conflicting interests and opinions. The complexities revealed in consideration of use of a single mineral resource would be multiplied in the development of a national policy for the fuels industries. The Paley Commission, however, challenged the nation to develop a fuels policy for a future span of time. The Supreme Court recently held that the Federal Power Commission was authorized to consider end uses of gas in certification proceedings.[41] The commission is thus obligated to develop one element in a national fuels policy. But ultimately it may be necessary to develop a national fuels policy relating to all sources of energy. To accomplish this, some new organization, such as a Department of Conservation or a presidential staff agency, would apparently be required. Its function would encompass in some manner activities now scattered in such agencies as the Department of Interior, the Atomic Energy Commission, the Army Engineers, the Federal Power Commission, and the state commissions. We are brought to the same position as in the conclusion on transportation.[42] Integration in planning and policy development may be an imperative for the future; yet such integration is impeded by the complexities of interest and opinion, and by the substructures of organization and relationships which have developed for the separate energy resources.

[40] Arthur Maass, review of *Resources for Freedom, American Political Science Review,* **XLVII** (March 1953), pp. 206–210, at p. 207.
[41] *Federal Power Commission v. Transcontinental Gas Pipe Line Corp.,* 365 U.S. 1 (1961).
[42] Pages 422–424.

Chapter 22. Agriculture

IN SPITE of the persistent drift from a predominantly agricultural to a predominantly industrial economy, governmental policy on agricultural matters remains an important facet of the political and economic life of this country.

NINETEENTH-CENTURY POLICIES[1]

The origins of several public policies toward agriculture are traceable to the early years of the republic. The Western lands owned by the national government were sold in the early years to civilians and given to war veterans. The gift of 160 acres for those who settled on the land and tilled it appeared in the 1860's, and continued until the tillable lands were gone. This policy certainly encouraged westward movement and settlement on the land. By the end of the century some of the consequences of the rapid settlement were signalling their appearance in a variety of demands on government.

The development of an administrative agency of the national government with a constituency in agriculture began in the 1860's and emerged as a full cabinet-level office in 1889. The grant of lands to the states to encourage the creation of colleges to instruct and develop the agricultural and mechanical arts opened the way to technological developments that have altered the character of the agricultural economy. The railroads were stimulated by land grants to provide transportation facilities to the new agricultural lands, and, in turn, their lands were opened to settlement. By the end of the century railroads were available for transport throughout the area. Early in the twentieth century, as the arable lands disappeared, Congress created the Reclamation Bureau. This Bureau encouraged the development of water

[1] A comprehensive account of the history of agricultural policies is available in Murray R. Benedict, *Farm Policies of the United States* (New York: Twentieth Century Fund, 1953). An evaluation of the recent programs has been made by the same author: *Can We Solve the Farm Problem? An Analysis of Federal Aid to Agriculture* (New York: Twentieth Century Fund, 1955). These two studies for the Twentieth Century Fund are resource books as well as discussions of the issues and problems. A brief introduction to the problems may be found in A. Andrews, *The Farmer's Dilemma* (Washington, D.C.: Public Affairs Press, 1961). An excellent summary of postwar developments may be found in *U. S. Agricultural Policy in the Postwar Years, 1945–1963* (Washington, D.C.: Congressional Quarterly Service, 1961). Recent publications are: J. O. Coppock, *North Atlantic Policy: The Agricultural Gap* (New York: Twentieth Century Fund, 1963) and D. E. Hathaway, *Government and Agriculture: Economic Policy in a Democratic Society* (New York: The Macmillan Company, 1963). The Solicitor's Office in the Department of Agriculture publishes, from time to time, a handbook on agricultural legislation. That inexpensive volume is the most convenient reference on such legislation.

resources to irrigate the rich but dry areas not yet settled and to increase and stabilize productivity in the settled areas.

Land and transportation were important, but access to markets was also an imperative for the agricultural output that had to move eastward. As industrial development expanded in importance, the impact of the accompanying crises in markets—recurrence of overproduction and its accompanying unemployment—had its devastating consequences on the prices of raw materials, including agricultural output. The customary reaction of the farmer to lower prices was to produce more. That in turn depressed prices more. With large parts of the world population inadequately fed and clothed, more agricultural production seemed to be what was needed, yet the paradox of agricultural surpluses and an ill-fed and ill-clothed world to this day has not been adequately resolved.

In the late nineteenth century there were two explanations for a decline in agricultural prices: (1) that the increasing size of business firms with an accompanying ability to control prices operated to the disadvantage of the farmer in the prices of the things he bought, and (2) that the elevators that stored the grain pending shipment, and the railroads that transported it, combined to charge higher and higher prices for their services. The cost of the goods and services, it was reasoned, were then deducted from the market prices of the agricultural commodities, thereby reducing the net return to the farmers. Adding these increased costs to the costs of mortgages (these also loaned by alien and national large business firms), the farmer began to see himself as the victim of eastern monopolists or oligopolists. The national government, to which he looked for a way out of the cul-de-sac, answered with the Interstate Commerce Act of 1887 and the Sherman Act of 1890. That legislation followed, in time, an effort by the farmers to use the state governments to regulate the practices and prices of the elevators and the railroads.

Another minor feature of the legislation bearing on agriculture came in 1893. The Congress passed an act requiring that all meat to be shipped to Europe should be properly inspected. The European countries had indicated that meat imports from the United States would be banned unless adequately inspected. These customers had their way, although domestic customers were not so protected until 1906, and then only on meat shipped interstate. Intrastate slaughter and sale is still subject only to state policy.

THE TWENTIETH-CENTURY SURPLUS

The support for research in agriculture has paid off handsomely in this century. The scientists in the Department of Agriculture and in the agricultural colleges have developed plants with greater productivity and more desirable characteristics, they have made it possible to produce livestock that meet larger and changing consumer demands, and they have increased the knowledge of soils and farming practices.

Along with the increase in agricultural knowledge, new machinery has been developed in the agricultural implement firms to increase the efficiency of each person employed in the farming enterprise. The result has been an enormous increase in agricultural output, an output that has increased much more rapidly than the population. The result has been that when the total output of food and fiber is divided by the expanded population, the per-capita quotient is larger than it has ever been. Moreover, agricultural products have an inelastic demand curve (to use economic terminology); there is not an equivalent increase in demand as the price decreases. Shifts of demand between commodities may occur with differences in national income, but the total need for agricultural products does not increase.[2] There are economic and political consequences of such shifts, however.

The Secretary has tersely summarized the story of production in a way that manifests its consequences for the demand for labor:

In 1900 37.5 percent of our labor force was in agriculture. In 1960, only 8.6 percent. A century ago one worker on the farm supplied less than 5 persons—hardly more than his own family. It took nearly eighty years for this number to double, and by 1940 the number of persons supplied by each farm worker had risen to 10.69. Five years later, during the war years, that 10.69 figure had risen to 14.55; but the five post war years saw little change—14.56 by 1950. But note the rate of increase during the decade of the 50's. By 1955 each farm worker supplied more than 19 people. By 1960 it was more than 26. Today it is more than 27. And the rate will continue to increase.[3]

The increase in output has been accompanied in recent years by a decline in the total number of farms in the United States; that is, the farm units are becoming larger and have been for many years, and each of these units has increased its contribution to the total output. Such data are average, of course. There are still 5 million farming units, but about 60 per cent of them produce about 13 per cent of the total output. The remaining 40 per cent produce the other 87 per cent. The large, highly mechanized units utilize the best seeds, the best farming practices, and the best livestock for the particular purposes, and are, in some instances, very nearly factories in the field.

These developments have come simultaneously with substantial changes in the markets and in the productivity of other areas in the world. The increase in the use of mechanical energy has nearly eliminated the horse and mule as a consumer of agricultural products. The remainder of the world has increased its production of agricultural supplies, and new sources of such commodities have emerged in the Americas, Africa, and Australia.

---

[2] It may properly be argued that the above statement does not take into account the very poor, particularly not in any precise way. If this segment of the population had an effective demand (that is, an income), the output of the farms would still be in exces of food needs. For an excellent description of these poor, see Dwight Macdonald, "Our Invisible Poor," *New Yorker,* January 19, 1963.

[3] Address by Orville Freeman, Secretary of Agriculture, to the American Political Science Association, September 7, 1962.

The shift in demand has affected the various agricultural commodities differently. In the United States the change from starches as a large part of the diet to a diet with substantially more green vegetables, fruits, and meat has had serious implications for several regions of the country.

Changes have come steadily throughout the century, but there were two sudden changes that merit brief attention. In World War I the United States became the supplier of its allies. Trench warfare and the loss of men to the military services in the European countries provided a market in which the seller could command high prices; and to meet that demand, there was an enormous expansion of the land under cultivation in this country. As the European countries restored their productive capacity in the twenties, the demand for the products that were so important in the preceding decade weakened. Those countries that had experienced wartime shortages developed agricultural policies that would furnish more local supplies. The result was depression in United States agriculture with, again, an effort to use the government to effect better conditions. The formulas for the "solution" of the problems reflected several themes.

(1) Since the farmer was deprived of proper financial returns through marketing practices, it was the duty of the government to regulate middlemen who dealt with the farmer and his selling organizations. (2) Since the middlemen had special advantages flowing from their capital and credit facilities and from the dependence of the farmer-seller on their services, an organization should be created with the ability to act on their behalf. Cooperatives for marketing purposes were conceived as an answer to this need, and in some formulations it was recommended that the cooperatives be developed into a scale of organization that would enable them to counterbalance the middlemen with equal financial resources and expertise in market analysis. (3) Farmers should be placed in a position of equality with other groups in the economy. Initially, this was a demand for the equivalent of tariff protection for industry. In the early stage this meant placing tariffs on the import of agricultural commodities, but later the idea was expanded to protect export products more effectively by protecting the domestic market and at the same time dumping surpluses abroad—a two-price system. Still later, the concept of parity prevailed,[4] and with it production control and other measures designed to maintain equality for agriculture.

These themes clearly have interrelationships, and it requires simplification of complex discussions to make the materials fit this pattern. However, a pattern or framework of analysis is needed before description of the complex experiences can go forward. These three themes will form the pattern of the discussion in following sections.

[4] It had emerged as early as 1922 in a pamphlet by George S. Peek and Hugh S. Johnson, *Equality for Agriculture.*

REGULATION OF MIDDLEMEN

PACKERS AND STOCKYARDS ACT. As the title of the act [5] indicates, two kinds of activity are brought under the controls of the national government. The act has been amended a few times since 1921, and it operates on an industry that is still regulated in some of its parts by some states. This will not be examined. The main goal of the legislation in the states is to protect the producers in the marketing of their animals. The national law extends to the stockyards of 20,000 square feet or more in which livestock, meats, meat food products, livestock products in manufactured form, and poultry or poultry products are sold to the public. Unless a given market's facilities meet the area requirement, it is not subject to national regulation. State regulation presumably applies in the smaller yards. If the yard meets the national standards, then it can be "posted"; that is, it may be subjected to the regulations of the act. In the early years of the act all such yards were posted. In recent years, with the development of means of transportation alternative to the railroads, there has been an increase in the number of markets eligible for posting, and the administration of the act has not maintained the percentage of posted markets.

In a posted market or yard, the statute requires all packers, stockyard operators, dealers, and commission men to register with the Packers and Stockyards Division of the Department of Agriculture. They must also file reports on their operations annually. These include information on ownership, organization, financial condition, services performed, and total number of livestock handled. In poultry markets, dealers, agencies, and handlers must meet the same obligations.

Two kinds of control are imposed. One is aimed at the honesty and fairness of the practices of those who perform services in the yards such as unloading, weighing, feeding, watering, and, in general, caring for the animals accepted for selling. The rates charged for these services are subject to regulation as to amount, methods of payment, and related features. The proceedings to determine rates are typical of that type of order: rates or charges must be on file, changes are subject to approval, and rebates are prohibited. Intrastate rates may be controlled in order to protect interstate commerce against discrimination.

The second group of regulations derives from the antimonopoly theme in United States legislation. At the time of the enactment of the legislation in 1921, there were four major packers, and most livestock was marketed at the yards where these packers were located. Congressmen, expressing the views of their constituents, thought of the packers as monopolists who were exploiting their livestock producers at one end of the marketing process and the consumers at the other. Efforts made to apply the Sherman Act to the

[5] 42 Stat. 159 (1921).

packers had met with limited success. The legislation of 1921 was an effort to provide a special means of enforcing an antimonopoly policy against the packers and the stockyards.

In execution of this policy the act prohibits unfair, discriminatory, and deceptive practices, unreasonable preferences to persons or to localities, trading between the packers in a manner to apportion or divide the market among themselves, manipulation of prices in the markets, monopolizing the market, and engaging in conspiracies on such matters as apportionment of territory, purchases, and sales.

In the course of the application of this legislation the term "packer" came to include the buying of livestock for purposes of slaughter and the manufacturing or preparing of meats or meat food products for sale or shipment in interstate commerce. The administration of the act includes any firm engaged in these activities. A chain grocery that packs its own meats is a packer regardless of the significance of the meat in its total operations. A company engaged in marketing dairy products, if it also owns a meat company, is under the control of the agency administering this law. The significance of this fact rests in the provision that exempted all firms under the Packers and Stockyards Act from the administrative regulation of the Federal Trade Commission. This clause was amended in 1958 to provide for the division, between the Federal Trade Commission and the Department of Agriculture, of administrative control over firms which, absent this clause, would be subject to regulation by the Federal Trade Commission. Agreements between the two agencies have to be made in order to divide the activities of a regulated firm between them.

The enforcement policy of the Department of Agriculture has left much to be desired by some members of Congress and by other interests outside of Congress. The act included all those who packed meat, and some enterprises used this as a means of escaping the competitive controls of the Federal Trade Commission. There have also been a number of rate cases, some of which took exceedingly long periods to resolve. The major complaint, however, has been the failure of the department to post all the markets that come within the terms of the act. The usual explanation has been that the lack of funds has prevented adequate staffing of the agency for administration in all markets. The department has sought to accomplish the purposes of the legislation through consultation and requests for cooperation, and it has been satisfied with the results. The outcome is somewhat surprising, since the department is especially concerned with farmers and livestock producers, and is regarded as their spokesman in the area of agricultural policy. Extenuating circumstances are the rapid growth of alternative means of marketing livestock through local markets and direct buying by the packers from the producers.

COMMODITIES EXCHANGES. The markets for many commodities are highly centralized, with quick transfer of information between markets in different parts of the country. These markets provide prompt and accurate information on current prices of the commodities traded upon the exchange or board of trade. The exchange or board of trade—the names differ from place to place—provides a body of specialized traders who keep abreast of developments and who often estimate the future differently, so that these buyers and sellers create the demand-and-supply situation through the sequence of transactions. In addition to providing prices for cash or spot transactions, the markets also provide a futures market; that is, transactions are made at the present time for the future delivery of the commodities.

Trading between brokers and commission merchants on the floors of the exchanges occurs in specified units and qualities of commodities. That is, wheat, cotton, and some other commodities have grades or standards fixed by law or regulation. Where the grades are specified, the commodities are graded under government supervision. Storage of such commodities in supervised warehouses open to inspection is usually concomitant with these markets.

The prices at which buying and selling occur on the exchanges are constantly circulated by radio and telegraph to the various places in which local sales of the commodities are made. The Department of Agriculture provides such a news service. The significance of the prices at which exchange trades are made is broadened by the use of those prices in local transactions; that is, prices everywhere in the United States, and even in the world, are tied into a single market through the practice. There are variations between the prices of the different markets that are related to shipping costs between the markets or to temporary dislocations. It should be noted that different prices in different markets may also involve interest on the investment for the time interval of shipping. Even more important, they may involve tariff and other trade regulations as between the location of such markets internationally.

Finally, the exchanges are the sources for prices of commodities in future delivery. It is often asserted that it is the setting of future prices that makes the markets of greater policy concern than would spot prices, but it is not necessary to decide such a complicated question. The markets to be examined here are those in which future transactions take place. These transactions are especially important for those engaged in processing commodities for future delivery. Not wishing to run the risk of fluctuating prices between the time a contract is made and the time of delivery, such a processor will "hedge" himself against fluctuation by currently purchasing the amount needed to fill his contract and contracting to sell an identical amount of the commodity. If the price of the one contract varies in the future, that of the other varies in the same direction, so that the losses or the gains on the one will be offset by the equivalent losses or gains on the other. The men who engage in the buying and selling of such contracts are speculators in future prices. They are futures merchants, and they operate on the exchanges.

There are instances in which the speculators have manipulated the prices of commodities in their behalf, and the preservation of an honest market has been deemed an essential element of public policy. At the same time, it has been deemed desirable to have speculators available who are willing to take the risks of the speculation from those firms primarily engaged in processing commodities. There is also a suspicion on the part of the policy makers that if such speculation is not permitted in the open markets, it will take place in secret, and thereby merely enhance the possibilities of manipulating market prices. The result has been the regulation of the markets so as to make them open and honest, and the regulated commodity exchange is the outcome.

The basic national legislation on this matter is the Commodity Exchange Act of 1936.[6] This act was a revision of the Grain Futures Act of 1922.[7] The basic principles of the controls have remained the same through the years. The markets are declared to be of national public interest, and thereby become public utilities. Congress relies on its authority from the commerce clause as the constitutional basis for its actions. The change in the title of the act indicates a broadening of the commodities brought under supervision. The markets on which the following commodities are traded come within the regulations: wheat, cotton, rice, oats, barley, rye, flaxseed, grain sorghums, mill feeds, butter, eggs, Irish potatoes, wool tops, corn, fats and oils (including lard, tallow, cottonseed oil, peanut oil, soybean oil, and all other fats and oils), cottonseed meal, cottonseed, peanuts, soybeans, and soybean meal. Onions were included for a brief period, but were later dropped.

Boards of trade or exchanges that wish to operate as a site for futures trading must be registered as a contract market with the Commodities Exchange Authority in the Department of Agriculture. Persons or firms wishing to operate as floor brokers or future commission merchants, either in their own behalf or in the execution of orders for others, must also be registered with the authority. Specific details for the registration in the different classes are provided in the regulations of the Commodities Exchange Commission. Regulations are also made prescribing in detail the information that must accompany the act of registration in both instances. The board of trade or exchange must undertake to supervise the conduct of its members and discipline them to trading practices that conform with the statutory requirements. Proper accounts must be kept, they must be open to inspection, customer's funds shall not be intermingled, deceptive and fraudulent practices are prohibited, limits on the amount of speculative trading may be imposed, and there may be regulations of delivery on contracts. In short, the aims of the statute are to assure a market that accurately represents the actual amount of trading in the various commodities and honest dealing with the clients of the firms that compose the boards of trade.

The enforcement of the act is divided among the departments of Justice, Commerce, and Agriculture. The act makes some of the malpractices listed above crimes against the United States, and the prosecution of those is vested in the Department of Justice. The heads of the three departments make up

[6] 49 Stat. 1491.
[7] 42 Stat. 998.

the Commodities Exchange Commission, which has the power to issue regulations of various kinds under the act after hearings. The regulations are binding rules, and are enforced administratively by the Commodities Exchange Authority, a subdivision of the Department of Agriculture. Exchanges may have their status as contract markets rescinded, and floor commission merchants and brokers may have their registration cancelled, for practices in violation of the statute and regulations. In general, these actions are taken for false statements and manipulation of market prices. Such actions are infrequent, but are nonetheless an important facet of the total marketing situation.

PERISHABLE COMMODITIES. The marketing of perishable agricultural commodities was not aided in the preceding legislation, and there was (and is) a major problem of maintaining honesty in such markets. The major problem has been in the rejection of perishable fruits and vegetables. The producer or farmer shipped his products to an agency in the cities to sell, and he necessarily had to depend on the probity of his agent to return to him the proper and honest amount. Often the agent was thousands of miles from the point of shipment, so that reshipment or reconsignment was not feasible. If the agent reported the fruits or vegetables to be in poor condition, or the conditions of the market to be such as to reduce returns to the shipper, the latter either accepted the report or sought to prove otherwise in a lawsuit distant from his base of operations.

The first legislation at the national level on this matter was the Produce Agency Act of 1927.[8] The main burden of the law was to make it a crime against the national government for a firm receiving fresh fruits or vegetables in interstate commerce to destroy, abandon, discard, or refuse them without adequate cause, to make false reports about the shipments to the shipper, and knowingly to make false reports about the produce. The law was aimed at the agency and at the malpractices, but the results were not satisfactory, although the act was and is still used. Since this is criminal legislation enforcement is in the hands of the Department of Justice.

The second effort to correct the difficulties was in the Perishable Agricultural Commodities Act of 1930.[9] This act is administered by the Department of Agriculture in considerable part, though criminal prosecution is in the Department of Justice. The act is aimed at the same "evils" as the Produce Agency Act, but reliance is placed more on administrative supervision of the market. The act makes a number of specific practices illegal—such as making fraudulent charges for marketing services; the failure to take delivery of perishables without just cause; dumping or discarding such commodities without just cause; making misleading statements about, and incorrectly accounting for, commodities; altering or removing notices as to grade, quality, and origin of commodities on railroad cars or containers if they have

[8] 44 Stat. 1355.
[9] 46 Stat. 531.

been placed there by a federal or state inspector; and prohibiting any changes by commission merchants, dealers, or brokers of officially inspected lots of perishables, except for re-sorting and discarding inferior produce. Violations of these prohibited practices are subject to disciplinary action by the Secretary of Agriculture. The commission merchants, dealers, and brokers cannot legally operate without licenses from the Secretary. Disciplinary action could result in suspension or cancellation of the licenses. Disciplinary actions are taken after hearings and with other protections against arbitrary action by the Secretary. The obvious aim of these provisions is to provide honest practitioners in the market.

In addition to these controls, the act went further and provided that any commission merchant, dealer, or broker who violated the above prohibitions was liable to the injured party or parties for the full amount of the damages suffered. The injured party could proceed in a regular court, or he could institute proceedings for reparation before the Secretary. The award of the Secretary is not automatically effective. It may be taken before a district court, where a *de novo* trial is had. In the trial, however, the facts as found by the Secretary are given prima-facie standing. Failure to pay proper awards subjects one to the disciplinary proceedings before the Secretary.

The act has been amended in several details since 1930, usually with the effect of increasing the obligations of commission men to shippers. The act is admittedly a tough one as regards the liabilities it imposes.

FOOD AND DRUG LEGISLATION. No effort will be made to survey the vast array of controls that now exist in this area. In its early development legislation on these matters vested administration in the Department of Agriculture. With the creation of the Department of Health, Education and Welfare in 1953, the administrative responsibility was transferred to that department. The transfer signified to some degree a shift in the focus of the policy from its consequences to the farmers and producers toward a more general concern with consumers generally. It was always something of an anomaly that the administration of the legislation was in the Department of Agriculture, and there are those critics who suggest that the administration was lodged there to protect producers against the more rigid safeguards that a representative of the consumers might support.

The legislation on meat inspection, adulteration of foods, and other matters involved in the manufacturing processes of foods had obvious implications for agricultural producers. More recently, the use of pesticides that persist through the cleansing processes that precede marketing, the use of chemical or other colors to make the agricultural products more like the "image" the advertising pictures present, and the use of chemical curing processes and chemical preservatives, as well as the development of antibiotics, have posed problems that take on a general character and are obviously of great importance to consumers. The goal of much of the legislation is non-economic; that is, it is related to the maintenance of minimum standards of health protection. The economic struggle, it is hoped, takes place above the minimum standards that the legislation seeks to establish. It costs in labor and products to improve standards, and enterprises engaged in profit-seeking are not above finding that goal and the goal of pure food and drugs occasionally inconsistent one with the other.

COOPERATIVES FOR FARMERS

Despite the assistance of the marketing legislation, the agricultural producer desired additional help in the marketing process. He was, on the one side, a purchaser of commodities such as fertilizer, agricultural equipment, feeds, and other supplies, and on the other, a seller of his produce. In both activities there were sponsors for the notion that if the farmers combined to consolidate their transactions, they could eliminate some of the costs and charges for the middleman's stage, and also increase their bargaining position through the size of their purchases or sales. On the purchasing side, brokerage and commissions that would otherwise be paid to intermediaries would be saved, and the ability to shift patronage from one supplier of farmers' needs to another probably would bring lower prices. In short, the farmer would obtain some of the advantages of the oligopsonist and monopsonist. On the selling side, the same sort of advantages could be estimated. That would especially be the case if the selling agency had capital or could obtain low-cost credit to carry the products from the harvesting period to later periods of the year. The farmers would become oligopolists or monopolists. The means to these bargaining advantages were potentially available through cooperatives.

A cooperative could be chartered as a corporation with a separate legal personality. The farmers would become the stockholders in the corporation, and the latter would act as a purchaser or seller as need indicated. The gains from the advantageous bargaining position would become earnings of the farmer-owned enterprise, and these earnings would be distributed to the stockholders in proportion to their purchases and sales through the common agency. The capital for the operating cooperative would come from the stock purchases of the farmer owners. The cooperative would be able to secure credit for short-term transactions at cheaper rates than would the individual members. In the most optimistic formulations of the theme, the farmers would be able, through the cooperative, to gain the benefits of large-scale enterprise and yet remain independent farmers. A visible gap in that optimistic outlook lay in the antitrust laws, for the cooperative had all the appearances of a combination in restraint of its members. The solution of that shortcoming was legislation by Congress granting the cooperatives exemption in legitimate operations from the application of the Sherman Act, and placing them under the supervision of the Secretary of Agriculture. The Secretary may issue orders restraining them from unreasonable practices, a rarely used grant of authority. The exemption was granted for non-stock and nonprofit organizations in the Clayton Act of 1914,[10] and the Capper-Volstead Act of 1922 [11] widened the exemption to include those associations whose dividends were limited to 8 per cent on share capital, with the major portion of their business being done for members, each member exercising only one vote. Other legislation has prohibited business practices that discriminate against the cooperative; for example, the Packers and Stockyards Act requires the operators of covered facilities to permit cooperatives to utilize the facilities. The Commodities Exchange Act entitles cooperatives to transact business on the exchanges. Many of the states also have granted farmer cooperatives exemptions from their antitrust legislation. More recently, national legislation has utilized cooperatives in marketing agreements under legislation to be discussed below.

EQUALITY FOR AGRICULTURE

The campaign for "orderly marketing," the original label for the broad hopes of the cooperatives, was unable to prevent the great slump in agricultural prices that followed World War I. Many remedies were suggested in many quarters. These were finally united in a goal that may be called "equality for agriculture." In an early and unsuccessful step, tariffs were provided to protect the American market for American agriculture, but higher tariffs in the legislation of 1922 still did not provide a solution to the problem. An alternative suggestion foresaw a two-price system: one for domestic markets and another for foreign markets. The Congress enacted such legislation twice in the 1920's, only to have it vetoed by the President. A variation was the export-debenture scheme, which depended on the reservation of the United States market for United States farmers, and on subsidization of exports with contributions from sales in the U.S. markets and with the revenues from tariffs on imports. The justification was found in the view that business and industry benefited from protective tariffs that made costs higher to farmers. Farmers should participate in the protective policy, and the two-market, two-price system was a means of doing it.

The pressure for governmental aid for agriculture in the early 1920's came especially from the midwest and its wheat producers. Toward the end of the decade, as the remainder of the world recovered from the war, cotton began to feel the competition from expanded foreign production. A congressional coalition between midwest and southern representatives was able, with some auxiliary assistance, to attain what the midwest alone had not been able to accomplish earlier in the decade. The victory of the coalition was signalled by a statute, adopted at a special session of Congress in 1929, which declared it to be national policy to attain "equality for agriculture." A Farm Board was created and given $500 million to check the price depression in agricul-

[10] 38 Stat. 730.
[11] 42 Stat. 388.

ture that had persisted through the 1920's. The depression that started in late 1929 frustrated the Farm Board and led to the political overturn in 1932. The new administration in Washington in 1933 moved a step further toward control of production in its early agricultural programs, but now the goal was to be "parity" for the farmer. A variety of techniques was made available to attain that goal. In a small way, each had already been subject to experiment, the single exception being direct governmental control of the quantities that legally could reach the markets for sale. The New Deal set out to try this, too. At present, agricultural policy still embodies all the strands of 1933.

PARITY. The Agricultural Adjustment Act of 1933 stated that it was the policy of the United States to ". . . give agricultural commodities a purchasing power with respect to articles farmers buy, equivalent to the purchasing power of agricultural commodities in the base period 1909–1914." For tobacco, the base period was the period 1919–1929. Usually the requirement about purchasing power in the 1933 (and subsequent) legislation is translated to mean that the prices per unit of commodity in the present period ought to yield a purchasing power equivalent to the purchasing power for that unit in the base period. Some sections of the legislation speak of parity income for farmers. Parity income sets as a goal the principle that income to individuals on farms shall bear the same relation to income of non-farm individuals as the relation was in the same base period. The latter principle, in some circumstances, could lead to different results than the former; however, little use has been made of the parity-income principle, and regulatory activities have been focused mainly on the maintenance of parity prices.

The Department of Agriculture computes the parity prices. Statutory changes have been introduced in the definition of such prices since World War II, with the intention of modifying the earlier parity prices. Several changes have been made: first, taxes and wages have been incorporated in the formula, the outcome being to increase the base parity price. Second, changes were introduced to calculate individual parity prices for particular commodities based on more recent price trends. The effect of such changes was to guide agricultural production toward those commodities in demand currently, and to discourage the production of commodities in less demand that had been popular in the base period. This "modernized" parity has been a feature of recent agricultural policy.

"Parity" has not been a precise concept. There are mathematical difficulties in computing price relationships in past periods and in arriving at the other figures required in statutory definitions. Law goes further in this instance than in rate-making and price-fixing statutes generally. In those statutes only a general guide is given, while in the agricultural legislation the statutory standard is defined specifically. But what, on its face, is specific may lack preciseness in application. Moreover, the parity concept has been engulfed in macropolitics. The issues referred to above—price parity or income parity, inclusion or noninclusion of tax and wage costs in computation of parity, the base period to be used as the standard—have been subjects repeatedly of intense legislative conflict.[12]

Parity prices are maintained in two ways: by reducing production, and by withholding commodities from the market, either by shipping outside the domestic market or by giving them within the country to segments of the population that were not actual participants in the market for price-making purposes—for example, relief recipients and school children. The last means were congenial with attitudes that favored raising the living conditions of the poorest part of the population and improving the health of the people through better diets. Ingenuity in devices has been helpful. Recently, Public Law 480 has authorized a variety of sales to foreigners that private profit-making enterprises could not indulge in, and the program is labelled "Food for Peace." As a counter to communism in the lesser developed countries, among other things, it gains political support from the proponents of foreign aid. The devices of control are numerous and complex, and only the basic features can be described here.

PRODUCTION CONTROLS OF BASIC COMMODITIES. The New Deal agricultural legislation of 1933, 1934, and 1935 provided for adjustments to be made in acreage of basic commodities.[13] The controls of acreage were tied in with a tax, collected by processors, equal to the difference between the current market price and the parity price. The proceeds from the tax were to be used by the Secretary of Agriculture to pay farmers for reductions in acreage. The Supreme Court held the scheme unconstitutional in *United States v. Butler* in 1936.[14] Congress immediately enacted the Soil Conservation and Domestic Allotment Act to fill the gap until a new program was devised.[15] Additional legislation was enacted in 1937 and 1938.[16] The basic scheme of production controls was delineated in these enactments. National allotments (explained later) were to be made for soil-depleting crops, and payments were to be made to cooperating farmers for soil-conserving practices. A section of the 1933 legislation providing for marketing agreements of agricultural commodities was renewed. The latter type of regulation will be described below. This section will be devoted to marketing controls for the basic commodities. A generalized account of the pattern of control will be given. The changes in detail of the legislation through the years are very great, and it is impossible in a brief account to give an exact report for each commodity. It may be said that the annual amendments almost make the agricultural committees of the two houses of Congress planning agencies for the commodities included within the controls, and

---

[12] See "The Parity Concept and Its Relation to the Farm Problem," Appendix A in Murray R. Benedict, *Can We Solve the Farm Problem? An Analysis of Federal Aid to Agriculture* (New York: Twentieth Century Fund, 1955).
[13] 48 Stat. 31 (1933); 48 Stat. 528, 598, 670, 1275 (1934); 49 Stat. 163 (1935).
[14] 297 U.S. 1.
[15] 49 Stat. 1151.
[16] 50 Stat. 246, 52 Stat. 31.

that the legislation represents the coalition of the regional crop representatives that is necessary to gain a majority vote in Congress.

The basic commodities are cotton, corn, wheat, rice, peanuts, and tobacco. The administrative controls begin with the setting of national acreage allotments for each crop. The Secretary of Agriculture sets the allotments. He adds estimated domestic consumption, normal exports, and normal reserve supplies to get the total needed supply of the commodity. The carry-over from the previous year is subtracted, and the remainder is the national need. He then determines the number of acres which will produce the annual need. That figure becomes the national acreage allotment. The national acreage is next distributed to the states in accordance with past proportions of national acreage. The state acreage is then subdivided to counties and within counties to farmers on the basis of past production records. The scheme, it will be noted, grants advantages to farms and regions with past production records, and the ability of newcomers to enter the production of the basics has been regulated, usually by withholding a small proportion of the acreage allotments from assignment to those with records. Newcomers could produce acreage to the minimum permitted number of acres without penalty. In part, the potential injustices or restrictions on new areas have been met generally by imposing acreage controls only on the commercial-crop-growing counties. A commercial-crop county was one that produced more of the commodity than it consumed—that is, exported the commodity.

Annually the Secretary makes the calculation of the availability of supplies and the potential demand. If the excess of carry-over into the new crop year exceeds the level specified in the statute, the Secretary announces the fact and determines the national acreage that will be needed to meet the market demands and provide parity prices. At this stage two possible lines of policy are open. First, if the excess is not large, the Secretary can announce the acreage and authorize allotments to each farm. Under the soil-conservation section, he will announce payments for compliance with soil-conserving practices and the amount of such payments per acre. Farmers who comply with the acreage restriction and engage in the soil-conserving practices get income for better farming practices, and also are entitled to price supports on the produce from the allotted acreages. (The operation of the price-support scheme will be described later.) This arrangement is voluntary, since the farmer can comply or not with his allotment. Failure to comply means that he takes what the market offers. Compliance assures him of support prices. The conservation payments improve his soil and presumably increase its long-run productivity. This phase of the program was expanded beyond its original boundaries in the soil-bank policy of the Eisenhower Administration. With that expansion, payments are made for rotating productive acreage to soil-building crops and taking it out of production for longer periods of time. Payments in this scheme are closely related to the loss of income to the farmer from not producing the basic commodity. The development in policy was designed to pull more acreage out of production than smaller payments for soil-conserving practices had been able to motivate. However, the latter were not discontinued.

When the carry-over or surplus exceeds certain limits, the Secretary calls for a referendum on the imposition of compulsory control for the basic commodity. The referendum is conducted among the commercial growers of the basic commodity, and if two-thirds vote in favor of imposition of compulsory controls, the Secretary imposes quotas on each commercial grower. The quota allows the farmer to market the output of a specified number of acres, and marketing in excess of the quota is subject to fairly drastic penalties. If the voters in the referendum fail to approve quotas, the Secretary then has to rely on the first or voluntary scheme. Support prices usually will be dropped substantially below what they would have been with the compulsory controls. Under the compulsory arrangement, the marketing of the commodity is limited to those with a quota. This arrangement has been applied, off and on, to the basic crops, and most consistently applied in the control of tobacco.

The administration of the programs has usually been in the hands of a subdivision of the Department of Agriculture. The labels have differed through the years. Currently, the agency is the Agricultural Stabilization and Conservation Service. This administration allots the acreage to a state committee, which in turn allots it to a county committee composed of farmers in the county assisted by an administrative officer and staff. There have been frequent controversies over the centralization and/or decentralization of control. A great deal of talk and writing has focused on the influences upon the committees and the possibilities of favoritism in their actions. The county agency is the one that allots the acreage to the farmers and does the measuring to check the compliance with allotments.

CONTROLS FOR NONBASICS. The legislation in 1938 provided that the Secretary of Agriculture, with the approval of the President, should instruct the Commodity Credit Corporation (CCC) to make loans on agricultural commodities. The loans on the basic commodities were obligatory in accordance with the provisions of the legislation in effect for that year. Loans by the CCC on other commodities, including dairy products, depended on the availability of funds and policy decisions in the Secretary's office. The Agricultural Act of 1949 [17] extended this activity and authorized and mandated the Secretary to make price-support loans for wool, tung nuts, honey, Irish potatoes, milk, butterfat, and the products of milk and butterfat under specified conditions. He was also authorized to make loans at his discretion for any other nonbasic agricultural commodity. The loans in this last group were to be made after funds were found to be available for the basics and the mandatory nonbasics. The prices of competing commodities being supported were to be taken into consideration in the making of the discretionary loans.

[17] 63 Stat. 1051.

Mandatory loans on the nonbasics were to be made between 60 per cent and 90 per cent of parity prices at a rate determined by the Secretary as necessary to assure an adequate supply. Loans and supports on the discretionary commodities were to be made at a percentage of parity (75–90), depending on the supply at the beginning of the year. As the supply percentage increased over 102 per cent, the support percentage declined; that is, the loans varied inversely with the supply within the statutory ranges.

In general there was a requirement that the commodities were storable as security for such loans, and the effect was to limit the availability of price-support loans to storables. Obviously, it was hoped or expected that as the support price or loan declined, the quantities produced would decrease, and vice versa.

In the late 1950's the competitive feed grains gave serious trouble to the operation of support prices. These grains—oats, barley, rye, and grain sorghums—were competitive with corn and wheat as sources of food for livestock under certain price situations. In general, as the prices of corn and wheat increased, these competitive grains increased in acreage. The restrictions of the acreage in wheat and corn merely increased the acreage available for these competitive grains. After 1958, corn acreage was unrestricted, too, but wheat continued to be a major problem of surplus supply. Support and control of these competitive feed grains became essential if any semblance of the usual proportions between the grains was to be maintained. The 1961 emergency legislation tried to reduce the supply by making reduction in plantings more attractive through payments for diverting acreage.[18] It was essential, also, to prohibit the unused acreage from being used for competing crops. The Secretary was instructed by Congress to make payments to farmers for reducing the acreage of such commodities by 20 per cent. Another 20 per cent reduction in acreage was made attractive by authorizing the CCC to give certificates to cooperating farmers claiming commodity instead of cash payments. Thus, the farmer could obtain the commodity to sell if the price increased as a result of the drop in acreage. It was expensive to operate the program, but the alternative of supporting prices under existing legislation was regarded as more expensive and not likely to achieve any reduction in surpluses.

COMMODITY CREDIT CORPORATION. This corporation is the agency the Department of Agriculture uses in the performance of the duties assigned to the department in the support and maintenance of agricultural prices. The corporation has legal personality, and operates on funds appropriated to it by Congress and on borrowings that Congress authorizes it to make. Another source of funds is from the sale of commodities to which it has acquired title. Congress has provided in legislation that a percentage of the proceeds from tariffs on imported commodities shall be allocated to the CCC for the promotion of domestic use of agricultural commodities—a

---

[18] 75 Stat. 6.

remnant of the earlier view that agriculture ought to have the equivalent of industry's benefit from tariff. The losses that may ensue on the difference between the purchase or support price and sale price is later made up by an appropriation from Congress. This is a form of "backdoor spending" that is occasionally regarded unfavorably by members of Congress and others outside Congress.

The CCC executes the policy decisions of Congress embodied in the legislation for that particular year. Congress may have legislated rigid or specific prices that the CCC must maintain, or have authorized support at flexible prices. In the latter case, the statute instructs the CCC to maintain support prices within a specified range. The CCC has statutory directions to take into account the supply in relation to demand, the price levels, the availability of funds, the perishability of the commodity, and other standards. In the performance of these duties, it announces the price supports for the various commodities at the beginning of the crop year.

Two procedures for supporting prices prevail. In the one case the farmer will go to his bank and borrow on his commodity as security. The amount of the loan will be related to the support price. Later, the farmer may repay the loan and regain the commodity. Presumably, he will do this if the market price of the commodity increases, and in this situation the CCC is not involved. However, if the market price remains below the support price, the farmer will take the debt to the CCC, which will pay off the loan at the bank and take title to the commodity that served as security. There are rules that govern this kind of transaction.

The second means of price support by the CCC is through purchase from cooperating farmers at the prices specified in the program. The farmer is not obligated to sell to the CCC, but the CCC is obligated to purchase from the cooperating farmer the amount he wishes to deliver. The CCC's action may have the consequence of bolstering the price of the commodity so that the support price and the market price are identical. If the market price is higher than the support price, the farmers will obviously sell at the market price. However, if the market price is lower, the cooperating farmer will deliver his commodity to the CCC and receive the support price.

It is noteworthy that a market price below the support price is a possibility because of noncooperating farmers who are not entitled to support prices, cooperating farmers who are unable to arrange for storage of their commodities, the authority of the CCC to sell commodities under specified conditions, commodities not meeting specifications for CCC loans, and other reasons.

From time to time, the CCC may be ordered to stabilize prices. In this case, it may sell from its stocks to maintain the market price at a specified level. Stabilization also will require the CCC to withhold commodities from the market at other times in order to maintain prices. In order to prevent the CCC from depressing the market price, it is usually prohibited from selling, unless the market price has reached a specified percentage of the support level. The level has usually been 105 per cent of the support price.

The CCC is also permitted or instructed to sell or give away its commodities from time to time. The CCC is the intermediary in the execution of the obligations of the United States under the International Wheat Agreement, to be described below. It has also been authorized to furnish food to schools under the national school-lunch program, to veterans' hospitals, to the military services, and to agencies for distribution to needy and aged people in this country. The commodities in the possession of the CCC are also being used in conjunction with the Food for Peace, foreign-aid programs, disaster-relief grants to foreign countries, and in international barter agreements. In short, any desirable project at home or abroad that can absorb agricultural surpluses is a potential recipient. The deficit in the CCC accounts that may grow out of such programs is made up ultimately from appropriations by Congress.

The CCC, through its support programs, has become a large owner of agricultural commodities, and since it cannot sell except under limited conditions, it maintains a large storage operation. The storage facilities are owned by the government or rented from private owners. The cost of the storage facilities has become a very large annual charge in the agricultural program. To facilitate the storage operation, the CCC has been authorized to sell stocks in order to keep the stored supplies in good condition. As it sells, it must buy equivalent quantities so that market prices are not disturbed. All of the operations of the CCC take place in accordance with legal grading standards. Only commodities that meet the specified standards of cleanliness and other qualities in the regular commodities markets are eligible for the privileges.

MARKETING AGREEMENTS AND ORDERS. The agricultural legislation of 1933 contained provisions authorizing the Secretary of Agriculture to enter into agreements with producers and processors of agricultural commodities. Under specified conditions, licenses for handling the commodities could be required. The legislation was amended in 1935 and revised in 1937 in the Marketing Agreement Act of 1937.[19] This act anticipates agreements between the handlers and processors of any agricultural commodities and the Secretary of Agriculture. If such agreements are reached, they are exempt from the provisions of the Sherman Act. The agreement becomes a restraining set of conditions on those who are party to it. Presumably, the operation of the agreement will improve the income and prices of the producers of the products included in the agreement. These agreements may be used to supplement the controls described above.

The statute also provides for the issuance of orders by the Secretary of Agriculture that will govern the operation of the marketing practices of the commodities included within its terms. The order has binding effect, and violations of it are violations of law. Usually an agreement accompanies an

[19] 50 Stat. 248.

order, the handlers of 50 per cent of the commodities within the order having agreed to the terms of the proposed order. Hearings must be held in which producers, handlers, processors, and consumers are entitled to appear and present their arguments pro and con the proposal. The 50 per cent requirement may be by-passed with the determination of the Secretary and the President that the policy of the act will be defeated without the order. However, the statute requires the proposed order to be approved by two-thirds of the producers, or the producers of two-thirds of the commodity, before it may be issued by the Secretary. Larger proportions of the producers are required in the case of California citrus products. (Special terms that apply to milk will be described below.) The order must contain provisions prohibiting unfair methods of competition and trade practices; it must also provide that sales shall be at prices not less than those filed by the handlers; and it must provide for the selection by the Secretary of an administrator or administrative board to administer the order, to investigate alleged violations and report them, and to recommend amendments. The order may include provisions for the handling and marketing practices, such as limiting and/or specifying the grades of the commodity that may be sold, supervision of the rate at which the marketing takes place, or borrowing money to make advances to producers pending the final sale of the producers' commodities. Clauses of this type are intended to maximize returns through controlled marketing. This prevents the price depression that results from large quantities reaching the market at the same time. Some agreements may prohibit the marketing of inferior grades and may provide ways of removing some quantities from the market in the expectation of holding prices higher and increasing net income. There are a fairly large number of these agreements and orders in effect for citrus, nuts, raisins, avocadoes, and other products. Usually there is a cooperative marketing agency that acts for the various producers. State legislation often buttresses the federal order, since the latter is limited to interstate transactions and transactions that affect interstate commerce. California and Florida have legislation on the marketing of citrus fruits, and the California Pro-Rate Act has been used in conjunction with marketing orders and agreements on other commodities.

The most extensive use of the marketing order has been in the marketing of milk. The statute from the outset has had a special provision permitting minimum prices for milk. A substantial portion of the milk sold for consumption as fresh milk is marketed under these federal orders. The national government does not regulate the retail distribution of milk for human consumption, but many of the states have elaborate programs for such controls. In fact, milk may properly be considered a public utility in many states. The state regulation supplements the national marketing orders. Indeed, the latter are often essential to prevent the state regulations from suffering a competitive situation that would make state controls ineffectual.

Federal milk orders are used rather than agreements, for the reason that not all handlers will sign agreements. The order is applicable to all who handle milk in a given market. The usual procedures preceding an order are applicable—that is, the hearing and the proposal of an order. The order must be approved by the required number of producers for the market in which it applies. Usually milk is sold through cooperative marketing, and the administrators of the cooperative vote for its producing members on their volume of supply; that is, there is no referendum among the individual farmers who belong to the cooperative. This practice probably simplifies the getting of the requisite majorities. The Secretary then designates an administrator for supervision of the market.

The market is usually an urban community in which distinguishable producer boundaries may be determined with some confidence. The dairies that supply milk to that market are brought within the terms of the order. All handlers, whether cooperatives or private, are supervised by the administrator as to accounts and sources of supply. The terms of the order may vary in detail, but the purpose is to obtain a minimum price for milk to the producers; some orders establish market-wide pools that include all suppliers of milk; and some establish handler pools that include all suppliers of a handler. In the latter case there must be a second pooling as between handlers to reach the minimum price paid to the suppliers. The goal is to get the proceeds from the sale of milk into a common fund. From that fund are deducted the costs of administering the program, and the remainder is available for distribution back to the farm producers. Each producer will receive his proper proportion based on contribution of milk to the common milk pool.

The order usually designates Class I as milk sold for human consumption. It brings the highest prices. In a sense, the major purpose of the control is to divide the fresh-milk market among all the dairy producers so as to enable each to gain his share of that market. The proceeds from the sale in this market go into the pool to be shared among all the producers. The milk not sold for Class I use is then sold for other uses, and usually the price in the alternative markets is lower. The quantity of milk sold as Class I bears the brunt of maintaining the minimum price payable to the dairies. The alternative markets involve ice cream, canning or condensing, drying, and other uses.

The administration of the order requires the various handlers to keep accounts as to sales for the different purposes, to keep records of the source of the milk they receive, and to distribute money properly to the farmers.

The Kennedy Administration proposed a substantial revision of the approach to attaining agricultural goals, and the mainspring of that change was to broaden the use of the marketing agreement and orders to include all agricultural commodities, and to discontinue some of the controls applied to basics and nonbasics. Congress was unwilling to accept the change, but the Agricultural Act of 1961 did expand the commodities that could be brought within the controls of the marketing orders. It remains to be seen whether the opportunity will be taken. The legislative discussion clearly indicated that there are some sectors of agriculture in which some of the producers resist the possibility of orders. There are other sectors in which this possibility is looked on with favor, and there are still other sectors in which producers have no clear view as to advantages and disadvantages.

SUGAR. The special policy toward sugar is found in several statutes: the tariff law, the tax law, the Sugar Control Act of 1948 as amended,[20] and the treaty including the International Sugar Agreement. Both the tariff and the tax features go back to the beginning of national policy, for the levies on sugar provided a substantial portion of national revenues through the nineteenth century. The act of 1948 was a revision of an earlier act of 1937, which in turn was a revision of the act of 1934. The controls in these three acts are alike, and are geared into the tariff and excise-tax provisions.

In contrast with the previous commodities, sugar is a deficit commodity; that is, imports from foreign countries provide about half the sugar consumed in the United States. The International Sugar Agreement represents the cooperation of the United States with the other countries that export and import sugar. Sugar also has the distinction of being controlled in most countries of the world. The controls usually are designed to protect the domestic market from outside competition, but in the countries that have surpluses there are also controls to help maintain the prices for the producers.

The basic sugar law provides that the Secretary of Agriculture shall determine in December of each year the basic sugar needs for the following year. A hearing precedes the determination. Currently, the total quantity is about 9 million tons. Of this amount, about 53 per cent is allocated to producers in the producing states, plus Puerto Rico and the Virgin Islands. There are some twenty-two mainland states that produce sugar from beets, and two that produce it from cane. Hawaii joins the latter two. About one-third of the needed sugar has traditionally come from Cuba, and some 10 to 11 per cent from the Philippine Islands. The remainder is allocated among other producing countries. Recently the severing of sugar trade with Cuba made its quota available for allocation among other nations. There has been a considerable effort on the part of the producing states within the U.S. to gain a larger share of the former Cuban allotment.

The International Sugar Agreement approves the current practices of the United States, and it does not have much importance for the United States market. That agreement allocates quotas among the producing member states and the importing member states. Usually the agreement allocates the markets that are over and beyond that supplied by the domestic industry.

The amount of sugar allocated in the U.S. to domestic production is in turn allocated to farms in the various producing states. Each farm is entitled to its "proportionate share," and in making this determination, the Secretary must take into account the amount of carry-over each area may have,

---

[20] 61 Stat. 922.

as well as the past production and the ability of the farm. Small producers and new producers also are entitled to consideration by the Secretary. The farms are not obligated to stay within "proportionate shares," but if they do, they are eligible for conditional payments. These payments come from the U.S. Treasury, and are conditional on the farmer-processors' paying fair prices to other growers, on paying the workers in the fields a fair wage as determined by the Secretary, and on not employing children under the age of 14, or those between the ages of 14 and 16 more than eight hours a day. Penalties are provided for growers who do not comply with the child-labor regulations. Since the payments are a sizable factor in the incomes of the growers, most of them comply. The basic payment is 80 cents per hundred pounds of raw sugar for the first 350 tons, and it varies downward for larger tonnages. The act also provides payments for disaster losses.

There is an excise tax of 5 cents per pound paid on all imported sugar sold in the U.S.; the proceeds from this tax exceed the conditional payments.

The stated goals of sugar policy are to make the U.S. independent of foreign sources to a considerable extent, to provide a stable price for consumers, and to maintain national defense. Presumably, these goals are maintained in the operation of the existing patterns of relations, for there is little opposition to them in the Congress. The availability of the Cuban quota may stimulate more pressure to increase the percentage produced in the mainland states; it is already reported that more acreage has gone into cane planting in Florida, but the granting of additional acreage to Florida probably depends on the future of Castro's regime.

WOOL. Wool, like sugar, is imported in large quantities. Congress considers both commodities to be "essential and strategic commodities," and it believes that the nation ought to be considerably self-sufficient in supplies. A special program has been worked out that provides incentive payments through the Commodity Credit Corporation for wool and mohair grown in this country. The statute authorizes the use of revenues from import duties to be used to make payments to those farmers who cooperate with the program. In this program, the CCC does not undertake to maintain the market price of wool at the support level, but the wool growers market their commodity, and the CCC pays to the grower the difference between the price he receives in the market and the guaranteed support price. This policy differs markedly from the support-price policy in other commodities.

The operation of the wool program requires the growers and the Secretary to agree on the price at which the commodities will be supported. That price will be a percentage of the calculated parity price. The goal is to encourage the production of not more than 360 million pounds of shorn wool, but the total payments to that end shall not exceed 70 per cent of the proceeds from the import duties on wool and wool products. The payments plan is designed to increase the returns to the more efficient farmers. The payments are based on the difference between the national average price received for wool and the support price, so that the wool grower who receives higher than the national average price because of the quality of his product will still receive the difference between the national average and the support price. The statute authorizes other means of support for wool prices, but the payments arrangement is the one that has been used consistently. The original legislation was adopted in 1954; it was renewed in 1958 and again in 1962.[21] The present expiration date is 1966.

The Western states have been strong supporters of this policy toward wool, but political support is found in many other states. Sheep and goats are grown in many parts of the country, and all producers of these are eligible for the benefits that the legislation provides.

COMMENTARY

The programs that have developed in recent years for the agricultural commodities described in the preceding pages have been concurrent with the cultivation, from many sources, of an ideology which envisages the American economic system as a free economy, and which therefore looks on the government as a potential threat to economic productivity and private enterprises. The rationale of supporting agriculture has been the task of those members of Congress that come from the crop-producing areas, and they have obviously been equal to the task. Despite the ideological opposition to the programs, Congress, and usually the President, have not swerved from their goal. Yet there is some evidence that the strength of the political support for the programs is weakening. The Secretary of Agriculture under President Eisenhower pressed successfully for a new definition of parity that would be a moving average of the commodity prices in the past ten years. The new parity opened the way to allowing changes in the demand for agricultural commodities to influence the level of parity. The tendency of the Secretary to use the lower side of the percentage for support prices also pressed in the same direction as the moving average price. In the mid-fifties, something of a break in the solidarity of the farm-voting bloc began to show in the Congressional battles of 1954. President Kennedy proposed a greater use of the marketing-agreements pattern, and supply management through such agreements. He also proposed quantity limits rather than acreage limitations. Congress did not fully grant these requests, but the avenue to a wider use of agreements was opened.

The surpluses that have been most persistent have been limited to a few commodities, and there have been unexpected escapes from burdensome surpluses in the past. The droughts of the middle thirties and the needs for food and fiber in World War II and the Korean crisis have removed insupportable surpluses at periodic intervals. The late fifties and early sixties have not provided any such escape. The Food for Peace program in this last

---

[21] 68 Stat. 910, 72 Stat. 994, 75 Stat. 294.

period has furnished substantial markets that otherwise would not have been available. So far, that program has not been able to absorb the surpluses, and there is clear evidence that foreign countries do not find the exports of these commodities an unmixed blessing. Protection of domestic markets for domestic agriculture is not limited to the United States.

On occasion, the support programs have created surpluses in additional commodities or have increased existing surpluses in a commodity. The support programs have usually been restricted in their operation to the commercial crop areas—that is, the areas that produce more than they consume. The commercial growers of the controlled commodity would then restrict their acreage to comply with the control, and the growers in noncommercial areas would increase acreage in the controlled commodity. Often, acreage restriction results in freeing land for planting in another crop that competes in some measure with the controlled commodity, thereby increasing the output. For example, corn, oats, rye, barley, and grain sorghums are substitutable in great measure for each other as feed for animals. The reduction of corn acreage might lead to increased acreage in the others, with the result that production of competing crops would counter the purposes of the acreage reduction of corn. A way out of this difficulty is to require cross-compliance; that is, no controlled crop should be grown on acreage that was released by the imposition of controls. A few efforts have been made to obtain cross-compliance, but the administrators of the programs were unable to maintain the requirement. The soil-bank program in the 1950's sought to avoid some of the consequence of the absence of cross-compliance by making payments for soil-conserving practices. This involved taking the acreage out of the production of any commercial crop. The payments had to be large enough to persuade the farmer that not using the acreage was almost as profitable as using it. The cost of such payments are high, and might go higher if the acreage becomes more productive in subsequent years. A further development of this principle provided payments for letting a minimum percentage of productive acreage lie fallow. The CCC also granted commodities as an alternative to cash payments for retiring a still larger percentage of the productive acreage. The costs of such programs were high, but there was the possibility also of reducing the carrying charges of the CCC. Despite these efforts, the surpluses are continuing to pile up, and it seems likely that the urban representatives in Congress might ultimately openly rebel at such obvious largesse to a small portion of the population.

In setting out the agricultural controls in the 1930's, policy makers were deeply concerned with the consequences of the reduction of acreages on tenants and sharecroppers. In the absence of provisions for their protection, owners of land would reduce their acreage simply by reducing the number of sharecroppers or tenants who farmed the land. The results would likely be inequitable and unjust. The early programs brought the renter of agricultural land into the program by entitling him to share in the payments and other benefits. This practice has persisted throughout the years.

A perennial topic in the dialogues about agricultural policy is consumer prices. The curve has been upward, and simultaneously the farmers have complained of declines in their selling prices. The usual explanation of the seeming paradox has been that the consumer is receiving in the product a great many more services than the farmer sells: the cleaning and processing is more complete than in earlier years, and the processors or manufacturers are furnishing more preparation of the foods for consumption than in times past. These preparations take place after the products leave the farm. The services are expensive and are often performed in urban communities by organized labor. The processing requires heavy capital investment and skilled labor, both of which add to the final selling price. This matter is not especially an agricultural question, although uninformed urban consumers may attribute the situation to governmental policy. True, the prices of some agricultural commodities are higher as a result of the programs, but not all of the increases in price are attributable to agricultural policy.

A more persuasive criticism of the general policy of price maintenance is to be found in the fact that the policy holds up consumers' prices, while at the same time consumers as taxpayers are required to make up out of tax receipts the losses in the operations of the CCC. This burden is a general one, and is difficult to trace out to its end result. The theoretical situation can be shown easily. The CCC buys up supplies of the commodities and either gives them away or sells them at lower prices domestically or abroad. Two situations are possible. In one, the CCC competes with other sellers of commodities and operates as any businessman; in the other, it disposes of its commodities to consumers who are not participants in the usual businessman's market.

If the CCC's commodities are distributed to people who would not have an impact on the market, then there is no downward pressure on the price. Such consumers would be the indigent and relief cases, whose dietary levels would be raised by the "gifts" or "charity" of the CCC. The CCC ultimately would need to have its treasury replenished by an appropriation from Congress. If the distribution of CCC commodities were to those who otherwise would purchase in the usual markets, then the impact would be felt in reduced demand. If, for example, the Defense Department received quantities of its food needs from the CCC, or if the state welfare institutions received similar gifts of food that as a result removed these agencies from the demand side of the markets, the effect would be to reduce demand in the markets and thereby reduce prices. However, if the gifts were foods that would not otherwise be bought by these agencies, the consequences would be different and more difficult to trace out. In short, the effectiveness of the price-support policy depends on preventing the controlled commodities from depressing prices. Selling or giving the supported commodities to foreign markets has exactly the same economic consequences as in the domestic markets. Selling abroad at a price less than domestic market prices constitutes "dumping." Also, the two-priced system is likely to generate international friction.

Insofar as prices are held higher than they would be otherwise, the consumers in the United States are paying higher prices than they would have to pay in a competitive market. In the long run, if prices were not supported, output presumably would decrease, and a balance between demand and supply at a satisfactory price to suppliers and buyers would be achieved. With the support-price policy that holds the price above such a hypothetical competitive price, the losses must be made up by the CCC, and these losses are borne by the taxpayers through Congressional appropriations. The final economic burden then falls on the taxpayers in accordance with the operation of the principles of the incidence of taxes. The taxpayer pays once as a consumer and again through his contribution to the Treasury for appropriation to make up CCC losses. Obviously, not all persons contribute proportionally to the Treasury's funds. No effort will be made here to trace out the equity of the tax incidence and its relation to the support price.

This double payment has not seriously disturbed policy makers for agriculture, but there have been occasional comments and suggestions about it. The outstanding suggestion has been dubbed the Brannan Plan. Charles F. Brannan, Secretary of Agriculture briefly under President Truman, proposed that the national government engage in a support policy toward perishable agricultural commodities. Producers of such commodities would sell them at the market price. The department would pay a subsidy equal to the difference between the market price and parity or support price. The consumer would buy at the going market price, which probably would be lower than the support price. The taxpayer would make up the difference through subsidy payments. However, he would pay only one subsidy, and he would also get the benefit of lower market prices. It should be noted that Secretary Brannan did not propose that this policy be applied to the basic commodities. Yet the principle of the plan could be extended to those commodities as well as the perishables. The principle, it should be recalled, is applied in the current wool program, under which the rancher receives direct payment from the government. Whatever the reasons, Congress would have none of Brannan's plan at the time of its proposal, and has not relented in its opposition to it. One of the alleged grounds of opposition is the high visibility of the subsidy.

The controls that apply in agriculture have continued in the directions that have been evident for many years. The antimonopoly provisions continue, the supervision of the marketing processes continue, and the cooperatives continue to be aided in their undertakings. Credit is extended in order to maintain prices and to enable farmers to acquire land.[22] Substitutes for tariff protection are found. Nonetheless, agriculture continues to receive devoted attention from the committees of Congress, from Congress, and from the Department of Agriculture.

It is clear that public policy attributes great value to the maintenance of

[22] On the latter, see pages 604–605.

a sound agriculture. The justification for the continued solicitude is found in the contributions that a profitable agriculture make to the well-being of the economy, both as a customer for industry and as a source of supplies for the magnificent industrial development. It is said also that the rural areas provide moral as well as economic resources. Many of the desired rules of human behavior are traced to the characteristics of the farm family, and those same families have been a constant source of population for the cities and industry.

Finally, the complex market controls have directly benefited owners and operators of about 2 million farms. Owners of the other 3 million have not strenuously objected to controls, nor have most of the urban representatives in Congress found the agricultural programs unbearable.[23]

[23] For indirect benefits, see E. Higbee, *Farms and Farmers in an Urban Age* (New York: Twentieth Century Fund, 1963).

Chapter 23. Financial Institutions and Markets

IT IS NOT NECESSARY for a student to review in detail and comprehensively every field of government legislation on economic matters in order to obtain a perspective on trends, methods, and problems in the political economy. To attempt completeness in knowledge through full examination of every clump of trees would lead at some point to diminishing returns and to an inability to view the forest. For these reasons, in certain final, though important, fields of government regulation, this book seeks only to reveal the outstanding features of the regulatory pattern. This is done for three fields of regulation: commercial banking, insurance, and security markets.[1]

COMMERCIAL BANKING

Commercial banking is one of our most fully regulated industries. Regulation is both comprehensive and intimate. Also, banking has been subject to regulation for a longer period than any other American industry. Regulation is traditional, and no issue of its necessity is now presented.

The dominant objective in regulation is safety. The solvency of banks is a matter of concern to depositors, stockholders, and the communities they serve, and much bank regulation is designed to serve this end. Another objective is adequacy. The existence of adequate bank credit and services, conveniently located, is an aid to industry, trade, and personal business, and achieving this is an objective parallel to, and sometimes conflicting with, that of safety. A further objective in recent years has been economic stabilization and growth. The contraction or expansion of bank credit so vitally affects these objectives that its regulation is an essential part of government's macro-economic policy.

The chief peculiarity of banking regulation is that it has allowed the development of a dual banking system—that is, one in which there are both state and national banks. In no other regulated industry is each company allowed to choose the jurisdiction (state or national) to whose supervision it

---

[1] For additional discussion of financial institutions, see Chapter 9 on "Monetary and Fiscal Policy" and pp. 603–606 on "Credit" in the Chapter on "The Scope of Public Enterprise."

will be subject. The reason for this unusual situation is historical. Banks were licensed regularly by states long before the national government enacted its statute in 1863 providing for the licensing of national banks. The national statute left it optional with existing or new banking associations to obtain national charters.

The establishment of banks had gone through transitions similar to those for business generally. Until near the end of the eighteenth century, most banks were private, unincorporated, individual proprietorships or partnerships. Charters were granted to a small number of banks by the states in the late eighteenth century, and by Congress to the Bank of North America in 1782 and to the first Bank of the United States in 1791. In the nineteenth century, creation of banks by special legislative acts granting charters became common. Then, beginning with a New York statute in 1838, "free banking" began to be substituted for special-charter grants. "Free banking" was the term applied to a system under which charters were granted under general law to all associations which met legal requirements. The result was more than a triple increase in the number of state (that is, state chartered) banks in the approximately twenty-five years prior to the Civil War.

Banking was, however, different from other businesses. Its distinctiveness in the early years of our country lay in the note-issuing function. Banks issued paper money and loaned it, thus performing both monetary and credit functions. From early in the nineteenth century, however, banks began a shift to deposit banking, in which funds for credit were obtained from customer deposits.

These methods of banking were significant with respect to the fate of state banks. In 1865 Congress levied a 10 per cent annual tax on state bank notes. This made state bank-note issue unprofitable, and added impetus to the conversion of state banks to national-bank status. The rate of conversion was so great that it appeared for a time that the desire of Secretary of the Treasury Chase for an exclusively national system would be realized. It soon became apparent, however, that state banking, based on deposits, could survive without the note-issuance function. The number of state banks began to increase again after 1869. The dual banking system is now firmly established, there being at the end of 1962 nearly twice as many state banks as national banks. National banks, however, held substantially more than 50 per cent of the deposits.

The dual banking system has offered temptation for "competition in laxity" between state and national jurisdictions, and such competition has existed, though with much greater effects in some periods than in others. Nowadays, the effects are greatly reduced—first, by the standardization of national and state bank supervisory practices, and second, by the partial subjection to national controls of state banks which elect to become members of the Federal Deposit Insurance system or also of the Federal Reserve system.

This reference to partial subjection illustrates still further the peculiar "line of federalism" in banking. Nearly all of the state banks in the country in 1962 were members of the Federal Deposit Insurance system, and those holding approximately two-thirds of state bank deposits were members of the Federal Reserve system. A further peculiarity of the relationship between state and national authority is that Congress has permitted national banks to establish branches under conditions similar to those established for state banks by the particular state in which the bank operates. In effect, Congress has delegated some of its policy function over its own banks to the states, and has made its jurisdiction—complete, partial, or nonexistent—dependent upon private choice. Such delegations result in decentralization and diversity in banking policy and supervision.

The diversity is reflected in numerous laws and in the degree of tightness of bank supervision in the many jurisdictions. It is most clearly seen in the different laws relating to bank structure. Statewide branch banking was permitted in 1963 in the seven most westerly states in the continental United States, and in Alaska, Hawaii, Vermont, Connecticut, Rhode Island, Delaware, Maryland, the District of Columbia, North Carolina and South Carolina. Unit banking—that is, by single bank offices only—was required under the laws of all the states (except Louisiana) westward from the Mississippi River to the boundaries of Idaho, Utah, and New Mexico, and is also required in New Hampshire, Kentucky, and Florida. Branch banking restricted to the county in which the bank's head office is located, or to contiguous counties, was allowed in the remainder of the states, including most of those east of the Mississippi River, Louisiana, and New Mexico. In general, the Far West is an area of branch banking, the East an area of limited branch banking, and the Trans-Mississippi Midwest an area of unit banking.[2]

The outstanding feature of national banking regulation is the division of administrative responsibility among three bank supervisory agencies. The first of these is the Comptroller of Currency. This agency is a single-headed, semi-independent bureau within the Treasury Department. It has developed a strong tradition of independence, and the law provides only that it shall function "under the general directions of the Secretary of the Treasury."[3] Created in 1863, it was the only national bank supervisory agency until the creation of the Federal Reserve Board in 1913. The Federal Reserve system is now directed by an independent seven-man board of governors appointed by the President, with senatorial confirmation, for overlapping terms of fourteen years. The third agency is the Federal Deposit Insurance Corporation, established by statute in 1933. Management of the corporation is vested in a board of directors of three members, two appointed by the President with senatorial confirmation, and the third being the Comptroller of the Currency.

[2] The data is from "Changes in Banking Structure, 1953–62," *Federal Reserve Bulletin*, **XLIX** (September 1963), pp. 1191–1198.
[3] Reorganization Plan No. 21 of 1950. USC, Title 46, Ch. 27 (following Sec. 1111).

The primary powers of national bank supervision are vested in the Comptroller. His initial function with respect to a bank is approval of its charter. This in itself is a distinctive feature of national regulation, for "the only appreciable or long-time experience of the national government with the use of incorporation as a device for controlling private enterprise" is in the history of banking supervision.[4] Approval depends upon the Comptroller's judgment concerning community need for additional banking facilities, sufficiency of capital and prospects of earnings of the proposed bank, and the character, experience, and financial standing of the organizers.

A second function of the Comptroller is approval or disapproval of changes in bank status. He must approve changes in capitalization or in title and location, and also reorganizations and mergers of national banks. He may also, either because of insolvency or violation of banking laws, force liquidation of a bank. In case liquidation is forced, the Federal Deposit Insurance Corporation acts as receiver under the direction of the Comptroller.

The Comptroller is responsible for continuous supervision of national banks. He exercises supervision partly through reports required of banks, but mainly through bank examinations. In no other field of regulation has public examination of the records of private business been important over so long a period. The detailed operations of banks (whether state or national) are subject to continuous scrutiny by public officials. The bank examination, conducted periodically—and additionally, as need requires—is the chief instrument for such scrutiny. The examiner appraises the assets of the bank, studying loans and investments, and looks into the policies and acts of the management. As a result, either he or his superiors may make criticisms and urge corrections in bank practice. The Comptroller has a battery of weighty legal sanctions which he can use to overcome deficiencies of various sorts in bank management. These include forced receivership, suit for forfeiture of charter, publication of reports of examinations, institution of proceedings for removal of officials, and other measures. These are, however, so drastic that he relies on extralegal sanctions, such as persuasion and pressure, and more frequent examinations.[5]

The functions of the Federal Reserve system, heretofore discussed with respect to the monetary system and economic stabilization, are of special significance for commercial banking. The Federal Reserve performs central banking functions for banks which are members of the system, including all national banks and about fifteen hundred state banks. The member banks in each of twelve Federal Reserve districts "are under a Federal Reserve

---

[4] Guy Fox, "Supervision of Banking by the Comptroller of the Currency," in Emmette S. Redford (ed.), *Public Administration and Policy Formation: Studies in Oil, Gas, Banking, and Corporate Investigations* (Austin, Tex.: University of Texas Press, 1956), p. 121. This section on banking supervision relies heavily on Fox's analysis and the longer dissertation on the subject prepared by him at the University of Texas.

[5] For a perceptive treatment of the powers and practices of the Comptroller, see Fox, *ibid.*, pp. 119–188.

bank, which holds most of their legal reserves, discounts their commercial paper, collects their checks and other credit instruments, issues Federal Reserve notes to them, and acts as their financial adviser." [6] These are service functions which increase the credit resources of the member banks and provide clearing-house and collection services for them. They make tolerable for the banks the regulatory functions of the system, which include the setting of reserve requirements and the discount of commercial paper.

The third agency of bank supervision in the national government, the Federal Deposit Insurance Corporation (FDIC), has the sole function of guaranteeing bank deposits. Bank failures, which had been so common in our history, were at a high peak between 1920 and 1934. There were less than half as many commercial banks in this country in 1934 as in 1920, and undoubtedly a major cause was the large number of bank failures. To give greater security for stockholders, Congress has provided for insurance of bank deposits of $10,000 or less in an insured bank. All national banks and most state banks are members. Over 96 per cent of the nation's banks and about three-fifths of all bank deposits are insured. The FDIC is under legal obligation to insure only sound banks. It generally accepts the reports of the Comptroller on national banks, and of the Federal Reserve system on state banks that are members thereof, but makes its own examinations of state nonmember banks.

The distribution of controls over banking within the national government may be illustrated by reference to two recent acts. The Bank Holding Company Act of 1956 [7] requires bank holding companies (companies having controlling stock interest in commercial banks) to register, provides for their examination, proscribes certain types of transaction between holding companies and their subsidiaries, requires divestiture by holding companies of nonbanking interests, and requires approval for future banking acquisitions and holding-company mergers. The agency of administration is the Federal Reserve Board. Before giving approval to acquisitions and mergers, the board must obtain the recommendations of the Comptroller of the Currency if national banks are affected, and of the supervisory state authority if state banks are affected; if either of these opposes approval, then the board must hold hearings before making its decision. Amendments to the bank merger laws in the Bank Merger Act of 1960 [8] allocate control on merger of federally insured banks as follows: to the Comptroller of the Currency for resulting national banks, to the Federal Reserve Board for resulting state member banks, and to the FDIC for resulting insured, nonmember state banks. To insure uniformity of decisions, the appropriate agency must (unless immediate action is necessary to avoid a bank failure) secure advisory opinions from the two other banking agencies. The act provides also for the

---

[6] Charles L. Prather, *Money and Banking*, 7th ed. (Homewood, Ill.: Richard D. Irwin, Inc., 1961), pp. 256–257.
[7] 70 Stat. 133.
[8] 74 Stat. 129.

advisory opinion of the Attorney General on "the competitive factors involved." The criteria of decision in the two acts of 1956 and 1960 are the same—solvency, convenience, and competitive effect.

The accumulation of banking controls in the legislation of 1863 and 1865 setting forth the Comptroller's basic powers, the statutes of 1913 and 1935 governing the Federal Reserve, the law of 1933 establishing the FDIC, the Bank Holding Company Act of 1956, the Bank Merger Act of 1960, and other legislation results in an extensive system of controls over national banks. The controls extend to such things as rate of interest, capitalization, bank investments, kinds and amounts of loans, quality of loans, loans to executive officers, amount of reserves, rediscount rates, branch banking, mergers, and holding-company controls.

The structure of banking supervision which has developed in this country raises three significant questions. The first is whether all commercial banks should be placed under national supervision. There would be positive advantages in a single system of bank supervision. First, the "competition in laxity" existing under the dual system would be eliminated. Second, the duplication in banking supervision, which now exists when a state bank is also a member of the FDIC and perhaps, too, of the Federal Reserve system, would be terminated. Third, "a unified system would permit the establishment of a national policy on many matters of nation-wide importance such as credit, branch banking, par clearance, and elimination of the causes of banking disturbances." [9]

It cannot be expected, however, that the historically developed dual system will be changed to a unified national system unless some unusual set of events occurs which reveals weaknesses in state controls. The influence of state banks and state banking authorities, and the widespread appeal of decentralization in government, operate toward the retention of the dual system.

The second question is whether the dispersion of authority among three national bank supervisory agencies should be eliminated or reduced. Two task forces of the first Hoover Commission favored unification of national controls. The Task Force on Regulatory Commissions recognized that the most "glaring inefficiencies of duplication" had been eliminated by cooperative arrangements. It saw, nevertheless, not only some duplication, but, more important, differences in supervisory standards. It recommended consideration of transfer of all functions of the Comptroller and the FDIC to the Federal Reserve Board, except that the FDIC, divested of supervisory authority, would remain as an insurance corporation.[10] The Task Force on Lending Agencies thought that all functions of the FDIC should be placed under the Federal Reserve Board.[11]

[9] Fox, *op. cit.*, p. 182.
[10] *Task Force Report on Regulatory Commissions* (Washington, D.C.: Superintendent of Documents, 1949), pp. 116–117.
[11] *Task Force Report on Lending Agencies* (Washington, D.C.: Superintendent of Documents, 1949), p. 53.

There are undoubtedly important effects of the dispersion of controls. State banks may escape Federal Reserve requirements on reserves by remaining out of the system, and yet be members of the FDIC. The examination policies of the Comptroller and the credit policies of the Federal Reserve Board may differ. Whether such differences should be avoided is a matter on which there is difference of opinion. Some think that safety should be the sole objective of bank-examination policy, while others believe that bank examination should be made a credit-control device by raising or lowering banking standards to counteract cyclical movements in the economy. A competent authority has concluded that the justification for consolidation of the Comptroller's and the Federal Reserve's functions should rest on a judgment on this issue.[12]

The third question is how bank supervision, particularly as it is exercised through the Federal Reserve Board, should be coordinated with the functions of the Treasury Department and the Council of Economic Advisors, and with the policy of the President. This important problem of coordination of over-all economic policy has been treated generally in Chapter 9.

REGULATION OF INSURANCE

RISE AND CONTINUATION OF STATE REGULATION. The regulation of insurance is unique in the extent to which it is a responsibility of the states. For banking, securities issuance, utilities, transportation, employer-employee relations, and commerce in general, there is division of regulatory power between the national and state governments, and often cooperation among separate jurisdictions. For the business of insurance, national law permits virtually complete control by the several states.

The explanation for this unique allocation of responsibility to the states, like that of divided responsibility in banking (discussed above), is historical. Initially, the business of insurance was largely a local business and came under state regulation. In the first half of the nineteenth century, states began to exercise a modicum of control through requirements for reporting, special charter provisions, and designation of supervisory officials. In the decade following 1850, a number of states created an insurance commissioner, or commission, and this initiated the pattern of administrative regulation which has been used to this date. In *Paul v. Virginia* in 1869, the Supreme Court sustained a state regulatory statute because, it said, "issuing a policy of insurance is not a transaction of commerce." [13] The system of state legislative-administrative control was thereby validated judicially, and for nearly seventy-five years it was not seriously questioned.

In time, the interstate character of the insurance business became apparent, and the broadened interpretation of the commerce clause of the Con-

---

[12] Prather, *op. cit.*, p. 246.
[13] 8 Wall. 168, 183.

stitution made it inevitable that the issues of state and national jurisdiction would be reconsidered. This occurred in *U. S. v. South-Eastern Underwriters' Association* in 1944.[14] The Supreme Court held in this case that insurance was commerce, that the Sherman Act applied to the business of insurance, and that a rate-making agreement of the defendants violated the act.

This decision produced consternation in the state regulatory agencies and the insurance industry. It brought into question the regulatory and tax laws of the states. The insurance industry, which had often contested state laws on the ground that they were regulations of, or burdens on, interstate commerce, now feared a more stringent national regulation—particularly the application of the national antitrust laws to the activities of rate bureaus operated by the industry. Joined by the state commissioners and other state officials, the industry pushed for congressional legislation to validate state regulation.

There were some in Congress who favored national regulation. Congress, however, passed the McCarran Act,[15] which, although apparently a compromise between national and state control, actually yielded almost complete control to the states. The act stated that "continued regulation and taxation by the several states of the business of insurance is in the public interest." It provided that the business of insurance should "be subject to the laws of the several states." It exempted the business of insurance from the Sherman, Clayton, Federal Trade Commission, and Robinson-Patman acts "to the extent that such business" is regulated by state law,[16] except that the Sherman Act should remain applicable to boycotts, coercion, or intimidation.

Having obtained this act, the industry then desired such legislation in the several states as would remove any threat of national regulation. An "All-Industry" bill (including provisions favorable to rate bureaus) was prepared for recommendation to the states. It was substantially adopted in most states.

PURPOSES AND CONTENT OF REGULATION. As in banking, the primary objective of insurance regulation is solvency—that is, the continued ability of companies to fulfill the commitments in insurance contracts. "Their efficiency . . . and solvency are of great concern," said Justice Mc-

---

[14] 322 U.S. 533.
[15] 59 Stat. 33 (1945).
[16] Where advertising matter was shipped to agents in a state and distributed by them, regulation of advertising by the state in which the agents resided excluded Federal Trade Commission jurisdiction. *FTC v. National Casualty Company*, 357 U.S. 560 (1958). On the other hand, where the only applicable state regulation was that of a state in which a corporation was domiciled, and the corporation did a mail-order business throughout the country, the Supreme Court noted that the citizens of the several states who were targets of advertising were not protected by the state law, and held that the business was not regulated in such a way as to exclude the jurisdiction of the Federal Trade Commission with respect to advertising. *FTC v. Travelers Health Association*, 362 U.S. 293 (1960).

Kenna.[17] A leading author has called this "the principle of solidity," and has identified the purpose with the success of the insurance enterprise itself.[18] To assure solvency, states have set capital requirements, prescribed "legal reserves," regulated rates to insure their adequacy, regulated investments of companies, prescribed accounting methods which would reflect accuracy in accounts, and provided for public examination of accounts.

A second objective in regulation is fairness. To attain the objective, states seek to prevent rates from being excessive or discriminatory among groups of purchasers. They regulate the terms of insurance policies to protect purchasers from technicalities and sleepers in the fine print of policies. They try to insure fairness in the payment of claims. They seek to prevent dissipation of assets through payment of excessive executive salaries or unsafe payment of dividends to stockholders. They license agents and brokers to assure their integrity and competence, and regulate their practices to prevent unfair dealings. They prohibit rebating of premiums to customers, misrepresentation, and "twisting" (inducing a policy holder to transfer his policy from one company to another).[19]

To safeguard the diverse groups having interests in the solvency and fairness of the insurance business, state laws have become complex and intricate. There is often, however, a wide gap between the requirements of law and the provisions for administration. Some states—for example, New York and Wisconsin—have provided for adequate administration, while others have only a semblance of regulation. A study, made within the last decade, of insurance regulation in one of the smaller states showed that less than $30,000 was expended annually by the state for regulation of insurance, and that the main duties of regulation were vested in a commissioner with a salary of $6,000 and two deputies with salaries of $4,800 and $4,500.[20]

THE ISSUE OF RATE REGULATION. There has been one issue of state policy that has produced much controversy. This is the issue of competition versus publicly supervised industry cooperation in the setting of insurance rates. Before the end of the nineteenth century, rate bureaus had developed in the industry, and their activities became a matter of public concern. They operate in fire and casualty insurance, but not in life insurance.

---

[17] *German Alliance Insurance Company v. Lewis*, 233 U.S. 389, 413 (1914).

[18] See Spencer L. Kimball, "The Purpose of Insurance Regulation: A Preliminary Inquiry in the Theory of Insurance Law," *Minnesota Law Review*, **XLV** (March 1961), pp. 471–524. Good summaries of regulation are contained in this and the same author's book on *Insurance and Public Policy: A Study in the Legal Implementation of Social and Economic Public Policy, Based on Wisconsin Records, 1835–1959* (Madison, Wis.: University of Wisconsin Press, 1960).

[19] On such matters, see Spencer L. Kimball and Barrett A. Jackson, "The Regulation of Insurance Marketing," *Columbia Law Review*, **LXI** (February 1961), pp. 141–200.

[20] Spencer L. Kimball and W. Eugene Hansen, "The Utah Insurance Commissioner: A Study of Administrative Regulation in Action," *Utah Law Review*, **V** (Fall 1957), pp. 429–455; and **VI** (Spring 1958), pp. 1–22.

The arguments in support of joint rate making through rate bureaus rest primarily on two bases. First, the argument is made that there is a public interest in the solvency of companies, and in rates which will be adequate to guarantee this interest. It is contended that cutthroat competition can undermine the rate structure and threaten the continued solvency of companies. Second, it is argued that rates must be based on actuarial experience —on data concerning average losses and average costs—and that the experience of a single company does not provide a sufficiently broad base of data. Rate bureaus can accumulate and average the data, and thus provide a sound accounting base for rate determinations.

Prior to 1944 fire-insurance rating bureaus had been recognized in most of the states and subjected to varying degrees of supervision. Casualty-insurance bureaus were less widely recognized in law.

Following the decision in the South-Eastern case in 1944, an All-Industry Committee recommended state supervision of joint rate making. The All-Industry Bill recommended the following features for state legislation: (1) that rates meet a statutory standard—they could not be "excessive, inadequate or unfairly discriminatory"; (2) that companies be permitted to join licensed rate-making bureaus; (3) that the bureaus file rates with the insurance commissioner, who would have authority to disapprove any of them. Protections would be given to "independents" in the industry. They could fail to join a bureau and file their own rates with the state commissioner, or they could join a bureau but file with the state "deviations" from bureau rates. In the latter case the bureau could contest the "deviation." In either case, the burden on the individual company was greater than if there were no bureau: in the former instance it would operate without bureau data; in the latter, it would carry the burden of justifying the deviation.

Most states adopted the All-Industry recommendations. Nevertheless, considerable variations in philosophy on competition and flexibility in rates are reflected in state laws. In a few instances, no filings are required or rate-adherence agreements permitted. On the other hand, in a small number of states membership in a rate bureau is mandatory on companies—a requirement which operates toward complete rate uniformity; and in some other states, approval is required prior to rate changes, which results in rate inflexibility. In Texas, and in a few other states for some lines of insurance, uniformity is the result of direct state regulation of insurance rates similar to that usually provided for utility rates. It may be concluded that the decision of the states has leaned toward public supervision of joint rate making, but that many of the states try to preserve some freedom for competition and also opportunity for flexibility in insurance rates. Also, it can be stated that the capacity of the state commissioner to exercise effective supervision for the protection of insurance buyers may be, with the appropriations and staff supplied to him, quite limited.

NATIONAL REGULATION. Insurance companies are subject to regulation in every state in which they do business. This multiple regulation, and the diversity of state laws, impose cost burdens upon the companies, for they must have knowledge of and meet the varying state requirements. States have sometimes placed burdensome restrictions on out-of-state insurance companies, the most glaring instance perhaps being the Texas requirement for over fifty years that an out-of-state company invest in Texas a stated proportion of its revenue from Texas business. Administration of laws is weak in some states, and scandals occasionally occur. Yet neither the burdens imposed on business nor the inadequate protection to the buyer of insurance has led to a movement for national regulation. There is virtually no support for national regulation within the industry, and only scattered support from academic sources and buyers of insurance. There is, it should be added, one protection for the insurance buyer, even though he lives within a state with ineffective administration; if he buys from a company operating nationally, he gets protection from the supervision by the states which regulate most effectively. Federalism, in this instance, results in extraterritorial protection, and is some compensation for the weakness of the many states in the action of the few which impose tight requirements.

THE SECURITIES MARKETS

MARKET FUNCTIONS. Discussion of regulation of the securities markets must be preceded by an analysis of the functions performed in the markets. The initial step in the creation of a market is the decision of a corporation to issue securities. In the language of the securities markets, the corporation is the issuer. The issuer may make arrangements with an investment banker for sale of the securities. The investment banker is the securities middleman. He normally "underwrites" the securities issue; that is, he guarantees the corporation that on a given date he will deliver to it a definite sum of money for the block of stocks being issued. Large investment banking houses arose in the nineteenth century to serve as underwriters for the securities of the emerging and expanding corporations. Nowadays, however, many blocks of securities are "privately placed"—that is, sold directly by the corporation to insurance companies, other large investors, or its own stockholders, rather than through underwriters in a public sale. In addition to sales for issuers, underwriters may make what is called "secondary" distribution, which is a sale for a non-issuer of a large block of stock—for example, sale for the Ford Foundation of a block of Ford Motor Company stock.

The underwriter may arrange with other banking houses to take a portion of an issue, in this way reducing its own risk. It will also use "dealers," or "broker-dealers," across the country as retailers of the security.

A continuous market for securities is provided through facilities called exchanges, and through the activities of dealers, brokers, and broker-dealers. Sales of securities may be made in unorganized markets, but sales are facilitated through organized markets or exchanges. These are associations of member brokers, dealers, and other traders. The broker buys and sells for others for a commission; the dealer trades in securities himself; the broker-dealer does both.

Many of our large cities have exchanges, but the two most familiar ones are the New York Stock Exchange and the American Exchange in New York. Trade exists on exchanges only for "listed" securities. "Unlisted" securities are sold in the "over-the-counter" market—that is, by brokers or dealers in their offices. Bank stocks, insurance-company stocks, and state and municipal bonds are normally sold in the over-the-counter market, as well as a large portion of U.S. Government securities and corporate bonds.

THE ADVENT OF REGULATION. The first noteworthy fact about regulation of security transactions is the lateness of its advent. Until well into the twentieth century, the only protection of the investor against fraud and misrepresentation was through suit under the common law. State regulaion of security issues began with a Kansas statute in 1911, which was followed by enactment of laws in many other states within less than a decade. The national government provided in 1920 for regulation of railroad security issues by the Interstate Commerce Commission, but did not follow this with any other regulation of security issues until the New Deal. The Holding Company Act of 1935, and some other regulatory acts, provided for commission regulation of certain types of securities. Except for the prohibition over use of the mails to defraud, general regulation over securities issues and over securities exchanges began at the national level in 1933 and 1934, respectively.

The state laws have been called "Blue Sky" laws, because they were aimed at speculative ventures which someone said had no better financial basis than "so many feet of blue sky." They have included three main types of provisions. First, there is an almost universal requirement for registration of securities with a state agency prior to sale. Second, most states require also that dealers in securities obtain licenses. Third, a small number of states have anti-fraud laws, under which investigations may be conducted and injunctions issued, or other remedies applied, against fraudulent sales. These three types of regulation are generally referred to as registration laws, dealer-licensing laws, and fraud laws.

The inherent weakness of state regulation lay in a multitude of legal questions about jurisdiction over sales by persons in one state to those in another, and in the practical difficulties of enforcement of a state's laws on persons within other states. In addition, in many of the states the laws were weak and enforcement lax.

Although bills proposing national regulation had been introduced many years before, the Great Depression precipitated the first and main pieces of national legislation. The Securities Act was passed in 1933 [21] and the Securities Exchange Act in 1934.[22] The first was enforced initially by the

---
[21] 48 Stat. 74.
[22] 48 Stat. 881.

Federal Trade Commission, but in the second a Securities and Exchange Commission (SEC) of five members appointed by the President, with approval of the Senate, was created. It has been, since 1934, the chief agency for administration of the 1933 and 1934 acts and their amendments, and several other acts. The purposes, main provisions, and chief features of administration will be set forth for these two basic acts and the Maloney Act, which amended and extended the Securities and Exchange Act.[23]

REGULATION OF SECURITIES ISSUES. In recommending legislation on sale of securities, President Roosevelt said,

> This proposal adds to the ancient rule of *caveat emptor,* the further doctrine, "Let the seller beware." It puts the burden of telling the whole truth on the seller.

The Securities Act has been called the "truth-in-securities act." The government does not pass upon the soundness of securities, but requires full disclosure to the potential purchaser of relevant facts about them. The means employed is to deny the use of the mails or interstate commerce for sale or offer of sale of securities unless a registration statement has been filed with the SEC and is in effect, and unless the prospectus (description and advertisement) sent to the potential purchaser contains all the data set forth in the act or required by the SEC. These two documents are in practice prepared jointly, and the prospectus contains information drawn from the registration statement.

The technique of enforcement is a veto power in the SEC. The registration statement becomes effective twenty days after filing, unless within the twenty days the SEC refuses to permit its effectiveness or "at any time" (before or after twenty days) issues a stop order. The "stop order" is a new term for an administrative cease-and-desist order. It can be issued, after notice and opportunity for hearing, if the registration statement "includes any untrue statement of a material fact or omits to state any material fact" necessary to prevent the statement from being misleading.

The most distinctive feature of national regulation of security sales is the informal administrative arrangements to adapt regulation to the requirements for successful marketing. The formal procedure of notice and hearing provided in the act is not congruent with efficient marketing of securities. When plans have been made by issuer, underwriters, and dealers to market a security, prompt execution of these plans is essential to assure success in the sale. Delays in an administrative bureaucracy would be intolerable. Moreover, a hearing on a security would raise questions in the investor's mind about its soundness. To meet these practical considerations, the SEC devised a unique procedure. It examines a registration statement upon its receipt, then notifies the issuer or underwriter by a "deficiency letter" of inadequacies in the statement. The underwriter then amends

---

[23] Not discussed here are other acts administered by the SEC for protection of investors: the Trust Indenture Act of 1939, the Investment Company Act of 1940, the Investment Advisers Act of 1940, and Chapter 10 of the Bankruptcy Act.

his statement to include the additional facts. This is all done within nineteen days so that the statement can go into effect and sales be legal on the twentieth day.

Two other adaptations in procedure contribute to the benefits of the informal process. The SEC may accelerate its clearance of the security, thus allowing a quicker registration. Also, amendments to the act in 1954 allow distribution of preliminary prospectuses to interested parties and allow offers to sell prior to SEC action, though without any consummation of sale. It is apparent that the process of regulation has been adapted both to the needs of investor protection and to success in the marketing of securities.

In addition to the registration requirements, the Securities Act prohibits fraudulent practices in the sale of securities in interstate commerce or by use of the mails. Criminal penalties are provided for any willful violation of the act or of rules of the SEC promulgated under authority of the act. Moreover, persons responsible for false or misleading statements in a registration statement, prospectus, or other communication are liable to suit by any person acquiring the security.

The registration requirements of the act are inapplicable to some types of securities. Included, among others, in the exemptions are securities issued by governments, issues of securities in small amounts if exempted by SEC rules, and securities sold to persons within a single state by persons within that state. The last exemption includes sales by corporations chartered by, and doing business within, the state.

An interesting feature of securities regulation is the duplication of national and state controls. Although purely intrastate sales within a single state are exempted from the national registration requirements, they are not exempted from the anti-fraud and civil-liabilities provisions of the Securities Act. Sellers of securities within a state in which they reside may, therefore, be subject to both state and national laws. More significant, however, are the complexities arising as a result of the growing interstate nature of securities sales and the express saving of state jurisdiction in the Securities Act. State security laws are applied to sales by persons in one state to those in another. An underwriter will, therefore, conform to the requirements both of national and state laws.[24] This means registration in each state in which he plans to sell that requires registration, as well as registration with the SEC. The difficulties are partly met by arrangements for "coordination" of state and national action. Under these arrangements, copies of the registration statement filed with the SEC are sent also to state commissioners, and these latter follow the practice of allowing the registration statement to become effective under state law at the same time it be-

---

[24] See Edward M. Cowett, "Federal-State Relationships in Securities Regulation," *George Washington Law Review*, **XXVIII** (October 1959), pp. 287–305.

comes effective under the national law, unless substantive provisions of state law are violated.

There is argument among experts as to whether it is not desirable for the national government to pre-empt the entire field of securities legislation.[25] Arguments for this change are that securities sales are becoming increasingly interstate, that the state laws impose diverse requirements, and that state regulation is really inefficient in view of the many legal uncertainties and practical difficulties. On the opposite side, it is argued that the responsibilities of the national government, particularly because of many small issues, would be too heavy to permit their effective discharge, that states should have the power to give added protection to their citizens through dealer registration or other requirements not imposed by, or more stringent than, those imposed in national regulation, and that the answer to the problem lies in uniform state laws and effective coordination. A uniform state securities law in four sections has been prepared by an expert committee—three sections on registration, dealer licensing, and fraud, and one on enforcement. A state can adopt the sections which parallel its own type of regulatory law. The hard facts are, however, that on the one hand, national pre-emption is not likely to be imposed in an area where state regulation is so prevalent, and on the other, that the uniform code asks states with weak laws to strengthen them and states with strong laws (for example, California) to adopt lower standards. Nevertheless, the uniform code provides the pattern toward which efforts will be directed by most of those dissatisfied with present arrangements.

THE SECURITIES EXCHANGE ACT. Whereas the Securities Act regulates initial distribution of securities, the Securities Exchange Act deals with trading of securities. The act was passed after thorough investigations by House and Senate committees and a recommendation from President Roosevelt for legislation for better supervision of purchase and sale of "all property dealt with on exchanges" (for legislation on commodity markets passed in 1936, see page 506). The objective was to check the "naked speculation" which the President said had been "far too alluring and far too easy."

The Securities Exchange Act imposes a complex system of regulation over a highly intricate marketing mechanism. Yet the basic features of the regulatory system are describable in brief compass. The first feature is requirement of registration of security exchanges and of listed securities. Exchanges must register, unless exempted because of limited size, with the SEC. To register, an exchange must file with the SEC a statement which includes (1) an agreement to comply with and enforce the provisions of the act and regulations of the SEC thereunder, and (2) comprehensive

---

[25] See Louis Loss, *Securities Regulation,* 2nd ed. (Boston: Little, Brown & Company, 1961), 1, pp. 90–107.

data on its organization, rules of procedure, membership, and other matters. The registration will not become effective unless the rules of the exchange provide for the expulsion, suspension, or disciplining of members whose conduct is inconsistent with "just and equitable principles of trade," including such principles as are embodied in the act and in the regulations of the SEC in conformity with the act. No security (with minor exceptions) can be traded on an exchange unless it is registered. Registration is effected by a company filing information similar to that required for issuance under the Securities Act. The information is filed with the exchange and the SEC. The information must be kept up to date by periodic reports.

The SEC may grant or, after appropriate hearing, deny registration of an exchange. It may also, after notice and hearing, and upon a finding of violation of the act or rules and regulations thereunder, suspend or withdraw registration of an exchange or a listed security, or suspend or expel a member or officer of an exchange. It may, summarily and with the consent of the President, suspend trading of a security for a period not exceeding ten days, or all trading on an exchange for a period not exceeding ninety days. Review of orders of the commission may be obtained in a U.S. Court of Appeals.

The second feature of the regulatory pattern is prohibition of specific types of transactions that had been the subject of abuse. These prohibitions affect dealers and brokers primarily, though not exclusively. There is an attempt to prevent speculative profits by persons having inside information about corporate policy and prospects; profits realized by "insiders" —for example, officers and directors—may be recovered in suits brought by the issuing corporation or by any of its security holders. There is credit regulation, both by regulation of margin trading by the Federal Reserve Board (see page 160) and by additional restrictions on borrowing by members of exchanges and by brokers and dealers. There are provisions with respect to proxies, and to various forms of manipulative and deceptive devices.

A third feature of the regulatory pattern is a large delegation of rule-making authority to the SEC. The practices regulated are so complex, and the markets so intricate and sensitive, that Congress found it necessary in almost every section of the act to delegate power to the commission to make "rules and regulations." There is probably no regulatory program in this country in which more (or even equally) extensive use is made of administrative rule making. To a large intent, the SEC is, in this and other programs under its jurisdiction, administering its own regulations— issued in conformity with governing acts, but nevertheless under broad discretionary authority.

The final feature of security-exchange regulation is self-regulation under public supervision. Exchanges originated as "private clubs" of traders; the act and the SEC have made them quasi-public institutions. While exchanges had previously, on their own initiative, made rules on membership and on conduct of trading through their facilities, they were now placed under a public obligation to enforce standards of a public act and rules of a public agency. An exchange could be registered only if it agreed to assume this obligation; it could be suspended or its registration withdrawn if it failed in the obligation. More than this, the SEC preferred that desired reforms be made through action of the exchanges themselves. It made a report to Congress in 1935 in which it urged changes in government of the exchanges.[26] It brought pressure on the New York Stock Exchange to revise its rules in order to provide for a paid presidency, for public representatives on its governing committee, and for other changes. Through arrangements for self-government the enforcement task of government has been reduced, the cooperation of the exchanges obtained, and severe strains between traders and the government avoided.

This does not mean that all problems in offering effective protection to the public have been solved. As this book is being completed, the SEC is engaged in a mammoth investigation of trading practices; this investigation may lead to new steps in national regulation.

THE MALONEY ACT.[27] Brokers and dealers who are members of exchanges may also sell securities over the counter; also, some brokers and dealers are not members of an exchange, and thus sell only over the counter. The latter group, by an amendment to the Securities Exchange Act in 1936, were required to register with the SEC as a condition of using the mails or the facilities of interstate commerce. Both groups are subject, in their over-the-counter dealings, to various provisions of the Securities Exchange Act and to state laws.[28] Regulation of practices in over-the-counter sales was nevertheless, even after 1936, far less adequate than that obtained through the self-policing of the exchanges.

The Maloney Act—Section 15a of the amended Securities Exchange Act —was intended at least partially to fill this gap. In considering legislation, the congressional committees decided against comprehensive, direct SEC controls over the minute operations of several thousand over-the-counter dealers. They chose instead, and Congress enacted, a plan

of cooperative regulation, in which the task will be largely performed by representative organizations of investment bankers, dealers, and brokers, with the government exercising appropriate supervision in the public interest, and exercising supplementary powers of direct regulation.[29]

The act authorized registration of national securities associations. Such registration would be approved by the SEC if the rules of the association

---

[26] *Report on the Government of Securities Exchanges,* H. Doc. 85, 74th Cong., 1st Sess.
[27] 52 Stat. 1070 (1938).
[28] For a view of the full scope of regulation, see Alexander Hamilton Frey, "Federal Regulation of the Over-the-Counter Securities Market," *University of Pennsylvania Law Review,* **CVI** (November 1957), pp. 1–51.
[29] H. Rept. 2307, pp. 4–5, Sen. Rept. 1455, pp. 3–4 (75th Cong., 3rd Sess., 1938).

allowed admission of all reputable brokers or dealers (or all within districts, for types of business, or on other bases approved by the SEC), assured internal democracy in its affairs, promoted just and equitable principles of trade, prevented fraudulent and manipulative practices, provided for disciplining of members, and contained other specific provisions. Appeal to the SEC in cases of disciplinary action was provided by the act. The act not only authorized registration of one or more associations, but encouraged this by allowing no discounts in sales to any except members.

Pursuant to the act, a National Association of Securities Dealers, Inc. has been formed. Its membership includes about 95 per cent of the brokers and dealers in the country. It functions through a national, elected board of governors and fourteen district offices. It has facilitated trade by furnishing quotations on prices. It has adopted rules of fair practice, conducts examinations of its members' books, has sought to establish guides on commission rates, and has taken disciplinary action against members. This is indeed self-regulation and self-policing, but subject to public requirements and restrictions, and without relaxation of direct public regulation as contained in provisions of law other than Section 15a.

CONCLUSION. From the foregoing discussion several features of regulation of securities markets can be set forth by way of summary:

1. Registration under specified conditions and prohibition of fraudulent practices have been the chief elements in the system of regulation.

2. National and state governments both exercise jurisdiction over distribution of securities, which frequently results in regulation by many jurisdictions over the same issuances.

3. Informal administrative practices have largely taken the place of statutory formal procedures in the administration of the Securities Act.

4. The adjustment of regulation to the intricacies of the securities market is achieved, in considerable measure, through issuance of administrative rules and regulations.

5. The adjustment is further achieved by sharing the regulatory function with quasi-public market institutions operating under public supervision.

Part V. The Regulatory System

Chapter 24. The System of Administrative Regulation

THE READER of the preceding parts of this book will have seen that, by and large, the function of making basic economic policy has moved from the judiciary to the legislature. The responsiveness of legislatures to movements of opinion, and the utility of legislation as a means of making new policy in a dynamic society, have placed legislatures in the forefront. The Supreme Court, by its restoration of the early interpretation of due process and its construction of other constitutional limitations, yielded to legislatures the choices on public policy; and by its reinterpretation of the commerce power and its decisions on the extent of other delegated powers, it centered judgment on economic policy in the Congress.

The legislatures, and Congress in particular, have in turn established administrative agencies to give continuous attention to the matters on which laws are passed. These agencies, upon establishment, stand at the center of the stage on the matters delegated to their respective jurisdictions. The results of public intervention in the economy will depend in large measure on their operations.

One feature of these agencies is dominant. They have been established on the basis of the function to be performed or the industry to be regulated, not on the basis of the type of governmental power which was to be exercised. An agency was established to prevent "unfair methods of competition" and other undesirable trade practices. With respect to this function, investigatory, prosecutory, judicial, and perhaps legislative powers could be exercised. An agency was established to handle railroad problems, another to handle communication problems, another to regulate power transmission and sale, and in each case it was given legislative, judicial, and executive functions. Unity in regulation has been sought, and to attain this end, departures have been made from the separation-of-powers doctrine. It has been said that the administrative process "presents an assemblage of rights normally exercisable by government as a whole." [1]

There is, however, much variation among the agencies in the types of functions exercised. Some are primarily, or to a great extent, engaged in law enforcement. These may, like the Food and Drug Administration and

---

[1] James M. Landis, *The Administrative Process* (New Haven, Conn.: Yale University Press, 1938).

the Antitrust Division, enforce by carrying cases to the courts; or they may, like the Federal Trade Commission, the National Labor Relations Board, and the Securities and Exchange Commission, hear and decide cases themselves, subject to appeal to the courts. A second type of agency operates primarily through rule-making and policy decisions. The plainest example is the Federal Reserve Board, whose enforcement and enforcement-judicial functions are small in comparison with its rule-making and policy functions. A third type of agency is distinctive in the extent to which it exercises broad discretionary and supervisory powers over particular industries by a variety of methods. Included are such well-known agencies as the Interstate Commerce Commission, the Civil Aeronautics Board, the Federal Maritime Commission, the Federal Communications Commission, the Securities and Exchange Commission, and the Federal Power Commission. These may have operating, policy-making, investigatory, and adjudicatory functions. Finally, some agencies have advisory functions. The U.S. Tariff Commission and the Civil Aeronautics Board (when passing upon certificates for foreign air transportation) serve as advisers to the President.

Although these and other diversities exist, a system of administrative regulation has developed in this country. The system consists of the patterns of organization, the powers and procedures, and the lines of responsibility which have grown up and from which choices and combinations can be made in establishment of regulatory arrangements for a particular industry or aspect of economic activity. This chapter describes the system, and the following one analyzes problems arising in its use. The system itself is a highly legalized one, and must be described for the most part in legal terms.[2]

ADMINISTRATIVE AGENCIES

COMMISSIONS. The American regulatory commission originated in the states with the establishment of state railroad commissions after the Civil War. Congress, which had provided for a single administrator for banking regulation in 1863, established a regulatory commission for railroads in 1887. House leaders preferred executive action before the courts, rather than decisions by a commission. Senate leaders desired a commission. In the compromises between the houses, the Senate won on this issue. An Interstate Commerce Commission (ICC) of five members, appointed by the President with confirmation of the Senate and serving for staggered terms, was created.

The board or commission has been the favored form of organization for

---

[2] Much of the material in this chapter is condensed or adapted from the discussion of administrative regulation in Emmette S. Redford, *Administration of National Economic Control* (New York: The Macmillan Company, 1952).

The System of Administrative Regulation 549

regulatory activities. Congress has established new commissions as it extended regulation to new fields. It created the Federal Reserve Board (now called the Board of Governors) in 1913, the Federal Trade Commission (FTC) and the U.S. Shipping Board in 1916, the U.S. Tariff Commission in 1916, a Federal Power Commission (FPC) in 1920, and a Federal Radio Commission in 1927. In the flush of regulatory acts during the New Deal, new commissions were created and new functions delegated to old commissions. The Securities and Exchange Commission (SEC) and the Federal Communications Commssion (FCC—replacing the Federal Radio Commission and assuming functions from the Interstate Commerce Commission) were created in 1934, the National Labor Relations Board (NLRB) in 1935, and the Civil Aeronautics Board (CAB) in 1938. The functions of motor-carrier regulation and domestic water regulation were given to the ICC in 1935 and 1940, the FPC received expanded functions over power in 1935 and the function of regulating natural gas in 1938, and a Federal Maritime Board (now called Commission) replaced the U.S. Shipping Board in 1936.

Although there may be some difference of opinion on what agencies should be listed as regulatory commissions, the following list is presented, with date of creation and present fields of regulatory activity.[3]

Interstate Commerce Commission	1887	Railroads, motor carriers, domestic water carriers, oil pipelines
Civil Aeronautics Board	1938	Air carriers
Federal Maritime Commission,	1961	Oceanic transportation
Preceded by U.S. Shipping Board,	1916	
U.S. Maritime Commission, and	1936	
Federal Maritime Board	1950	
Federal Reserve System	1913	Credit Control
Federal Power Commission	1920	Hydroelectric power, electric energy, natural gas
Federal Trade Commission	1914	Antitrust, trade practices
Securities and Exchange Commission	1934	Security issues, security exchanges, power and gas holding companies
Federal Communications Commission,	1934	Telephone and telegraph, radio and television
Preceded by Federal Radio Commission	1927	
National Labor Relations Board	1935	Labor Relations
Federal Home Loan Bank Board, Preceded by a board in an executive agency	1955	Credit for home financing

The two features of the commission system are plurality and independence. It is administration by boards rather than by single administra-

---

[3] The Atomic Energy Commission is not included because its functions are primarily developmental and operational, nor the U.S. Tariff Commission because it has advisory functions only. The listing is taken from the author's report on *The President and the Regulatory Commissions*, prepared for the President's Advisory Committee on Government Organization in 1960. Portions of this chapter draw heavily from this report.

tors. They vary in membership from three (Federal Home Loan Bank Board) to eleven (ICC since 1920) with the most common number being five. They are said to be independent. By this is meant that they are not subject to the direction of the President in the same way that departments and nondepartmental single-headed agencies are. They are not, however, completely independent from the President.

Several factors make for independence. First, appointments are for definite, staggered terms. The terms range from four years for the Federal Home Loan Bank Board and the Federal Maritime Commission to fourteen for the Board of Governors, though the normal term is five to seven years. Second, for most of the commissions the law provides that no more than a majority of the members may be from the same party. Although a president may not find it difficult to locate persons in the opposition party who share his points of view, this provision does insure a lack of partisan responsibility. Third, for most of the commissions, statutes provide for removal only for neglect of duty or malfeasance in office, or for these causes or inefficiency, or for cause. Often, limitation on the power to remove is "thought of as the distinguishing mark of the independent commission." [4] Congress has limited the President's power of removal of members of the Federal Trade Commission to cases of "inefficiency, neglect of duty, or malfeasance in office," and this was upheld by the Supreme Court in the Humphreys case.[5] The decision meant that Congress could limit the President's power of removal concerning agencies whose functions were quasi-legislative and quasi-judicial. It has also been held that where an agency's functions are judicial, the President could not remove even if there were no statutory provision limiting removal.[6] Fourth, the President lacks the authority to designate the chairman of the Interstate Commerce Commission; and since the commission selects its own chairman, the President may lack a friendly channel of contact with it. Fifth, procedural features limit the President. Where decision must be made on the basis of the record made in hearings, an overhead directive power is necessarily excluded, except as to choice and prosecution of cases. Moreover, the tendency of the commissions to operate through case-to-case proceedings obscures the opportunity to develop policy by overhead directives. Sixth, the commissions' close association with their clienteles, and their cultivation of channels of contact with Congress, have tended to insulate them against novel or disturbing influence from the chief executive.[7] Finally, tradition has contributed to the development of a theory of independence.

---

[4] Task Force of the Commission on Organization of the Executive Branch of the Government, *Regulatory Commissions* (Washington, D.C.: Superintendent of Documents, 1949), p. 14.

[5] *Humphrey's Executor v. U.S.*, 295 U.S. 602 (1935).

[6] *Weiner v. U.S.*, 357 U.S. 349 (1958).

[7] See James W. Fesler, "Independent Regulatory Agencies," in Fritz Morstein Marx, *Elements of Public Administration,* 2nd ed. (Englewood Cliffs, N.J.: Prentice-Hall, Inc., 1959), p. 195.

L. D. White has said, "The gulf between the Interstate Commerce Commission and the President has been worn deep by usage of more than a half century." [8] The example of the traditional immunity of the ICC has helped set a pattern in men's thinking about regulatory commissions generally.

On the other hand, there are many ways by which the President can exert control or influence over the commissions. First, the commissions are subject to the President's managerial powers. Civil Service rules apply to commission personnel, budgets must be channelled through the Bureau of the Budget, legislative proposals must be referred to it also, and the Bureau may make studies of administrative management. Second, the President still has significant control over membership of commissions. The power of appointment is a means of influencing the trend in regulation, particularly because of the frequently rapid turnover in membership, and the power of reappointment may also be effective where members desire to remain. The President can designate the chairman for most of the commissions, and it may be presumed that he can remove such a chairman from his duties as chairman. For the FPC, the SEC, and the FCC there are no statutory limitations on his power of removal. Also, a President may make a finding that a commissioner is inefficient, and presumably a court would not consider whether such a finding had basis. Third, there are several statutory provisions that confer the power of presidential approval or disapproval of specific commission decisions. Fourth, the President may appoint study commissions or recommend legislation to Congress concerning matters on which the commissions have been delegated authority. Finally, in conference or otherwise, he may communicate his views to the commissions. This may vary from mere interchange of views to strong pressure to follow a presidential policy.

DEPARTMENTAL AND PRESIDENTIAL AGENCIES. Much regulatory legislation is administered by agencies which have single heads and are subject to executive supervision. Normally, such administration is by bureaus or other divisions within departments. Outstanding examples are the vast controls over agriculture by units within the Department of Agriculture, the consumer-protection functions of the Food and Drug Administration of the Department of Health, Education and Welfare, and the regulation of banking by the Comptroller of the Currency—a bureau within the Treasury Department. Sometimes, however, administration is located in nondepartmental agencies reporting directly to the President. A current example is the Federal Aviation Agency, which has extensive regulatory functions with respect to flying. During the New Deal, World War II, and the Korean affair quite a number of regulatory agencies were established outside the departments and under the control of the President.

---

[8] Leonard D. White, *Introduction to the Study of Public Administration*, 4th ed. (New York: The Macmillan Company, 1955), p. 116.

552   *The Regulatory System*

Usually, functions which are not distinctly temporary are placed in departments or commissions.

Functions very similar to those of the commissions are exercised within departments, and occasionally in permanent presidential agencies. Licensing of national banks and their examination to determine conformity with law and sound banking practice is done by the Comptroller of the Currency, who is, however, subject only to "general directions of the Secretary of the Treasury." [9] The Packers and Stockyards Administration of the Department of Agriculture has rate-making authority for stockyards. It also performs the same types of functions—investigation, complaint, hearing, and decision on unfair trade practices—with respect to packers that the FTC does for industry generally. The Department of Agriculture and a commission composed of three executive officials—the secretaries of Agriculture and Commerce and the Attorney General—exercise controls over commodity exchanges and commission merchants similar to those exercised over security exchanges and dealers by the Securities and Exchange Commission. The Department of Labor determines prevailing minimum wages for payment by public contractors—a function similar to rate determination. The Federal Aviation Agency has extensive rule-making powers which, though related to safety, also have an economic impact on persons and companies.

Although there are some substantial differences between commission and departmental administration, the acceptability of departmental administration of economic regulatory functions may be attributable in part to the fact that functions will be exercised in much the same way regardless of where they are placed. Both types of administration are affected by the legalization of the process of regulation. The elements of legalization will appear in the subsequent discussion.

ADMINISTRATIVE DEVELOPMENT OF REGULATORY PROGRAMS

ADMINISTRATIVE DISCRETION. Congress has found it necessary to legislate in broad terms and vest responsibility in agencies for development of the substance or content of regulatory policy. One author has summarized the reasons for this development as urgency, lack of time, technicality, and the need for experimentation; [10] to these may be added need for adaptation to particulars and continuity, for even the process of legislation now requires flexible and continuous procedure.

The administrative responsibility is given in a set of directives. Sometimes such directives may come from the President or from a high ad-

[9] Reorganization Plan No. 21 of 1950, U.S. Code, Title 46, Chapter 27 (following Sec. 1111).
[10] F. J. Port, *Administrative Law* (London and New York: Longmans, Green & Co., Inc., 1929), pp. 137–146.

ministrative authority, but their original source is usually a statute or series of statutes. The directives may include as many as five things: (1) a statement of purposes; (2) a statement of subjects on which action must be taken; (3) a prescription of standards or guides to govern action on the stated subjects; (4) a group of restrictions on scope or exercise of the delegation; (5) a set of requirements on administrative methods, extending perhaps to organization, techniques of application, and procedural processes.

The most significant aspect of statutory directives on economic policy is the extent of discretion left to agencies for program development. Some directives are very specific. Sometimes the initial directives are general, and specificity is added as experience is gained. Professor Hyneman has concluded that this is the history of much of our legislation, and that the experience of the administrative department is itself incorporated into legislation.[11] An example of increasing specificity is seen in our labor legislation, which has spelled out the original prohibition in the Railway Labor Act of 1926 forbidding "interference, influence, or coercion" of laborers in the choice of their representatives for collective bargaining. Sometimes, however, the appearance of specificity is deceptive. This was true, for example, of the rule of "annual . . . fair return upon the aggregate value" in the Transportation Act of 1920. It was equally true of the directive to the President to "equalize . . . costs of production" at home and abroad in the Tariff Act of 1922, for it has been concluded that "the ascertainment of actual costs of production is in many countries an impossibility"[12] and that there was no guide to the Tariff Commission concerning which of the many items on the customs list should be investigated.[13]

Actually, generality is the characteristic of much of our economic legislation. Thus, certificates are to be granted if they are in the "public convenience and necessity," and rates are to be "fair and reasonable." Multiple guides are given, with the result that a number of considerations must be reconciled in the development and application of policy. Sometimes even conflicting guides are given, and the agency is, in effect, asked to strike a balance between them. An example is the provision for the ICC, in fixing railroad rates, to consider the need for revenues and the effect on movement of traffic, for high rates bring revenues and low rates bring traffic. Justice Roberts once said of a statute on agricultural prices that it required the Secretary of Agriculture "to form a judgment by balancing a price-raising policy against a consumer-protection policy ac-

[11] Charles S. Hyneman, *Bureaucracy in a Democracy* (New York: Harper and Row, Publishers, Inc., 1950), pp. 88–89.
[12] John Day Larkin, *The President's Control of the Tariff* (Cambridge: Harvard University Press, 1936), p. 71.
[13] See E. E. Schattschneider, *Politics, Pressures, and the Tariff* (New York: Prentice-Hall, 1935), p. 25, and E. Pendleton Herring, *Public Administration and the Public Interest* (New York: McGraw-Hill Company, Inc., 1936), Chapter 6.

cording to his views of feasiblity and public interest."[14] Much legislation is, in fact, a "dilatory compromise,"[15] for it contains a formula, expressed in generalities, which reconciles diverse claims of interest for the purpose of the statute, but which postpones and hands to the administrators the task of reconciliation on specifics.

Not all responsibility is delegated to the administrator. The courts have their power of interpretation. The discretion of administrators may be circumscribed by historic views of the courts on what constitutes "fair and reasonable," on the tests of the "public convenience and necessity," or on the meaning of other language. Also, the courts may substitute their own judgment for that of agencies on the substance of new directives. And the Congress can at any time retrieve what it has delegated, or amplify the directives it has given.

The Supreme Court was reluctant to accept the delegation of law-making power to the executive branch of the government. It declared that the principle that Congress could not delegate legislative power to the President was "universally recognized as vital to the integrity and maintenance of the system of government ordained by the Constitution."[16] But it also proclaimed, relative to the issue of delegation, "The Constitution . . . does not demand the impossible or the impracticable."[17] Hence, legislative power can be delegated to the President, commissions, or executive departments *"when it is necessary to do so in order to achieve the results* which it [Congress] desires."[18] The legal link between the doctrine that legislative power cannot be delegated and the practical fact that it can is that there must be a standard to guide the delegee. But this link is a slender one. After holding invalid two delegations in 1935,[19] the Supreme Court accepted guides for administrators which were as general as any advocate of program flexibility could desire. Delegation is now accepted as one of the ordinary facts of government.

MEANS OF POLICY DEVELOPMENT. Administrative agencies may make use of various means for developing the substantive content of their programs. The means employed will be dependent upon statutory authorizations and the circumstances affecting the program.

One method is the issuance of legislative rules. Such rules, when issued in

[14] *H. P. Hood & Sons, Inc. v. U.S.*, 307 U.S. 588, 605 (1939).

[15] This useful term was employed years ago by Professor Carl J. Friedrich in lectures on constitutions.

[16] *Field v. Clark*, 143 U.S. 649, 692 (1892). The principle is not stated in the Constitution. It was part of a political tradition which channeled through Locke—*Second Treatise on Government*, Chapter XI—and a legal doctrine coming, it appears, from Bracton through Story and Kent—Patrick Duff and Horace E. Whiteside, "Delegata Potestas non Potest Delegari: a Maxim of American Constitutional Law," *Cornell Law Quarterly*, **XIV** (1929), p. 168.

[17] *Yakus v. U.S.*, 321 U.S. 414, 424 (1944).

[18] E. S. Corwin, *The President: Office and Powers*, 4th ed. (New York: New York University Press, 1957), p. 125. Corwin's italics.

[19] *A. L. A. Schechter Poultry Corp. v. U.S.*, 295 U.S. 495 (1935), *Panama Refining Co. v. Ryan*, 293 U.S. 388 (1935).

accord with statutory delegation, have legal force and effect. They are binding on private parties in the same way that statutes are. This is subordinate, or delegated, legislation in its purest form. The method is authorized in many statutes, and is used regularly by some agencies.

Somewhat different is the interpretative rule. Whereas the legislative rule creates new law, the interpretative rule declares the meaning of existing law. The correctness of the interpretation may be challenged in any court proceeding in which its application is questioned. An outstanding example is the interpretatve bulletins of the Wage and Hour Division of the Department of Labor.

Different in form and somewhat difficult to classify legally is the policy statement which fixes the standards the agency will apply in particular cases. An example is the chain-broadcasting regulations of the Federal Communications Commission. These regulations stated the policy that no license would be issued to a station having specified relationships with networks.[20] Similar were the policy standards developed in the Office of Price Administration to guide those within the agency in the framing of regulations. These policies guided the rule-makers in the several divisions of the agency.

The rule or standard gives an advance guide for action. Although the Administrative Procedure Act [21] recognizes rules of specific applicability (comparable to the local or special law passed in legislatures), the characteristic use of rule making is by general rules applicable to a category of situations. The rule or standard may, therefore, be the means of making a very large and broad step forward in policy.

Agencies may also develop policy through case-to-case administration. As in courts, policies evolve in the decisions on specific situations. A first rule of sound administration is that discrimination among persons in like situations should be avoided, and the courts will regard such discrimination as arbitrary and unsustainable. Hence, decisions build precedents and create law. Cumulatively, they build a structure of policy.

Still another means of developing policy is through the operating decision. The Federal Reserve Board in 1923 announced a policy of coordinating through a committee the open-market operations of the Federal Reserve Banks, and thus made a big leap forward in its program. The Federal Trade Commission in the twenties inaugurated the trade-conference procedure. Agencies make decisions on enforcement policies, choice of matters to be given attention, choice of cases to be initiated. In these several instances, no rules having the force of law are created and no decisions establish legal precedent, but decisions of an operating nature fix the trend of policy.

A final means of policy development is through recommendation to the legislature of amendments to the directives under which the agency operates. A large part—perhaps the major portion—of modern legislation is proposed

---

[20] For further treatment of the methods just discussed, see Kenneth Culp Davis, *Administrative Law* (St. Paul, Minn.: West Publishing Company, 1951), pp. 194–200.
[21] 60 Stat. 237 (1946).

by administrative agencies. Agencies see imperfection and incompleteness in their statutory authorizations, and seek corrective or expansive legislation. Legislatures expect those who deal continuously with problems to suggest improvements. There is, as noted many times in the preceding pages, a continuous working relationship between the agencies and the committees of Congress. Part of this relationship is in the flow of suggestions for legislation from agency to Congress, either on its own initiative or in response to inquiries from Congress.

EVOLUTION OF REGULATORY SYSTEMS. There evolves in each area of regulation a system of control. Its foundations are in legislation, but much of the superstructure may be administratively built. Illustrative is the edifice built by the CAB. It determined the classifications of carriers to be certificated; it decided to issue temporary certificates to some of these, and stuck with this policy until Congress changed it; it determined to keep local service and trunkline carriage separate; it developed the conditions of grants; it determined to use a quasi-judicial procedure for determining the needs of communities for air service; it evolved the necessary procedures for handling informally many types of petition. It has, in fact, fashioned both the airline structure and, to a considerable extent, the procedure for expanding it. Or note may be taken of the initiative of the Federal Power Commission in establishing the acceptability of "actual legitimate cost," and later of gaining acceptance for area pricing for producers of natural gas. Or reference may be made to the ICC's contribution of the structure of motor-carrier grants, or to the SEC's arangements for self-regulation of exchanges. This, of course, is only one side of the picture. Politics presses in from outside and limits—even overrules—agency decisions, and the courts perform a similar function. Nevertheless, the agencies are more than managers of public business; they are placed in a position where they must create policy through their own decision.

ADMINISTRATIVE PROCEDURE

President Kennedy said that the objectives of procedure are "efficiency, adequacy, and fairness." [22] It should be efficient in the sense of getting work done without unnecessary delay and expense to the government and parties, adequate for the attainment of the goals set for the agencies, and fair to the parties affected.

Prior to 1946, the procedures of national administrative agencies developed under three kinds of influence. To a large extent, the procedures were worked out by the agencies in response to the types of situations with which they dealt. Agencies with similar functions borrowed from each other's experience. The second kind of influence was the requirement of due process

---

[22] Executive Order 10934, April 13, 1961.

of law and other constitutional provisions as defined by the courts. Third, Congress made some prescriptions with respect to procedure. In 1946, after years of discussion, the veto of one bill by President Roosevelt, and a mammoth study by an Attorney General's Committee on Administrative Procedure, the Administrative Procedure Act was passed. It is the organic act on procedure. However, it leaves some discretion to agencies to adapt procedure to needs as they see them, leaves much room for judicial interpretation, and does not govern all agencies or all types of administrative action. Procedure is so complex in its varied uses that it can best be discussed by illustrations, followed by comments on outstanding features.

The first illustration is from the Federal Trade Commission. It can issue cease-and-desist orders—a function delegated to a considerable number of agencies, most notably the National Labor Relations Board. The order is issued after a determination that law has been violated, and this determination must be made after a judicial hearing. But there are pre-judicial phases that lead in some cases to complaints, and there is a prosecution function as well. The combination of these several aspects in the over-all procedural pattern is an interesting development in public administration, and especially in the growth of regulation of economic interests. The staff of the commission is divided in three parts for the separate tasks of preliminary investigation, prosecution, and hearing. There is a large group of officials within the commission who consider complaints received from the public alleging violation of law, and who, on their own initiative, examine newspaper, magazine, radio, and television advertising copy. A company may learn that its advertising or other practices is being questioned, and may come to the commission offices for conferences with the staff. It may change its advertising copy or discontinue a practice in order to cut off a recommendation by the staff that a complaint be issued. But staff investigation may lead to a recommendation to the commission that a complaint be issued. The commission, with assistance of legal and other staff, will decide whether to issue it. Prior to this, parties may sign an agreement to cease and desist and bring the case to a close. If not, the case goes to the hearing or judicial stage. There is within the commission a core of independent judicial officers, called hearing examiners, who serve under the direction of a chief hearing examiner and perform no functions except those of hearing examiner. When the complaint is docketed, the chief hearing examiner assigns it to an examiner. The examiner will set a date and place for hearing. He will "hold court" in much the same manner as if he were a judge. The officials within the commission's staff who have the responsibility for prosecution will have noted the docketing of the case and will appear to support the charge in the complaint. The Administrative Procedure Act requires complete separation of the prosecuting and examiner corps, and prevents the examiner from consulting with either parties prosecuting or defending unless notice and opportunity is given to the other to participate. The examiner takes testimony in open hearing, receives briefs from attorneys, hears oral arguments, and in due time thereafter makes an initial decision. This decision stands unless the parties appeal to the commission, in which case it will receive various motions, pleas, and attorneys' briefs, hold an oral hearing, and ultimately decide upon the issues. Defendants, if losing, may then appeal for a reconsideration by the commission, and if denied, or if losing on reconsideration, may appeal to a Court of Appeals.

A second illustration is from the CAB. It relates to the performance of a function which is common to many of the agencies that regulate industries—the grant of a certificate of public convenience and necessity.[23] There are two elements in the decision to be made on the application of an airline for a certificate to render service between two cities. One is the need for the additional service, and the other is whether this or some other airline shall be granted a certificate. Both questions are considered in the same proceeding. It begins with the receipt and docketing of one or more applications for service. Sometimes a number of airlines will make applications for the same or related service. The board will determine what applications shall be consolidated into a single proceeding. This may be a very difficult decision, and may result in a very large case. This was true, for example, of the Chicago–New York Service case decided in 1955. It resulted from the consolidation of a large number of applications relating to service between eastern and midwestern points. The commission may wait for years before it consolidates a set of applications for consideration. Ultimately a case is docketed, and the chief examiner assigns it to an examiner. A bureau within the agency will assign attorneys to participate. They will present data and analyses, but in cases of this kind they may or may not take a position on the issue.

The examiner will take steps to simplify and expedite the complex proceeding. He will hold a prehearing conference attended by the parties to the proceeding. Following this, various motions will be made, and these must be decided by the examiner or referred to the board. The examiner will set guidelines for the proceeding, dates when successive steps will be taken, and requirements concerning the submittal of evidence. Evidence will be submitted in written form, and rebuttals also. Thereafter there will be oral hearings, with questioning of witnesses, and then filing of briefs and oral argument. The examiner will make a decision which may be appealed to the board.[24]

These are examples of judicialized proceedings. They are typical for proceedings called "adjudication" in the Administrative Procedure Act, and for rule making where the statute requires that rules be based on a record made in a hearing. The typical rule-making proceeding will be less involved

---

[23] For detailed summary of the procedure, see Winston M. Fick, *Administrative Procedure in a Federal Regulatory Commission: The Civil Aeronautics Board and the New York–Chicago Case* (University, Ala.: University of Alabama Press, 1964).

[24] For fuller summary, see Winston M. Fick, *ibid.*

in procedural requirements. Illustrative is the procedure for Regulation No. ER-381 adopted by the CAB on June 17, 1963. The board published in the Federal Register, and circulated to the industry, a Notice of Proposed Rule Making, proposing an amendment to the Board's Economic Regulations to require carriers to issue passes, except in emergencies, to all persons accorded free or reduced-rate transportation. In response to the notice, comments were received from a number of persons. In light of these comments, the board modified the proposed rule and issued a statement of reasons for the rule. This illustrates the three requirements of the Administrative Procedure Act with respect to rules not based on a record after hearing: (1) notice in the Federal Register of a proposed change; (2) opportunity to interested parties to present written data and arguments, with or without oral presentation; and (3) a concise statement, along with the rule adopted, of its basis and purpose. However, even these requirements do not apply where the agency finds that "notice and public procedure . . . are impracticable, unnecessary, or contrary to the public interest"; nor do they apply to "interpretative rules, general statements of policy, rules of agency organization, procedure, or practice," nor to military, naval, or foreign affairs, nor to matters of agency management, personnel, public property, loans, grants, benefits, or contracts.

There are many types of decisions of administrative agencies which are neither adjudicative nor rule making. The decisions are purely administrative or operative in nature. An illustration is the procedure of the Board of Governors in making open-market decisions. Every two weeks the seven members of the Board of Governors and the twelve presidents of the Federal Reserve banks meet in Washington to discuss open-market purchases. They have the benefit of data assembled by staffs, and of their own knowledge and experience. The members of the board and five of the presidents designated for this purpose determine by vote the policy to be followed. Other examples of operating decisions are those on management and personnel, on choice of matters to be given attention, on deployment of resources toward the selected objectives, and on loans, grants, and contracts.

It may be concluded that although much of the regulatory work is done under judicialized procedures, there is some variation in the patterns of use of these procedures, and there is a considerable volume of regulatory work which, because it is preliminary or because its nature does not permit judicial methods, is done by the more flexible process of rule making or by administrative processes similar to those used in other organizations.

There are, nevertheless, certain general features of the American system of regulatory procedure which merit attention. One is the office and position of the examiner. When formal hearings are held, the hearing examiner is the center of the administrative process. The large volume of work in holding hearings and making initial decisions is delegated to examiners. The examiner is an officer of the agency, and will be overruled if he does not follow its decisions and policies. On the other hand, he is guaranteed substantial independence through provisions which prevent his removal without charges proven before the Civil Service Commission.

A second feature is informal process. By this is meant any type of process or method of settlement of particular cases without a formal hearing. It has been appropriately referred to as "the lifeblood of the administrative process." [25] Informal process reduces the burden of procedure for agency and affected parties, and it may make regulation much more palatable for the latter. An illustration is the procedure on prospectuses filed with the SEC. The commission can issue a stop order against sale of a security issue in interstate commerce or through the mails. Such an order would have a disastrous effect on the stock sale and on the company and its underwriting house. To avoid the overly adverse effects of formal action, the commission has worked out procedure for contact with the parties and for their amendment of the prospectus to meet the requirements of law and policy. We have noted the oportunities offered to persons to consult with the staff of the FTC, and to modify practices against which a charge of illegality might be made. Another advantage of informal procedure is that it may facilitate prompt decision. An example is the announcements of the CAB during consideration of the General Passenger Fare Case that it would approve certain temporary increases if these were requested.

Another feature is institutional process. The term may be used in both a broad and a narrow sense. The student of administrative science will think of all the ways in which an agency gets its work done—of its operation as an institution. The student of legal methods or of decision making will think of the ways in which the various experts within an agency cooperate in the making of a decision. Agencies are institutions which must sort out and delegate their tasks and establish means of direction, correction, and coordination. They also make institutional decisions—that is, decisions which accumulate the wisdom of the different types of experts in the agency. Law, however, places some restrictions on institutional decision making. Examiners in certain types of cases are prohibited from consulting *ex parte* with any "person or party." Their contacts with other parts of the agency are normally "on the record." The examiner's decision, like that of a judge, is a personal decision. Moreover, the Taft-Hartley Act prohibited members of the National Labor Relations Board from obtaining assistance from anyone except their legal assistants. In general, however, it may be said that the commission members have a great deal of freedom to consult with experts. In some cases, as in motor-carrier certification in the ICC, there is an extensive system of review of examiner's decisions before the case is decided. Usually, commissions obtain aid from a general counsel's office, personal attorneys, and from opinion-writing staff. On the other hand, they are careful in some types of cases to avoid consultation with other experts. There are, in

---

[25] *Final Report of the Attorney General's Committee on Administrative Procedure* (Washington, D.C.: Superintendent of Documents, 1941), pp. 58–59.

other words, limitations both in law and in practice on the combination of institutional resources in the handling of matters on which decision is to be based on a record.

ELEMENTS OF ADMINISTRATIVE STRENGTH

The strength or weakness of administrative agencies in the development and administration of regulatory programs—the extent of their ability to have an impact upon the shape of things—will be dependent upon many factors. Upon the basis of the immediately preceding discussion and supporting analyses in earlier chapters, three of these may be summarily noted. The first is the adequacy of substantive authority in terms of the situations to be confronted. Substantive authority has often been unequal to problem challenges. Utility commissions labored to protect the consumer on rates and service without collateral authority over utility finance and organization. The FTC found that its power over purchases of stock could be avoided through the escape hatch of mergers and, since having been granted power to attack mergers, has found that these can be consummated without notice and before commission action is possible. The ICC was granted authority with respect to consolidations, but without the power of compulsion that would have been necessary to carry out a consolidation plan. On the other hand, the SEC had a plenitude of power with respect to holding-company reorganization and simplification, which enabled it to attain the objective set forth in legislation. Usually, agencies will find their substantive delegations to be inadequate in terms of initial or subsequently developed situations, and, if they are to be measurably effective, will need to return to the legislature for additional authority.

Also, strength will be dependent upon the availability of suitable technique. If rule making is a suitable approach in policy development, then the agency will need authorization for use of the method. If advance check is more suitable than later corrective intervention, then some form of licensing may be required. Normally, in addition to such legislative authorizations of technique, an agency will find it necessary to discover and create special techniques applicable to its task.

Technique merges into procedure. To be effective, an agency will need to be able to use procedures which are efficient as well as fair. This requisite of efficiency will be considered further in the next chapter.

Two additional types of factors are important. The first are legal in nature, and may be referred to as facilitative arrangements; the second are legal and political, and may be discussed as external support.

FACILITATIVE ARRANGEMENTS. Seven types of auxiliary support for agencies may contribute to their success. First is the authority to obtain information. Facts—lots of facts, facts about the details of industry operation—are the *sine qua non* of intelligent public control. To meet this need, agencies may be given, according to the requirements of their programs, such powers as the following: to require regular and special reports; to prescribe forms of accounting and examine accounts; to inspect premises and products, test equipment, or analyze samples; to require submission, perhaps under oath, of specific information, and to require attendance of witnesses; to conduct special or general investigations. According to an old bit of dictum in a Supreme Court decision, national agencies cannot compel production of papers or testimony by administrative process;[26] they must go to a court to enforce a subpoena. In the past, agencies faced some difficulties because of Supreme Court attitudes on compulsory production of papers, but today the chief judicial requirement is for a showing that what is demanded by the agency is relevant.

Second, agencies normally need authority to act on their own initiative. Only if they have this authority can they deploy their resources where they will be productive. They should have information which will enable them to know what investigations should be made and what complaints should be filed. Usually, agencies are given this authority, though statutes also allow complaints from outside the agency.

Third, the agency needs in most instances to have exclusive original jurisdiction. This element of administrative authority was first stated by the Supreme Court in 1907 in the famous Abilene case,[27] in which it was held that a shipper could not resort to a court for reparations for an alleged unreasonable charge when a charge had been filed with the ICC and no decision had been made by it on the issue of reasonableness. Justice Brandeis stated the reasons for such a judicial doctrine: the need for uniformity in decisions, and the need for decision on technical matters by experts.[28] The doctrine is not always applied, but it is now a general rule of practice.

Fourth, a closely related doctrine is that of exhaustion of administrative remedies. According to this doctrine, a person must exhaust all his remedies before an administrative agency that has jurisdiction before he can resort to the courts. Together with the doctrine of exclusive original jurisdiction, it enables an agency to complete its process before court intervention will occur. It also protects the courts from an excessive number of interventions. The doctrine, though a general rule of administrative law, is not applied in all circumstances, for courts—though sensitive to needs for administrative effectiveness—are also sensitive to threats of real injury during pendency of administrative proceedings.

Fifth, the agency needs to be able to build the final and complete record on which decision is made. It has been noted in an earlier chapter that the ICC's effectiveness was impaired initially by the courts' acceptance of new evidence on appeal.[29] The practice today is different. Most of the na-

[26] *I.C.C. v. Brimson*, 154 U.S. 447 (1894).
[27] 204 U.S. 426.
[28] *Great Northern Ry. Co. v. Merchants Elevator Co.*, 259 U.S. 285, 291 (1922).
[29] See page 374.

tional regulatory statutes provide that appeal shall go from the agency of administration to a Court of Appeals (an appellate, not a trial, court), and that if there is additional evidence which is material and which could not reasonably have been presented to the agency at its hearing, then the court shall remand the case to the agency for further consideration. Also, some statutes provide that no contention shall be raised at the judicial stage which was not made at the administrative stage, or which was not presented without good cause for failure to do so.

Sixth, agencies need to be able to make authoritative decisions. It has long been settled that an administrative rule may be given the force and effect of law, with violators being subject to penalty for violation of a valid rule.[30] It has also been the general practice to give administrative rules automatic legal effect. It has been noted, however, that orders of the ICC and the FTC did not initially have legal force. This was corrected for the ICC in 1906, and for the FTC in Federal Trade Commission Act cases in 1938 and Clayton Act cases in 1959. Statutes now generally provide that administrative orders issued after hearing shall have legal force and effect until and unless set aside by a court.

Seventh, an agency will need appropriate sanctions for its decisions. The main problem is to find the sanction which has the correct amount of severity. Some agencies are provided with sanctions which are so heavy that they will not be used. For example, until recent years, the only sanctions available to the Comptroller of the Currency in case of violation of banking laws were appointment of a receiver or proceedings in a federal district court to dissolve a banking association. Obviously, these sanctions are too drastic for the thousands of minor violations of law. Agencies may have to add unofficial sanctions, as did the Comptroller. His chief sanctions have been "moral suasion" by bank examiners, and the annoyance of more frequent examinations. Ordinarily, an agency needs a scale of sanctions. It should be noted that, although some administrative sanctions exist, sanctions are ordinarily applied by courts, and this is especially true of fine and imprisonment.

EXTERNAL SUPPORT. Even with all the elements of strength which have been sketched, an administrative agency may have small impact if it does not have external support. One source of support must be the judiciary. Even though administrative orders have legal force and effect on persons unless set aside, they will be accepted and complied with only if they carry weight in reviewing courts. The courts scotched the ICC and the FTC in the first phases of their existence. They throttled the utility commissions for years. They have, on the other hand—partly in obedience to statutes and partly in recognition of the needs filled by administrative agencies—relaxed their controls over the administrative process. The result is that the agencies may now expect that most of their decisions will be accepted without appeal to the courts.

---

[30] *U.S. v. Grimaud,* 220 U.S. 506 (1911).

Agencies must also have political support of various types. This is the ultimate source of power on which their ability to perform will be dependent. Without political support, legal power will not be granted, or will be withdrawn, or will not be usable. Administration either has a political base, or it disappears or fades into insignificance. "There is," as Norton Long wrote, "no more forlorn spectacle in the administrative world than an agency and a program possessed of statutory life, armed with executive orders, sustained in the courts, yet stricken with paralysis and deprived of power." [31]

From where does the agency draw this support? It may draw it from the groups it regulates. The Federal Reserve Board draws support from bankers, the Department of Agriculture from farmers, the Texas Railroad Commission from oil men. The ICC is accepted by the railroads and truckers as a satisfactory moderator of their interests, and the CAB by the established airline industry as its protector. Agencies which have to administer programs which impinge on entrenched interests, such as the FTC, the Antitrust Division of the Department of Justice, and the Food and Drug Administration, often have a more scattered support. They may find it in professional groups —lawyers for the Antitrust Division, scientists for the Food and Drug Administration, in a variety of interests whose support is latent and subject to being aroused, and in the general ideological consensus of society.

An agency will reach to the centers of power in the committee system of Congress that are strategic with respect to its operations. Links will be established with those committees which handle an agency's legislation and appropriations. Stronger links will be sought with strategically located members of Congress who are friendly to the agency and its program. An agency's ability to continue with its established program will depend upon the development of a triangle of relations among itself, the committee system, and the supporting clienteles.

The agency will also need to draw support from the presidency. Their lack of support in the Bureau of the Budget can cost them a great deal, as was evident in the low budget recommendations of the bureau for commissions' budgets during the Eisenhower Administration. Lack of presidential interest can cost them support when they are on the defensive, and can rob them of help when they seek to be aggressive. In fact, agencies are not likely to adopt an aggressive stance unless appointments have been made with this idea in mind.

Agencies will try to win a favorable public image on their operations. It has been noted how the Office of Price Administration struggled for the support of public opinion.[32] The operations of most agencies do not touch the daily lives of people so directly and intimately, and at so many points; hence they have more difficulty in obtaining public attention. Their access is largely restricted to their clienteles and some other specially interested

---

[31] Norton E. Long, "Power and Administration," *Public Administration Review*, IX (Autumn 1949), p. 257.
[32] See pages 340–341.

groups. The trade press is reachable, but the general press is crowded by competing pressures for publicity. Also, an agency may face criticism if it moves positively into the public arena. It moves, therefore, for support for established lines of activity in the triangular substructure of which it is a part, and through established lines of contact with department heads and the presidency. If it must buck strong interests, or proposes to cut new paths in policy which will have divisive tendencies among the interests, it may shortly find that it is in macropolitics, where battles are won or lost by presidents and the other party leaders; it may also find that in such a struggle, its own survival is threatened.

RESPONSIBILITY

Administrative power is balanced by safeguards. By and large, power and safeguards against power grow out of the same relationships. Courts, Congress, President, and the public give power and check power, and the giving and the checking is in the same process.

What are the purposes of safeguards? There are four.

First, that the exercise of power shall be confined within the limits of the delegations. Action should not be ultra vires. Second, that power shall be exercised in a reasonable and non-arbitrary manner. This means that decisions should be made on the basis of data, in accord with proper purpose, and in an even-handed manner. Third, that power shall be exercised effectively. This means success in doing jobs assigned in directives. Fourth, that power shall be exercised under conditions of democratic responsibility. This calls for accountability to the public and its representatives.[33]

One line of safeguard is the courts. Court review of administrative decisions extends to three things: "procedure, law, and facts. Were the proceedings 'conducted lawfully'? Was there error in the application of law? Was there adequate basis in fact for the decision?" [34]

Court review on questions of law, once frequently based on constitutional doctrines, is now largely for the purpose of construing the meaning and purpose of statutory language. Similarly, on procedure, court review is now largely for the interpretation of the requirements of the Administrative Procedure Act and other statutes. Judicial review of facts on economic matters now usually follows the substantial-evidence or rationality test. The agency's decision on facts will not be looked at to see if it is right or wrong; the court will review to determine whether there is substantial evidence to support the conclusion of the agency—or differently stated, whether there is in the record of facts rational basis for the conclusion. But the Administrative Procedure Act does not allow the judge to look at only a bit of the

---

[33] Emmette S. Redford, *Administration of National Economic Control* (New York: The Macmillan Company, 1952), p. 325.
[34] Redford, *ibid.*, p. 327.

record to find there some evidence to support the conclusion, without seeing if there is some evidence to point the opposite way; the judge, says the act, must "review the whole record or such portions thereof as may be cited by any party."

Judicial review is one effective safeguard, but it is not by itself enough to insure responsible action. First, some types of administrative decision, even on questions of law, have been held to be final and nonreviewable in courts.[35] Second, there are many decisions which lie outside the purview of courts. They cannot determine which cases will be prosecuted, nor can they reach those situations where men choose to compromise with government. They cannot force decisions within the realm of discretionary authority—the President to make a trade agreement, or the Department of Agriculture to make a marketing agreement. They cannot affect decisions of the Federal Reserve and the Treasury, as on open-market negotiations, the level of margins for trading on stock exchanges, or the timing and manner of distribution of government bonds. They cannot correct laxness in bank examinations or other inspections, nor can they adequately protect men's interests from the effects of administrative delay. Third, the courts have been forced, by the need for expert judgment on intricate and technical economic data, to yield a large measure of finality to administrative decisions. Finally, most men will accept the decisions of agencies rather than go to the courthouse for contest.

Of greater importance are the internal safeguards within agencies. The lawyers inhabit administrative agencies in great numbers, and they keep the agencies close to their statutory objectives and constantly warn against discriminatory or arbitrary action. Other experts, loyal to professional standards, offer guidance toward wise decision. Procedural safeguards protect men's rights to a fair administrative hearing. The institutional process insures that things move through many pieces of organization, that many minds contribute to solutions, that things will be traced out in many directions.

Another line of safeguard is in the work of Congress. The Constitution gave it four levers for control of administration: the legislative power, the appropriations power, the Senate's power of confirmation of appointments, and the impeachment power. Although it contained no express provision for congressional inquiry into the conduct of administration, practice has filled the gap. Congress exercises surveillance over administration in many ways; and an administrative agency is forever conscious of this fact, and of the possibilities for favorable or adverse congressional action. This control, as has been shown in Chapter 3, is exercised normally through legislative committees and members who occupy strategic positions in the committee system. There is continuous contact between each agency of administration and the committees which consider legislation and appropriations relating to its

---

[35] See Kenneth Culp Davis, *Administrative Law* (St. Paul, Minn.: West Publishing Company, 1951), Chapter 19.

work. In addition, other standing committees (such as the committees on Government Operations in the two houses) and special subcommittees (such as the recent Legislative Oversight Committee) may inquire into the operations of administrative agencies. The powers of support and restraint in the congressional committee system, although fragmentary and intermittent with respect to particular subjects, are so extensive and pervasive as to result in a considerable sharing of responsibility for administration of regulatory programs between the agencies and the congressional committees.[36]

Note has been taken of the considerable powers of the President with respect to the agencies. Also, the limitations on him with respect to the independent commissions have been noted. There are limitations also on the span of attention of the President, and there are gaps in the organization of the top structure of the government which prevent continuing attention to regulatory policy.

There are many checks on the agencies from the society of which they are a part. The trade press, the interest groups, and the practitioners before the agencies have their eyes on them continuously. The news reporters and commentators have an ear tuned for matters of general interest. The members of the agencies share the attitude of the public of which they are a part, including even the ideas that public administration should operate with restraint and with recognition of the diverse rights and interests which will be affected.

In sum, administrative regulation operates in a pluralistic society and in a pluralistic government. It is restrained from many directions. It may be argued that the negative safeguards—those against arbitrary and capricious action—are fully adequate. There may be question, however, whether positive safeguards exist for wise decision and effective performance. This question will serve as a transition to the next chapter.

[36] For illustration of the extent of the sharing, see William E. Rhode, *Committee Clearance of Administrative Decisions* (East Lansing, Mich.: Michigan State University, 1959).

Chapter 25. Problems in Regulatory Administration

WITH THE BACKGROUND of basic information about the regulatory system provided in the last chapter, it is now possible to concentrate attention on the criticisms of, and misgivings about, the system and the ways people have thought it could be improved. The problems of the system will be discussed under four headings: Internal Process, Organization and Responsibility, Interest Associations, and Public-Private Balances.

It should be said in the beginning that there has been quite a babel of discordant voices on the merits, demerits, and means of improving the regulatory system. The conflicts of opinion about features of the system have existed from the beginning.[1] The discussions have had continuity since the thirties. Those on the first two problems—internal process, and organization and responsibility—have often been merged in a chain of discussion which began in 1933. In that year the American Bar Association created a Committee on Administrative Law, which has since devoted its attention to procedure, organization, and responsibility. In 1937 the President's Committee on Administrative Management, in its proposals for improvement of administration, included proposals for drastic reorganization of the regulatory system.[2] In 1940 an Attorney General's Committee on Administrative Procedure, after an exhaustive study of about forty agencies, made a report on internal processes.[3] Congress legislated comprehensively on the matter in the Administrative Procedure Act of 1946.[4] Both the first and the second Hoover Commissions gave attention to the problems.[5] The House of Repre-

---

[1] For illustration, see the summary of conflicting opinions on the regulatory commission in James E. Anderson, *Emergence of the Modern Regulatory State* (Washington, D.C.: Public Affairs Press, 1962), Chapter VII.

[2] President's Committee on Administrative Management, *Report with Special Studies* (Washington, D.C.: Superintendent of Documents, 1937), including, in addition to recommendations in the Committee's Report, a study by Robert E. Cushman on "The Problem of the Independent Regulatory Commissions."

[3] *Final Report of the Attorney General's Committee on Administrative Procedure* (Washington, D.C.: Superintendent of Documents, 1941).

[4] 60 Stat. 237.

[5] Commission on Organization of the Executive Branch of the Government, *Regulatory Commissions* (Washington, D.C.: Superintendent of Documents, 1949), and Task Force of the Commission, *Regulatory Commissions* (Washington, D.C.: Superintendent of Documents, 1949). Also, Commission on Organization of the Executive Branch of the Government, *Legal Services and Procedure*, House Document No. 128 (84th Cong., 1st Sess., 1955),

sentatives created a Legislative Oversight Committee in 1957 to study the operation of regulatory agencies, and the Senate Judiciary Committee also became active on the subject. In 1960, President-Elect Kennedy appointed James M. Landis to make a study.[6] Administrative conferences, composed of governmental and private parties, conducted studies in 1953–55 and 1961–62. These are only the highlights of the discussions. They are mentioned here to show the continuity of interest and, furthermore, because most of them will be referred to (some of them repeatedly) in the ensuing analysis.

The discussions on interest associations may be said to have their origins in a book by Pendleton Herring on *Public Administration and the Public Interest* in 1936. It has undoubtedly received impetus from the revival of interest in Bentley's *The Process of Government*[7] and from certain instances of improper conduct on the part of public officials. There has been much less official discussion of this problem than of the first two listed above.

One looks in vain for comprehensive discussion of the fourth problem. It is so important, however, that the author offers some random comments on it.

INTERNAL PROCESS

All would accept President Kennedy's listing of the objectives of process: "efficiency, adequacy, and fairness." Men differ on the weight to be given to each objective and on the means of attainment. It is perhaps not oversimplification to say that there are two moods from which an approach is made to the problems of process.

One mood results from a suspicion of processes of decision concerning men's rights and interests which are not like those used in courts. The central feature of the judicial process is a hearing. The judicial hearing is an adversary process in which opponents in interest present testimony. The basic essentials are notice to affected parties, opportunities to know the claims of the opposition and meet these with evidence and argument, and decision on the basis of the record made in the hearing. The decision is a personal decision of an impartial judge. It is presumably made on the basis of standing law and legal standards or concepts, though this view overlooks the uncertainties in the content and application of law. Those who share this mood may have an antagonism to legislation, or they may believe that administrative legislation does not have the safeguards for men's interests which characterize the legislative process. They may, therefore, desire that admin-

---

and *Task Force Report on Legal Services and Procedure* (Washington, D.C.: Superintendent of Documents, 1955).

[6] James M. Landis, *Report on Regulatory Agencies to the President-Elect*, Committee Print, Committee on the Judiciary, U.S. Senate (86th Cong., 2nd Sess., 1960).

[7] A. F. Bentley, *The Process of Government* (Chicago: University of Chicago Press, 1908).

istrative rule making, as well as administrative adjudication, shall be done with the safeguards believed to inhere in judicial process. The motive is fairness, and to this is wedded the idea that fairness will be attained best, or perhaps only, by judicial processes.

The other mood results from the desire that government be effective in the tasks it undertakes. The essential requirement, from this view, is adaptation of process to function. Judicial process should be used where it is appropriate, but other techniques may be more useful than judicial methods, and equally fair. When making general rules, administrative agencies may find staff studies and general hearings of a legislative type more satisfactory than judicial-type hearings. In considering various types of applications, combinations of administrative and judicial process will be useful. Government must get its total job done, and must make particular decisions with reasonable promptness. This calls for a search for means of simplifying procedure. Decisions must be made expertly, and this may call for group collaboration rather than personal decision. The motive is efficiency and adequacy, and this can be achieved only if there is willingness to innovate.

Fortunately, most people share something from both moods. There will be some among those representing private interests who will desire that government be ineffective, and there will be some among administrators who in their zeal overlook requirements for fairness. But the practitioners of the law, who desired judicialization, and the agencies, which desired managerial efficiency, reached agreement on the Administrative Procedure Act. They had been assisted by a study made by the Attorney General's Committee which showed the elements of validity in the rival contentions. Yet neither side was completely satisfied, and new movements for reform began about a decade later.

One movement for reform came from those who wanted further judicialization of the administrative process.[8] It began with a Task Force Report on Legal Services and Procedure of the second Hoover Commission. The keynote was: "The more closely that administrative procedures can be made to conform to judicial procedures, the greater the probability that justice will be attained in the administrative process. . . ."[9] The spearhead of the movement was to be the American Bar Association. Most of the recommendations made by the second Hoover Commission and the Bar Association are too technical for analysis in this discussion, but their general import may be indicated.[10] The proposals were in the direction of formalization of the rule-making process. The Bar Association's proposed Code of Federal Administrative Procedure would accomplish this in part by redefining rule making so as not to include rate making, corporate reorganizations, and

---

[8] For summary, see Ferrel Heady, "The New Reform Movement in Regulatory Administration," *Public Administration Review*, **XIX** (Spring 1959), pp. 89–100.

[9] *Task Force Report on Legal Services and Procedure, op. cit.*, p. 138.

[10] The Bar Association's Proposed Code of Administrative Procedure was incorporated in S. 1070 (86th Cong., 1959).

many other matters when they relate to particular corporations or individuals. An effect would have been to make the stricter requirements of the Administrative Procedure Act on adjudication applicable to these things. Hearing examiners would make the initial decisions, and they would be insulated from consultation with agency economists, engineers, and other specialists. In addition, the code provided, on rule making, among other things, that agencies prescribe in advance in each instance the procedure to be followed, issue a concise statement (if requested) of the matters considered in adopting or rejecting a rule, and give reasons for denial of any petition for issuance, amendment, or repeal of a rule. Such things would obviously take away some flexibility in rule making, and increase enormously the burden on agencies. Furthermore, the proposals looked toward closer similarity between administrative adjudication and adjudication in courts. For example, both the Hoover Commission and the Bar Association code proposed that rules of evidence and requirements of proof conform to those in civil, non-jury cases in district courts. Moreover, both of these looked toward further independence of the examiners from the agencies. The Hoover Commission would have placed the selection and supervision of such officials in the hands of a Chief Hearing Commissioner who would be located in the judicial branch, and the Bar Association proposed that such function be placed in an independent office.

Such proposals have not been carried out, undoubtedly because of the opposition of the Department of Justice and other agencies, and because of the adverse comment of many legal scholars. The proposals show, however, that the desire to judicialize administrative processes is still very much alive. It is apparent also that such proposals meet the opposition of those who believe that "the virtues of full hearing in most types of economic regulation have been so enthusiastically embraced that the administrative process in this area . . . now moves with the mammoth gradualness of cinemascope in slow motion." [11]

Another movement for reform has come from those who have looked at the management aspects of regulation. In 1959 the author of this chapter wrote as follows:

> It was natural that lawyers should demand judicialization of the administrative process. On the other hand, it may now be time for a new look at this trend to determine if it is not robbing us of the opportunity for effective administrative regulation. One of the advantages which has been asserted for the process is expertness. But do statutory and administrative restrictions on use of staff aid limit the attainment of this advantage? Another asserted advantage is expeditious settlement. Today, however, the most frequent complaint against the commissions is delay in reaching decisions.[12]

---

[11] Nathaniel L. Nathanson, "Law and the Future: Administrative Law," *Northwestern Law Review*, **LI** (1956), p. 174.
[12] Emmette S. Redford, *National Regulatory Commissions: Need for a New Look* (College Park, Md.: University of Maryland Press, 1959), pp. 9–10.

In his report to the President-Elect in 1960, James Landis, formerly Dean of the Harvard Law School and member of three regulatory commissions, spelled out the problems of the administrative process. "Inordinate delay characterizes the disposition of adjudicatory proceedings before substantially all of our regulatory agencies." The costs of proceedings are so great that "in many situations the small businessman is practically excluded from an opportunity to compete." The Administrative Procedure Act, "with its emphasis on 'judicialization' has made for delay in the handling of many matters before these agencies." Viewing the possibility of new methods, Landis commented:

> Very recently suggestions have been advanced that due to modern techniques for the assemblage of facts, the older "judicialized" forms may well be supplanted. The exact technology applicable to such a process has not as yet been clearly articulated. But if judgments of regulatory agencies in many fields such as rates are, in truth, business judgments rather than judgments conforming to a legal theory, techniques which do not rest upon the tedious process of examination and cross-examination and which underlie honest business judgments made by the industries may have a value in the handling of substantially the same problem by the agencies.

With respect to airline certification, Landis said that the "inordinate delay . . . arises out of the procedures," in which "issues with regard to the desirability of new routes and new services are commingled with issues as to what carriers should fly what routes," and all the issues are "handled by the lengthy process of examining and cross-examining witnesses." He suggested that issues on the need for new routes "be determined beforehand by less legalistic and reasonably scientific methods, leaving for a 'judicialized' hearing only the issue as to which of the competing carriers is to be selected for certification on any particular route." [13]

The chief recommendation by Landis on the administrative process was for delegation within the agencies. He recomended that the President propose reorganization plans "providing for the delegation to panels of agency members, single agency members, hearing examiners or boards of employees for final determination all adjudicatory matters subject only to discretionary review by the agency *en banc* on petition by a party in interest." [14] Although Landis did not explain the advantages of such a step, it was obviously a means of preventing delays. The proposal is appealing for other reasons also. Those who favor judicialization of processes will regard this as a means of strengthening the prestige and power of the examiner, whom they would like to see occupy a stronger position. It has been suggested also as a means of freeing commissions from some of the burden of decision on particulars so that they would have time and freedom to consider policy.[15]

[13] The quotations are from James M. Landis, *Report on Regulatory Agencies to the President-Elect*, Committee Print, Committee on the Judiciary, U.S. Senate (86th Cong., 2nd Sess., 1960), pp. 5, 10, 16, 17, 41, 42.
[14] Landis, *ibid.*, p. 85.
[15] Emmette S. Redford, *National Regulatory Commissions: Need for a New Look* (College Park, Md.: University of Maryland Press, 1959), p. 17.

Landis also recommended that the President establish a second Administrative Conference, similar to the one which studied administrative procedure from 1953 to 1955. This President Kennedy did. The conference, composed of eighty-eight representatives of agencies and outside professional groups, functioned from mid-1961 to the end of 1962. Its recommendations showed awareness of the managerial approach, and of due-process considerations as well. Probably its most important recommendation was for delegation. It modified the Landis proposal somewhat. As did Landis, the conference proposed that examiners' decisions be accorded finality unless reviewed by the agency. But whereas Landis would have made review entirely discretionary with the agency (as it is with the Supreme Court where review is by the writ of certiorari), the conference proposed appeal if the party desiring it made a showing of prejudicial error in the proceeding before the presiding officer, or a showing that the subordinate decision contained (1) a finding of material fact which was clearly erroneous, or (2) an erroneous conclusion of law, or (3) involved an exercise of agency discretion, or (4) involved an important decision of law or policy.[16] President Kennedy had already proposed, in reorganization orders, that certain agencies be given authority to accord finality to decisions of those presiding at hearings, and such orders had been approved for the Federal Trade Commission, the Civil Aeronautics Board, and the Federal Maritime Commission. These agencies in making rules for delegations, and the President and Congress in making authorizations for future delegations, will undoubtedly consider the conference's suggestions for qualification of delegation. Nevertheless, although delegation may be limited, it may be hoped that steps taken in that direction will reduce the length of many proceedings, and will allow more time for agency consideration of policy.

Among other things, the conference attacked the problem of delay in rate-making cases. Its recommendations favored simplification of adjudicatory proceedings. It proposed that evidence be submitted in advance in writing. It urged examiners to use conference procedures to the maximum extent possible and to limit cross-examination. It recommended also that agency staff members participate in rate making, and that the examiner be allowed to obtain specialized expert assistance in analyzing data and reaching his conclusion. Although such recommendations accept continued use of a judicial framework in rate making, they include modifications designed to expedite proceedings and to take advantage of institutional expertness.

The Landis report and the work of the Administrative Conference show a shift from the movement toward further judicialization to interest in simplification, expedition, and use of expert aid. Whether this new ferment will lead to substantial modifications of administrative process is, of course, uncertain.

One specific suggestion for improvement merits special attention. It has

---

[16] *Final Report of the Administrative Conference of the United States* (Dec. 15, 1962), pp. 13–15.

been suggested that where an agency is applying a general standard prescribed by Congress, it should spell out by rules or policy standards the content of the statutory standard so that decisions in particular cases would be fairly predictable. This suggestion is not new, but was renewed by Judge Henry J. Friendly in the Holmes Lectures at Harvard in 1962.[17] There has been much criticism of agencies such as the Federal Communications Commission and the Civil Aeronautics Board because their standards for granting licenses or certificates are not specific. Actually, the agencies have a number of standards, and it is impossible to predict which of these will dominate in the decision in a particular case.

The many advantages of clear standards have often been repeated. One brief summary will suffice here:

First, they inform the regulated companies and give them a measure of certainty on which to base their plans. Second, they inform examiners and thus increase their opportunities to make decisions which will not be appealed or will stand upon appeal. Third, they inform the staff, facilitate delegation, and lay the basis for responsible evaluation of policies. Finally, miscellaneous advantages include conservation of time of administrators, reduction of expense and delay, and limitation of opportunities of private persons to gain special favor through influence and pressure.[18]

The issue is one of feasibility. On the surface, it appears desirable that judicial interpretations—for example, of antitrust standards—should be more definite, that statutes should be more specific, that administrative agencies should develop clear standards. But beneath the surface are hard realities. Some flexibility must be allowed because factual situations to which standards are applied are different. The courts, Congress, and agencies may not be able to foresee all the competing interests which will be involved. The appellate courts, Congress, and commissions are composed of groups of men whose consensus is limited, and who will be replaced by other men who will balance things differently. Generality of standards is in large part the result of these factors of complexity and diversity of factual situations, competing interests, and lack of agreement among officials. Yet it may be due also to the fact that administrative agencies have become engulfed in case-to-case proceedings and have not tried to extricate themselves by concentrating on policy development.

The discussion of standards to guide in the decision of particular cases is part of the broader discussion of the relative usefulness of rule making and adjudication as means of developing policy. The latter is a slow, piecemeal, and indirect method of making policy. It may lead administrators so deep into particulars that they fail to see general interests and considerations—may lead to what Dean Landis has called "Administrative myopia that fails

---

[17] Henry J. Friendly, *The Federal Administrative Agencies: The Need for Better Definition of Standards* (Cambridge, Mass.: Harvard University Press, 1962).
[18] Redford, *National Regulatory Commissions*, op. cit., p. 14; see also Friendly, *ibid.*, Ch. I.

to see the woods because of the abundance of the trees." [19] It is a method which encourages the administrator to take the easy road of deciding only the issues presented, rather than the hard road of finding fundamental solutions for economic maladjustments.[20] Rule making may be a means of leaping forward with program at a pace comparable to that with which the economy moves. This opportunity for achievement may be of much greater significance than the advantages in internal process set forth above in the discussion of standards. Although it would be unwise to require that all general statutory provisions should be implemented by rule making, it is desirable to emphasize the need for appropriate use of the instrument to enable policy to keep pace with change.

ORGANIZATION AND RESPONSIBILITY

Although the commission has been the favored form of organization for economic regulation, there has been much discussion of whether it is the best form, and of whether changes should be made in its position and operation if it is retained. Discussion of these questions may appropriately begin with a summary of the reputed advantages and weaknesses of the commission system of economic regulation.

ADVANTAGES AND WEAKNESSES OF THE COMMISSION SYSTEM. A task force for the first Hoover Commission presented four arguments for the independent regulatory commission.[21] First, there is need for impartiality. Favoritism and unfairness in administration are serious risks because of the wide discretion of public officials and the political strength of the regulated interests. Hence there "is a vital necessity for assuring that such regulatory agencies are insulated from partisan influence or control to the maximum extent feasible." Second, there are advantages in group policy making and decisions. The "combined judgment of the group . . . provides both a barrier to arbitrary or capricious action and a source of decisions based on different points of view and experience." Third, there is need for expertness. A commissioner gains expertness because of "fixed terms of reasonable duration, and the tradition of reappointment," and because of the assistance of other members who have served for some time. Fourth, another essential is continuity of policy. Private industry should have the benefit of stability and uniformity in policy. This objective is sought through "long terms expiring at staggered intervals," "restraints on removal," and "group consultive action." The Task Force admitted that group action

[19] James M. Landis, *The Administrative Process* (New Haven, Conn.: Yale University Press, 1938), p. 68.
[20] For comparative advantages of adjudication and rule making as means of developing policy, see Emmette S. Redford, *Administration of National Economic Control* (New York: The Macmillan Company, 1952), pp. 112–120.
[21] *Task Force Report on Regulatory Commissions* (Washington, D.C.: Superintendent of Documents, 1949), pp. 19–25.

could be slow and time-consuming, that "the main source of expertness in a commission must lie in its staff," that there had sometimes been "excessive turn-over of members," and that "in practice, the commissions have fallen short" of the ideal of continuity and stability in policy. It concluded, nevertheless, "that the independent commission has an essential place for certain types of governmental regulation," [22] and the Hoover Commission accepted the conclusion.[23]

Although they are not so neatly summarized in one place, the weaknesses of commissions are reiterated in the literature on economic regulation.[24] First, it is said that the commissions have reflected the usual weaknesses of boards in management. The first Hoover Commission emphasized these weaknesses, particularly the lack of delegation and the failure to concentrate responsibility for administrative work. To correct the latter failing, it recommended placing administrative responsibilities in the chairman.[25] This has been done in some measure for most of the commissions, but it has not removed the feeling of the members that they share responsibility. Second, the board system contributes to delay in the making of decisions on substantive matters. Time is lost while members and their aides complete their studies, and further time is often lost because of disagreements. The commission system itself contributes to the lack of sensitivity on time passage, which can weaken administrative effort. Third, it is contended that the combination of judicial functions with other functions impairs the independence which should exist for the judicial functions. The adjudicator, it is argued, should have no other functions. Fourth, it is said that the plurality and independence of the commissions impedes executive coordination and leadership. The traditional assumption has been that the commissions handled problems which could be dealt with in isolation, often by judicial process, and that political leadership and executive coordination were both unnecessary and dangerous. It is now argued that new developments call for a reversal of thinking—that executive coordination is necessary, and political leadership vital. It is argued that a prolonged conflict in policy between the Federal Reserve Board and the Treasury would be intolerable, that there is need for a coordinated transportation policy and a coordinated fuels policy, that there is need for over-all communications planning, and that overlapping jurisdictions on monopoly and trade practices call for coordination in this area. It is argued further that leadership for coordination and for policy

[22] Task Force Report (Superintendent of Documents), *ibid.*, p. 28.
[23] The Commission on Organization of the Executive Branch of the Government, *The Independent Regulatory Commissions* (Washington, D.C.: Superintendent of Documents, 1949), p. 3.
[24] See especially Robert E. Cushman, *The Independent Regulatory Commissions* (New York: Oxford University Press, 1941); James W. Fesler, *The Independence of State Regulatory Agencies* (Chicago: Public Administrative Service, 1942); Marver H. Bernstein, *Regulating Business by Independent Commission* (Princeton, N.J.: Princeton University Press, 1955), Chapter 5; Emmette S. Redford, *Administration of National Economic Control* (New York: The Macmillan Company, 1952), Chapter 10.
[25] *The Independent Regulatory Commissions, op. cit.*, p. 5.

planning can come only from the President and those who represent him. Fifth, it is argued that regulation cannot be nonpolitical in its policy aspects, and that the issue is what kind of politics shall prevail. The point was stated pungently in *Fortune:* "The facts of political life in Washington are that if a regulatory agency does not get guidance and support from the White House, it gravitates toward its 'clients,' that is, toward the industry it is supposed to regulate or toward some sections of that industry." [26] The point might be restated in terms of language used in this book: divorce from macropolitics means marriage to the politics of subsystems. It is argued that the effort to free vast policy-making functions from control by the top political officers of the government is undemocratic. Sixth, the fourth and fifth arguments—coordination and political responsibility—are joined with the ideal of the public interest in the arguments of a leading authority. Marver Bernstein, like the author in *Fortune,* sees a gravitation of the regulatory commissions toward the interests they regulate. He argues that the public interest cannot be adequately protected by agencies confined to the limited spheres of experience characteristic of the commissions. He concludes, "The public interest can scarcely be identified and defined short of effective coordination of the various regulatory programs with each other and with national economic policy." [27] Finally, it is argued that regulation obtains strength from political support. The agency that lacks a pipeline to the White House will be weak. Regulation which lacks the continuous invigoration of politics will become traditional in approach, narrow in point of view, and weak in overcoming resistance.

PROPOSALS FOR SEPARATION OF FUNCTIONS. One proposal that has issued from the criticisms of the regulatory commissions is that functions should be reassigned in line with the separation-of-powers doctrine. The proposal first came from the Bar Association's Committee on Administrative Law, which in 1934 suggested that an effort be made to divorce judicial functions from legislative and executive functions, and that the former be placed in special courts and the latter in executive departments responsible to the President.[28] Three years later, the same recommendation was made by the President's Committee on Administrative Management. It described the independent commissions as "miniature independent governments," constituting "a headless 'fourth branch' of the Government, a haphazard deposit of irresponsible agencies and uncoordinated powers." It saw a fundamental defect in the commission system:

They suffer from an internal inconsistency, an unsoundness of basic theory. This is because they are vested with duties of administration and policy determination with respect to which they ought to be clearly and effectively responsible to the

---

[26] George Bookman, "Regulation by Elephant, Rabbit, and Lark," *Fortune,* **LXIII** (June 1961), pp. 137–139, 232, 237.
[27] Marver H. Bernstein, *Regulating Business by Independent Commission* (Princeton, N.J.: Princeton University Press, 1955), p. 163.
[28] *American Bar Association Report,* **LIX**, pp. 539–540.

President, and at the same time they are given important judicial work in the doing of which they ought to be wholly independent of Executive control.[29]

The proposal, or a part thereof, recurs from time to time. The second Hoover Commission, the House of Delegates of the American Bar Association, and bills introduced in Congress have in recent years proposed some transfer of judicial functions to an administrative court or other form of judicial tribunal. Such proposals ordinarily relate to labor or trade practices. Louis J. Hector, in a memorandum to the President at the time of his resignation from membership on the Civil Aeronautics Board, recommended a reorganization which would "transfer to an appropriate executive department the functions of policy-making and administration, to an administrative court or courts the adjudicatory responsibility in major litigated cases and appeals from administrative actions, and to the Department of Justice the prosecution functions." [30]

Such proposals were debated extensively following the Committee on Administrative Management's report in 1937. The recommendations drew more criticism than support. Many thought that the criticisms of the committee were extravagantly stated and overdrawn; after all, responsibility is enforced on commissions by courts, Congress, and the President. Some attacked the conclusion that policy-making functions should be placed in executive departments, arguing instead that the commissions were and should remain "arms of Congress." Some thought that the committee had failed to show the feasibility of its solution, for while it spelled out in detail how the division of functions would be consummated for the Federal Trade Commission, it did not show how the scrambled egg of regulation in such an agency as the Interstate Commerce Commission could be unscrambled into a judicial white and an administrative and policy-determining yellow. Still more basic was the argument that the regulatory task was a unity, and could be performed successfully only if all parts of it were performed in an agency which was responsible for total results. Dean Landis condemned the attempt to fit the solution of twentieth-century problems into the "triadic contours" of Montesquieu's thought.[31] Finally, the Attorney General's Committee on Administrative Procedure believed that the division of prosecuting and adjudicatory functions would impair the informal processes of settlement of cases.[32]

In no case has a commission been abolished and its functions reassigned in line with the precise proposals of the committee. There have been some

---

[29] President's Committee on Administrative Management, *Report with Special Studies* (Washington, D.C.: Superintendent of Documents. 1937), pp. 39–40.

[30] "Problems of the CAB and the Independent Regulatory Commissions," September 10, 1959, reprinted *The Yale Law Journal,* **LXIX** (May 1960), pp. 931–964. Quoted words at p. 960.

[31] James M. Landis, *The Administrative Process* (New Haven, Conn.: Yale University Press, 1938), p. 10.

[32] See *Final Report of the Attorney General's Committee on Administrative Procedure* (Washington, D.C.: Superintendent of Documents, 1941), pp. 57–59.

separations of functions. In 1938 an administrator was given certain executive functions over civil aeronautics, but a board retained the policy-making and judicial functions. As for safety matters (but these only), the division of functions is now substantially what the committee recommended, for policy-making and executive functions are under the administrator of the Federal Aviation Agency and judicial appeals go to the Civil Aeronautics Board. In maritime regulation, certain functions have been placed under an administrator, but not all policy-making functions. In another instance there has been a separation of prosecuting from judicial functions. In the Taft-Hartley Act of 1946 prosecuting functions were placed in a General Counsel responsible to the President, and judicial functions left in the National Labor Relations Board; the two were independent of each other. Experience under the arrangement has not been happy. This has been due in part to a kind of joint control of the two authorities over field personnel, and in part to fundamental differences between the two over policy. An advisory panel of labor experts has proposed that a solution be sought by placing full control over personnel in the General Counsel, thus fully consummating a separation similar to that recommended by the President's Committee in 1937. On the other hand, the Bureau of the Budget recommended a return to the union of functions which existed prior to 1946, and Dean Landis believes that the frictions over policy cannot be reduced without such a reunion of functions.[33]

The unhappy experience with the incomplete separation of functions in labor-relations administration may not be sufficient basis for conclusions on the merits of proposals for separation in other agencies. The strongest argument can be made for separation in agencies which carry enforcement and judicial functions. But it may be many years before anyone can conclude with confidence whether the model of the Federal Trade Commission, which adjudicates, or that of the Food and Drug Administration, which goes to court for enforcement, is superior for enforcement in sensitive fields. The attempt at separation is not likely to be made for agencies with a more complex assortment of functions. The arguments in favor of separation should, however, be given careful consideration when agencies are constructed for new fields of regulation in the future.

IMPROVING THE COMMISSION SYSTEM. Assuming retention of some or all (and possible creation of new) commissions, what are the routes to most satisfactory performance? There are four kinds of answers given to this question. They comprise some of the lines of suggestion stated earlier in this chapter, but extend beyond these. Most authorities will see some value in each type of answer, but there is much difference of opinion on details and on the relative merits of the four approaches.

One kind of answer starts with the assumption that the commissions' tasks

---

[33] For the various proposals, see James M. Landis, *Report on Regulatory Agencies to the President-Elect*, Committee Print, Committee on the Judiciary, U.S. Senate (86th Cong., 2nd Sess., 1960), pp. 58–65.

are primarily judicial. They do and must operate largely through case-to-case proceedings. Parties should have an opportunity for a judicial-type hearing in such cases. To insure fairness, the agencies should have the maximum amount of independence from political influence. It is often suggested that terms be lengthened, and even sometimes that members of commissions have the same tenure that judges have. The President should not be able to remove commissioners. The examiners within the commissions should also have protections comparable to those of judges. The chief corrective for administrative decision should be judicial review. Congress should change statutes which make administrative decisions nonreviewable, and should give the courts a broader rule of review than the substantial-evidence rule.[34]

An opposed view is that the dominant need is for the commissions to give greater attention to procedural simplification, internal management, and policy development. The real tests of the commissions are their ability to shape policy within statutory limits to meet changing economic conditions, and their ability to get their jobs done expeditiously. Commissions should show more initiative and boldness in procedural simplification. They should give more attention to the development of policy standards. They should make use of techniques of planning and policy development familiar to administrators in other fields. One technique would be to delegate more work so that they would not be bound to the in-basket of petitions. Another would be to make use of policy planning staffs. Internal management should be the responsibility of a single official—the chairman.

A third answer emphasizes the role of Congress. It is argued that commissions are primarily engaged in the elaboration of legislation. They should, therefore, be regarded as "arms of Congress." Congress should maintain continuing supervision over them, and give them direction through new legislation.

A fourth answer emphasizes the role of the President. It is argued that the interest and leadership of the President is vital to the success of regulation. Through his leadership, new policy suggestions can be made, the commissions can be periodically reinvigorated, and steps can be taken as needed for the coordination of policies. His responsibility for leadership arises out of his constitutional position as head of the executive branch and his political position as the people's representative and the agent of the nation as a whole. He should, through his powers of appointment and removal, see that the commissioners are men of competence and integrity and that designees for chairmen have leadership ability; it is appropriate, also, that he consider whether they will be sympathetic to the directions of policy favored by his administration. He should, through his position of general manager,

---

[34] The usual suggestion is for substitution of the "clearly erroneous" for the substantial-evidence test. "Clearly erroneous" on the whole record is the test now used for appellate review of non-jury district-court determinations of facts. Those favoring the substitution believe that it would give the courts more opportunity to substitute their judgments on facts for those of the agencies.

see that there is good management on the commissions, using for this purpose his controls over personnel administration and budget policy and his authority to designate the chairman of most commissions. He should initiate policy studies through departments, his own staff, or special study groups. He should recommend legislation to Congress on economic policy. He should bring to the attention of the agencies urgent public needs, relevant facts, and policy considerations, as he sees fit. This he should do by written or oral communication, according to his choice. All of these have been done in some measure by all presidents of the past thirty years.[35] The suggestions are for more vigorous and continuing leadership. To provide this, suggestions are advanced that provision be made to strengthen the arrangements for study and policy consideration in the departments and the President's office.[36] For example, the Landis study for President-Elect Kennedy recommended creation within the Executive Office of separate offices for coordination and development of transportation policy, communications policy, energy policy, and an Office for Oversight of Regulatory Agencies. An office to coordinate certain aspects of communication policy was established by President Kennedy, and Landis himself served as an advisor on regulatory problems in the President's office in 1961–62.

There are hazards to be avoided on any of the four paths toward improvement. The view that the commissions' functions are primarily judicial can narrow the opportunities for achievement through the regulatory process. The departure from judicial methods in the work of commissions, the supervision of Congress, and the initiative of the President can lead to improper outside influences below the level of policy (a topic to be discussed presently).

A CONCLUDING COMMENT. Many of the problems of operation, direction, and responsibility will be the same whether a commission or a bureau-departmental system of administration is used. Unavoidably, there will be much mixture of functions in administration. Agencies will have adjudicatory, legislative, and executive functions, and combinations or even fusions of these. Whatever was meant in the comment that "an administrative agency" is "part elephant, part jack rabbit, and part field lark,"[37] it is

---

[35] One of the outstanding examples of coordination by the President is the regular Monday morning conferences held for some time in President Eisenhower's office and attended by the Secretary of the Treasury, the Chairman of the Board of Governors of the Federal Reserve, the Chairman of the Council of Economic Advisers, and the President's Economic Adviser.

[36] The President's position is discussed in an unpublished study by Emmette S. Redford on *The President and the Regulatory Commissions* for the President's Advisory Committee on Government Organization in 1960. The suggestion is also made that the President could be given authority to issue directives in certain areas of public policy to implement general statutory objectives and standards. Although this suggestion is not likely to be adopted for general use, it is noteworthy that President Eisenhower—without specific statutory authority, but to meet urgent public needs—issued a formal statement of approved policy standards to guide the agencies in their statutory responsibility of promulgating operational standards for protection against radiation hazards (*Federal Register*, May 18, 1960).

[37] These words in the title of the *Fortune* article, referred to above, were, according

clear that modern administration in general, and modern regulatory administration in particular, has been built in response to situations, not to the separation-of-powers theory. Hence, whatever the type of agency, search for solutions to the problems of administration will carry one down a number of lanes, not a single broad highway. The procedural problems will exist somewhere. The issue of scope of review will remain. Congress will probably act much the same way toward bureaus and commissions. Bureaus and commissions will both be parts of political subsystems, struggling for both independence and support from macropolitics. The President will be limited in his control both of commissions and bureaus, in part because of the limits on his span of attention, and in part because they are operating within their own subsystems. Plural headship and the tradition of independence add some difficulties for the President in giving guidance to commissions, but he is not without encumbrances in asserting leadership over bureaus. The fact is that in the American system of government, where power is widely distributed and integrative forces are weak, it is difficult to obtain coordination and leadership in policy both for bureaus and for commissions.

INTEREST ASSOCIATIONS

In contemporary America law and opinion set high standards for public officials. Public office is regarded as a high public trust to be used only for public purposes. Officials are not to profit economically from the activities of their agencies, and they are to be immune from improper influence and improper bias. The bias of the official is to be grounded in the policies of the law and the standards of the public interest embodied therein. Bias toward persons or toward interests, except in accord with these policies and standards, is improper. Also, not merely evil, but the appearance of evil, is condemned.

The public official, however, operates in constant contact with interested parties. This is part of the necessities of administration: he must have information from them, he must often obtain their cooperation, he must know the limits on his own action set by their attitudes. It is also the result of action of the parties. Individually or as groups, they will be pressing the agencies to avoid unfavorable, or to obtain favorable, response.

In this setting of administrative necessity and pressure of parties, there is danger that the high ideal of public office will be breached. This may occur through favoritism in particular cases or through the regulators' acquiring attitudes overly reflective of those of regulated interest groups. To meet these dangers, and to maintain the ideal of independence in official

---

to that article, used by Judge Prettyman in a series of lectures at the University of Virginia.

position, safeguards of various kinds are built into the system of administration.

Efforts to influence public officials, or appearances of such efforts, are occasionally brought to public attention. The effect is to emphasize both the hazards and the standards expected by the public. The most spectacular set of recent events involved Sherman Adams, commonly referred to as Assistant to the President during the first five years of President Eisenhower's Administration. It developed, in congressional hearings in the summer of 1958, that Adams had received expensive gifts from Bernard Goldfine, a manufacturer who had been a friend since Adams' days as Governor of New Hampshire. Adams had communicated with regulatory agencies on matters affecting Goldfine's business affairs. Adams resigned and, in a television address to the Nation, admitted the imprudence of his actions. Shortly before this, a congressional committee uncovered evidence indicating that Richard E. Mack, member of the Federal Communications Commission, had received loans from an attorney for a successful applicant for a very valuable Miami television channel. Mack had voted for the award to the attorney's client. Upon the suggestion of the Chairman of the House Committee on Legislative Oversight and on the request of the President, Mack resigned. The investigations of the Federal Communications Commission at the time revealed a web of efforts to exert influence on the commission through congressmen and other well-connected persons.[38]

There are some solid protections against influence. Where a decision is to be made on the basis of a formal record, it is regarded as improper for a party to discuss the merits of the case with those who must decide it. Examiners and commissioners will resent any such effort. There have been many bills introduced in Congress in recent years to strengthen the protection against *ex parte* contacts. Some of these would have required that the deciding official place in the record the substance of any communication with him about the case. Yet many decisions affecting individuals—for example, whether to initiate a complaint, or what company shall get a contract—are not required to be made on the basis of a record. In such cases, however, there are protections in the complexities of administrative process. An item of business moves through channels, it goes over the desks of many officials, and it is checked and counterchecked at many points; a number of people share the responsibility of the ultimate decision. Quite infrequently is a single official in a position to make a decision contrary to the facts accumulated and the judgment of others participating in the process of decision. Moreover, men participating in the process have professional pride, they are interested in the integrity of the operations in which they work, they realize

---

[38] See Victor G. Rosenblum, "How to Get Into TV: The Federal Communications Commission and Miami's Channel 10," in Alan F. Westin, *The Uses of Power* (New York: Harcourt, Brace & World, Inc., 1962), pp. 173–228; and Bernard Schwartz, *The Professor and the Commissions* (New York: Alfred A. Knopf, Inc., 1959), *passim*.

that the pinprick of influence can shatter the balloon of public policy, and they have put on an armor of resistance against influence. The result is that repeatedly in the daily affairs of administration, individuals are pushing to exert influence, and their efforts are absorbed like a rock dropping into quicksand.

The greatest danger is that people of great power and influence will be able to make use of high political officials in advancing their interests. It seems clear that a telephone call from the White House is constraint on a public official. It appears, therefore, that the rule which should prevail is that no person connected with the Executive Office of the President should contact agency officials on decisions that are committed to the responsibility of the agencies and that apply law or policy to particular persons. It has been suggested above that it is appropriate for the President to communicate his views on policy to agencies, whether these are bureaus or commissions; but the high office of the President should not be used to influence decisions on individual petitions or other matters relating to specific individuals.[39]

The situation of the congressman is more difficult. The citizen uses his congressman as an aid in dealing with administrative agencies. The congressman may be asked to find out why an application is delayed, or to inform the citizen on what action he can take before an agency. The line which separates the appropriate action of a congressman in finding out the status of a constituent's business with an agency, and the inappropriate action of trying to influence the decision, and the line which separates the congressman's proper concern with policy and efficient administration and his improper concern with special favor for his constituent, are guides for his action, but his constituent may be pressing him to step over either line. Nevertheless, the congressman may be restrained by his view on what is proper, or his influence come to naught because other interests will be opposed and because the administrative process is so efficient in the absorbing of particular pressures.

More difficult than the problem of protecting against influence in particular cases is that of developing a public-interest orientation in the official position. One means of seeking this is through the non-interest principle. This is the principle that the public official should have no personal interest in matters subject to his control as an official. The narrow meaning of the principle is that a man should not gain in a pecuniary way from his own actions as an official, but the broader significance is that it is one means of immunizing the official against biases narrower than those embodied in legally defined policy. The principle was included in the Interstate Commerce Act of 1887, which prohibited commissioners from having any official relationship with, owning stocks and bonds of,

---

[39] It must be noted that the line may sometimes be a hard one to draw, and that there are special problems in those several cases where commission decision is subject to presidential approval.

or having any pecuniary interest in a railroad.[40] Subsequent regulatory statutes sometimes broadened the prohibitions. The Communications Act of 1934 extended the prohibition to interest in any business closely related to communications,[41] acts of 1935 and 1937 on bituminous coal prevented members of the commission or the Consumers' Counsel from owning interests in coal or the competing oil, gas, and hydroelectric power industries,[42] and an act of 1935 prevented appointment of persons to the Maritime Commission who had had excluded interests during the three preceding years.[43] Such provisions have not been included in statutes relating to commissions whose activities affected a span of industries, such as the Federal Trade Commission, the National Labor Relations Board, and the Federal Mediation and Conciliation Service. It would be expected that a public official in such agencies would disqualify himself if a case arose in which he had a personal interest.

Similar restrictions have been applied by some of the Senate committees in considering confirmation of appointees. The Senate Armed Services Committee forced the sale by Charles E. Wilson, of General Motors Corporation, of 39,470 shares of General Motors stock as a condition of confirming his appointment, believing that the Secretary of Defense should not own stock in a company which received large contracts from the government. The same non-interest principle was not applied, however, to George M. Humphrey, who was appointed Secretary of the Treasury. Actions in this position could affect industry generally and the value of any stocks and bonds. Over the years the non-interest principle has been strengthened, particularly in the Senate Armed Services Committee.[44]

There has been much concern that strict application of the non-interest principle to all situations may prevent the government from obtaining qualified personnel. Herring long ago questioned the desirability of restrictions on financial interest of heads of regulatory agencies. The commissions, he thought, needed men of experience, not as spokesmen for business, but to bring to commissions knowledge of "the methods and values of the business world." "One or two such men on each board would make these commissions more balanced and better armed to face all comers."[45] In the wartime emergency many agencies found it necessary to employ persons without requiring that they resign from or give up financial interest in companies affected by their official positions. Special prob-

[40] Section 11.
[41] 48 Stat. 1064, 1066–1067.
[42] 49 Stat. 991, 992–993; 50 Stat. 72, 73–74.
[43] 49 Stat. 1985.
[44] See Association of the Bar of the City of New York, Special Committee on the Federal Conflict of Interest Laws, *Conflict of Interest and the Federal Service* (Cambridge, Mass.: Harvard University Press, 1960), Chapter V.
[45] E. Pendleton Herring, *Federal Commissioners: A Study of Their Careers and Qualifications* (Cambridge, Mass.: Harvard University Press, 1936), pp. 24 and 28.

lems arise with respect to temporary or intermittent consultants and to "without compensation" officials. The problem is particularly acute with respect to scientists who serve on boards in government which make research awards to universities and other institutions with which they have connections. It has been argued that in our mixed economy the blending of public and private endeavor requires reassessment of the assumption that government and business can operate as separate compartments.[46]

Immunization against narrow or improperly biased viewpoints may not be achieved merely by enforcing a personal non-interest principle. Persons who divest themselves of investments or official connections may still have close associations with, or biased attitudes toward, groups with which they were previously connected. There must be hope that occupancy of official position creates new attitudes about responsibility. One idea is that to insure a broader view of responsibility direct representation of regulated interests in administrative positions should be avoided. The issue arises most frequently with respect to board membership. Many persons believe that members of boards should not be appointed as representatives of particular-interest viewpoints. They may, however, regard it as proper to try to get a board with balanced experience. The line between representation and balanced experience may be illustrated by the history of the Federal Reserve Board. President Wilson rejected banker nominations to the Board.[47] However, the Federal Reserve Act of 1913 provided that the President, in making appointments, should "have due regard to a fair representation of the different commercial, industrial, and geographical divisions of the country," [48] and an amendment in 1922 added "agricultural" to the list of interests.[49] Despite the provision, a member of the board declared that its members "without exception, regard themselves as representative not of any group or class interest, but of the common interest and the public welfare." [50]

There are some devices for reconciling opposed needs. One is the use in advisory capacity of persons who have the needed qualifications but are associated with affected private concerns. In this way responsibility for decision can be retained in persons who can meet the strict requirements of the public-service ideal. Another is to place persons who have been associated with regulated industries in subordinate positions. Donald Nelson, head of the War Production Board in World War II, checked the

---

[46] Association of the Bar of the City of New York, *op. cit.*, Chapters VII, VIII, and IX. President Kennedy said, "This need to tap America's human resources for public purposes has blurred the distinctions between public and private life." Message to Congress, April 27, 1961, *Congressional Record*, **CVII**, p. 6454.

[47] Carter Glass, *An Adventure in Constructive Finance* (Garden City, N.Y.: Doubleday & Company, Inc., 1927), pp. 115–116.

[48] Section 10.

[49] 42 Stat. 620.

[50] Address of Chester C. Davis, quoted by Avery Leiserson, *Administrative Regulation: A Study in Representation of Interests* (Chicago: University of Chicago Press, 1942), p. 106.

actions of industry men in the agency by appointing men with broader viewpoints to higher positions.

President Kennedy attacked some of the many problems of interest association and ethical conduct in a message to Congress and an executive order in 1961. In the message he recommended revision of the seven conflict-of-interest statutes of general applicability, five of which had been passed before 1873.[51] Congress did pass a new comprehensive statute dealing with such things as bribery, receipt of outside compensation by an official on any matter on which the United States was a party before a department or agency, receipt of any salary from outside sources for compensation for official services, and disqualification of former government employees acting as agents or attorneys before government on matters connected with their former duties.[52] Following the President's recommendation the new law relaxed the prohibitions for temporary and intermittent personnel. The President also recommended that Congress pass legislation requiring each agency to promulgate a code of behavior governing *ex parte* contacts. The President himself designated a single person in the Executive Office to be responsible for coordinating action on ethical conduct in agencies and reporting to the President. In an order applicable to heads and assistant heads of agencies, full-time members of boards and commissions appointed by the President, and members of the White House staff, he prescribed certain standards. He prohibited incompatible outside employment, receipt of compensation or anything of monetary value except from the government for official services, or taking of gifts under defined inappropriate conditions. The order required each agency to revise or issue similar orders governing its personnel.[53]

Legal standards and protections in administrative process against influence in particular cases, though necessary and beneficial, will not by themselves solve the problem of obtaining independence in official position, either for decision of particular cases or for making policy. The problem is basically one of attitudes and breadth of viewpoint. To retain a perspective as broad as the public interest is difficult for the regulator. For one thing, his agency may have mixed regulatory and promotional activities. The Department of Agriculture, Labor, and Commerce are promotional departments; for this reason they may find it difficult to think in terms larger than the interests of special clienteles in exercising regulatory functions. This was the reason for separation of the conciliation service from the Department of Labor and for moving the Food and Drug Administration from the Department of Agriculture. But promotional and regulatory activities are often inseparable, as in the regulation of civil aeronautics. Moreover, the health of regulated industries is so important a consideration in regulation that the administrator may tend to be fearful of innovations

---

[51] *Congressional Record*, **CVII**, p. 6454.
[52] 76 Stat. 1119 (1962).
[53] Executive Order No. 10939, May 6, 1961, 26 FR 3951.

which will disturb the status quo. Also, he operates in a circle of influences in the subsystem of which his agency is a part. The need, however, is for the broad and the long view. To obtain this, it appears to be necessary to search for men for top administrative positions who have broad experience and wide vision. It may be necessary also to strengthen the policy-planning functions in the office of the President. This is to say that the tug toward clientele viewpoints in the agencies may be counteracted in part by interest in regulatory policy in the spot (the presidency) where all competing interests have to be considered.

PUBLIC-PRIVATE BALANCES

Administrative regulation is a system in which public authorities stand above private management to restrain or direct its action. It is a system which concentrates certain decisions and activities in public agencies and leaves the remainder to private directorates. It will be well, largely by way of summary and extension of previous discussion, to comment on the factors affecting the impact of the public agencies in this system.

It has been noted that regulation may be comprehensive in scope, may extend intimately into details, and may penetrate deeply into policy and management (pages 368ff.). There has been explanation of the means developed to strengthen the authority of these agencies (especially pages 561ff.). It may be concluded also, on the basis of the earlier chapters and particularly the immediately preceding one, that the nation has evolved a system of regulatory techniques upon which the policy makers of the future can draw for almost any type of contingency. The technology—comprising substantive approaches in policy, administrative techniques, organizational devices, and power allocations—has been accepted in the legal system and the customs of the nation.

There are inherent limitations on such a system. One is that in a system of centralized control over many and diverse private decisions means of economizing administrative intervention must be found. The decisions of the small units, or the minor decisions of the large ones, may be exempted, overlooked, or treated in some general manner. A roving power of intervention and bridgehead decisions on rates, rather than approval or disapproval of each rate, may be necessary. This, it will be recalled, has been the technique in regulation of railroad rates. A generalized form of rate decision may be deemed essential. This, the reader will remember, is what the Federal Power Commission did in area pricing for natural gas, and what the Office of Price Administration did in using margin pricing. Some arrangement with the regulated to obtain their cooperation may be employed. This is what the SEC did for security exchanges, and what the FTC tried to accomplish through trade conferences. Use of the rule-making power may be a means of escape from detail. This, it will be remembered, is what the War Production Board did in World War II. One challenge to regulators may be to seek bridgeheads of control and to find means of withdrawing or handling other matters with near automaticity. In doing so, they may be bowing to the necessity for some looseness in the system of regulation.

Second, the regulator will be limited by dependence upon private initiative and decision. It has been shown that much of the action of regulators is taken on petition. This is obvious where the technique of control is licensing, as in communications, airlines, motor carriers, professional occupations, and other areas. It is also true where the agency governs by order or rule, but must depend largely on persons adversely affected to bring matters to its attention. Provision may, of course, be made for agency initiative on some matters. But then there will be limits on what can be gained by compulsion. Private parties must make the decisions on whether they will make investments, on what and under what conditions they will buy and sell, or loan or borrow, and on whether they will consolidate properties or make other changes in ownership and operation.

Third, the regulator will be limited by interest group opinion. Some of those who are regulated may desire a strong policy to curb other groups, but most of the regulated will want regulation that is moderate or easy in approach. To insure this, they will seek balances in their favor within the administrative system. They will want a form of organization which appears safe—a commission or a friendly department. They will be fearful of aggressive personnel, and will watch for upsetting tendencies in the behavior of regulators. They will want to establish for themselves a position in the regulatory subsystem—to make it a triumvirate of administrators, congressmen, and private interests. They will want limitation of agency powers and safeguards on their exercise. To attain these ends, they will shop at any counter where favorable returns may be obtained. They may work within the subsystem, go the courts, reach to the President and other party leaders, or appeal to the public. This public appeal may be openly aggressive, or it may be as subtle as a whisper through the press that government is antagonistic to business, labor, or whatever group believes that its position is threatened.

In view of the limitations in a free society on administrative regulators, we may refer to the question raised by Merle Fainsod as to whether the regulatory machinery may be able to tilt the scales in the conflict of interests.[54] It may be asserted confidently, as Fainsod did, that they can do so. But whether they can move mountains or merely shift a little soil will be dependent upon their power position. The first sinews of strength are in the evolved administrative system—the powers and techniques which have been developed for administrative agencies. A second element in power

[54] "Some Reflections on the Nature of the Regulatory Process," in C. J. Friedrich and Edward S. Mason, *Public Policy, 1940* (Cambridge, Mass.: Harvard University Press, 1940), Chapter 10.

will be acceptance, satisfaction, and support among some interests with strength.[55] With these two elements an agency may tread the mill in an established pattern. But if it is to have the opportunity to move to another treadmill—or changing the metaphor, to establish a new beachhead—it will, it seems, have to obtain the broad interest support reflected in macropolitics. The strength may come from the initial political force reflected in the passage of regulatory legislation and the establishment of the agency. Often this is the agency's great moment for creativeness and impact; it may be the only great moment it will have.[56] Or new surges of political vigor in the presidency and Congress may revive the potentialities for substantial effects. Perhaps also, the energy and imagination of one or more new administrators will contribute to the revival of strength, but such contribution may be expected to wither quickly if not watered through a pipeline from sources of political power.

In sum, in the system of public administrative regulation of private enterprise, the public-private balances will be dependent upon the system of administrative technology, the inherent limitations on regulation as a device, and, beyond all else, on the coagulations of political power and influence.

[55] See comments on E. Pendleton Herring's conclusions, pages 50–51.
[56] See Marver H. Bernstein's chapter on "The Life Cycle of Regulatory Commissions," in his *Regulating Business by Independent Commission* (Princeton, N.J.: Princeton University Press, 1955), Chapter 3.

Part VI. Public Enterprise

Chapter 26. The Scope of Public Enterprise

PUBLIC ENTERPRISE is the supply of a commodity or service to producers or consumers by government. Illustrative are sale of power, lease of lands, loan of money, insurance against hazards, education of youth, operation of an air-traffic system, and construction and maintenance of highways. *Public enterprise contrasts with unregulated private enterprise and with the dual system of regulated private enterprise.* It is often, however, part of the system of promotion of private enterprise. Examples are highways or port facilities for aid of commerce, lease of public lands for grazing of livestock, and operation of credit facilities to aid private entrepreneurs.

Public enterprise may be operated in conformance with the welfare (social service), economic, or mixed model. The welfare model is service without charge. Courts largely, and relief for indigent persons necessarily, are free services; education is usually entirely free at the elementary and secondary levels. The economic model is service for a charge. Power, credit, and insurance are examples of areas of public enterprise operating on this model. The mixed model is service for a price which pays only part of the cost. The postal system has long been an example of this type; education at the college level, when tuition pays part of the cost, is another example.

The term "public enterprise" is sometimes (even quite commonly) used narrowly to apply only to so-called business-type enterprise—that is, to that which operates exclusively or primarily on the economic model. This is, however, a purely artificial restriction of the term "public enterprise." A highway or a bridge may be offered by the public for use free, for a charge which pays the full cost of construction, maintenance, and operation, or for a charge which defrays part of the cost; in any of these cases it is public, not private, enterprise. What is today a business-type operation of government may become tomorrow a social-service type, or vice versa. Thus, bridges are now much more generally supplied free of charge than once was true, and, in contrast, a decision in the author's city in 1961 changed garbage disposal from the welfare to the economic category. There is a social-service objective in most public enterprise, and government has a choice of means, only one of which is business- or commercial-type operation.

As defined above public enterprise includes a large part of the public sector of the economy. It is distinct from the kind of things discussed in Part III—promotion of growth and stability in the economy, maintenance of competition, and regulation of the employment relationship. It contrasts with the regulation of industries, discussed in Part IV, though no fine distinction can be drawn between promotion of private industries and public enterprise. In public enterprise we see government as itself the manager of enterprises. This chapter deals with the full scale of such managerial activity, and the following chapter will give special attention to problems in business-type operations.

It should be noted in advance that in addition to private management and public management, there are diverse forms of mixture of public and private management. A final section of this chapter will present illustrations of the forms of mixture in this country.

ARGUMENTS AND MOTIVATIONS

The argument of the state socialist that public ownership of the means of production and distribution is necessary to correct injustices of the capitalist system has never had wide appeal in this country. The primary reason is that the American has not seen injustices on a scale which would make him interested in changing the basic system of dependence on private enterprise. Capitalism in this country has exhibited results far different from those postulated in socialist theory. The existence of a large middle class, the ability of the unions to obtain high wages under capitalism, the corrections of evils through regulation, the redistribution of income through taxation and social expenditure, and the social mobility allowed under existing institutions have combined to prevent any large-scale attack on private enterprise. Even the Negro in his awakening finds no fault with the economic system, but desires only access to it. Probably the largest assault on the system was the agrarian socialism promoted by the Nonpartisan League in 1919 in North Dakota. Legislation in the state provided for the establishment of a state bank, the manufacture by the state of farm products and machinery, the operation of mills, elevators, and warehouses, and the establishment of a Home Building Association to provide homes for residents of the state. Yet this program of legislation was designed to help the dominant private economic enterpriser of the state—the farmer. It was a subsidiary socialism to promote the primary system of private agrarian enterprise.

On the other hand, the existence of private savings and the daring of the American entrepreneur made unnecessary the reliance on public investment which is manifest today in underdeveloped countries. In these countries the shortage of private capital, and the indigenous nationalism which fears control by foreign capitalists, lead to reliance on public capital on a scale which was never contemplated in this country.

The American has sought remedies for the problems he saw in his economic and social system in a greater diversity of approaches than was contemplated in socialist theory. He has used public enterprise on a large scale. In fact, public enterprise in education is one of the most notable characteristics of the American social system. Yet he has great faith in regulation, a greater faith than has existed in most other countries. In the case of labor he has sought to strengthen self-help. Where slack has appeared in desired developments, he has frequently resorted to promotion of private enterprise. More lately, he has used the contract system for production of defense and space goods. He has not accepted the dogmatism of socialist theory about public ownership; he has, though often repeating dogmatically the doctrine of the superiority of private capitalism, adjusted his approaches to the particular situations with which he has been concerned.

What other arguments are made for or against government enterprise? One argument is that government enterprise is justified when private enterprise is deficient for the task. This was the standard of decision offered by Adam Smith. He wrote that the sovereign had:

. . . the duty of erecting and maintaining certain public works and certain public institutions which it can never be for the interest of any individual, or small number of individuals, to erect and maintain; because the profit could never repay the expense of any individual or small number of individuals, though it may frequently do much more than repay it to a great society.[1]

Some modifications of Smith's statement may be required to make it an acceptable test of the "duty" of government in the twentieth century. First, Smith did not have any conception of the great growth of corporate enterprise to come. He speaks of "any individual, or small number of individuals." Unless one were to take the view that large private corporations were undesirable, he would say that Smith's test should be restated in terms of the ability of private enterprise in any of its forms, including the corporate. Yet the ability of modern corporations to perform great tasks is tremendous. The limitation on their adequacy seems not to be one of size of the undertaking, but only of opportunity to make a profit. Perhaps a trip to the moon is beyond private abilities, but certainly it is beyond private interests because of the lack of promise of profit. The test that Smith offers would become, for most people at least, one of the adequacy of corporate enterprise.

Second, the test appears meaningless unless related to the scope and terms of the service supplied. Private enterprise can supply education, but

[1] Adam Smith, *An Inquiry into the Nature and Causes of the Wealth of Nations*, edited by Edwin Cannan, 6th ed. (London: Methuen and Co., Ltd., 1950), II, p. 185.

can it do so on terms which will make universal education possible? Private enterprise could today run a postal system, but would it give universal service? Would it, for example, have set up rural free delivery? Private enterprise might build a road system, but would it build one which ran to less profitable or to no-profit locations? The question becomes one of what areas or how many people shall be served. The decisions may be made as value judgments, or they may be made as political judgments—that is, in terms of the pressure of interests and the anticipated response of the voters.

An alternative to public supply is, of course, private supply with a subsidy. There are, with respect to housing, for example, three alternatives, one, two, or all of which may be selected: full employment with good incomes, and perhaps also with government support for low interest and long payment periods; government housing to those unable to pay for adequate private housing; government subsidy to private housing developments. Subsidy was not mentioned by Smith. There is a tendency to condemn it in principle, and accept it in practice only in circumstances regarded as exceptional.

Undoubtedly there are some who would prefer subsidized private enterprise to public enterprise, at least in some areas of economic activity. Others may regard Smith's test as a good and sufficient one, and still others will think of it as only one useful test. John Stuart Mill added another kind of argument, and discussed it in broad and restricted terms. He raised the issue of the comparative advantages and disadvantages of corporate and government enterprise. He thought there would be in free countries "greater publicity and more active discussion and comment" with regard to government affairs than there would be among stockholders with respect to corporate affairs. This was a way of saying that stockholder enforcement of responsibility of corporate directors would not be as great as public enforcement of responsibility of government. He concluded that the defects of "government management do not seem to be necessarily much greater, if necessarily greater at all, than those of management by joint-stock." Nevertheless, he preferred corporate management because of the dangers of overloading the chief officers of government and diverting their attention from duties which they alone could perform; of "swelling the direct power and indirect influence of government," and of multiplying collisions between the government and its citizens; and of "concentrating in a dominant bureaucracy all the skill and experience in the management of large interests," and all the organized action in the community.[2]

A twentieth-century American, with knowledge of the triumphs and defects of corporate management and of the accomplishments and hazards of government management, could expand the arguments on the relative

[2] John Stuart Mill, *Principles of Political Economy*, 7th ed. (1871), W. J. Ashley (ed.) (New York: Longmans, Green and Co., Inc., 1909), Chapter 11.

efficiency and responsibility of each. Undoubtedly, however, most Americans would find Mill's arguments for leaving economic enterprise generally to private corporations convincing. His arguments against overloading government and in favor of a pluralistic society have even stronger force than when he advanced them.

But Mill continued the discussion with a more restricted focus. He saw that there would be monopolistic enterprises. In such instances it would be necessary to have either government enterprise or *regulated* private management. He himself thought the reasons were preponderate in favor of local public ownership for gas and water companies, and that regulation was better in the case of roads and canals.

What Mill did was to raise the issue of choice between regulation and ownership, an issue which has been debated in this country in a multitude of forums. Because of monopoly, oligopoly, or other factors in certain industries, it becomes necessary to impose detailed and comprehensive regulation or to establish public ownership. For many persons the issue is not, then, one of ability of private enterprise to supply the service, but one of choice between two techniques.

The issue might be approached coldly and deliberately, as an English nonsocialist Liberal lecturing in this country suggested it should, as quest for "a technical answer to a technical question." If so, one will find that when the technical or specific facets of the question are defined and considered, the answer is definitely a nontechnical judgment on uncertainties. In both regulation and ownership a burden is placed upon government. There is one initial advantage in ownership: capital can be obtained cheaply. Capital in a government enterprise is normally bonded debt. Where the ratio of capital investment to sales is high, as in some public utilities, then this advantage is substantial. Yet it can be dissipated if there is inefficiency or political spoils. American history reveals much inefficiency and political spoils in government bureaucracies, and at the same time it reveals much spoliation of consumers by utility companies. In either case it can be anticipated that the gross excesses of the past will probably not exist in the future, for government bureaucracy is now more efficient, and private bureaucracy is more adequately regulated. One of the strongest arguments for public enterprise is the record of deficiencies in regulation; but this contention may be countered by the claim that these deficiencies, though to some extent inherent and incorrectable, are now sufficiently corrected to make regulation a reasonably satisfactory method. An argument may be made that in public enterprise it is too easy to adopt pricing policies which result in deficits, but this may be countered by the argument that in private ownership it is too difficult to expand service to as many persons as should have it. The answer on this question may be the critical one in one's judgment on public or private enterprise in a particular area of service, and the issue of deficit or nondeficit service is considered separately in the next chapter. Ultimately, as the technical aspects are isolated, one reaches the question of progressiveness in policy and management. How can one have assurance of research on new technique, readiness to innovate, vision of opportunities, and efficient internal management in either private or public monopoly? Where it is a national monopoly, as in the postal and telephone systems, one may make a guess as to whether the pressure of politics or the opportunities for gain will offer a surer route toward these advantages. Where the service is decentralized to many systems, as in power and education, it may be hoped that the pluralism of the situation will produce centers of initiative and innovation, whether the service is publicly or privately supplied, or in part by each method.

The generality of these considerations is removed only when they are brought to focus on a particular situation. Attitudes may be developed by reason and prejudice, but decisions are made in response to situations. Events may have fixed a pattern of private or public ownership for supply of a service which it would be unreasonable, even fantastic, to consider abandoning. Only at particular times, in certain places, and in the course of a sequence of events will the issue become relevant. A proposal to adopt government ownership of railroads would present a different balance of considerations in the 1960's than it did when the Windom Committee proposed a competing government transcontinental line in 1874. The development of a new multipurpose river project provides a different setting for consideration of the issue of public power than exists in other situations.

There are many special factors which lead to government enterprise. Governments may try to economize on their own costs. As a result the United States and some states governments run their own printing establishments, many public institutions operate their own laundries, and many other miscellaneous enterprises are conducted. Public schools operate cafeterias or dormitories for the convenience and economy of students. Some states operate liquor-distribution stores in order to provide a tight control over liquor sales or to obtain revenues. Some cities apparently operate power plants for the profit to be obtained therefrom. Finally, public enterprises may be established merely because this seems to be the necessary or appropriate way to extend a service to the community generally. Examples are the public schools and public park and playground facilities.

The relation of the above arguments and motivations to experience in the United States can be briefly summarized. In the United States there has been no widespread sentiment for government enterprise because of the belief either that the capitalistic system produces injustices or that government enterprise was generally preferable to corporate enterprise. The opposed opinion on both of these points has dominated. Consideration of public enterprise occurs in narrower focus. One criterion for determining in a mixed economy what commodities and services government should supply directly is whether private enterprise is deficient for a specific task to be undertaken. Undoubtedly this is a weighty, and normally the dominant, factor in a decision to adopt public enterprise. Another approach is a comparison of the relative advantages of the dual system of regulation of private corporations and the direct system of government supply in those areas of service where one or the other of these methods must be chosen. Such comparison may influence men's judgments, but only within a narrow part of the area within which decisions for public enterprise are made. There are, in addition, a variety of special factors leading to public enterprise, and in many cases it appears that public enterprise is selected for the sole reason that it appears to be the necessary or most practicable means of supplying an important public service on the scale, terms, and conditions deemed to be in the public interest.

AREAS OF PUBLIC ENTERPRISE

It is difficult to find any scheme for classifying the areas of public enterprise. It will be sufficient if the discussion shows the broad scope, the major variations, and some of the features in important areas.

SOME OBVIOUSLY PUBLIC AREAS. We may begin by mere notation of some areas in which private enterprise seems most clearly an impossible or unlikely substitute. These are national defense, maintenance of domestic peace, fire protection and traffic control, establishment of a comprehensive system of aid to the indigent, and exploration in space. Note may be taken also of the diversified public undertakings in conservation of natural resources, extending to forests, land and minerals, water, and fish and wildlife. Much of the program of conservation is on the nation's own property, particularly in the western part of the country. Some of the program has regulatory features, and for oil and soil they have been described in earlier chapters. In addition to the regulatory activities and to conservation on government property, there are extensive service, promotional, and developmental functions. Examples of the service function are the activities of the states, with national assistance, in forest-fire prevention, and the arrangements in the states, again with national assistance, for county agents to aid farmers and for resident foresters to help forest owners. Illustrative of promotional activities are those for the creation of soil-conservation districts in which farmers participate in conservation programs. Illustrative of the development functions are the irrigation and flood-control projects of the national government. Taken in combination, these various natural-resource functions reflect a large mixture of public with private enterprise in this nation's development.

Flowing from the government's proprietary position with respect to land and other resources are some commercial-type operations. Government sells water for irrigation. It takes bids from private operators for timber-cutting rights. It leases lands to ranchers for livestock grazing. It leases land also for development of oil and gas resources.

SOME OUTSTANDING AREAS OF SOCIAL SERVICE. Note may be taken next of four areas of public enterprise which are conducted predominantly on the welfare model. The first is education. Next to national defense, this is the largest undertaking in the nation. Some features of the system are noteworthy in this summary. Government does not carry the whole burden of education, for parochial and other private schools and colleges maintained under various auspices provide a choice of educational facilities. The system is decentralized in operation, the growing national aid not having supplanted state and local responsibility. As a result of these two features, the safeguards of pluralism are present in education. Yet government seeks to provide universal opportunity. Hence, education is supplied either free of charge, or at a tuition charge which meets only a fraction of the cost. The second is hospitals and associated medical care. Governments, especially the state governments, have maintained hospitals for treatment of special kinds of illness, such as tuberculosis and mental illness. They have, particularly through city and county governments, maintained general hospitals, at which they supplied both paid and charity care. The national government maintains hospitals for members of the armed services and an extensive hospital system for veterans who can meet the requirements for admission. Hospital care, like education, is supplied by both public and private enterprise. This pluralism in supply is maintained by the Hospital Survey and Construction (Hill-Burton) Act, under which national funds are made available through the state governments for construction of public and private hospitals and other health facilities. The third area is recreation. Cities maintain parks, playgrounds, and other recreation centers, and state and national governments provide a vast system of parks. There are some charges for services supplied, but these are nominal with respect to the total value of the services. The fourth area is transportation facilities. This includes streets, roads, canals, port facilities, and river navigation developments. All levels of government are involved. Charges may be made for port facilities or for transportation over toll roads or bridges. By and large, however, the public expenditures are recouped by taxation, as in the case of other social services.

COMMERCIAL-TYPE OPERATIONS. We come now to those areas where commercial-type operations are dominant in government enterprise. The summary will show a considerable variety and extent of such operations.

The Post Office. There comes to mind, first, the largest commercial-type government operation in the Western world. The Post Office carries the mail and distributes it through some 40,000 post offices and a system of home and office delivery, and operates a savings-bank system for small depositors. It is more than a business operation. From time to time it performs services for the government—for example, registration of aliens in World War I, and sale of bonds in both world wars. It may be regarded also as a facility to commerce because of its dependable service, low rates on advertising through second- and third-class mail, and universal delivery and pick-up, and also as a social-service institution because of the cheap distribution of newspapers and magazines and the universal service, extending to almost every hamlet and farm. These things create or contribute to deficits, and give rise to issues of public policy (to be discussed in the first section of the next chapter).

Electric-Power Sales. One of the most persistent conflicts over public policy in the twentieth century has been that between public and private power advocates. The conflict is exhibited in community struggles over whether supply should be through public or private generating and distributing facilities; state struggles over whether rates of public enterprises should be regulated by state commissions; local, state, and national struggles over expansion of public facilities; and national struggles over whether preference should be given to public and cooperative agencies in sale of power from multipurpose river projects. The results in the first three of these struggles have varied from place to place; the answer on the last has generally been, except for certain events in the Eisenhower Administration, toward preference to public and cooperative undertakings. Certain features of the resulting system are significant. First, public and private enterprise have divided the field, roughly in a four-to-one ratio, between private undertakings on the one hand and public and cooperative undertakings on the other, as determined on the basis of kilowatt-hours supplied by each to ultimate consumers. Second, public supply has been rendered through every kind of area organization, including municipalities, states, local power districts, regional authorities, and national agencies, and often through the cooperative effort of two or more of these. Third, the largest public power enterprises are those developed as part of river projects where power generation and sale is only one among a number of public objectives.

Municipally owned power utilities exist in about two thousand cities in the United States and Canada. The cities range across the spectrum in size— up to cities the size of San Antonio, Seattle, and Los Angeles. The local systems may exist independently of any other power developments, but sometimes are combined in power pools, or purchase power from large public power administrations.

Public power projects have been developed in the states in other ways than through the cities. An author found in 1951 that the laws of twelve states provided for public power districts.[3] These districts have potential advantages over municipal systems in that they can provide for integrated supply to city and rural purchasers and can operate over large areas. In Nebraska, where all electric power is publicly supplied, the power districts cover most of the state. Power districts may, as in Washington, be a means of taking advantage of the opportunity to purchase low-cost power at whole-

[3] See "Power Districts: An Emerging Device for Low Cost Electricity," *Yale Law Journal,* **LX** (March 1951), pp. 483–505.

sale from national projects. Another device used in the states is the river authority. In Texas the state river authority is a standard device for public power projects. One of these, the Lower Colorado River Authority—a multi-purpose river project—developed a public power monopoly over ten central Texas counties. The New York Power Authority, in contrast, is a large single-purpose agency. A creature of state law, it has been licensed, under congressional directive, by the Federal Power Commission to develop, in partnership with Canada, the power potentials of the Niagara and St. Lawrence rivers. It has, in cooperation with the Hydro-Electric Power Commission of Ontario, harnessed sections of the river and constructed generating plants, and has built transmission lines to carry power to cities, rural electric cooperatives, the state of Vermont, private utilities, and basic industries to which it has marketed power.[4]

In the national government, power facilities are constructed by the Army Engineers, the Bureau of Reclamation, and the Tennessee Valley Authority (TVA). It is marketed by four units in the Department of Interior—namely, the Bonneville Power Administration, the Southwestern Power Administration, the Southeastern Power Administration, the Bureau of Reclamation—and the TVA.

The Bonneville Power Administration (BPA) is the marketing agency for power generated at dams in the Columbia River basin. BPA serves an area of 220,000 square miles covering Oregon, Washington, Northern Idaho, Western Montana, and a small corner of Nevada, with a population in excess of 5 million people. During the fiscal year 1962 BPA supplied slightly over half of the total energy generated by major utilities in this area. In fiscal year 1962 power sales totaled 29.2 billion kilowatt-hours for $68,900,000. Of this total, 43.4 per cent was to publicly owned utilities, 10.8 per cent to privately owned utilities, 30.1 per cent to the aluminum industry, and 15.7 per cent to other industries and federal agencies. Its low rates have resulted in residential and farm use of electricity two and a half times the national average at one-half the national average price. In addition to marketing power generated by the Bureau of Reclamation and the Army Engineers, it has constructed a high-voltage grid system to carry power from public and private generating stations to the region's major load centers. On this grid, nonfederal power is transmitted under long-term "wheeling" contracts. In a study completed in 1961 it was found to be feasible to construct high-voltage transmission lines into California with mutual benefit to the Pacific Northwest and the Pacific Southwest, but action on the proposal awaits congressional appropriation.[5]

The Southwestern Power Administration markets public power generated in the Southwest. Dams are constructed in Arkansas, Missouri, Oklahoma, and Texas. During the fiscal year 1962 this administration marketed ap-

[4] See Robert Moses, "The Niagara Power Project," *State Government,* **XXXV** (Summer 1962), pp. 155–157.

[5] Recommended by President Kennedy in his budget message of January 17, 1963.

proximately 2⅓ billion kilowatt-hours for almost 16 million dollars. Of the revenue dollar, 56 per cent was from sales to cooperatives, 13 per cent from sales to municipalities and public authorities, 12 per cent from sales to the aluminum industry, and 19 per cent from sales to private utilities.

The Southeastern Power Administration markets power generated at Army Engineers' dams in Alabama, Georgia, Tennessee, Kentucky, Virginia, and North Carolina. In fiscal 1962 it sold power for over 23 million dollars to fifty-two public bodies, seventy-four rural cooperatives, one national agency, and four privately owned utilities.

The Bureau of Reclamation itself markets power generated in the Missouri River Basin, at the Falcon Dam on the Rio Grande River, and at certain other dam sites under bureau jurisdiction.

The largest marketer of power in the national government is the TVA. Its hydroelectric system generates less power than is sold by the Bonneville Power Administration, but this system now produces only about one-third of TVA's electricity. Initially only a hydroelectric system, TVA now gets about two-thirds of its power from seven steam plants. In 1962 its revenue from power sales was approximately a quarter of a billion dollars, obtained from sale of over 60 billion kilowatt-hours.

TVA's power sales have had both a social and a military significance. Upon creation in 1933, TVA embarked on an aggressive program to promote the use of electricity in the Tennessee Valley. This was part of its program for development of better living standards in the region. It adopted promotional rates on sales to municipalities and rural cooperatives. It gave managerial aid to its buyers, required that they pass on low rates to consumers, demonstrated uses of electricity on farms, and negotiated with manufacturers for better prices on electrical equipment for households and farms. Its latest success involving electricity has been in multiplying the use of electricity for home heating. It developed a regional public power area, and by 1962 supplied 102 municipalities, 51 cooperatives, and 2 small privately owned utilities. Electricity use in the region is far above the national average, and the average cost is approximately 40 per cent of the national average. TVA went further than this; it set out to establish a yardstick on the proper charge for electricity. (This effort and the finances of TVA will have further attention in the next chapter.)

The military significance of TVA is registered in the sales to the Atomic Energy Commission, the National Aeronautics and Space Administration, other public agencies, and to private industries contracting with the government. Its sales to public agencies have recently exceeded those to municipalities and cooperatives.

Credit. The national government has been especially active in rural electrification. It does not itself operate facilities and sell power. Its chief function is to loan money to rural cooperatives to finance their power projects. This function is carried out by the Rural Electrification Administration (REA) in the Department of Agriculture. The administration has not been a passive banker. It has promoted the formation of rural cooperatives and given technical assistance to them. Its efforts have received support from the national power-marketing agencies, which have made power available to rural cooperatives. In 1935, when REA was established, only about 11 per cent of the farms of the country had electricity; today more than 95 per cent receive electricity, and the use of electricity on farms is constantly expanding. The initiative for this development came from REA, and even today more than half the electrified farms are served by power systems financed through REA loans. Today loans are made also to independent telephone companies and cooperatives for extending rural telephone service.

The longest continuous experience of the national government in supply of credit is in the programs now operated by the Farm Credit Administration. In 1916, when a 10 per cent interest rate was common on loans to farmers, Congress provided for the establishment of the Federal Land Banks, through which long-term mortgages could be financed at low interest rates. Beginning in 1923 with the establishment of the Federal Intermediate Credit Banks, provision was made for loans to meet other needs. Today the system has three parts, operated primarily through three sets of banks located together in twelve district cities. The first is the land-bank system. Farmers desiring to obtain long-term credit through this system join one of the nearly eight hundred local land-bank associations affiliated with the twelve district Federal Land banks. The second is the production-credit system, through which loans up to a maximum period of seven years are made. Farmers borrowing through the system become members of, and obtain credit from, one of nearly five hundred production-credit associations. The regional Federal Intermediate Credit Banks discount paper for, and make loans to, the associations, to other agricultural corporations, and to state and national banks which lend to farmers. The combined share of total loans to farmers of the land-bank and production-credit institutions on January 1, 1962, was 17.6 per cent. The third part of the system is credit for cooperatives. Agricultural cooperatives borrow money from the twelve district banks for cooperatives. A Central Bank for Cooperatives participates in larger loans and makes direct loans to the district banks. The whole system is really a mixed system of government and farmer cooperation. Although the national government was once the largest stockholder in the Federal Land banks, all the capital stock of the banks and of the associated federal bank associations is now owned by farmer borrowers. Additional capital is obtained by sales of bonds to investors. The government still in 1962 owned stock in Federal Intermediate Credit banks, banks for cooperatives, and a few production-credit associations; but legislation in 1955 and 1956 provides for gradual retirement of the government's investment.[6] Ultimately, the government's position is to become entirely one of supervision and regulation of a system which it established and initially financed.

Still another part of the agricultural credit system is the Farmers Home

[6] 69 Stat. 655, 70 Stat. 659.

Administration. Established during the Depression to assist operators of family-size farms, its loan program has been expanded through the years. It has viewed its function in broader terms than the supply of credit, and has provided technical farm and money management assistance to borrowers. The core of its original program was loans for up to forty years and at low interest rates to purchasers of family-size farms. In addition to these loans, it now makes operating loans for purchase of machinery, livestock, fertilizer, and like needs; for construction and maintenance of farm buildings; for re-establishment of normal operations after flood, drought, or other disasters; for soil and water conservation, and for watershed protection and flood prevention. The allowable services were expanded in the Housing Act of 1961,[7] including the extension of housing loans to residents of rural communities. This administration combines social objectives with banking operations to a greater extent than its strictly banking sister, the Farm Credit Administration. Moreover, its operations are not as extensive as those of FCA, for in 1962 it financed slightly less than 4 per cent of farm debt.

The final part of the government's agricultural credit activity is loans made to farmers by the Commodity Credit Corporation. This is part of the program of stabilization of agricultural prices, and has been discussed in the chapter on agriculture.

Although business credit is not now one of the large programs of government, it once was. For over twenty years the Reconstruction Finance Corporation (RFC) was the nation's largest banker. It was created in 1932 to avert bankruptcies by loans to railroads, banks, insurance companies, and industrial corporations. In 1938 it was authorized also to purchase securities and other obligations of business enterprises. During the Depression it assisted in the financing of various relief and recovery operations. It also was used as an instrument for making loans to other government credit agencies, to state and local governments, and to foreign governments. During World War II it financed the construction, often through subsidiary corporations, of public and private plants engaged in production of armament and strategic materials. It was also responsible for the operation of the government-owned synthetic-rubber plants and tin-smelting facilities, and for lease of certain other government properties. In 1947 it was given the responsibility of making loans to small businesses. After loaning approximately 49 billion dollars, the RFC went out of existence in 1954.

The small-business loan activities of the RFC were transferred to the Small Business Administration, created by the act of 1953 which provided for liquidation of RFC. It can make loans to small businesses, either directly or with participation of banks or other private lenders. It is delegated special authority to make disaster loans and to assist small companies in obtaining government contracts.

The government is engaged in a variety of other business-credit opera-

[7] 75 Stat. 149.

tions. The Export-Import Bank, established in 1934, makes loans to finance export and import trade. The Maritime Administration holds mortgages on ships sold after World War II and under the Merchant Marine Act of 1936. The Veterans Administration makes loans to veterans for purchase of farms, construction of homes, and other purposes. A number of other agencies make miscellaneous types of loans.

Insurance. The United States government is the largest insurer in the nation. Its insurance programs are designed to stabilize and support finance and business, and to protect individuals from the hazards of life.

Bank deposits up to $10,000 for each depositor are insured by the government-operated Federal Deposit Insurance Corporation, created in 1933. Investor accounts in federal savings-and-loan associations and approved state-chartered institutions are insured by the Federal Savings and Loan Insurance Corporation, established in 1934 and operated as part of the quasi-independent Home Loan Bank system.

Loans for construction, improvement, and purchase of residential property, either owner-occupied or rental, are insured by the Federal Housing Administration (FHA). This is done under a number of separate programs, which vary in detail. At the end of 1961 FHA-insured loans on single-family residences were about 30 billion dollars, or 19 per cent of the total mortgage debt on nonfarm homes; on multifamily projects they were about 6.5 billion, or 30 per cent of the outstanding mortgage debt. The Veterans Administration also insures or guarantees loans for such purposes as construction or purchase of a home, and conduct of farming or business operations. In 1962 such guarantees extended to about 5 per cent of the nonfarm mortgage recordings of $20,000 or less, and a few years earlier the percentage had been as high as 16. These programs of the FHA and VA are supported by the activities of the Federal National Mortgage Association, which buys and sells mortgages in order to support a secondary market for these and maintain their prices.

Personal insurance extending to retirement, disability, and survivors' benefits is carried by the Social Security Administration for the major portion of the population. Life and disability insurance is carried by the Veteran Administration for approximately 6 million policy holders. Unemployment insurance is provided under a joint national-state program. Workmen's-compensation insurance is provided in some states by a government insurance agency.

Housing. Particular note should be taken of the government's role in construction and rental of residential housing for low-income persons. During the Depression the Public Works Administration constructed and administered over fifty housing projects in scattered American cities. These were subsequently transferred to municipal ownership and administration. A long-range program was established by the United States Housing Act of 1937, and expanded in the Housing Act of 1949.[8] The program established is one

---

[8] 50 Stat. 888, 63 Stat. 413.

of national-municipal cooperation. A Public Housing Administration obtains funds through government-guaranteed bonds and notes. It makes loans at low interest rates to municipalities and also grants annual subsidies to these. The cities construct housing facilities and rent them to persons of low income. They must also make a contribution to the projects to enable them, with the national subsidy, to operate at low-rent levels. Under the program about half a million units had been constructed in more than 1,500 communities by 1962.

Under the Housing Act of 1949 and subsequent amendments thereto, there has been national-municipal cooperation in an urban-renewal program. The national government makes grants to assist cities in planning for redevelopment of slum areas. It also grants to cities amounts up to two-thirds of the cost, and in smaller cities up to three-fourths, for acquiring blighted areas, clearing or rehabilitating obsolete or dilapidated structures, and making sites available for new development. The redevelopment may include betterment of existing properties or their destruction to make way for new ones; the redeveloped area may be devoted to industrial and commercial as well as residential uses. The sites may be made available for private development, or may be used for public projects. The national phases of the program are administered through the Urban Renewal Administration. By the end of 1961 about five hundred cities had participated in the expanding program, and some one hundred projects had been completed.

Notice should be given also to the Community Facilities Administration (in the Housing and Home Finance Agency) and the programs it administers. It makes loans for college housing, public facilities, housing for elderly persons, public and private nonprofit organizations to assist in industrial expansion in redevelopment areas, and for other purposes.

MISCELLANEOUS ENTERPRISES

It has been noted that state and local governments may operate hospitals on a commercial basis, though providing some charity care. It has also been noted that highways, bridges, and port facilities may be operated as business-type enterprises. One of the most notable and largest business-type public enterprises in the United States is the Port of New York Authority, which, as representative of the states of New York and New Jersey (under a compact between them), constructs and operates bridges, tunnels, terminal facilities, and airports. Recently, the states in the Delaware River Basin joined in a compact to establish an agency to control the use of water from the basin, prevent water pollution, provide flood protection, generate and transmit hydroelectric power, develop recreational facilities, to provide watershed management, and to borrow money for these purposes; a unique feature is the representation of the United States government through an appointee of the President on the interstate commission established to plan and administer the extensive program contemplated by the compact. Airports have generally been built by state and local governments, normally with national aid in accordance with the provisions of the Federal Airport Act. In about one-third of the states, packaged liquor sales are made by the states, either at wholesale or retail, or both.

The cities are engaged in many types of commercial enterprises in addition to power, public housing, airports, and port facilities, already mentioned. Almost seventy urban transit systems are government-owned in the United States and Canada together; in 1961 six additional transit systems were acquired by cities in the United States. Of the twelve largest cities in the United States, six own and operate transit systems. In 1961 there were about six hundred municipal gas utilities, over four hundred of which had been formed since 1950. Water is normally supplied by the city, and this is almost universally true of large cities. Garbage disposal is a normal city function, and may be done for a charge. Among other enterprises operated on a commercial basis by some cities are slaughter houses, coal yards, ice plants, laundries, swimming pools, golf courses, and cemeteries.

MIXED ENTERPRISE

In many areas of the economy there is so much interaction between and complementary performance by private and public enterprise that the resulting system can be described most accurately as one of mixed enterprise.

This may be the result of promotional activities of government which support the expansion of industries. Viewing the broad span of American history, one may witness certain large increments in the ways of promoting industries. First, there was subsidy, which may be witnessed initially in the grants to railroad corporations and which has now branched out along other lines to additional industries. Next, there was conservation of resources, which now assists the development of many industries. Then came government credit, guarantees of loans, insurance of assets and credits, expanding from the Farm Credit Act of 1916 into a maze of credit and insurance functions for industries. Finally has come research and accompanying large-scale developmental projects, opening up large opportunities for private enterprise in areas as diverse as drugs, electronics, and atomic energy. And beyond all of these one may witness the early birth and the vigorous growth of public education—the most significant of all means for supporting the growth of enterprise.

One may look, in addition, at particular industries for illustrations of the mixture of public and private enterprise. Public promotion is well illustrated by the airline industry. There is a commercial-transportation industry, and back of that a manufacturing industry. The foundation for both, in addition to the daring enterprise of private entrepreneurs and flyers, is cooperative research and development on new types of planes by government—chiefly through the military—and manufacturers, the direct public subsidization of a commercial air-transport industry, the public development of air-traffic controls, and the public construction of airports and ground facilities. The service the public gets flows from the combination of public and private activities.

One of the most familiar illustrations of mixed enterprise is the Federal Reserve System. It has been described "as a pyramid having a private base, a mixed middle level and a public apex." [9] The private base is formed by the commercial banks. The public apex is a Board of Governors of seven members appointed by the President with Senate approval. At the mixed, middle level are the Federal Reserve banks. They perform a public role as members of the central banking system. Also, five of their presidents are voting members, along with the seven Reserve Board members, of the Federal Open Market Committee. Each Federal Reserve bank has a board of nine members, six elected by the member commercial banks of the district and three (including the chairman and deputy chairman) appointed by the Board of Governors. The president of the bank is selected by this mixed board of nine members, subject to the veto of the Board of Governors. Formally, the functions of the Federal Reserve System are distributed in this mixed mechanism; in actual practice, however, there has been a tendency toward centralization in the public portion (the Board of Governors) and in the mixed public-private portion (the Open Market Committee).[10]

Another illustration is in the mixed enterprises supplying agricultural credit. The credit institutions operating under the Farm Credit Administration have largely been mutualized; that is, the stock is owned entirely, or to a large extent, by borrowers. Capital is also obtained through the sale of bonds on the private market. But government organized the system, owns some of the stock in some of the institutions (and once owned more), and supervises it and participates in the management. There is, in this instance, a combination of public, borrower, and investors' capital, and of borrower and public management.

Still another illustration is in the multiple forms of enterprise in the supply of housing. The housing industry is still dominantly private. Private contractors build the units, and private lenders supply the capital. But the government has set up a system of Home Loan banks, similar to the Federal Reserve banks, to provide a credit reserve for savings and home-financing institutions; and the banks, like the Federal Reserve banks, can be viewed as neither strictly public nor private institutions. It has insured loans, maintained a secondary market for mortgages, and insured deposits in savings-and-loan institutions. It is providing financial aid in the redevelopment of slum areas. Cities build and rent some housing units. Though dominantly private,

[9] Michael D. Reagan, "The Political Structure of the Federal Reserve System," *The American Political Science Review*, **LV** (March 1961), pp. 64–76.
[10] For details see Reagan, *ibid*.

housing construction and repair, in its total aspects, is both public and private enterprise.

In different ways, health illustrates a similar combination of public and private activity. Through the National Institutes of Health alone government expenditures on health research are approaching the billion-dollar-a-year figure. This money is channeled to a multitude of public and private researchers. Public medical schools parallel private ones. The national government, through the Veterans Administration, the armed services, and other agencies maintaining hospitals, is the nation's largest hospital supplier. States and cities also supply hospital services, and the national government now helps finance both public and private hospital construction. Government health services to the public are numerous and diversified. Medical assistance is now given to some of the needy aged in some states through a national-state program. Charity care to the aged and others through public institutions is extensive. On the other hand, medical practice is still dominantly private, and insurance of medical costs is also private. Government enterprise in this field, in contrast to housing, is predominantly on the social-service model.

Still another, and largely different, combination of public and private enterprise has developed in atomic energy. The atomic bomb was developed in the Manhattan Project, in which there was planning and direction by the government (the Manhattan Engineering District of the Army Corps of Engineers), with most of the work being contracted to industrial corporations, universities, and research institutes. This contract system was continued by the Atomic Energy Act of 1946. The dominance of military objectives and the uncertainties concerning the possibilities for peaceful uses, the need for secrecy so that the American monopoly of atomic weapons could be perpetuated, and the requirements for safety controls all combined toward the view that the government should retain its monopoly of fissionable materials and production facilities. But nearly all the funds applied to the enterprise continued to be expended through contractors. Even the large plants at such locations as Oak Ridge and Hanford were operated by private corporations. The Atomic Energy Commission, created by the act of 1946, directed the operations. It was also authorized to lend or lease fissionables for research and medical therapy, and to license industrial uses, subject to the requirement in the latter case that it report to Congress and delay the effectiveness of licenses for ninety days. In 1954 the President proposed that the prohibitions in the act against private ownership of fissionable materials, productive facilities, and patents be relaxed. Amendments to the act later in the year allowed private construction and operation of atomic power plants, private possession of fuel, and private sale of by-product material under license from the commission. It also allowed patents to be granted to private persons. The commission, in accordance with the purpose of the 1954 amendments, has assisted in the development of private capabilities for peaceful uses.

Especially significant are cooperative activities in nuclear-power development. The commission has estimated that with the anticipated solution of technical difficulties and reduction of costs to make production economically feasible, the annual savings by the end of the century in generation costs of electricity through use of nuclear power will be four to five billions of dollars. Moreover, nuclear power could be produced at essentially the same cost everywhere, removing the disabilities of high-cost power areas. In view of such possibilities, it is not surprising that the traditional conflict between public and private power interests and advocates was reopened in 1954. The control of so important a resource could determine the dominance of public or private enterprise in the power industry of the future. The private power interests won a considerable victory in 1954 in the prohibition of generation and commercial disposition of power by the AEC, except as a by-product or from demonstration projects. Yet the victory could not, under the circumstances, be complete. The need for security and safety precautions would necessitate strict public control, and the tremendous costs of experimental development would require government leadership and financial participation. Government monopoly over the fuel was still retained, though the commission has now recommended that private ownership of special nuclear materials be authorized. Reactors would be developed under government license and with government subsidy.

The commission has considered that its function was to accumulate basic technology, develop and improve nuclear reactors and associated facilities, and improve the safety of nuclear-reactor operations. By 1962 there were thirty experimental or developmental reactor projects, with eleven reactors being owned by the national government, twelve being developed with cost-sharing between the national government and a public or private utility, and seven being developed by private industry on the basis of government-developed technology.

The struggle over public or private power erupted again in the eighty-seventh Congress. The Kennedy Administration proposed that 95 million dollars in national funds be used to construct a generating plant at the Hanford, Washington, site; but this was fought by the coal and oil industries and private utilities. The House, after rejecting the proposal three times, accepted a Senate compromise in 1962. AEC was authorized, contingent upon making certain findings, to contract with the Washington Public Power Supply System (representing sixteen utility districts in Washington) for the sale of by-product steam from the Hanford reactor, and the construction and operation of electric facilities to use the steam. But the WPPSS was to pay the costs of generating facilities and of any reactor modifications required for power production, and it was required to offer 50 per cent of the electricity generated to private utilities and users on a nondiscriminatory basis. Thus a balance was maintained between public and private use.[11]

The contract system used by the Atomic Energy Commission is illustrative

[11] 76 Stat. 599.

of the largest single development toward mixed enterprise that has existed in this country. About 80 per cent of the national government's expenditures for research and development is made through nonfederal institutions. "Contracting out" of research and development is practiced by the Department of Defense, the National Aeronautics and Space Administration, the Atomic Energy Commission, the National Institutes of Health, and, on a smaller scale, by other departments and agencies. Although some of these funds go to state universities and other public institutions, the largest proportion goes to private corporations. As Don Price has said, some nine-tenths of the Atomic Energy Commission's employees work for private corporations, from three-fifths to five-sixths of the budgets of leading private universities come from government, and entirely new private corporations (such as the RAND Corporation, the Institute for Defense Analysis, and the Aerospace Corporation) have been created to undertake government business. He concludes that the government contract has become a new type of federalism. This new government-industry federalism, as Price shows, is very different from both socialism and *laissez faire*.[12] The government has become dependent upon private institutions for its operations; and, as a recent government report said, "a large group of economically significant and technologically advanced industries depend for their existence and growth not on the open competitive market of traditional economic theory, but on sales only to the U.S. government." [13] Truly, what could have been exclusively a government function, and what could not have been exclusively a private one, has been made a joint government-private undertaking.

A final illustration of mixed enterprise is the Communications Satellite Act of 1962.[14] For development and management of a satellite system there was created a corporation. Its governing board is composed of twelve members selected by private stockholders and three appointed by the President with Senate approval. It will operate with the cooperation of the National Aeronautics and Space Administration, under regulatory controls exercised by the Federal Communications Commission, and subject to supervisory and directory powers of the President.

CONCLUSION

When one views the American economy in its segments, he sees almost infinite complexity. Public enterprise exists by the side of private enterprise. Public enterprise is supplied on the welfare model, on the economic model, and with a mixture of these. Moreover, in area after area, the consumer's service is the result of a mixture of public and private enterprise. There

[12] Don K. Price, "The Scientific Establishment," *Proceedings of the American Philosophical Society*, CVI (June 1962), pp. 235–245.
[13] *Report to the President on Government Contracting for Research and Development* (the Bell Report), Sen. Doc. No. 94 (87th Cong., 2nd Sess., 1962).
[14] 76 Stat. 421.

appears to be, in addition, a strong trend toward increase of mixed enterprise in a variety of patterns.

The motivations governing men in the choice of methods differ with the circumstances in the several areas of service. A preference for private enterprise is strong, but a willingness to use public enterprise also exists. The preference for private enterprise may be overcome by a conviction that under the existing circumstances, direct operations are preferable to regulation, or to regulation and promotion. Or deficiencies of private enterprise for the task on the scale and terms desired may be seen to exist. Or special advantages may be recognized in public enterprise in particular circumstances. The choices between public enterprise and private enterprises, and in the combinations of the two, reveal a pragmatic approach toward appropriate solutions for particular needs, including search for solutions which compromise contending interests.

The response to the combined technical and institutional features and the configuration of interests—general and particular—can be witnessed in bold and clear revelation in the new fields of atomic energy and communications satellites. It is a response which mixes public and private enterprise in special patterns adapted to special circumstances. The responses in other fields where policy is not yet fully fixed, such as low-cost housing and health care, will be made in other patterns adapted to the different circumstances.

Chapter 27. Policies and Methods in Business-Type Enterprises [1]

THIS CHAPTER deals with business-type public enterprises. Even this limited portion of public enterprise exhibits many diversities. Business enterprises engage in many different types of activities. They exist in the full range of government organization: local, special district, state, regional, national. They reflect separately the special conditions, motivations, and pressures which account for their existence. They embody different mixtures of social-service objectives with business operations. They vary in organization and relationship to the other parts of government.

No pattern of common characteristics can be presented. Moreover, no balance sheet on such enterprises as a group will be attempted, and probably none would be possible. Results of the enterprises would vary, standards of judgment would be debatable, and the balances among the successes and the failures would be impossible to assess. What can be done is to present some issues of policy and of method which arise in the conduct of business enterprises.

FINANCE

The central issues in business enterprise are those of finance. There are distinctive aspects and some peculiar problems of finance in business enterprises.

Two aspects of financing business enterprises are distinctive. First, where an enterprise sells commodities or services or makes loans, it is possible to run revenues into a revolving fund so that these revenues can be re-used to supply another round of commodities, services, or loans. This ability to reapply operating revenues provides dependability for a minimum quantity of continuous service. Second, in government enterprises of a commercial type the revenues of the enterprise can be made the basis of capital financing.

[1] Portions of this chapter were originally published in the *Revista de Ciencia Sociales*, University of Puerto Rico, **III** (June 1959), pp. 173–199, and are reprinted here with permission of the editor.

Capital financing on a large scale is normally required, but this may be achieved by pledging the revenues of the enterprise to payment of debt. Moreover, if the legislature has authorized borrowing authority up to a stated maximum sum, then the authority can be used and re-used to supply the basis for long-range, continuous service.

These capacities for re-use of revenues, and use and re-use of borrowing authority, create opportunities to make a commercial enterprise independent from general governmental controls. It can be freed from the appropriations process as the means of obtaining funds for expansion and operation, and this freedom can lead to other types of autonomy.

These possibilities have given rise to the issue of whether these enterprises should be autonomous. Should they be given a grant of initial capital and borrowing power and then be allowed to operate without report to the executive and the legislature, without authorization of use of money through appropriation acts, and without controls by the central accounting and auditing offices? If controls are established, should they be different from those established for other agencies? It will be seen in the next section that these questions are answered in different ways by governments.

One question is whether the general government should guarantee the bonds of the commercial enterprise. In countries where such enterprises have been given substantial independence from political control, the enterprises have established a credit standing which may be stronger than that of the government which organized them. In the states and cities the establishment of an independent authority may be a way of escaping the legal limitations on the borrowing power of the general government; in such a case, a guarantee would not be possible. As for the United States government, its credit is good, and there are no limitations on its borrowing authority except those set by Congress. It has guaranteed the bonds of many corporations established by it to operate business enterprises. This may strengthen them in financial markets; it may also diminish their independence from central controls. Perhaps the guiding consideration in determining the issue of guarantee is that these enterprises are created to supply services deemed to be of high social value; this being true, it would appear to be illogical for government to deny to the recipients of the services any advantages which would accrue from the sharing of the credit of the government.

The most significant issues on finance relate to the profit-and-loss calculation. Should a business enterprise operated by government pay all of its expenses out of its revenues? Can subsidies to business enterprises, and through them to their customers, be justified? Or, is it justifiable to use business enterprises as a means of obtaining profits to pay general government expenses?

Subsidy may be defined as any payment to, or immunity from payment by, an enterprise which releases it from the obligation to pay its total expenses, including its capital and operating costs and also its fair share of the costs of social services of government. Subsidies may accrue to business enterprises in a number of ways. First, they may come from tax exemption. Normally a government will not tax its own enterprises. They may pay taxes to other jurisdictions—for example, a state enterprise may pay taxes to local government—but this, too, is unusual. A government enterprise may make payments in lieu of taxes, as the Tennessee Valley Authority does to local jurisdictions. In such an event, the payments may be less than those which would be paid by a private enterprise. Second, subsidy may be the result of government supply of capital at less than cost. This is now true, for example, of the Rural Electrification Administration. It loans money at 2 per cent interest, which is less than the cost of capital to the United States government, which supplies its funds. During the last years of the Eisenhower Administration a move was initiated to discontinue loans at less than cost of capital, but the political power of the electric cooperatives was sufficient to prevent change in the law which provides for 2 per cent loans. Third, subsidy may result from miscalculation of benefits and costs. The Reclamation Project Act of 1939 [2] requires, with respect to proposed projects, that the Secretary of the Interior report to the President on costs to be allocated to (and probably to be repaid by users of) irrigation, power, and municipal water supply, respectively. The Flood Control Act of 1944 [3] provides, in effect, that costs of electric energy generated at projects under the control of the Army Engineers shall be repaid by rates on power. The Tennessee Valley Authority Act contains provisions which have been interpreted similarly. In multipurpose projects there are two elements of calculation of significance. One is of total costs and benefits of proposed projects. Some students have concluded that the calculations of benefit-cost ratios made by the agencies tend to overestimate financial benefits and underestimate costs of projects.[4] There is political pressure from communities, benefiting groups, and congressmen for relaxation of standards, and for congressional approval of projects whose benefit-cost ratio is low. The other element in calculation is the allocation of costs among the purposes of the project. There may be inaccuracy in these economic calculations, though a great amount of expert attention has been given to their perfection over a period of years. Fourth, subsidy may be the result of rate policies. This has already been noted with respect to REA loans. Other examples may be cited. Postal rates do not cover all costs of operation, even excluding tax equivalents and building costs. Subsidies are provided for newspaper and magazine readers (or for publishers) and for parcel-post customers. One group of users may be subsidized by rates for another group, as in those cases where a portion of the irrigation costs is paid from power revenues.

[2] 53 Stat. 1187.
[3] 58 Stat. 887.
[4] See Otto Eckstein, *Water Resources Development: The Economics of Project Evaluation* (Cambridge, Mass.: Harvard University Press, 1958). Reviewed in *Public Administration Review,* **XIX** (Spring 1959), pp. 114ff. Task Forces of the first and second Hoover Commissions cast doubt on allocations of cost: *Revolving Funds and Business Enterprises of the Government* (1949), *Water Resources Projects* (1949), and *Water Resources and Power* (1955).

Rather than subsidy, revenue for general purposes may be obtained from operation of a business enterprise. Thus, some cities obtain a profit from utility or other enterprises.

Operation for a profit is rare, however. The issue on whether to earn a profit is equivalent to that on apportionment of taxes, for a profit bears a resemblance to a sales tax. The more frequent issue is over subsidy. This issue, like others in government, will be resolved differently for different enterprises, both on rational grounds and in response to interest pressures. Considered on rational grounds, there is apparently basis for a preconception in favor of an enterprise paying its costs, or its costs with tax exemption. When service is sold, or money is lent, to one group at less than cost, then the uncovered cost must be paid by other members of society. The shift of income from one group to another may be on a geographical basis, as when a project serves one geographical area, or on a group basis, as when farmers are loaned money or mail is carried at a loss. On the other hand, unless one adopts the view that no redistribution of income should be made by government and that no efforts should be made by it to provide universal benefits, then he may have to admit the appropriateness of subsidy in particular instances. Subsidy is characteristic of government. The adoption of the form of business enterprise may not mean that some form of subsidy is not justified. The answer is dependent upon the value placed on the service. Society may place a high value on reading of periodicals, or on extending electricity use to all, in the same way that it does on education or health, and choose to adopt a middle road between service completely on the welfare model and completely on the business model.

The decisions will not be made on rational considerations alone. As on other issues, the resolution will be made in a political context. Groups will struggle for benefits at low cost, and other groups will oppose government enterprise in this direction. Each group will seek to identify its special interests with the general interest. Its success may be dependent solely on its strength and bargaining power, or also on other groups accepting its argument that the position taken is identified with public interests.

The opportunity for infusing rational considerations into the decisions will be enhanced to the extent that accounting judgments can be accurately made and information on these widely diffused among those who will influence the decisions. Accounting judgments must, however, be made on three levels, and the judgments become more difficult as one moves in a certain progression up these levels. The first level is financial accounting, which is the calculation of expenditures, revenues, fund uses, and other items which normally appear on profit-and-loss statements, balance sheets, and financial reports. Such accounting can go beyond that in private enterprises and show what would have been the results if costs not charged to the enterprise, such as taxes or free building space, had been made to it. The second is efficiency accounting. Efficiency accounting includes the isolation, measurement, and estimate of factors affecting the efficiency of the management of the enterprise. It may include such factors as internal procedural flows, modernization of equipment, personnel policies, pricing policies, promotional methods, and leadership. It is obvious that this kind of accounting or auditing for either a private or a public enterprise is more difficult than financial accounting. Anyone who has turned from the annual profit-and-loss statement to the question of whether actions could be taken which would increase revenues and decrease costs knows that the tools of analysis for efficiency auditing are far less precise than those for financial auditing, and hence that conclusions are less definitive. Third, there is welfare accounting. This is accounting which looks at the totality of social costs and social benefits. Such accounting is analysis of total input and output, and also of the transfers of income from group to group. Such analysis cannot be definitive in the sense that all who pursue it will agree on the conclusions, for not only are methods of analysis inadequately refined for consensus, but judgments on results will be based on value assumptions. It may be possible to estimate whether there is a dollar loss on carriage of newspapers in the mails; it may be less possible to determine whether the loss can be reduced by more efficient post-office management; it will most certainly be less possible—apparently impossible—to decide to all persons' satisfaction whether there was social gain greater than social loss in the enterprise.

In spite of the potential spread of issues in particular situations, it is possible either to form reliable conclusions or to narrow the range of judgment by use of financial and welfare accounting. This is true whether one is evaluating past operations or determining a future course of action. All would agree that the Home Owners Loan Corporation was a successful enterprise. Created during the depression to make loans to homeowners threatened with foreclosure, it loaned for this purpose and for home repairs approximately 3.5 billion dollars to over a million borrowers. When it was liquidated it showed a surplus of about 14 million dollars. It had been narrowly successful on the tests of financial accounting, and had a fat surplus by the tests of welfare accounting, for it enabled many families to retain their homes. Similarly, the Reconstruction Finance Corporation concluded its operations with a surplus, and in addition had contributed materially to arresting bankruptcies and salvaging assets in American business. The Rural Electrification Administration, in its early years, loaned money at a rate commensurate with the cost of the capital and at the same time ameliorated the living conditions on farms and improved economic operations thereon; only after the postwar increase in government's interest rate did the accounting data present any meaningful policy issues. In the case of the Tennessee Valley Authority accounting data show that the costs of building and operating power-generating and -distributing facilities are covered by rates, and the disputes are thus slightly reduced to the issues relating to dam-construction costs, tax payments, economic and social development, and the intangible values of public and private enterprise. In the consideration of future river developments, the practice of estimating benefits and costs to be anticipated, and particularly of estimating expected revenues of and costs attributable to irrigation and power portions of the proposed projects, have the effect of excluding some projects from consideration, placing others on a priority list on rational considerations, and making it more difficult for others to get through the authorization and appropriation process.

It may be concluded, therefore, that it is important to have accurate and adequate information with respect to business enterprises. The core of such information, though not necessarily the whole of it, is the financial data. It appears to be desirable to build into the decisional process means of insuring that the most adequate financial data are developed and brought to focus in the process. Business enterprises differ from others in the greater opportunity to make use of such data. Means now available in the national government for bringing such data to attention include reports of the enterprises, the reviews by the Bureau of the Budget, the audits and studies by the General Accounting Office, and the requirements for benefit-cost estimates on river projects.

ORGANIZATION

There are two main methods of administration for business enterprises. One is through a department or bureau, the other through a government corporation or authority. Both are used in most parts of the world. The corporate device has been used in countries with such diverse cultural, political, and administrative traditions as the United States, Canada, Australia, Great Britain, France, Italy, Germany, Puerto Rico, India, Burma, the Philippines, Turkey, Pakistan, the U.S.S.R., and those in Latin America. On the other hand, the departmental system is also used for business enterprises—examples being the postal systems of the United States, Great Britain, and Germany, and the railway systems of Canada and Sweden.[5]

In the United States, the cities have in the main used the same system of administration for business enterprises as for other services—a department headed by a single official or board; there are, however, many municipal authorities. The states have also used the departmental system primarily, but there has been in recent years a large growth of authorities. Notable examples are the New York Port Authority and the Lower Colorado River Authority of Texas. The former, as noted in an earlier chapter, constructs and operates bridges, port facilities, and airports;[6] the latter is the little TVA of central Texas, operating for flood control, irrigation, power generation and sale, and recreation.[7] In the national government, in addition to

---

[5] For experience with the government corporation, see W. Friedmann (ed.), *The Public Corporation: A Comparative Symposium* (Toronto: University of Toronto Press, 1954).

[6] On the long-range prospectus, see its comprehensive analysis, *Metropolitan Transportation—1980* (New York: New York Port Authority, 1963).

[7] See Comer Clay, "The Lower Colorado River Authority," in Emmette S. Redford (ed.), *Public Administration and Policy Formation: Studies in Oil, Gas, Banking, River Develop-*

the Post Office, such large business enterprises as the Bonneville, Southwestern, and Southeastern Power administrations are operated on the departmental or bureau pattern. On the other hand, the characteristic form of organization for business enterprises has been the government corporation, including among others such terminated corporations as the First and Second United States banks, the Reconstruction Finance Corporation and a number of subsidiaries, the Home Owners Loan Corporation, and the Inland Waterways Corporation, and such existing corporations as the Tennessee Valley Authority, Saint Lawrence Seaway Development Corporation, Federal Deposit Insurance Corporation, Export-Import Bank of Washington, Panama Canal Company, Public Housing Administration, Federal Prison Industries, Inc., Commodity Credit Corporation, and the federal home-loan banks, federal land banks, federal intermediate-credit banks, and banks for cooperatives.

Much of the discussion of business enterprises in this country during the past thirty years has centered on the use, financing, and relationships of the government corporation, in the same way that much of the discussion about regulation has been concentrated on the commission system. The corporations vary in their functions, powers, and form to such an extent that one author has said that all they have in common "is the name." [8] Typically, however, the government corporation exhibits the following attributes:

1. It operates business-type enterprises.

2. It is an instrument of government, operating a public service on behalf of the government.

3. It has an independent legal existence, with legal powers and liabilities similar to those of private corporations, including the right to make contracts and to sue and to be sued in its own name.

4. It is a separate financial entity with revenues obtained from sale of its services.

5. It has a separate administration, often combining a policy board and a director of operations.

6. It has a measure of operating independence, usually greater than that of departmental bureaus.

Claims of advantage for the government corporation over the government bureau have been confidently asserted, particularly in the decade of the thirties when many new national corporations were formed. The arguments of advantage have had a negative and a positive character. The negative way of putting the argument was to emphasize the utility of the corporate

---

ment, and Corporate Investigations (Austin, Texas: University of Texas Press, 1956), Chapter IV.

[8] V. O. Key, "Government Corporations," in Fritz Morstein Marx, *Elements of Public Administration* (Englewood Cliffs, N.J.: Prentice-Hall, Inc., 1946), p. 240. See also on the same point, C. Herman Pritchett, "The Paradox of the Government Corporation," *Public Administration Review*, **I** (Summer 1941), pp. 381–389.

device as a means of escaping from traditional rules and practices which would encumber a commercial undertaking. The archaic rule that a government cannot be sued without its consent, and the cumbersome methods and delays in giving such consent, have seemed to be particularly illogical for a public commercial undertaking. The limitations of the annual appropriation process, the accumulation of rules on contracting and purchasing, the lack of flexibility in civil-service rules and of initiative in civil-service administration, and the tightness of overhead controls in departments of government have all been listed as encumbrances which would prevent the government from operating commercial enterprises successfully. Also, the possibility that political interferences and direction would lead to inefficiency and to supply of service on an uneconomic basis has been in the minds of many who favored the corporate device. These several arguments on legal archaisms, bureaucratic encumbrances, and political direction have all seemed to support the conclusion that a special type of organization was required for commercial enterprises.

The positive way of putting the case for a government corporation was to contend that it would be a means for attaining the flexibility and initiative needed in a commercial undertaking. Thus, for example, President Roosevelt in 1933 recommended TVA as "a corporation clothed with the power of government but possessed of the flexibility and initiative of a private enterprise." [9]

The flexibility and initiative could result from the greater independence of the corporation than of the bureau. Authority to re-use its revenues and to borrow money would prevent or limit dependence on appropriations. Special exemption from rules on purchasing, personnel, and other matters could be granted. Responsibility could be placed directly and largely, perhaps almost exclusively, on corporate boards and managers.

TVA presented an opportunity to apply these ideas. It was provided with a broad and general assignment which gave large scope for initiative. On funds it had a dual position. It could re-use its revenues from power and fertilizer sales, and it could borrow within a stated limit, but it also had to obtain appropriations. It has had to rely mainly on congressional appropriations for capital funds, but it had the advantage that authorization for projects could be made by appropriation committees alone rather than by these and legislative committees. It was exempted from civil-service laws, except on such matters as veterans' preference and noncommunist oaths. The alternate safeguards were provisions prohibiting any political test or qualification for office and empowering the President to remove any official violating the prohibition. It could sue and be sued through its own counsel. It was freed from disallowance of its expenditures by the General Accounting Office, and until 1945 used outside auditors. Administration was vested in a board of directors who were independent from any departmental supervision.

[9] Message from the President, April 10, 1933 (73rd Cong., 1st Sess.), *Congressional Record*, **LXXVII**:2, p. 1423.

The results have justified the expectancies of those who advocated the corporate form. Leadership has been aggressive, and the staff has felt a sense of mission. The agency's accounting system was termed "excellent" by the head of the General Accounting Office. It developed collective-bargaining procedures for construction employees and a merit system for the usual type of government employee which has been widely studied and acclaimed. While successful in these administrative features, it has also attracted attention both at home and abroad for its substantive achievements. It was the pioneer in application of multipurpose engineering to a whole river system. It has expanded the use of electricity on farms and in households by its low wholesale rate and its requirement in contracts with municipalities that they earn no more than a return on their investments and, in lieu of taxes, a fair share of the cost of government. It has supplied power directly to industries, and materially assisted national-defense and atomic-energy projects. While the allocation of costs to power has been disputed, it has earned an annual return of approximately 4.5 per cent on the allocation. Though criticized for compromise with local ideas and interests through its efforts to "co-opt" their support,[10] it has presented an example of cooperative engagement with local governments and local interests. It has, above all, stimulated the development of the region and raised the status of a depressed area.[11]

These accomplishments do not, however, present a conclusive case for corporate autonomy. TVA has been substantially dependent upon appropriations. The President was forced to intervene in a dispute among board members, removing the chairman of the board in 1938. The Authority has not, it is clear, been completely independent. In fact, its early progress was attributable in large part to the interest of President Roosevelt and supporters in Congress. Initiative and zeal have been revealed in the operations of many other new agencies, corporate or otherwise, and only time will show whether TVA retains these qualities in its mature stage.[12] Moreover, the independent multipurpose river authority presents so many problems of coordination with the bureaus and departments of the government concerned with forests, lands, river development, and other matters that it is not likely to be the pattern of organization in the future. In fact, the TVA may not be a good example of appropriate use of the corporate device, because its business operations (power generation and sale primarily) were, under its en-

[10] On co-optation, see Philip Selznick, *TVA and the Grass Roots* (Berkeley, Calif.: University of California Press, 1949).

[11] The literature on TVA is voluminous. The most useful source is Roscoe C. Martin (ed.), *TVA, The First Twenty Years: A Staff Report* (University, Ala. and Knoxville, Tenn.: University of Alabama Press and University of Tennessee Press, 1956). Also useful are Herman Pritchett, *The Tennessee Valley Authority: A Study in Public Administration* (Chapel Hill, N.C.: University of North Carolina Press, 1943); David E. Lilienthal, *TVA, Democracy on the March* (New York: Harper and Row, Publishers, Inc., 1944), and Norman I. Wengert, *Valley of Tomorrow: The TVA and Agriculture* (Knoxville, Tenn.: University of Tennessee Press, 1952).

[12] A question raised by Roscoe C. Martin, *ibid.*, pp. 270–271.

abling act, subsidiary to such stated social and nonbusiness functions as flood control and navigation.

The reputed advantages of the corporate device may themselves be questioned. Many of the weaknesses of government subsumed under the argument for the business enterprise are equally significant to government bureaus. One answer to the problems would be to attack the weaknesses in government rather than search for new forms of independence. This has, in fact, been the trend in the national government. The Federal Torts Claims Act of 1946 [13] provided for suits against the government. The government personnel system has been so radically improved, particularly in decentralization of civil-service operations to the agency level, that it bears little resemblance to the system which existed in the early thirties. The restrictions of the General Accounting Office, which so seriously invaded the area of executive responsibility, have been relaxed. On the other hand, the trusteeship position of government and the need for public faith in its operations call for stricter rules on government purchasing and contracting than prevail in most private business, and the need for the safeguards are as great in business as in other types of government operation. The real difference in the business enterprise, as noted in the beginning of this chapter, is the opportunity afforded to relieve the enterprise from its dependence upon the annual appropriation bill. It may be concluded that the need for flexibility in operations is a need for all agencies, and that the special problem of the business enterprise lies in the peculiarities of its financing.

Beyond these separate questions of government liability, personnel, and financial accountability is the broader one of whether corporate management should be free from direction and supervision on business policy and operations from the executive officials of the government. Some of the outstanding authorities on government corporations have pressed an argument for the autonomous corporation—that is, for autonomy with respect to executive controls. Thus, Marshall Dimock, author of several books on government corporations, while recognizing that practice differs widely with respect to the autonomy of government corporations, makes autonomy the basic essential for an "authentic" corporation. He would place the control of corporations in corporate management, corporate boards, and the legislature.[14] On the other hand, other authorities have argued for executive supervision. William A. Robson, the outstanding English authority on government corporations, has concluded: "Parliament will not be able to exercise effective control or supervision over the operations of the public corporations. . . . For the task of general supervision and direction on questions of major policy we must look to ministers and their depart-

---

[13] 60 Stat. 843.
[14] "Government Corporations: A Focus of Politics and Administration," I and II, *American Political Science Review*, **XLIII** (October 1949), pp. 899–921, and (December 1949), pp. 1145–1164.

ments." [15] Harold Seidman of the United States Bureau of the Budget has gone further: "Making government corporations full-fledged members of the government team is to the advantage both of the corporation and of the government as a whole." [16]

Another American authority, V. O. Key, spots rival needs: "The solution lies in better appreciation of the need for creative freedom of public management buttressed by full responsibility—and for forms of control appropriate to this fundamental approach." [17] There are two themes here: freedom and responsibility of management, and appropriate forms of control. With the changes in government which have occurred since the beginning of the Depression, these can be seen as needs existing throughout the government structure. If not freedom, at least initiative and sense of responsibility is needed in such diverse units as the Bureau of Public Roads, the Atomic Energy Commission, and the Office of Education. On the other hand, their activities need to be coordinated with the objectives and operations of the government as a whole. This need may also exist for corporations. The business enterprise does need independence for operating decisions. Thus, loans or sales should be made without political influence through an executive superstructure. But the grant of patents by the Patent Office, the prescription of standards by the Bureau of Standards, and many other decisions in bureaus should be made without political influence. The rival needs referred to by Key may be achievable in a departmental structure if the overhead direction is limited to general policy. It is possible that for business enterprises, as for regulation, the autonomy (or independence) to be sought is relative and discriminate, not absolute and general.

In the American national government, the position of the government corporation seems to have been conclusively determined between 1935 and 1945. After the flush development of new corporations with substantial independence, parallelling the rash of other agencies poorly coordinated within the executive structure, a trend toward assimilation of the government corporations into the executive structure emerged. In general, they were attached to departments or agencies for general supervision, civil-service rules were extended to them, administrative expenses were required to be substantiated before the Bureau of the Budget in annual submittals, and the jurisdiction of the General Accounting Office was established over them. The TVA remained free of these controls, except for the submission of administrative budgets to the Bureau of the Budget and subjection to accounting controls of the General Accounting Office. Finally, in the Government Corporation Act of 1945 [18] the position of the corporations with re-

---

[15] "The Administration of National Industries in Britain," *Public Administration Review*, **VII** (Summer 1947), p. 168.

[16] "The Theory of the Autonomous Government Corporation: A Critical Appraisal," *Public Administration Review*, **XII** (Spring 1952), p. 90.

[17] V. O. Key, in Fritz Morstein Marx, *Elements of Public Administration* (Englewood Cliffs, N.J.: Prentice-Hall, Inc., 1946), p. 263.

[18] 59 Stat. 597.

spect to their establishment and their finances was regularized. There were four important provisions in the act with respect to corporations "wholly owned" by the United States government. First, corporations could be created only under the authority of national law and could not receive charters from the states, as some had in the past. Second, the Treasury was given control over issuance of bonds, notes, and debentures, including forms and denominations, maturities, interest rates, terms and conditions, and offering dates. These provisions enable the corporations to have the benefit of Treasury counsel, and enable the Treasury to coordinate the marketing of corporate securities with those of other government securities. Third, the corporations were required to submit "business-type" budgets annually to the Bureau of the Budget. Fourth, although the General Accounting Office could not disallow items of expenditure, it would make "commercial-type" audits of corporate accounts and would report irregularities to Congress.

Some separate explanation of the budget requirements is needed. The corporations usually submit budgets of their administrative expenses for annual congressional authorization. As for program activities, these are presented in the business-type budget. The budget is a report to be considered by the Bureau of the Budget, the President, and Congress, and not a request for an appropriation, for the corporation is allowed to re-use revenues in accordance with its statutory authorizations. The key schedules in the budget report are similar to those prepared regularly in private corporations. They include three statements, showing respectively sources and application of funds, income and expenses, and financial condition.[19]

In conclusion, it can be said that the government corporation in the national government is a chartered entity which can sue and be sued in its own name, and thus can have somewhat greater freedom than other agencies in making contracts and disposing of property; that statutory authorizations provide for re-use of revenues and issuance of bonds up to stated limits; that accounting, budgetary, and auditing requirements have been adjusted to the peculiar features of a business operation; but that the corporations are usually subject to numerous government regulations with respect to such matters as personnel and financial accountability, and also to general direction and supervision of a cabinet or other high executive official (for example, the Administrator of the Housing and Home Finance Agency).

It is impossible to state similar comprehensive conclusions about state and local corporations—usually called authorities—except to say that they are quite generally more independent from the general government than are national corporations. This independence is implicit in the definition of an authority given by Nathaniel S. Preston: "a non-taxing gov-

---

[19] For fuller discussion of budgets, see Chapter 16 on "The Budgeting and Control of Public Enterprise," in Jesse Burkhead, *Government Budgeting* (New York: John Wiley & Sons, Inc., 1956).

ernment agency having an identifiably separate existence from its parent government, and financially independent to the extent that it determines its own budget and sets its own prices for the services it performs, subject only to general limitations expressed in law or fixed by regulatory agencies." [20] Preston distinguishes a number of kinds of existing authorities. The type with the largest range of administrative and policy responsibilities is the standard authority. "It can plan, finance through revenue bonds, construct or purchase, maintain, operate or lease, and support through rates, tolls, rentals or other charges, any project which can be made to pay its way." [21] Included, among others, are some 689 local municipal utility authorities, state-established power or multipurpose river authorities, and toll-road and bridge authorities. Another type is the building authority, which may plan, finance, and construct public buildings for rental to public agencies. Still another type is the managing authority. It operates, and perhaps constructs, facilities and collects charges from the public; but it does not, as do standard authorities, provide the financing. Examples are the New York City Transit Authority, the Boston Arena Authority, and the Greater New Orleans Expressway Commission. Distinguishable also is the joint authority—that is, one established by two or more governments. The New York Port Authority is a joint, standard authority operating for the states of New York and New Jersey.

The usual claims of advantages and disadvantages are made for these authorities. There are, however, some peculiar reasons for establishment of some of them. They may be established to escape tax or debt limitations on local or state governments, or they may be created to serve an area for which there is no general government—an area smaller than the state, but comprehending a number of local government areas. Where the latter reason exists, the authority is likely to be almost completely free of control from any governmental jurisdiction. The most notable disadvantage revealed in the authorities is found in the transportation function. Authorities are not integrated into a total scheme of transportation planning, and they are likely—because they are pressed by the necessity of making revenues cover costs—to engage in cream-skimming operations, leaving to the communities the construction and operation of less remunerative projects. This illustrates the fact emphasized earlier in our discussions (Chapter 26) that a government, even when it establishes business enterprises, may not find it expedient to render the total amount of service required through business-type operations.

[20] Nathaniel S. Preston, "Public Authorities Today," *State Government*, **XXXIV** (Summer 1961), p. 205. The author is indebted to Preston's article for much of the information in this discussion of state and local authorities.
[21] Preston, *ibid.*, p. 206.

MISCELLANEOUS ASPECTS

It will be recalled that Mill pointed to the dangers of overloading government and of concentrating all the skill of the community in government as reasons for avoiding government enterprise. To a substantial extent these dangers have been avoided by the methods used in business enterprise. There is pluralism in the organization of these enterprises, some being local, some state, some district or regional, some national. The authority in the states and localities, and the corporation to a lesser extent in the national government, has provided means of relieving the load on general governments. Although some business enterprises, such as the Post Office and the RFC, have been of necessity highly centralized operations, decentralization and a measure of autonomy have been usual characteristics of government enterprise. TVA, Bonneville Power Administration, the New York Power Authority, and other large power-generating administrations are themselves decentralized units of organization, and in turn sell power to smaller retailing systems. On the other hand, the power district and the regional, state, or national authority or administration have been means of achieving the size of operations required for efficient project development. In such areas as rural electrification and farm credit other devices for decentralization have been developed to fit special circumstances. The difficulties of achieving the proper balance between centralization and decentralization, and of maintaining a pluralistic administration of economic affairs, may not be greater in this country in public than in private enterprise.

For each of the major groups in the population some special problems may arise from the existence of government's business enterprises. Especially in construction activities, the enterprises may come into contact with organized labor. Some of these may refuse to engage in collective bargaining; others, such as TVA, may embrace it. Normally, either because of the essential nature of the service or the position of government, strikes will not be tolerated on maintenance activities, nor for long on construction activities.

Consumer pricing problems will exist in public enterprises. In public power, for example, there is the problem of rate relationships in the rate structure. There is a somewhat greater use of flat rates for all consumers —regardless of distance of transmission—in public power enterprises than in private ones. There is also a somewhat greater tendency to use promotional rates in public enterprises. The drive to lower rates is often a major element in the movement to establish a public enterprise.

There has been much discussion of government rates as yardsticks of the appropriate rate of charge by private companies. Government enterprises may demonstrate that it is possible to supply service at lower rates than have prevailed, and may cause private concerns to lower their rates. This happened on interest rates for agricultural loans after the Federal Land banks were created, and has often followed the creation of public power projects. On the other hand, strict comparability of rates is feasible only where the conditions of service are the same. Private power companies never accepted the argument that TVA rates were a standard for private rates, always insisting that there were circumstances favorable to TVA which did not exist for private companies. Some other public power authorities have deliberately avoided any argument that their rates were a standard for private power rates in their area or any other.

Business interests often complain that public enterprise is competitive with private enterprise. Frequently, public enterprise is not competitive with respect to the particular service rendered. Neither the Post Office nor a municipal power plant is competitive with a private organization supplying the same service. The government may either have a monopoly in the geographical area served, or be supplying a service different in some respect from that supplied by private concerns. On the other hand, competitive factors do exist in much government enterprise, whether conducted on the business or the welfare model. Federal Land banks are competing with commercial banks, Military Air Transport carries passengers whom the commercial airlines would like to carry, and even public colleges compete with private ones. Private enterprise will, however, accommodate itself to the situation and adjust to the opportunities which remain for it. Moreover, public enterprise has, in one area of service after another, been a service to the private sector of the economy. For example, the public bridge is a boon to the economy, though one of the most famous cases in American constitutional law turned on the issue as to whether a public bridge could be built in competition with a private bridge. In a mixed economy public enterprise and private enterprise may both flourish, and though some entrepreneurs may lose opportunities to public enterprises, others will find that in many situations it is part of the service rendered by government to all or a part of the private sector of the economy.

Part VII. Summary and Conclusions

Chapter 28. Final Observations

REALITIES OF OUR TIME

One major reality of our time colors the screen on which events are revealed: Man uses the processes of government as part of his effort to make the conditions affecting his existence more beneficent. The changed economic and social conditions coerce him in this direction. The ease of his access to government in a democratic society provides opportunities for its use. The widening of access through universal suffrage and interest coagulations has extended the opportunities both vertically to the poor and horizontally to the functional groups. The development of organizational centers, both outside and within government, through which pressure can be exerted and within which search for solutions to problems can be sought has raised man's expectancy that solutions be found. Human needs have come to be regarded as social problems for which existing or new organizational centers should find solutions.

The assumptions underlying *laissez faire* have been rejected. A cosmic philosophy of *laissez faire* assumes that there is an orderliness and regularity in a self-operating economy, and that human agency should not interfere with the operation of the system, either because it is beneficial or because it is inevitable. This philosophy is implicit in many pronouncements of men in high position, but it is doubtful whether there is any interest group in society which can present it without hypocrisy. The resort to politics is a common feature of group action, and the resort is taken by groups for positive ends, not merely for defense against other groups.

The resort to politics is no longer impeded by constitutional doctrines. The due-process barricade against political decision on economic policy, erected by the Supreme Court by a merger of higher law doctrines and economic philosophy, has been destroyed. Legislatures are sovereign with respect to economic policy. Likewise, the states-rights barricade, either erected or supported by the Supreme Court in such decisions as those in the Sugar Trust and Child Labor cases, has been torn down by later decisions. The sovereignty of legislatures usually rests in the Congress whenever it chooses to assume it. The Grand Pattern of the Constitution, which made this country one and under which the economy developed as a unit, ultimately became one in which political sovereignty was coterminous with economic structure and process.

Rejection of *laissez faire* as the working creed of the nation has not been paralleled by the development of any arching and all-encompassing philosophy. The simplistic, dogmatic doctrines of theoretical socialism, and the visions of complete economic planning, with their implicit totalitarianism, have had meager acceptance. What characterizes American governmental interventions in the economy is empirical response to particular situations, problems, or pressing human needs. Philosophical justification has been found in the general and vague notion of the public interest. There has been, in addition, an assumption, like that of idealist thinkers, that the intervention would be most likely to work in the public interest if the political system were democratic. At the same time, the notion of the public interest has been qualified by recognition of private rights and interests, and the development of democratic forms has left scope for pluralistic societal organization reaching upward into the structure of government.

In recent years, as the departure from *laissez faire* and the complexities of the economy and government alike have become apparent, some new descriptive concepts which explain the realities of our time have emerged. One enrichment of thought was embodied in such terms as imperfect competition, monopolistic competition, oligopolistic competition, and workable competition. These terms all evidence recognition of varieties and complexities within the economy. They also show recognition that the internal operation of the economy does not always correspond with the simplistic model of free competition. Another concept is that of Boulding, the economist, and March, the political scientist, concerning the politicalization of economic processes. As used by them, the terminology recognizes that the processes of politics have invaded the internal structure of the economy. The economy and government reveal similar processes, though in somewhat different contexts. Parallel to enrichments of thought about current realities in economic life are those about realities in government. The concept of group politics has led to clearer perception of the nature of political decision making, and has even led to inquiry into the meanings conveyed by the term "public interest." The concept of political subsystems, with triangular influences within, has modified the hierarchical notions about the governmental system. In addition to new concepts about realities within the economic and political systems, there have been new concepts about the relation of government to the economy. One of these is the idea of continuities, advanced by the economist Lindblom and the political scientist Dahl. The idea will be a constant reminder of the varieties of approach used by government in its empirical response to situations, and of the fruitlessness of bipolar concepts of *laissez faire* and economic planning as approaches to understanding of public policy. There is also the widely used and broadly encompassing term "mixed economy," which capsules better than any other now available the real nature of an economic system within which economic and political processes both operate.

PUBLIC POLICY IN THE MIXED ECONOMY

Two basic ideals in the American vision of a good economy were set forth in Chapter 5. One is the opportunity ideal. America has been a "land of opportunity" where liberty itself was "freedom to grasp opportunity." The other is the ideal of material well-being. This has become a land of plenty, an affluent society. These two ideals, combined into one—plenty within the grasp of all—will be the goal of public policy for the economy.

The two ideals were incorporated in an official statement in the Employment Act of 1946. "Maximum employment, production, and purchasing power" were stated as "continuing policy" of the national government. Lately, the aims have tended to be assimilated into that of economic growth. Stability has also been discussed as a related objective. Stability would not, however, be accepted as a goal if it were not conceived to be related to long-run attainment of opportunity and material well-being. National defense will be a superordinate goal, but efforts will be made to ensure that domestic economic welfare and opportunity are not impeded by allocation of resources to defense. There are many subordinate and instrumental goals explicitly set forth or implicit in the policies of government, but the ultimate test of public economic policy in the minds of people generally will be whether it contributes to the twin goals of opportunity and material well-being.

In a mixed economy these goals are to be attained by a combination of public and private action. The Employment Act explicitly set forth the joint responsibility of public and private organizations. It thus recognized the essential pluralism of the American politico-economic system.

More than this, American public policy is based on the assumption that private enterprise will be the normal means of supplying goods and services to the public. Public-policy interventions are corrective and supplemental.

Much of the policy in the mixed economy is directed toward the objectives of preserving the private economy and restricting the intervention of government. Certain large policy concepts and approaches of government have a double aspect: they extend government power, but they also economize the use of government. Probably the most significant concept of public policy today is that of compensatory action. The concept assumes a private economy with supplemental government action. In implementing the concept in a depression or recession, government seeks to revive and stimulate the private economy; and in an inflationary period, it seeks to conserve the values of such an economy. Another concept—that of competition—is one of the oldest and most persistent in American policy. It has become clear that the maintenance of competition through antitrust is an alternative to the extension of regulation to additional industries. The essence of the antitrust policy is the maintenance of market controls over the allocation of resources and the avoidance of overhead regulation of price, entry, and other key decisions in industry. The complementary concept of countervailing power assumes, as does the ideal of competition, the advantages of control through internal checks and balances within the economy rather than through overhead regulation. The concept of collective bargaining, though it has brought a redirection and amplification of government intervention, presents an alternative to, and the last stand against, government decision on wages and other benefits for labor. For industries presenting special problems, regulation rather than socialization is the usual choice. Whether regulation imposes smaller burdens on government than does socialization may be debatable, in some instances at least; but it is an approach which preserves private enterprise. Recently, the choice of private contracts as means of carrying out the government's research, defense, and space responsibilities has preserved the mixed nature of the political economy.

Even in social legislation, in which government redirects the flow of income, government action has been restricted to the setting of minimum standards. Private decision determines benefits above the minimums. Both the policies on labor-management relations and those in social legislation preserve balances between public and private action.

In the mixed economy much of what government does has the purpose and effect of promoting private enterprise. There is, however, so much discussion of the restrictive or regulative aspect of government intervention that the promotive aspects are sometimes overlooked. The fact is that private suppliers of goods and services demand action that is promotive of their interests, and resist actions that they regard as overly restrictive. If one glances at the history of American policies, he sees a struggle of economic groups for promotion of their interests through public policies on such matters as public lands, credit, tariffs, conservation and use of resources, limitation of entry or of production, minimum prices, and insurance of assets. Government, in response to these efforts, has intervened to promote the interests, not alone of consumers, but also of producers, distributors, and financial groups.

In a mixed economy regulation itself may be initiated for promotion of the interests of the control groups within industries as well as for protection against them. Legislation ranges from the outright prohibition of industry action for the protection of consumers to the guardianship of industries. Whatever the motivation, the controls may be restricted or comprehensive in scope, remote or intimate in the degree to which they impinge on managerial decisions, dependable or variable in their content. The control by government may hang loosely and be imposed intermittently over an industry or industries, or it may be strict and continuous.

Public policy in general moves between two poles. On the one hand, there is the tendency, initially or over a period of time, to make the controls as comprehensive and detailed as is necessary to achieve the objectives of policy. On the other hand, the controls will be limited to what is feasible in a system of overhead public control of private enterprise. Reliance must still be placed on private initiative primarily, and much of what government does will be through approval or disapproval of private action, or will be accomplished by the support of private individuals and groups. Moreover, the regulated interests will be ingenious in finding ways of obtaining regulation favorable to their interests, or of moderating those elements which are unfavorable. Ultimately, public policy can be interpreted from some new set of balances between public and private action, resulting from the acceptance of control by the regulated interests, or the yielding of government to them, or more likely by compromise between the two.

Although in American public policy regulation has been highly favored in comparison with public enterprise, there has nevertheless been a considerable amount of the latter. The most notable development of public enterprise in the nation's history has been public education, offering opportunity to all, and the most striking recent development of such enterprise has been government insurance, providing security both to individuals in their personal life and to certain groups of entrepreneurs and absentee investors in their businesses. Public enterprise often supplies service free of charge, sometimes for charges sufficient to sustain the enterprise, and sometimes for a charge which pays part of the cost.

Whether the goal of plenty within the grasp of all will lead to large new adventures in public policy in the near future will depend upon changes in conditions and upon the demands of groups. In the background are two important factors: the continuing conquest of nature through science and technology, and the uncertain impact of international politics. Although the range of effects of these two factors are uncertain, both may be expected to lead to adjustments, perhaps expansions, in public functions in future years. In addition to these broad factors, some specific conditions which could give rise to demands for public action can easily be foreseen. One is unemployment. If the unemployment rate remains high or rises, then questions about training, make-work projects, reduction of hours, increase of public expenditures, and stimulation of the private economy through tax reduction or other means will be forced upon public policy makers. A second is slums, poor housing, delinquency, and dependency in cities. The conditions are present now and will undoubtedly receive more attention in the future, particularly as reapportionment and redistricting for legislatures force attention to the problems of the cities. A third is the new conditions in agriculture. Whether the means now used will carry the nation successfully through the period of transition resulting from the burgeoning increase in farm productivity and the lack of markets is uncertain. A fourth would be public dissatisfaction over industry price policies or the results of collective bargaining. The President's action on the steel-price increase of 1962, the repeated threats of the serious stoppage of industry and commerce, and the discussions of cost-push inflation are indications that new policies which would alter the present balances between public and private responsibilities may be more seriously considered in the future than in the past. A fifth would be a severe economic recession, and a sixth would be the threat of such a recession from a cold-war thaw and a consequent large reduction of defense expenditures. Such events would call for consideration of compensatory policies, and might lead to a permanent expansion of public economic functions. A seventh would be mobilization requirements of such extent as to put a strain on the economy, or bombings of the country, either of which would lead to extraordinary, though perhaps temporary, controls. An eighth would be a continuation of the dollar deficit in the nation's international accounts on a scale sufficient to require major changes in foreign trade, capital export, or other policies.

The mere listing of so many possibilities shows that the horizons of the future are uncertain, and that public policies will be dependent upon the directions and force of change.

THE PROCESSES OF GOVERNMENT

For a long time the judiciary occupied the central position in the making and application of public economic policy. It developed policy by expansion of the common law and by interpretation of the Constitution. It applied policy, when called upon to do so, in private suits. It extended its function in the late nineteenth century, and for about fifty years set the bounds of economic policy. It restricted legislatures, confined administrators, and applied through its own decisions the policies it evolved. The preceding chapters have shown how in two areas especially—labor relations and utility regulation—it built and applied its own set of policy norms. These were, however, only the most spectacular examples of judicial supremacy in matters of economic policy.

The judiciary has now withdrawn from the Olympian position it once took on economic policy, and consequently the role of other parts of the government has been expanded. The centerpieces of economic policy are made by legislation, and the responsibility for elaboration and application is normally in administration. The judiciary still performs a role, but only in interpretation of legislation, correction of administrative error, and adjustment and application of common law rules.

Even with legislative supremacy established, large alternatives of methodological approach on policy development exist. Never in our history have these been so clearly focused as in the debates of the three national leaders—Roosevelt, Taft, and Wilson—on antitrust methodology a little more than a half-century ago. One method advocated was general law interpreted by courts, with the administrative hand present only in the form of enforcement action. Another was specific law applied in the courts, again with administration present only in enforcement. The third was general law given specific content by administration, with the courts remaining in a corrective position.

All three of these methods are used. In antitrust, the first of the three (general law interpreted in courts) is the primary method, and the second (specific legislation) is its chief supplement. Nevertheless, for economic policy generally, the trend has been toward the third method (general law elaborated through administration). Moreover, executive or administrative agencies usually have the dominant role in enforcement, whichever of the three methods is used. Public responsibility in enforcement has to a large extent supplanted private responsibility.

As a result, when one looks at economic programs of government, he normally turns his attention to the work of administrative or executive agencies. He then witnesses a tremendous development of administrative technology which can be used in application of economic legislation, particularly regulatory legislation. The regulatory technology is in large measure described in the literature of administrative law, which deals with the functions, procedures, and limitations of administrative agencies. The regulatory technology includes such things as rule making, orders, and licenses, various forms of implementing arrangements, and the operating processes of agencies—all described in detail in Chapter 24. They offer a great variety of technical instruments from which choices and combinations can be made by the maker of economic policy.

Although there is a comprehensive battery of regulatory tools for general use, special techniques adapted to particular needs have been created in almost every area of regulation. The Federal Reserve Board used the open-market operations, the Federal Trade Commission the trade conference, the Federal Power Commission area pricing for natural gas, the Atomic Energy Commission and the Department of Defense the contract, and the wartime agencies the various methods of allocation and price control. The opportunities for creativity in discovery of applicable technique have been great.

Administrative organization has been a significant aspect of technique in the legislative-administrative state. For regulation, the commission has offered an alternative to the bureau or department, as has the corporation or authority for the business enterprise conducted by government. Experience has shown that variations in internal structure and in relationships with other parts of the government can exist when either the commission or the corporation is used. In the national government the corporation has been largely assimilated into the structure and normal operations of the general government, while in the states and the cities the authority usually is autonomous. As for the national regulatory commissions, their structure and relationships are still debated, but tendency is fixed toward some measure of responsibility on each of three lines—to Congress, to the President, and to the judiciary. It is apparent that, with respect to organization, there is room for choice among methods, and that choices must be made when new programs are instituted.

Although independence or autonomy of some kind has been sought for many of the administrative agencies, and although there has been a great measure of success in insuring such independence or autonomy with respect to certain specific functions, the agencies will not operate in isolation from the forces of politics. An agency becomes a part of a universe (or area) of social action. Within this universe there will be an interplay of pressures and influences, and a development of strategic centers through which pressures and influences can be exerted. The strategic centers for a particular universe of action can be classified as administrative or executive centers, congressional centers (including particularly committees and committee chairmen), and affected clientele organizations outside government. A whirlpool of activity develops among these centers, and a subsystem of politics related to the functions performed in the universe arises. The interrelations within the subsystem are continuous. The agencies struggle both for independence and for support, the outside interests seek both to avoid and to control agency power, and the congressional units in the subsystem strive to establish and maintain their influence.

In a large and broad sense, the independence that exists in modern government is the independence of function. It is the operation of each category of government activity—whether education, health, railroad regulation, agricultural stabilization, or a multipurpose river project—in substantial independence from other functions and from overhead control from the top political officials and the general public. This results from the specialization and separation of functions, the limitations on the span of attention of the public and its representatives, and the concentration of attention on particular functions by those who are affected by them.

Agencies of administration do not escape, however, from that larger arena of politics which we have called macropolitics. They must work within the total political system as well as within their subsystems. Many things may draw them into the larger vortex. They may be subjected to attack from outside their subsystems. They may need support from outside in order to sustain their power within the systems. They may need to broaden support for their appropriations, their legislative proposals, or new policy objectives. Their functions may bear so close a relationship to the functions of one or more other subsystems that coordination is essential. The President or other top political leaders may take an interest in their performance.

Interventions from the macropolitical arena may, nevertheless, be infrequent or have low impact. The President is so busy with so many matters, and particularly with foreign affairs and national defense, that his attention to matters of policy in many areas of economic control will be limited and occasional. The decentralization of functions within the Congress makes it difficult to lift particular matters of economic policy to consideration by the membership and leadership of the houses as a whole. Moreover, the problems became so complex that careful congressional consideration may be possible only in committees. And new directives to administration, or new appointees to it, may be absorbed into the existing system without having material effect upon it.

Yet interventions from macropolitics do have effects. Studies, investigations, and criticism generate new consideration of policies in agencies. Legislation adds new policy. The attention of the President increases or decreases the vigor of administrative effort. Although these may disturb the status quo only rarely, they do have a substantial impact at times.

The complexities and the diversities of the governmental process unfolded above and in the preceding chapters may make it impossible to set forth broad generalizations about the effects to be anticipated from governmental intervention in the economy. The political process, like the economic, yields different results in different situations. It is possible, however, to discern problems about which men should be concerned. Three of these deserve mention at the close of this book. The first is the problem of improving administrative technology and management. There is need certainly for developing more expeditious forms of procedure. There is need also to discover means by which more attention can be given by administrators to policy objectives. There is need, in general, to bring more expertness, more flexibility, and more energy to the administrative process. The second is the problem of establishing means to view emerging problems with a broad perspective. The problems often cut across the subsystems which have been set up for handling particular functions. Or they need to be reconsidered from perspectives larger than, or different from, those which have come to prevail in the existing organizations. The means by which emerging problems can be discerned and analyzed with fresh and broad perspectives have not been adequately established. The third is the inclusive problem of the political system. It is the problem of combining responsiveness and rationality in decision making. The American political system operates in a pluralistic society in which economic interests have easy access to government; a high degree of responsiveness to separate demands of groups is therefore insured. There is also much provision for expert search for reasonable and effective solutions to economic problems. The means of making the responsiveness broad enough in terms of all the interests involved, and the solutions expert enough to meet their needs, is the problem which should concern all those who recognize that the economy is, and will remain, a political economy, and who are interested in its beneficial operation.

Selected References

CHAPTER 1

Dodd, Edwin M. *American Business Corporations until 1860 with Special Reference to Massachusetts.* Cambridge, Mass.: Harvard University Press, 1954.

Haines, Charles Grove. *The Revival of Natural Law Concepts: A Study of the Establishment and of the Interpretation of Limits on Legislatures with Special References to the Development of Certain Phases of American Constitutional Law.* Cambridge, Mass.: Harvard University Press, 1930.

Handlin, Oscar, and Mary Flug Handlin. *Commonwealth: A Study of the Role of Government in the American Economy: Massachusetts, 1774–1861.* New York: New York University Press, 1947.

Hartz, Louis. *Economic Policy and Democratic Thought: Pennsylvania, 1776–1860.* Cambridge, Mass.: Harvard University Press, 1948.

Heath, Milton Syndey. *Constructive Liberalism: The Role of the State in Economic Development in Georgia to 1860.* Cambridge, Mass.: Harvard University Press, 1954.

Primm, James Neal. *Economic Policy in the Development of a Western State: Missouri, 1820–1860.* Cambridge, Mass.: Harvard University Press, 1954.

Taussig, F. W. *The Tariff History of the United States,* 7th ed. New York: G. P. Putnam's Sons, 1923.

Williamson, Harold F. (ed.) *The Growth of the American Economy: An Introduction to the Economic History of the United States,* 2nd ed. Englewood Cliffs, N.J.: Prentice-Hall, Inc., 1951.

CHAPTER 2

Berle, Adolf A., Jr. *Power without Property: A New Development in American Political Economy.* New York: Harcourt, Brace & World, Inc., 1959.

——— and Gardiner C. Means. *The Modern Corporation and Private Property.* New York: The Macmillan Company, 1933.

Boulding, Kenneth E. *The Organizational Revolution: A Study in the Ethics of Economic Organization.* New York: Harper and Row, Publishers, Inc., 1953.

Burnham, James. *The Managerial Revolution: What Is Happening in the World.* New York: John Day Company, Inc., 1941.

Dimock, Marshall E. *The New American Political Economy: A Synthesis of Politics and Economics.* New York: Harper and Row, Publishers, Inc., 1962.

Eells, Richard. *The Government of Corporations.* New York: Free Press of Glencoe, Inc., 1962.

———. *The Meaning of Modern Business.* New York: Columbia University Press, 1960.

Hacker, Andrew. *Politics and the Corporation.* New York: Fund for the Republic (pamphlet), 1958.

Kaplan, A. D. H. *Big Enterprise in a Competitive System.* Washington, D.C.: Brookings Institution, 1954.
Kaysen, Karl, and Donald F. Turner, *Antitrust Policy: An Economic and Legal Analysis.* Cambridge, Mass.: Harvard University Press, 1959.
March, James G. "The Business Firm as a Political Coalition," *The Journal of Politics,* 24 (November 1962), pp. 662–678.
Mason, Edward S. (ed.) *The Corporation in Modern Society.* Cambridge, Mass.: Harvard University Press, 1959.
Maurer, Herrymon. *Great Enterprise: Growth and Behavior of the Big Corporation.* New York: The Macmillan Company, 1955.
Means, Gardiner C. *Industrial Prices and Their Relative Instability.* Washington, D.C.: Senate Document 13, 74th Cong., 1st Sess. (January 1935).
Moore, Wilbert E. *The Conduct of the Corporation.* New York: Random House, Inc., 1962.
Reagan, Michael D. *The Managed Economy.* Oxford: Oxford University Press, 1963.
Report of the Federal Trade Commission on Changes in Concentration in Manufacturing, 1935 to 1947 and 1950. Washington, D.C., 1954.
Steiner, George A. *Government's Role in Economic Life.* New York: McGraw-Hill Company, Inc., 1953.
Thompson, Victor A. *Modern Organization: A General Theory.* New York: Alfred A. Knopf, Inc., 1961.
Turner, Frederick J. "The Significance of the Frontier in American History," *Annual Report of the American Historical Association for the Year 1893* (Washington, D.C., 1894), pp. 197–227.
Webb, Walter P. *The Great Frontier.* Boston: Houghton Mifflin Company, 1952.

CHAPTER 3

Fainsod, Merle. "Some Reflections on the Nature of the Regulatory Process." In Friedrich, C. J., and Edward S. Mason, *Public Policy, 1940.* Cambridge, Mass.: Harvard University Press, 1940.
Freeman, J. Leiper. *The Political Process: Executive Bureau–Legislative Committee Relations.* Garden City, N.Y.: Doubleday & Company, Inc., 1955.
Herring, E. Pendleton. *Group Representation before Congress.* New York: McGraw-Hill Company, Inc., 1929.
———. *Public Administration and the Public Interest.* New York: McGraw-Hill Company, Inc., 1936.
Holcombe, Arthur N. *The New Party Politics.* New York: W. W. Norton & Company, Inc., 1933.
———. *The Political Parties of Today.* New York: Harper and Row, Publishers, Inc., 1924.
Key, V. O., Jr. *Politics, Parties, and Pressure Groups,* 4th ed. New York: Thomas Y. Crowell Company, 1960.
Leiserson, Avery. *Administrative Regulation: A Study in Representation of Interests.* Chicago: University of Chicago Press, 1942.
Lubell, Samuel. *The Future of American Politics.* New York: Harper and Row, Publishers, Inc., 1951.
Maass, Arthur. *Muddy Waters.* Cambridge, Mass.: Harvard University Press, 1951.
Redford, Emmette S. "The Never-Ending Search for the Public Interest" (Chapter 5), *Ideal and Practice in Public Administration.* University, Ala.: University of Alabama Press, 1958.

———. "The Protection of the Public Interest with Special Reference to Administrative Regulation," *American Political Science Review,* 48 (December 1954), pp. 1103–1113.

Schattschneider, E. E. *The Semisovereign People: A Realist's View of Democracy in America.* New York: Holt, Rinehart & Winston, Inc., 1960.

Schubert, Glendon. *The Public Interest: A Critique of the Theory of a Political Concept.* New York: Free Press of Glencoe, Inc., 1960.

Sorauf, Frank J. "The Public Interest Reconsidered," *The Journal of Politics,* 19 (November 1957), pp. 616–639.

Truman, David B. *The Governmental Process: Political Interests and Public Opinion.* New York: Alfred A. Knopf, Inc., 1951.

Wright, Benjamin Fletcher (ed.) *The Federalist.* Cambridge, Mass.: Harvard University Press, 1961, No. 10.

CHAPTERS 4 AND 5

Clark, J. M. *Social Control of Business,* 2nd ed. New York: McGraw-Hill Company, Inc., 1939.

Dahl, Robert A., and Charles E. Lindblom. *Politics, Economics, and Welfare.* New York: Harper and Row, Publishers, Inc., 1953.

Dewey, John. *The Public and Its Problems: An Essay in Political Inquiry.* New York: Holt, Rinehart & Winston, Inc., 1927.

Dicey, A. V. *Lectures on the Relation between Law and Public Opinion in England.* New York: The Macmillan Company, 1905.

Ebenstein, William. *Man and the State.* New York: Holt, Rinehart & Winston, Inc., 1947 (a collection of readings).

Friedrich, Carl J. "The Political Thought of Neo-Liberalism," *American Political Science Review,* 49 (June 1955), pp. 509–525.

Galbraith, John Kenneth. *The Affluent Society.* Boston: Houghton Mifflin Company, 1958.

Hansen, Alvin H. *Economic Policy and Full Employment.* New York: McGraw-Hill Company, Inc., 1947.

Harris, Seymour E. (ed.) *The New Economics: Keynes' Influence on Theory and Public Policy.* New York: Alfred A. Knopf, Inc., 1947.

Hayek, Friedrich A. *The Road to Serfdom.* Chicago: University of Chicago Press, 1944.

Hobhouse, L. T. *Liberalism.* New York: Holt, Rinehart & Winston, Inc., 1911.

Hofstadter, Richard. *Social Darwinism in American Thought,* rev. ed. Boston: Beacon Press, 1955.

Hoover, Calvin B. *The Economy, Liberty and the State.* New York: Twentieth Century Fund, 1959.

Mayo, H. B. *Democracy and Marxism.* New York: Oxford University Press, 1955.

Mill, John Stuart. *Principles of Political Economy,* 7th ed. (1871), Ashley, W. J. (ed.). New York: Longmans, Green and Co., Inc., 1909.

Myrdal, Gunnar. *The Political Element in Development of Economic Theory.* Cambridge, Mass.: Harvard University Press, 1954.

Potter, David M. *People of Plenty: Economic Abundance and the American Character.* Chicago: University of Chicago Press, 1954.

Reagan, Michael D. *The Managed Economy.* New York: Oxford University Press, 1963.

Rossiter, Clinton. *Conservatism in America.* New York: Alfred A. Knopf, Inc., 1955.

Ruggiero, Guido de. *History of European Liberalism,* Collingwood, R. G., translator. New York: Oxford University Press, 1927.
Simons, Henry C. *A Positive Program for Laissez-Faire.* Chicago: University of Chicago Press, 1934.
———. *Economic Policy for a Free Society.* Chicago: University of Chicago Press, 1948.
Smith, Adam. *An Inquiry into the Nature and Causes of the Wealth of Nations,* 6th ed., Cannon, Edwin (ed.). London: Methuen and Co., Ltd., 1950.
Steiner, H. Arthur. "Fascism in America?" *American Political Science Review,* 29 (October 1935), pp. 821–830.
Taylor, O. H. *Economics and Liberalism.* Cambridge, Mass.: Harvard University Press, 1955.
Watson, Donald Stevenson. *Economic Policy: Business and Government.* Boston: Houghton Mifflin Company, 1960. Chapters 2, 3, 4, and 5.
Wilson, Woodrow. *The New Freedom.* Garden City, N.Y.: Doubleday & Company, Inc., 1913.
Wootton, Barbara. *Freedom Under Planning.* Chapel Hill, N.C.: University of North Carolina Press, 1945.

CHAPTERS 6, 7, AND 8

I. General

Corwin, Edward S. *The Constitution and What It Means Today,* 11th ed. Princeton, N.J.: Princeton University Press, 1954.
Croskey, William W. *Politics and the Constitution in the History of the United States.* Chicago: University of Chicago Press, 1953, 2 Vols.
Kelly, Alfred H., and Winfrey A. Harbison. *The American Constitution: Its Origins and Development,* rev. ed. New York: W. W. Norton & Company, Inc., 1955.
McLaughlin, Andrew C. *A Constitutional History of the United States.* New York: Appleton-Century-Crofts, Inc., 1935.
McCloskey, Robert G. (ed.) *Essays in Constitutional Law.* New York: Alfred A. Knopf, Inc., 1957.
Schwartz, Bernard. *The Supreme Court: Constitutional Revolution in Retrospect.* New York: Ronald Press Co., 1957.
Swisher, Carl B. *American Constitutional Development,* rev. ed. Boston: Houghton Mifflin Company, 1954.
———. *The Growth of Constitutional Power in the United States.* Chicago: University of Chicago Press, 1946.
Warren, Charles. *The Supreme Court in United States History.* Boston: Little, Brown & Company, 1926, 2 Vols.

II. Chapter 6

Frankfurter, Felix, and James M. Landis. "The Compact Clause of the Constitution—A Study in Interstate Adjustments," *Yale Law Journal,* 34 (May 1925), pp. 685–758.
Jackson, Robert H. *Full Faith and Credit: The Lawyer's Clause of the Constitution.* New York: Columbia University Press, 1945.
Wright, Benjamin F. *The Contract Clause of the Constitution.* Cambridge, Mass.: Harvard University Press, 1938.

III. CHAPTER 7

Corwin, Edward S. *Liberty against Government: The Rise, Flowering and Decline of a Famous Juridical Concept.* Baton Rouge, La.: Louisiana University Press, 1948.
———. "The 'Higher Law' Background of American Constitutional Law," *Harvard Law Review,* 42 (1928–1929), pp. 149–185, 365–409. Reprinted Ithaca, N.Y.: Cornell University Press, 1955.
———. *The Twilight of the Supreme Court: A History of Our Constitutional Theory.* New Haven, Conn.: Yale University Press, 1934.
Haines, Charles G. *The American Doctrine of Judicial Supremacy,* 2nd ed. Berkeley, Calif.: University of California Press, 1932.
———. *The Revival of Natural Law Concepts.* Cambridge, Mass.: Harvard University Press, 1930.
Hamilton, Walton H. "Affectation with Public Interest,"*Yale Law Journal,* 39 (June 1930), pp. 1089–1112.
Mendelson, Wallace. *Capitalism, Democracy, and the Supreme Court.* New York: Appleton-Century-Crofts, Inc., 1960.
Warren, Charles. "The 'New Liberty' under the Fourteenth Amendment," *Harvard Law Review,* 38 (February 1926), pp. 439–465.
Wright, Benjamin F. *American Interpretations of Natural Law.* Cambridge, Mass.: Harvard University Press, 1931.
———. *The Contract Clause of the Constitution.* Cambridge, Mass.: Harvard University Press, 1938.
———. *The Growth of American Constitutional Law.* New York: Holt, Rinehart & Winston, Inc., 1942.

IV. CHAPTER 8

Commission on Intergovernmental Relations. *A Report to the President for Transmittal to the Congress.* Washington, D.C.: Superintendent of Documents, 1955.
Corwin, Edward S. *The Commerce Power versus States Rights.* Princeton, N.J.: Princeton University Press, 1936.
Frankfurter, Felix. *The Commerce Clause under Marshall, Taney and White.* Chapel Hill, N.C.: University of North Carolina Press, 1937.
Hamilton, Walton H., and Douglass, Adair. *The Power to Govern: The Constitution—Then and Now.* New York: W. W. Norton & Company, Inc., 1937.
Kallenbach, Joseph E. *Federal Cooperation with the States under the Commerce Clause.* Ann Arbor, Mich.: University of Michigan Press, 1942.
Pritchett, C. Herman. *The Roosevelt Court: A Study in Judicial Politics and Values, 1937–1947.* New York: The Macmillan Company, 1948.
Welborn, David. "National-State Cooperation in Regulatory Administration," *State Government,* 33 (Summer 1960), pp. 199–207.

CHAPTER 9

Bach, George L. *Federal Reserve Policy Making.* New York: Alfred A. Knopf, Inc., 1950.
Bailey, Stephen K. *Congress Makes a Law: The Story Behind the Employment Act of 1946.* New York: Columbia University Press, 1950.

Bator, Francis M. *The Question of Government Spending*. New York: Harper and Row, Publishers, Inc., 1960.
Commission on Money and Credit. *Federal Credit Programs*. Englewood Cliffs, N.J.: Prentice-Hall, Inc., 1963.
Dale, Edwin L. *Conservatives in Power: A Study in Frustration*. New York: Doubleday & Company, Inc., 1960.
Dillard, Dudley. *The Economics of John Maynard Keynes*. Englewood Cliffs, N.J.: Prentice-Hall, Inc., 1948.
Goldenweiser, Emanuel A. *Federal Reserve System in Operation*. New York: McGraw-Hill Company, Inc., 1925.
Gross, Bertram, and Wilfred Lumer. *The Hard Money Crusade*. Washington, D.C.: Public Affairs Institute, 1954.
Keynes, John Maynard. *The General Theory of Employment, Interest and Money*. New York: Harcourt, Brace & World, Inc., 1936.
Reagan, Michael D. "The Political Structure of the Federal Reserve System," *The American Political Science Review*, 55 (March 1961), pp. 64–76.
Reed, Harold L. *Federal Reserve Policy, 1921–1930*. New York: McGraw-Hill Company, Inc., 1930.
Saulnier, Raymond J.; Harold G. Halcrow; and Neil H. Jacoby. *Federal Lending and Loan Insurance*. Princeton, N.J.: Princeton University Press, 1958.
Smithies, Arthur. "Uses of Selective Controls," in *United States Monetary Policy*. New York: The American Assembly, 1958.
Staff Report on Employment, Growth and Price Levels. Prepared for the Joint Economic Committee. Washington, D.C.: Superintendent of Documents, 1959.

CHAPTER 10

Adelman, Morris A. *A & P: A Study in Price-Cost Behavior and Public Policy*. Cambridge, Mass.: Harvard University Press, 1959.
Heflebower, Richard B., and George W. Stocking, (eds.) *Readings in Industrial Organization and Public Policy* (published for the American Economic Association). Homewood, Ill.: Richard D. Irwin, Inc., 1958.
Jones, Eliot. *The Trust Problem in the United States*. New York: The Macmillan Company, 1921.
Machlup, Fritz. *The Political Economy of Monopoly: Business, Labor and Government Policies*. Baltimore, Md.: Johns Hopkins Press, 1952.
Mason, Edward S. *Economic Concentration and the Monopoly Problem*. Cambridge, Mass.: Harvard University Press, 1957.
Massel, Mark S. *Competition and Monopoly: Legal and Economic Issues*. Washington, D.C.: Brookings Institution, 1962.
Neale, A. D. *The Antitrust Laws of the United States of America: A Study of Competition Enforced by Law*. Cambridge, England: Cambridge University Press, 1960.
Report of the Attorney General's National Committee to Study the Antitrust Laws. Washington, D.C.: Superintendent of Documents, 1955.
Stocking, George W., and Myron W. Watkins. *Monopoly and Free Enterprise*. New York: Twentieth Century Fund, 1951.
Taft, William H. *The Anti-Trust Act and the Supreme Court*. New York: Harper and Row, Publishers, Inc., 1914.
Wilson, Woodrow. *The New Freedom*. Garden City, N.Y.: Doubleday & Company, Inc., 1913.

CHAPTER 11

Adams, Walter, and Horace M. Gray, *Monopoly in America: The Government as Promoter.* New York: The Macmillan Company, 1955.
Blaisdell, Thomas C. *The Federal Trade Commission: An Experiment in the Control of Business.* New York: Columbia University Press, 1932.
Delivered Pricing, set of articles in *Law and Contemporary Problems.* Durham, N.C.: Duke University, **15** (Spring 1950), pp. 123–313.
Dirlam, Joel B., and Alfred E. Kahn. *Fair Competition: The Law and Economics of Antitrust Policy.* Ithaca, N.Y.: Cornell University Press, 1954.
Edwards, Corwin D. *The Price Discrimination Law: A Review of Experience.* Washington, D.C.: Brookings Institution, 1959.
Hall, Hugh M., Jr. "The Investigatory Function of the Federal Trade Commission, 1933–1952," in Redford, Emmette S. (ed.), *Public Administration and Policy Formation: Studies in Oil, Gas, Banking, River Development, and Corporate Investigations.* Austin, Tex.: University of Texas Press, 1956.
Heflebower, Richard B., and George W. Stocking (eds.) *Readings in Industrial Organization and Public Policy* (published for The American Economic Association). Homewood, Ill.: Richard D. Irwin, Inc., 1958.
Henderson, Gerald C. *The Federal Trade Commission: A Study in Administrative Law and Procedure.* New Haven, Conn.: Yale University Press, 1925.
Latham, Earl. *The Group Basis of Politics: A Study in Basing-Point Legislation.* Ithaca, N.Y.: Cornell University Press, 1952.
Lyon, Leverett S., et al. *The National Recovery Administration: An Analysis and Appraisal.* Washington, D.C.: Brookings Institution, 1935.
Machlup, Fritz. *The Basing-Point System: An Economic Analysis of a Controversial Pricing Practice.* Philadelphia: Blakiston Company, 1949.
Massel, Mark S. *Competition and Monopoly: Legal and Economic Issues.* Washington, D.C.: Brookings Institution, 1962.
Neale, A. D. *The Antitrust Laws of the United States of America: A Study of Competition Enforced by Law.* Cambridge, England: Cambridge University Press, 1960.
Palamountain, Joseph C. *The Federal Trade Commission and the Indiana Standard Case.* University, Ala.: University of Alabama Press, 1964.
———. *The Politics of Distribution.* Cambridge, Mass.: Harvard University Press, 1955.
Report of the Attorney's General's National Committee to Study the Antitrust Laws. Washington, D.C.: Superintendent of Documents, 1955.
Stocking, George W. *Basing Point Pricing and Regional Development: A Case Study of the Iron and Steel Industry.* Chapel Hill, N.C.: University of North Carolina Press, 1954.
——— and Myron W. Watkins. *Cartels or Competition? The Economics of International Controls by Business and Government.* New York: Twentieth Century Fund, 1948.

CHAPTER 12

Berle, Adolf A. *The 20th Century Capitalist Revolution.* New York: Harcourt, Brace & World, Inc., 1954.
Chamberlain, E. H. *The Theory of Monopolistic Competition: A Re-orientation of the Theory of Value.* Cambridge, Mass.: Harvard University Press, 1933.

Clark, J. M. "Toward a Concept of Workable Competition," *American Economic Review,* **30** (June 1940), pp. 241–256.
Eckstein, Otto, and Gary Fromm. *Steel and the Postwar Inflation.* Joint Economic Committee, 86th Congress, 1st Session (November 6, 1959).
Galbraith, John Kenneth. *American Capitalism: The Concept of Countervailing Power,* rev. ed. Boston: Houghton Mifflin Company, 1956.
Kaplan, A. D. H.; Joel B. Dirlam; and Robert F. Lanzillotti. *Pricing in Big Business: A Case Approach.* Washington, D.C.: Brookings Institution, 1958.
Kaysen, Karl, and Donald F. Turner. *Antitrust Policy: An Economic and Legal Analysis.* Cambridge, Mass.: Harvard University Press, 1959.
Lilienthal, David E. *Big Business: A New Era.* New York: Harper and Row, Publishers, Inc., 1952.
McConnell, Grant. *Steel and the Presidency, 1962.* New York: W. W. Norton & Company, Inc., 1963.
Oppenheim, S. Chesterfield. "Federal Antitrust Legislation: Guidepost to a Revised National Antitrust Policy," *Michigan Law Review,* **50** (June 1952), pp. 1139–1244.
Quinn, T. K. *Giant Business: Threat to Democracy.* New York: Exposition Press, 1952.
Reagan, Michael D. *The Managed Economy.* New York: Oxford University Press, 1963.
Redford, Emmette S. *Potential Public Policies to Deal with Inflation Caused by Market Power.* Joint Economic Committee, 86th Congress, 1st Session (December 11, 1959).
Robinson, Joan. *The Economics of Imperfect Competition.* New York: The Macmillan Company, 1933.
Rostow, Eugene V. *Planning for Freedom: The Public Law of American Capitalism.* New Haven, Conn.: Yale University Press, 1959.
Stocking, George W. "On the Concept of Workable Competition as an Antitrust Guide," *Antitrust Bulletin,* **2** (September 1956), pp. 3–39.

CHAPTER 13

Berger, Morroe. *Equality by Statute: Legal Controls over Group Discrimination.* New York: Columbia University Press, 1952.
Commons, John R., and John B. Andrews. *Principles of Labor Legislation,* 4th rev. ed. New York: Harper and Row, Publishers, Inc., 1936.
Dodd, Walter F. *Administration of Workmen's Compensation.* New York: Oxford University Press, 1936.
Harrington, Michael. *The Other America: Poverty in the United States.* New York: The Macmillan Company, 1962.
History of Labor in the United States, 1896–1932. New York: The Macmillan Company, 1935.
Leek, John H. *Government and Labor in the United States.* New York: Holt, Rinehart & Winston, Inc., 1952.
Mendelson, Wallace. *Discrimination: Based on the Report of the United States Commission on Civil Rights.* Englewood Cliffs, N.J.: Prentice-Hall, Inc., 1962.
Ruchames, Louis. *Race, Jobs, and Politics: The Story of FEPC.* New York: Columbia University Press, 1953.
Somers, Herman M. and Ann R. *Trends and Current Issues in Social Insurance.* Berkeley, Calif.: University of California Press, 1957.
———. *Workmen's Compensation: Prevention, Insurance, and Rehabilitation of Occupational Disability.* New York: John Wiley & Sons, Inc., 1954.

U. S. Department of Labor, Bureau of Employment Security, *Comparison of State Unemployment Insurance Laws as of January 1, 1962.*

Wilcock, Richard C., and Walter H. Franke. *Unwanted Workers: Permanent Lay-offs and Long-Term Unemployment.* New York: Free Press of Glencoe, Inc., 1963.

CHAPTER 14

Aaron, Benjamin. "The Labor Injunction Reappraised," *Labor Law Journal,* **14** (January 1963), pp. 41–81.

Berman, Edward. *Labor and the Sherman Act.* New York: Harper and Row, Publishers, Inc., 1930.

Bernstein, Irving; Harold L. Enarson; and R. W. Fleming (eds.) *Emergency Disputes and National Policy.* New York: Harper and Row, Publishers, Inc., 1955.

Bradley, Philip D. (ed.) *The Public Stake in Union Power.* Charlottesville, Va.: University of Virginia Press, 1959.

Braun, Kurt. *Labor Disputes and Their Settlement.* Baltimore: Johns Hopkins Press, 1955.

Clark, John M. *The Wage-Price Problem.* New York: American Bankers Association, 1960.

Frankfurter, Felix, and Nathan Greene. *The Labor Injunction.* New York: The Macmillan Company, 1930.

Gregory, Charles O. *Labor and the Law,* rev. ed. New York: W. W. Norton & Company, Inc. 1949.

Lecht, Leonard A. *Experience under Railway Labor Legislation.* New York: Columbia University Press, 1955.

Lindblom, Charles. *Unions and Capitalism.* New Haven, Conn.: Yale University Press, 1949.

Mason, Edward S. *Economic Concentration and the Monopoly Problem.* Cambridge, Mass.: Harvard University Press, 1957, Chapter 10.

McNaughton, Wayne L., and Joseph Lazar. *Industrial Relations and the Government.* New York: McGraw-Hill Company, Inc., 1954.

Millis, H. M., and E. Brown. *From the Wagner Act to Taft-Hartley: A Study of National Labor Policy and Labor Relations.* Chicago: University of Chicago Press, 1950.

Reynolds, Lloyd G. *Labor Economics and Labor Relations,* 3rd ed. Englewood Cliffs, N.J.: Prentice-Hall, Inc., 1959.

Stephens, Elvis C. "The No Man's Land of Labor Relations Remains Unoccupied," *Labor Law Journal,* **14** (February 1963), pp. 192–200.

Taft, Philip. *The Structure and Government of Labor Unions.* Cambridge, Mass.: Harvard University Press, 1954.

Taylor, George W. *Government Regulation of Industrial Relations.* New York: Prentice-Hall, Inc., 1948.

The Public Interest in National Labor Policy, by an independent study group. New York: Committee for Economic Development, 1961.

CHAPTER 15

Chandler, Lester V., and Donald H. Wallace. *Economic Mobilization and Stabilization: Selected Materials on the Economics of War and Defense.* New York: Holt, Rinehart & Winston, Inc., 1951.

Connery, Robert H. *The Navy and the Industrial Mobilization in World War II*. Princeton, N.J.: Princeton University Press, 1951.

Fesler, James W., et al. *Industrial Mobilization for War: History of the War Production Board and Predecessor Agencies, 1940–1945, Vol. 1, Program and Administration*. Washington, D.C.: Superintendent of Documents, 1947.

Gitlow, Abraham L. *Wage Determination under National Boards*. New York: Prentice-Hall, Inc., 1953.

Gulick, Luther. *Administrative Reflections from World War II*. University, Ala.: University of Alabama Press, 1948.

Harris, Seymour E. *The Economics of Mobilization and Inflation*. New York: W. W. Norton & Company, Inc., 1951.

Hart, Albert G. *Defense and the Dollar: Federal Credit and Monetary Policies*. New York: Twentieth Century Fund, 1953.

———. *Defense without Inflation*. New York: Twentieth Century Fund, 1951.

——— and E. Cary Brown. *Financing Defense*. New York: Twentieth Century Fund, 1951.

Mansfield, Harvey C., and Associates. *A Short History of OPA*. Washington, D.C.: Office of Temporary Controls, 1947.

Metz, Harold W. *Labor Policy of the Federal Government*. Washington, D.C.: Brookings Institution, 1945.

O'Brian, John Lord, and Manly Fleischmann. "The War Production Board Administrative Policies and Procedures," *George Washington Law Review*, 13 (December 1944), pp. 1–60.

Scitovsky, T.; E. S. Shaw; and L. Tarshis. *Mobilizing Resources for War*. New York: McGraw-Hill Company, Inc., 1951.

Somers, Herman M. *Presidential Agency: The Office of War Mobilization and Reconversion*. Cambridge, Mass.: Harvard University Press, 1950.

The Economics of National Defense, Fifth Annual Report to the President by the Council of Economic Advisers. Washington: D.C.: Superintendent of Documents, 1950.

U.S. Department of Labor, *A Short History of the War Manpower Commission* (June 1948).

U.S. Department of Labor, Bureau of Labor Statistics, *Problems and Policies of Dispute Settlement and Wage Stabilization during World War II*, Bulletin No. 1009. Washington, D.C.: Superintendent of Documents, 1950.

Wallace, Donald H. *Economic Controls and Defense*. New York: Twentieth Century Fund, 1953.

CHAPTER 16

Anderson, James E. *The Emergence of the Modern Regulatory State*. Washington, D. C.: Public Affairs Press, 1962.

Anshen, Melvin, and Francis D. Wormuth. *Private Enterprise and Public Policy*. New York: The Macmillan Company, 1954, Part II.

Blachly, Frederick F., and Miriam E. Oatman. *Federal Regulatory Action and Control*. Washington, D.C.: Brookings Institution, 1940.

Clark, J. M. *Social Control of Business*, 2nd ed. New York: McGraw-Hill Company, Inc., 1939.

Freund, Ernst. *Administrative Powers over Persons and Property*. Chicago: University of Chicago Press, 1928.

Graham, George A., and Henry Reining, Jr. *Regulatory Administration: An Exploratory Study*. New York: John Wiley & Sons, Inc., 1943.

650 Selected References

Koontz, Harold D. "Extent of Administrative Regulation in Economic Affairs," *The Annals of the American Academy of Political and Social Science* (May 1942).

Redford, Emmette S. *Administration of National Economic Control*. New York: The Macmillan Company, 1952, Chapters 1 and 2.

CHAPTER 17

Benson, Lee. *Merchants, Farmers, and Railroads: Railroad Regulation and New York Politics, 1850–1887*. Cambridge, Mass.: Harvard University Press, 1955.

Bigham, Truman C., and Merill J. Roberts. *Transportation*, 2nd ed. New York: McGraw-Hill Company, Inc., 1952.

Cherington, Charles R. *The Regulation of Railroad Abandonments*. Cambridge, Mass.: Harvard University Press, 1948.

Cushman, Robert E. *The Independent Regulatory Commissions*. New York: Oxford University Press, 1941, Chapter 3.

Fair, Marvin L., and Ernest W. Williams, Jr. *Economics of Transportation*, rev. ed. New York: Harper and Row, Publishers, Inc., 1959.

Latham, Earl. *The Politics of Railroad Coordination, 1933–1936*. Cambridge, Mass.: Harvard University Press, 1959.

Locklin, D. Philip. *Economics of Transportation*, 5th ed. Homewood, Ill.: Richard D. Irwin, Inc., 1960.

Mansfield, Harvey C. *The Lake Cargo Rate Controversy*. New York: Columbia University Press, 1932.

McFarland, Carl. *Judicial Control of the Federal Trade Commission and the Interstate Commerce Commission, 1920–1930*. Cambridge, Mass.: Harvard University Press, 1933.

Meyer, John R.; Merton J. Peck; W. John Stenason; and Charles J. Zwick. *The Economics of Competition in the Transportation Industries*. Cambridge, Mass.: Harvard Universty Press, 1959.

National Transportation Policy, Report by Special Study Group on Transportation Policies in the United States. Committee on Commerce, U.S. Senate. 87th Cong., 1st Sess., 1961.

Sharfman, I. L. *The Interstate Commerce Commission: A Study in Administrative Law and Procedure*. New York: Commonwealth Fund, 1931–1937, Vols. I, II, III-A, III-B, IV.

Westmeyer, Russell E. *Economics of Transportation*. New York: Prentice-Hall, Inc., 1952.

CHAPTER 18

Beard, William. *Regulation of Pipe Lines as Common Carriers*. New York: Columbia University Press, 1941.

Bigham, Truman C., and Merill J. Roberts. *Transportation*, 2nd ed. New York: McGraw-Hill Company, Inc, 1952.

Caves, Richard E. *Air Transport and Its Regulators: An Industry Study*. Cambridge, Mass.: Harvard University Press, 1962.

Cherington, Paul M. *Airline Price Policy: A Study of Domestic Airline Passenger Fares*. Boston: Division of Research, Graduate School of Business Administration, Harvard University, 1958.

Cookenboo, Leslie, Jr. *Crude Oil Pipe Lines and Competition in the Oil Industry*. Cambridge, Mass.: Harvard University Press, 1955.
Dearing, Charles L., and Wilfred Owen. *National Transportation Policy*. Washington, D.C.: Brookings Institution, 1949.
Fair, Marvin L., and Ernest W. Williams, Jr. *Economics of Transportation,* rev. ed. New York: Harper and Row, Publishers, Inc., 1959.
Keyes, Lucile S. *Federal Control of Entry into Air Transportation*. Cambridge, Mass.: Harvard University Press, 1951.
Locklin, D. Philip. *Economics of Transportation,* 5th ed. Homewood, Ill.: Richard D. Irwin, Inc., 1960.
National Transportation Policy. Report by Special Study Group on Transportation Policies in the United States. Committee on Commerce, U.S. Senate. 87th Cong., 1st Sess., 1961.
Redford, Emmette S. *The General Passenger Fare Investigation*. University, Ala.: University of Alabama Press, 1959.
Rostow, Eugene V. *A National Policy for the Oil Industry*. New Haven, Conn.: Yale University Press, 1948.
Westmeyer, Russell E. *Economics of Transportation*. New York: Prentice-Hall, Inc., 1952.
Williams, Ernest W., Jr. *The Regulation of Rail-Motor Rate Competition*. New York: Harper and Row, Publishers, Inc., 1958.
Zeis, Paul M. *American Shipping Policy*. Princeton, N.J.: Princeton University Press, 1938.

CHAPTER 19

Barnes, Irston R. *The Economics of Public Utility Regulation*. New York: Appleton-Century-Crofts, Inc., 1942.
Bauer, John, and Nathaniel Gold. *Public Utility Valuation for Purposes of Rate Control*. New York: The Macmillan Company, 1934.
Elsbree, Hugh L. *Interstate Transmission of Electric Power: A Study in the Conflict of State and Federal Jurisdiction*. Cambridge, Mass.: Harvard University Press, 1931.
Glaeser, Martin G. *Public Utilities in American Capitalism*. New York: The Macmillan Company, 1957.
Huitt, Ralph K. *National Regulation of the Natural Gas Industry* (Ph.D. Dissertation). Austin, Tex.: University of Texas, 1950.
Lyon, Leverett S., and Victor Abramson (eds.). *Government and Economic Life,* Washington, D.C.: Brookings Institution, 1940, Vol. 2, Chapter 21.
Mosher, William E. "Public Utility Regulation," in Graham, George A., and Henry Reining, Jr., *Regulatory Administration: An Exploratory Study*. New York: John Wiley & Sons, Inc., 1943.
Mosher, William E., and Finla G. Crawford. *Public Utility Regulation*. New York: Harper and Row, Publishers, 1933.
Ruggles, C. O. *Aspects of State Public Utility Commissions*. Cambridge, Mass.: Graduate School of Business Administration, Bureau of Business Research, Harvard University, 1937.
Troxel, Emery. *Economics of Public Utilities*. New York: Holt, Rinehart & Winston, Inc., 1947.

CHAPTER 20

Archer, Gleason L. *Big Business and Radio.* New York: American Historical Company, Inc., 1939.
Danielian, Noobar R. *American Telephone and Telegraph.* New York: Vanguard Press, 1939.
"Direct Regulation of American Telephone and Telegraph Company," *Yale Law Journal,* 48 (1939), pp. 1015.
Hagan, Charles B. "The Bell System and a Decade of Regulation," *Current Economic Comment,* 17 (1955), p. 38.
Regulation of Broadcasting. A Study Made for the Committee on Interstate and Foreign Commerce, House of Representatives. Washington, D.C.: 85th Congress, 1st Session, 1958.
Report of the President's Communication Policy Board, *Telecommunications: A Program for Progress.* Washington, D.C.: Superintendent of Documents, 1951.
Rosenblum, Victor G. "How to Get into TV: The FCC and Miami's Channel 10," in Westin, Alan F., *The Uses of Power.* New York: Harcourt, Brace & World, Inc., 1962.
Wall, T. H., and J. B. Jacob. "Communications Act Amendments 1952—Clarity or Ambiguity," *Georgetown Law Journal* (1953), pp. 135–181.
White, L. *The American Radio.* Chicago: University of Chicago Press, 1947.

CHAPTER 21

Bartley, Ernest R. *The Tidelands Oil Controversy: A Legal and Historical Analysis.* Austin, Tex.: University of Texas Press, 1953.
Carper, Edith T. *Lobbying and the Natural Gas Bill.* University, Ala.: University of Alabama Press, 1962. Reprinted in Bock, Edwin A., and Alan K. Campbell, *Case Studies in American Government.* Englewood Cliffs, N.J.: Prentice-Hall, Inc., 1962.
Cassidy, R., Jr. *Price Making and Price Behavior in the Petroleum Industry.* New Haven, Conn.: Yale University Press, 1954.
"FPC Regulation of Independent Producers of Natural Gas" (unsigned note), *Harvard Law Review,* 75 (January 1962), pp. 549–568.
Hardwicke, Robert E. *The Rule of Capture and Its Implications as Applied to Oil and Gas.* Chicago: American Bar Association, 1935.
Huitt, Ralph K. "Federal Regulation of the Uses of Natural Gas," *American Political Science Review,* 56 (June 1952), pp. 455–469.
———. "National Regulation of the Natural-Gas Industry," in Redford, Emmette S. (ed.), *Public Administration and Policy Formation: Studies in Oil, Gas, Banking, River Development, and Corporate Investigations.* Austin, Tex.: University of of Texas Press, 1956.
Johnson, Nicholas. "Producer Rate Regulation in Natural Gas Certification Proceedings: CATCO in Context," *Columbia Law Review,* 62 (May 1962), pp. 773–820.
Mills, Warner E., Jr. *Martial Law in East Texas.* University, Ala.: University of Alabama Press, 1960.
Roberts, John S. *Primer of Oil and Gas Law in Texas.* Bellaire, Tex.: Belltex Publishing Company, 1955.

Rostow, Eugene V. *A National Policy for the Oil Industry.* New Haven, Conn.: Yale University Press, 1948.
Watkins, Myron W. *Oil Stabilization or Conservation? A Case Study in Organization of Industrial Control.* New York: Harper and Row, Publishers, Inc., 1937.
Willbern, York Y. "Administrative Control of Petroleum Production in Texas," in Redford, Emmette S. (ed.), *Public Administration and Policy Formation: Studies in Oil, Gas, Banking, River Development, and Corporate Investigations.* Austin, Tex.: University of Texas Press, 1956.
Zimmermann, Erich W., *Conservation in the Production of Petroleum: A Study in Industrial Control.* New Haven, Conn.: Yale University Press, 1957.

CHAPTER 22

Andrews, A. *The Farmer's Dilemma.* Washington, D.C.: Public Affairs Press, 1961.
Benedict, Murray R. *Farm Policies of the United States, 1790–1950: A Study of Their Origins and Development.* New York: Twentieth Century Fund, 1953.
———. *Can We Solve the Farm Problem? An Analysis of Federal Aid to Agriculture.* New York: Twentieth Century Fund, 1955.
Coppock, J. O. *North Atlantic Policy—The Agricultural Gap.* New York: Twentieth Century Fund, 1963.
Hathaway, D. E. *Government and Agriculture: Economic Policy in a Democratic Society.* New York: The Macmillan Company, 1963.
Higbee, E. *Farms and Farmers in an Urban Age.* New York: Twentieth Century Fund, 1963.
U.S. Agricultural Policy in the Postwar Years, 1945–1963. Washington, D.C.: Congressional Quarterly Service, 1961.

CHAPTER 23

Contemporary Problems in Securities Regulation (a symposium). *Virginia Law Review,* 45 (October 1959), pp. 787–1072.
Cowett, Edward M. "Federal-State Relationships in Securities Regulation," *George Washington Law Review,* 28 (October 1959), pp. 287–305.
Fox, Guy. "Supervision of Banking by the Comptroller of the Currency," in Redford, Emmette S. (ed.), *Public Administration and Policy Formation: Studies in Oil, Gas, Banking, and Corporate Investigations.* Austin, Tex.: University of Texas Press, 1956.
Frey, Alexander H. "Federal Regulation of the Over-the-Counter Securities Market," *University of Pennsylvania Law Review,* 106 (November 1957), pp. 1–51.
Kimball, Spencer L. *Insurance and Public Policy: A Study in the Legal Implementation of Social and Economic Policy, Based on Wisconsin Records, 1835–1959.* Madison, Wis.: University of Wisconsin Press, 1960.
———. "The Purpose of Insurance Regulation: A Preliminary Inquiry in the Theory of Insurance Law," *Minnesota Law Review,* 45 (March 1961), pp. 471–524.
Loss, Louis. *Securities Regulation,* 2nd ed. Boston: Little, Brown & Company, 1961, 3 Vols.
Patterson, Edwin M. *The Insurance Commissioner in the United States: A Study in Administrative Law and Practice.* Cambridge, Mass.: Harvard University Press, 1927.

Prather, Charles. *Money and Banking,* 7th ed. Homewood, Ill.: Richard D. Irwin, Inc., 1961.
Regulation of Insurance (a symposium). *Law and Contemporary Problems,* 15, No. 4 (Autumn 1950).
Sawyer, Elmer W. *Insurance as Interstate Commerce.* New York: McGraw-Hill Company, Inc., 1945.
The Insurance Industry, Report of the Committee on the Judiciary, United States Senate, 87th Congress, 1st Session, Report No. 831 (1961).
"Twenty-Five Years of Federal Securities Regulation," *Columbia Law Review,* 59 (May 1959), pp. 697–747.

CHAPTERS 24 AND 25

Administrative Regulation, Symposium in *Law and Contemporary Problems,* 26 (Spring 1961), pp. 179–346.
Association of the Bar of the City of New York. Special Committee on the Federal Conflict of Interest Laws. *Conflict of Interest and the Federal Service.* Cambridge, Mass.: Harvard University Press, 1960.
Bernstein, Marver H. *Regulating Business by Independent Commission.* Princeton, N.J.: Princeton University Press, 1955.
Bookman, George. "Regulation by Elephant, Rabbit, and Lark," *Fortune,* 63 (June 1961), pp. 137ff.
Commission on Organization of the Executive Branch of the Government. *Legal Services and Procedure.* House Document, No. 128, 84th Cong., 1st Sess. (1955).
———. *Regulatory Commissions.* Washington, D.C.: Superintendent of Documents, 1949.
———. Task Force Report, *Regulatory Commissions.* Washington, D.C.: Superintendent of Documents, 1949.
Cushman, Robert E. *The Independent Regulatory Commissions.* New York: Oxford University Press, 1941.
Davis, Kenneth Culp. *Administrative Law.* Saint Paul, Minn.: West Publishing Company, 1951.
Fainsod, Merle. "Some Reflections on the Nature of the Regulatory Process," Chapter 10 in Friedrich, C. J., and Edward S. Mason, *Public Policy, 1940.* Cambridge, Mass.: Harvard University Press, 1940.
Fesler, James W. "Independent Regulatory Commissions," Chapter 10 in Marx, Fritz Morstein, *Elements of Public Administration,* 2nd ed. Englewood Cliffs, N.J.: Prentice-Hall, Inc., 1959.
———. *The Independence of State Regulatory Agencies.* Chicago: Public Administrative Service, 1942.
Fick, Winston M. *Administrative Procedure in a Federal Regulatory Commission: The Civil Aeronautics Board and the New York-Chicago Case.* University, Ala.: University of Alabama Press, 1964.
Final Report of the Attorney General's Committee on Administrative Procedure. Washington, D.C.: Superintendent of Documents, 1941.
Friendly, Henry J. *The Federal Administrative Agencies: The Need for Better Definition of Standards.* Cambridge, Mass.: Harvard University Press, 1962.
Gellhorn, Walter. *Federal Administrative Proceedings.* Baltimore, Md.: Johns Hopkins Press, 1941.
Heady, Ferrel. *Administrative Procedure Legislation in the States.* Ann Arbor, Mich.: University of Michigan Press, 1952.

———. "The New Reform Movement in Regulatory Administration," *Public Administration Review*, **19** (Spring 1959), pp. 89–100.
Hector, Louis J. "Problems of the CAB and the Independent Regulatory Commissions," *Yale Law Journal*, **69** (May 1960), pp. 931–964.
Herring, E. Pendleton. *Public Administration and the Public Interest*. New York: McGraw-Hill Company, Inc., 1936.
Jaffe, Louis L. "The Effective Limits of the Administrative Process: A Reevaluation," *Harvard Law Review*, **67** (May 1954), pp. 1105–1135.
Landis, James M. *Report on Regulatory Agencies to the President-Elect*. Committee on the Judiciary, U.S. Senate. 86th Cong., 2nd Sess. (1960).
———. *The Administrative Process*. New Haven, Conn.: Yale University Press, 1938.
President's Committee on Administrative Management. *Report with Special Studies*. Washington, D.C.: Superintendent of Documents, 1937.
Redford, Emmette S. *Administration of National Economic Control*. New York: The Macmillan Company, 1952.
———. *National Regulatory Commissions: Need for a New Look*. College Park, Md.: University of Maryland Press, 1959.
Rosenblum, Victor G. "How to Get into TV: The Federal Communications Commission and Miami's Channel 10," Chapter 4 in Westin, Alan F., *The Uses of Power*. New York: Harcourt, Brace & World, Inc., 1962.
Schwartz, Bernard. *The Professor and the Commissions*. New York: Alfred A. Knopf, Inc., 1959.

CHAPTERS 26 AND 27

Birkhead, Jesse. *Government Budgeting*. New York: John Wiley & Sons, Inc., 1956, Chapter 16.
Ciriacy-Wantrup, S. V. *Resource Conservation: Economics and Policies*. Berkeley and Los Angeles, Calif.: University of California Press, 1952.
Clay, Comer. "The Lower Colorado River Authority," in Redford, Emmette S. (ed.), *Public Administration and Policy Formation: Studies in Oil, Gas, Banking, River Development, and Corporate Investigations*. Austin, Tex.: University of Texas Press, 1956, Chapter 4.
Commission on Organization of the Executive Branch of the Government. *Business Enterprises*. House Document, No. 162. 84th Cong., 1st Sess. (1955).
———. Task Force Report on *Lending Agencies*. House Document, No. 107. 84th Cong., 1st Sess. (1955).
Dimock, Marshall E. "Government Corporations: A Focus of Politics and Administration," *American Political Science Review*, **34** (October and December 1949), pp. 899–921, 1145–1164.
———. *Government-Operated Enterprises in the Panama Canal Zone*. Chicago: University of Chicago Press, 1934.
Eckstein, Otto. *Water Resources Development: The Economics of Project Evaluation*. Cambridge, Mass.: Harvard University Press, 1958.
Friedman, W. (ed.). *The Public Corporation: A Comparative Symposium*. Toronto: University of Toronto Press, 1954.
General Accounting Office. *Reference Manual of Government Corporations*. Senate Document, No. 86. 79th Cong., 1st Sess. (1945).
Key, V. O. "Government Corporations," in Marx, Fritz Morstein, *Elements of Public Administration*, rev. ed. Englewood Cliffs, N.J.: Prentice-Hall, Inc., 1959, Chapter 11.

Kleinsorge, Paul L. *The Boulder Canyon Project: Historical and Economic Aspects*. Stanford University, Cal.: Stanford University Press, 1941.

Lilienthal, David E. *Democracy on the March*, rev. ed. New York: Harper and Row, Publishers, Inc., 1953.

Martin, Roscoe C. (ed.). *TVA, The First Twenty Years: A Staff Report*. University, Ala., and Knoxville, Tenn.: University of Alabama Press and University of Tennessee Press, 1956.

McDiarmid, John. *Government Corporations and Federal Funds*. Chicago: University of Chicago Press, 1938.

McKinley, Charles. *Uncle Sam in the Pacific Northwest: Federal Management of Natural Resources in the Columbia River Valley*. Berkeley and Los Angeles, Calif.: University of California Press, 1952.

Port of New York Authority. *Metropolitan Transportation—1980*. Published by the Authority, 1963.

Preston, Nathaniel S. "Public Authorities Today," *State Government*, **34** (Summer 1961), pp. 205–211.

Price, Don K. "The Scientific Establishment," *Proceedings of the American Philosophical Society*, **106** (June 1962), pp. 235–245.

Pritchett, C. Herman. "The Paradox of the Government Corporation," *Public Administration Review*, **1** (Summer 1941), pp. 381–389.

———. *The Tennessee Valley Authority: A Study in Public Administration*. Chapel Hill, N.C.: University of North Carolina Press, 1943.

Redford, Emmette S. "Reexamen de la Corporation Publica," *Revista de Ciencias Sociales*, **3** (June 1959), pp. 173–199 (University of Puerto Rico).

Report to the President on Government Contracting for Research and Development. The Bell Report, Senate Document No. 94. 87th Cong., 2nd Sess. (1962).

Seidman, Harold. "The Theory of the Autonomous Corporation: A Critical Appraisal," *Public Administration Review*, **12** (Spring 1952), pp. 90–96.

Thomas, Morgan, in collaboration with Robert M. Northrup. *Atomic Energy and Congress*. Ann Arbor, Mich.: University of Michigan Press, 1956.

Thurston, John. *Government Proprietary Corporations in the English-Speaking Countries*. Cambridge, Mass.: Harvard University Press, 1937.

Table of Cases

Adair v. U.S., 208 U.S. 161 (1908), 130, 132, 297
Adams v. Tanner, 244 U.S. 590 (1917), 130
Addyston Pipe and Steel Co. v. U.S., 175 U.S. 211 (1899), 141
Adkins v. Children's Hospital, 261 U.S. 525 (1923), 130–131, 285, 366
A. L. A. Schechter Poultry Corp. v. U.S., 295 U.S. 495 (1935), 144, 241, 287, 554
Allen-Bradley Co. v. International Brotherhood of Electrical Workers, 325 U.S. 797 (1945), 309
Amalgamated Ass'n. of Street, Electric Railway and Motor Coach Employees of America, Division 998 v. Wisconsin Employment Relations Board, 340 U.S. 383 (1951), 145
American Column and Lumber Co. v. U.S., 257 U.S. 377 (1921), 198, 199
American Communication Ass'n. v. Douds, 339 U.S. 382 (1950), 134
American Newspaper Publishers Association v. NLRB, 345 U.S. 100 (1953), 314
Apex Hosiery Co. v. Leader, 310 U.S. 469 (1940), 187, 308–309
Appalachian Coals, Inc. v. U.S., 288 U.S. 344 (1933), 95, 186, 196–197, 200, 207
Arrow, Hart & Hegeman Electric Co. v. FTC, 291 U.S. 587 (1934), 227
Arver v. U.S., 245 U.S. 366 (1918), 271
Ashwander v. Tennessee Valley Authority, 297 U.S. 298 (1936), 149
Associated Press v. NLRB, 301 U.S. 103 (1937), 145
Atchison, T. & S. F. R. Co. v. Rr. Comm., 283 U.S. 380 (1931), 113
Atlantic Refining Co. v. Public Service Commission, 360 U.S. 378 (1959), 490
Atlantic Refining Co. v. Railroad Commission, 346 S.W. 2d 801 (1961), 483
Automatic Canteen v. FTC, 346 U.S. 661 (1953), 217

Bailey v. Drexel Furniture Co., 259 U.S. 20 (1922), 138, 286
Bank of Augusta v. Earle, 13 Pet. 519 (1939), 107
Bank of U.S. v. Deveaux, 5 Cr. 61 (1809), 107
Barnard v. Monongahela Natural Gas Co., 65 Atl. 801 (1907), 476
Bedford Stone Co. v. Journeymen Stone Cutters' Ass'n., 274 U.S. 34 (1927), 299, 323
Bement v. National Harrow Co., 186 U.S. 70 (1902), 204
Block v. Hirsh, 256 U.S. 135 (1921), 365
Briscoe v. Bank of Kentucky, 11 Pet. 257 (1837), 110
Brown v. Maryland, 12 Wheat. 419 (1827), 126
Brown Shoe Co., Inc. v. U.S., 370 U.S. 294 (1962), 225, 230
Brundred Bros. v. Prairie Pipe Line Co., 68 ICC 458 (1922), 416
Buck v. Kuykendall, 267 U.S. 307 (1925), 113, 399
Bunting v. Oregon, 243 U.S. 426 (1917), 285, 286

Calder v. Bull, 3 Dall. 386 (1798), 15–16, 64, 123, 125
California v. FPC, 369 U.S. 482 (1962), 241–242
Carter v. Carter Coal Co., 298 U.S. 238 (1936), 144
Charles River Bridge v. Warren Bridge Co., 11 Pet. 420 (1837), 124
Chicago Board of Trade v. Olsen, 262 U.S. 1 (1923), 143, 145
Chicago Board of Trade v. U.S., 288 U.S. 344 (1918), 196

658 *Table of Cases*

Chicago, M. & St. P. R. Co. v. Minnesota, 134 U.S. 418 (1890), 129
Cin., N. O. & Tex. Pac. Ry. v. ICC (Social Circle case), 162 U.S. 184 (1896), 374
City of Detroit v. FPC, 230 F. 2d 810 (1955), cert. denied, 352, U.S. 829 (1956), 491
Claire Furnace Co. v. FTC, 285 F. 936 (1923), 210
Class Rate Investigation, 1939, 262 ICC 447 (1945), 387
Columbia Broadcasting System v. U.S., 316 U.S. 407 (1942), 467
Commonwealth v. Hunt, 4 Met. 111 (1842), 296
Commonwealth v. Pouiliot, 198 N.E. 256 (1935), 271
Continental Paper Bag Co. v. Eastern Paper Bag Co., 210 U.S. 405 (1908), 203
Cooley v. Board of Wardens of the Port of Philadelphia, 12 How. 299 (1851), 113
Coppage v. Kansas, 236 U.S. 1 (1915), 130, 132, 297, 303
Corfield v. Coryell, 6 Fed. Cas. No. 3,230 (1823), 106
Corn Products Refining Co. v. FTC, 324 U.S. 726 (1945), 234

Daniel Ball v. U.S., 10 Wall. 557 (1871), 140
Dartmouth College v. Woodward, 4 Wheat. 518 (1819), 111, 123
Davidson v. New Orleans, 96 U.S. 97 (1878), 128
Dayton Coal & I. Co. v. Barton, 183 U.S. 23 (1901), 270
Dayton-Goose Creek Ry. v. U.S., 263 U.S. 456 (1924), 380
Deering & Co. v. Peterson, 77 N.W. 568 (1898), 138
Doherty & Co. v. Goodman, 294 U.S. 623 (1935), 107
Dorchy v. Kansas, 264 U.S. 286 (1924), 130
Douds v. Metropolitan Federation of Architects, 75 F. Supp. 672 (1948), 317
Dr. Bonhams Case, 8 Co. 118a (1610), 129
Duplex v. Deering, 254 U.S. 443 (1921), 299, 307, 309, 323

East New York Savings Bank v. Hahn, 326 U.S. 230 (1945), 111
Electric Bond and Share Co. v. SEC, 303 U.S. 419 (1938), 436
Ely Lilly & Co. v. Sav-on-Drugs, Inc., 366 U.S. 276 (1961), 238
Erie Railroad v. Tompkins, 304 U.S. 64 (1938), 117
Erie Railroad Co. v. Public Utility Commrs., 254 U.S. 394 (1921), 113
Erie Railroad Co. v. Williams, 233 U.S. 685 (1914), 270
Ethyl Gasoline Corp. v. U.S., 309 U.S. 436 (1940), 204
Exquisite Form Brassiere v. FTC, 301 F. 2d 499 (1961), 220

Farmer's Educational and Cooperative Union v. WDAY, 360 U.S. 525 (1959), 472
Fashion Originators Guild of America v. FTC, 312 U.S. 457 (1941), 216
FCC v. Allentown Broadcasting Corp., 350 U.S. 1015 (1955), 469
FCC v. Pottsville Broadcasting Co., 309 U.S. 134 (1940), 464–465, 466
FCC v. Sanders Bros. Radio Station, 309 U.S. 570 (1940), 465–466
FPC v. Hope Natural Gas Co., 320 U.S. 591 (1944), 50, 133, 444–447, 487, 491
FPC v. Transcontinental Gas Pipe Line Corp., 365 U.S. 1 (1961), 498
FTC v. A. E. Staley Mfg. Co., 324 U.S. 746 (1945), 219–220, 234
FTC v. American Tobacco Co., 264 U.S. 298 (1924), 210
FTC v. Anheuser-Busch, Inc., 363 U.S. 536 (1960), 217
FTC v. Cement Institute, 333 U.S. 683 (1948), 214, 235, 261
FTC v. Claire Furnace Co., 244 U.S. 160 (1927), 210
FTC v. Curtis Publishing Co., 260 U.S. 568 (1923), 223
FTC v. Maynard Coal Co., 22 F. 2d 873 (1927), 210
FTC v. Morton Salt Co., 334 U.S. 37 (1948), 218
FTC v. National Casualty Co., 357 U.S. 560 (1958), 534
FTC v. National Lead Co., 352 U.S. 419 (1957), 236
FTC v. Raladam Co., 283 U.S. 643 (1931), 215

Table of Cases 6 5 9

FTC v. R. F. Keppel & Bro., 291 U.S. 304 (1934), 215
FTC v. Simplicity Pattern Co., 360 U.S. 59 (1959), 220
FTC v. Standard Oil Co. (Standard Stations case), 335 U.S. 396 (1958), 220, 261
FTC v. Travelers Health Association, 362 U.S. 293 (1960), 534
Field v. Clark, 143 U.S. 649 (1892), 554
Fletcher v. Peck, 6 Cr. 87 (1810), 111, 123
Fly v. Heitmeyer, 309 U.S. 146 (1940), 465
Fong Yue Ting v. U.S., 149 U.S. 698 (1893), 150
Frost Trucking Co. v. Railroad Commission of California, 271 U.S. 583 (1926), 398

German Alliance Insurance Co. v. Lewis, 233 U.S. 389 (1913), 365, 535
Gibbons v. Ogden, 9 Wheat. 1 (1824), 112, 114, 139
Goodyear Tire and Rubber Co. v. FTC, 101 F. 2d 620 (1939), cert. denied, 308 U.S. 557 (1939), 219
Great Northern Ry. Co. v. Merchants Elevator Co., 259 U.S. 285 (1922), 562
Guss v. Utah Labor Relations Board, 353 U.S. 1 (1957), 317

Halbouty v. Railroad Commission, 357 S.W. 2d 364 (1962), 483
Hammer v. Dagenhart (Child Labor case), 247 U.S. 251 (1918), 143–144, 147, 286, 631
Hampton & Co. v. U.S., 276 U.S. 394 (1928), 139
Hartford Empire v. U.S. 323 U.S. 386 (1945), 206
Hawkins v. Bleakley, 243 U.S. 210 (1917), 277
Heaton-Peninsular Button Fastener Co. v. Eureka Specialty Co., 77 F. 288 (1896), 203
Heim v. McCall, 239 U.S. 175 (1915), 272
Helvering v. Davis, 301 U.S. 619 (1937), 133, 137
Hess v. Pawloski, 274 U.S. 352 (1927), 107
Hitchman Coal and Coke Co. v. Mitchell, 254 U.S. 229 (1917), 297
Holden v. Hardy, 169 U.S. 366 (1898), 285
Home Building & Loan Association v. Blaisdell, 290 U.S. 398 (1934), 111, 133, 165
Hoover v. Intercity Radio, 286 F. 1003 (1923), 460
Houston, E. & W. T. R. Co. v. U.S., 234 U.S. 342 (1914), 143
H. P. Hood & Sons, Inc. v. U.S., 307 U.S. 588 (1939), 554
Humphrey's Executor v. U.S. (Rathbun v. U.S.), 295 U.S. 602 (1935), 550

In re Debs, 158 U.S. 564 (1895), 297
International Brotherhood of Teamsters v. Vogt, 354 U.S. 284 (1957), 134
International Business Machines Corp. v. U.S., 298 U.S. 131 (1936), 223
International Salt Co., Inc. v. U.S., 332 U.S. 392 (1947), 203, 224
ICC v. Alabama Midland Ry. Co., 168 U.S. 144 (1897), 375
ICC v. Brimson, 154 U.S. 447 (1894), 562
ICC v. Cin., N. O. & Tex. Pac. Ry. Co. (Maximum Freight Rate case), 167 U.S. 479 (1897), 374, 376
Interstate Natural Gas. Co. v. FPC, 330 U.S. 852 (1947), 487
Ives v. South Buffalo Railway Co., 201 N.Y. 271 (1911), 277

Julliard v. Greenman, 110 U.S. 421 (1884), 110

Keokee Consolidated Coke Co. v. Taylor, 234 U.S. 224 (1914), 270
Knoxville Iron Co. v. Harbison, 183 U.S. 13 (1901), 270

La Tourette v. McMaster, 248 U.S. 465 (1919), 107
Legal Tender Cases, 12 Wall. 457 (1871), 110 U.S. 421 (1884), 110, 139

Lichter v. U.S., 334 U.S. 742 (1948), 149
Lincoln Federal Labor Union v. Northwestern Iron and Metal Co., 335 U.S. 525 (1949), 133
Loan Association v. Topeka, 20 Wall. 655 (1875), 128, 138
Local 537, International Brotherhood of Teamsters v. NLRB, 365 U.S. 667 (1961), 316
Lochner v. New York, 198 U.S. 45 (1905), 130, 131, 132, 285
Loewe v. Lawlor (Danbury Hatter's case), 208 U.S. 274 (1908), 195, 298, 299, 323
Louisville Joint Stock Land Bank v. Radford, 295 U.S. 555 (1935), 111, 165
L. P. Steuart & Bro., Inc. v. Bowles, 322 U.S. 398 (1944), 149

McCulloch v. Maryland, 4 Wheat. 316 (1819), 110, 136, 139
McLean v. Arkansas, 211 U.S. 539 (1909), 270
Maple Flooring Manufacturers' Association v. U.S., 268 U.S. 563 (1925), 198–199
Marbury v. Madison, 1 Cr. 137 (1803), 122
Market Street Railway Co. v. Railroad Commission of California, 324 U.S. 548 (1945), 449
Maryland and Virginia Milk Producers Ass'n., Inc. v. U.S., 362 U.S. 458 (1960), 240–241
Massachusetts v. Mellon and Frothingham v. Mellon, 262 U.S. 447 (1923), 138
Matter of Packard Motor Car Co., 61 NLRB 4 (1945), 312
Mennen Co. v. FTC, 288 F. 774 (1923), cert. denied, 262 U.S. 759 (1923), 218
Mercoid Corporation v. Mid-Continent Inv. Co., 320 U.S. 661 (1944), 203
Michigan Public Utilities Commission v. Duke, 266 U.S. 570 (1925), 398
Missouri v. Holland, 252 U.S. 416 (1920), 150
Missouri v. Kansas Natural Gas Co., 265 U.S. 298 (1924), 431
Morehead v. N.Y. ex rel Tipaldo, 298 U.S. 587 (1936), 285
Mountain Timber v. Washington, 243 U.S. 210 (1917), 277
Mugler v. Kansas, 123 U.S. 623 (1887), 129
Mulford v. Smith, 307 U.S. 38 (1939), 146
Muller v. Oregon, 208 U.S. 412 (1908), 77, 284
Munn v. Illinois, 94 U.S. 113 (1876), 77, 128, 129, 365, 398, 438, 449

National Biscuit Co. v. FTC, 299 F. 733 (1924), cert. denied, 266 U.S. 613 (1924), 218
NLRB v. Denver Building & Construction Trades Council, 341 U.S. 675 (1941), 317
NLRB v. Friedman-Harry Marks Clothing Co., 301 U.S. 58 (1937), 145
NLRB v. Fruehauf Trailer Co., 301 U.S. 49 (1937), 145
NLRB v. Gamble Enterprises, Inc., 345 U.S. 117 (1953), 314
NLRB v. Jones & Laughlin Steel Corp., 301 U.S. 1 (1937), 133, 145, 311
NLRB v. Mackay Radio and Telegraph Co., 304 U.S. 333 (1938), 312
Nebbia v. New York, 291 U.S. 502 (1934), 133, 366
New Jersey v. Wilson, 7 Cr. 164 (1812), 123
New State Ice Co. v. Liebmann, 285 U.S. 262 (1932), 130, 132, 366
Noble State Bank v. Haskell, 219 U.S. 104 (1911), 132
Norman v. Baltimore & Ohio Ry., 294 U.S. 240 (1935), 133, 165
North American Company v. SEC, 327 U.S. 686 (1946), 437
Northern Securities Co. v. U.S., 193 U.S. 197 (1904), 141, 185, 189, 195, 225, 257, 380
N.Y. v. U.S., 331 U.S. 284 (1947), 387

Ohio ex rel Clarke v. Deckebach, 274 U.S. 392 (1927), 272
Oyama v. California, 332 U.S. 633 (1948), 272

Pacific Telephone and Telegraph Co. v. Tax Commission, 297 U.S. 403 (1936), 108
Palmer Oil Corp. v. Amerada Petroleum Corp., 343 U.S. 390 (1952), 483

Palmer Oil Corp. v. Phillips Petroleum Co., 321 Pac. 2d 997 (1951), 483
Panama Refining Co. v. Ryan, 293 U.S. 388 (1935), 484, 554
Patterson v. Stanolind Oil and Gas Co., 77 Pac. 2d 83 (1938), appeal dismissed, 305 U.S. 276 (1939), 483
Paul v. Virginia, 8 Wall. 168 (1869), 107–108, 533
Peik v. Chicago & N. W. R. Co., 94 U.S. 164 (1876), 372
Pennsylvania Gas Co. v. Public Service Commission, 252 U.S. 23 (1920), 431
Peonage Cases, 123 F. 671 (1903), 271
Perry v. U.S., 294 U.S. 330 (1935), 111, 165, 169
Phillips Petroleum Co. v. Wisconsin, 347 U.S. 672 (1954), 35 P.U.R. 3d 199 (1960), 489, 492
Pipeline Cases, 234 U.S. 548 (1914), 415
Prentis v. Atlantic Coast Line Co., 211 U.S. 210 (1908), 376
Public Utilities Commission for the State of Kansas v. Landon, 249 U.S. 236 (1918), 431
Public Utilities Commission of Rhode Island v. Attleboro Steam and Electric Co., 273 U.S. 83 (1927), 431

Railroad Commission v. Rowan and Nichols Co., 310 U.S. 573 (1940), 474, 482, 485
Reduced Pipeline Rates and Gathering Charges, 243 ICC 115 (1940), 416
Reagan v. Farmers' Loan and Trust Co., 154 U.S. 362 (1894), 438
Ribnik v. McBride, 277 U.S. 350 (1928), 77–78, 130, 366

Santa Clara Co. v. S. P. R. Co., 118 U.S. 394 (1886), 129
Schaffer Transportation Co. v. U.S., 355 U.S. 83 (1957), 403
Schwegmann Bros. v. Calvert Distillers Corp., 341 U.S. 384 (1951), 238
Scott v. Sandford (Dred Scott case), 19 How. 393 (1857), 126, 140
Signal Oil and Gas Co., 14 FPC 134 (1955), affirmed, 238 F. 2d 771 (1956), cert. denied, 353 U.S. 923 (1957), 490
Slaughterhouse Cases, 16 Wall. 36 (1873), 111 U.S. 746 (1883), 106, 127, 129
Smith v. Alabama, 124 U.S. 465 (1888), 113
Smith v. Cahoon, 283 U.S. 527 (1931), 398
Smyth v. Ames, 169 U.S. 466 (1898), 133, 440, 444–445
Southern Pacific Co. v. Arizona, 325 U.S. 761 (1945), 113
Southgate Brokerage Co. v. FTC, 150 F. 2d 607 (1945), 219
Southwestern Bell Telephone Co. v. Public Service Commission of Missouri, 262 U.S. 276 (1923), 441
Special Equipment Co. v. Coe, Commissioner of Patents, 324 U.S. 370 (1945), 203
Spring Valley Water Works v. Schottler, 110 U.S. 347 (1884), 438
Sproles v. Binford, 286 U.S. 374 (1932), 113
Sprout v. South Bend, 277 U.S. 163 (1928), 108
Stafford v. Wallace, 258 U.S. 495 (1922), 143, 145
Standard Fashion Co. v. Magrane-Houston Co., 258 U.S. 346 (1922), 223, 224
Standard Oil Co. of California v. U.S., 337 U.S. 293 (1949), 224, 225
Standard Oil Co. of Indiana v. U.S., 283 U.S. 163 (1931), 205, 206, 207
Standard Oil Co. of Indiana v. FTC, 340 U.S. 231 (1951), 219
Standard Oil Co. of New Jersey v. U.S., 221 U.S. 1 (1911), 187, 189–190, 225
Standard Sanitary Manufacturing Co. v. U.S., 226 U.S. 20 (1912), 205
State v. McClure, 105 Atl. 712 (1919), 271
State v. Nelson, 45 N.W. 33 (1890), 138
State v. Osawkee Township, 19 Am. Rep. 99 (1875), 138
State of Missouri ex rel. Southwestern Bell Telephone Co. v. Public Service Commission of Missouri, 262 U.S. 276 (1923), 369
State of Wisconsin v. Phillips Petroleum Co., 205 F. 2d 707 (1953), 489

6 6 2 *Table of Cases*

Stephenson v. Binford, 287 U.S. 251 (1932), 399
Sterling v. Constantin, 287 U.S. 378 (1932), 479
Stettler v. O'Hara, 243 U.S. 629 (1917), 285
Steward Machine Co. v. Davis, 301 U.S. 548 (1937), 133, 137
St. Louis & O'Fallon R. Co. v. U.S., 279 U.S. 461 (1929), 383
Stone v. Farmers' Loan and Trust Company, 116 U.S. 307 (1886), 438
Stone v. Mississippi, 101 U.S. 814 (1880), 128
Stout v. Pratt, 85 F. 2d 172 (1936), 145
Sugar Institute, Inc. v. U.S., 297 U.S. 553 (1936), 200, 233
Swift v. Tyson, 16 Pet. 1 (1842), 117
Swift & Co. v. U.S., 196 U.S. 375 (1905), 142, 195
Swift & Co. v. FTC., 272 U.S. 554 (1926), 226–227

Tampa Electric Co. v. Nashville Coal Co. et al., 365 U.S. 320 (1961), 224–225
Terral v. Burke Construction Co., 257 U.S. 529 (1922), 107
Texas & N. O. R. Co. v. Brotherhood of Railway & S. S. Clerks, 281 U.S. 548 (1930), 133, 303, 311
Texas & Pac. Ry. v. Abilene Cotton Oil Co. (Abilene case), 204 U.S. 426 (1907), 377, 562
Textile Workers Union of America v. Lincoln Mills of Alabama, 353 U.S. 448 (1957), 302
Thatcher Mfg. Co. v. FTC, 272 U.S. (1926), 226–227
Theater Enterprises, Inc. v. Paramount Film Distributing Corp., 346 U.S. 537 (1954), 202
Thornhill v. Alabama, 310 U.S. 88 (1940), 134
Toomer v. Witsell, 334 U.S. 385 (1948), 107
Triangle Conduit & Cable Co. v. FTC (Rigid Steel case), 168 F. 2d 165 (1948), upheld, 336 U.S. 956 (1949), 202, 235, 261
Truax v. Raich, 239 U.S. 33 (1915), 272
Tyson v. Banton, 273 U.S. 418 (1927), 77–78, 130, 366

United Mine Workers v. Coronado Coal Co., 259 U.S. 344 (1922), 297, 299, 308
U.S. v. Addyston Pipe and Steel Co., 85 F. 271, 175 U.S. 211 (1898), 185, 195, 200
U.S. v. Alkali Export Ass'n., Inc., 58 F. Supp. 785 (1944), affirmed, 325 U.S. 196 (1945), 237
U.S. v. Aluminum Company of America (Alcoa case), 148 F. 2d 416 (1945), 191–192, 207, 261
U.S. v. American Linseed Oil Co., 262 U.S. 371 (1923), 198–199
U.S. v. American Tobacco Co., 221 U.S. 106 (1911), 189, 190, 192, 201–202, 261
U.S. v. Atlantic Refining Co., Civil Action 14060, D. Col. (1941), 416
U.S. v. Borden Co., 308 U.S. 188 (1939), 239
U.S. v. Brooks, 147 F. 2d 134 (1945), cert. denied, 324 U.S. 878 (1945), 271
U.S. v. Butler, 297 U.S. 1 (1936), 137, 144, 512
U.S. v. California, 332 U.S. 19 (1947), 494
U.S. v. Columbia Steel Co., 334 U.S. 495 (1948), 193–194, 200, 247
U.S. v. Curtiss-Wright Export Corp., 299 U.S. 304 (1936), 148, 150
U.S. v. Darby, 312 U.S. 100 (1941), 147, 287
U.S. v. Doremus, 249 U.S. 86 (1919), 138
U.S. v. E. C. Knight Co. (Sugar Trust case), 156 U.S. 1 (1895), 140–141, 189, 225, 631
U.S. v. E. I. du Pont de Nemours, 353 U.S. 586 (1957), 336 U.S. 316 (1961), 228–230
U.S. v. General Electric Co., 273 U.S. 476 (1926), 204–205, 206, 207
U.S. v. Grimaud, 220 U.S. 506 (1911), 563
U.S. v. Hutcheson, 312 U.S. 219 (1941), 308–309, 323

U.S. v. International Nickel Co. of Canada, 203 F. Supp. 739 (1962), 210
U.S. v. Kahriger, 345 U.S. 22 (1953), 139
U.S. v. Lehigh Valley Railroad Co. (Anthracite Coal case), 254 U.S. 255 (1920), 191
U.S. v. Line Material Co., 333 U.S. 287 (1948), 202, 205–206
U.S. v. Louisiana, Texas, Mississippi, Alabama, and Florida, 363 U.S. 1 (1960), 494
U.S. v. Masonite Corp., 316 U.S. 265 (1942), 202, 204–205
U.S. v. New York Great A. & P. Co., 173 F. 2d 79 (1949), 193, 250, 251
U.S. v. Paramount Pictures, Inc., 334 U.S. 131 (1948), 198, 200–201, 204, 225
U.S. v. Parke, Davis & Co., 362 U.S. 29 (1960), 238
U.S. v. Pewee Coal Co., 341 U.S. 114 (1951), 325
U.S. v. Philadelphia National Bank, 374 U.S. 321 (1963), 231, 242
U.S. v. R. C. A., 358 U.S. 334 (1959), 241, 470
U.S. v. Reading Co. (Anthracite Coal case), 253 U.S. 26 (1920), 191
U.S. v. Sears, Roebuck & Co., 111 F. Supp. 614 (1953), 165 F. Supp. 356 (1958), 232
U.S. v. Socony-Vacuum Oil Co., 310 U.S. 150 (1940), 197–198, 200
U.S. v. South-Eastern Underwriters Association, 322 U.S. 533 (1944), 151, 534, 536
U.S. v. Storer Broadcasting Co., 351 U.S. 192 (1956), 468
U.S. v. Texas, 339 U.S. 707 (1950), 340 U.S. 848 (1950), 494
U.S. v. Trans-Missouri Freight Association, 166 U.S. 290 (1897), 186, 187, 195, 380
U.S. v. Trenton Potteries Co. (Trenton Potteries case), 273 U.S. 392 (1927), 196–198, 204, 207
U.S. v. United Mine Workers, 330 U.S. 258 (1947), 308
U.S. v. United Shoe Machinery Corp., 110 F. Supp. 295 (1953), affimed per curiam, 347 U.S. 521 (1954), 188, 192
U.S. v. U.S. Steel Corp., 251 U.S. 447 (1920), 190–191, 197, 199, 225, 229
U.S. v. Wrightwood Dairy Co., 315 U.S. 110 (1942), 147
U.S. v. W. T. Grant Co., 245 U.S. 629 (1953), 232
U.S. v. Yellow Cab Co., 332 U.S. 218 (1947), remanded, dismissed, 80 F. Supp. 936 (1948), affirmed, 338 U.S. 338 (1949), 193–194
U.S. v. Zenith Radio Corporation, 12 F. 2d 616 (1926), 460
U.S. Shoe Machinery Co. v. U.S., 258 U.S. 451 (1922), 223
United Steelworkers of America v. American Mfg. Co., 363 U.S. 564 (1960), 302
United Steelworkers of America v. Enterprise Wheel and Car Corp. (Steelworkers' Trilogy case), 363 U.S. 593 (1960), 302
United Steelworkers of America v. Warrior & Gulf Navigation Co. (Steelworkers' Trilogy case), 363 U.S. 574 (1960), 302

Van Camp & Sons Co. v. American Can Co., 278 U.S. 245 (1929), 218
Veazie Bank v. Fenno, 8 Wall. 533 (1869), 110, 139
Virginia Railway Co. v. System Federation No. 40, 300 U.S. 515 (1937), 303–304

Wabash, St. Louis & Pacific Railway Co. v. Illinois, 118 U.S. 557 (1886), 22, 372
Ware v. Hylton, 3 Dall. 199 (1796), 64
Waters-Pierce Oil Corp. v. Texas, 177 U.S. 28 (1900), 107
Weiner v. U.S., 357 U.S. 349 (1958), 550
West v. Chesapeake & Potomac Telephone Co. of Baltimore City, 295 U.S. 662 (1935), 444
West Coast Hotel Co. v. Parrish, 300 U.S. 379 (1937), 133, 285
West River Bridge v. Dix, 6 How. 507 (1848), 124
White v. New York Central Rr. Co., 243 U.S. 188 (1917), 277
Wickard v. Filburn, 317 U.S. 111 (1942), 146
Wilkinson v. Leland, 2 Pet. 627 (1829), 122, 123
Williams v. Standard Oil Co., 278 U.S. 235 (1929), 130

Wilson v. New, 243 U.S. 332 (1917), 286, 365
Wisconsin v. FPC, 373 U.S. 294 (1963), 492
Wisconsin R. Comm. v. Chicago, B. & Q. R. Co. (Wisconsin Rate case), 257 U.S. 563 (1922), 143, 145, 146
Wolff Packing Co. v. Industrial Court, 262 U.S. 522 (1923), 267 U.S. 552 (1925), 130, 286, 366
Worthen Co. v. Kavanaugh, 295 U.S. 56 (1935), 111
Wright v. Vinton Branch of Mountain Trust Bank, 300 U.S. 440 (1937), 165
Wynehamer v. State of New York, 13 N.Y. 378 (1856), 125

Yakus v. U.S., 321 U.S. 414 (1944), 554

Index

Adams, John, 15, 121
Adams, Sherman, 583
Adamson Act, 286
Administration: improper influences, 582 ff.; informal, 539–540; policy standards, 574–575
Administrative agencies: and Congress, 590; commissions, 548–551, 575 ff.; congressional control, 567, 580; creativity, 556; departmental and presidential agencies, 551–552; facilitative arrangements, 561–563; features, 581–582; internal safeguards, 567; judicial review, 563, 565–566, 580; operating decisions, 555; political support, 564–565, 589–590; recommendation of legislation, 555; rule making, 554–555; types, 637–638; types of functions, 547–548; union of functions, 547; *see also* President and commissions
Administrative conference, 569, 572
Administrative discretion, 552–554
Administrative orders, authoritativeness of, 212, 374, 376
Administrative procedure: adjudication, 571; delays, 572, 573; delegation, 572, 573; illustrations of, 557–559; informal process, 560; institutional process, 560; objectives, 556, 569; position of examiner, 559; reform, 569–570, 580; rule making, 570–571, 574–575
Administrative Procedure Act, 555, 557, 558, 559, 565, 568, 571, 572
Administrative regulation, inherent limits on, 588–589
Agricultural adjustment, constitutionality, 137, 145–146
Agricultural cooperatives, 239–240, 241, 509
Agricultural employment, 23
Agricultural Marketing Act of 1937, 147
Agricultural paradox, 500
Agricultural parity, 511
Agricultural policies, 502; in 19th century, 499–500
Agricultural policy, comments, 522 ff.
Agricultural technology, 501
Agriculture: basic commodities, 513; bureau-committee-clientele relations, 61; equal-

Agriculture (*Cont.*):
ity with industry, 510 ff.; non-basic commodities, 514
Air carrier regulation: expertness and responsiveness, 412; management of competition, 406, 407–409; origins, 404–405; politics and economics, 412–414; procedure, 558, 559; purposes, 405–406; rates, 409–412; safety, 405, 406–407
Air Transport Association, 406
Aitchison, Clyde B., 389n
All channel television sets, 463
Allocation of scarce materials, 148
American Bar Association, 568, 570, 577, 578
American Farm Bureau Federation, 44, 48
American Federation of Labor, 298, 311, 312
American Federation of Labor-Congress of Industrial Organizations, 27
American Revolution, economic importance, 6
American Telephone & Telegraph, 453–454, 455; Long Lines Department, 455
Anti-Peonage statute, 271
Antitrust: abuse of power, 193; basic purpose, 633–634; coercive acts, 189, 190, 191; common law, 186–187; compliance, 254; conscious parallelism, 202, 235; consent orders, 213; conspiracies, 201–202, 235, 236; constitutional questions, 140–142; delivered pricing, 232; division of market, 195; effect of intent, 188, 189, 190, 192; effect of size, 190, 200; effects of, 206–207; efforts to strengthen, 208; enforcement, 227, 242, 253–258; evil intent, 191; exclusion of competitors, 192; exemption of insurance, 534; loose and close associations, 197; market analysis, 224, 257; methods used, 637; open-price associations, 198–200; penalties for violation, 253; *per se* doctrine, 188, 197, 198, 203, 204, 224, 256, 260, 262; possession of power, 192; price agreements, 196–198; purposes, 94–95; quantitative test, 224–225, 229–230; rate-making associations, 195; relevant market, 229, 230, 255; rule of reason, 187; size, 229; suggestions for policy change, 260–265; tests of market effects,

665

666 *Index*

Antitrust (*Cont.*):
    256; uncertainties, 185–186, 256; weakening influences, 260; *see also* Antitrust and labor, Antitrust and regulatory acts, Antitrust Division, Attorney General's National Committee to Study the Antitrust Laws, Celler-Kefauver Act, Clayton Act, Competition, Corporate concentration, Exclusive dealing, Export associations, Federal Trade Commission, Federal Trade Commission Act, Federal Trade Commission and Department of Justice, Holding companies, Imperfect competition, Monopolies and monopolizing, Price discrimination, Prices—administered, Sherman Act, Tying agreements, Workable competition
Antitrust Division, 55, 56, 227, 228, 241, 242, 254, 255, 257, 308
Antitrust and labor, 195, 239, 297–300, 308–309, 324
Antitrust and regulatory acts, 241–242
Appleby, Paul, 50, 51
Arbitration, compulsory, 136
Atomic energy, 149, 610–612
Attorney General's Committee on Administrative Procedure, 557, 560n, 568, 578
Attorney General's National Committee to Study the Antitrust Laws, 186, 213, 224, 241n

Bailey, Stephen K., 178
Banking: Congress' power, 139; dispersion of controls, 532–533; dual system, 527 ff.; regulation, 231n, 242, 527–533, Chapter 9 generally
Barnes, Irston R., 444n
Baruch, Bernard, 346
Bauer, John, 442n
Beard, Charles A., 10
Bell, Alexander Graham, 453, 458
Bell System, 454
Bentham, Jeremy, 65, 66
Bentley, A. F., 569
Berle, Adolf A., Jr., 23, 24, 31, 248, 249
Berman, Edward, 298n, 299n
Bernstein, Irving, 319n, 325n
Bernstein, Marver, 577, 590n
Beveridge, A. J., 10
Bigness, good or bad?, 247–249
Blachly, Frederick F., 370n
Blough, Roger, 265
Bluestone, David W., 420n, 421n
Bonneville Power Administration, 602
Bookman, George, 577n
Boulding, Kenneth E., 29, 30, 632
Brandeis, Louis D., 77, 191, 299, 441, 446
Brannan, Charles F., 525
Bureau-committee relations, 55–57

Bureau of Corporations, 190, 209, 210
Bureau of Mines, 481
Bureau of Reclamation, 602–603
Bureaucracy, effects of, 81
Burkhead, Jesse, 625n
Burnham, James, 21, 80n
Business conscience, 248–249
Business cycle, 158–160, 180

Cables, 458–459
Capitalism, strength of, 83
Case, Senator, of South Dakota, 489
Caves, Richard E., 412n, 413, 414
Cease-and-desist orders, 212
Celler-Kefauver Act, 227
Chain broadcasting, 466–468
Chain store investigation, 217
Chandler, Lester V., 343, 344
Chase, Samuel, 15, 16, 64, 125
Child labor prohibition, constitutionality, 138, 143–144, 147
Child Labor Tax case, 138
Churchill, Winston, 333
Civil Aeronautics, *see* Air carrier regulation
Civil investigative demands, 258
Civil rights legislation, 134, 275
Civil War, economic significance, 7
Clark, J. M., 261
Clark, Tom, 225
Class struggle, 82–83
Classes, middle, 82, 83
Clay, Comer, 619n
Clay, Henry, 15
Clayton Act, 207, 208, 214, 242; and labor, 298–299, 306; enforcement, 212 ff.; Section 2, 216 ff., 232; Section 3, 222 ff.; Section 7, 191, 195, 225–231, 231n, 241, 242, 264, 380; Section 8, 231, 232
Closed shop, 314, 316, 323
Cohen, Benjamin, 435
Cohn, Herbert B., 448n
Collective bargaining, 133, 318, 319, 323, 327, 328; basic policy, 296, 300; duty of parties, 301, 304
Combination, illegality of, 191, 192, 194–195, 264
Commerce: acts affecting, 140 ff., 146–147; and production, 140, 143–147; and property ownership, 140; congressional silence, 112 ff.; current of, 142, 147; intrastate sales, 142–143, 147; state powers, 112–115, 144; state regulation, 140
Commission on Organization of the Executive Branch (Hoover Commission), 532, 550n, 569, 570, 571, 575, 576, 616n
Committee for Economic Development, 97
Commodities clause, 416
Commodity Credit Corporation, 34, 515

Commodity exchanges, 504
Commons, John R., 270
Communications, development of, 22
Communications Satellite Act, 612
Communist Manifesto, 82
Compensatory policy, 97–98, 633
Competition: arguments for, 244–245; issues on, 246
Comptroller of the Currency, 55, 161, 242, 530, 531–533
Compulsory settlement of labor disputes, 286, 304, 325 ff.
Congress: effects of silence of, 112–114; functions of committees, 55–56, 61; role in macropolitics, 60
Congress of Industrial Organizations, 27, 311, 312
Consent settlement, 213
Conservatism, 85, 87, 89, 101
Constitution: economic importance, 6; "grand pattern," 106, 109, 154, 631–632; Chapters 7–9, generally
Controlled Materials Plan, 337–338
Cook, Donald C., 448n
Cooley, Justice, 126, 131
Coolidge, Calvin, 493
Corcoran, Thomas, 435
Corporate charters, 8, 107
Corporate concentration, 23–25
Corporate development, 5, 16
Corporations: comity clause, 107; early views toward, 13; government of, 29 ff.; interlockings, 25; politicization, 29 ff., 632; protections for, 129; state power, 107–108
Corwin, Edward S., 132, 554n
Council of Economic Advisers, 179, 327
Countervailing power, 249–252, 634
Cowett, Edward M., 540n
Cox, Archibald, 325n
Crawford, Finla G., 442n
Credit conditions: 1920's, 164–166; 1930's, 165–166
Credit controls, selective, 170–171
Credit for special purposes, 171 ff., 181, 367–368
Credit, public agencies, 171 ff., 367–368, 603–606
Cross of Gold, 158
Cullom Committee, 372

Dahl, Robert, 94, 632
Davis, Chester C., 586n
Day, William R., 132, 133, 191, 297, 303
Declaration of Independence, 64, 65
Defense Production Act, 355
Defense Production Administration, 353
Delaware River Basin, 607
Delivered pricing systems, 232

Democracy and equality, 76, 99
Democracy and freedom, 76, 79, 86
Democracy: moderated, 52, 91; pluralistic, 47, 62, 90
Depreciation, telephone regulation, 457
Depression, money and credit conditions, 164–166
Dimock, Marshall, 623
Dirlam, Joel B., 256n, 262n
Discount rate, 160
Discrimination in employment, 272 ff.
Dodd, Walter F., 275n, 276n
Doherty, Henry L., 483, 496
Douglas, Paul, 491
Douglas, William O., 194, 247, 445, 446

Eastman, Joseph B., 385, 399, 406
Eccles, Marriner, 177n
Eckstein, Otto, 267, 616n
Economic fluctuations, 157, 180
Economic growth, 4–5
Economic individualism, 120
Economic investigations, 210
Economic paternalism, 120
Economic planning, 62, 89, 93
Economic Report, 179
Economic Stabilization, Director of, 351
Education, as public enterprise, 600
Educational television, 463–464
Edwards, Corwin, 221–222
Eells, Richard, 32n
Eisenhower, Dwight D., 180, 316, 320, 321, 423
Electric power, public supply, 601–603
Elsbree, Hugh L., 432
Emergency Planning, Office of, 355, 356
Empirical approach, 76 ff., 91
Employment Act of 1946, 37, 92, 177 ff., 633
Employment agencies, 78
Enarson, Harold L., 319, 325
Engels, Friedrich, 82
Entry into business, restrictions on, 130
Exclusive dealing, 222–225
Exclusive original jurisdiction of agencies, 377
Export associations, 236

Fact finding, 303, 326
Fact-finding boards, 301, 319, 321
Fact-finding processes for price increases, 267–268
Fainsod, Merle, 51, 589
Fair competition, 215, 242, 283
Fair Labor Standards Act, 147, 287; amendments of 1961, 288
Fair, Marvin L., 420, 422n
Fall, Albert B., 493
Farm Board, 511
Farm Credit Administration, 604–605
Feasibility dispute, 334

Federal Aviation Agency, *see* Air carrier regulation
Federal Deposit Insurance Corporation, functions, 531–533
Federal Incorporation Act, 208
Federal Mediation and Conciliation Service, 318
Federal Power Act, 152, 153, 430–433, 444
Federal Power Commission, 152, 153, 241, 430–433, 444, 497, 498; jurisdiction over producers prices, 486 ff.
Federal Reserve Board: Clayton Act cases, 232; coordination with other agencies, 533; operating decisions, 559; procedure, 559
Federal Reserve System, 157, 158–159, 160–162, 176, 180; as mixed enterprise, 609; banking regulation, 530, 531–533
Federal Trade Commission, 25, 202, 207, 227, 434; basing-point pricing, 233; enforcement by, 220, 232; enforcement function, 212 ff., 227, 228, 253, 254; export trade associations, 236–237; investigatorial function, 209 ff.; length of cases, 257; procedure, 557
Federal Trade Commission Act, 202, 207, 208, 209 ff., 310
Federal Trade Commission and Department of Justice, 214–215
Fesler, James W., 336n, 550n
Financial regulation, 367
Fiscal policy, emergence, 164 ff.
Flammable Fabrics Act, 213
Fleming, R. W., 319n, 325n
Flood Control Act of 1944, 616
Food and Drug legislation, 508
Fortune, 577, 578
Fox, Guy, 530n
Frankfurter, Felix, 50, 443n, 445, 467
Freeman, J. Lieper, 57n
Freeman, Orville, 501n
Freund, Ernst, 361
Friedrich, Carl J., 554n
Friendly, Henry J., 574
Fromm, Gary, 267
Frontier, 3, 17–19
Frontier, The Great, 17, 19
Fuel policy, 497–498
Fur Products Labeling Act, 213
Future transactions, 505

Galbraith, John Kenneth, 20, 91n, 249, 250, 251, 252, 265
Gaus, John M., 17
General Telephone Company, 458
General Welfare provision, 137
Gerry, Elbridge, 111
Gold, Nathaniel, 442n

Gold revaluation, 169
Gold Standard Act of 1900, 158
Goldfine, Bernard, 583
Gompers, Samuel, 298
Gore, Senator, 267
Government action: rationality, 53, 57, 59–60, 62, 99, 639; responsiveness, 53, 57, 59–60, 62, 81, 99, 639
Government enterprises, measurement of success, 617–619
Government contracts, 35, 368
Government Corporation Act, 624–625
Government corporations, 619 ff.
Government decision-making, tests, 98–99
Government functions, traditional, 7–8
Government service, 93, 96
Grain elevator charges, 77
Grain Futures Act, 143, 145
Granger legislation, 372, 373
Gregory, Charles O., 307
Griffith, Ernest S., 57
Groups: contacts with bureaus and committees, 56–57; limits on, 47 ff.; representation of, 45 ff.

Hagan, Charles B., 453n
Hall, George R., 228n, 230n
Hall, Hugh, 210n, 211
Hamilton, Alexander, 13, 14
Handler, Milton, 214n, 228n
Hansen, Alvin, 97
Harbrecht, Father, 31
Hard money, 158, 180
Harding, Warren G., 493
Hardwicke, Robert E., 482n
Harlan, John M., 187
Harris, Joseph P., 488n
Hartz, Louis, 4, 8, 9, 13
Hayek, Friedrich A., 88, 89
Heady, Ferrel, 570n
Health, public enterprise in, 610
Hector, Louis J., 578
Hepburn Act, 375, 416
Herring, E. Pendleton, 45–46, 50, 51, 569, 585, 590n
Higher law, 12–13, 16, 123, 129
Heldebrand, George H., 327
Hobhouse, Leonard T., 75–76, 90, 92, 101
Holcombe, Arthur N., 42, 43
Holding companies, 190, 208, 225, 231n, 386, 433 ff.
Holmes, Oliver Wendell, 65, 77, 78, 123, 131, 132, 185, 248, 257n, 299, 366
Home Owners Loan Corporation, 618
Hoover Commission, *see* Commission on Organization of the Executive Branch
Hoover, Herbert, 493
Hospitals, government, 600

Hours legislation, 130, 131
Housing, government enterprise in, 606–607, 609
Hughes, Charles Evans, 95, 132, 133, 186, 297, 303, 311, 428
Huitt, Ralph K., 437
Huntington, Samuel P., 393n
Hyneman, Charles S., 553

Imperfect competition, 245–246
Implied powers, 136, 148
Individualism, 13, 15, 63 ff.
Industry Guide Program, 214
Industry planning, 384–386, 390, 391
Inflation and countervailing power, 252
Inflationary price increases, 267
Inherent powers, 148, 150
Insurance: government enterprise in, 34–35, 368, 606; national regulation, 536–537; purposes of regulation, 534–535; rate regulation, 535–537; state powers, 151
Interlocking directorates, 231
Interlocking relations in railroad contracts, 231
Interstate Commerce Commission: criticisms of, 392–393; nature of its performance, 390 ff.; organization, 391; powers, 143, 207, 474; see also Air carrier regulation, Motor carrier regulation, Pipeline regulation, Water carrier regulation, Chapter 17 generally
Interstate Oil Compact, 480, 485
Iredell, James, 123, 132

Jackson, Barrett A., 535n
Jackson, Robert H., 491
Jefferson, Thomas, 14, 15
Johnson, Elizabeth Sands, 283n
Johnson, Lyndon, 275
Johnson, Nicholas, 492n
Joint Economic Committee, 179
Judicial, legislative, and administrative methods, 258
Judicial review, 122–123, 129, 134, 136
Judicial review of administrative decisions, 207, 374–375, 377
Judiciary, role in economic policy, 53–54, 631, 636–637

Kahn, Alfred E., 256n, 262n
Kaplan, A. D. H., 23
Kaysen, Carl, 24, 262, 263, 264
Kennedy Administration, 518
Kennedy, John F., 182, 267, 275, 320, 393, 421, 556, 569, 581, 587
Kent, Chancellor, 15, 122, 125, 131
Kerr, Robert S., 488

Key, V. O., 56, 620n, 624
Keynes, John Maynard, 166, 166n, 167, 167n
Keynesian theory, 97, 166 ff.
Kimball, Spencer L., 535n
Knight, Frank, 88
Korean War: price controls, 248–249; production controls, 335; wage stabilization, 352
Kuznets, Simon, 333, 334

Labor: basic policy, 96, 269, 296, 323; communist associations, 321; corruption, 315–316; draft of, 342; emergency disputes, 301, 304–305, 318 ff., 324 ff.; growth of unions, 18, 26; injunction, 297, 305 ff., 319, 320; interests of parties, 295, 323; monopoly, 323–324; no-man's land in labor law, 317–318; organization reports, 321; patterns of public policy in disputes, 301–303, 319; political contributions, 321–322, 323; Reporting and Disclosure Act, 27, 313, 317, 322; right to strike, 295, 312, 319; rights of employers, 314, 315, 323; seizure, 324–325, 326; setting guide-posts, 327; slave or free, 11–12; types of legislation, 269; see also Antipeonage statute, Antitrust and labor, Closed shop, Collective bargaining, Compulsory settlement of labor disputes, Discrimination in employment, Employment agencies, Fact finding, Fact-finding boards, Fair Labor Standards Act, Federal Mediation and Conciliation Service, Labor regulations—early state, Labor regulation—administration in, Labor unions, Manpower controls in wartime, Manpower Development and Training Act, Minimum labor standards—problems in maintaining, National Labor Relations Act, National Labor Relations Board, National Mediation Board, National Railroad Adjustment Board, National Wage Stabilization Board, National War Labor Board, Norris-La Guardia Act, Picketing, Railway Labor Act, Secondary boycotts, Taft-Hartley Act, Unemployment, Union shop, Unionization, Unions, Wage controls in wartime, Wage dependency, Wage Stabilization Board, War Labor Board, War Labor Disputes Act, Wartime wage control, Work-or-fight order, Yellow-dog contracts
Labor regulations, early state, 9
Labor relations, administration in, 579
Labor unions, fascist view, 84

6 7 0 *Index*

Laissez faire, 13, 15, 16, 64, 66, 79, 88, 126, 307, 631–632
Laissez faire economics, 67 ff., 85
Laissez faire with exceptions, 130
Landis, James M., 547n, 569, 572, 573, 574, 578, 579n, 581
Landis Report, 491
Landon, Charles E., 233n
Larkin, John Day, 553
Latham, Earl, 235n, 386n
Lecht, Leonard A., 304n
Legislative Oversight, Committee on, 569, 583
Leiserson, Avery, 51
Lewis, John L., 307
Liberalism, 85–89, 101
Liberty of contract, 130, 131–132
Liberty, views on, 67, 72, 73, 75, 86
Licensing, 9, 361–362
Licensing and patents, 203–206
Lilienthal, David E., 247, 248, 260, 622n
Lindblom, Charles, 94, 632
Lippmann, Walter, 41
Little Steel Formula, 351
Loans on business securities, 163–164
Lobby, 46
Locke, John, 13, 28
Long, Norton E., 564
Loss, Louis, 541
Lower Colorado River Authority, 602

Maass, Arthur, 498n
McCabe, Thomas B., 177n
McCarran Act, 534
McClellan, John, 322
McFarland, Carl, 375n, 377n
Machlup, Fritz, 236n
Mack, Richard E., 583
McKenna, Joseph, 534–535
McLaughlin, James A., 187, 226n
Macmahon, Arthur W., 53n
McReynolds, James C., 191
Macropolitics, 58–60, 236, 324, 392, 412, 413, 417, 450, 590, 638–639
Madison, James, 10, 14, 41, 42, 47, 111, 121, 135
Malthus, Thomas, 12, 18, 20
Mann-Elkins Act, 377
Manpower controls in wartime, 341–342
Manpower Development and Training Act, 281
Mansfield, Harvey C., 338n, 349n, 392n
March, James G., 29, 632
Marketing agreements and orders, 517
Marshall Court, 123
Marshall, John, 64, 112, 114, 122, 123, 126, 129, 137, 139
Martin, Roscoe C., 622n
Martin, William McC., Jr., 177n

Marx, Karl, 41, 82, 83
Marxism, 86
Mason, Edward S., 262n, 263n
Massel, Mark S., 256n, 262n
Material well-being, as ideal, 91, 93, 633
Maturity thesis, 168, 181
May, Stacy, 333
Means, Gardiner C., 23, 24, 30
Mergers, 188, 227, 258, 386; *see also* Antitrust
Military Air Transport, 59
Milk marketing orders, 518
Mill, John Stuart, 47, 71–74, 89, 90, 92, 93, 131, 596–597, 627
Miller, Samuel F., 106, 127
Miller-Tydings Act, 243
Mills, Warner E., Jr., 478n
Minimum labor standards, problems in maintaining, 291–294
Minimum standards legislation, 96
Minimum wages, 92, 130, 131, 133, 289–290
Minority rights, 91
Mixed economy, 39, 90, 92 ff., 101
Monetary powers of Congress, 139
Money, early policies, 11
Money and credit system, 158
Monnet, Jean, 333
Monopolies and monopolizing, 186, 188–189, 190, 191–192, 194, 201; *see also* Antitrust
Morse, Samuel F. B., 451
Moratorium laws, 133
Mosher, William E., 442n
Motor carrier regulation: by states, 398–399; common carriers, 400; contract carriers, 400; looseness in, 400–401; management of competition, 399, 402 ff.; problems, 401 ff.; rate regulation, 400, 403
Municipal enterprises, 608

Nathan, Robert R., 333
Nathanson, Nathaniel L., 571n
National Association of Manufacturers, 25, 44, 48, 316
National Association of Railroad and Utilities Commissioners, 153, 399, 429, 432
National budget, 38, 173–174, 182
National Industrial Recovery Act, National Industrial Recovery Administration, 234, 240–241, 243, 301, 309, 366, 493
National Labor Relations Act, 26, 27, 145, 152, 310, 313 ff., 318, 321
National Labor Relations Board, 310–312, 315, 316, 317
National Mediation Board, 301, 304, 305
National Musicians Union, 44
National Railroad Adjustment Board, 301
National-state cooperation, 152–153
National supremacy, 112, 116–117, 137

Index 671

National Wage Stabilization Board, 313
National War Labor Board, 313
Natural Gas Act, 152, 153, 430–433, 486, 487, 490
Natural gas: jurisdiction to regulate, 486–489; pricing problems, 489–492; *see also* Utilities, Utility holding companies
Natural rights, 13, 15–16, 63–65, 85, 129
Nelson, Donald, 333, 334, 586
Neoliberalism, 88–90, 245
New Deal credit policies, 168
New York Port Authority, 602
Norris-La Guardia Act, 306–308

Oatman, Miriam E., 370n
Office of Defense Transportation, 353–354
Office of Economic Stabilization, 354
Office of Price Administration, 149, 340, 341, 346, 347, 348, 350, 353
Office of War Mobilization and Reconversion, 354
Open market operations, 160–161, 170, 175, 176
Oppenheim, S. Chesterfield, 260, 261, 264
Opportunity ideal, 90, 633
Organization behavior, 28 ff.

Packers and stockyards, 143, 145, 503
Palamountain, Joseph C., 257n
Panics, 157, 158
Perishable commodities, 507
Petroleum Administrator for War, 340, 353
Petroleum, import regulation, 494–496
Petroleum industry: taxes, 494; types of regulation, 474
Petroleum, Naval Reserves, 493
Petroleum production: advent of regulation, 477–480; comments on regulatory system, 480–486; correlative rights, 476–477, 480, 482–484; features of regulation, 480 ff.; interests in, 477; physical conditions, 475–476; unit development, 483–484, 496
Petroleum, tideland controversy, 494
Phillips, Charles F., Jr., 228n, 230n
Picketing, 133–134, 323
Pipeline regulation, 415–416
Pittsburg plus, 233
Planning, limits on, 62
Pluralistic society, 73, 75, 80, 93
Policy development, methods, 636–637
Political process, *see* Politics, Government action, Groups
Political system, pluralism of, 62
Politics: class, 43; functional, 44; macro, *see* Macropolitics; micro, 58; nature of, 41, 51; of function, 57, 58–59, 61; of subsystems, 54 ff., 392, 412, 417, 632; sectional, 42

Port, F. J., 552
Port of New York Authority, 607
Positive government, 93, 100
Post Office, 21, 600–601
Postal Telegraph, 452
Potter, David M., 20, 90
Prather, Charles L., 531n, 533n
President and commissions, 550–551, 564, 567, 577, 580–581, 590
President, function in regulation, 59
President's Committee on Administrative Management, 568, 577, 578
Price agreements, 204; *see also* Antitrust
Price control in wartime, 344 ff.
Price discrimination, 216–222
Price, Don K., 612n
Price fixing, test for, 77–78
Price regulation, 130, 132, 133, 365–366
Prices, administered, 30
Pritchett, C. Herman, 620n, 622n
Private economy, policy toward preserving, 633–634
Private enterprise, promotion of, 634–635
Private-public balances in regulation, 390, 419
Processing tax, 137
Production control, 366–367; *see also* War Production Board
Production controls in agriculture, 512
Promotion of industry, 8, 9, 10, 13, 38, 362, 367
Public authorities, 619, 626
Public enterprise: competition with private, 628; constitutionality, 132; meaning, 593–594
Public interest, 49 ff., 58, 81, 91, 126, 128, 130, 266, 323, 327, 632
Public policy, future problems, 635–636
Public power agencies, 601–603
Public utility, characteristics of, 425 ff.
Public Utility Holding Company Act, 255n, 259, 263, 430
Pump priming, 167–168
Puritanism, 12, 128, 131

Radio broadcasting, 459–461
Radio licenses: competition, 464–466; renewals, 470; transfers, 470
Radio networks, 466–468
Radio programs, 470–473
Railroad combinations, 141
Railroad industry, economic features, 372
Railroad regulation: comprehensiveness, 382, 389, 390; holding companies, 386; initial weaknesses, 374–375; long-short haul provision, 373, 374, 377, 379; policy toward cooperation and consolidation, 380–381, 384–386, 387; pooling, 373–374, 375, 380; pragmatic nature, 390; pur-

Railroad regulation (*Cont.*):
poses, 378; rates, 22, 373, 374 ff., 379, 382–384, 387, 391; recapture clause, 379–380, 384; regional discrimination, 386; safety, 381–382; securities, 381; service, 381; transportation policy, 387–388; valuation of properties, 382
Railroads: financial difficulties, 378, 385, 388; seizure of, 304; state ownership, 9
Railway Labor Act, 300 ff.
Rationing systems, 338–341
Rayburn, Sam, 435
Reagan, Michael D., 161n, 609n
Reclamation bureau, 499
Reconstruction Finance Corporation, 605, 618
Redford, Emmette S., 38, 62n, 406n, 411n, 548n, 565n, 571n, 572n, 574n, 581n
Regulation: agencies, 362–364 (chart); early state, 9; expansion, 359–361, 362–364 (chart); features, 634–635; purposes, 95; recommendations for relaxation, 393; state cooperation, 540; technology, 637, 639
Regulation and management, 369–370, 389
Regulation and politics, 392
Regulation as remedy for private power, 252
Regulatory commissions, *see* Administrative agencies, commissions
Regulatory Commissions, Task Force Report, 532
Renegotiation Act, 149n
Rent control, 349–350
Representation: class, 44–45; functional, 45–46; sectional, 45
Resale price maintenance, 237–239
Research, 19–20, 368
Reserve requirements, 160, 174, 177
Resources, conservation, 18–19, 599
Reuther, Walter, 320
Ripley, William Z., 384
Roberts, Owen J., 466, 553
Robinson-Patman Act, 217 ff., 234, 243, 250
Robson, William A., 623
Roosevelt, Franklin D., 273, 333, 540, 541, 557, 621
Roosevelt, Theodore, 18, 187, 208, 248, 258, 267, 380, 381, 637
Röpke, Wilhelm, 88
Rosenblum, Victor G., 583n
Rostow, Eugene V., 254n, 264n, 496
Rousseau, Jean Jacques, 28, 47
Rural Electrification Administration, 603–604, 616, 618
Rüstow, Alexander, 88

Scitovsky, T., 339n
Schubert, Glendon, 49n
Secondary boycotts, 298, 299, 314, 315, 317, 323
Securities: marketing of, 537; national-state cooperation, 152, 540; state regulation, 538
Securities Exchange Commission: over-the-counter markets, 430; regulation of exchanges, 541 ff.; regulation of holding companies, 435–437; regulation of securities issues, 539–541; state cooperation, 152
Securities market, forms of regulation, 544
Seidman, Harold, 624
Seizure of plants, 149
Senate Armed Services Committee, 585
Sharfman, I. L., 377n, 390, 391n
Shaw, E. S., 339n
Shaw, Justice, 125, 296
Sherman Act, 187, 212, 216, 223, 232, 233, and Chapter 10; *see also* Antitrust, Antitrust and labor
Simons, Henry C., 88
Sinclair, Harry, 493
Small Business Administration, 605
Smith, Adam, 20, 28, 67–71, 89, 90, 99, 129, 595–596
Smith, Harold D., 38
Social Security Act, constitutionality, 137
Socialism, democratic, 86
Sociological jurisprudence, 77
Somers, Herman M., 354n
Somers, Herman M. and Anne Ramsay, 275n, 276n, 277n, 278n, 279n
Sorauf, Frank J., 49n, 50, 51
Southeastern Power Administration, 603
Southwestern Power Administration, 602–603
Splawn, Walter M. W., 435
State bank notes, 139
State banks, 152
State policies, before Civil War, 8–9
State powers: commerce, 112–114, 144; delegated by congressional acts, 152; police, 126; types of, 151
State regulation: banking, 527; early types, 22; commerce, 140; insurance, 533 ff.; securities, 538
State regulatory commissions, 372
States and emergency planning, 355
States: cooperative activities, 152–153; uniform laws, 115
Statism, fear of, 80
Stephens, Elvis C., 318n
Sterling, Ross, 499
Stocking, George W., 192, 203, 206, 233n, 236n, 251, 261, 262n

Williams, Ernest W., Jr., 420, 420n, 421n, 422n
Williamson, Harold F., 4, 5
Wilson, Charles E., 585
Wilson, Woodrow, 94, 208, 209, 225, 231, 243, 258, 381, 586, 637
Wool Products Labeling Act, 213
Workable competition, 261

Work-or-fight order, 271
Wright, Benjamin F., 111n, 122, 126
Wyzanski, Charles E., Jr., 188

Yellow-dog contracts, 132, 297

Zimmermann, Erich W., 475, 480n

Stone, Harlan F., 77, 78, 366
Story, Joseph, 12, 137
Subsidies, 345, 367, 408, 409, 615–616
Sugar regulation, 520
Sutherland, George, 150

Taft-Hartley Act, 27, 313 ff., 316, 317, 318, 321, 579
Taft, Robert A., 321
Taft, William Howard, 143, 146, 185, 187, 208, 258, 637
Taney Court, 123–124
Taney, Roger B., 125
Tariffs, 11
Tax reduction, 181
Technological change, 4, 19–21, 36
Telegraph: early legislation, 452; existing legislation, 452; invention, 451; merger of Western Union and Postal, 452
Telephone: capital costs, 455–456; early development, 453; exchange rates, 457–458; long distance service, 456; power to regulate, 454; rate proceedings, 455
Telephone cooperatives, 458
Television licensing, 462–464
Telstar, 36, 612
Tennessee Valley Authority, 93, 149, 602, 603, 616, 621–623, 628
Texas Railroad Commission, 143, 474, 478–480, 481, 482, 483, 484, 485
Textile Fiber Products Identification Act, 213
Thompson, Ernest O., 480, 484, 485
Thompson, Victor A., 21, 80n
Thorp, Willard, 23
Trade conferences, 213–214
Transportation: development of, 21; exemptions from control, 401, 415, 418; expansion or contraction of regulation, 420–422; extent of regulation, 390; minimum-rate regulation, 421; policy, 387–388; policy coordination, 418, 422–424; relative position of different modes, 396–397; *see also* Air carrier regulation, Interstate Commerce Commission, Motor carrier regulation, Water carrier regulation, Chapters 17, 18 generally
Treaty-making power, 149, 150
Truman, David, 47–48
Truman, Harry S., 177n, 179, 313, 320
Turner, Donald F., 24, 262, 263, 264
Turner, Frederick J., 17, 18, 43
Tying agreements, 203, 222–225

Unemployment, 280, 635
Uniform state laws, 115
Union shop, 301, 314, 316, 323
Unionization, legality of, 296

Unions: growth and membership, 26–27; internal operations, 27; liability to suit, 297; power of, 27; right not to join, 314; right to join, 130, 297, 309, 310, 319; rights of members, 322
United Automobile Workers, 48
United States Chamber of Commerce, 25
United States Steel Corporation, 190, 194, 234, 251, 265
United Steelworkers of America, 48
Utilitarianism, 65–66, 85
Utilities: rate regulation, 430–432, 438 ff.; types of regulation, 433; valuation, 440 ff.
Utility, concept of, 425–427
Utility holding companies, 433 ff.

Valuation: railroads, 382; utility properties, 440
Value of service, telephone, 455
Vertical integration, 189, 193–194, 201, 228, 251
VHF-UHF controversy, 462–464
Vocational rehabilitation, 271

Wage controls in wartime, 350–352
Wage dependency, 23
Wage Stabilization Board, 353
Wallace, Donald H., 332n, 336n, 343
War and the economy, 147–149
War Food Administration, 340, 353
War Labor Board, 347, 351, 352, 353
War Labor Disputes Act, 149n, 312
War Manpower Commission, 341, 342
War powers, 148–149
War Production Board, 148, 333, 336, 337, 338, 353
Wartime controls, elements of, 331
Wartime credit, 176
Wartime price control, 344 ff.
Wartime rent control, 349–350
Wartime wage control, 350 ff.
Water carrier regulation, 414–415
Watkins, Myron W., 192, 203, 206, 237n
Webb-Pomerene Act, 236, 243
Webb, Walter P., 17, 19, 86
Webster, Daniel, 15, 122
Welborn, David M., 403n
Wengert, Norman I., 622n
Western development, policies on, 11
Western Electric Manufacturing Company, 454, 456
Western Union, recent developments, 453
Western Union Telegraph, 452
Wheeler-Lea Act, 212, 213, 215, 234, 242
White, Edward D., 185, 187
White, Leonard D., 551
Willbern, York, 485, 486,

DATE DUE

HIGHSMITH #45230   Printed in USA